This study conducts a lively and innovative exploration of the traditional Indian religions and cultures – an area that has both fascinated and puzzled the West for centuries. Friedhelm Hardy aims at presenting the widest possible range of themes that have preoccupied traditional Indian culture. He uses a great variety of sources, in various languages, and listens not only to what the learned philosopher or theologian in the classical Sanskrit texts has to say, but also to what folk and regional cults and cultures express in stories, myths and poetry. The result is a personal and entertaining portrayal of the colourful world of India which will have great appeal to the non-specialist. By making the three universal human drives of power, love and wisdom his focal points, Hardy seeks to guide the reader through an alien world which is nevertheless recognizably human. This book will be required reading for all those interested in India and its culture.

CAMBRIDGE STUDIES IN RELIGIOUS TRADITIONS 4

THE RELIGIOUS CULTURE OF INDIA
POWER, LOVE AND WISDOM

CAMBRIDGE STUDIES IN RELIGIOUS TRADITIONS

Edited by John Clayton (University of Lancaster), Steven Collins (University of Chicago) and Nicholas de Lange (University of Cambridge)

1. *Religion and the individual: a Jewish perspective*
   Louis Jacobs
2. *The body divine: the symbol of the body in the works of Teilhard de Chardin and Rāmānuja*
   Anne Hunt Overzee
3. *The feminine principle in the Sikh vision of the Transcendent*
   Nikky-Guninder Kaur Singh
4. *The religious culture of India: power, love and wisdom*
   Friedhelm Hardy

The Religious Culture of India

Power, Love and Wisdom

FRIEDHELM HARDY

Reader in Indian Religions, King's College, University of London

CAMBRIDGE
UNIVERSITY PRESS

Published by the Press Syndicate of the University of Cambridge
The Pitt Building, Trumpington Street, Cambridge CB2 1RP
40 West 20th Street, New York, NY 10011-4211, USA
10 Stamford Road, Oakleigh, Melbourne 3166, Australia

First published 1994
Reprinted 1996

Printed in Great Britain at Woolnough Bookbinders Ltd, Irthlingborough, Northants

A catalogue record for this book is available from the British Library

Library of Congress cataloguing in publication data

Hardy, Friedhelm,
The religious culture of India: power, love and wisdom / Friedhelm Hardy
p. cm. – (Cambridge Studies in Religious Traditions; 4)
Includes bibliographical references and index
ISBN 0 521 44181 1 (hardback)
1. India – Religion. I. Title. II. Series.
BL2001.2.H37 1993
294 – dc20 93 – 12492 CIP

ISBN 0 521 44181 1 hardback

Dedicated to
P. Georg Mühlenbrock SJ

Contents

Illustrations

PLATES

(*All photographs taken by the author*)

FIGURES

(*All figures drawn by Isobel Balakrishnan*)

Preface

There are many crimes a scholar can commit. Inaccuracy and sloppiness are two of them, and the imposition of his own ideas (for the sake of originality, fame, or whatever) is another. But collectively the scholarly community knows of one unforgivable crime: to make a fascinating subject boring. Thereby it prevents future generations from deriving the delight and edification they are entitled to from it.

In the following pages I have tried to demonstrate that the study of the traditional Indian religions can be delightful and edifying. Mountains are simply there, justifying the climbing of them. But books can be justified only if they have not been there before. For many years I have found it disconcerting to be asked by friends, acquaintances and strangers what the study of Indian religions is all about, why I enjoy doing it and what possible benefits could be derived from it. I was unable to refer them to a single book that might provide them with some representative ideas about it. The opportunity to remedy the situation arose when I was invited to deliver the Wilde Lectures in Comparative Religion at the University of Oxford over the period of 1985 to 1987. These lectures are open to all members of the university and the general public. Given that I had to address specialists in my own discipline, colleagues learned in other subjects, undergraduates and a variety of interested non-academics, I had in front of me an ideal cross-section of curious humanity whom I could, once and for all, convince of the virtues of my own subject. The twenty-four hours allotted for this task provided an opportunity unmatched by two minutes at a sherry party. So it will not require many pages' reading to realize that what is offered here is not a textbook about Indian culture nor a learned monograph. What follows is unashamedly subjective and personal. But to the extent that something like a typology, illustrating the wide range of Indian religions, might emerge from the present venture, some objective usefulness is perhaps not altogether absent.

That the chapters of the book are essentially similar to those lectures will explain some of their idiosyncrasies. The lectures had to be delivered over a period of three years to three substantially different audiences – hence the three key themes and the relative independence of the three parts. Painful though it has been, some fortuitous chronological coincidences are not retained in the present version. As it happened, Canetti's *Auto da Fé* was originally published precisely fifty years prior to my referring to it in my first lecture; when I talked about the transcendental dimensions of love (in lecture 12), it was St Valentine's day; and when I quoted from Mr Hatterr in my seventeenth lecture 'two years this Thursday', this happened to be accurate down to the day. Similarly a persistent textual scholar might still be able to trace allusions to the political and social climate during which the lectures were produced. Those allusions have been toned down here, not because that climate itself has since then fundamentally changed, but because they will be of little interest to a future reader. Some lectures were illustrated with slides; comparable literary illustrations have been substituted for them where possible.

It is with pleasure that I express here my gratitude to a host of people who, in one way or another, have been of help and comfort to me (though they cannot be held responsible for any shortcomings.) The rather unconventional ideas about religion of Dr Henry Wilde himself are briefly discussed on pp. 426f below; I would like to thank the Electors of the Wilde Lecturer for the unique opportunity they have offered me. I am indebted to Professors M. Wiles, B. Mitchell and the late B. Motilal, to Fr N. Tanner SJ, G. Lienhard, Jacky and Peter Mackridge, P. Clarke, F. Zimmermann and A. Sanderson for their hospitality and thought-provoking discussions during my stays in Oxford. R. Norman presented me with the font used in this book. The British Academy provided me with two research grants to visit India in 1982 and 1988 and some of the materials gathered there have been incorporated here. S. Chandra, S. Collins, M. Cooper, Bonny and William Crawley, F. Gros, J. Hardy, R. King, Gyan and Gitanjali Pandey, G. Parrinder, the late A. K. Ramanujan, Narayan Rao, C. Shackle, D. Shulman, D. Smith, S. Sutherland and K. Ward provided encouragement, friendship and useful, though sometimes painful, criticism. But sadly G.-D. Sontheimer never saw any of this, though I would have welcomed his comments. I take the opportunity here to thank Peter Byrne for assistance that has remained unacknowledged so far. Linda Antoniw, Isobel Balakrishnan, Jo and Ian Dennis, Roger Jones, Renate Ogilvie, Rosslynne Hefferan and, above all, Janet Banks, have been involved in the process of giving shape to the book. Jenny and Mike Walker cheered me up on many occasions and so did Jartua's friendly smile. Maya and Uday Narkar, Shankar Gopal Tulpule and Sunanda Krishnamurti assisted me with difficult passages in Marathi and Bengali. For many years Gopala Chakravarthy has been a source of knowledge, a reliable travel companion and a friend. I owe special thanks to Sanjukta and Richard Gombrich who supported the present venture in quite a variety of ways, not least through their enthusiasm. Fr G. Mühlenbrock SJ, to whom I dedicate this book, created for me years ago an atmosphere in which the seeds of the present exploration were sown and allowed to grow. I hope that he would not totally disapprove of it, were he ever able to read it.

Whatever the outcome of this attempt at entertaining may be, it is with great regret that I have to apologize already at this stage for a failure. There is one friend who, perhaps more than all others, would deserve to be given the finished product for her enjoyment and edification. Instead my wife Aruna had to suffer for years the agonies of seeing me prepare and then deliver the lectures and then write the following pages. To a slightly lesser degree this also applies to my children Nikhil and Monika. As well as thanking them for their patience, I would like to ask their forgiveness for diverting so much of my time away from them.

PART ONE

Power: the challenges of the external world

CHAPTER 1

Consulting the oracle once again

Let me introduce you to José Arcadio Buendía – adventurer, colonist and founder of a lineage that is to last for a hundred years. Somewhere in a fictionalized Colombia and isolated from the rest of the world, a dynastic history unrolls that is filled with violence, mercenary sex and frustrated love. It is an earthy history that is subject to an inexorable and cruel fate and that condemns five generations of Buendías to lives of mental and emotional solitude.

José Buendía, we are told, had been a friend of Melquíades, a gypsy who, shortly before his death, had left José a parchment purporting to reveal to him the future destiny of his descendants. And a mysterious destiny it was to be! Pure lust and strict adherence to a code of wifely duty, but never love, motivated the procreation of Buendía children. For the family was bedevilled by a strange fascination – that of nephew for aunt and of aunt for nephew. As the generations passed, this obsession came increasingly close to realization in an act of physical love. But the dread of producing a child 'with a cartilaginous tail in the shape of a corkscrew and with a small tuft of hair on the tip' [1] prevented this time and again. Yet during the last phase of the Buendías' history, such a child was actually produced – 'the only one in a century who had been engendered with love'.[2] This culminating event in the family's history coincided with the decipherment (by the boy's father, Aureliano) of the mysterious manuscript.

Caught up in the predicament of being forced into a love that the threat of disaster frustrated, previous members of the Buendía family had tried to decipher the text and so to unravel the mystery of their fate, but to no avail. 'The letters looked like clothes hung out to dry on a line and they looked more like musical notation than writing.'[3] The breakthrough came only when Aureliano discovered that it was written in Sanskrit – a language he then learnt. But the moment he had read the last line of the text and uncovered the secrets of the Buendías' fate, their history came to an end: the boy with the pig's tail died. The final comprehension of the alien writing put an end to the isolation and solitude of the Buendías.

This powerful and uncanny story is told in the novel *One hundred years of solitude* by Gabriel García Márquez. It is not difficult to see in the figure of the gypsy, Melquíades, and his Sanskrit manuscript, a metaphor of India as the oracle that the West has been consulting in ever so many ways (I shall return to these at a later stage). At the same time, this metaphor allows me to suggest in a rather colourful manner what the following pages will be about. Specifically, it is about the religious culture of India and, more generally speaking, about that mysterious relationship between the development of one culture and the exploration of another. At the same time, speaking of metaphor here puts up a clear warning sign against taking the symbol of the oracle literally. The allegory tells us that an understanding of the mysteries of the East, of the oracle that contains the revelation of our destiny, or, in even more naive terms, of the truth, will only become possible at the moment when our destiny has itself reached its inexorable fulfilment; that the solitude of our own world can only be removed by our growing ability to divine our innermost drives; and that there can be no short-cut from lived, physical reality to an abstract code that anticipates its course. But in that case, an opponent might object, is not the real message to be derived from the allegory a different one? Does it not simply tell us that all the effort spent by the Buendías on deciphering the manuscript was merely a waste of time? What is the use of searching for the truth 'out there', if we can find it only by previously realizing it within ourselves? A fair comment, it would seem, and deserving of closer attention. But further opponents have gathered and insist on being heard first.

We live in the age of the computer, one of them tells us, where creativity is made available to us of such a totally different and superior kind that anything that the ancient cultures of the world have to offer dwindles to insignificance. Just look at the way we have broken down form and sound to their most atomic components, in the video and sound chips, and how we can dominate these in total freedom. Look at how completely new worlds have opened up – the culmination of a scientific culture! Ks and bytes and go-toing, saving and killing, software and disc drives are as much part of the everyday vocabulary of seven-year-olds as comics, lollies and Meccano were in a less modern age. Even the politicians are prepared to acknowledge that this is one of the very few areas where education can be relevant and useful. And, indeed, the educational advance here is staggering. As it said in one computer magazine: 'The eight- to ten-year-old kids of today prefer to write their own games' software than to depend on the old-fashioned stuff produced by senile fifteen-year-olds.' Thus, what possible relevance could such unscientific and obsolete matters as Indian religions have to the concerns of our society?

Further voices of opposition, particularly from the so-called Third World, make themselves heard. Some point out that the whole Orientalist enterprise is a Western, colonialist, capitalist affair. Advocates of the grand 'West=materialistic' versus 'East=spiritual' theory see it as basically analytical and incapable of reaching out to the inner, spiritual heart of the Eastern traditions. Or, related to this, the methods of scholarship are criticized. Our text-critical and historical approach is felt to impose a normative rigour ('the critical edition of the ur-text') on a live and multifarious development ('later interpolations that misunderstand and distort the original'). Others have seen it as escapism on our part: we pick and choose what we like, particularly 'safe' subjects like names of plants, inscriptions, or bits of old pottery, and call that 'studying another culture', without ever allowing ourselves to be challenged in our ways of looking at the world. From a different angle, the ridicule implied in the notion of 'primitive people' and in the way that live human beings have been treated like puppets or cog wheels in a machine, was seen as parallel to the degradation resulting from political and economic exploitation. Similarly, a link between this form of exploitation and our modes of research has been pointed out. We come, endowed with generous grants, look around and generally have a good time, and disappear to celebrate our victory with fame and fortune derived from the 'subject' we have researched. Others again resent our focus on spiritual matters and support the advocates of science and of progress. And perhaps most pressing in this array of voices is the resentment expressed against concepts like 'multi-culturalism', 'cultural development', 'acknowledging separate cultural identities' – for this is used in the propaganda of apartheid.

On the surface, many of the points made are contradictory, and some reveal, when analysed, a hidden basis in precisely the Western attitudes that are being criticized. But it would be obnoxious to try and play the *divide et impera* game here, by playing one against the other and letting them cancel each other out. Behind it all remains the irrefutable truth of a divide between a First and a Third World, an inequality in terms of power and standard of living between the two, and even a contempt of one for the other.

The traditional Indian art of disputation would require me to look at each of these objections, demolish them by means of clever counter-arguments and, somewhat repetitively, follow this up by stating my own position. I shall not do so here. For, had we questioned a Buendía about the value or usefulness of deciphering the manuscript, he would have answered: give me time, until I know what it actually says. Thus it is clear that the task being undertaken here – the exploration of the religious culture of India – will itself be part of any final counter-argument. Until that task is completed, we must shelve those objections, although some preliminary comments will be made in the course of this first chapter.

Unlike the Buendías, who as amateurs had to create their own methods of decipherment, anybody setting out to explore Indian culture can, and in fact must, make use of the tools that are already available. But this leads me to a semantic difficulty: how to label in more precise terms the discipline responsible for such an enterprise? Terms like indology, Indian Studies, Orientalism tend to confuse more than they clarify. Thus it is perhaps not surprising that sometimes it makes me wish I were a spy, secret agent, detective, doctor, second-hand-car dealer, don, or whatever. Not only because through endless works of fiction and films about such heroes of modern society everybody knows what they are doing and has a secret or open admiration for them. But also, because – on a more serious level – society has reflected on the role of these professionals and has laid out a range of observations as to the ethics or purpose of their occupation. No identity crisis here, but an enormous amount of often stimulating ideals! But there is no use in lamenting the absence of a thrilling TV series or popular novel on the work of an indologist or Indian anthropologist or comparative religionist. Instead, let me turn to the one novel that I do know and with which I have been confronting myself for more than twenty years now. Let me introduce you to Professor Peter Kien, by means of a pastiche of quotes and paraphrases.

He was 'a tall, emaciated figure, man of learning and specialist in sinology'.[4] Like a hermit, he kept himself aloof from the trivialities of ordinary life and common people. 'Knowledge and truth were for him identical terms. You draw closer to the truth by shutting yourself off from mankind. Daily life was a superficial clutter of lies.'[5] 'He knew more than a dozen oriental languages' – not to mention the European ones – and 'no branch of human literature was unfamiliar to him. He thought in quotations ... Countless texts owed their restoration to him.' When he encountered bad readings or corrupt passages 'in ancient Chinese, Indian or Japanese manuscripts, as many alternative readings suggested themselves for his selection as he could wish. Other textual critics envied him; he for his part had to guard against a superfluity of ideas. Meticulously cautious, he weighed up the alternatives month after month, was slow to the point of exasperation.'[6] Many chairs of Oriental philology were offered to him, but 'the genuine, creative research worker' that he was, he contemptuously left them to the 'unproductive popularizers'.[7] Equally contemptuous he was of those 'beer-swilling dullards, the general run of university students'.[8] Naturally he refused to attend conferences. But what he regarded as the greatest threat of all to the pursuit of serious scholarship was – woman. 'Kien repudiated the idea of a wife. Women had been a matter of indifference to him ... a matter of indifference they would remain.'[9] That is why he held nothing but contempt for his gynaecologist brother, George, who had turned psychiatrist. In his eyes, George lived for sensations, was a womanizer who chased from one novelty to another, without ever reaching any depth. When the brothers met, soon before the tragic climax of the novel, Peter told George: 'That is the difference between you and me. You live by your lunatics, I by my books ... I could live in a cell, I carry my books in my head. You need a whole lunatic asylum.'[10]

But it was Peter who was insane, and the steady growth of the mental disorder and delusion in this 'head without a world'[11] is the theme of Elias Canetti's novel. It was published originally (in 1935) in German under the title *Die Blendung* ('The Blinding'); the English translation of 1946 is called *Auto da Fé*. Professor Peter Kien is pure intellect, but deprived of application and impotent in more than one sense of the word. All his knowledge, all his books serve him to no further end than to lock himself up more and more hermetically in his own ego. The wisdom of the East is merely a tool in his hands to protect himself against the intrusions of the outside world. Thus, over more than eight pages,[12] he can quote all the Eastern classics on the pernicious role of woman. Yet the traumatic intrusion of the alien outside world he cannot prevent.

It all started with one fundamental miscalculation. For eight years Kien had kept Therese as a housekeeper, employed exclusively to dust his books. When he surprised her wearing gloves while reading the filthiest book in his large library – some kind of pulp novel from his early student days – he was so impressed by her combined respect for his books and zest for the learning contained in them, that he decided to marry her. After the perfunctory ceremony, so much of practical wisdom was left in his mind, that he remembered: marriage also involved consummation. To delay matters as long as possible, he filled the couch – the only place in his flat where such an event was practical – with lots of books. But Therese 'held up her little finger, crooked it menacingly and pointed at the divan. I must go to her, he thought, and did not know how ... What was he to do now – lie down on the books? He was shaking with fear, he prayed to the books, the last stockade. Therese caught his eye, she bent down and, with an all-embracing stroke of her left arm, swept the books on to the floor. He made a helpless gesture towards them, he longed to cry out, but horror choked him ... A terrible hatred swelled up slowly within him. This she had dared. The books!'[13] This was the shock from which he never recovered. The one thing he held sacred and loved, his books, had been violated, by the one thing he resented most: a woman. After that, this marriage turned into a nightmare for Kien. His obsession with the safety of first his, and then all books, increased steadily. His nightmares became filled with the sight of burning books, and in his attempts to save books from the devil – for he it was who burnt and ate books – he compared himself to the saviour Christ.[14] Were one to define the ultimate in absurdity, it would be – in the words of George Kien – Peter setting fire to himself and all his books.[15] Yet this is what happens at the end. George, who had come all the way from Paris to look after his ill brother, recreated the ideal external circumstances for Peter to carry on with his researches. However, the threats of the outside world became unbearable to Peter and the fire he lit to ward it off consumed him and his whole library.

Into this history of the madness that consumed an impotent, pure intellect, Canetti has woven further characters who realize their complementary nature to Peter Kien's. At a certain stage of their bizarre interactions, Therese actually threw Kien out of the flat, into 'the headless world'. Oblivious to his environment, he landed in the seedy underworld filled with prostitutes and crooks and people with their own bizarre dreams, delusions and fears. A hunchback, Fischerle – pimp, misogynist like Kien, shrewd and worldly-wise, competent chess-player with the ambition of becoming the world-champion and ultimately prevented by his own meanness from fulfilling his dream – attached himself to our lost professor. Protecting him in one way and exploiting him in another, he allowed Kien one insight which nevertheless remained without consequence: 'that Fischerle possessed precisely what he himself lacked, a knowledge of practical life, to its last ramifications'.[16] Shortly before his own murder, Fischerle sent a telegram to George in Paris, with the wonderfully simple message: 'Am completely crackers. [*Bin total meschugge.*] Your brother.'[17]

Peter's brother was a highly successful psychiatrist. His success derived from his remarkable talent of empathy. 'A rapid glance was enough. When he saw the slightest alteration, a mere crack which offered a possibility of sliding into the other's soul, he would act at once. Thus he lived simultaneously in numberless different worlds. Involuntarily he behaved to women as if he loved them. Surrounded and spoiled by innumerable women, all ready to serve him, he lived like Prince Gautama before he became the Buddha. He found the way to the wilderness in his twenty-eighth year.'[18] That was when he encountered a mentally ill man and was so impressed by him that he changed over to the study and cure of mental diseases.

Thus George is introduced to us as a man singularly endowed with the talent of entering into the minds of others and acting according to their liking – the gift of the playboy as much as of the psychiatrist. The title of the third part of the novel, 'The world in the head', might be meant for him. He himself offers us a comparison between George and Peter. 'If I were to ask you,' said George to his brother, '"tell me now, how did you fall into the hands of that woman [Therese]?", that you would not be able to do. You see it is just this kind of memory, which you lack, and which I possess – a memory for feelings, as I'd like to call it.'[19]

Thus, like Fischerle, but in a different way, George's personality is complementary to Peter's. But Canetti, at least in the subsequent words of George, goes further: 'Both together, a memory for feeling and a memory for facts – for that is what yours is – would make possible the universal man … If you and I could be moulded together into a single being, the result would be a spiritually complete man.'[20] But in the end, neither George nor Fischerle could help Peter.

I think what we have here are the outlines of a programme, both of its method and its possible contents. Behind the different complementary characters lies the problem of the relationship between intellect and emotion, between reflection and experience, and between the abstract, absolute and the concrete, particular. Once again we encounter here the dichotomy between the quest for truth or understanding or knowledge, and the realities of actual human life. An imaginary and obviously non-existent fourth part of Canetti's novel, which by the logic of the titles of the first three ought to be called 'Head in the world', suggests a kind of synthesis. Meticulous and accurate scholarship, combined with a playful imagination and empathy, and directed towards the 'practical life, to its last ramifications' – this would make the ideal indology. 'Head in the world' would mean: an analytical, engaged and self-reflecting preoccupation with the lives of real people and their pursuits of power, love and wisdom. It would mean to aim for the moment of total decipherment, when love replaces lust and coercion, when the walls of solitude come crumbling down and when self-destructive madness is averted through total self-reflection.

It is a grand and fascinating programme that could be extricated from Canetti's novel. To this kind of empathetic scholarship few people could object. It is also an ideal that nobody can actually achieve. Nevertheless, like the belief that the manuscript could explain the agonizingly mysterious fate, or the belief in some ultimate, immutable truth 'out there', such an ideal methodology might stimulate aspirations towards it. In the course of moving closer towards it, something of what is aimed for might become actualized. It is easy enough to see where Peter Kien went wrong. But it is much more difficult to do better than him. How can we empathize with a totally alien culture? How can we prevent ourselves from imposing an order, a structure, a rigidity upon it that is merely the product of our own solitary or neurotic minds? It seems worth looking at these questions in greater detail, for it would be disappointing if, at the end of our journey, we found that we had missed most of the important sights, or discovered that we had got completely lost. At the same time, it is only fair to tell any potential traveller, before he begins the journey, what to expect and what the route is going to be.

The journey will take us to India, the original home of the gypsy and of Sanskrit, the language he chose for his secret message – the India also of many of the texts so ingeniously reconstructed by Professor Peter Kien. That it is not the whole of India, or all of its cultures, will become apparent presently. Nor will it be each and every facet of this fascinating country that we shall be looking at. Neither its steam-engines, nor its many kinds of exotic birds; neither the motifs on its many types of saris, nor its immensely variegated cuisine will be our concern. Our journey will take us into the religions native to India.

Now it is easy to point at a particular building and state that it is a Hindu temple. But the minute we start asking questions, we seem to be drawn into a bottomless pit. 'What is the difference between a "temple" and a "church"?' 'What makes a Hindu temple different from a Jain one?' 'What is the "philosophy" of temple worship?' 'Why does a Hindu go into a temple?' 'What is the meaning of life for a temple-visiting Hindu?' By now it should be clear that by choosing religion, instead of looking at saris or travelling in steam-trains, we have chosen the most difficult of all possible topics.

One difficulty lies in the fact that the 'religious individual' is a totally closed book to us. We cannot directly look into the mind or heart of a Buddha, a Śaṅkara, or of any other person we may see visiting a temple or meditating. But here something can come to our assistance – what I shall call 'culture'.

The religious individual is not closed off against the world and the society in which he lives. In a dual manner, he is open in relation to these. Logically, prior to any 'religious experience', he has received from society a whole host of symbols, concepts and spontaneous emotive associations connected with these. They flow into his experience and flavour it and provide a social or 'cultural' dimension to it. Nobody could even identify in his own consciousness a religious experience, had he not learnt from society the words, and their meaning, of 'experience' and 'religious'. This example also shows that, naturally, 'culture' encompasses a much wider range of words, concepts and symbols than what we would call 'religious'.

But many such religious individuals do not merely draw on their culture; they also attempt to express something of their own inner life (the area closed to any direct observation) to that culture. In simple terms, they speak and tell others about it, and thus once again make use of such cultural factors as language and symbols. In addition, they may well subtly alter something in that culture itself. But we can envisage much more complex cases of such a radiation of the religious life into society and its culture. Many individuals, operating in the same milieu, may well give rise to very elaborate new cultural expressions, for example the construction of temples along with the development of the concept 'temple' that presupposes such building activities.

It is not difficult to see how culture in this situation can be made use of for our purpose of exploring religion. Unlike the inner life of the religious individual, these cultural surroundings allow for at least a partial scrutiny by us. Thus, like Aureliano, we could learn Sanskrit, and there are more Indian religious texts in our libraries than we can hope to read in a lifetime. Here lie the print-outs of the system's input and output, and by studying them carefully we should be able to gain an understanding of the system itself.

While in principle such an approach appears feasible, we must face up to some technical problems. As defined here, culture is the wider term: out of all possible cultural features, only a limited amount would be 'religious'. We might now be tempted to impose uncritically the criteria of our Western culture as to what is religious and what is not, on to the Indian cultural material. But even if we assumed that we could thereby discover immediately obvious correlations, we still ought to ask the question whether this does justice to the ideal scholarly programme established previously. That means – if I am permitted to play with words – we ought to consider the possibility that the dichotomy of (secular) culture versus the 'religious' is itself in that form a culture-specific affair. In other words, it might well be possible that, to an Indian, cultural features are in fact 'religious' which our criteria would pick up as 'secular'. The fact that so much written about Hinduism or Buddhism in books of the 'Religious Studies' genre reads like a parody of some form of Christianity may well be due to such a naive projection of our criteria on to the Indian material. At the same time, let me emphatically state that nothing like the equally naive claim that every aspect of Indian culture is 'religious' is implied in this.

This is the second instance where homing in on 'culture', and not directly on 'religion', will prove its usefulness. In order to avoid missing out on important and fascinating aspects of what, to the Indian, would belong to the religious dimension of his culture, but not by our standards of neatly compartmentalizing the secular and the religious, I shall survey the widest possible range of cultural constructs. If I have erred, I hope it is on the side of offering more than what an Indian may regard as strictly religious. Detours that are enjoyable in their own right are preferable to neurotic revulsion at the unfamiliar.

At this point it may be appropriate to look more closely at what I actually mean by this apparently quite useful entity 'culture'. In the widest and most generous application given to the term here, it denotes all forms of human interaction with, and imposition of control upon, the natural environment, motivated by the need for survival and security. Moreover, it denotes the pursuit of comfort and pleasure and, at its highest, least physical level, the quest for understanding and for the meaning of this whole enterprise. It is easy enough to see how for our purposes we can derive from this the three themes of power, love and wisdom. Were we to regard merely the third theme as directly related to religion, we would miss out most of the material found in the sections on love and power – a considerable loss in my opinion. How this could work in practice, and also how this relates to the problematic relationship between the secular and the religious, the following example may illustrate. It is the famous or notorious 'caste-system'. It certainly fulfils our definition of a cultural phenomenon. It offers a well-demarcated place for an individual and defines his individual responsibilities, rights and religious role. Thereby it protects him against an environment that otherwise would threaten his identity and his very survival. Thus it can be described as a socially evolved and shared mode of coming to terms primarily with survival and security. But the role of religion in this is quite ambivalent. On the one hand, it appears to justify the system, which refers to it as its authorizing agent. (Chapter 4 will furnish material for this.) But, on the other hand,

India did not have to wait until the arrival of Christian missionaries to produce critics of the system. From within the Indian tradition, religious personalities and movements arose that for *religious* reasons rejected the system – the Buddha, the Mahāvīra, Basavaṇṇa, Cakradhar and Gurū Nānak, to name but a few. Given this position of the 'religious' *vis-à-vis* the caste-system, it appears appropriate to keep the two separate, naturally with the corollary that the 'religious' itself has to be further differentiated in such situations.

It may be asked whether I am using a 'native category system' when speaking of the themes of power, love and wisdom. The answer is simple: I am not. Anybody even vaguely familiar with Indian material will feel sympathy for the agonies of somebody trying to present material on India in three parts. Groups of three complementary concepts are legion in Indian thought, and it would have been so obvious to use one of them. After endless trials, I gave up and decided on the present classification. Naturally, there are many other ways of dissecting the reality in which we live and, accordingly, innumerable other ways of organizing our Indian sources. My concern has merely been to find something that allows for easy access and identifiability. Even without demonstrating it here, the two novels I have referred to could profitably be analysed with the help of our three key concepts. That, I believe, demonstrates their usefulness. And there is one advantage in not using a native schema of classification. Traditionally, our view of the Indian material has been through the package that the Indian pundits of the eighteenth and nineteenth centuries put together in their attempt to conceptualize their heritage. It has served us well, but the time has come to try to go beyond it. We have come to realize that what they gave us possesses an in-built ideological bias – it was normative, not descriptive. Moreover, it was extremely selective. By ignoring here the various '-isms' and classifications we have become used to, it becomes possible to bring together once again the India of the indologist and the India of the anthropologist – that means the high and the low, the supra-regional and the local –which were at the point of becoming mutually unrecognizable. Also, it can only be hoped that the India of much of the current Religious Studies enterprise eventually finds its way back to the reality which it claims to depict.

The programme suggested here aims to study the widest possible range of the Indian religions empathetically. But it is clearly difficult for us to make sense of, or relate to, a god who has a blue complexion, commits adulterous love with hundreds of women, and creates replicas of all of them to keep their own husbands happy in bed. Or a god who runs around naked, chasing the innocent wives of pious ascetics and reveals his full manliness in the process. Or the opposite, for which we are even less prepared: god as a woman. A woman so horrific that she uses blood as her make-up, bones as her ornaments, drinks out of a skull as her cup, and carries a severed head in her hand. No, I agree, it is not easy to relate to this kind of material. We have known about it for nearly two hundred years, and have tried hard to discover its meaning and significance. There is no need here to mention the well-known general interpretations in terms of 'worship of personified natural forces', 'celebration of tribal cohesion', 'totemism', or 'projection of a stern father-figure'. Different modes of potty-training have been adduced as explaining different cultural developments, and the relatively late weaning of Indian children has been suggested as the cause of the Goddess's gruesome nature. Structuralism in its various forms – which are now almost as numerous as the sand grains on the bank of the Ganges – has been projected on this kind of material. – Yet can it be said that we 'understand' it now? That we can actually enter into the minds and hearts of those Hindus to whom those gods and goddesses were meaningful? I don't think it can; or better, I think there is still considerable scope for improvement, and the present exploration aims to contribute to it.

For here we can see the third instance of the usefulness of culture. The mind of a Buddha may be as incomprehensible to us as the Sanskrit manuscript was to the first Buendías, the god figures mentioned may be as revolting to some as Therese was to Peter Kien, but surely nobody could deny that power, love and wisdom are categories of universal human experience. However much the study of the finer details in different cultures may take us apart, at least we find here some initial common ground and a real basis for empathy. In that case, the Orientalist's methods would cease to be humiliating for the 'subjects' that he studies, and divisive due to a dichotomy between the different humanities of 'modern' and 'primitive' man. Thereby we would take seriously the critique some of the opponents brought to bear on our enterprise.

At this point let me introduce two actual travellers and eavesdrop into their conversation about other cultures. That they are Indians (though not quite in the normal sense of this description) and actually commenting on Western culture, should make it all the more interesting for us. At least in fiction, India knew of the aeroplane or, better, something like our helicopter, because it was possible to see things on earth while travelling in one of these machines (called *vimāna*). One day two superhuman beings, two *yakṣas*, decide to go sightseeing and take a good look at the world of men. They make a weird pair, complementing the cynicism and emotional rigidity of the one (Kṛśānu) with the almost romantic enthusiasm and exuberance of the other (Viśvāvasu). When they have traversed, in an extraordinary criss-cross pattern, northern India (fuel prices did not affect the workings of such a *vimāna*), they arrive above the town of Madras. Since the poem – *The Mirror of the World's Qualities* (*Viśvaguṇādarśa-campū*) – was written around 1650, it is the Madras that has recently made the acquaintance of the British, after an occupancy of the Portuguese. Viśvāvasu, being a religious person, delights in the sight of Pārthasārathī, that is, Kṛṣṇa in the famous temple of that name. It is his praise of the learned brahmins associated with the temple that makes the bilious Kṛśānu disagree with him. He points out that the place is not at all idyllic and wonderful and suffers from one fundamental disease. 'It is far too close to the town crowded with undesirable people – with Huns [Hūṇas, *sic*!] totally devoid of any good qualities. It is almost impossible on earth to find people more despicable than these Europeans. Knowing no compassion, and without respect for the brahmins, they are vile, and their vices go beyond all words.'[21]

He puts the blame in no uncertain terms on the Creator who brought about a situation where 'incomparable rulership over the earth is given to the filthy Hūṇas, and the righteous and learned have to beg for a living'.[22] An early statement of the colonial experience, you might call this. But our poet makes Viśvāvasu reply to this. 'Now look! Even among those people you find virtue acknowledged. They do not steal from, nor do they tell lies to, each other. They have their own rules for punishing those who commit crimes. You must accept these qualities – however much they may be contemptuous of virtue otherwise!'[23]

That means, look at them in their own right, on their own terms, and you will find an ordered society there, an autonomous cultural system. This is indeed a fine example of a balanced assessment of an alien world! Viśvāvasu has one more point to make, and unknowingly hints at the one factor that, more than any other, accounts for the misery of the Third World. What he invites his pessimistic friend to admire is that these Europeans 'build wonderful things'[24]. It may not have been the computer of the twentieth century but the mechanical clocks of the seventeenth, not Exocet missiles but firearms, not the Rolls-Royce or the Mercedes but a musical box – yet the fascination for these wonders of science is there. It is only a short way from such a fascination to the readiness to buy them at great cost. (For the record it should perhaps be mentioned that our two aerial travellers do not land in Madras and sign some development contract or enter into an arms-deal. Instead they do what all good tourists in Madras do even today: they proceed to look at the temples in Kāñcīpuram.)

Before we can begin our own adventure trip, some loose ends will have to be tidied up. Precisely what kind of India are we going to explore? What kind of route can we derive from the three themes of power, love and wisdom? And what can we do about the voices of opposition that, at least for the time being, ought to be quietened?

There are many Indias, and we shall not pass through all of them. It would easily fill a whole chapter just trying to define the different kinds of levels and regional variations in Indian culture and to circumscribe the different periods in its history and the interaction with and absorption of new, alien elements that characterize these periods. Such influences have come from the Greek world and from Central Asia, from the Christian and Jewish Near East, quite significantly from Islam, and finally from Europe. For reasons of my own competence, no such ambitious project is envisaged here. Thus what we shall be looking at is 'traditional', in the sense of 'pre-Islamic', India. However, this is not simply a chronological definition, for even today such an entity can still be observed in certain milieux of the country. There are many more religions in India than the following pages will deal with; to 'traditional India' belong those that have been native to the country. Popularly though misleadingly, these native religions are gathered together under the three headings of Hinduism, Buddhism and Jainism. But these three '-isms' are not particularly useful as signposts for our journey. In fact, one of the main purposes of the present exploration is to substitute for them a genuine *typology*. We shall soon find that for each of our three themes of power, love and wisdom a whole series of clearly distinct types of religious beliefs and practices can be gathered together, types for which labels like 'Hindu' or 'Buddhist' provide merely secondary subdivisions. Thus what follows is not yet another futile attempt at stating what 'the Hindu' or 'the Buddhist' believes and does in his religion. Instead, it wants to establish a spectrum of the whole range of different types of religious pursuits. But let me warn you: the result of this undertaking does not produce a neat and tidy situation, with all the different types hanging like different dresses from a rail. They are far more like features of a landscape that gradually change their appearance as we walk through it. The three themes make up the route we shall follow through this landscape.

But what about those voices of protest which still deserve to be taken into consideration? These were the issues they raised: the relationship between the Orientalist enterprise and the Third World, the relevance of 'pre-modern' matters in a scientific age, and – on the most abstract level – the problem of an incomprehensible truth 'out there'. They are actually so closely intertwined that I shall look at them together.

For the Buendías, the Sanskrit document written by Melquíades was like an oracle; yet their attempts to read it, to find out about their destiny from it, bore success only at the point when that destiny itself had been lived through. But this is the point at which a paradox appears. For those endless days spent in the gypsy's old room by members of the last two generations poring over his ancient text – those days and all their struggle and frustration were themselves part of that destiny. Similarly, Western civilization has been involved in 'deciphering' Indian culture for hundreds of years. Most of the testimony of this shared destiny may still lie buried in learned journals or in the unconscious recesses of our minds, but it is abundant. What would our childhood have been like without the stories of Sindbad the Sailor? Yet what we get here is an Arab transmission of Indian sea-farer tales, minus the ideological, religious frame in which India has preserved them. Many other stories have entered our literature, without ever being acknowledged as having an Indian origin. Thousands and thousands of pages of this material is available, and yet the Penguin Classics include not a single work. Or what about the spices that impelled a fifteenth century Europe to find a way to India, and the fundamental changes this produced in our own world? Tantalizing visions might open themselves up about the impact of Buddhist philosophy on the shaping of a Muslim theology, which then in the company of Aristotle travelled to Spain and triggered off medieval scholasticism. Could a comparative philology, or even general linguistics, have been developed without the acquaintance of a purely descriptive and totally formalized, not to say computerized, Sanskrit grammar produced by Pāṇiṇi in the fourth century BC? History of religion and comparative religion have drawn heavily on the Indian material. Or look at the elaborate discussions of the nature of religion which have been brought about by the troublesome outsider, Buddhism (or, even more so, Jainism, had this latter religion been taken into consideration)! Must not the work of Richard Burton and Arthur Avalon have had an influence on creating a milieu in which it was possible for D. H. Lawrence, Henry Miller, James Joyce and many others to write and explore an area of human nature that until then 'one did not talk about'? These ramifications are more important for the texture of European civilization than the colonial experience that has found such lavish treatment in British literature. The success of recent films like *Gandhi* or *Passage to India* demonstrates that, even at present, Britain draws on India, just as a sizeable group of people in the West looks at forms of Indian religion as providers of ultimate meaning and fulfilment. And as a final point: the Indian reality has moved right on to our own doorstep, through the presence of real live Indians who are now full members of our society. Their children, born here, go to school and are being taught by their teachers what it means to be a Hindu or a Sikh. Thus is it necessary to labour the point that a preoccupation with India is a relevant and useful enterprise?

On a superficial level, this multifarious interaction with India has given rise to a mystique of things Indian that may express itself in the belief that India has preserved the primordial, eternal truth. Such a perception literalizes the allegory of the oracle (against which I warned earlier). Let us nevertheless see what happened at the ancient oracle. Well, it may have provided specific messages, but its overall programme was proclaimed in writing and clearly visible to all who came to consult it: *gnõthi seautón* – 'come to know yourself'. This is our grand paradox: fulfilment can only lie in what we are (and that also in a very down-to-earth sense), and yet the realization of this needs an outsider to tell us – the oracle, the novelist, the experience of an alien culture and religion. Were the outsider we had to face nothing but our own mirror image, we could learn nothing. Thus the modern India with its atomic bombs, factories, its belief in science, and its brides burnt in faked accidents due to an unharnessed obsession with consumer goods, is remarkably like our own world. (On the other hand, the mystique of the totally other, incomprehensible East makes it so different that we cannot expect to learn anything from it.) The India of the pre-modern age is indeed different enough and yet not, as my programme wants to show, totally alien, to provide the *thaumázein*, the 'being wonder-struck' which is the beginning of philosophy according to the ancient Greeks. I hope that the following pages can spread out a vista of wonders which is sufficiently striking to make us reflect on our own pursuits of power, love and wisdom. For that is what the *philosophía* of the Greeks wanted to be: critical self-reflection.

Now such a self-exploration must involve, as one of the central questions, the role of science in our culture. The philosophers of science, its historians, the post-structuralists – however much they may differ between themselves – have begun to tell us that science lies with us firmly embedded in a non-scientific ground. This does not invalidate the scientific method, if by this we mean a rational and healthy interest in exploring things systematically, reflecting on them logically, and aiming at an accurate, empathetic, understanding. But it means that 'science' cannot be made into a final goal or isolated absolute. A clear example is our computer buff. The enormous fascination the home-computer has generated, which makes psychologists already talk about the danger of addiction in school children and of marriages ruined by it, is not 'scientific'. The thrill of writing a program or of playing a computer game is something totally non-scientific. And I cannot help feeling that those other computer specialists who work on a different kind of Star Wars game, share that same primal and non-scientific thrill. Neither the imaginative dreams that trigger off the pursuit of science, nor the use to which we put the end-product (such as the computer in my example) could be described as 'scientific'. Given the fact that there is already a computer game called 'Arabian Nights', one could speculate that Indian material also is on the verge of becoming respectable in the imaginative drive of our computer expert. In that case we are surely allowed to explore it for more serious matters!

All this talk of 'self', of 'our' and of 'we' may sound very egocentric. What about the predicament of the Third World? Instead of getting committed, we seem to be drawing on it again merely for our own enrichment and pleasure, just as we use India as an exotic backdrop for the heroic feats of a James Bond or an Indiana Jones. But I believe that such an increasingly critical self-awareness, which is envisaged here, will automatically have an increasingly positive effect on the Third World. Not just in terms of more charity, of doing more things there but, far more importantly, in terms of learning where not to mess around and interfere, of learning to accept differences as legitimate alternatives in a common human pursuit and not demolishing them as Satanic creations.

This whole discussion can actually be reduced to a single issue. The study of another culture must not be like the analysis and description of a piece of stone, but like listening in to a conversation.[25] But by listening to what others have to say to each other and, I dare add, by studying the modes in which they carry out their own critical self-reflection, we may well achieve something of the *gnõthi seautón* of the ancient oracle. Nobody, in whatever social or political climate, could argue that a culture without self-reflection would be worth living in. At the same time, as I have claimed earlier, culture encompasses more than such abstract matters of the mind. It offers also enjoyment, and I hope that journey to mysterious worlds undertaken here will support us with nourishing sips from an ocean of milk and a sea of treacle.

CHAPTER 2

Oceans of milk and treacle

In 1835 the historian Macaulay investigated whether there was anything in the traditional Indian systems of learning and education that could be used in the training of native personnel. In fairness to Mr Macaulay, we must remember that those were days long before the writings of a Tolkien or a Mervyn Peake. He came to the devastating conclusion that people who believe in oceans of milk and treacle had nothing to offer to a modern system of education. A straightforward, realistic assessment in an age that believed in science and realism! The effects were far-reaching. Traditional Indian ways of looking at the world were written off as obsolete. India was provided with three universities (Calcutta, Bombay and Madras, founded in 1857) as the hothouses to nurture a custom-built, English-speaking Indian intelligentsia. A new age began for India, and two of its inevitable consequences were the demand for independence and the production of atomic bombs and satellites by the post-independent Bhārat.

Historical developments carry their own justification and I am not going to argue with Mr Macaulay. Instead, I would like to introduce you now to a lady. Perhaps in a different age and with the feminine touch she may bring to bear on the issue, our own perception of those marvellous oceans might be different. It is the World Woman, as she is known among the Jains. In terms of our own metaphorical journey, this is one way of presenting the 'landscape' that we are going to explore, as seen through the eyes of the 'natives' (see Figure 1). Our earth is located in the centre, precisely in the lady's middle. The upper half of her body contains increasingly ethereal realms which we might want to call 'heavens'. Her head reaches up to the top of the universe. Below her middle lie many levels of underground realms and of infernal torture chambers.

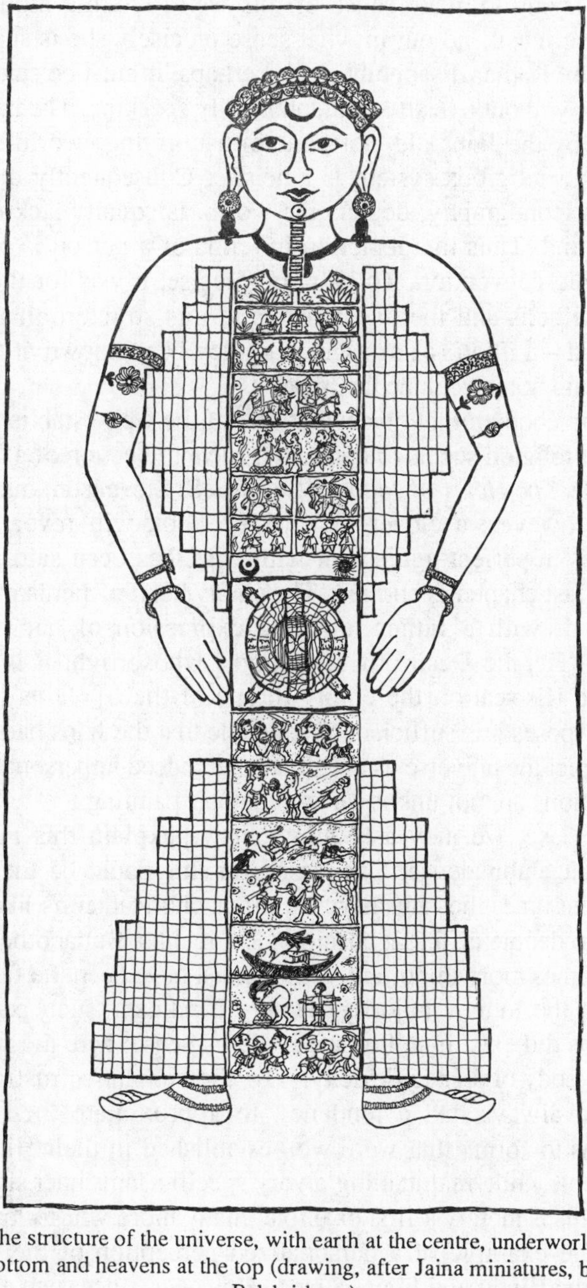

Figure 1. The structure of the universe, with earth at the centre, underworlds and hells at the bottom and heavens at the top (drawing, after Jaina miniatures, by Isobel Balakrishnan)

Before trying to make sense of this weird-looking model of the universe, we must find out in what sense precisely she is supposed to be a woman. Rather disappointingly, perhaps, it must be said that she is a woman without a heart – metaphorically speaking. The universe as envisaged by the Jains did not contain a unifying 'world-soul', for Jainism as a religious system is atheistic. Consequently the woman that, in its iconography, depicts the world, is equally lacking in any divine ground. Thus the depiction in terms of a person is merely an iconographic convention. To be more precise, it was for the sake of locating the hells and the underworlds in this structure that a 'skirt' was required – a *dhoti* (or trousers, had they been known at that time) simply would not have done the trick.

Now somebody might object that one of the well-established books on the Jain religion seems to contradict such a rejection of a 'heart' by its very title *The Heart of Jainism* (by Mrs S. Stevenson, published in 1915).[1] However, a closer look at the book will reveal that the authoress is in perfect agreement with what has been said about the Jains. Her last chapter is entitled 'The empty heart of Jainism', and she concludes it with a rather touching expression of her hope that eventually 'He, the Desire of all nations, whose right it is to reign, [shall] take His seat on the empty throne of their [=Jains'] hearts'.[2] For our purposes it is sufficient to conclude that the Jains had really no need to depict the universe as a woman, and indeed impersonal, abstract representations are not unknown among their paintings.

In that case, we may ask, how can we explain this misleading iconographic ambivalence? One reason for this could be the fact that since ancient times the Jains have used metaphorical terms like 'middle' or 'head' to denote different cosmological realms. But another, and for medieval times more important, reason must have been the fact that on the side of the Indian majority, namely Hinduism, such personalized conceptions did exist in a thoroughly literal sense: here the world was indeed the body of a specific deity.[3] To the scholar's frustration, the Jains have always had a tendency to approximate their external expressions to forms that were well-established in their Hindu (etc.) environment, while maintaining a very specific Jain inner significance of them. This is merely a first example; many more will follow. Figure 2 offers one example of a personalized perception of the universe, involving the Hindu god figure Kṛṣṇa. However, since such a vision of

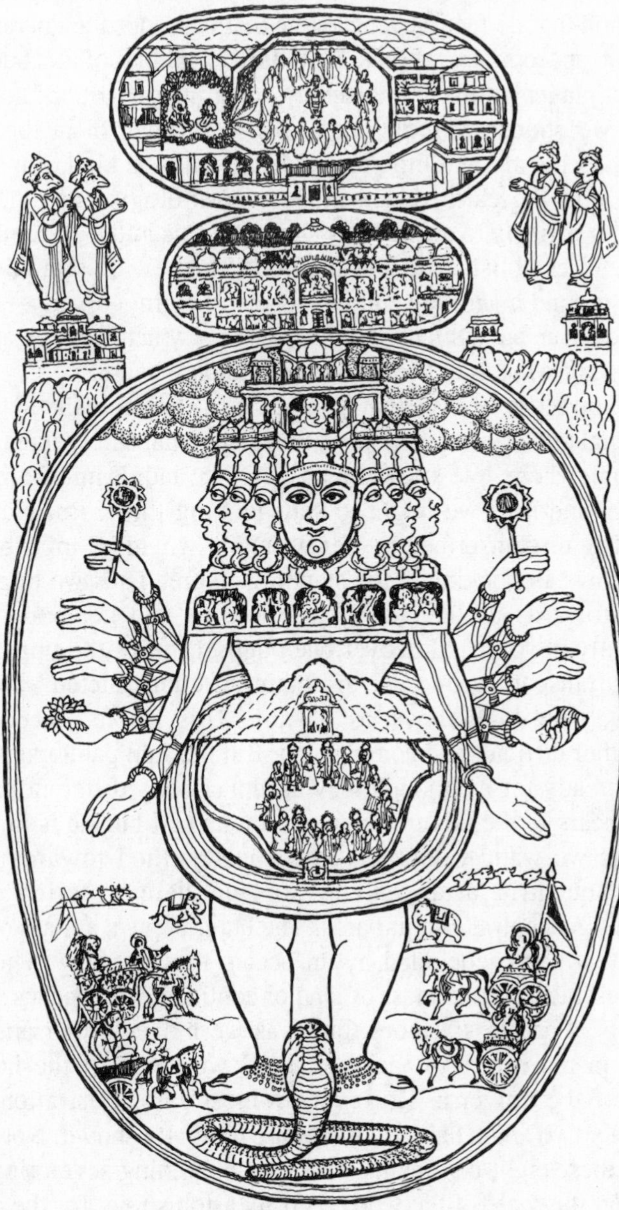

Figure 2. The cosmic Kṛṣṇa, showing earth (in the region of his stomach) and the heavens at the top, both with their (earthly and eternal) round-dances (drawing, after Hindu miniatures, by Isobel Balakrishnan)

the cosmos as the god's body implies the presence of a pulsating heart or soul, and that de facto means a love that pervades the universe, such images are appropriately discussed in the second part of this book.

A first glance at this extraordinary construction (it does not matter, whether we choose to look at the World Woman or at the abstract diagram) seems to yield little resemblance with the kind of map of the universe and the earth that a modern cosmologist, astronomer, or geographer is likely to draw. Thus already at this initial stage, the grand programme established in the previous chapter, of searching for a common ground in an alien culture, seems to be in jeopardy. However, all it needs is an adjustment of the angle from which we look at it and a knowledge of what finer details we should home in on.

Common sense tells us that it might be rather unrealistic to expect to find England or Europe on this ancient map; but surely India ought to figure somewhere. We know already that the lady's middle represents our earth, and thus we ought to start looking there. But clearly this central disc circumscribed by her waistline would be invisible to us, given that we are looking at the standing figure. Thus we ought to tilt the lady towards us, her head closest to us and her body floating horizontally in space. Moreover, we ought to make the upper half of her body transparent, in order to obtain an unobstructed view of her waist-disc from high above, as it were. This whole procedure may sound rather difficult and complicated. But the Jain painters have done all this already for us, though they used a slightly different procedure. What appears in the picture as an enormous belt buckle is in fact that same disc we want to look at, conveniently tilted towards us. In a neatly concentric arrangement, we see here a series of rings surrounding a central circular area. The latter depicts a mass of land, a continent, which is encircled by an ocean, the first ring. The second ring represents a second mass of land or continent, and oceans and ring-continents alternate six more times, as we move further and further away from the centre of the disc, until we come to the horizontal frontier of the universe. However, in most Jain illustrations of the genre, only two and a half continents are normally shown. Not only the shape of these eight continents with the intervening seven ring-oceans is striking: the scale of the whole is truly astonishing, for the diameter is measured in many millions of miles.

Clearly the scale of this map is far too large for our purposes, and we must focus on a much smaller segment. Figure 3 offers us such a greatly enlarged section. All ancient maps from different parts of the globe tend to depict a central area that is fairly accurate in geographical terms, because it corresponds to the known and travelled realm of the cartographer. Around this we find increasingly spurious and imaginary areas known only from hearsay or derived from pure speculation. But if

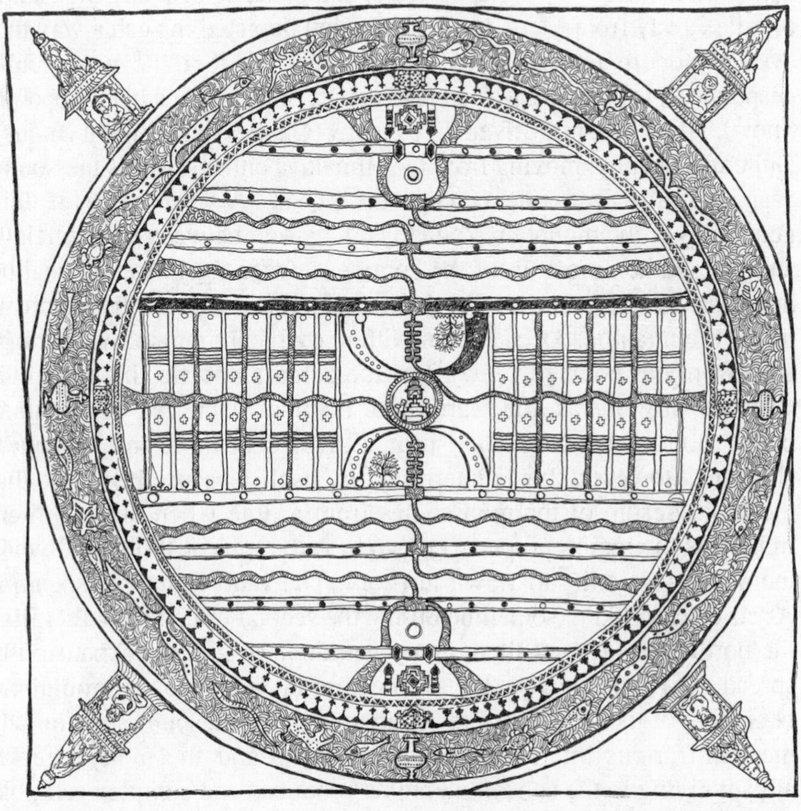

Figure 3. Map of the central portion of earth (drawing, after Jaina miniatures, by Isobel Balakrishnan)

we applied this principle to our map, we would end up in a most extraordinary region which would yield no more to our present search than the name of the whole central disc-continent. Here, at the centre of the whole earth, stands a gigantic mountain (called Meru or Sumeru) which props up the heavenly realms above and which is many millions of feet high. An equally gigantic rose-apple tree (*jambu*) grows on a secondary mountain near Meru, and it is from this tree that the whole central continent derives its name: Jambudvīpa, the 'Island [=continent] of the Rose-Apple Tree'.

Instead of focusing on the centre, we have to search for India in a location of extreme marginality: in the far south of the disc (the directional orientation of the map happens to coincide with the conventions of our own maps). Here, at a distance of many thousands of miles away from Meru, we find a region depicted in such a way that even a modern tourist could find his way on it, if he were really desperate. It is here that we can read names of mountains like 'Abode of Snow', Himalaya, or of rivers like Gaṅgā (Ganges) and Sindhu (Indus). Quite realistically, moving from the Himalaya either towards the south-east or south-west, one reaches the ocean. A peculiarity of Jain geography is the mountain Vaitāḍhya, half-way between the Himalaya and the southernmost tip of the continent. Once again we are dealing here less with resonances of vague travellers' accounts of the Vindhyas or the mountainous Deccan than with a mythical, imaginary realm (at least from our point of view). For the Jains associate this mountain with the *vidyādharas*, the 'carriers of magical sciences', superhuman beings about whom we shall hear a great deal more in subsequent chapters. However, this is interesting by itself, because it reveals that the basic design of the map comes from a time when only northern India was the region properly known in geographical terms and when the south was still unknown territory. The Indo-European-speaking Āryas entered India (sometime during the second millennium BC) from the north-west. It took them many centuries of gradual expansion to spread their culture over the whole region, which only around the beginning of the Common Era began to include the south. It is, in fact, the multifarious interaction of these Āryas and the many peoples already living in the subcontinent that produced the complex religious culture we are exploring here.

The enormous mass of land of the central continent of Jambudvīpa is divided by impassable mountain ranges (the Himalaya is one of them) into *varṣas* or 'regions'. The land south of the Himalaya, where we could discover India, is called Bhāratavarṣa, the country of the mythical culture-hero Bharata.[4] Given that the ancient map for this region encompasses an area far wider than what is commonly called 'India', the territorial claims implied in the modern name of the state of Bhārat are somewhat ambitious!

The whole of Jambudvīpa is surrounded by an ocean; nothing special about this one, because it consists of salt water. Islands with strange people are scattered over it. This ocean is now, in turn, surrounded by more land, this time in the shape of a ring-continent. The same pattern repeats itself seven times, and it is here that the oceans become interesting. Consecutively, they are supposed to contain: black water, crystal-clear water, rum, milk, ghee, and treacle. That on most of the pictures only two and a half of these continents are shown has its rationale in Jain belief that these are the only areas where proper human beings can live. Naturally, all the ring-continents have names, and innumerable details about their trees, animals, inhabitants, conditions of life, geography, etc. are mentioned in the texts. Only then do we come to the end of the world, where the earth touches the non-world. However, this is not merely empty space, for, according to Jain belief, the whole cosmic woman is enclosed by layers of matter.

Whether we look at Jain or Hindu or Buddhist maps of the earth, the details may vary, even within each tradition. But the basic ideas, the shapes of the regions, and even many names, are similar or identical. So we may briefly turn to a prestigious Hindu text, in order to explore a little further those magical *varṣas* beyond the Himalaya, without thereby leaving our basic cultural construct. Here[5] we are told that the central mountain Sumeru is surrounded by four less lofty secondary mountains. Each one has a gigantic tree growing on it. Thus Mount Mandara (towards the east) carries a mango tree; its enormous fruits, when fully ripe, drop to the ground and, squashed by their fall, give rise to a large stream of mango juice that runs all the way to the eastern ocean and, naturally, delights all beings that live in the *varṣas* through which it flows. Similarly, from the cavities of a gigantic *kadamba* tree towards the west of Sumeru originate five streams filled with honey. But truly paradisiacal is the river that flows out of the trunk of the banyan tree towards the northern sea. Every imaginable luxury item can be fished out of its waters, from milk, sugar and rice to clothes, jewellery, chairs and sofas. But what about us who live in the realm south of Sumeru? We also get at least a hint of those paradises beyond the Himalaya. From the fruits of the rose-apple tree already mentioned springs forth a mighty river whose water, when dried up, becomes the gold we all cherish so much. Thus gold is the one link we have with those other *varṣas* which are appropriately called 'heavens on earth'. Yet it is only here in Bhāratavarṣa, where life is anything but paradisiacal, that man has any control over his fate. What gold, the residue of paradise, may be for the powerful men of the world, the chance to gain the ultimate power over our destiny, is here the privilege of everybody.

There is no need to prolong this brief excursion to a Hindu variation on our theme; the details we could look at would reveal no more than minor differences (our text tells us that only in one *varṣa*, and not in three, man has influence over his destiny; that there are nine, instead of seven, *varṣas*; and that it knows of an ocean of curds and another of wine). So let us return to the Jain World Woman. We can now tilt her middle back to its natural horizontal position and venture a look at other parts of her anatomy; we may begin by moving upwards.

Ascending the enormous Meru mountain, we find steep slopes alternating with flat plateaux. The latter are covered with wonderful parks and heavenly palaces. Different types of non-human beings live here – the lower classes of the *devas*. To translate *deva* as 'god' and the palaces and parks in which they live as 'heavens' is more misleading than helpful. Religious connotations are evoked for something which, on the Indian side, is understood to belong to the natural order. The inordinate fun the poets seem to be making of these 'gods' because of their often all-too-human follies and weaknesses is ample proof of this. Human beings are permitted into these regions on Mount Meru only in quite exceptional circumstances; the *devas*, on the other hand, pay frequent visits to the world of man, often very much in the manner of a Zeus.

When we approach the peak of Meru, we enter the realm of the sun and the moon, the planets and the stars. Although they form the object of study of the astronomer, they are not liveless chunks of matter, but embodied beings – beings who have the power to influence and to interfere with the lives of men. The higher we move upwards, beyond the realm of the stars, the more ethereal and incorporeal everything becomes. This can already be seen by the fact that female *devas* (*devīs*) are born only into the two lowest storeys. They can still visit the *devas* as far up as the eighth storey. But the 'gods' of the ninth to twelfth storeys do not require their physical presence any longer. Thinking about them in their minds is sufficient for them to obtain total satisfaction. Incidentally, it may be mentioned here that on the Hindu side such overt sexism is at least minimally compensated for in another realm. In one of the 'heavens on earth' (the Ilāvṛtavarṣa) only women are allowed to live. Any man trying to enter will instantly turn into a woman.[6]

With the twelfth storey we have reached the lady's neck. Quite appropriately, the next nine higher 'heavens' are called Graiveyakas, 'realms of the neck'. Still higher up, we enter into realms that prepare us for the qualitative leap from the natural order (defined by space, time and matter) to the transcendental. At the same time, Hindu mythology locates the source of the river Ganges here.[7] When the eggshell-like enclosure of the universe cracked, the waters that surround the world began to gush inside, to fall down the billions of miles on to earth.

Reserving a discussion of the religious significance of the 'transcendental' for later, we may now retrace our steps and let the Ganges carry us back to earth. Surprising though it may sound, some of the splendour of the inaccessible realms above can be found even here. For the nooks and crannies, the caves and cavities of earth are the openings into splendid lower regions. That does not mean that these splendid realms stretch downwards all the way to the feet of the cosmic lady: we shall presently hear about very different kinds of subterranean chambers. However, in these 'underworlds' (for which the generic term Patāla is frequently used) we encounter a wide range of other non-human beings. Since such apertures into Patāla are found all over the earth – unlike the inaccessible approach to the 'heavens' via Meru – it need not surprise us to detect some form of empirical basis for such beings. The *nāgas*, when they show themselves to humans, tend to take on the shape of serpents. Moreover, popular literature finds it easy to talk about the underworld and its beings. Fragments from two such 'travelogues' may convey some impressions of the underworlds.

There was a king, Ploughman, who was desperately in love with Princess Playful. But since it seemed that he would be unable ever to win the girl, who lived far away, he considered suicide. His spiritual adviser Nāgārjuna, however, admonished him and suggested an alternative.

'Don't you realize that he who dies in the course of his transmigration is gone for good? Ask yourself how the dead could meet again with their beloved ones?

So why should you want to commit suicide, which serves no purpose and is done only by unsophisticated persons? If you are not interested in kingship here, come on then: let us both go into the underworld (Patāla)! For there can be found by wise people pleasures eight times greater than in the heavens, and uncountable thousands of years without any disease or death.'

When the king had listened to this, he pondered for a very long time over it; finally he agreed to the monk's suggestion. When the next morning arrived, he handed over his kingship to his son and set out from his capital. Eventually he reached the bank of the river Godāvarī. Accompanied by skilled and devoted knights, he came to the opening of a cave, the doors of which were guarded by a lion. Although that mighty beast emitted a terrifying, loud roar from its wide-open mouth, they ignored it and went inside.

After about half a mile they saw a second door that was guarded by a goblin of Śiva and blocked up with a large slab of rock. But it opened up for the king instantly. Another half mile further they saw a temple of Śiva. It was shaded by shrubs that, as their name suggests, surpass pearl with whiteness. The ground around it was decorated with the petals of fully open lotuses used in worship. The tree-arbours were reverberating with the musical humming of swarms of honey-intoxicated bees. The cooing of the cuckoos could be heard far away. Any king who can visit such a heavenly park indeed obtains great fortune!

Then they praised Śiva and proceeded. After a short distance they saw a third gate. It was firmly shut by means of a golden bolt across its golden door-panels; a host of serpents blocked the access to it. There the king saw a handsome man who was fettered with many rope-like snakes and thus totally powerless. He called out to his companions: 'Come and look! Here is a man who wanted to go into Patāla but got bound by vicious serpents!'

But as the king was saying this, all the snakes let go of the youth and fled in all directions. Then that attractive man spoke: 'Well-done, well-done, king! Who but you could have brought to an end another person's evil predicament? Nobody else is found in this world as skilful as you or as helpful to somebody else or as instinctively compassionate. But what am I saying? What is and what will happen to somebody like me, who got rescued from this misfortune, lies entirely in your hands.'

But the king answered: 'How could there be anything happening to you which is not the consequence of some good deeds done in your past! So tell us now why you are here?'[8]

We need not go into the details of the prince's adventures or identity. It was discovered that his adventure was intimately connected with the king's own quest for the Princess Playful. But we may note that the unexpected flight of the serpents turned out to be due to the king carrying a ring which, unknown to him, had the magic property of warding off all the possible dangers that can come from snakes/*nāgas*.

Then the golden door-panels were opened from inside, and two beautiful girls came walking towards the king and spoke to him: 'Your majesty, please enter this palace of Jewel-Lustre, our mistress. Only through you can her lonely heart find comfort.'

When the king heard this invitation, he replied politely by making Nāgārjuna speak his words: 'That marvellous palace of Jewel-Lustre you mention is indeed an incredibly rare find. Yet I am forced to refuse, since another matter demands my attention. As long as this prince, our good friend, has his wishes unfulfilled, it would not be fitting for me to indulge in such great wonders.' At this reply the two girls went back into the palace. But the king turned to leave the underworld.[9]

Underground caves and serpents can easily be accommodated in our picture of the earth; Patāla and *nāgas* are their mythical expansion. And how they were expanded: we hear of palaces and parks, beautiful (*nāga*) girls and an alluring (*nāga*) queen, of golden gates and 'pleasures eight times greater than those found in the heavens'. The theme that destiny keeps such treasures in store for the lucky man is amplified in the following story.

Snake-Prince met in the course of his adventurous travels a merchant whom he asked whether he knew of any strange or wonderful things. The merchant told him of an amazing Jina temple in the middle of the jungle not too far away. What made the temple even more remarkable was the fact that a wild tribesman stayed there who 'wields a bow and arrows, is decorated with peacock feathers and is constantly crying out unrestrainedly, while tears which he does not bother to wipe off are running from his eyes'. This aroused the knight's curiosity and he marched off with his entourage to that peculiar place. When he had found the temple and had worshipped in it, 'he saw the tribesman: his mind appeared in a state of depression and his body was burning from the fire of separation from his wife. "Help! Help!" he kept on shouting, so that all who heard him felt great pity.'

Then the prince asked him: 'Tell me why you are deafening the very forest with your screams.' And the tribesman replied: 'Here in this Cave of Death lives a terrifying ogre. He has abducted my beloved wife – whose eyes are as large and as curved as the petals of a lotus flower. Noble lord! Help a wretched man. If it is within your power, then bring her quickly back to me.'

Snake-Prince consented to the man's request, but first gave him something to eat. He too ate, and then, after his meal, entered into the underworld (Patāla). There he saw the demon's palace: it was more wonderful than anything he had seen before. It was decorated with banners, the cloth of which was dyed in five different colours. A whole series of intricate designs were laid into its walls with bits of pearl. Its arches were made of the tender branches of wish-yielding trees. When the hero had admired all this, he was able to enter the palace without hindrance, for the guardsman stood at the gate silently, his sword drawn but motionless as if life had left him. The prince went inside and soon found his way to the demon's throne-room. To see him better, the *asura* stretched his neck, and he who had not yielded a foot in hundreds of battles that he had fought with the *devas*, folded his hands at him and rose up, not staying seated on his throne. He offered him a seat and began to converse with him.

'A fine sword that neither hero nor *deva* would find fault with, a couch called Treasure-Trove, and this sensuous, amorous woman with arms like an elephant's trunk and flowing over with passion – take, take them all! I have been guarding them for you. In fact, that I abducted the tribesman's wife was merely in order to attract you here – think about this!'

Then the prince replied: 'In that case, please give me back the beautiful tribal woman who gives such pleasure to her husband.' Immediately she too was handed over to him, and when the tribesman saw her, he beamed with delight. Snake-Prince established a bond of friendship with the terrifying *asura*; he made him happy in his mind and spoke words that charmed the ears and the heart. Then he walked out of the Cave of Death. He marched along a wide jungle path where lion cubs were chasing stags. Then he discovered a strange cave and made enquiries about it.[10]

This turned out to be the Gold-Cave where a *devī* presented him with magical sciences. Twice more the prince got drawn into the mysterious realms of the underworld. In the subterranean realm of the Vetāla of Death he found treasures, and then 'he entered into the cave of the Tree-*Rākṣasa*. Playfully he kicked against the demon made of wood, and it fell to the ground and broke to pieces.'[11]

Of interest here is not just the wider range of wonderful things to be found in these underground realms (including 'magical sciences') or further species of ogre-like beings (the original actually lists *asuras*, *vetālas*, *piśācas* and *rākṣasas*), but also the seemingly smooth transition from the world of man to those mysterious realms. Already the jungle with its wild tribesmen symbolizes in the Indian imagination a realm outside, or at least at the very margin of, human culture which is thus basically frightening. Yet Snake-Prince realizes a common bond of empathy with the tribesman's suffering, just as he can talk to the *asura* and make friends with him in the much more alien world of Patāla. While this can be regarded as indicative of how much the underworlds are regarded as part of the natural order, we shall have ample opportunity to note the dangers lurking here for ordinary mortals.

These underworlds with all their splendour and terror occupy no more than a narrow slice just under the middle of the World Woman. The bulk of the space denoted by her skirt is filled with realms far more terrific: the hells. The idea of such underground torture chambers is certainly not exclusive to the Jains (who tend to list seven hells), as a look at a Hindu text[12] will make clear (where twenty-one plus seven are given). The names alone can convey strong impressions of what is going on in these realms – they are like the plates on the doors that lead into the various torture chambers. With some poetic licence we can translate a selection of such names as 'Gloomy', 'Furnace-Cooking', 'Worm-Food', 'Pincers', 'Red-hot Iron', 'Diamond-Thorns', 'Pus-River', 'Slaughterhouse', 'Impaling', 'Solitary Confinement', 'Spinning-Wheel', 'Cruncher', 'Frying-Pan', etc. It does not require much imagination to figure out what is going on here. People are driven insane by total darkness and isolation, boiled alive in cauldrons filled with boiling oil, driven past trees with leaves and thorns as sharp as knives, squeezed through machines, gnawed at by worms, pinched with tongs, rubbed up and down the stems of thorny silk-cotton trees, flung into rivers of pus and other foul substances such as excreta, urine, saliva, mucus, blood and fat, cut into small bits, made to drink from pits filled with saliva, have molten iron poured into their throats, imprisoned in cells that have red-hot iron walls and floors, pierced with needles like a pin-cushion or lacerated with iron spikes.

Often the type of punishment meted out shows a logical connection with the type of offence committed on earth in one's former life. For slaughtering and boiling or roasting an animal for food one has to suffer the same fate; the man unwilling to share his food with others gets both gnawed at by worms and is made to eat nothing but worms; false evidence in court is punished by being flung into a lake, the waves of which are equally 'false' – they are solid rock. A brahmin who during sexual intercourse with his wife makes her swallow his semen is cast into a pit full of saliva (in one interpretation) or semen (in another).[13] As can be seen from all this, the tortures envisaged here are on the whole straightforward physical punishments. But occasionally a more psychological approach is used. The notion of the hell called 'Avīci' belongs to one of the most ancient strata of infernal speculation. The original meaning of the name (perhaps to be connected with 'southern', the region of the dead) was lost, and 'non-waves' was substituted for it. Imaginative ingenuity then tried to make sense of the word. In this hell, it tells us, the culprit is taken up a high cliff. In front of him appears what looks like the sea. As he is pushed down, for those few seconds of his fall he may well take comfort at the idea of diving into water. But alas! The ripples he sees are 'not waves' – they are made of solid rock.

A fair number of the offences to be punished in one of these hells will not surprise us (like murder). In some cases only our own most recent secular sentiment would disagree (as in the case of adultery). In many other cases, the offence is culture-specific (like drinking alcohol or threatening behaviour towards brahmins). But in a few instances we may register positive or negative surprise: when the instigation of inter-religious animosity is regarded as an offence, or the feeding of a *śūdra* (the lowest and most down-trodden member of Indian society).

It is clearly impossible to list here all types of hellish tortures and all forms of human beastliness to be punished by them. But let us satisfy our curiosity at least in one case: what is the gravest offence to be punished in the lowest of all hells? If we applied to the name of the hell, 'needle-tip' (Sūcīmukha) some lateral thinking (the camel and the needle), we might actually pick up the right associations. People's bodies are treated here like a canvas, to be stitched all over with sharp needles. This is the punishment reserved for people who took pride in their wealth, hoarded it like their dear life, spent all their energies on increasing it, and treated others with contempt because of it.[14]

While it was possible to regard the caves and underground cavities of the earth as a realistic starting point for the vastly expanded vision of Patāla, etc., these hells seem to derive their existence exclusively from sadistic imagination. Yet this is not the case, for even here it is possible to discover a basis in real life. Even here the familiar has been expanded imaginatively. For instance, we hear in a text[15] that the seducer of a virgin was forced to embrace the red-hot iron statue of a woman. Yet it was a king, in real life on earth, that meted out this punishment, and the culprit did not have to wait till after his death to be tortured like this in the Taptasūrmi ('Heated Metal-Image') hell reserved for seducers and adulterers.[16] A brahmin who has drunk certain types of alcohol can expiate this violation only by drinking boiling-hot liquor (which will kill him) – thus to prevent having molten iron poured down his throat in the Ayaḥpāna ('Iron-Drink') hell.[17] It would not be difficult to enlarge such a list of real punishments and tortures inflicted on criminals by kings, the guardians of law and order. The horrors of hell are thus but a vastly enlarged version of the nightmares caused by the brutality real man is capable of inflicting on others, or on himself (see the example of the alcohol). There is only one major difference. Since this is the realm of death, dying does not exist as a relief for the tortured culprits. Whether he is smashed to pieces on the rocks of the Avīci hell, or flattened like a piece of sugar-cane in the 'hog's-mouth' machine, instantly he comes back to life, which is to say, his body gets reconstituted, and the same is repeated. However, unlike the Christian idea of hell, there will be an end to these tortures, even in the deepest and most severe of hells. For whatever offence was committed in a lifetime, it never constitutes a qualitative leap (into eternal – timeless – punishment), but remains a specific quantum which gets gradually exhausted, as it were, by means of the tortures. Incidentally, the same principle applies to the pleasures of the 'heavens' enjoyed by the *devas*; once the store of their 'merit' has been exhausted, they die. The details of such a striking conception of religious reward and punishment will be given in another chapter.

After this initial and cursory exploration of the world as envisaged by the Indian imagination, we may wish to reflect on what we have seen (and probably also to turn to less startlingly concrete matters than the tortures of hell). To begin with, some comments on Jainism seem appropriate, although a more detailed account will have to be reserved for subsequent chapters. After all, normally very little is said about the Jains. This is regrettable, and I shall try my best to demonstrate in the course of the following pages how interesting and useful Jain material can be. From a practical point of view, the advantage of Jain material is that it has undergone fewer historical developments and transformations than other forms of the Indian religions, and that due to an intensive and zealous patronage of copying manuscripts and producing illustrations in them, we have a disproportionate amount of Jain visual material available. This is particularly useful, since textual studies of Hindu and Buddhist material reveals that we are dealing here with no more than variations on pan-Indian themes. In terms of chronology, we are dealing with a conception of the world that at least prior to the sixteenth century, had remained, in essence, the same for fifteen hundred years.

Having said 'of the world', I have to qualify this now. The Jains do indeed assume that the structure we have been looking at represents the universe in its totality. Some Hindu traditions believe in more than one *brahmāṇḍa*, 'cosmic egg', although this plurality has remained without any religious and literary importance. With the Buddhists, such an idea of many world-systems (called by them *buddhakṣetras*, 'Buddha-fields') has found its culmination. While their number itself may be astronomical, an extensive literature does describe (some of) those other worlds and, moreover, explores the theme of 'interstellar' communication between the various Buddhas found there. Thus, in fact, we find a fluctuation between a conception of one universe that is geocentric (the Jain situation, with the sun revolving around Meru) and a vision of many world-systems (particularly with the Buddhists) in which, moreover, no superiority is attributed to our own. In fact, where Buddhist texts deal with the world of the Buddha Amitābha, our own world is regarded as decidedly inferior and marginal.

There are now a number of more theoretical issues that we shall have to look at, before we can turn to the 'life' that pulsates through the universe. It is not difficult to see that all three structures derive from the same archetype. The world is divided into three spheres: the underworld, the earth, and the sky/heavens. The classical name is *trailokya*: the three realms of living beings. Depending on how we stretch it or mould it, we end up with an egg-shaped, or a woman-shaped affair. The egg-shape can claim to be more original, because in our everyday awareness we see a flat earth in front of us, and a hemispherical sky that stretches out far above us, but touches the earth at the horizon. But more interesting than to ask what the possible origins of this conception of the world and the factors accounting for the remoulded shape of a 'person' could have been, is to determine the nature of the conception itself. Given that the different Hindu, Buddhist and Jain traditions draw on a recognizable archetype, it must be interpreted as a culturally evolved phenomenon upon which the religious significance was imposed only subsequently and in a differentiated manner. This is remarkable, for certainly in the Judaeo-Christian tradition we take it for granted that 'religion' determines how we imagine the world to look. In the present case, religion does no more than to produce its own specific interpretation and evaluation for the shared archetype.

However, to distinguish the cultural from the religious in this way does not yet fully determine the role of this model of the world in Indian culture as such. For there remains to be investigated the relationship between empirical evidence and imagination. There are definite areas in this structure of the world which are open to empirical evidence, and others that at least allow for a more analytical investigation. For example, the realm of what I would love to call by its German name '*Himmel*' (which is both 'sky' and 'heaven') is, among other things, the area in which the sun and the moon, the planets and the stars, move about: thus it presents itself as open to the empirical knowledge of astronomy. And the Indians were no mean astronomers. The reason for this is known: they were very interested in astrology, and horoscopes played an important role, for example in arranging marriages. Moreover, we seem to have a definite history of astronomy, while the structure of the world as depicted here stayed relatively unchanged over almost two thousand years. Before drawing any conclusions from this bifurcation, let us look at a second example.

Certainly during the third century BC and later, at least two empires carried on trade connections with places as far away and as far apart as Rome and China (the Śātavāhanas in the north and the Pāṇḍyas, etc. in the extreme south). Pālī, the language of the Buddhist Canon preserved in Sri Lanka, and Sinhalese, spoken on the same island, are both North Indian dialects. We call parts of Asia Indo-China and Indonesia. What this all means is simple enough: right through the first millennium AD and presumably some centuries before that, Indians travelled in considerable numbers over a wide area and to many other countries. Had they followed the kind of map of the earth which is shown in Figure 3, their fate would have been worse than that of Columbus. Again we must assume that a far more 'scientific', 'empiricist' kind of information was available in India at the time, which did not get reflected in the view of the world as presented in the present context. To call India 'unscientific' because the maps used by sailors have not survived would be ludicrous. But it would be equally ludicrous to assume that, since a map of the world such as that in Figure 3 shows an ocean full of milk, Indian literature would contain accounts of frustrated attempts to get there. However well known some groups of Indians may be as adventurous business people, there are no hints in the texts of anybody trying to set up a profitable milk (or treacle or rum) business by constructing a pipeline to one of those oceans.

So what can we conclude from these considerations? Simply, that the structure of the world, as presented here, is – quite consciously – not meant to be 'scientific'. It is employed as a religious model of reality, in which real islands like Sri Lanka or Indonesia figure merely as dots, marked at random, in the salt ocean. A model of the world like the Jain Lady does not exhaust what other strands of Indian culture have to say about it which have, through their empiricism, bypassed such a religious construction.

At this point I may add one further consideration. What happened when analytical philosophy got hold of this view of the world? Let me remind you what happened in Christian Europe: we had to undergo the traumatic experience of the 'modernist heresy' and all the bad blood this produced. In some parts of the world they are still fighting court-cases over it! As it happens, India took a lively, critical interest in the nature and structure of the concrete world. Let us call this nature-philosophy. The earliest documented version is Jainism itself, to be followed by systems like the Sāṃkhya, Vaiśeṣika and the Buddhist Abhidharma. Each one operates with a concept of atomism, although the details vary enormously. In this enterprise, the whole wonderful edifice is cut down to its smallest components – material atoms and (to account for phenomena such as organic growth, consciousness and will) live-cells (*jīvas*, etc.).

This seems extremely brutal, yet it did not, and did not want to, invalidate the picturesque world displayed by our illustrations. The whole with all its wonderful realms and strange beings, could still be explained in terms of material atoms and *jīvas*, and could still be envisaged, as a grand meta-meta-combination of atoms and *jīvas*, in the shape and structure presented here. To the Jains right from the beginning, and to the Buddhists and Hindus slightly later, the *devas*, *nāgas* and denizens of hell were heaps of very many atoms and a *jīva*! Thus no modernist clash of views and interests could occur here, because the two systems, the analytical and the religious, understood each other as complementary, or – with reference to astronomy and real geography – as belonging to different 'modes of discourse'.

Thus the model of the world presented here reveals itself as far more complex than a naive, literalist interpretation (of the Macaulay kind) could accommodate. Three examples may briefly illustrate to what extent the Indian traditions themselves reflect such a variety of attitudes towards the basic archetype. The examples are: the symbol of the milk-ocean, the *deva–asura* antagonism, and the function of the hells in relation to the underworlds.

The milk-ocean as a mythical, religious and poetic topic was a particular favourite of Hindu culture. Yet what range of meanings is found here! At the earliest stage, it is almost a creation myth. The two classes of non-human beings, the *devas* and *asuras*, churned it and produced the essence of all good and bad things in the cosmos: the 'nectar' – drink of immortality and pure being – and a world-destructive poison. Later, theistic Hinduism added to the event Viṣṇu, who took on the form of a tortoise to support the mountain serving as the churning stick. Another mythological strand envisaged a further role for this *deva.* Here Viṣṇu took on the form of an extremely attractive woman, to cheat the *asuras* out of their share in the nectar. Folk-religion used it to add respectability to the local god Aiyappaṉ: when Śiva saw this Viṣṇu-woman his passion was aroused, and from their brief and rather violent union, a son was born – Aiyappaṉ. The deflation of the religious symbolism is reached with medieval poets:

> The women living at the shore
> of the milk-ocean praise Rādhā:
> the heat of Lakṣmī's sighs
> has turned the milk into butter.[18]

(Rādhā and Lakṣmī are rivals for Viṣṇu's affection. The burning sighs of jealousy of the latter affect her father, the milk-ocean, so much that he/it all 'knots up and curdles', thus yielding a free supply of butter for the women, without the laborious task of having to churn the milk themselves. All this is thanks to Rādhā's power over Viṣṇu's heart!)

The myth about the churning of the milk-ocean reveals the *devas* and *asuras* partly as antagonistic and partly as complementary towards each other. They may be pulling at opposite ends of the rope but, as it is wrapped around the mountain used as the churning-stick, this produces precisely the backward and forward motion required to keep the mountain spinning clockwise and anticlockwise. Thus *devas* and *asuras*, in spite of the visual antagonism, are integrated into one concerted effort. It is only when the *devas* cheat the *asuras* out of their legitimate share of the nectar that a real antagonism is revealed. Yet the *asuras* are no angels either: other myths tell us about their attempts to oust the *devas* from their heavens.

We have here a direct parallel to the relationship between the heavens and the underworlds on our cosmic map, which are the abodes of the *devas* and *asuras* respectively. Visually antagonistic, they nevertheless constitute complementary spheres, like the two halves of an egg or the upper and lower parts of a human body. Both are filled with equally splendid palaces and parks, miraculous treasures and wonderful women. But now a puzzling further feature is introduced: the hells.

It is very tempting to assume that they are a secondary addition to the archetype. Unlike heaven/sky, earth, and underworlds, these are definitely not pleasant places to be in. They are institutions of punishment, cruelty and torture. But what need is there for them? After all, all three '-isms' can accommodate them easily in human life on earth, where they are executed efficiently and to the full, by human beings inflicting this on each other, as will become clear in the following chapters. Thus is it possible to assume external influence here, the variegated adoption of a fascinating, but unnecessary, conception typical of some other culture? I do not know the answer. But what ought to be mentioned here is that, for other reasons, in some forms of later Buddhism, an influence from Iran (Zoroastrianism, Manichaeism?) has been suspected.[19] In these almost monotheistic cults of Amitābha and Avalokiteśvara, the world is depicted as black and white, heaven and hell, and Avalokiteśvara as busy diving deep down into these hells and saving suffering souls. Whatever the truth may be, 'the hells' of our system possess a definite ethical character which is totally absent in the other realms.

This juxtaposition of the hells and their moral implication with the *trailokya* that is totally and blissfully non-moral, has been an important source of misunderstanding and distorted interpretations of traditional Indian religions. The distinction between underworlds and hells was not realized, so that the denizens of the former were equated with the torturing agents of the latter and set in stark contrast to the *devas* living in the realm above. Thus the *devas* became 'gods', the denizens of the world below (*asuras*, etc.) 'devils' and, to the utter consternation of all who saw it that way, the 'gods' weren't good – at least not all the time, and sometimes very bad indeed – and the 'devils' or 'demons' did all kinds of very decent things, like being deeply religious. Similarly, when forms of monotheism were developed in Hinduism, the God-concept was linked with the side of the *devas* and with the heavens, and consequently the *asuras* and their underworlds acquired 'demonic' properties.

But whatever the historical layers and different cultural components of the map may be, we would expect it, as a religious model, to make statements about man's ultimate destiny. The Jains in their usual literalism build human fulfilment beyond space, time and matter right into their system – the anti-structure is still contained within the structure. The very top of the World Woman's head – and they do call it the 'head of the universe' – marks the realm in which the totally emancipated *jīvas* live, completely cut off from the realm of concrete form and time. Thus although on the pictures it looks like part of the whole, it is understood as the opposite to the rest. On the Hindu side, things are more complex and variegated and I shall not side-track here by entering into a discussion of those variants. Just one or two interesting points may be mentioned here. A very ancient Hindu view is that the egg within which we live (the *brahmāṇḍa*) has a hole at the very top, and that emancipation takes place by passing through that hole into a realm outside the universe.[20] Alternatively (as we see in Figure 2), a heaven (in our sense of the word) may be located at the top of the universe, in the 'head of the deity', as it were. With the Buddhists, things are again different and no less difficult. While, as we have seen, early Buddhism drew on the same archetype of the structure, it makes a special point of refusing to locate emancipation within it (although there are traces of an attempt to correlate stages of meditational advance with cosmological spheres). *Nirvāṇa*, the ultimate spiritual realization, cannot be defined within the terms of a space–time–matter continuum. Certainly later Indian Buddhism goes further in this direction: it produces a total re-interpretation of the concept of the *trailokya*. It now denotes three levels on a scale from the material to the ethereal, and from the physical (=sexual) to the mental (=Platonic). In turn it is followed in this view by later schools of Hindu thought, just as the Jains had already prepared it by envisaging the love-life of the higher *devas* in rather ethereal, Platonic terms. Yet it is absolutely clear that, whether or not one was prepared to locate ultimate spiritual fulfilment on a map, it did not create problems as far as the understanding of that fulfilment itself is concerned. Just as the top of the Jain lady's head depicts a realm outside space and time and matter as we know it, the very top of the cosmic Kṛṣṇa wants to depict the same thing, formulated more than a thousand years later, or in the heaven of Viṣṇu's Vaikuṇṭha. But what I find even more remarkable is the fact that here we have a religious culture that does not place itself in the centre of things and, moreover, is capable of living in – by which I mean, mentally and emotionally able to accept and happily envisage itself in – a universe so enormous, so vast, that even our modern astronomy cannot quite compare with it. There are not many Christian theologians who are involved in accommodating the Christian belief system within the structure of the universe as suggested by modern astronomy, yet in the case of the ancient Indian model we are dealing with precisely such an integrated conception, and that on a comparable scale. This I think is quite remarkable, not because it anticipates 'scientific' insights, but because it demonstrates an impressive talent of the mind and the imagination to conceive, in religious terms, of a very vast world indeed, and of man's minute and marginal role in it.

By emphasizing that the map of the world discussed here is an archetype developed along more specific lines by Hinduism, Jainism and Buddhism, we have pretended that as such it is known to all religious traditions of India. At this point we must realize that this is certainly not the case. Many a religious tradition was aware of and concerned itself with a much smaller image of the world. This now allows us to make very practical use of the World Woman. For it becomes possible to use her as a 'yard-stick' or a 'scale' to assess and measure such different religious traditions from a typological point of view. As we have defined 'power' as control over man's destiny, we can enter into our map the individual range that is encompassed by a specific tradition. This device will be explained in due course, but meanwhile there are further aspects connected with the World Woman that we shall have to explore. She may be without a heart, but she is filled with 'life' in other senses – the living beings themselves, and a pulse of 'history' beats in her. These themes take us away from an ocean filled with milk to the much more painful metaphorical ocean of earthly existence.

CHAPTER 3

Navigating the sea of earthly existence

The two major symbols used in the construction of our cosmic map – those of the egg and of the person – both suggest some form of growth, organic development, or life. Although literally this is the case in only a few instances of monotheistic belief, we can nevertheless speak of cosmic 'life' in two senses of the word. Clearly, the different kinds of beings, the *devas*, *nāgas*, *asuras*, animals and humans, are alive. But, in addition, the cosmos itself is perceived by the Indian traditions to be 'alive' in the sense of having a history, a growth and a decay. We shall see in due course that cosmic history and the life-story of the individual being are much more closely interwoven than it would appear at first sight. Thus what seem to be two separate topics of discussion in this chapter will reveal themselves as a single, though complex, theme: the pulsation of life to the rhythm of time. Let us begin our exploration by looking at the cosmic scale of this pulse, that is to say, at 'world history'.

'Time' can be broken down into five components: beginning, past, present, future and end. In our view of things, reflections on the beginning and the end are the concern of cosmology and theology; those on the past are the concern of history, archaeology, etc.; those on the present, the concern of journalists, moralists and politicians; and finally those on the future, the concern of astrology and futurology. In traditional India, this whole complex is treated as one grand and coherent whole.

None of the Indian systems knows of an absolute beginning nor of 'creation' in the strict sense of the word. The world is not created *ex nihilo*, because it exists eternally. But it is not a static affair: it pulsates on a vast scale, fluctuating between periods of evolution and dissolution, of differentiation and contraction, or, in metaphorical terms, between cosmic days and nights. In this imagery we find a hint of the 'origin' of such a conception. The fluctuation of days and nights, the phases of the moon, the four seasons and the progression from man's youth to his old age can all be represented as emboxed cyclic events on an increasingly large time-scale. From this was then extrapolated, as the most extreme form of cyclic pulsation, cosmic time, on a time-scale so fantastic that it involves millions of billions of years. (When we cut up this process into smaller segments, we obtain the cosmic time-units or aeons – *kalpas*, *yugas*, etc.) It is with reference to such a cycle that we can speak of a beginning and an end. Given that any account of such a beginning has to remain relative, we need not be surprised to find a sheer unlimited variation of the theme. So-called creation myths are legion, and a vast range of symbols is used: organic processes like germination of a seed, fertilization of an egg, the breaking up – into man and woman – of an originally unified being, or human procreation through incest. All this may make fascinating reading, but it cannot be given a significance comparable to the account of creation in the book of Genesis. In that sense, the Indian traditions do not possess a myth of creation.

In fact, the aspect of the five components of time which most fascinated the Indian imagination, was not the beginning, but the past. Such a fascination is easily explained. The structure of the world, in which man experiences the present, has been decided in the past: here the blueprint of man's destiny has been laid out. The beginning is merely the event constituting past history, and the end simply the start of an interlude before another beginning. The future is primarily the outcome of decisions taken in the present, derived from guidelines offered by the past. If this nexus of ideas is correct, one interesting corollary emerges. A civilization that can merrily speculate on milk and honey flowing in imaginary oceans surrounding equally imaginary continents might be expected to expand this game by envisaging the future. That such detailed prognostications about future historical events have not been put forward suggests that the future – and that obviously includes man's destiny – is not decided. This, I think, throws a rather new light on a tradition which is normally seen as backward-looking, in the sense of being bogged down by the past. By keeping the future open and undetermined, fatalism is clearly avoided and an arena for real decision-making is accepted. The only thing that is regarded as definite in this vision is the end, on a global, cosmic scale, and this as the night before another beginning. I would have no hesitation to regard this conception as extremely optimistic and allowing for real human freedom.

So what happened in this apparently all-important past of cosmic history? As the central theme we hear about a series of powerful humans who were born, lived and then died – in quite a normal manner. But these people had such an enormous impact that the destiny of man was affected by their presence on earth. Having started with the Jain conception of the universe, we might as well repeat this and begin with the Jain version of the history of the world. As always, this has the advantage that we can start with something neatly defined and systematized.

The Jains tell us of sixty-three staff-men (*śalākapuruṣas*), who are divided into five categories. Actually, the Śvetāmbara faction includes among these men one woman (Princess Mallī);[1] moreover, in reality we are dealing with only sixty persons, because three men belong to two categories at the same time. Having dealt with the problems of gender and number in the expression 'sixty-three men', we can now turn to these colourful figures themselves. First and foremost are twenty-four *tīrthaṅkaras*, 'creators of fords (or better, religious communities)'[2] who are directly connected with the history of the Jain religion, as the Jains themselves envisage it. At twenty-four points in the history of the world, a *tīrthaṅkara* appeared and re-established Jain teaching. The second group is that of the twelve *cakravartīs*, 'wielders of the discus', in other words, of universal rulership over the earth. Thus we are dealing here with secular figures, whose influence concerns the political and social structures of the past. In three instances[3] now, a man first became a universal emperor and then discarded all his political power and the luxuries of worldly life and succeeded in becoming a *tīrthaṅkara*. This illustrates that *cakravartī* and *tīrthaṅkara* are seen as two sides of the same coin. Particularly gifted individuals have the choice of rulership over the earth or power over man's ultimate destiny. Finally we have three complementary groups, with nine persons in each. These are the *vāsudevas*, *baladevas*, and anti-*vāsudevas*.

A brief look at how this system was constructed will allow us, at the same time, to add some colour to the bare outlines given so far. The raw material is taken from ancient Indian folklore, legends, and mythologized historical memories. Were one rash enough to put dates against this material, 800–400 BC might not be totally unrealistic, as far as the beginnings of these stories are concerned. It is during this period that the Mahāvīra lived – who from our Western point of view was the historical founder of Jainism (and whom the Jains regard as the twenty-fourth *tīrthaṅkara* of their list). And it is during this period that we ought to place the kings whose exploits and battles are dealt with in heroic poetry: Kṛṣṇa (=Vāsudeva), his half-brother Baladeva, and their arch-enemy, Jarāsandha. These figures served as the starting point of the system, which was developed by projecting it back into the past and duplicating our heroes. Still within the range of historicity, though very much at the borderline, appears Pārśva, the twenty-third *tīrthaṅkara*. Jain sources tell us that the Mahāvīra actually reformed a movement which had been created by a Pārśva, and some historical truth might lie in this.[4] But with the second set of *vāsudevas*, etc. we definitely cross the boundary into the realm of myth. The story of Rāma, who was exiled along with his half-brother Lakṣmaṇa and his beautiful wife Sītā (whom the Digambara-Jains regard as Rāvaṇa's lost daughter), provides the raw material here. In the forest, Sītā got abducted by Rāvaṇa, a non-human being (a *vidyādhara* among the Jains, and a *rākṣasa* with the Hindus), and was taken to the island of Laṅkā. After a lengthy military expedition, Rāma succeeded in defeating Rāvaṇa and in gaining Sītā back. Though she had faithfully resisted Rāvaṇa's advances, doubt about her chastity lingered on, and in disgust she cast herself into the fire. Rāma, Lakṣmaṇa and Rāvaṇa here make up the second set of *vāsudeva*, *baladeva* and anti- *vāsudeva*. By drawing on story material of a similar kind, seven further sets were produced. Many of the figures found here reappear on the Hindu side as god-figures – a point to be discussed later on. In the same way, from the life stories of the Mahāvīra and Pārśva, twenty-two further biographies are created and cast into the distant past. Thus the Jains believe that religious truth suffers a decline in the course of human history and requires an ever-new proclamation.

Less easily identifiable is the origin of the category of *cakravartī*, passionate and often extremely violent men who ruled the earth. Brahmadatta, the last of the twelve, who ruled between the twenty-second and twenty-third *tīrthaṅkaras*, is not known from other sources. A brahmin had insisted on eating this emperor's food, in spite of being warned that it was far too strong for him. This made him a raving sex-maniac, and he took his revenge on Brahmadatta by shooting the latter's eyes out. The blinded emperor then spent the rest of his days squashing between his fingers what he thought were people's eyeballs.[5] But the first *cakravartī*, Bharata, is well known and provided the Bhārata-varṣa with his name. Thus, in this case, the construction must have taken place in the opposite direction, by deriving from Bharata eleven *later* figures. What the Jains have created here is, on the one hand, a grand vision of the past history of the world and of the Jain religion and, on the other hand, an encyclopaedic synthesis of Indian myth, legend, historical recollections and literature.[6]

A glance at the chronology of this literature reveals relatively late dates (the earliest Jain work containing the whole system is from AD 892). But what we have here is no more than the final literary expression of a much older process during which individual figures and groups of these were dealt with separately. Ultimately, the structure goes back, by centuries, into the BC era.

All this would be relatively interesting, but of little pan-Indian relevance, if it was only the Jains who expressed ideas of this kind. But, just as in the case of cosmography, we are dealing here with no more than a Jain variation on an Indian theme. For various reasons, among the Buddhists the system is far more unsettled and often far simpler. Chronology is obviously one reason: we have extremely little popular Buddhist literature preserved from the AD period. But in spite of this scarcity of sources, it is clear from both the Pālī tradition and extant Indian works like the *Lalitavistara* and *Mahāvastu*, that the Buddha of our historical perspective was regarded as no more than the penultimate representative of a set of individuals known as *tathāgatas*, *jinas*, or *buddhas*. The number of these varies, but Indian texts may list hundreds. Another interesting difference to the Jain system is the addition of one further *buddha* who is still to appear on earth, sometime in the rather distant future – the *buddha* Maitreya. Cases of millenarianism associated with this *buddha* are attested from Burma and Japan, but I know of no Indian examples – which might corroborate my previously stated view of the Indian attitude towards the future.

When turning to the 'Hindu' side of things, we again enter deep and muddy waters. Once more, as in the case of cosmography, it is the splendid work of W. Kirfel[7] that allows us to make some sense of this incredibly diffuse and complex material. Kirfel discovered that the second primary building-block of the vast literature known as the Purāṇas was an originally independent treatise on the history of the world. He called it the '*Purāṇa-Pañcalakṣaṇa*', the 'Ancient Account of the Five Themes'. Thanks to his painstaking text-critical work it is possible to discern a number of historical layers and resultant interesting historical developments of ideas. At its earliest stages, the world history depicted here possesses an even more secular flavour than the Jain version. The *ṛṣis* or 'seers' appear here as 'religious' figures, but not really outside the arena of ordinary human life, and only during the earlier phase of the past. Besides, we find universal rulers who institute the human race – consecutively – and society with its customs. These are the Manus. Another important theme running through this work is that of the origin and past history of various dynasties (in which Kṛṣṇa also figures).[8] In this form the system must be very ancient, definitely earlier than the AD era. Subsequent developments grafted on to it new figures and a new orientation. These are the famous *avatāras* of the Hindu god Viṣṇu, incarnations 'descending' (the literal meaning of the word *avatāra*) from the realm of eternity into the world of man and history. Again, it is the figure of Kṛṣṇa who initiated the process. It was probably during the fourth or fifth century AD that Kṛṣṇa became regarded as an *avatāra* of Viṣṇu. The pattern could then be extended, for instance by including Rāma, until (by about the ninth century AD) a classical number ten evolved as at least partially established. As with the Buddhists, one of these *avatāras* is still to come. This is Kalki, who will initiate the collapse of the current cosmic order. Perverse though it may seem, it must be stated that the 'religious' role of these divine 'incarnations' is far less obvious or central than that of the *tīrthaṅkaras* and *buddhas*. (Part two will concern itself with this problem.)

Thus as part of cosmic history extraordinary persons have appeared on earth who have consecutively laid the foundations for human culture, religion and 'history' in the narrower sense of the word. On the grand stage of the world these persons engaged in the play of the passions, of lust and hatred, and pursued their quest for pleasure and power – be it over the world or over man's ultimate fulfilment. The stories that could be told here about their exploits are innumerable, and the amount of textual material dealing with them is incalculable. Space does not permit us to pursue them here. Instead we ought to step back and reflect on the grand edifice itself.

First of all, attention ought to be drawn to the underlying similarities found in the conceptions of the different religious traditions. Thus once again, as in the case of cosmography, we may speak of a cultural construct that predates specific religious interpretations. Without much difficulty we could abstract from this a trifurcation, three roads leading away from the common basis into the Jain (*śalākapuruṣas*, including the *tīrthaṅkaras*), Buddhist (*tathāgatas* or *buddhas*) and Hindu (Manus, *avatāras*) directions. But what is perhaps more interesting is the fact that even after this parting of the ways the three main traditions interconnect and refer or allude to each other. One example is the figure of Kṛṣṇa who is known to all three traditions. Another is the work of Jinasena and his disciples which, completed in AD 892, is one of the earliest full accounts of Jain world history and its sixty-three mighty persons. It is clearly an attempt to argue the Jain case against an increasingly powerful Hinduism in South India.[9] On the other hand, the Tamil *Periya-Purāṇam* (of the eleventh century) can be assumed to be playing with Jain themes when it narrates the stories of sixty-three South Indian saints devoted to the Hindu God Śiva. Its anti-Jain intentions are particularly manifest in the story of one of them who had thousands of Jains put to death through impalement.[10] Another highly influential work from South India, the ninth- or early tenth-century *Bhāgavata-Purāṇa*, provides a Hindu counterattack by dealing with figures like the first Jain *tīrthaṅkara*, *cakravartī*, etc. in a deprecatory manner.[11] On the other hand, in its version of the life of Kṛṣṇa, it draws positively on material specific to the Jains. The same text is also one of the first to mention the Buddha as one of the *avatāras* of Viṣṇu. Thus the differentiation did not take place in isolation, and it might be appropriate to speak here of a particular type of discourse, in which the three '-isms' participated over a period of hundreds of years. But apart from such polemics, what could be the purport of such a discourse? It is clearly meant to locate a specific religious system in the wider context of universal history. This self-reflection looks back into the past for its 'origin', but not to point at some specific, unique event. It sees itself continuously founded and renewed, through the work of outstanding human personalities, people of flesh and blood. A generosity reveals itself here, which we encounter also in the equally generous scattering of *tīrthaṅkaras* over the other one and a half continents inhabited by humans, and of *tathāgatas* over unnumbered further world-systems. The truth proclaimed by these is eternal, but can only be realized in the space–time–matter continuum, and thus has to be brought back into it, time and again, given that all human endeavour suffers decay in the course of time. No event in the future can add anything to this. The future *avatāra* of Kalki is altogether irrelevant in this context, and Maitreya, the *buddha* to come, simply makes sure that people far away in the future, after the inevitable decline of the teaching, will receive it again. What matters most is that it has been made available *here and now*.

Secondly we might ask what the textual relationship is between our cosmographic archetype and that of world history. As far as the Hindu Purāṇas are concerned, Kirfel[12] has shown that the two core treatises were originally independent. Yet in the actual Purāṇas, in most cases they are in close proximity, if not fully integrated. With the Jains (where the texts are also called Purāṇas), both constitute one unit. The *Mahāvastu*[13] can profitably be analysed in terms of the same structure: starting with a 'beginning', it provides an account of cosmography (the emphasis being on the hells), and turns to world-history with the many *tathāgata* figures it knows of, and culminates in the life of the 'historical' Buddha.

A third point worth investigating is whether the series of *buddhas*, *tīrthaṅkaras* and *avatāras* or Manus reveal some inner coherence or structuring, some form of overarching rationale, or whether each appearance constitutes a separate, discrete event. It is easy to show that the former alternative applies.

Each system of 'heroic men' indeed produced its overarching coherence. Marīci was the son of Bharata, the first Jain universal emperor. He made a nuisance of himself by giving up the right religion and creating perverse things, such as Hindu philosophy, etc. Duly punished for all this in further rebirths, he then was reborn as the sixth *vāsudeva* Three-Backs (Tripṛṣṭha). Involved in a war of imperial proportions over the possession of a charming park, he had to face once again many ups and downs in further existences, eventually to be reborn as the last *tīrthaṅkara* of our aeon, the Mahāvīra. As told in works like the *Mahāvastu*, the penultimate of the *buddhas* of our aeon, the 'historical' Buddha developed the first inklings of buddhahood in front of the *tathāgata* Dīpaṅkara. Through innumerable further lives, as animal, human being, etc. this initial commitment was strengthened and developed. Similarly with the Manus: for example, the seventh Manu of our aeon at a much earlier stage in his career laid the foundations for his grandeur, when as exiled monarch he learned to worship the Goddess.[14] Or with the *avatāras*: certain *asuras*, defeated by one *avatāra*, after many subsequent rebirths make the descent of another *avatāra* necessary. The classical system of the ten *avatāras* also knows of a further feature of overarching coherence. It begins with the ocean, the Fish-*avatāra*, to continue with the Turtle-*avatāra* and an amphibian creature, the Boar (renowned for its wallowing in muddy patches). Once on the dry land, the next *avatāra* is half man, half lion. A deformed human, the Dwarf follows, and only then are our *avatāras* fully human. In all but the last of these instances, it is the theme of rebirth which creates the coherence in the systems. In the case of the *avatāras*, we notice a similar concern to encompass human and animal forms of life. It goes without saying that for many of our 'heroic persons' a series of previous lives will be told; for the Buddha such stories (called Jātakas) are particularly numerous. The bulk of such material is astronomical, and there is no way that even a glimpse of it could be conveyed here.

Inadvertently, it seems, we have come upon a new and, to us in the West, quite unfamiliar topic: that of transmigration or rebirth. Yet as far as the Indian traditions are concerned that speculated on the structure of the universe and world history, it is a universal phenomenon that applies equally to all forms of life in the cosmos. The time has come to investigate this theme in greater detail.

Let us first cast a brief glance over the range of what are regarded as living beings. There are usually five categories listed. The first comprises human beings. Little needs to be said here about them, since to the ancient Indians it was as obvious as it is to us what this means. The only point of interest is perhaps the fact that when we travel to some of the islands in the salt-ocean, we encounter rather strange-looking creatures, with one leg only, with a head located in the chest, with two heads, or with four legs. These are mythical residues of seafarer tales about other faraway lands. The second class, animals, still presents few surprises, except for a range of – predictably – sea-monsters. The third category consists of denizens of the hells. On the whole, though I doubt that we can postulate a hard and fast rule, these are realms reserved for human beings after their death. After all, the name *naraka* is derived from *nara*, 'human being'. As we have seen in the previous chapter, imagination has run overtime to depict the various tortures inflicted here and the weird-looking creatures that perform such services as sawing people into half. But in remarkable contrast to the overheated imagination at work on the infernal details, no specific information is found as to the rationale behind the creatures that inflict the tortures. Is this the reward for merits acquired by KGB or CIA interrogators? Various demonic and other powerful, and often dangerous, non-human beings constitute a fourth category. These include such beings as the *nāgas*, *vetālas*, *rākṣasas*, *asuras* and *piśācas* whom we have encountered in the previous chapter. We might add to this list the *yakṣas* (and their females, the *yakṣiṇīs*) who are tree-spirits, *bhūtas* ('demons') and *pretas* ('ghosts'). Other such beings belong to realms that, from above, touch upon the world of man: *gandharvas* (heavenly musicians), *kinnaras* (centaurs), *apsarases* (nymphs, usually associated with ponds and rivers), and – for the Jains the most important category – the *vidyādharas*, the 'bearers of magic lore'. Whether male or female, they all have the power to change their form at will. Thus the *nāgas* tend to show themselves in the form of snakes in the world of man, but occasionally a person catches a glimpse of their real, overpoweringly beautiful and attractive form. The beauty of the *apsarases* is again proverbial. Most of these beings are in closest contact with the world of the humans, threatening them, trying to devour them, accounting for a variety of events in human life (like madness, illness, conception) and on occasions offering them untold treasures. The fifth category is that of the *devas* who live in the realms above the earth which we would style sky and heavens. Of marginal interest in the general context of the Indian religions is the Jain belief that plants also have a 'soul' and thus ought to be included in the catalogue of living beings.

What holds these five categories together? There is obviously the fact of being alive – a fact that is envisaged as a constant antagonism, a power-struggle between various categories. Big fish eat small fish, man eats the meat of animals, *asuras* strive to obtain the position of *devas*, *piśācas* and *rākṣasas* love to eat up human beings, and the denizens of the hells are constantly out to catch more victims for their tortures.

Then there is the fact of death. When Canetti asks (in one of his aphorisms of the year 1943) 'And what is the original sin of animals? Why do they suffer death?'[15] he is questioning one of the fundamental premises of the Judaeo-Christian tradition. Human death is seen here as the consequence of the original sin of Adam and Eve, and the salvation in a new life, after the resurrection of the dead, similarly focuses exclusively on man. What Canetti is hinting at is a vision of life that derives from the common fate of all life-forms and does not erect an *a priori* demarcation line between human and all other beings. This is precisely what the Indian concept of transmigration or rebirth does. Not only are there envisaged five distinct categories of beings, but beings of each category can, after death, move into any of the other four (until another death occurs). In fact, the common term *pañcagati* denotes the 'five possible directions' of rebirth after a death. Life is not a discrete event limited in time from the moment of conception to the moment of death. Life is eternal, which, in our present discussion, means it stretches back into the past without encountering a border there, and stretches out into the future, again without theoretically running into any fence. If we ignore here the way scholastic Buddhism would analyse this process further, we can employ a less vague language and talk about a 'soul' or a 'self', a permanent and autonomous core in each living being that courses in this way through time. A further pulse in the cosmic rhythm emerges: each core takes on a body of five fundamentally different kinds, spends one life-time in this physical form and dies, to pick up the next body, in a potentially endless series. It is here that all those different categories of beings become relevant, however fantastic and picturesque they may have appeared. It is here that the grand structure of the universe with its different layers becomes relevant. For the type of body taken on by a 'soul', and the realm where it is to spend one life, is catalogued here. These are the possibilities on offer: from the highest heavens down to the darkest of hells. This movement from life to life, potentially across the whole structure of the universe, is called *saṃsāra*.

One of its most commonly used metaphors is that of the ocean of earthly existence, and we shall presently see that much of the fear and horror that real sailors and merchants felt at travelling across the real ocean has flowed into the emotive associations of this metaphor. *Saṃsāra* encompasses all living beings in the world, the high and mighty as much as the low and humble, animal as much as god. We already caught glimpses of how this worked in the case of the extraordinary persons of world history. But in the light of the present observations, we have to ask now in what sense we can still speak of them as 'extraordinary'. First of all, they are required as catalysts of certain historical processes. Kalki is the most obvious example: he initiates the collapse of the world at the end of our present cosmic cycle. Other *avatāras* are shown to perform some 'cosmic repair work', such as rescuing the earth when she (*sic*) had sunk to the bottom of the ocean. It is only in these cases of the *avatāras* that their birth, life and death are not subjected to the laws of *saṃsāra*; monotheistic beliefs override the otherwise universal applicability of *saṃsāra*. Secondly, the extraordinary persons of world history act as 'culture-heroes', laying down, after periods of anarchy and lack of civilization, the blueprints of culture. Bharata is here the most obvious example. Then we have the 'religious' figures – from which we should exclude the *avatāras* for the moment. One of their essential functions is to reveal to mankind precisely the structure and nature of the universe in which we live, and to expound the laws that govern in it – transmigration. But they do not do this as outsiders, as 'exceptions to the rule', for they are subject to the same laws. This is where the remarkable ambivalence of a *cakravartī* and a *tīrthaṅkara* or a *tathāgata* becomes significant. On one level, these powerful rulers illustrate, on a grand scale, through their lusts and passions, their cravings for power and their violence, the very nature of what it means to be alive. Thus they are the exemplars of life, the pictures on the screen a *buddha* or a *tīrthaṅkara* can point at during his teaching. On the other hand, they are people who can make the qualitative leap and turn into *buddhas* or *tīrthaṅkaras* themselves. Again, at least with the human *avatāras*, the same fusion of the 'secular' and the 'religious' can be observed. They may bring some teaching, or may convey the grace of some God, but invariably they lead an ordinary existence on earth and may well illustrate, in their actions, the same features as a *cakravartī*. To state it differently: with the exception of some *avatāras*, or some interpretations of them, these history-makers are human beings and essentially illustrate what human nature is capable of. In that sense there is no qualitative difference between them and ordinary folk. They are subject to the same fundamental laws of being alive in this world.

But what precisely are these laws? So far the process of transmigration has appeared as a random affair – which is certainly not the way it is conceived of in our texts. Here these laws are seen as ruthlessly applicable to all forms of life with an inexorable logic: they are the laws of retribution. Each and every act performed in this pulsating universe constitutes a cause which inevitably produces an effect. Such an effect must be measured against a scale of values, from positive to negative, and the corresponding value then determines the nature of the act itself. As an act on the positive side, it requires reward, on the negative side, punishment. In the course of a lifetime, innumerable acts are performed, innumerable values stored up. The final total will determine the next rebirth: a preponderance of rewards acquired will allow for an upward movement of the soul, into one of the splendid realms of the sky and of the heavens. A preponderance of punishments necessary will push the soul downwards, in the extreme case right into the darkest of hells. The overall term used for this is *karma* – the residue of the act which demands subsequent treatment (reward or punishment). Now a distinction is drawn between different parts of the whole cosmic structure. In some realms, as in the heavens, in the *varṣas* outside Bhārata, or on the other continents – wherever we find paradisiacal conditions – only rewards can be enjoyed, and in the painful abodes such as the hells, only punishment can be suffered. No new *karma* is accumulated. At the same time, through the enjoyment of rewards or the suffering of punishment, old *karma* is used up. And when the store is exhausted, hell comes to an end just as heaven does. A new life, in a new embodiment of the soul, has to be faced, with the new acquisition of *karma*, in the realm called therefore *karmabhūmi* – the 'land of action' in which all of us live. To reveal the laws of *karma* and illustrate its operations is the task of our great men; to be subject to them is the fate of every living being. To draw any practical consequences from this knowledge is, properly speaking, only possible to the human being, and thus it is logical and necessary to have human beings who reveal these laws to other human beings. (The Jains also allow for some rudimentary religious insights among certain animals.)

In two ways, all this has been expanded: through scholastic systematization and through stories. Let me illustrate this very briefly here from Jain sources – after all, the Jains are the grand masters of *karma* speculation![16] The Jain scholastics list 148 varieties of *karma*, which are gathered together in eight larger groups. Some of these eight destroy qualities innate to the soul, others impose extraneous qualities on them. Some type of *karma* accounts for the fact that we cannot read other people's thoughts; another one, that instead of the soul's innate bliss we experience but transient joy and sadness. A knowledge of the truth and the style of living that corresponds to it is innate to the soul, but various varieties of *karma* obscure this through anger, greed, disgust and sexual desire. A further type of *karma* determines the life-quantum (which means the length of one's life is not fixed, but is subordinate to the 'intensity' of our living). Particularly interesting and scholastic is the sixth category, concerning the physical characteristics of an individual being. Its ninety-three varieties fix in minute detail the type of living being one becomes after death, how one gets to the place of one's rebirth, what species one enters, how the inherited *karma* merges with the *karma* acquired afresh from the moment of birth, how beautiful or handsome one becomes, what colour skin one has, how the joints are formed, etc. The joints are important here: only four of the six possible formations allow for sustained meditation, and only one allows for *tīrthaṅkara*-hood! In the final category we find a *karma* that causes impotence and other physical handicaps. In true scholastic fashion, all these varieties of *karma* are specified as to the kinds of actions that will generate them, and are quantified. Moreover, their interaction is described with almost mathematical precision. But I think there is no need here to provide further details. After all, my intention is merely to give some idea of what is, and what is not, determined by *karma*. It may prevent one from becoming a *tīrthaṅkara* in a given life, but it will never make certain basic moral decision impossible – the whole teaching of *saṃsāra*, as controlled by the laws of *karma*, necessitates the assumption of a morally responsible and free individual. Our next example will show this with all clarity. So, after a glance at scholasticism, let us explore how *saṃsāra* is dealt with in a story. I would like here to summarize a famous cultural construct, at least as far as the Jains (who after all were great story-tellers) are concerned: the story of Fame-Bearer (Yaśodhara).[17]

Once upon a time there lived a king, Fame-Bearer, whose days were filled with the enjoyment of making love to his chief queen, Full-of-Nectar. They had a son Fame-Minded. One night, when the king could not sleep, he saw his queen sneak off to make love to a revoltingly ugly and cruel servant of the stables, after receiving a harsh whipping from him. Deeply upset and depressed by this, he was unable to tell his mother the reason for his depression. However, at her suggestion, he performed a sacrifice, using a cock, but one of dough instead of a real one. Soon after that, Full-of-Nectar killed both husband and mother-in-law with poison, in order to give her lover undivided attention.

Fame-Bearer was reborn as a peacock, his former mother as a dog, and, in consequence of their connection in their previous existence, both ended up as pets of the son, Fame-Minded, who had now become king. Suddenly the peacock remembered his past life and, seeing his former wife making love to the same revolting man, he tried to kill them. Wounded by them, he crawled towards the king, but the dog bit him to death. Angry over this and his mind distracted, the king killed the dog. When it dawned upon him that his two favourite pets were now dead, he had them cremated with the finest wood, their ashes scattered into the Ganges, and a sacrifice performed so that their rebirth should take place in heaven.

Far from this, Fame-Bearer became a vicious porcupine, who ate up his former mother, now a cobra – to be bitten to death himself by a hyena. He who had been Fame-Bearer and the son was reborn as a fish, and his former mother as a terrifying crocodile, in the same river. When the reptile was about to gobble up the fish, one of the king's favourite dwarf women fell into the water and was eaten up instead. The enraged king had the crocodile hunted and slowly tortured to death. Soon after that, the fish was caught and was then fried alive. This was intended to be a sacrifice in honour of the king's dead father – the fish!

Now things became more complicated. Both souls were re-embodied as goats, mother as mother and son as son. When the billy-goat had mounted the she-goat and fertilized her, another ram gored him to death. The mother, pregnant with the soul of the billy-goat (Fame-Bearer), was shot by the king while hunting, but the kid was taken out of her cut-open belly. She herself was reborn far away as a buffalo. The goat was kept in the palace. One day the king performed a large sacrifice of buffaloes. When the meat began to smell, the goat was brought to purify it [apparently some superstitious belief]. For the second time the goat (Fame-Bearer) remembered his former lives. Unfortunately for him, the king's mother – his former adulterous wife – did not feel like buffalo meat, and the lazy cook just cut a slice off the goat. The rest of the goat, still alive, was designated as gift for the brahmins by the king, Fame-Minded, for the benefit of his dead father! Just then his favourite horse was gored to death by a buffalo, which was no other than the former mother. As punishment, the buffalo (together with the goat) was roasted alive.

They were reborn in a filthy hamlet of untouchables as a pair of fighting-cocks. Cruel-Deeds looked after them, when he had made a gift of them to the king. One day the king and his favourite queen were making love in a park pavilion. The cocks were kept nearby. Cruel-Deeds was having a chat with a Jain monk who used the past history of the cocks as an example to illustrate how cruelty produces bad *karma*. Once again the animals remembered their former lives and now converted to the Jain religion. They uttered a crow of delight, which was heard by the king in the middle of his sexual activities, and in order to show off his skill in archery, he took his bow and shot them dead merely by aiming at the sound they had made. Their souls entered his presently impregnated queen (who had thus conceived her own father-in-law and her husband's grand-mother!). The ensuing human birth of the twins, a boy and a girl, was the reward for their act of faith in the Jain religion when as cocks they had listened to the monk's sermon. As adolescents, they accompanied their father hunting and heard from a Jain monk about their past lives. Struck by an acute loss of interest in the affairs of the world, they joined the Jain order. As novices, wandering in a different country, they were caught by a king's henchmen, to be given in sacrifice to the blood-thirsty goddess Vicious-Murderess. But their resoluteness and their account of their past lives succeeded in converting all present, including the goddess, who threatened to kill anyone who from then onwards should think of performing a bloody sacrifice in her honour.

This is rather gruesome and gory stuff, and it is meant to be! There are a number of further themes which I have not mentioned in my very brief summary of the story and which will have to be looked at in different contexts. But the overall theme is clearly that of violence and cruelty which generates *karma* that necessitates further violence. The starting point seems innocuous enough: a purely symbolic animal sacrifice, encouraged by the mother and carried out by Fame-Bearer himself. What follows makes it clear how strongly the Jains felt about even such a residue of cruelty. Both persons involved in the act inflict punishment upon each other or have to suffer similar acts of cruelty committed by their son and grandson respectively. What adds irony to the events, and must have increased the mental agony of the victims, is the fact that time and again such cruelty was committed with the conscious intention of doing something good or pleasant to the dead Fame-Bearer and his mother. Only when they are once again human and find themselves in the position of their former (symbolic) victim, does the *karma* caused by the initial 'animal sacrifice' get exhausted. Incidentally, the whole story is filled with polemical attacks on various types of Hindu sacrificial practices. Yet it is made abundantly clear that Fame-Bearer cannot search for excuses by pointing out that he only did what others were also doing. But what happened to the adulterous queen and her sadistic lover? The latter is altogether ignored, and Full-of-Nectar reappears at some stage suffering from leprosy, and after death ends up in a hell – punishment for her on a much larger scale.

A second major theme is woven into all this, which we shall have to analyse in greater detail in Part two, under the heading of Love. Notice that the initial act of violence of the king is motivated by intense jealousy and disappointment; his depression is the result of what, at least in his eyes, was the collapse of a life filled with passionate love. This element of sexual lust is apparent in the whole series of rebirths and, as we shall see at a later stage, is central to the sacrifice of a pair of all living beings that the other king is involved in. To the Jains, the pursuit of power and of violence is intrinsically connected with love and sexual passions.

This all leads up to the insight that within each human being an arena similar to the grand cosmic one is contained, on which the battle of a miniature power-struggle rages. Part of our personality draws on the forces that pervade the universe – lust, passion, violence, craving for power – and another part attempts to counteract these. Each minute facet of this continuous war is subject to the laws of *karma*, and will bear fruit in the different kinds of future existence. At the same time, each moment is conditioned by past *karma*. Yet no fatalism is implied in this. For each present act may be conditioned by *karma*, but this conditioning does not eliminate the chances of genuine decision-making. That freedom is left intact, and thus each act is ambivalent as to the kind of *karma* it will generate. This does not now imply that the rationale of all conditioning factors is known. I may fall down and break my leg, and this is *a priori* due to past *karma*. But what precisely this may have been cannot be determined by ordinary people. Thus we hear of the *adṛṣṭa*, the 'unseen' (and thus unknowable); *daiva* (fate, divine ordinance); and '*ē pāvam*', which in Tamil means more or less 'alas!', 'what a misfortune!', though etymologically it derives from *pāpa*, negative *karma*. As the story makes clear, occasionally the individual can remember his past lives; but ordinarily this information can only be obtained from Jain sages. Thus on a small scale such a sage repeats what the *tīrthaṅkara* does on a cosmic scale: reveal the laws that govern *saṃsāra* and thereby teach people the consequences of it. We shall presently return to this theme.

Coursing through this complex maze of different life-forms was, by the testimony of the Indian traditions, a painful and horrifying experience. The story of Yaśodhara has made this, at least emotionally, clear. How could hell be worse, one could ask? Perhaps the hells are no more than quantitatively different, to wear out much worse *karma*. Even so, on the surface rebirth might still sound rather like fun – like an esoteric and exquisite form of tourism, conducted tours through the heavens and the underworlds – some intimate hours with our favourite pets within their world! Naturally this is so only as long as we can explore the pleasant and enjoyable sides of it. Standing at the outside, we do not quite understand all the fuss the Indians made about it. But then we might come across William Burroughs' *Cities of the Red Night*,[18] and terror will strike into our hearts. I doubt that there is anything in the Indian texts I could quote here that could recreate in *our* minds and hearts the terror that traditional, normative Indian awareness associated with *saṃsāra*. My intention is not to explore *Cities of the Red Night*, nor to do justice to Burroughs' work. It is a nightmare of a novel, and to me quite unpalatable. So let it be mentioned here just for the record as the only Western work known to me that explores the theme of transmigration and rebirth. One could be facetious and argue that, if you write about some form of suicidal sexual perversion, you would not get much of a story if you did not allow your heroes to be reborn time and again. Be that as it may, the effect of Burroughs' novel is, at least on my mind, identical to the effect of *saṃsāra* on the Indian mind. Moreover, if only in the form of a way-out avant-garde novel, Western culture does express here an imaginative interest in the idea of rebirth.

Filled with sea-monsters, whirlpools, treacherous rocks and unpredictable storms (as popular ditties would describe it metaphorically), this 'ocean of earthly existence' must have been a powerful symbol at a time when luxury cruises were unheard of. The various '-isms' provide a more detailed and searching analysis of it. According to Buddhism, it is, in essence, suffering, because nothing lasting (and what is pleasure, if it does not last?) can be found in it. Yet what keeps up the eternal life-pulse of this universe? Thirst, craving, desires – the drive towards external objects, as if they could enrich the subject driving towards them and the will to live and to continue living – are the answers. And almost identical answers are given on the Jain and the Hindu side. This adds a new dimension to our understanding of the general conception: not only is the universe the battle-field of different powers and forces, but, it is implied here, it pulsates in time because of the desires that initiate those battles. Yet it is important to note that this all-pervasive Thirst or Desire is not hypostatized. It does not exist independently of the individual beings in which it occurs. This is the point at which all this teaching expounded by *tīrthaṅkaras*, *tathāgatas*, *ṛṣis* (and some *avatāras*) becomes positive and optimistic. Escape from the 'ocean of earthly existence', from the hell that means being alive in the universe, is possible. It is possible by turning against this thirst or desire that, found within ourselves, can never be stronger than us, and by initiating a battle against it, not through it. This is where the ambivalence of *cakravartī – tīrthaṅkara*, as the two sides of one coin, becomes significant. The former searches for power in and over the external world, the latter, within himself. This is the significance of the 'religious heroes' referred to frequently, on the most profound level: that is what they carry into the world of man, the analysis of the world as governed by desire, the assurance that escape is possible, and the path leading towards that escape.

One of the important issues raised by these reflections concerns the authority on which the general theory of rebirth and the retribution of *karma* is based, and that includes, as integral component, the assumption of a unity of all life. Here we notice rather interesting variations in the different '-isms', together with a common assumption. The latter entails that these beliefs are empirically verifiable, at least for certain outstanding persons.

With the Buddhists, the standard description of what happened during the Buddha's enlightenment includes two insights. First, the Buddha is supposed to have seen that particular chain of causes and effects which made up his previous existences and led up to his present embodiment. Secondly, he is said to have then seen the general laws operating not merely on this specific, individual history, but on all human lives: the law of *karma* and of the desire that motivates it. With the Jains, similar insights are not reserved for such a peak experience by comparable exalted figures. Minimally they allow for the possibility that even the most incidental event or item in a person's life can trigger off a recollection of one's past experiences (this is called *jātīsmara*, a term used frequently in the story of Fame-Bearer). Similarly, equally innocuous happenings, such as a beautifully decorated maypole falling into a manure heap, may trigger off an experience of *vairāgya*, of losing interest in the worldly life (as happened to the twins in the story of Fame-Bearer). To see the whole structure with all its laws and all its individual pasts, is nevertheless reserved for the spiritually perfected (the Jain monk in the same story). Moreover, *jātīsmara* and *vairāgya* do not happen at random: only when past *karma* has created the right opportunity for it do they occur. On the Hindu side, it is similarly the *yogī* who can verify the truth of the system.

This now seems to be the point at which this whole conception closes itself off against our comprehension. Obviously we all know the fairy-tales of the brothers Grimm in which people seem to be able to transform themselves into animals and vice versa. If we stay up long enough in the evening and are bored enough, we can without difficulty watch werewolves in action – in a Hammer film. Witches, ghosts, giants and ogres fill our folklore, and during a seance we may be able to communicate with a deceased person, at least according to those who believe in them. But the mainstream Judaeo-Christian tradition has built very strong walls against all this, to protect its assumption of the uniqueness of the human soul and of the uniqueness of human life on earth. I have no intention of knocking all these walls down; instead, let me merely list some further interesting points that might turn out to offer promising new avenues of exploration.

Without doubt the idea of rebirth has in recent years acquired a more widespread currency, so that it can be seriously discussed even in popular magazines like *The Reader's Digest* or *The Sunday Times Colour Supplement.*[19] Thus Burroughs' novel cannot be written off as a totally solipsistic adventure, and I have heard even a Christian theologian reflect on the possibility of transmigration. But on the whole such current speculations restrict themselves to human rebirth – a possible past or future as animal (or ogre or 'god') lies generally outside the interest of popular Western discourse. Hypnosis is employed to unearth past embodiments – a Mr Smith is made to speak under hypnosis as a Napoleonic soldier who he is understood to have been in the past. Without wanting to deny that hypnosis is generally a fascinating subject of study, I feel that there are a number of problems associated with this application to rebirth. First of all, we are still far removed from possessing a comprehensive psychological and philosophical theory of what hypnosis precisely is and does. Secondly, there have been suggestions that a striking correspondence can be detected between the kind of persons unearthed by a hypnotist and the latter's own personal interests and predilections. Thirdly – and that is really what matters in our present discussion – no Indian theory could actually accommodate such a phenomenon. Ideas, sentiments, language and speech are regarded here as intrinsically connected with a specific and unique embodiment. Once a person has died, that particular constellation disintegrates and as such is irrevocably lost. Only an 'omniscient' mind can still know of it, but even he cannot recreate that constellation. In other words, even though the Buddhist Jātakas tell us about the Buddha's past existences in the form of animals, under no circumstances could Buddhism envisage that, say in the course of one of his sermons, the Buddha suddenly 'reconstructs' one such past embodiment and begins to roar like a tiger (or whatever).

Concern with our animal past or with the 'animal in all of us' occurs in other areas of discussion. For example, we have the fascinating mixture of the occult with the visual arts that goes by the name of atavism. Yet the interpretations of the relevant phenomena vary enormously, from cults of possession to self-hypnosis, and from unblocking forgotten childhood dreams and fears to recovering past existences. Only the last case would be interesting in our present context, but it has in fact been dealt with above.

No doubt it is possible that further systematic studies of hypnosis, possession, unconscious survival of childhood memories and atavistic practices will throw interesting light on details of the Indian experiences. But as far as the grand intellectual edifice that the Indian religions have established is concerned, the study of animal behaviour seems to me to be the most immediately relevant avenue of exploration. Research over many years into the behavioural patterns of chimpanzees[20] appears to suggest that our charming 'neighbours' can produce murderers and are capable of long-term hatred and revenge. The theory of evolution may explain all this, but as far as our ordinary understanding of human nature is concerned, I venture the suggestion that we regard, for instance, animal aggression and violence merely as an epiphenomenon. In this sense, the theory of *saṃsāra* and *karma* locates the animal drives which we have inherited through evolution much more solidly in the centre of our persons. Aggression and violence generate *karma* that must be 'worked off' – see the story of Fame-Bearer – and cannot simply be contained by a 'nice' home, or a 'caring' social service, or a 'moving' sermon. Does that make the Indian traditions more pessimistic? Clearly not, as we have seen earlier on. Man alone among the five categories of beings has the actual chance to do something qualitatively different about his destiny in *saṃsāra*. It is simply more difficult than we might initially imagine, since he is so much more solidly tied to the instincts and drives of animals (and ogres, 'gods' and demons) than we would accept.

On this basically optimistic note we may conclude the discussion of the present cultural construct with its three closely interlinked aspects: the structure of the universe with its layers of different life-forms, the cosmic transformations in time, and the laws governing the lives of all individual beings within this structure and revealed to them at particular points during world history. Now it would be a serious mistake to regard this whole conception as universally applicable to all types of Indian religion. This is certainly not the case. Instead, we shall use it as a mental map to explore the theme of power, by looking at types of religion that aim to encompass increasingly large and more comprehensive segments of it. In its extreme form, religious power will want to control the whole of human fate and destiny. It will want to cross over the 'ocean of embodied existence' altogether and make the qualitative leap into the realm beyond space, time and matter. But not all religion necessarily has such ultimate, transcendental ambitions; it may well content itself with the manipulation of this continuum and with the pursuit of much more limited and earthly goals. But minimally, power concerns itself with the most basic aspect of human culture, which is to survive and to create a small but secure environment for man to live and flourish in. So let us leave the grand cosmic scale and begin the exploration of power by focusing on the small and seemingly simple safe havens that religion wants to establish in this frightening universe.

CHAPTER 4
Safe havens

We have been looking at a view of the universe on a grand scale, where only the imagination sets the limits. It is a world filled with weird and wonderful beings and powers and held together through the common fate of transmigration. In many ways it is a terrifying world, frightening not only because of its enormous proportions, but also because it is pervaded by violence and a constant struggle for power between the different beings. Here is one example of how the popular imagination has envisaged such threats and power struggles. It takes us back to King Ploughman, whose adventures we have heard about previously. After his generous refusal to accept the amorous pleasures offered to him by Jewel-Lustre in her underworld palace, the king arrived at an ascetic's hermitage near the confluence of the 'seven Godāvarīs' with its temple of Śiva, and was welcomed there. But disaster had struck the seemingly idyllic place, as the ascetic told him.

'During the day, the *devas* play music for Śiva [in his temple]. But once they have left, ogres [lit. 'night-wanderers'] roam about during the night. The leader of these demons is called Horror-Face, and the visiting sages are so terrified of him that they do not dare stay here even for one day. But I know that tonight you will fight a battle with him. So take from me this *mantra*, with which you will be able to see, even in the dark of night, the body of any ogre (*rākṣasa*), even those concealed through magic. And once you have spotted such a wicked creature, let him find his death!'

When the king heard this, he laughed and exclaimed: 'Your reverence! This night will indeed be his last!' After this pledge the king accepted the *mantra* with wide-open eyes and agreed to do battle with the ogres. When the day was drawing to a close, the sage, who had bestowed many honours on the king, dismissed him, and he returned to his camp.

When the moon had set and the world was in the power of darkness, when the people were happily asleep and midnight was approaching, the leader of the demons, who took great pride in the valour and aggression of his own force, sent out two *rākṣasas* as messengers to the king. They spoke to him: 'King!

We have been sent as messengers. So listen to what our king has to tell you. "Because the two final watches of the night are meant for my pleasure, whatever living creature remains here [during that period] will serve me as my food. So if you desire to save yourself, then give me as an offering a hundred knights, a hundred rutting elephants and a thousand men, horses and heads of cattle!"' Hearing this, the king replied to the messengers in a rage: 'Be off! Go back and pass on my message to your lord. Tell him: "Ogre! Come here, so that I can make an offering of your flesh to the dogs and crows that scavenge in my royal camp!"' In this and many further ways the king in his fury shouted insults and then drove the two *rākṣasa* messengers back.

After they had left, he ordered the guard of the camp not to permit anyone to leave the camp before dawn. 'A thousand princes and knights will be enough for us, though I understand that the demon's army is ten thousand strong.' Such were the orders he gave, and thus he marched out of his camp to fight the ogres, surrounded by a thousand heroes.

Soon the *rākṣasa* army fell upon the king. They were impossible to look at because of the blazing fire that shot out of their gaping, monstrous mouths. They turned the surface of the sky dark-red with the sparks of the fire from their deadly daggers. Their loud shrieks and howls made the world reverberate. The flames shooting from their eyes dispelled the darkness and illuminated their own forms. Their massive thick, rough, red hair was tied up with 'garlands' in the form of blood-dripping entrails. Strung-up human heads served as belts around their gruesomely clad hips. Their appearance was blackness – as of a bee, or wild buffalo, or a cloud filled with rain, or the *tamāla* tree, or a cuckoo, or of collyrium.[1]

We can leave out the details of the terrific battle that sets in; eventually it seems that the ogres are winning.

When the king saw his army being decimated by those demons who concealed their bodies under magic, he remembered the *mantra*. Now wherever he could thereby spot a demon, there and then in his fury he cut him instantly in two. Thus although Horror-Face's forces outnumbered his own many times, in no time the king was able to 'clip his wings'. Soon the army of the *rākṣasas* was in a state of disarray: the piles of cut-off feet, hands, legs and heads began to attract hordes of *piśācas*, it allowed *vetālas* to wallow in the mud caused by the abundantly flowing streams of warm blood, and it echoed with the howls of the jackals that came in the entourage of hundreds of witches (*ḍākiṇīs*).[2]

At this point the king of the ogres himself attacks Hāla who, naturally, kills him.

There cannot now be any doubt that for most people a view of the world filled with such horrific beings would give rise to agoraphobia. There is in most of us an inbuilt need for some far more limited and homely environment in which we feel safe and protected. These are, in terms of my previous ocean metaphor, the relatively cosy 'safe havens' of ordinary life. In modern literature, both Western and Indian, such 'safe havens' against a threatening world often appear in the guise of the 'room': an enclosed space within which some person locks himself and tries to protect himself hermetically against the unbearable terror of the outside world. Examples could be quoted from Grass, García Márquez or Rushdie; here are two lines by the Maharashtrian Dilip Chitre found in his *Travelling in a Cage* – a collection of poems pervaded by 'room symbolism':

> What kind of wind was making love to leafless trees
> Outside the door I was always afraid to open?[3]

In this chapter I would like to take a closer look at types of religion that concern themselves with the construction, maintenance and defence of spaces enclosed by boundaries. To label these 'timid' is perhaps unfair, since there is obviously a deep need in human nature for such protectionism. But in contrast to the adventurousness and bravery to be explored at a later stage, this label might not be too misleading or unfair. As a further introduction to the subject let me quote from Adil Jussawalla:

> It has been said that the Indian personality isn't well integrated, and that, unlike the Western, it fails to make a coherent synthesis of different elements in its experience. It must be remembered that the elements the Indian is expected to synthesize are more various and further apart from one another than any within the national experience of a contemporary Westerner.[4]

Mutatis mutandis this observation could be applied to traditional India with its equally enormous range of elements – part of which we have already had the opportunity to come to know. The view of the world we find in the isolationist structures, in the safe havens built and guarded by religion, may be more amorphous and far narrower than the one discussed previously, but they share a fair amount of the different types of beings populating it and, above all, the perception of threatening powers of violence and destruction. Thus an enclosed space is created, with clearly demarcated boundaries, and ritual serves as the protective device to keep up these boundaries, maintain the safe inner space and ward off intruders from the outside. Equally important are similar rituals and other religious protective devices that allow for a safe crossing from one protected realm to another. With the help of this model such a large segment of Indian religious traditions can actually be encompassed, that it is clearly impossible to do anything more here than illustrate this type of religious mentality and its range, using a few examples.

Possibly the smallest enclosed space we can imagine is that of the individual person, the body itself acting here as the boundaries. By now, enough material has accumulated to prepare us for the fact that the traditional Indian perception of what could threaten the safety and well-being of the person differs from our own explanation in terms of bacteria and viruses, lack of hygiene and childhood traumas. Thus we find, for instance, a widespread belief in the 'evil eye', in malice or jealousy or envy that can magically substantialize itself, as it were, and inflict harm on the person who is its target. Logically, the defence may involve tattooing the body or marking it in some other form. The shape of the tattoo may then suggest something 'auspicious' (like a conch or certain flowers or trees) and repel the danger by virtue of its own non-dangerous, auspicious nature. Or such a tattoo may be the image, symbol or name of a particular *deva* who is then assumed to guard his 'property' thus marked and identified as such. Equally logical is the wearing of mirrors, for in them the glances of the evil eye are cast back upon itself. Related to this are rituals in which a dazzling bright light – demons belong to the night and, like Count Dracula, hate the light – is waved in front of a person. Here the relevant lines of an old South Indian song, meant to be sung as part of such a daily rite for young boys, may be quoted. (That the setting for the song itself is mythical – Yaśodā calling her adopted son Kṛṣṇa – need not concern us in the present context.)

Lovely twilight has arrived –
            Come here that I may 'protect' you!
I am waiting here, calling you –
    all the cows and calves
    have gone into their stables
    and are lowing!
You must not stay at the crossroad
    when it is twilight –
I am telling you for your own good!
            Come here that I may 'protect' you!
I may have spoken scolding words

when you kicked in the girls' sand-castles
(and you ran off without your dinner),
but now I won't do anything like that to you –
Come here that I may 'protect' you!
There are rumours that an ogress
with red hair and poisonous breasts
is on her way to harm you!
So I am terrified that you stay there.
Come here that I may 'protect' you!
Your bed-time has come –
Come here that I may 'protect' you!
Look! There is horrific Kāpāli!
Come here that I may 'protect' you!
Don't roam about at twilight!
Just listen for once to what
your mother is telling you!
I am holding a twilight lamp
to give you sacred protection
and let your body light up
in all its splendour:
Come here![5]

What could be closer to a scene from everyday life? – a rather naughty boy, chasing the girls and fooling around, the sun setting and his mother calling him home for dinner, threats and cajoling words, and inexhaustible patience! But the whole is pervaded by deeply ingrained beliefs in the dangers lurking at crossroads and at twilight (two areas of transition from one boundary system to another) and in ogres and ogresses and the terrifying *devī*, Kāpāli. A lamp – presumably burning camphor – will be waved in front of the child to 'protect' him, which is to say create a shield against the evil eye and whatever other evil forces may be lying in wait to harm him.

From the person we can move to the village, an area with boundaries in the most literal sense. For we come across, for instance in Tamil Nadu, images in stone or terracotta of beings variously called 'guardians', 'deities', or 'goddesses' 'of the village boundary'. *Rākṣasas* and *piśācas* and similar ogre-like figures crave for the human flesh of the village people; other such non-human beings may be responsible for illnesses and epidemics, or for the droughts and diseases that can destroy the crops in the fields. Among the many protective devices employed, we find in the same Tamil Nadu very impressive arrays of sometimes gigantic terracotta horses which are often explained as the mounts used by (the 'god') Aiyaṉār in the night to ride out against dangerous demonic beings (see Plates 1f). But my favourite example consists of a whole pile-up of protective images: Aiyaṉār himself, a soldier and a policeman, a dog and a watchman (see Plate 3)![6]

Plate 1. Terracotta figures, near Salem, Tamil Nadu

It follows from the definition of a safe haven as a place of life and security that death is its direct opposite. Accordingly, the cremation ground where corpses are cremated (and criminals used to be executed) lies outside the village boundaries and appears in the popular imagination as the epitome of everything that is horrific, dangerous and deadly. Haunted during the night-time by the most vicious and blood-thirsty of creatures, it conjures up a foretaste of the hells and symbolizes forbidden territory. Not surprisingly, images of vicious-looking beings are installed here which are identified as 'guardians of the cremation ground', whose role must be to keep an eye on the demons, ghosts and goblins that gather here at night and block their entry into the village.

To the uninformed traveller, the visual appearance of the statues of these different kinds of guardian figures will be quite disconcerting. What could be more horrific than these creatures? Such a question fails

Plate 2. Terracotta figure, near Mayil āṭu tturai, Tamil Nadu

Plate 3. Terracotta figures, near Villupuram, Tamil Nadu

to see the logic behind the situation. Precisely because these guardian figures are so terrifying, they are able to instil fear into other dangerous beings; like the mirrors, they reflect horror back on to the dangers lurking outside. In fact, we might as well simplify matters and acknowledge that no real qualitative difference exists between them. That means, they are like mercenaries hired by two different factions and fighting against each other. These guardians have been taken into the employment of the villagers, and as long as they receive their desired rewards, they will continue to protect them. Terminology typical of learned discourse is inapplicable to this level of perception. Thus when one observes the loving devotion offered to a statue outside the main shrine at Jejurī in Maharashtra, it is clear that this figure is perceived and treated as a loyal protector and not as the image of the evil demon that the god Khaṇḍobā of the temple killed, according to the textual interpretation of the sight.[7]

If some non-human beings can be hired as guards for a village, what are the rewards paid to them for their services? Moreover, what would happen if these village protectors were not properly paid for their labours? The latter question is easier to answer: they will revert to being precisely what other members of their species have been all along: dangerous, destructive and causing all kinds of disasters. Epidemics or droughts may thus be regarded as caused by some dissatisfied, ignored, insulted, enraged protective figure (see Plate 4). Thus the village will have to offer to him or her on a much larger scale the sort of things which normally keep the protecting beings favourably inclined to the village. Now what are such rewards? There is nothing mysterious about the way such protective beings are shown the villagers' gratitude: they are all the things appreciated among the humans. Thus they may be given pieces of clothes and jewellery (particularly for the females among them); milk and water (to drink, or as a refreshing bath); sweet-smelling substances such as camphor, perfume and incense, beautiful flowers; and rice, vegetables, sweets, fruits and pan nuts, and, on special occasions, meat and alcohol. Among the gestures of honour and respect we may mention clockwise circumambulations and singing, dancing and general festivity on certain days of the year. The technical term used for all these types of honouring and rewarding is *pūjā* (see Plate 5).

Plate 4. 'Shrine' of Māriāī, a typical epidemic *devī*, outside a Harijan village, between Pune and Jejurī, Maharashtra

Plate 5. *Pūjā* in the Viṣṇu temple of Nantipura-viṇṇakaram, Tamil Nadu

From the village and its 'veneration' or 'payment' of the non-human guardians it is only a very small step to the temple. There are various continua which make this transition so easy. First, there is the housing of such respected protective agents: as a special reward a village may well decide to build a special abode for one of them, and whether we call them huts or shrines or temples or palaces is really only a question of scale. Secondly, the same applies to the treatment offered – in the temple this may well approximate the luxuries with which a king is wont to be surrounded. Finally, the royal scale of many a temple continues one of the essential aspects of the king himself: to be the 'protector of the earth', a function attributed to the non-human being abiding in the temple.

In many ways now the complex cults practised in the temples elaborate on the themes of protection and power. In a direct reversal of the idea of the evil eye, the beneficial effect of the *darśana*, the 'sight' of the protector, is developed. To see the *deva* in his temple means to absorb through the eyes, as it were, his protective powers (see Plate 6). Since Viṣṇu temples in Tamil Nadu house the *deva* in a dark, windowless inner shrine, the priest actually lights a piece of camphor on a tray and moves along the statue, so that the devotee can see every detail of the figure. Although the learned frown upon this, ordinary people will then place their hands over the same camphor and touch their foreheads with them. In Kerala, the image is visible only during brief periods of the day; the dramatic moment when the doors are flung open by the priests is prepared for through long waiting, while wind and percussion instruments play an increasingly fast tune. Finally the *deva* can be seen – drowned in the dazzle of hundreds of oil-lamps.

A very similar substantialized conveyance of protection can be seen in the *prasāda*. This is a food offering which, by contact with the temple image, becomes imbued with special powers and is then returned to the devotee, to be consumed by him. We may note here that in monotheistic traditions the same word *prasāda* denotes 'divine grace'.

Another mode of offering respect and receiving the desired assurance of well-being and prosperity in return derives from the social custom of prostrating before a respected person and touching his feet with one's forehead. Among the Todas in the Nilgiri hills, the women still greet the men in this fashion. In ancient days this may have been the custom also in the temples: people could approach the statue and put their head

Plate 6. Bronze figure of Viṣṇu in Nantipura-viṇṇakaram, Tamil Nadu

on its feet. But for unknown reasons (and it may well have been the abrasive effect this had on the finely carved statue) this custom became obsolete, the inner shrine being closed off to all devotees. Now an ingenious solution was produced: if you can't get at the *deva*'s feet, let them come to you. Thus in the Viṣṇu temples of Tamil Nadu, a bell-shaped metal object with a pair of feet and ankles on its top (which can be seen in Plate 5) is brought by the priest to the devotee and placed like a crown for a moment or so on the devotee's head.

And here is another example of comparable ingenuity. At most times it will be sufficient for the guardian of the village or town to reside in his temple-palace and hold audiences for his protégés who, in the various ways mentioned, take his protective power home with them. But on some occasions the reverse situation is called for, when the protector goes out of his palace, visits his protégés, casts his protective glance more directly over the fields and houses, and reiterates his claims over the territory he is supposed to be guarding. As long as the physical image of the protector is a piece of stone or a small terracotta figure, this can be carried out without difficulty. But what happens when the statue is of solid granite and more than life-size? So the category of the 'image that moves' was developed: a second statue of much smaller size and of metal which can be taken out of the temple in procession through the streets and fields (see Plate 7).

Although, in theory, Jain doctrine cannot accommodate the temple as a meaningful component, on the popular level we nevertheless find an understanding of the temple expressed which resembles the one discussed so far. Let me illustrate this from a moralistic tale.

Once upon a time there lived a pious merchant whose wife Jina-Gift was barren and therefore cajoled him into a second marriage. He chose her half-sister Gold-Lustre by the same father, but a different mother called Kin-Lustre. One day the latter arrived for a visit and rather delicately asked her daughter whether everything was all right in her marriage. The incongruous reply was anything but delicate and ran along the following lines:

'My husband has remained completely infatuated by that bitch! Those two think of nothing but having sex and spend day and night in the Jina temple!'

Back home, Kin-Lustre remained filled with fury and tried to figure out a way of destroying Jina-Gift. Then one day a *kāpālika* ascetic called Vicious-Killer arrived (Caṇḍamāri). He was carrying a skull-topped stick and resembled

Plate 7. Procession in Tiruveḷḷakkuḷam, near Tirunakari, Tamil Nadu

Death himself. Kin-Lustre, whose heart was devoted to Śiva, was sitting at the door and saw him. 'I have seen many *kāpālikas*, but this one has something unique about him. Surely it will be from him that I shall obtain the fulfilment of my desires, and through him that that useless creature will be removed!' With these thoughts in mind, every day she gave him many kinds of food as his alms. That rogue in turn realized that through the overabundance of her devotion his own aims could be furthered. So one day he addressed Kin-Lustre:

'Little mother! We possess magical powers (*vidyās*) and accomplishments (*siddhis*) and spells (*mantras*) powerful from meditation and *yoga*. There is nothing in the world which I cannot accomplish. If there is any business you would want me to do for you, you must tell me!'

When that stupid and evil-minded old woman heard this, she cried out and said: 'Oh, you God-sent gift! How kind you are! Through your favour I could achieve anything! Yes, my son, there is a weighty matter ... Your sister is endowed with incomparable qualities; her name is Gold-Lustre and she has a lovely body. I was cheated by a wicked woman who practises magic, and married her to that woman's own husband. And now the girl remains fettered by an evil spirit. Day and night she stays in her own room, and that damned woman does not let go of her husband even for a moment. Her name is Jina-Gift, and she is of evil character. If that wicked woman could be killed in some way – you could stay in my house permanently ... '

'If, by conjuring up the *vetāla-vidyā*, that powerful magic spell which subdues the three worlds, I do not succeed in leading that evil woman to the town of Death, I shall hand over my own body to the fire.'

That night Caṇḍamāri went into the cremation ground, with all the paraphernalia and utensils he needed. He (who had studied books about casting spells) sat down in the lotus position, clasped a dagger in his hand, worshipped the goddess and recited *mantras*. He was sitting on a corpse. Terrifying like Death himself, he emitted from his mouth flames of fire that proceeded to stand in front of him.

'Give us, oh master!' it spoke, 'a mission, a task to fulfil according to your orders! Whom do you want to send out?' Then Vetālinī, the *vidyā* of horrific form, manifested herself before him in the guise of a corpse. He commanded her: 'Go and kill in the temple of the Jina the pious co-wife of Gold-Lustre!'

Obeying the command of the *kāpālika*, she went to the Jina temple where Jina-Gift was praying. But she was unable to enter the shrine, repelled by the power of the *deva* and, humiliated, remained standing at a distance. Since the mere mention of the *deva*'s name makes demons (*grahas*), ogres (*rākṣasas*) and ghosts (*bhūtas*) flee and lasting peace is secured, how could that wicked, impure, evil-minded and damned ogress have gained entrance into his temple! Since she was unable to find a way inside, she lost her lustre and, emitting a loud roar, returned to the cremation ground. She fell down before Vicious-Killer, but his spells forced her up again and immediately he sent her out a second time. She who could not normally be subdued by anyone, failed in her task, going out and returning three times. Yet, worried about the oath he had uttered, he did not give up, and sent her out once again, after telling her: 'I want you to kill the one of the two co-wives who possesses an evil character and has fallen from good conduct and bring her here!' Consequently that evil creature went into the house and, after killing Gold-Lustre, returned. When Vicious-Killer saw the *vetālinī*'s dagger smeared with blood, he dismissed the conjured-up ogress and left the cremation ground. Pleased with himself, he returned to his own abode.

Even Kin-Lustre was pleased for a while in anticipation, but when she discovered that it was her own daughter who had been killed by the spirit she rushed off to the king and accused Jina-Gift of the murder. But both the evil ascetic and Kin-Lustre began to be haunted by demons and were chased through the town, and thus were made to confess their crime. Thus Jina-Gift's devotion to the Jain religion protected her against all these evils.[8]

This charming and edifying tale brings together a number of the themes we have explored previously: the cremation ground and its dangers for the village or the town, the ambivalent powers of the 'holy man' or evil ascetic, who through his association with the beings lurking in the cremation ground has acquired their malevolent or benevolent powers; terrifying non-human beings who harm or protect humans; spells and magic lore as the means of conjuring up such beings and controlling them; and the temple as a safe haven which is guarded against intruders by a, or the, *deva*. (However, attention must be drawn to the fact that in a specifically Jain manner all this is superseded by locating the rationale for Jina-Gift's protection in her own piety and moral purity. While popularly the temple's *deva* may be identified with the Jina himself, a more sophisticated interpretation can avoid such a non-orthodox view by speaking of a *deva* installed there as the guardian.)

But in the general context that we are exploring, ambivalence remains and, in a sense, itself constitutes a major threat of insecurity. Let me illustrate this from two examples. The first one is still directly connected with the temple, and the second concerns the ambivalent function of certain 'goddesses'.

From one angle, the temple may be the seat of the village's or town's protective power; but from another angle, it must itself be protected so as not to lose its protective faculties. A particularly striking expression of this idea can be observed in Kerala. Here balls of sandal paste are given by the priests as *prasāda*, to be rubbed over the chests and shoulders of the devotees. Yet instead of handing these balls over to them, the priest flings them into their hands – a striking way of avoiding contact with dangerous powers outside the boundaries of the temple. I have mentioned already that in the Viṣṇu temples of Tamil Nadu (as also in Kerala and other regions) the inner shrine is closed off to the devotees. In the same Tamil Nadu we witness the development of the famous *gopurams*, 'temple towers', which in the course of the centuries have reached gigantic proportions and totally dwarf the original central shrine. They are erected over the entrance gates, but otherwise no architectural or ritual function for them has so far been discovered. The only explanation that appears to make some sense of this enormous construction effort is that these towers block off, in all four directions, the sight of the central shrine from demonic beings. The temple bells have a clearer function – their ringing puts panic into the hearts of demons. And a third feature must probably be included under the heading of protective mechanisms: obscenity (see Plate 8). Far from showing that in India sex in all its varieties has been celebrated as a religious act and that even houses of worship are decorated with scenes of such celebrations, such erotic images (and

Plate 8. Govindarāja temple, Tirupati, Andhra Pradesh

some of them can be very gross indeed) have been explained to me as protection against interference by demons. Nudity is generally a public taboo in India and far more so the obscene nakedness of couples and groups of people involved in all kinds of less-than-straightforward sex. Like the mirrors and the terrifying faces of the guardian-demons, such images repel dangerous beings by casting their own obscene nature back at them. (Certainly, for southern India I believe this to be the only valid explanation. At most one could assume the survival of archaic ideas about fertility and prosperity linked with the seat of security and life; but this could hardly include the more 'pornographic' scenes found at some temples.) But the most obvious and best-known illustration of the idea that the temple itself requires protection lies in the strict rules that apply to those who are allowed to enter into it. Until very recently, no untouchables (and still today, in some cases, no Muslims or Indian and European Christians) were allowed inside a major, orthodox Hindu temple. Should such an incident happen, enormously complicated rituals have to be performed to restore the protective power of the temple.

So far I have tried to avoid using commonplace labels and categories and instead have spoken of 'protective beings', etc. At this point I would like to introduce some more specific material, which happens to be associated with two different *devī* figures. The first example comes from north-eastern India (Bengal and neighbouring regions) and involves the goddess Manasā.

The *devī* Manasā, blind in one eye, realized that she alone among the *devas* was not worshipped by men. So she set out to enforce her cult in the human world. In the shape of an ancient brahmin woman she approached some cowherds and asked them for milk. When they refused, Manasā stole their cattle. To placate her, they began to make offerings to what they now realized was a powerful being.

But there had been a prophecy that only if and when the rich merchant Chando offered her *pūjā*, would her worship on earth become established. Chando's wife had learnt the secrets of Manasā's *pūjā* from fishermen whose enterprise had begun to flourish as soon as they began to worship the *devī*. But when Chando discovered that his wife was indulging in this (what he regarded as) most vulgar and despicable rite, he kicked over the vessel sacred to Manasā, hit the *devī* with a stick on the hip, so that she remained lame thereafter, and beat up his wife. Naturally, Manasā became furious. She destroyed Chando's plantations, deprived him, in the guise of a prostitute, of his occult powers, killed his *guru*, and finally his six sons.

But a seventh son was born to him who, when he reached maturity, became betrothed to Behulā. Manasā instigated a row with Behulā, in the course of which she cursed her: her husband would die during the wedding night. In spite of putting the newly married couple into a sealed iron chamber, Chando could not prevent the curse from being fulfilled and one of Manasā's serpents succeeded in entering the chamber and killing the young man. Behulā put the corpse of her husband on to a raft, and for six months she floated with him down the Ganges. Then she encountered Manasā and made a deal with her: if she revived her husband (and his six brothers), Behulā would persuade Chando to venerate her. The merchant, after a lot of persuasion, finally and very contemptuously, payed his homage to the dangerous goddess.[9]

Before commenting on this story, let me turn to Maharashtra where we find another popular *devī*: Yellammā (see Plate 9). Time and again she shows herself in the world of man, but, unlike Manasā, these intrusions tend to be at first very innocuous, yet trigger off violent reactions. Humbly, Yellammā accepts all insults or impossible tasks demanded of her, and by carrying them out proves herself to be a very mighty lady indeed. It is only here that sometimes her violent nature comes to the fore. In one poem[10] her appearance threatens *devas* and *asuras* alike who force her to prepare a meal for them out of nothing. She succeeds, but poisons them all. In another poem[11] she humbly asks a gardener for a slice of onion, but he refuses, and when her request is repeated, he gives her a severe beating. Now Yellammā has had enough:

Plate 9. Yellammā, Jejurī, Maharashtra

Her head reached up to the sky,
her feet pressed down into the earth,
and each of her eyes
she made big like a cart-wheel –
certainly a whole hand
was not enough to measure them!
Pus welled forth from her eyes,
and running down on her body
it flowed towards the gardener's garden.
From her necklace of cowrie shells
she brought forth turmeric powder.
She scattered it over his body
so that it flared up with inflammation.
Boils appeared on his body,
each the size of a capsicum –
certainly a whole hand
was not enough to measure them!
Blood and pus began to drip to the ground.
People who were passing by
had to hold their noses closed.[12]

The people of the village make him an outcaste and he has to live outside the village boundaries. After a while, Yellammā approaches him once again, in the garb of a female religious mendicant (*jogtīṇ*). The gardener has learnt his lesson; he falls down before her and begs for forgiveness.

Then all malice went away from her heart.
She scattered *bel* leaves
and turmeric powder over him,
and put her hand on his head.
She placed her mouth on his body
and sucked up all the blood and pus.
Then she stepped back,
smacked her lips and belched.
In this manner she brought back
to life the gardener.[13]

In another poem a British Colonial officer, who treated her with contempt and believed her to be merely a silly superstition, is granted a vision of her having a bath and dressing herself. This sight makes him lust after her, but she punishes him with blindness.[14]

These stories and poems require some 'decoding'. Initially it is easy enough to recognize familiar themes like the struggle for power. These *devīs* want to receive honours and benefits from people, are ready to use all kinds of malice and violence to enforce their demands, and in turn are prepared to guard people's well-being and prosperity. Cowherds and fishermen, merchants and gardeners, increase their business through a *devī*'s favours, but at the same time the stories illustrate very dramatically the fears in people's minds of their destructive violence, were Manasā or Yellammā not rewarded properly, or were anyone to question their powers (as the Colonial officer did). But the destructive power is only partially illustrated in the stories, through the association of the *devīs* with serpents, poison, eczema and blindness. Behind these images are hidden a much more generic, general connection with disease, illness and epidemics. When the *devī*'s 'havoc' is mentioned,[15] this is idiomatic for an outbreak of cholera, typhoid or smallpox. To make matters more complicated for us: this is not understood merely as something caused by the *devī*; rather, she has physically come and entered people. The boils or whatever on people's bodies are the signs that she is dwelling in them. Thus special rites must be performed to placate her anger and make her resume her protective role – in other words, to make her leave people's bodies and return to her own shrine. Often this nexus of ideas is complicated further by becoming associated with 'possession' as a consciously manipulated phenomenon (after all, the presence of the *devī* in a person as a disease like smallpox is also a kind of possession, just as mental disorders tend to be interpreted as another, involuntary and individual type of possession by special spirits). In this case rituals are performed by means of which a non-human being is made to enter into a medium and is made to speak through him about the causes of a personal or a public disease, identifying the particular agent present in the person or in the people. Alternatively, there may be rituals through which the disease-causing agent itself is made to reveal her identity and proclaim the cause of her displeasure and the means of placating her.

Thus more than just being devotional stories or mythical reflections on the origins of a particular religious cult, these accounts of *devīs* intruding into the world of man seek to explain the mechanisms by which misfortune and disease, drought and illness, can be avoided. Temple worship, *pūjā* and the performance of special rites (like the cults of possession) are some of the means advocated in order to maintain or restore a healthy equilibrium between human and non-human interests. But the story of Yellammā introduces a further feature. In Maharashtra and Karnataka, Yellammā has her special 'holy men' and 'holy women', the *jogtīs* and *jogtīṇs.*[16] Note that the *devī* herself went to the gardener in the guise of a *jogtīṇ*. These men and women, who as children have been handed over to the *devī* and her temple (the girls might well serve as 'temple prostitutes') go on regular alms rounds. Any offering made to them is an offering and sign of respect for the *devī* Yellammā, and any insult to them will provoke her rage. As in the Jain story about the 'holy man' who tried to commit murder, our conventional terminology is clearly incapable of coping with such a situation.

Finally, we must cast at least a cursory glance over a much more complex illustration of a 'safe haven' – that of the Vedic tradition. What makes this example more complicated than the ones we have been looking at previously is the fact that the label 'Vedic tradition' gathers together a whole cluster of different protected realms: a sacred scripture, a social group, the individual person, ritual events, and a 'religion'. The historical starting point for all this (around 1200 BC) was something very concrete: the creation of a 'safe haven', in a quite literal sense, by one small group of immigrant people (the Āryas) in an alien, threatening and enormously variegated country (India). Their perception of the peoples whom they found living there and whom they endeavoured to subjugate in the course of the following centuries may well have flowed, as the real basis of subsequent imaginative expansion, into the conception of such beings as *rākṣasas* and other demonic creatures. They expressed their religion in an oral literature called the Veda ('Sacred Knowledge'); thus the phrase 'Vedic tradition' is meant to denote here the religion that developed from it. Whatever may have happened over the millennia to the Āryas in a purely physiological, racial sense, it was due to the effort particularly of their priests, the brahmins, that their religious heritage could be protected against all erosion in the course of time. The method employed is strictly exclusivist and it is here that we encounter some initial instances of the protective attitudes listed above.

Even long after other religious traditions were writing down their scriptures, the brahmins persevered in transmitting their Veda exclusively through oral means. Without doubt this was partly due to the belief that an Ārya could only realize his true brahminhood by physically, as it were, absorbing the Veda from the mouth of his teacher, via his ears, into his mind and heart and by expressing it in turn through his own lips. But this was partly a protective device. There may well have been economic and professional factors involved in this, but it is the religious factors that are relevant in the present context. The Veda is something that has to be protected against an outside interference that would damage its own protective power. The oral method of teaching made it possible to apply a stringent control to the selection of people admitted to the years of studying the Veda and to exclude all non-Āryas (and women) from coming into any kind of critical contact with it.

Nominally on the basis of the Veda, the tradition developed extraordinarily complex rules for the true Vedic life, rules that were spelled out in the Dharmaśāstras. This literature offers us fascinating insights into further aspects of protective methods. First of all, it envisages a rigidly compartmentalized society, cut up into Āryas and non-Āryas (the *śūdras*, 'untouchables', etc.). The latter must have always constituted the vast majority of the Indian populace, of perhaps eighty per cent or more. Furthermore, the Āryas themselves are divided into three groups – the brahmins or priests, *kṣatriyas* or warriors, and *vaiśyas* or 'settlers' (farmers and traders). The assumption put forward here is that each of the four basic groups lead separate and different lives, fulfil different roles in society, and do not intermarry. The boundary separating the Āryas from the non-Āryas is drawn in a particularly emphatic manner.

But over and above such concerns for social 'apartheid', the Dharmaśāstras attempt to regulate a whole range of group-internal matters and desire to protect the individual against various kinds of harm. On the whole, the perception of what could be harmful involves less personalized and concrete forces of danger than those we have encountered in our previous examples. But as we shall see, we are clearly dealing here with a continuity. For example, the treatise ascribed to Manu deals in the following manner with the problem of how to choose the right kind of wife.[17] Overriding constraints demand that, ideally, she belong to the same social group and is not related to the man (according to a complex set of criteria which, on the whole, are wider than our own definition of what constitutes a 'relative'). That the girl may belong to a rich and powerful family must not be a primary concern, for other factors may make such a family unacceptable as one's in-laws. Manu lists ten such factors, which include the neglect of Vedic rituals, lack of interest in studying the Vedas, and the absence of male offspring. Moreover, individual members of the family under scrutiny must not suffer from epilepsy, leprosy, a weak digestion, haemorrhoids, or an overabundance of body hair. Now follows the examination of the girl. She must have a brother, and her father must be known. She must not have any of the following features: red hair or red eyes, no hair on her body or too much of it, a redundant limb; and she must not be sickly or garrulous. She must not be named after such things as trees or rivers or birds or snakes. Instead, she should possess fine bodily characteristics, an auspicious name, moderate hair on her body, small teeth, soft limbs and she should walk with the elegance of a goose or an elephant. We may note that some of the undesirable features allude to the demonic creatures we have encountered at the beginning of the chapter – the *rākṣasas* too have red hair and red eyes, rough skin and large teeth!

Marriage is also in our perception an important crossroad in a person's life and filled with many potential dangers (even though we might employ somewhat different criteria in the choice of the right partner). But there are other such boundaries that an individual has to cross that are rather more culture specific, like sexual intercourse that penetrates a person's bodily boundary, eating and drinking that lets external substances enter into the body, defecating and urinating as the reverse process, and death as the crossing over into another realm. For all these events and acts, the Dharmaśāstras spell out detailed sets of rules, particularly with reference to who is permitted to be involved or participate or witness, in order to guard the individual against any harm that might arise from such dangerous crossings.

Finally we shall cast a brief glance over a particular ritual, the *śrāddha*.[18] By means of this offering, food is intended to be conveyed to the 'fathers' (*pitṛs*), namely dead ancestors, to nourish them and to prevent them from turning into ghosts (*pretas*, *bhūtas*) that are out to devour human beings. In that sense, it is another protective device. But in other ways, it has to be protected itself, so that the food actually finds its way to the desired goal. Thus Manu lists about a hundred different types of people who must not be invited to the ritual or who must not be permitted to come anywhere near it. For their presence would transform the desired beneficial effect of the sacrifice into a negative effect, destructive to the sacrificer. Here, as also in the previous examples, the emphasis is less on the correct performance of something and more on excluding certain kinds of people and beings from it who are perceived to have a negative effect. This, I think, suggests a communal fear in an alien and threatening environment. In the same way as the food sent out to the fathers will only reach them by avoiding endless obstacles on its way, man (and I am afraid, as far as the Vedic tradition is concerned, the emphasis of the word is heavily on the male gender) walks through a world, most of which is dark, pernicious jungle, on a narrow path lit up for him by the torch of Veda. Like the *mantra* given to king Ploughman, it reveals the powers of destruction among the crowds of potentially dangerous beings, which in certain circumstances may include other men with weak digestion, women with red hair, *śūdras*, certain animals and *rākṣasas* or *piśācas*. As such, the Veda itself has to be guarded against the forces of darkness that threaten to extinguish it. Thus the Veda evolved as a powerful symbol by means of which a particular religious tradition could defend itself against other religions that deny the Veda's validity, with the 'defence of the Veda' as the slogan on its banners.

By now a very wide range of material has been presented here which I have endeavoured to explain in terms of a conceptual framework involving terms like safe haven, boundaries, protective devices and dangerous forces. For a number of reasons, such an enterprise will require some justification and further discussion. The concepts used are not the ones usually employed in the analysis of some of the material looked at and the range of material gathered together here would normally be dealt with under a variety of different headings that are derived from distinct locations on the social map of India (and have traditionally been dealt with by the different disciplines of indology and anthropology). Moreover, we have to investigate to what extent we have been looking at realities or wishful thinking and to what extent the known facts themselves require us to add an element of flexibility or openness to the hermetically closed safe havens. I have treated together types of ritual practices which Indians would distinguish conceptually as *grāmya*, 'vulgar', literally 'belonging to the village'; as āgamic or tantric (and thus connected with enormously complex and rich textual traditions that also contain philosophy and theology); and thirdly as *vaidika*, or belonging to the tradition of the Vedas. Moreover I have treated myth and reality as if they shared a common logic. And finally, I have been using a terminology (boundaries, etc.) which may not be very familiar to the student of Indian material. I have assumed that all this can be treated as a system that is complete and coherent in itself.

Let me begin by looking at the terminology used here. The criterion cannot be whether it is true or false, right or wrong, but merely, whether the conceptual framework expressed through it proves useful or not. 'Useful' should mean being able to gather together as wide as possible a range of phenomena that share a common nature. The exercise of spreading out such phenomena has already been completed. If after some explanation this is felt to be convincing, the 'usefulness' would have been proved. The conceptual structure involving boundaries and so on has been used by social scientists. But in the case of India, a different framework has more typically been employed: that of purity and pollution. In a sense this is very useful, for it avoids a directly ethical, moral, or even theological association (good versus evil, or sacred versus profane). On the other hand, it still does give rise to wrong associations, particularly when pure or polluting substances are regarded as innately or essentially pure or polluting. This has given rise to considerable confusion, since the pure or the polluting, as far as the Indian material is concerned, can only be defined contextually or relationally, while the substances tend to be ambivalent (see the case of the untouchable Muli to be discussed below). All this is avoided when we talk of protective boundaries, set up to ward off dangerous powers and threatening and potentially lethal beings. These powers and beings can now be, and behave, precisely as described previously: violent, struggling for dominance and destruction, and at the same time controllable through gifts, flattery and mechanistic ritual means – very much like ourselves. It does not imply an 'objective' evaluation; we have already encountered enough examples of 'nice' demons and friendly ogres and benevolent *devīs*. Babb, in his *Divine Hierarchy*, seems to be at the threshold of realizing the usefulness of this descriptive technique, but goes no further than to list both terminologies as complementary to each other – certainly a most confusing solution! He mentions as the rationale of ritual action in the villages of Madhya Pradesh he has studied: 'that there are profoundly malevolent forces that constantly impinge on human existence'. Rituals are thus 'efforts to counteract these forces by opposing them with protective and benevolent forces'. In this context he mentions also that his malevolent/benevolent distinction is not a good one and adds that 'there is another assumption of profound importance ... the idea of purity and pollution'.[19] He sums up his views (and clearly combines both explanatory frameworks) by saying that 'pollution and danger are the main themes'[20] of ritual. In fact, concepts like 'pollution' are system-internal – they are typical of the language used in the Dharmaśāstras – but it is difficult to imagine that someone in a village would call the *devī* Yellammā 'polluting'. For that reason (and that means, wider, value-neutral applicability) it seems preferable to talk about boundaries and protection.

This now raises the question of whether it is actually permissable to link together phenomena that are quite clearly formally and socially distinct. In our case this means *inter alia* three different types of worship: *grāmya* or village religion, āgamic/tantric, and *vaidika*. Even when we restrict ourselves to the ritual forms, and ignore the theology and philosophy which, certainly, the latter two types possess in abundance, we are surely dealing with different things. In the first case, in village religion, all kinds of beings are involved, like *bhūtas*, *asuras*, *yakṣas*, *nāgas* and *devīs* (and *devas* of a rather 'rustic' kind). Very much in the way that these beings themselves are envisaged, the rituals associated with them involve rather crude activities and objects. Thus village religion involves the drinking of alcohol; smoking of opium; shedding of blood; gruesome, self-inflicted tortures; killing animals and eating the meat; states of possession; sexual obscenities; and liberties of various kinds. These are *grāmya*, crude, boorish features, unacceptable to middle-class taste, and not just the middle classes of India. In contrast, the other two types of ritual are far more abstract and refined. They involve only *devas*, primarily the males, and *devīs* usually only if they behave properly, which means, are married and subject to, a *deva*. The offerings are without blood, vegetarian, and the ritual implies a sophisticated royal symbolism, at least in the temple varieties. In the strictly *vaidika* ritualism, the abstraction might be carried even further by regarding the fire sacrifice as an autonomous, self-effective affair without any reference to a purpose outside itself. Whatever the precise interpretation may be, the formal distinction certainly between *grāmya* and *vaidika*, boorish and Vedic, is maintained in a large corpus of polemical literature, in which, for example, the *vaidika* brahmin very vehemently distances himself not only from the vulgarities of the village cults, but also from the 'heterodox' traditions of temple worship.[21] But what are these differences of form in their essential nature? They derive from *social* differentiation and historical layering. They can be used to make *social* value judgements, or to improve one's status in relation to other social groups. But my point here is that primarily these distinctions are merely social, and do not essentially affect the content. As used and envisaged by the majority of the populace, all three types of ritual system are basically mechanistic, aiming at creating safe havens in a threatening and terrifying environment through a relatively regular execution of ritual acts and formalized behaviour. There are different approaches possible in an account of the Indian religions – historical, sociological and typological. The programme established for the present investigation comes squarely down on the side of typology.

As far as the question of 'real' versus 'mythical' levels is concerned, this is a problem of our own creation. The *devas* that cheat *asuras* and try to protect their realm against the latters' aggression, and the *asuras* that are 'pious' and perform religious rites, are all part of the natural order; they are all beings of the same fundamental nature: caught in a threatening world and trying to create safe havens.

'Safe haven' implies that here is a realm that is hermetically closed off against other realms, that is fixed and static. Moreover, it is not difficult to demonstrate that this is also precisely the intention of those people involved in the creation and maintenance of these protected realms. Finally, the conceptual distinction (along with its value judgement) of *grāmya* versus *vaidika* rests on the assumption that both are factually different, and that immutably. To postulate a typological comparability does not yet question the element of immutability, and even without any further investigation we can infer that this necessarily implies the end of our journey – we would have exhausted what Indian religions have to offer. The chapters that follow are only possible because within the Indian religious traditions themselves the wishful thinking in terms of protected realms has been questioned, or has been replaced by other modes of thinking. However, that means, objectively speaking, that none of the areas described in the previous pages constitute *de facto* closed realms or systems, but have remained flexible and fluid. I shall try and briefly show this using three examples: the enclosed social unit, the temple and the Vedas.

As conventionally understood, a social unit in India is very much smaller than the groups I have discussed so far; it is then called a 'caste'. 'Caste' is supposed to denote a group of people with three well-defined boundaries. These are endogamy – marriages take place only within that group; restricted commensurability – food is taken from and shared with a very limited range of other castes, or consumed exclusively within the caste; and narrow choice of hereditary, professional occupations. The crossing of each of these boundaries is unacceptable and is perceived as a dangerous threat to the whole social unit or caste (and indeed, to society at large). It is punished with expulsion from the caste. On the other hand, the meticulous execution of all the detailed rules of behaviour laid down for each caste separately ensures the protection of the individual by his fellow caste-men, and of the caste as a 'safe' social realm.

A very clear example of the mentality involved here is the story of Muli.[22] Muli is an untouchable – thus a member of the lowest rank in caste hierarchy – from Orissa. The American anthropologist Freeman met him, became fascinated by his life-story, and has recorded it in his book *Untouchable*. For much of his life Muli has been wanting to find acceptance by members of the higher castes. In various ways he has been trying to endear himself to them and gain their friendship. An external opportunity for this is provided by the fact that Muli works as a pimp, procuring women for high-caste engineers working on projects in Bhuvaneshvar. Many times he experiences the same: as long as these men are in need of his services, they are prepared to socialize with him, while he for his part goes to any length, including acting as nurse to a man suffering from VD, to turn this socializing into something like friendship. But then, once the men get their women through Muli, they cut off all contact with him. Keeping this ambition of Muli's in mind, we must turn to another incident in his life. Muli manages to acquire a small piece of land. But eventually a brahmin cheats him out of it. It comes to a court case. When it is obvious to all officials that Muli has indeed been wronged, the brahmin challenges him: if you are indeed telling the truth, then touch me! Muli cannot do so, and loses the case.[23] Why should this have happened, this inability to accept the challenge and touch the brahmin? I think the best interpretation is that Muli does not have the courage to cross one particularly thick and dangerous boundary: that between a brahmin and an untouchable, in a quasi-ritual context. Either side represents a grave threat and danger to the other. But while we all have heard about the brahmins fearing contact with the lower castes, nobody so far has told us that the same applies to the untouchable. This, in itself, shows that the conceptual framework suggested here is applicable to both extremes on the scale of social hierarchies: 'pollution' in the sense of the Dharmaśāstras would be merely a one-sided relationship.

Moreover, even if Muli's individual attempt at cross-caste intercourse fails, it cannot be used as generic proof of the rigidity of the caste system itself. Historical studies have revealed that we are by no means dealing with groups of people who are unified, since time immemorial, by common biological descent. As Conlon[24] has shown for the Chitrapur Saraswat brahmins, for example, families have constantly joined the 'caste', while others dropped out and changed over to another social grouping. Or we can refer here once again to 'castes' like those of the *jogtī/jogtīṇ*, where, on the one hand, caste members are the biological descendants of previous caste members, but, on the other hand, a continuous 'recruitment' takes place, as a consequence of babies being promised to the temple in fulfilment of a vow. A second aspect of caste dynamism is the ambition of a larger group of caste members to improve their own status in relation to that of other castes. Thirdly, the very rationale of a 'caste' is by no means static and fixed. As research is discovering, a great many factors can determine, individually or in combination, the *raison d'être* of a specific social group. Fourthly, commonly assumed defining characteristics like commensurability and endogamy fail to explain the social behaviour of groups like the Śrīvaiṣṇava brahmins of Tamil Nadu, or that of certain Jains and Hindu Banyas. In the first instance, both marriage and communal eating is restricted to a tiny segment of the Aiyaṅkār community. The trend is to arrange marriages very close to home; the result may well be uncle marrying niece, and thus her mother-in-law is at the same time her grandmother. Food will be consumed only if prepared by the Aiyaṅkār himself or his wife, and even witnessing its consumption is restricted to a very limited set of relatives. On the other hand, some Jains blithely intermarry with Hindu Banyas – money thus sanctifies and legitimizes the breaking of an otherwise very dangerous boundary!

What conclusions can be drawn from all this for the purpose of the present discussion? One, rather accidental, conclusion is quite clearly that the hallowed concept of 'caste' or 'caste system' must be abandoned. It all began with the Portuguese noting that Indian social structures were very complicated and that groups of people tended to stick very much to themselves, living in boxes, as it were. I think it is that meaning of the Portuguese word *casta* which was intended here. From there it was anglicized as 'caste', and generations of anthropologists have tried very hard to discover a real and definable entity out there in real life that corresponds to the concept 'caste', just as they have tried to find an Indian word for it. (In modern Indian languages, *jāti* tends to be a translation from the English!) The second conclusion to be drawn is the fact that although there are normative suggestions of a rigid social compartmentalization in the Dharmaśāstras, *de facto* concerns other than the 'protection' of the social group have maintained some flexibility and fluidity here.

What about the temple? So far I have described it as a closed system that requires protection, in order to grant protection. In this particular case it will not be necessary to investigate or criticize the concept of a 'temple' itself. But the form of temple worship covers up at least two major and, in many ways, contradictory systems. So the fact that I have been able to take photographs in such temples at all is entirely due to this second attitude being found there. As it is thoroughly theistic and centres around the idea of grace being communicated to the world via the temple, the proper place for a discussion of it will be in Part two. But in the present context it is worth noting that such a different conception is woven into the same fabric of temple worship, and this clearly demonstrates a further aspect of the dynamism I am exploring at present. On the level discussed so far, temple ritual is indeed mechanistic and aims at protecting boundaries, while being itself a bounded system. Moreover, the intrusion of threatening powers into the world of man, which, for instance, the figure of the *devī* Manasā has illustrated, can be set in relation to this same theism, where a similar intrusion is perceived not as threat and a demand for submission, but as love and a request for requital. Conventionally, a rigid distinction has been drawn between the gods of 'village-religion' as incapable of love and as unworthy of devotion, and the 'higher' gods that love and deserve love.[25] This distinction is not borne out by the facts (note the extent of Yellammā's love for the gardener!). A different distinction is all-important: whether or not any of these *devas* and *devīs* are merely treated as powers in a complex ritualistic system of controlling and using them, or whether they are envisaged as supreme, autonomous and self-controlling agents. In the first case, we are dealing with precisely the mentality I have been describing here. (In the second case, we are dealing with theism or even monotheism.) Thus what really matters here is a typological, not a social distinction.

Finally, the Veda. This appears at first sight to be the most firmly closed system of all. Yet even here a dynamic flexibility is not totally absent. Theistic illustrations – to be dealt with in greater detail in their proper place – are conceptions like that of a Tamil Veda, composed by a *śūdra*,[26] or of the *mantra Oṃ namo Nārāyaṇāya* containing the essence of the Vedas and being proclaimed (allegedly by Rāmānuja) from the tower of the temple in Tirukkōṭṭiyūr to all and sundry in the outside world. Non-theistic flexibility can be found in the comprehensive view of the world that the Mīmāṃsā developed around them, in speculations about the *śabda-* or the *nāda-brahman*. Naturally, the view of the world found in the Vedic hymns themselves constitutes a very different system indeed, but this really concerns a reconstruction of pre-Hindu Āryan religion, and has little to do with the way that the Veda has been used ritually over the past two thousand years. That such a neglect of the actual content could occur is another illustration of the flexibility of the seemingly rigid walls surrounding such a central symbol as the Veda.

I think the outcome of all this is clear: in order to link a variety of phenomena together in one common descriptive framework, it is essential to overcome the artificial boundaries that our conventional terminology (which is, after all, derived from internal value judgements and social hierarchies) has set up. Once this break has been made, very different religious attitudes can be discovered hiding behind a seemingly fixed form. By this token, I have been trying to extract boundary systems from a variety of elements, in order to demonstrate one particular religious attitude: to create a safe environment.

After these rather abstract considerations, let me return briefly to more concrete matters. Where should we locate this type of religion on

Plate 10. Upper-left section of Pāpūjī *pāṛ* (private collection)

our map? Clearly, we are dealing with a rather thin slice of the waist of the World Woman: earth with the immediately neighbouring sections of the underworlds and the sky/heavens. Moreover, the horizon certainly does not stretch as far as the seventh ring-continent. The cosmos envisaged in the stories and myths about Manasā and Yellammā is very much restricted to one small region of India. To assume that you can float down the Ganges for six months reveals a very narrow knowledge indeed of Bengal geography!

On the other hand, I have called the view of the universe which has been analysed previously a superstructure. And so we do find, sometimes rather amusingly, instances of a widening of the horizon due to the interaction of the two mental maps of the world. In the literature on Manasā, an increased geographical knowledge transfers the town of Ujani, where a lot of the action takes place, from Bengal to the famous Ujjain, hundreds of miles away, so that some versions now present the events in a pan-Indian context.[27] At some stage in the literary development of the story, a whole chunk was taken over from another story, the *Caṇḍī-maṅgal*, and Chando now travels to far away islands and continents.[28] In stories about Yellammā, Belgaun (very close to Saundatti, her central temple) turns into Bengal.[29]

But most amusing is the fate of the River Indus, in the story of the robber-knight and opium-smoker Pāpūjī who turned into a *deva.* While the oral Rajasthani epic still talks about the Indus River he once crossed, the cloth paintings of the story alter this and add grandeur to that deed: he is depicted as crossing over to Laṅkā and killing a ten-headed ogre, very much in the manner of the pan-Indian hero, Rāma, who killed the ten-headed Rāvaṇa (see Plate 10 above).[30]

But we are now talking already about a different type of person: the adventurer and hero, who sets out to cross the boundaries of the safe haven and who thereby yields to other human drives – violence and aggression – and aims at expanding the protected realm beyond the existing boundaries.

CHAPTER 5
Violence, aggression and heroism

It would not be difficult to derive, from the description of safe havens offered so far, rather romantic associations, for example of a homely, cosy environment pervaded by peace, tranquility, love and harmony. As we shall presently see, such a pastel-coloured picture has indeed been painted in certain quarters. However, let us first expose ourselves to some very different aspects of a world that endeavours to set up protected territories. Any such romantic image stands in remarkable contrast to the almost obsessive preoccupation of eighteenth- and nineteenth-century missionaries with the violence and cruelty they perceived, particularly in Hinduism. One of their favourite topics with which to illustrate this was the caste system. So let me quote a few sentences from the Abbé Dubois (who lived in Southern India between 1792 and 1823). He is talking here about a group of untouchables, the *paṟaiyār*, which, incidentally, gave rise to the English word 'pariah'.

> The contempt and aversion with which the other castes ... regard these unfortunate people are carried to such an excess that in many places their presence, or even their footprints, are considered sufficient to defile the whole neighbourhood. They are forbidden to cross a street in which Brahmins are living. Should they be so ill-advised as to do so, the latter would have the right, not to strike them themselves, because they could not do so without defilement, or even touch them with the end of a long stick, but to order them to be severely beaten by other people. A Pariah who had the audacity to enter a Brahmin's house might possibly be murdered on the spot. A revolting crime of this sort has been actually perpetrated in States under the rule of native princes.[1]

Dubois adopts here the terminology of the Dharmaśāstras that involves concepts like 'defilement' and 'purity'. Yet it is not difficult to explain what is going on here within the conceptual structure I have suggested in the previous chapter. The protective boundaries surrounding a given social group must be defended through ritual, formalized behaviour: to prevent the touch, physically and metaphorically, of an untouchable, is part of this ritual and maintains the status of both parties involved (note the example of the untouchable Muli).[2]

A second instance of aggressive violence generated by the belief system involving boundaries is the custom of animal and even human sacrifice. One of the earliest purāṇic passages translated into a European language is Chapter 75 of an otherwise extremely marginal work, the *Kālikā-Purāṇa*, which deals with human sacrifice.[3] Not too long ago the *Guardian* carried this small note:

> An Indian farmer kidnapped a four-year-old boy and sacrificed him to ensure a bumper harvest, a New Delhi newspaper said yesterday. The farmer carried the boy home in a gunny bag, fed him biscuits for four days, and sacrificed him to a god, by cutting off his head.
>
> (*The Guardian*, 5 February 1985)

To the author of this passage it was clearly a 'religious' act, but to infer from this that the recipient of the sacrifice was 'a god' begs the question. In another book by a missionary, Badley's *The Mela at Tulsipur*, we find a lengthy and blood-curdling description of animal sacrifice. As it is 'A Book for Children', all the events are presented through the eyes of a boy and a girl. So the detailed description of, for example, a man bashing a piglet to death on a stone platform,[4] is particularly nauseating.

Such accounts by missionaries may have their polemic rhetoric and may not accurately interpret the things they observe, but such biases do thereby not abolish the facts themselves. Given a view of the world as populated by all kinds of bloodthirsty beings, such sacrifices, as acts of pacification, follow logically.

We can observe here a ritualistic protection mechanism that operates through substitutions and replacements. The one sacrificial victim represents the whole group that could be devoured by our bloodthirsty friends, the demons, ogres and *devas*, were they not pacified. The blood shed and the pain suffered ritually is a partial concession to their demands. The safe haven can only be maintained by ritually enacting on one victim the full violence and harm that the rest of the community wants to protect itself against.

At the same time, this allows for a control to be exerted over internal violence. The ritual is the only legitimate place for this form of violence to take place – so the slaughter of animals intended to be eaten can only take place in a 'religious' context. This is another feature the missionaries failed to see: the act of killing is so dangerous that it can only be committed for the sake of a stronger being. The benefit is then twofold: a sacrificial pacification of the threatening powers, and safe meat to be eaten by man. By contrast, we have our battery-farms, abattoirs and slaughter-houses. Safely tucked away from our own eyes, it needs a poet like García Lorca to bring these places of killing back into our awareness:

> Slaughtered each day in New York are
> four million ducks,
> five million pigs,
> two thousand doves to please the palates of the dying,
> one million cows,
> one million lambs ...
> The ducks and the doves
> and the pigs and the lambs
> put their drops of blood
> below the multiplications
> and the terrific howling cries of the nearly crushed cows
> fill with pain the valley
> in which the Hudson gets drunk on oil.[5]

What applies to a group can also apply to an individual. A man in a desperate situation might well offer some of his blood or some part of his body in order to pacify a blood-thirsty powerful being from whom he then expects, as a reward, the protection of his own life or that of someone dear to him. Alternatively, such shedding of blood may be linked with ideas about the dangers arising for the agent causing, or permitting, such an act. Medieval literature is full of descriptions of (just as we have iconographic evidence for) threats, or real acts, of self-imposed mutilation as a means of forcing, for example, a *devī* to yield to a certain demand. When this is called 'devotion', the element of moral blackmail involved in such a threatening act gets obscured. An example from real human society may clarify this point. In Gujarat, Rajasthan and Sindh a particular group of people, the *cāraṇas*, used to be employed as guardsmen for caravans.[6] They were renowned for their readiness to commit suicide right in front of attacking brigands who tried to plunder a caravan guarded by them. The responsibility for such a suicide would fall on the brigands. To go into a *devī* shrine and threaten to cut off your arm, or even your head, implies an identical rationale.

It might well be objected now that all these examples stem from the lower strata of society. Surely in comfortable and more refined higher strata things must be different. What could be cosier and safer than the little world of a queen performing her *pūjā*, her fasting and other obligations faithfully every day? But then a Jain story tells us the following.

Formerly there lived a Buddhist king, Daṇḍaka. Impressed by the forebearance and deep knowledge of a Jain monk, he converted to Jainism. Once he invited a company of five hundred Jain monks to his city. His queen and his son, who had remained staunch Buddhists, conspired variously to incriminate the monks and reconvert the king. Eventually they arranged for the king to witness the queen being made love to by a beggar dressed up as a Jain monk. Taken in by this ruse, the king had all Jain monks executed by crushing them through a machine. The one monk who was accidentally saved became so enraged that the fire of his wrath consumed himself and the whole town with its inhabitants.[7]

Or we could look at another example, this time involving a Buddhist queen. The famous King Udeṇa had married the orphan girl Sāmavatī. Later he saw Magaṇḍiyā, fell in love with her and married her too. This girl had initially been offered to the Buddha but had been rejected by him. Ever since then she cherished a great hatred for Buddhism. When the Buddha visited the town, the first queen converted. Magaṇḍiyā, her old hatred having now found a new objective, schemed in various ways to get rid of her rival queen. Eventually she succeeded in murdering her by setting her palace on fire. When Udeṇa found out about this murder, Magaṇḍiyā in turn was tortured to death.[8]

A third example introduces us to the ninth century robber-knight Parakāla 'Death of his Enemies' whom the South Indian Śrīvaiṣṇavas venerate as a saint. Stories began to be composed about him from the twelfth century and, incidentally, are the earliest representatives of the detective story known to me from India. They report that he required large sums of money to build Viṣṇu temples and feed Viṣṇu devotees. When he ran out of funds, he blithely went off and stole, through trickery, a golden statue of the Buddha housed inside a Buddhist temple in Nāgapaṭṭiṉam. Through clever detective work the Buddhists of that town discovered who had committed the theft and followed him. But Parakāla managed to win the king over to his side and the Buddhists had to return empty handed.[9]

Even less lucky than the Buddhists of Nāgapaṭṭiṉam were the eight thousand Jains who, according to Śaivite hagiography, were killed in what surely must be one of the most gruesome manners of execution: impalement. This story is associated with the brahmin saint Tiruñānasambandhar who is presented as a lifelong antagonist of the Jains.[10]

Much more down-to-earth and set in real life is Bahiṇā Bāī. This brahmin girl of seventeenth-century Maharashtra tells us in her autobiography how she used to be beaten up by her husband who resented the innocent little religious world in which she tried to live. Whatever the personal factors may have been that were responsible for making the early years of the marriage so difficult, we can also identify more general principles at work here. While her husband, as a brahmin and professional priest, made a living by performing Veda-derived rituals, Bahiṇā Bāī cultivated a theistic and devotional form of religion which brought her into close contact with the lower castes.[11]

And as a final example, involving a Cōḻa king of South India, let us look at what is most likely a historical event. Outstanding personalities in the Śrīvaiṣṇava community, challenged to swear that Śiva is the absolute, preferred exile or being blinded to committing this act of betrayal. This event took place *c.* AD 1079 and is attributed to the Cōḻa king Kulottuṅga I. Two theologians of the Śrīvaiṣṇava movement lost their eyes, and Rāmānuja himself had to flee to the Hoysalas of Mysore.[12]

These examples have certain features in common: they all involve a new kind of threat which has so far merely been hinted at. This is the threat to one religious individual or group by another of a different religious tradition. It adds a new aspect to our present exploration of the violence contained in the construction of protected realms. What distinguishes these examples from the ones previously looked at, which on the whole were derived from 'folk religious' traditions, are the facts that, firstly, the 'religious' is not merely the means by which a protective mechanism is executed (e.g. by making an animal sacrifice to a *devī*), but the defining factor of what itself must be protected (e.g. the

'Vedic tradition') and that, secondly, the violence initiated by it is no longer merely a ritual substitution, but is quite real.

Let me summarize the observations made so far. The mentality that thinks in terms of safe havens and is eager to create these as rigid and immutable structures is caught up in the contradiction that the peace desired can only be bought at the price of (some form of) violence. The reason for this lies in the fact that it can fight the battle for security on the same level as the threatening forces fight theirs: if a *rākṣasa* can be pacified and turned into an agent of protection by an offering of blood, so blood has to be given to him. However, we saw in the previous chapter that what are desired safe havens to some are in fact fluid entities, for the simple reason that alternative religious interpretations are available. Thus the challenge and threat has been pushed on to a higher level: here the mentality itself is questioned. Thus it need not surprise us that such challenging alternative interpretations of reality are perceived to be more threatening than a *rākṣasa* and will generate not ritual (and limited), but real, violence in the pursuit of a safe haven for the established mode of thinking itself. Bahiṇā Bāī was beaten up viciously, with no ritual context intervening, rather because she frequented sessions of devotional hymn singing than because she had a nasty husband or because she crossed some minor boundary between castes. In the light of all this it is not necessary to enter into a discussion of trivial pronouncements, however popular they may be in certain quarters, about the 'tolerance' of the Indian tradition that can accept many alternatives as equally legitimate. Instead, let me briefly ask whether any of this bears any relation to our own experience.

Given the view of a world as threatening, dangerous and amorphous as the one sketched in the previous pages, we will not find it difficult to sympathize with people who prefer to abide in – potentially quite small – protected areas. This is the type of religion we, too, are familiar with in various forms. It is the religion of the Law, as pronounced in the Judaeo-Christian tradition; of enclosed sectarian groups that must guard their own state of salvation by avoiding contact with the rest of society; or of the Rules that in monastic life often turn into a self-fulfilling exercise. Ritual, whether in the more obvious sense of the word, or understood as conventionally defined behaviour, can be observed here, too, as the protective mechanism. While the dogma of '*extra ecclesiam nulla salus*' may now tend to be interpreted in a fairly innocuous institutional sense, that of 'Jesus alone saves' has produced a variety of mental blocks – another form of boundary. What differs in these cases from the Indian material is the more amorphous nature of how the threatening, dangerous powers beyond the boundary walls are envisaged. Satan and sin are prominent symbols in a more theological kind of discourse; Commies, Marxists and Reds in a more political-social context; while the kind of danger against which the man protects himself, whose life centres around the car and who faithfully washes, polishes, waxes and oils it every Sunday morning, still awaits exploration and definition. And we only have to look at the Inquisition or the destructive violence of the Spanish *conquistadores* (and more modern examples could be referred to) in order to find parallels for a situation in which violence is created because an established religion finds its boundaries threatened, or wants to expand its area of control.

The one area where Western thought has been most busily at work investigating religion as a boundary-protecting mechanism is that of class, primarily of the middle class or bourgeoisie, perceived to benefit most directly from religion. In turn, this approach has been applied to Indian material. Let me illustrate a particular direction that this critique of the bourgeoisie may take, from the pronouncements of Kosambi, a well-known Marxist writer. As joint editor of an anthology of Sanskrit poetry put together by a Buddhist monk around AD 1100 in Bengal, he also produced an introduction to the work. Little interested in a factual exploration of the poetry gathered together by Vidyākara, he concentrated here on spelling out the lack of guts and the effetism of the well-sheltered bourgeoisie. Protected by their own defence-mechanisms from the intrusion of reality, these middle-class poets, as much as their patrons, led a self-centred life of luxury and comfort.

> But we look in vain for Sanskrit military literature to match passages in Caesar's commentaries. Only Bāṇa's account of the army striking camp is impressive enough to make us wish that he had said something more about warfare. Who described the massed thunder of a cavalry charge, armoured elephants breaking through compact ranks of infantry?[13]

While this takes care of the middle-class Sanskrit poet, the supposed heroes of medieval India, the Rajputs, receive worse scorn. Of the various portraits of a king of Udaipur Kosambi says that, 'sporting luxuriant moustaches on a progressively fatter face with fatter body, [he looked] as unlike as possible to the romantic image of a dashing lover, headstrong fighter, heroic worshipper of the gods'[14] – effetism typical of the bourgeoisie even among so-called heroes! But in a footnote to this comment, a final link is established between Sanskrit culture and middle-class self-indulgence. Kosambi went through the library of our increasingly fat hero and found a volume in Sanskrit that 'showed considerable handling. The book, when I examined it, opened naturally to the *Anaṅgaraṅga*, on a page with the prominent sub-heading *liṅga-sthūlī-karaṇa*, so that knowledge of Sanskrit seems to have been put to practical use at court.'[15] He does not provide a translation of the Sanskrit phrase, so this in-joke would be lost on anyone who does not know that he is talking about 'how to produce an erection'. I am not pretending that Kosambi's logic is very perspicuous, but the overall affective impact he wants to generate by rather random images is clear. He wants to ridicule a particular class of traditional Indian society by making it appear 'impotent' in both senses of the word. Moreover, he tries to connect this self-indulgence and effetism with Sanskrit learning and religion.

A perception not unrelated to Kosambi's characterization of one class tends to occur in the Western image of India on a much larger scale. For example, Cyril Connolly (in a comment on Dom Moraes's film on India) could say: 'India's greatest virtue is its lack of the military; it is the sub-continent of wisdom, love, poverty and overcrowding.' This certainly annoyed Adil Jussawalla from whom I have been quoting Connolly, who remarked: 'it seems to represent the view of the liberal section of the British public to which Mr Connolly belongs. India: loving, wise, non-militaristic. (India has been to war four times since Independence and has the fourth largest standing army in the world but let such glaring disregard for facts pass.)'[16] I wonder what Jussawalla would have said about the film *Gandhi*!

It is now time to put the various bits and pieces together and, instead of convoluting the discussion further, to try and reduce it to its essentials. So far we have been exploring religion as a protective mechanism, as a defence against a great variety of threats, and as demarcating minute inner spaces. Kosambi has selected one single instance and, moreover, attached a definite value-judgement to it: protective enclosures imply lack of heroism, and that with a definitely militarist connotation. What Jussawalla styled 'the view of the liberal section' generalizes this much further by labelling the Indian tradition as such as 'peaceful'. The Western symbol of Gandhi and slogans about the 'tolerance' of Hinduism add a definitely religious dimension (a dimension Kosambi implied, in his case, by reference to Sanskrit learning). A very simple question arises from all this: can we really connect religion and lack of heroic guts in this global way? Gandhi's message of non-violence may be a most welcome gospel in a violent world in which arms are being sold to anybody prepared to mortgage the future of his people. But we must nevertheless ask the question – not whether there are hints of pacifism in the traditional Indian religions (there are) but – whether such a global characterization does justice to the overall picture. Let me begin answering such a question by returning once again to the rural scene.

Another missionary to India, Dr Duff, offers us in his *India and Indian Missions* a description of the *cakrapūjā* (*charak pujah*), the swing-festival, and many other self-inflicted tortures practised during this festival.

> An upright pole, twenty or thirty feet in height, is planted in the ground. Across the top of it, moving freely on a pin or pivot, is placed horizontally another long pole. From one end of this traverse beam is a rope suspended, with two hooks affixed to it. To the other extremity is fastened another rope, which hangs loosely to the ground. The devotee comes forward, and prostrates himself in the dust. The hooks are then run through the fleshy parts of his back, near the shoulders. A party, holding the rope at the other side, immediately begins to run round with considerable velocity. By this means the wretched dupe of superstition is hoisted aloft into the air, and violently whirled round and round. The torture he may continue to endure for a longer or shorter period, according to his own free-will.[17]

When Duff adds that everyone tries his best to prolong this as much as possible, this feature now introduces a definite element of the 'heroic'. This is the man's chance competitively to display his bravery, make 'a name' for himself, and actually challenge the *deva* or *devī* addressed in the rite. A mere quest for 'protection' is not a sufficient explanation. A man who undergoes such self-inflicted tortures is called a *vīra*, a 'hero', and this offers me the opportunity to introduce a conceptual framework which will remain with us until the end of this exploration of power.

There are various angles from which such heroism can be approached. Not everybody is happy to live in narrow, fenced-off and secure realms; some may well wish to stand out by virtue of their individual achievement (already suggested by the man swinging longer from the hooks than anybody else); they may well be curious about the world beyond the fences and wish to explore it. From a different angle it could be observed that enclosed systems show an inbuilt tendency to increase their protection by trying to expand their range of control and break down other boundaries that obstruct this expansion (hinted at in our examples of interreligious violence). Finally, it might well be possible to argue that all these – violence, aggression, heroism and adventurousness – are different expressions of one and the same primary human drive. The Indian religious traditions are aware of such a basic instinct, reflect on it, and utilize or channel it in a variety of directions. The concept of the *vīra*, 'the hero', gathers together most of these directions and we shall follow its ramifications. The map of the world initially sketched will allow us to measure the degree to which such adventurous, heroic pursuit of power, controlled by religion, encompasses the world. It seems natural to begin at the beginning and explore straightforward, concrete material of a secular nature that offers us an introduction to the images, terms, symbols and ambitions of a heroic culture. Against such a background we can then study the much more complex ways in which religion has built on this material.

Since we have talked so much about enclosed spaces, rooms, houses and homely environments, and are now planning to talk about the expansion into the outside world, it seems logical for us to begin with a look at a poetic tradition of heroism that uses precisely this symbolism to structure itself – '*caṅkam* literature'. This now takes us to South India, to the very beginning of the AD era. Here we find a poetic tradition in Tamil which in many ways can be regarded as autonomous, which means, uninfluenced by the northern cultures. In conceptualizing its own premises, it uses as an overriding division the categories *akam* 'house, home, inside', and *puṟam*, 'outside'. Let me hasten to explain that the first category actually has nothing to do with the bounded spaces we have been looking at previously, for *akam* denotes love-poetry. It does this not by virtue of the home in which amorous activities, we would expect, tend to take place – for the poetry talks a lot of bushes on a mountain side and of brothels with prostitutes who ruin a man's home. *Akam* is love-poetry because it deals with a person's inner, emotional life.[18] But the second category, *puṟam*, does deal with the matters we are exploring at present: it is heroic poetry.

The way in which this broad category is further divided, according to conventional sets of themes, gives us an indication of what is meant by heroism here. By abstracting from real geography, five different poetic landscapes were formulated which, through their various flowers, animals, inhabitants, modes of life and so on, denote five basic heroic situations. Three of these concern aggression of different types: (a) cattle-raids or, their reverse, the recovery of cattle stolen; (b) besieging an enemy's fort, with its reverse, the defence of one's own town; and (c) invading and conquering a neighbouring territory. The remaining two divisions deal with pitched battle scenes and with the celebration of victory. The praise of the brave hero is all-pervasive here.

These basic divisions were subdivided further into many 'themes' (in the technical sense of bardic poetry); depending on the poetician, one hundred and thirty-eight, or even two hundred and fifty-four, of them are listed.[19] A few examples will suffice to illustrate them: the claim over a territory not yet conquered; the greatness of the chieftain who sets out to accomplish what he desires; an attack on the enemy's fortress; the wealth of the king who is besieged; the sufferings inflicted upon him; his valour when he comes out to fight; the two armies fighting in the moats; the heroism of the one who scaled the wall; the conquest of the fort; the ceremony of bathing the victorious sword. Another set of such themes deals with the carving and erection of a 'hero stone' in honour of a brave warrior who lost his life in the defence of the cattle, and with the rituals accompanying it. Then there is the theme of praising a mighty king by conventionally envisaging his realm to stretch all the way to the Himalayas. The overriding rationale of all this poetry (well over four hundred such poems have survived)[20] is the desire for fame, to 'make a name', through displaying prowess and heroism.

There are a number of interesting points in this material. Above all, naturally, there is the fact that heroic actions are set before us as an ideal, and as a primary fact of human nature complementary to love. Then there is the idea that only through heroic action can a man make a 'name' for himself – in other words, become an individual person by acquiring a unique identity in his society and, through this name, survive after his death. This is the nearest the autonomous Tamil tradition came to the concept of immortality. Heroic poetry is itself one of the means of ensuring this survival of the name; another means is the erection of *vīra-kal*, 'hero stones', that commemorate heroic action in the place where they occurred. Such *vīrakal* can be found even today all over the Deccan.

Yes, but this was faraway and ancient Tamil Nadu, somebody like Kosambi might object. Had the latter bothered to explore Rajasthani literature, however, he might have encountered a work like the *Seven Hundred on the Hero* (*Vīr-Satsaī*, written by Sūryamalla Miśraṇ in Būndī as late as the nineteenth century AD!) Here we can read:

> It is fitting that the women
> in the house of him
> who without paying a penny
> can enjoy the possession of priceless elephants,
> should carry in their necklaces,
> as the symbol of their marital bliss,
> pearls from elephants' frontal lobes,
> and wear bangles made of ivory.[21]

Translated into more prosaic English this means: among the Rajputs, a happy love-life stimulates bravery, and that in turn yields, from killing battle-elephants, jewellery for the women. But there is more to it, for the stanza plays with, and in fact reverses, ideas expressed in another *Seven Hundred* of almost two thousand years earlier. In this collection, the marital bliss of a hunter's wife is revealed to the world by the fact that she has none of the jewellery just mentioned. He is far too busy with, and exhausted from, paying amorous attention to her, to go out and shoot elephants.[22] Thus, as far as the heroic poetry is concerned, only through prowess in fighting can amorous delight be obtained – heroism is set up as an ideal over and above love.

Or Kosambi could have looked at an anthology of Sanskrit poetry once again compiled in Bengal, around the year 1205. There he would have found long sections on bravery in battle and on heroism, with descriptions of armoured elephants, war horses, battleships, murderous swords, armies marching, the dust raised by their horses clouding the sky, trumpets blown, pitched battles, and demons gorging themselves when all is over. A third of the poems in this section deal with valour, manliness, heroism, and the fame and glory resulting from them.[23] That is, after all, what life was all about: to acquire a name through bravery! Or Kosambi might have read another, roughly contemporary, anthology in the semi-vernacular Prakrit, where we find quite extraordinary imagination at work. Here are some examples. A warrior is depicted, after completing his task with utter bravery, lying on an ivory palanquin and being fanned – but instead of having become a king, as this symbolism would normally suggest, he has been spiked on an elephant's tusk, and the fan is the animal's ear. Another brave warrior appears like a wild elephant that drags its broken chains behind – with his entrails dangling down to his feet, the hero still keeps on fighting. An amorous woman seems to be kissing and embracing another fallen hero – a jackal is licking at his wounds. Or, finally, the totally loyal soldier: in order that his master may find comfort from the flapping of a vulture's wings, lying next to him he keeps still and lets the bird pick at him.[24] This is obviously hyperbole at its Indian best! Can one detect irony here? I do not know, but what is interesting here is the fact that heroism can actually express itself within a framework of total and utter subjugation – in loyalty and devotion to a powerful master. This aspect of *bhakti*, of 'loyalty', is something that will have to be explored further in a different context.

But let me not be accused of trying to romanticize the issue at stake. For I have not yet mentioned one of the most unpalatable aspects of this type of literature: the relish at having inflicted destruction and cruelty. There is a special genre for this in Sanskrit court poetry, which concentrates on the enemy king's near and dear, to demonstrate the grandiose victory that the hero, the king flattered by the poet, has achieved. This gets particularly gruesome when sexual associations are woven into the build-up of images. Thus in one poem, the dishevelled and wretched appearance of a defeated king's queen is treated poetically like that of a woman in the middle of passionate love-making. Another unsavoury aspect of this genre are descriptions of the suffering endured by the defeated king's children.[25]

For those who are still unconvinced that India has encouraged the heroic, a look into the normative literature about statescraft, as much as that about social responsibilities of a *kṣatriya*, a member of the warrior class, should clinch the evidence. It is the duty of kings to expand their territory and fight wars, and it is the duty of warriors to rise to the utmost of their bravery and valour to fight in these wars. The Machiavellian nature of these treatises has been known for a long time and been discussed frequently.

Connected with this is a special symbolism, that of the conquest of the quarters, the *dig-vijaya*. These four quarters represent the earth on our map (not Jambudvīpa, but Bhāratavarṣa), and the idea is that a king can potentially rule over the whole realm, as one who covers the whole under one parasol – the insignium of royal power. This is the grand ideal; and again literature is full of instances where this ideal has been attempted, and naturally – since otherwise there would be no poem about it – achieved. The stereotyped pattern involves a clockwise movement by a king with his army over the whole of India and a series of defeats of recalcitrant local kings or of submission into vassalage by wiser ones. As a dream and as an ideal this idea of conquering and ruling the four quarters of the earth must have loomed over innumerable Indian kings, and must be regarded as motivation for the creation of a great many empires and many more wars. It is here that we find the origin of the concept of the *cakravartī*, the wheels of whose chariots never encounter any obstruction by enemies and who rules over the entire country from ocean to ocean and from the Himalayas down to the southern sea.

By now one thing should have become clear: there is no need to look very far in Indian literature, vernacular or Sanskrit, ancient or relatively modern, for a proclamation of the heroic ideal. The keywords here are *vīra*, 'the hero', and *dig-vijaya*, the conquest of the whole earth. And the imaginative exploration of violent aggression is a pronounced feature in all this literature. Were we to attempt a quantitative analysis of Indian literature, the amount that would appear under the heading of 'battle scenes' would be surprisingly large. To refer to the most obvious example: the world's largest epic, the *Mahābhārata*, two hundred thousand lines long (which corresponds to four or five thousand pages in print), developed around a battle that took eighteen days to finish. Similarly in the Purāṇas, descriptions of wars fought between the *devas* or *avatāras* and *asuras* fill thousands of pages. Any major poet, whether in Sanskrit or in any of the vernaculars, spent a considerable amount of energy on descriptions of armies, battle-scenes, and victories. Somewhat to our surprise, this includes Jain poets. A vast amount of medieval Jain literature is actually about battles. Imagine pious Jain ladies, renowned for their grief at harming a single living being, be it even a fly, sitting through hours and hours of descriptions of the most violent wars and fights, arms and legs and chopped-off heads flying in all directions, and streams of blood turning the ground into mud! Catharsis, you may say: the eradication of the last trace of violence by exposing oneself to endless symbolic representations of it. That may be the case. But then what do you make of the following example – violence in religious allegory? Madana, who prides himself at being irresistible to any woman on earth, hears that Siddhi is about to get married to Mahāvīra. This is a challenge to his honour and, using a variety of tactics, including sending his own wife Rati as go-between, he attempts to entice Siddhi out of her engagement and make her his own wife. When all this fails, he sets out in full battle array. A lot of limbs fly around, the inevitable heads get chopped off and the conventional headless trunks keep on fighting. To no avail: Mahāvīra defends the honour of Siddhi, and off he goes to marry her in great style.

What is all the fuss about, you may ask? So let me decode the story. Madana is the Indian god of love; Rati his wife, who symbolizes sexual passion. The virtuous Siddhi stands for final emancipation, gained by total rejection of all violence, according to Jain spirituality. Mahāvīra is himself, 'the great hero' who is the last of the twenty-four *tīrthaṅkaras* and, from our perspective, the founder of Jainism as we know it. Out of all possible Indian themes, the Mahāvīra, engrossed as he was in strictest celibacy and asceticism and striving for final emancipation from a violent world, seems the least likely subject for a 'heroic' description in terms of battle-symbolism and fighting over a woman. Yet Harideva achieved the sheer impossible, in his Apabhraṃśa poem *Mayaṇaparājayacariü*.[26] *Et tu, Jaina*! we might exclaim. After this, nothing will take us by surprise, like other respectable characters fighting in mighty allegorical battles. Thus to see Discrimination and Passion offering each other a duel in the allegorical drama *Sunrise of Determination* (*Saṅkalpasūryodaya*) can only come as an anticlimax to the Mahāvīra's valour in defending his fiancée Siddhi's honour and marrying her as his pure bride.

Some might argue that we can now discard once and for all the myth of the meek Indian absorbed in his own peaceful, pleasurable world. Yet the relevance for a deeper understanding of the religious traditions still seems totally elusive, in spite of a vague and metaphorical usage of 'war symbolism' even in religious contexts. So far all we need assume is that for propagandistic purposes the vulgar taste of the masses, who seem to relish descriptions of battle, violence and heroism, has been catered for. But that is all. In a sense such cynicism is not surprising, because after all, the association of the religious with the heroic is not popular with us. After endless war and anti-war novels and films, we are decidedly suspicious of anything smelling of 'heroics' and the military, particularly when it appears dressed up as religion. But whatever our own sentiments may be, we have to face up to the fact that, far beyond mere allegory or catharsis, links between aggressive heroism and religion were forged in India. It may be unpalatable to us, but there are many instances of a similar linkage in our own modern world. So let us be brave ourselves and look at some concrete examples.

When Yaśovarman, a king of Kanauj in the eighth century, set out on his *dig-vijaya*, he first paid a visit to the famous and particularly blood-thirsty *devī* 'living on the Vindhya mountains'. His musings in front of her image – at least as presented to us by the author of the epic that narrates the events (the *Gaüḍavaho* in the Prakrit language)[27], are filled with violent images that anticipate, as it were, the violence of the subsequent military encounters. The *devī* as the ultimate controller of this violence thus becomes the mistress of the king's own fate.

Already, this single example cannot be written off as an Indian version of attending mass before going into battle. For the religious reality that confronts the king (the temple with its statue and rituals and the mythical associations of the *devī*) are filled with the same kind of aggression and violence that he will meet again in battle. But let us look at another example, at a Tamil epic of the early twelfth century (the *Kaliṅkattupparaṇi*).[28] This is a eulogy of the Cōḻa king Kulottuṅga I (whom we have met earlier in this chapter, in connection with the persecution of the Śrīvaiṣṇavas) on the occasion of his devastating war against Kaliṅga (which on today's maps would be somewhere in Andhra Pradesh and Orissa).

After various introductory sections, this poem takes us into the wild jungle, where the *devī* Kālī and her hordes of demons abide. All further events are seen through their eyes, or are in fact narrated by them. These gruesome beings are in a famished state, which turns to frenzy when an old visiting demon conjures up a battle scene. But, he assures them, he is showing them a real event that is going to take place in the near future, and he begins to talk about Kulottuṅga and his imminent invasion of the country of Kaliṅga. Kālī herself confirms this.

A demon messenger arrives who informs everyone of the king's preparation for war and soon we hear about the devastating, bloody battle that is being fought. All rush off in a wild stampede, mouths watering, to the battlefield. When they have feasted on the abundant corpses lying all over the ground, they sing the praise of the Cōḻa king and acknowledge their gratitude to him for having provided them with such a lovely feast.

On the one hand, this can be connected with earlier ideas about protective realms and sacrifices: the battle is seen as the ritual guaranteeing Cōḻa dominance. On the other hand, boundaries are clearly crossed and moved outward: Kaliṅga is invaded and annexed. Moreover, the sacrifice is here more than a representational affair. It almost looks as if the veneration of the *devī* Kālī has triggered off a very peculiar form of heroic, cruel superabundance. But the poem certainly implies a religious dimension to Cōḻa expansionist imperialism. It is a military conquest of the world carried out within a religious frame: an act of worship or pacification of a singularly powerful *devī*, Kālī. But the emphasis in all this is still clearly on the idea of conquering new territories in the literal sense of political expansionism.

Let us now look at another set of examples. Here the relationship between aggressive heroism and the religious has a different emphasis again; it is neither merely allegory, nor does it just provide a superstructure for concrete exploits. For our first example, let us look at something extremely orthodox and respectable, and that means a theologian – Rāmānuja (who lived during the time and in the kingdom of Kulottuṅga I). The little sketch offered here derives from the analysis of a number of poems (in Sanskrit and in Tamil)[29] written in honour of this great man within his own tradition, paying attention to the symbolism that is used in them to assess his role and significance. These poems employ a decidedly 'heroic' symbolism. One carries this in its very title: the *Dhāṭī-pañcakam*, viz. '*Five Stanzas of Attack*'. Then we find phrases like the following (and this is merely a small selection): 'the great hero', 'the leader of the armies', 'who pitched a battle', 'shot his arrows', 'attacked and razed to the ground the fortress', 'cut to pieces with his sword', 'the embodiment of the five weapons of Viṣṇu'. As in real heroic poetry, this naturally leads to: 'the war-drum proclaiming his fame', 'a fame that fills the quarters and conquers them'. 'Through his valour and determination he has become the support of the earth'; 'he is a *cakravartī*.' While here the earth is certainly meant literally, the enemies and battles are metaphorical for Rāmānuja's disputations with adherents of other religious systems. According to hagiography, he actually went on a *dig-vijaya*, to conquer the earth through his teaching and his debates with other philosophers and theologians. This symbolism perseveres: three hundred years later a reorganizer of the Śrīvaiṣṇava community called his eight main disciples the *dig-gajaṅkaḷ*, 'the eight elephants supporting the quarters and intermediary quarters [of the earth]'.

Moreover, such symbols as *dig-vijaya* and heroic religious conquest are not unique to the interpretation of the role of Rāmānuja. A whole literature concerns itself with such expeditions of conquest by famous religious persons; often they carry the word in their titles. While in older material the route is stereotyped and corresponds very much to that of a king going on one of these 'conquests of the quarters', a new geographical awareness modifies this. So Gurū Nānak, the founder of the Sikh community, is presented as travelling over a somewhat different area, which now includes Mecca. That such religious conquests involve the breaking down of established boundaries is symbolized by an incident in Rāmānuja's life, when from the tower of the temple in Tirukkōṭṭiyūr he proclaimed to the world the *mantra* which was regarded as the essence of the Vedas. The same is apparent in the egalitarian design of the Sikh community: all men acquire the surname 'Singh', to abolish caste distinctions inherent in the older surnames; all members of the community share food, regardless of who prepared it.

For the Buddhists, a book title like *Meditation of the Heroic March*[30] may be but fanciful metaphor. But then we may find the following ideas: faced with the terrifying vastness of a world in which nothing is solid or permanent or reliable, the true Buddhist does not run scared but, protected by the armour of his own determination, mounts his battle chariot and drives out into this empty space, to fight all suffering.[31]

I think by now it does not require a lengthy justification when I want to conclude from all this that the heroic is more than a mere metaphor. The militaristic aspect of heroism and aggression is still extraneous to the religious heroism unrolled so far. But I am sure that the spirit of heroism, on a deeper level and relating to a basic human drive of aggression and adventurousness, is directly implied in this. I think this throws further light on the ambivalence of *cakravartī* and *tīrthaṅkara* or *tathāgata*. It is no accident, perhaps, that both the Buddha and the Mahāvīra belonged to the class of *kṣatriyas*, warriors. Certainly, the Jains make this a special issue. For they assume that the Mahāvīra was initially conceived in the womb of a brahmin woman. But this was just not right, and so the foetus of him who was to become the Great Hero was taken out and relocated in the womb of a *kṣatriya* woman who then gave birth to him. What lies behind all this is simple enough: religion here identifies itself with the heroic drive (in a non-metaphorical sense) and provides it with its own direction, channels and structures, within which valour can be displayed, fame gained, and a 'name' (and that means fulfilment) acquired.

But to draw on the heroic instincts in man and channel them towards primarily religious purposes (like spreading the true teaching and defending it against heretical doctrines or driving out into the vastness of a world to alleviate suffering) may in turn involve a decision as to how far those religious purposes can be pursued through 'heroic' means in a concrete, material sense. So let us look at some final examples where the emphasis is once again very much on the latter aspect.

In 1699 the tenth and last of the Sikh *gurus* instituted the *Khalsā*. This 'is best described as an order, as a society possessing a religious foundation and a military discipline'. Both had earlier existed in some form, but now the two get fused. 'Thus were the sparrows transformed into hawks. Thus was there forged a community dedicated to the defence of righteousness by the use of the sword, an invincible army of saint-soldiers destined to withstand the most fearsome of persecutions.'[32] Besides this well-known example, there are many more such militant monastic and non-monastic orders documented for Northern India during this period.[33]

Moreover, we cannot regard this religious militancy as a phenomenon merely of the post-fifteenth-century period – so that it would be tempting to connect it with a dominant Muslim presence in India. Already from the twelfth century, and from much further South (Karnataka, to be precise), such a case is known. That the group involved is generally known as the Vīra-Śaivas, 'the heroic devotees of Śiva', is particularly interesting in our present context. 'In the new egalitarian Vīraśaiva community a wedding took place between two devotees; the bridegroom was a former outcaste and the bride an ex-brahmin.' This offered the traditionalists, who had long been waiting for their chance to combat the new community, the opportunity to get the king on their side. 'So [king] Bijjala sentenced the fathers of the bride and bridegroom to death; they were dragged to death in the dust and thorn of the streets. The Vīraśaiva community, instead of being cowed by it, was roused to revenge and violence. Extremist youths stabbed Bijjala and assassinated him. Riots and persecution followed.'[34]

What can we make of all this? The boundary territories, particularly if evaluated in the light of modern literature ('the room') or even of eye-witnesses like the old missionaries, may be very unpleasant affairs. But the decidedly militarist associations of ways of breaking these boundaries, from the inside as much as from the outside, are, if anything, even more unpalatable to our tastes. So it is time to take a more positive angle on all this material. What was the message of Burgess' *Clockwork Orange*? I am still convinced, in spite of the scandal and the subsequent tendentious propaganda the film created, that the basic message of the book is this – that an amorphous aggressiveness is built into human nature, that this turns very nasty in a totally impersonalized environment which offers no chance of a positive channelling of this drive, and that a politically motivated eradication (the 'Law and Order' manifesto that may well resort to medical means) of this aggressiveness is a most inhuman and inhumane affair. Nobody, as far as the sources that I have presented so far are concerned, was fool enough to pretend otherwise. Either some kind of controlled, ritualized nominal execution of it was undertaken, or a whole-hearted endeavour of heroism was put forward as the ideal, both secular and religious, and that in a variety of ways, as we have seen.

It would not be difficult to list comparable phenomena from our own experience. Thus we could think of a perception of the world surrounded by Iron and Bamboo curtains, protected by Star Wars weapon systems, and the seed of Satan lurking beyond it – to be eradicated the first moment an opportunity arises. Or we could think of some of the modern religious movements which, to the young (and I am not commenting on the grey eminences controlling such movements), seem to offer an opportunity to be adventurous, by exploring and conquering the world. I have seen various brochures with pictures of members of the relevant movement sitting before a map of the world and eagerly planning future strategy for an expansion of the realm. In some of these groups we even find interracially arranged marriages. Or we could refer to somebody like Ignatius of Loyola, the founder of the *Compañía de Jesús*, the 'Battalion of Jesus', better known as the Jesuit order. This former soldier, who turned mystic, inspired a large number of people to go out into the world and break down the boundaries of known territory. And anybody reading the letters of followers of his, such as Francis Xavier, cannot fail to pick up their excitement at being sent out into the wide, unknown world on a particular type of conquest. A similar militarist symbolism is implied in the Salvation Army and, most recently, in the Jesus Army.

But I wonder whether, in the light of the material we have been looking at in the present chapter, it may not be appropriate to re-evaluate certain assumptions that are popularly made. Thus when, for example, 'brain-washing' is suggested as explanation for this outburst of heroic exuberance, it is at least worth asking whether factually this is always accurate or whether we are dealing with another version of the defence mechanism that labels as 'Marxist agitation' any movement that goes against the wishes of the bounded system we call establishment. What our Indian material is really saying is that religion can be liberating and adventurous, and can be a heroic affair in a unique way. Thereby it offers a critique and, as we shall see at a later stage, a very elaborately argued one, of the type of religion that concerns itself with the maintenance of boundaries. But what we have been looking at so far, this seemingly realistic material concerning a world very similar to the one we envisage, is from the Indian perspective merely on the surface – quite literally on the surface of the disc that constitutes the World Woman's middle. The Indian traditions offer us many further types of heroes who have the courage to move into realms much further down or higher up and who, not just content with dominating the odd *devī* or *rākṣasa*, desire to turn space, time and matter themselves into pliable entities.

CHAPTER 6

Manipulating space, time and matter

We sailed on, over seas still uncharted, with a following wind all the time. And then one night as we stood in the prow, watchful but carefree, a cloud appeared overhead, blacking out the sky. It was a monstrous, fearsome thing, and the sight of it filled our hearts with dread. 'Heavenly Power,' I exclaimed, 'what divine threat or mystery is this that the sea and the elements confront us with, for I am persuaded that it is something more than a storm?'

I had scarcely spoken when a figure took shape in the air before our gaze. It was of fantastic form and size and powerful build, with a heavy jowl, unkempt beard, and sunken eyes. Its expression was evil and terrifying, its complexion of an earthy pallor. Yellow teeth showed in its cavernous mouth, and its crisp hair was matted with clay.

And then it spoke, in a mighty, terrifying voice that seemed to come from the depths of the sea. Our flesh went creepy and our hair stood on end as we looked and listened.

'So, you daring race,' it said, 'bolder in enterprise than any the world has yet seen, tireless in the waging of cruel wars as in the pursuit of hopeless undertakings: so you have crossed the forbidden portals and presumed to sail on these seas of mine, that I have held and guarded for so long against all comers. You have come to surprise the hidden secrets of nature and of its watery element, that to no mortal, however great, however noble or immortal his deserts, have yet been revealed.'

The fearsome monster was proceeding, when I boldly interrupted. 'Who are you,' I asked, 'for proportions so outrageous take one's breath away?' It rolled its black eyes, contorted its mouth and, uttering a giant roar that filled me with terror, replied ...

There are three themes in this passage which I would initially like to draw attention to: sailing over uncharted waters, a grotesque 'supernatural' being, and the hidden secrets of nature. Now it is not difficult to accommodate the first in the wider framework of our discussion. In the previous chapter I developed the idea of the 'external drive' as a primary force in man's nature, and linked it with violence, aggressiveness and the heroic. Closely related to those aspects is the 'adventurous' drive. To set out and sail over uncharted seas is less a matter of conquest than of heroic exploration (whatever other motives may also be involved). Moreover, for us there is little new in this. Novel features enter when our realistic view of the world encounters the Indian one, which knows of many further types of being, besides animals and humans, in realms both below and above the earth. Thus an adventurous exploration of the world will inevitably, from the Indian point of view, involve a move into those mysterious realms, and a confrontation with those beings. This might even include the ambition to conquer some of those realms along with the creatures abiding there. But what do we do with the third theme, to 'surprise the hidden secrets of nature'? To us this would most naturally suggest the scientific exploration of the world – physics, chemistry, and so on. Only to the extent that some of these sciences require observation in exotic lands could we link them with the idea of 'adventurous heroism'. But to connect this with supernatural beings would be impossible, except for the medieval alchemist. Yet in the Indian context such a connection is a natural one. The key idea is that of *vidyā*, and the beings associated with it, like *nāgas*, *yakṣas*, and particularly the *vidyādharas*. To translate *vidyā* as 'magical lore' rather prejudices the issue; 'knowledge' is far too vague, while 'science' only partially covers what we mean by it. So let me be permitted to continue using the Sanskrit word to avoid unnecessary confusion. What is important for our purposes is that under the heading of *vidyā* we can explore a nexus of ideas that include aspects of the sciences and various supernatural beings.

Having thus introduced our conceptual framework, I ought to return to the passage with which I started. The reader may have taken it for granted that it is from an Indian text; in fact I have to confess that the work is actually a European one. The quotation comes from the Portuguese national epic, *The Lusiads* (*Os Lusiades*),[1] written by Luis de Camões in 1572. The grotesque ogre is none other than the personified Cape of Storms, soon renamed Cape of Good Hope, which was discovered in 1487 by Bartolomeu Dias (who is quoted in the epic as having had the terrifying vision). Ten years later, in 1498, Vasco da Gama passed it a second time and founded what in the eyes of Camões was a new Rome, the Portuguese colony of Goa on the western coast of India.

The epic of Camões is also interesting in the way in which historical events that gave rise to the first European sea-borne empire are presented in a mythical frame. Virgil's *Aeneid* is the model for such a frame. As we shall see later on, India has presented its own versions of the adventure story very much in terms of a classical model: the *Grand Story*. But before turning to this very complex cultural construct of India, let me first deal with a variety of smaller themes and summarize a few stories to illustrate these.

We have met King Ploughman on two previous occasions;[2] during his visit to the underworld, and when he was fighting the murderous *rākṣasa*. We can now sketch out the full story. It might surprise us to hear that he was desperately in love with Princess Playful, daughter of the king of Laṅkā, although he had never seen her; but Indian amatory psychology generally accepts the possibility of falling in love merely from hearsay. More interesting in our present discussion is the fact that a prophecy was attached to the girl: he who married her would become a *cakravartī* – nothing surprising, since her mother was half *yakṣiṇī*, half *vidyādharī* who had been cursed to live as a human. When later on Ploughman fights with the *rākṣasa* and defeats him, it turns out that he was not really an ogre at all, but a cursed *vidyādhara* who, grateful for his release, assists the king in his pursuit of the elusive princess. Naturally all ends well when Ploughman finally marries her and when his universal emperorship is established.

This story offers us an initial link between a heroic entrance into the underworld or a battle with a *rākṣasa*; and a quest for *vidyās*, encounter with *vidyādharas*, and the achievement of universal rule over the earth as a *cakravartī*. However, more typical of the literature under discussion is an accidental or circumstantial involvement in such adventurous journeys that yield extraordinary powers. Sometimes this is connected with the pregnancy longings of a queen. While pregnant with 'Scab-on-his-Hand' (Karakaṇḍu), his mother desired to ride in state, along with the king, on an elephant and get soaked in rain. Somehow this was contrived, in spite of the fact that it was the middle of summer. However, the animal decided to turn wild and run off into the jungle. The king managed to jump off, preserving himself for the benefit of his subjects, while the queen eventually found herself giving birth to Karakaṇḍu in a cremation ground. An untouchable attendant claimed the boy (revealing himself as a cursed *vidyādhara*), and the mother departed to become a Jain nun. Brought up in these spooky surroundings among untouchables and funeral pyres, Karakaṇḍu nevertheless succeeded in becoming king, being abducted by a *vidyādhara* princess who was impressed by his bravery, and conquering India.[3]

In another story, the queen, pregnant with Udayana (the Udeṇa of our previous Buddhist story),[4] desired to bathe in a pool of blood, dressed in a red garment. This attracted the attention of a mighty bird who swooped down, picked her up and, realizing its mistake, dropped her into the middle of a jungle. There she gave birth to Udayana and eventually found shelter with a hermit. Taught the arts by the sage and acquiring all kinds of *vidyā* from the *nāgas* he encountered in the wilderness, Udayana in the end returned to his rightful throne.[5]

In a third example the queen desired a ripe mango fruit, out of season. When nobody could find such a fruit, the king went himself into the forest where, while discovering such a fruit and sending it to the queen, he was converted by a Jain monk and turned ascetic. When the queen, in a rage about this rejection, had given birth to a son, she threw the baby away – to be snatched by a *vidyādhara*, who then taught him the *vidyās* through which he could recover his kingdom and also win the heart of many *vidyādhara* girls.[6]

Intrigues at court are another accidental cause of the hero's journey into the wild worlds filled with mysterious powers. It may be a minister or a relative of the king who succeeds in a *coup d'état* and then forces into exile the legitimate heir to the throne. In one example such a prince finds himself in the company of lepers and roams the country, eventually and inevitably to be wooed and married by a *vidyādhara* girl.[7]

But what is court life without the intrigues of the harem, the endless struggles of co-wives to gain some advantage over their rivals? When Hariṣeṇa's mother goes on hunger-strike after a co-wife had managed to cancel a religious festival she had planned, Hariṣeṇa runs off into the jungle. There, in a hermitage, he meets a princess whose future husband is prophesied to become an emperor. Caught in the act of making advances to her, he is expelled from the hermitage. But after he is abducted and married by a *vidyādhara* girl, the successful completion of his ambitions is assured.[8]

Or we can return to the story of Snake-Prince (Nāgakumāra). Due to a similar harem intrigue, as a baby he had fallen into a well, only to be rescued and brought up by *nāgas*. Roaming through the world, he shows extraordinary skill on the lute, in rousing passion in man-hating women, and in flying to faraway islands to rescue captive *vidyādhara* girls. And as we saw above, in a jungle he meets a wild and otherwise despised tribesman, whose wife he rescues from the underworld and with whose help he acquires many further *vidyās*.[9]

All this may strike us as rather fantastic. So it seems opportune to turn to more down-to-earth examples, taken from the world of seafaring merchants. Bhaviṣyadatta, 'Future-Given', had a happy childhood: he was handsome and intelligent. But then a rift set in between his parents, his father increasingly lost interest in wife and son, and in the end sent them back – disgraced and impoverished – to his parents-in-law's place, and married a second wife. Another son resulted from this union. When he had grown up, he wanted to go on a trading expedition across the seas. In spite of all entreaties to stay home and enjoy the parental wealth, he set out with his pauper half-brother. Cheated, betrayed, and brought close to death more than once by his half-brother, Bhaviṣyadatta nevertheless succeeded in returning home a rich and powerful man. An ordinary story, it would seem. But Future-Given's return would not have been possible, had not some *deva* entrusted a *yakṣa* to look after him, and had not he himself, in a previous existence, assisted a king. This king, reborn as a demon due to his excessive craving for revenge, had taken the life of a town on a faraway island where Bhaviṣyadatta was stranded. Only a pretty princess was left alive: when defending her against the onslaught of the demon, all was revealed, and both could marry.[10]

Or there is the story of Cārudatta, which must be one of the most realistic travelogues ancient India has preserved. Cārudatta was another merchant's son, happy to spend his days fooling around with his playmates. One day his mother made the mistake of arranging a marriage for him with his cousin. Not only did her husband, Cārudatta's father, resent this intrusion into his realm of responsibility, but also Cārudatta let his mother down by refusing to consummate the marriage (acquiring a few nasty names in the process from his in-laws). As an act of double revenge, the mother contrived to get Cārudatta entangled with a prostitute in a brothel. The fortune wasted there hurt his father, and it hurt Cārudatta too when one morning, hung over, he found himself destitute and penniless, thrown out on to a manure heap. That roused his adventurous spirits, and he set out into the wide world. His travels led him to exotic countries – and the way they are described suggests that some real person actually undertook them. Some of his adventures flowed into the narrative of Sindbad in the Arabian Nights, like the story about the traders hiding inside animal hides and being carried off by gigantic birds. In the end he returned a rich and successful man, and found his old prostitute sweetheart still waiting faithfully for him and serving his wretched mother and wife. So all ends well with a second marriage. But here again no such luck would have been possible without the help of a *vidyādhara* and a *deva*. The former had been attacked by a rival in the act of making love, and Cārudatta had freed him and cured his wounds. When all seemed lost and Cārudatta was certain to die in a mountain wilderness, they met again and Cārudatta was richly rewarded for his help. The *deva* who turned up on the same occasion and bestowed further riches on him, was no other than the reborn goat which Cārudatta had refused to kill, even at the risk of his life, and to which he had preached the essentials of Jainism.[11]

Or finally, what could be more realistic than a painter in charge of periodically repainting a *yakṣa* image? Yet this *yakṣa* had the nasty habit of eating the painter once he had done his job. When a particular painter, out of compassion for a weeping mother, substituted himself for her son to do the task, he managed through humility and skill to win the *yakṣa* over. Instead of devouring him, the *yakṣa* gave him the *vidyā* of being able to paint anything fully, even when merely a small part of it was visible. (This *vidyā* turned out to be a double-edged sword, as the painter found out when, from seeing a queen's ankle, he drew the whole of her figure in the flesh, including a birthmark on an intimate part of her anatomy.)[12]

All these different bits and pieces of story material have yielded various, rather consistent themes. There is the quest for powers which we would label 'supernatural' were they not connected with beings that are presented to us as irrevocably real and 'natural'. There is the association of the acquisition of such powers with realms beyond the boundaries of normal life: cremation grounds, the wild forest, caves that lead into Patāla, people with whom one would normally have nothing to do, exotic lands. Then, in most cases, the adventurous journey into those realms beyond these boundaries is triggered off by abnormal events.

But before I try to develop the interpretation of this material further, I must turn to the main story of this chapter which – appropriately it would seem – is called the *Bṛhatkathā*, the '*Grand Story*'. This work has been looming in scholarly literature for quite a while now, and more pages than it is long have been written about it. Not that its evaluation has been at the centre of the discussion – philologues and text-critics are not interested in that! So what did appeal to their particular form of imagination? It is a rather peculiar feature associated with the work: that it is supposed to be lost! But how can one write on a lost work, you may ask. The answer is simple: as always in India, things never come singly. By now we have identified about eight works[13] that are regarded as rewrites and adaptations of the supposedly lost original, in a variety of languages. It is on the basis of these that the reconstruction has been attempted. It is, however, worth keeping in mind that the greatest zeal was shown by scholars almost a century ago, when only three of the latest versions, all in Sanskrit, were known. It is also here that we hear something about the mythical origin of the *Grand Story*. Since this introductory story provides some interesting themes for our interpretation, let me summarize it briefly.

We are taken into the higher heavens, where the god Śiva claims to be telling his wife Pārvatī a unique story. Thus, not surprisingly, she considers herself made a fool of when later she hears the same story told by one of the heavenly *yakṣas*. The mystery is eventually solved: one of the *yakṣas* guarding the door of the heavenly palace has overheard Śiva tell his tale, and has then, in turn, told it to his wife. Since you do not make fools of *devas* like that, everyone involved in the incident gets cursed to be born on earth as human beings. An end to the curse will only be possible, if and when the *Story* is narrated to mankind. Down on earth things get very complicated, but the outcome of it all is that in the middle of the forest the last of our cursed *yakṣas* is seated in front of a fire, surrounded by birds and beasts. Unable to find ink in his wild abode, he has written the story on palm leaves with his own blood. He has been forced to use not a comprehensible human language, but that of demons – Paiśācī – and not surprisingly he has failed to find an audience. In despair he is now reciting each page, before throwing it in the fire. However, when only the last ten per cent are left, he does find a listener: the curse comes to an end and humanity has acquired the '*Grand Story*'.[14]

This story is interesting for two reasons. First of all, it has been the basis of the assumption that the original *Bṛhatkathā* has been lost – not because of the burnt ninety per cent, but because of the Paiśācī language. This has been assumed by our philologues and text-critics to be a real language. Since not a single line of any text[15] in this language has been preserved or can definitely be identified, it is argued that the whole literature that existed in the primordial past in this language, obviously including the *Bṛhatkathā*, must therefore have got lost. Secondly, it is interesting that the story's symbolism can immediately be connected with the stories told earlier on: it is a work of the wild forest, where blood serves as ink. It is a work connected with the human world via a hierarchy of supernatural beings: *piśācas*, then *yakṣas*, but in essence the product of a *deva* – thus a powerful and power-laden work indeed!

So what is it all about? While the aforementioned story would seem to prepare us for a grand tale of magic and mystery, this is not really the case. Putting all the pieces together, we are dealing with the family history, over four generations, of the kings of Kausambi. This seems a terrible anti-climax, but things are not that bad, for this history, at least in the third generation, includes the realm of the *vidyādharas*, and even earlier on some rather weird and wonderful things happen. But here again, things are probably not quite what they seem. Again, it is only the later versions that attempt anything like a coherent family chronicle, and that never quite in equal proportions. The earlier versions treat merely one or the other generation. Moreover, there is a marked difference in the literary genre of these two portions (only the second one deals with *vidyādharas* as its central theme). To make matters even more complicated, there is the story of Cārudatta, parts of which I narrated earlier on. This very long tale is included in the '*Bṛhatkathā*' complex. Our women-conquering hero – I am now talking about the third generation – meets Cārudatta (whose daughter Gandharvadattā he defeats at playing the lute and then – inevitably – marries) who narrates him his adventures. Many themes found here in a natural context, but repeated in other parts of the '*Bṛhatkathā*', in a rather artificial frame, must have had their origin in this story. So we would have to assume at least three, originally independent, source complexes.

However, the established opinion is that the late versions are relatively faithful adaptations of the original, while the early ones are all

Buddhist and Jain propagandist distortions. This reminds me of the Hittite calamity. When comparative philology had with great zeal reconstructed something like the common archetype of all known Indo-European languages, Hittite was discovered. This is a language far older than all those known until then. Unfortunately it is very simple in structure compared with the reconstructed version. Now just as this did not ruin the confidence of the comparative philologist, I am sure the theory of the original *Bṛhatkathā*, written in Paiśācī long before the AD era, will stay with us.[16] Yet it is only from the latter part of the first millennium AD that we find references to it. The suggestion that we might be overshooting our target by many centuries – and that the concept, and possibly an actual text, of the '*Bṛhatkathā*' only evolved sometime between what I have called the earlier and the later versions – is likely to leave the firmly rooted belief in a primordial *Grand Story* unshaken.

Be that as it may, for our purposes it is sufficient to have a vast amount of material that can be gathered together under this concept '*Bṛhatkathā*' – whether it is merely notional or real makes no difference. Now it would be extremely tiresome to provide the details here of the eight primary versions known to us. Let it suffice that Hindus, Buddhists and Jains have been at work here, that five languages are involved (Pālī, Prakrit, Sanskrit, Tamil and Apabhraṃśa), that almost fifteen hundred years of literary history in all parts of India are covered, and that the majority of these versions are incomplete even in terms of their own scope. Once again we are clearly dealing here with a grand cultural construct that logically predates its specific religious interpretations and adaptations.

Besides these primary texts, a number of dramas[17] deal with themes assumed to derive from the *Bṛhatkathā*. Finally, among the Jains many new stories were written on the basis of plot, symbolism and ideas (some of which have been summarized above). All this demonstrates the enormous appeal the *Bṛhatkathā* material has had for the religious imagination.

Events related to the first generation have already been narrated. There is the painter who gets punished because of his particular skill: the king (no other than Udayana's father) whose wife he has painted so true to life has the painter's fingers cut off, but in the end dies in a war which the painter instigates as his revenge. Then there is Udayana, brought up in the jungle and singularly talented at playing the lute. The same king who caused his father's death contrives to have him kidnapped. When the prince is out catching elephants, a particularly large, white specimen fails to fall for the entrancing music of the lute. Approaching him steadily, it reveals itself as a mechanical imitation made of wood that is filled with soldiers. Brought to the court of the king who then holds him captive, he teaches the lute to a princess: they fall in love, elope, and eventually have a son Naravāhanadatta. He now is the hero of the second part of the *Bṛhatkathā*. Nothing much happens during his childhood, until he falls in love with a prostitute, Madanamañcukā ('Casket of Cupid'). He does succeed in marrying her, but then it turns out that the girl is really a *vidyādharī* whom a *vidyādhara* abducts, since he regards himself as her legitimate bridegroom. The real adventure story begins when Naravāhanadatta himself is carried off by a *vidyādhara* girl. Three themes intermingle in the following events: Naravāhana's intense longing, in spite of acquiring a large number of further wives, for his first wife, from whom he is separated; his acquisition of *vidyās* with the help of the *vidyādharas* friendly to him; and his battles with his arch-enemy, the *vidyādhara* who has abducted Madanamañcukā and is keeping her captive. After the final battle, he is reunited with her and then becomes *cakravartī* over all the *vidyādharas* – the two realms of man and of *vidyā* are united, all through the heroism of a human being. Naturally all the wives our hero has married in the course of his adventures are brought together from their various homes. A quick glance at how he has acquired these ladies, human and *vidyādhara*, shows that three basic possibilities are involved here. First, it is Naravāhanadatta's personal skills, bravery, or *vidyās* that impress a girl or, more realistically, her father so much that a marriage is agreed upon. Secondly, without his own contrivance a girl – and here it is exclusively the *vidyādharīs* who are far more liberated and outgoing than their human counterpart – proposes to him. Thirdly, his arrival or his deeds in a particular place fulfil a certain prophecy that is connected with a particular girl. It is episodes of this kind that fill the interval between the abduction of and final reunion with Madanamañcukā.

At least one major variant to this second part of the *Bṛhatkathā* must be mentioned. This is a very old (third century AD?) Jain epic in Prakrit. Here we find basically the same pattern of amorous episodes and conquests as described for Naravāhanadatta, but attributed to Vasudeva, Kṛṣṇa's father. Two interesting peculiarities in this version, which was extremely influential on a large number of later Jain works, may be pointed out here. First, there is the cause of Vasudeva's adventure trip. He was so handsome that all the women in his town fell passionately in love with him. Naturally their husbands found this rather objectionable and complained to the king. The latter put Vasudeva under house-arrest. But in the dark of the night he managed to escape, faked a suicide, and swore to return only after a hundred years. From this, secondly, it follows logically that the theme of 'searching for the abducted beloved' is missing. Instead it is at the very end of this period, when Vasudeva had conquered the hearts of twenty-three or so ladies, that he encountered the two closest to his own heart: the mothers-to-be of Balarāma and Kṛṣṇa.

After all the build-up, this might be found to be disappointing. But then we have to explore the material further as to its symbolism and implications and avoid cutting out large chunks from it which, to the Indian audience, were significant. Inevitably, an evaluation must start with the *vidyās*. Now we find a certain ambivalence in all our sources about the location of such powers. On the one hand, this lies clearly beyond the boundaries of ordinary life, but on the other hand, we find the intrusion of *vidyās* into ordinary life. Specific places are identified as entrances into Patāla or as favourite hunting-grounds for *vidyādharas* keen on acquiring further *vidyās*. Yet most interesting, perhaps, is that our hero never really sets out with the specific aim of exploring those realms. Accidental or other undesirable circumstances impel him towards such an exploration. This suggests that as a cultural construct, our material does not present an ideal here, a blueprint for man to follow. While it is envisaged as quite possible to gain even total control over realms like that of the *vidyādharas*, we cannot find any overt suggestions as to the general method for doing so. This need not surprise us, for the religious traditions that have preserved the various versions of the *Grand Story* all have their own comments to make and, on the whole, would not be in sympathy with a religious pursuit that concentrates on the acquisition of *vidyās*. For these we shall have to look at rituals cultivated particularly in the esoteric traditions; such rituals will be discussed at a later stage.

Now what is the nature of these oft-mentioned *vidyās*? On the most concrete level, these are skills such as playing the lute well or painting interesting pictures; or crafts, like building mechanical dolls; or special talents such as winning the heart of a man-hating woman. The imagination expands this to include less 'realistic' skills, such as subduing elephants through lute-playing, painting a whole person from seeing merely a small part of the body, and so on. This gets further extended to include the construction of mechanical birds that allow one to fly, the ability to fly by oneself, to read people's thoughts, to change one's form at will, to become irresistible to any woman (or man – to do justice to our emancipated *vidyādhara* girls). To a small extent, these are actually available to us through our science and technology – I am thinking here of flying and also of similar skills the Indians did not, at that time, think about: the art of destroying the whole world of man with one massive bang. This now makes this material accessible to us: for in this conglomerate of skills, crafts, talents, 'magic lore' and sciences, some common ground with our own experiences and dreams can be discovered. I shall return to this presently.

Incidentally it may be of interest to draw attention to one of the sources on which the Indian imagination drew. In our material there are a number of references to Greeks and their special *vidyās*, such as building flying machines.[18] Beautifully illustrated Arab works that present us with developed versions of these Greek 'inventions' (like the famous *Book of the Knowledge of Mechanical Devices*)[19] reveal what is meant by those allusions: animated clocks, drinking vessels that make music when emptied, mechanical ducks on (real) ponds, etc. Since these are real devices that have also actually been reconstructed from those Arab manuscripts, once again we find ourselves at the threshold of real science. But let me return to the *vidyādharas* and their skills.

The possession of such *vidyās* is now controlled by certain factors that we must call ethical: strict rules apply even to the *vidyādharas* as to what they are allowed to do with their *vidyās*. Any breach of these rules brings about the automatic loss of these powers. Thus, for example, a *vidyādhara* can never actually rape a woman. But more important than the ethical restrictions is the purpose of it all. Particularly from the *Grand Story* one expects more than incidental results (like winning in a battle or conquering the heart of a woman). But here we encounter a more general problem: we can easily enjoy reading about adventures in pursuit of some quest, but when it comes to depicting the fundamental transformations in the hero brought about by the fulfilment of the quest, poets tend to be as much at a loss as the equally untransformed reader. To read about Parsifal after he found the Grail is as much of an anticlimax as reading about Naravāhanadatta after he became emperor of the *vidyādharas*. As the *Bṛhatkathā* tends to be presented as his own narrative, one would expect this to become a self-reflection and expression of his wisdom. This is not so, just as the circumstances that make him deliver the narrative are rather anticlimactic. In one version he wants to entertain his grandchildren, in another he has just acted as judge in a case brought before him that involves another man wanting to marry a *vidyādhara* girl. In a third version, the death of his father Udayana triggers off a reflection on the transience of all worldly power and pleasures.[20]

Yet this kind of argument does not do justice to how the material was perceived. The acquisition of skills, talents, and more super-ordinary sciences, is clearly a human ambition, a dream that Naravāhana could fulfil. Brought up in the European tradition of the *Erziehungsroman*, the novel that tells us about the inner character developments of a hero (or anti-hero) through encounters and through coping with external adventures, we want this spelled out to us in a similar manner for Naravāhanadatta. But I would have thought a man who has won the hearts of, made frequent love to, and related as person to person with, a large number of women (whether ten, twenty-five, five hundred and eighteen or seven hundred and seven makes no difference here), will have undergone a considerable development in his personality, quite apart from the *vidyās* he may have acquired in the process. Furthermore, we must not underestimate the importance of themes like searching for a love enjoyed initially and then lost, or finding after a long sequence of amorous conquest the one woman who completely fills one's heart (as in some versions of the *Bṛhatkathā* and secondary stories). These overarching features are complemented by those episodes in which our hero fulfils a prophecy. All in all, this could be phrased in terms of our hero fulfilling his destiny through his search and adventures, except that we are not prepared for such an overtly amorous nature of the quest!

Perhaps we ought to define the literary genre of our material further. Obviously we are reminded of our fairy tales; in addition, I am struck by the similarities with our science fiction. Neither category quite fits. In the former case we explore ourselves in relation to dreams and nightmares in our hearts, in the latter case in relation to the dreams and nightmares of a future technology. But to the Indian audience the *vidyās* were more than dreams: they were real, and where they went beyond the limits of empirical evidence, they still remained real by virtue of the real existence of the *vidyādharas*, *yakṣas*, etc., and the real possibility of a man actually encountering these beings. Thus our material is more than a dream: it is a definite view of the real world. Moreover, it has to do with science in some way. Now I have always been disappointed with science fiction, for the type of person envisaged in a futuristic setting has struck me as still identical to what I can see today in everyday life: motivation, values, interests, ambitions – the whole personality is unchanged. This is where the present material gets exciting, for here we find a very different personality in relation to the same sort of thing we try to explore through our science fiction or similar imaginative literature. So to the extent that sci-fi represents the direction of our whole scientific enterprise, our present material offers a different direction. One may find this very far-fetched. Nevertheless, I consider it worth our while to explore this further, under its proper heading of Love, as the relationship between an *eros*-centred culture and science.

All that has been said so far could not possibly make sense, to us as much as to the ancient Indians, were there not some empirical basis for it in human experience. As far as the travelogues are concerned, we need not pause, for it is well known that Indians travelled on a large scale, to very faraway places. But the weird beings we have been hearing about, and the *vidyās* associated with them, do raise problems in our minds. Let me therefore move away now from the type of literature discussed so far, to other matters.

We all know one type of magician: the man who pulls rabbits out of hats. This person is not unknown in ancient India; he is the practitioner of *māyā*.

> Standing at a crossroad, a skilled magician erects a pile of plants, leaves, twigs, gravel or sand, and then conjures up all kinds of magic objects: herds of elephants, horses, chariots, battalions of soldiers, heaps of precious stones, etc.

Similar passages talk about such a magician casting a rope into the air, sending his assistant up, following him, and then all bystanders see arms and legs fall down from the sky beyond the clouds.[21]

While our reaction would be to ask 'how did he do it?' or to try and take photographs of the tricks, to the average Indian audience these were quasi-real events, real transformations of the stones, etc. If you don't believe me, listen to the sequel of the first passage quoted.

Many spectators do not recognize the plants, leaves, etc. which the magician has been employing. Faced with those conjured-up objects, they think that the herd of elephants, of horses, etc. which he shows to them exist in reality. Relying on what they see and perceive, they firmly believe in that whole phantasmagoria and express themselves in the language of every day by saying: 'This is real!'[22]

This comes from a Buddhist text and is used as a metaphor for mistaken perceptions of the world. Thus, at least to the author of the passage, it is clear that no stone was actually turned into a horse, but also that most people did believe so.

Yet even our Buddhist author would not have rejected the reality of a different phenomenon: possession. This must be split up into two components: involuntary and controlled. The first variety of possession is used as the explanation of mental disorders – people going mad. Naturally the possessing agent tends to be identified with one of the more malevolent beings such as *bhūtas*, *piśācas*, *rākṣasas*. The second variety involves less destructive beings: *devīs*, *devas*, *yakṣas*, etc. This type of possession can be ritually induced and is thus a controlled affair, usually done by specialists in a village. The purpose of it is mainly to draw on the superhuman knowledge these beings possess. With reference to the past this means to find out the reasons for certain events (like droughts, illness, madness), and with reference to the future to learn about the next rainfall, whether or not the harvest will be good, and so on. To this we may add one further cause of worry: will she love me, or will she not? This, at least, is the problem of a young man in the Indian community of faraway Trinidad. With it, he approached the local *obeah*, who was happy to let the *devī* possess him and pronounce a favourable answer to the question – until he found out that the girl in question was his own daughter![23]

This now casts new light on the literature discussed previously: we are clearly dealing there with an imaginative abstraction from something that was actually happening in real life. What we are dealing with here shares a common frame of reference, something the title has already pointed at: a manipulation of space, time and matter. Just as the magician can turn stones into horses or elephants, knowing the right *vidyā* allows one to transform oneself from man into woman or vice versa, or from ugly into extremely handsome. Matter and form are pliable entities. Similarly time: past and future events can be revealed, and with the right *vidyā* can even be made manifest. Space can easily be crossed, in flying machines or on one's own. Now this brings all our material even closer to our own scientific enterprise, which in a similar manner attempts to turn the space–time–matter continuum into something pliable through human hands.

But what about real technology? It is clear that our general programme does not offer us the scope to discuss the details of traditional Indian technology. Let me, however, provide one illustration. Anybody who reads about the following incident found in a Prakrit drama[24] from Kerala will cease to doubt that ancient India was capable of applied science. A king had fallen in love with a beautiful young princess (who, incidentally, had been conjured up by a magician). His chief queen was obviously anxious to find out what was going on in the room where the king and the girl were having a private *tête-à-tête*. A tape-recorder or preferably a video-camera would have been ideal, but she thought of the best her medieval environment could provide. Thus you find her servant, next morning, walking across the stage carrying a statue that had been placed in the said room. From it the queen extricates a parrot that has learnt verbatim every word spoken by king and princess!

Our exploration has so far gathered together three types of material. The first kind of material deals with real-life phenomena that are perceived as modes of manipulating space, time and matter (like *māyā* or possession). Secondly, there is the equally realistic application of some 'scientific' principles to the construction, for instance, of mechanical elephants or artificial singing birds, or to the 'recording' of human speech. But the bulk of the material we have been looking at in this chapter belongs to a third category, the imaginative expansion of such realistic bases in the form of a world pervaded by *vidyās* and populated by *vidyādharas*. From all this arises a further basic question:

can we discover any kind of feedback on practical reality from this imaginative world? Generally speaking, the relationship implied in this could be seen as comparable to the effect the writings of H. G. Wells can be assumed to have had on the advance of real science. But in order to avoid getting drawn into a discussion of the history of Indian applied science, let me rephrase the question. Did Indian culture develop any generally available means of obtaining *vidyā*s? Let us recollect initially that none of the versions of the *Grand Story* nor any of the related stories, as discussed so far, offered any direct suggestions about such an access into the world of the *vidyās* and *vidyādhara*. But in two of the stories, those about the leper who became king and about 'Scab-on-his-Hand', we can find some clues.

Let me first return to the story of Śrīpāla, whom we left in the weird company of lepers, himself having contracted the disease. It now happened that a king wanted to get rid of one of his daughters whom he disliked intensely, and the leper Śrīpāla was chosen as her husband. However, this girl was a devout Jain laywoman, and not only converted Śrīpāla to Jainism, but also knew the cure for his disease. She taught him the *siddha-cakra*: a particular diagram, drawn, for instance, on the ground with powder, inscribed with potent words and then ritually treated. With the help of this tool, Śrīpāla succeeded later, during his adventure trip, in subduing a particularly nasty *devī* who had paralysed a fleet of merchant ships and demanded a human sacrifice.[25]

Further detail on what is meant by ritual here can be found in the story of Karakaṇḍu. When he had been abducted by a *vidyādharī*, his current wife

> invoked the *devī* Padmāvatī. She drew a beautiful diagram, and in the middle of it she installed the *devī*. She was made of red sandalwood besmeared with camphor, sandal paste and saffron. She made offerings of fruits, flowers and food. She recited the *devī*'s *mantra*. When thus thought of and invoked, Padmāvatī manifested herself before her. 'I grant you a wish – ask for whatever you want', she said, smiling sweetly.[26]

Then the princess consults the *devī* about the whereabouts of Karakaṇḍu. In the same way, our *vidyādharas* subdue and acquire their *vidyās* through the same kind of *mantras*-cum-ritual actions, which seem to include sexual abstinence.

It is important to remember that such ritual means as are described here represent specifically Jain reinterpretations of beliefs and practices found in less sophisticated, popular milieux. The latter are, however, not directly accessible to us, as far as the story material connected with the *Grand Story* is concerned. But it will be sufficient for our purposes to assume a basic compatibility between the Jain elaborations and the popular basis, so that by discussing the latter we are not actually leaving the world of the *vidyās* and *vidyādharas* behind altogether.

India has been aware of at least five facets of the human person which duplicate and reorganize our space–time–matter continuum: the dream, drawing or painting (the most obvious representational system), language, the body, and the mind. Alternatively we could speak of 'representational structures' that mirror the external world. (We shall return to this idea on a number of future occasions, so at this point I shall merely provide some relevant points.) What we have encountered as rituals in pursuit of *vidyās* can now be interpreted as the practical application of observations made in Indian culture about the role and function of such representation. The general idea is that by effecting change in the mirror-image of the world, the world itself can be affected.

In the present context, the first facet, dreams, can be dealt with briefly. The Indians conceptualized the nature of dreams as an alternative space–time–matter continuum; they located them as a midway house between everyday awareness and liberation; they utilized dreams in the prediction of future events. But they also realized that they are phenomena outside human control, and thus did not employ them in their ritual 'experiments'.

The case of language is different. Not only do words relate to objects, syntactical relations reproduce relationship between objects, and grammatical forms mirror our space–time continuum, words can also influence events. Commands uttered give rise to actions, knowing the name of a person singles him out from among a protective and anonymous crowd, and ordinary skills and crafts are acquired through the words of the teacher. In general, there is nothing here for which we could not easily find parallels in other cultures. What is remarkable is the degree of precision to which the structure of language itself has been analysed in ancient India, and the extent to which language as a command-system has been given philosophical exploration. But such matters lie outside our present context, and due justice will have to be done to them under the appropriate heading of Wisdom. On the other hand, there is another aspect which is relevant. This is the *mantra*, the 'spell' or formula, which consists of mainly meaningless syllables (which are nevertheless interpreted as 'representing' aspects of reality) and which, when accompanied by the right diagram or ritual actions, has influence over *vidyās* and beings associated with them. At the same time, they serve as the armour for the brave man who has gone out to face these forces.[27] We have encountered the usage of the *mantra* on a number of occasions previously.

Just as from real language powerful syllables can be abstracted that function in a *mantra*, from the immediately apparent representational properties of drawing or painting, abstract geometrical patterns are derived which, in sometimes very complex concatenations, are understood to function like the *mantra*. These diagrams are called *maṇḍalas* or *yantras*. It is no coincidence that the latter word *yantra* also means 'machine': like its mechanical counterpart, a diagram is thus perceived to 'operate' on normally invisible forces. As far as body and mind are concerned, we shall have ample opportunity to investigate their roles in representational systems at later stages. For the present discussion we need to take into consideration merely such aspects as the usage of gestures understood to mirror or effect real events and the mental concentration on a *mantra* or on the force 'represented' by it. A combination of these different features (language, gestures and concentration, together with the drawing of abstract designs) constitutes the kind of ritual we are discussing here.

Now it would seem to us that we have moved far away from 'science' in our sense and that the parallel I initially drew between it and the *vidyās* was no more than an ephemeral, rhetorical comment. But, in fact, it appears to me that in some basic sense we are indeed talking about comparable phenomena. For instance, what we would call 'experimentation' is not unrelated to what we can observe in the Indian material. I would not hesitate to call the enormous amount of effort and variation documented in the texts, concerning the design of such diagrams, formulae and ritual actions and utensils, a type of experimentation. In such a comparison we have naturally to exclude, or at least considerably modify, the element of verifiability. However, I think it is possible to draw a further parallel here between our Western delight in making use of our technology to produce ever new varieties of objects and an Indian fascination for a seemingly uninhibited proliferation of ritual materials. I am not drawing a parallel between, say, a car and a ritual. The comparison concerns the unrestrained creative exuberance and the spirit of experimentation underlying it. Surprising though it may sound, 'ritual' in India does not necessarily (and in fact, not that frequently) denote an ossified, mechanical action. Studying a single ritualistic text might still conjure up visions of the Roman Catholic Church, in which it was customary, once upon a time, to define the legitimate extent to which the priest's arms were allowed to move sideways while being raised during Mass. But reading more than one Indian ritual text even within the same tradition soon destroys such an association. Similarly, there is the consternation of the anthropologist who tries to compare the 'practice' with the 'text' it nominally derives from. The expression 'jungle-like growth' could hint at what is happening here, for unlike a carefully pruned rose-bush, an uncontrolled wild(er)ness manifests itself here.

Uninhibited proliferation can be observed in a threefold manner. There is, first of all, the staggering amount of manuscript material through which many generations of scholars had to cut a path in pursuit of more worthy matters (like philosophy). Indeed, it would be extremely unfair to raise my grand programme of the first chapter as the stick with which to castigate those scholars, for surely there cannot be anything more tedious than studying ritualistic texts. But we must not make the mistake of confusing textual study with actual ritual practice, which is really what this discussion is about, as we shall see presently. Secondly, we find that religious traditions, the longer they have developed, produce an increasing number of different ritual handbooks which, equally legitimately, inspire different sub-traditions. But thirdly – and this is the area where the rationale of the whole phenomenon reveals itself most clearly – we can see the principle at work even in a single text or rite. Logically, which means taking a purely utilitarian point of view, it is sufficient to make a single offering of flowers, pour out one libation of water, or recite a *mantra* once. But clearly the person actually involved derives a sensual delight already from the smells, sights, and rhythmic movements of his hands and the magic flow of language, and this shows itself in the tendency towards repetition. But it is more than mere repetition that is involved here. For new variations are introduced, new combinations emerge, and further details are added. One could call this creative experimentation. In fact, it is conceivable that were one to substitute musical notes for each discrete ritual item (e.g. scattering the petals of a particular flower), a musical structure might evolve. Such a structure extricated for an entire ritual event would then resemble a number of basic notes and discrete themes, and a set of increasingly complex variations on these themes. Thus on the one hand we are clearly dealing here with an aesthetic principle that underlies ritualistic proliferation. Such a 'self-authenticating' character may well explain the occurrence of ritual events in contexts that in terms of strict philosophy allow for no such practice (e.g. the Jain temple or the ancient Buddhist *stūpa*). But on the other hand – if I may continue with my musical metaphor – such ritual events are not like the fixed and 'authentically performed' musical compositions of our Western classical tradition. The phenomenon of uninhibited proliferation suggests instead a comparison with the improvisatory character of the Indian musical tradition, in which each performance appears as an extempore creation that is structured merely by some formal conventions and by the *rāg*. Such a principle of inventive creativity (or creative experimentation) could then also be recognized as underlying the proliferation of different makes and models of functionally practically identical objects (be they cars or cameras, leather-jackets, or hi-fi equipment). It is the proliferation of 'designs' (in both senses of the word, technical and aesthetic) that could justify the comparison initially drawn here; it is in the areas of application where the differences lie.

Thus we start off with a straightforward utilitarian design – of the car, for example, as a means of controlling space, or of a particular ritual action as a means of acquiring the *vidyā* of being able to fly through the sky. But this act of designing soon develops its own momentum and adds all kinds of further dimensions to itself and to the end-product. Control becomes elevated to pleasure, the pursuit of power turns into a quest for beauty. And in that sense Naravāhanadatta's or Vasudeva's amorous adventures in the world of the *vidyās* and *vidyādharas* begin to make some sense to us. If all this seems rather romanticized and sentimental, the next chapter will lead us into the realms of fear. There further kinds of heroes venture into the, as yet unexplored, territories of the forbidden.

CHAPTER 7

Entering forbidden realms

Although the last chapter dealt with deadly duels, bloodthirsty ogres and horrific sorcerers' battles, there cannot be any doubt that a romanticizing tendency was at work there. Our *vidyādharas*, *nāgas*, etc. are made to appear quite amiable on the whole. The odd man-eating *yakṣa* or demon may crop up, but there is always the chance of pacifying the creature and obtaining a *vidyā* from him, or of winning the love of a girl through him. As far as the *vidyās* are concerned, they are treated as related more to the 'battle' between the sexes than to anything really dangerous, such as the making of things by interfering in nature, breaking nature up and reconstituting it at will, or annihilating it altogether. This in turn means that, as far as the material discussed so far is concerned, the nightmarish fears which we find in our own imaginative projection of what *our vidyās* can do are not expressed. I am thinking here of all-pervasive themes like the mad German scientist or the 'Dr No's of our popular films and novels; of alien empires that must be destroyed through our futuristic weapon technology. Our Indian stories read much more like the exploits of modern heroes such as 007, although even here an unease about the role of science in the wrong hands does express itself.

Thus, to suggest against the background of Western fears and doubts a correlation of the *Grand Story* and its related material with Western science may not appear obvious. Other parallels from our own literary history come much more easily to mind, for example that of Dr Faustus or of the Golem. The learned doctor conjured up secret powers and was allowed to use them for as long as he remained dissatisfied and eager to pursue his quest for fulfilment. In his case, love-affairs did not provide that fulfilment, and the longing of his heart was appeased only when he became involved in a grand creative act – some large-scale dam-building project. It is then that he made the fatal request for the fleeting moment to stop.[1] Thus in his case it is the quest for creative power, not love, that reveals itself as the central driving force. But then he had exchanged his soul for his *vidyās* in a pact made with the Devil! Less subtly developed is the theme of the devilish aspects of a pursuit of power in the motif of the Golem which takes us back to the sixteenth century, to the East European Jews. Jewish folklore attributed the creation of this robot-like being to a Rabbi of Prague, and as one of its expressions we have a famous play in Yiddish by H. Leivick (written in 1920). No sooner has the Rabbi succeeded in creating the Golem, than he is addressed by him:

> I have come to warn you: create me not.
> Do not dislodge me from my rest.
> What my hand will touch,
> to dust and ashes it will crumble.[2]

And, indeed, in the end, this man-made man goes beserk with an axe and kills more people than could the enemy against whom he was designed to fight. From Leivick's play it is not far to Frankenstein and his monster; here a practically identical plot is merely given a 'scientific' setting. It is this continuity which I have felt tempted to explore for the Indian material on the *vidyās* and on manipulating space, time and matter.

Such examples imply that, somewhere along the line of pursuing power through rather esoteric means, a Dr Faustus or the Rabbi of Prague or a Frankenstein did something that was 'forbidden', something they ought not to have done. At some point they reached the boundary of what society regarded as permissible and crossed it. From this arises the question of whether or not something similar exists in the Indian traditions. Indeed, there is ample material which deals with expressions of nightmarish fears in connection with the cultivation of *vidyās* and related 'esoteric' powers. But what makes the situation here so much more interesting is the fact that enough material exists to allow us direct access into the minds of the heroes that cross into the realms of the forbidden. Thus we do not depend on a poet such as Goethe, Marlowe or Leivick to interpret for us the deeds and motivation of Dr Faustus, etc. On the other hand, the Indian material is much more complicated because we are not actually dealing with one society that globally agrees on what is forbidden. We are dealing with continua and many variations of what is forbidden in any one context, unlike the neat black-and-white contrast between religion and magic in traditional Western societies.

As an initial introduction to the realms of the forbidden, let us return to Naravāhanadatta. We find him in the pleasurable company of Cārudatta's stepdaughter whom he has recently married. He tells us:

When the first quarter of the night had passed, I went to sleep. But after a while I was awakened by the touch of a rough hand. In front of me I saw a man with open mouth. I understood that he must be some demon [various versions have: *preta*, *bhūta*, *vetāla*], animated by the power of sorcery, who wanted to carry me somewhere. He started to drag me forcefully up from my bed, and placed me on his hard, wood-like back. He carried me away from the inner chamber. I saw that the maid-servants were asleep and reflected: 'They must have been brought under the sleeping *vidyā*.' I was carried away to the cremation ground. There I saw jackals devouring flesh; they howled meanly and terrifyingly, when they were frightened by barking dogs. Somewhere I saw a circle of *ḍākiṇīs* [witches in the company of Kālī] dancing around a corpse. They wore no clothes, shook their arms wildly, and their hair was dishevelled. Somewhere I saw a man with a raised sword in one hand and holding a cup made of a skull in the other. He was shouting: 'Heroes! Buy human flesh!' Then I saw an old woman, seated under a banyan tree. She was pouring human blood into a fire while reciting spells. She was delighted to see the demon that had carried out her command. She rewarded him with offerings, and asked him to put me down.[3]

Similar scenes of ghostly and ghastly activities during the night in a cremation ground can easily be found in Indian literature, as, for example, in the classical Sanskrit drama *Mālatī-Mādhava*.[4] Two strange characters encounter each other during the night in the cremation ground just outside the temple of the *devī* Karālā 'Gaping-Mouth'. One is the hero of the play, Mādhava, who is in despair over the disappearance of his beloved Mālatī. As a last desperate means of recovering her, he has decided to come here and 'sell human flesh', which he holds in his left hand, 'thickish blood dripping down from it'. He is walking about, shouting out the ware he is offering for 'sale' to the *vetālas*, *bhūtas*, *piśācas*, *rākṣasas* and *pretas*, in exchange for the safety of his beloved. The second person is a woman-disciple of a sorcerer who is about to complete a lengthy course of rituals designed to gain him supernormal powers. She has been sent by him into the cremation ground to gather together various utensils required for the ritual. But she has also been ordered to capture, as the most important item, a faultless being. To Mādhava's horror he discovers that his beloved Mālatī is the being that is intended to be ritually killed. But naturally all ends well: the sorcerer is killed, and none of the demons do any harm to the hero Mādhava.

In the frame-story to a well-known collection of riddles, the *Twenty-Five of the Demon* (*Vetāla-pañcaviṃśati*),[5] another sorcerer (called *yogī*) enlists the help of a king for a similar cremation-ground ritual. This involves the fetching of a corpse dangling from a tree in the distance, to be used in the ritual. Fortunately for the king, a *vetāla* has taken up abode inside this corpse and reveals to him that the *yogī* is planning to use the king himself as a human sacrifice, in order to gain the eight perfect powers, the *siddhis*. At the same time he, the *vetāla*, would become the *yogī*'s slave. But if the king were to kill the *yogī*, he would not only save his own life, but also be able to make him (the *vetāla*) his loyal servant, if he offered him the *yogī*'s blood.

Here we find a further dimension of the world, and of the heroic quest for power. First, we encounter beings that are far less amiable than the *vidyādharas*: *bhūtas*, *pretas*, *vetālas*, *piśācas*, *rākṣasas*, *ḍākinīs* and cruel *devīs* such as Karālā 'Gaping-Mouth' and Kālī 'Black'. They are perceived as demonic creatures of a most vicious and dangerous kind. They frequent cremation grounds, and devour both the corpses found there and, under normal circumstances, any man who is fool enough to enter there at night; they can only be appeased with human blood and flesh. Secondly, we find that this setting is intentionally chosen by individuals called *vīras*, 'heroes', as the ideal place to perform certain rituals, which may include murder. The intention behind such rituals is, thirdly, the acquisition of powers (called *siddhis* in one instance). But fourthly, only in the first, very moderate, example is the usage to which the old woman has put the *vetāla* (whom she subdued with offerings of blood) not questioned. In the remaining two examples the respective authors clearly disapprove and therefore have the sorcerers killed as punishment for their evil designs. Also, other aspects of the tale definitely mention things forbidden in normal life: any contact with meat or blood, corpses and, above all, the act of gratuitously killing another person, just as normally nobody would dream of going into the cremation ground in the middle of the night.

In a nutshell, this new realm into which the hero moves symbolizes death. It lies beyond the boundary that contains life – ordinary, normal, day-to-day human life as much as 'life' in the abstract. It is here that, quite literally, the dead are taken to be cremated and where death lies in wait for the fool who ventures into it unprepared. Death is the all-pervasive symbolism associated with those terrifying beings and with the rituals we have heard about. And thus in the final analysis, the intention behind the same must be the defeat of death itself. This is clearly the one frontier of the space–time–matter continuum in which we live which is felt to be most urgently in need of removal. It would appear here that a conscious delving into the realm of death and ritual manipulation of its powers is regarded as the means to destruct this frontier which lies at the end of a man's life.

Now it is extremely important to make certain distinctions here, particularly in relation to material discussed in Chapter 4. A *yakṣa* or a *rākṣasa* who invades the territory of a community and demands a human sacrifice at regular intervals and threatens to kill everybody in that community if his demands are not met, is one thing. To find that a fleet of merchant ships cannot leave the harbour, because a *devī* wants a human sacrifice first (as we found in the story of Śrīpāla), is another thing, half-way between the first and the next example. For a man to perform certain rituals, which require a human victim, in order to enrich his own powers, is the third type. This is what we heard about in the frame-story to the *Vetāla-Riddles*, and in the drama about Mālatī and Mādhava. Similarly, in the story of Fame-Bearer (Yaśodhara), the purpose of the king's performing sacrifices with samples of all living beings was to gain the power to move through space at will – which effectively means, to acquire the properties of one of the *siddhis*. Thus, although on the surface these horrific rituals may appear identical, their motivation is clearly different. In the first instance, the sacrifice serves to re-establish protective boundaries around a *community*, while in the last two it is an act perceived (certainly by the writers depicting them) as breaking a boundary in order to draw, in a ritually controlled context, on the dangerous forces latent in the act, for the sake of *individual* increase of power. Ultimately this power appears envisaged as the transcendence of death by an individual, but is communally disapproved of.

At this stage it is necessary to make a brief excursion into a topic that, perhaps more than any other, fired the British imagination about India during the later part of the nineteenth century, and which, as a recent film has shown, even today still possesses great commercial potential. The film is *Indiana Jones and the Temple of Doom*, and the topic is *thuggee*. On the most popular and uninformed level, this evokes ideas like: India is filled with people called thugs – the original Hindostani word, *thag*, means 'robber' – who kill people in order to sacrifice them to the *devī* Bhavānī or Kālī. Accounts of the nineteenth century assume the existence of a particular religious sect which they generally locate in central and eastern North India.

The idea of tribal people living in the jungles and ambushing innocent travellers for human sacrifice is an ancient one. Medieval literature contains many illustrations, both imagined and presented as real events, of such dangers lurking in the forests. The existence of robbers, brigands, dacoits and other types of criminal outlaws is also attested from an early date. Moreover, the British administration suggested that certain social units were gangsters and had a variety of criminal activities as their specific and hereditary 'caste' profession – the 'criminal caste'. These various groups would relate to the rest of society in the way that gypsies are alleged to relate to ours. Just as the gypsies have their own religion (and, at least in films, *mafiosi* are religious), such socially organized groups of 'criminals' had their religion, because social cohesion is unthinkable in traditional India without a religious component.

However, the way the *thugs* are presented to us by the missionaries and colonial officers of the period differs from all this. In contradistinction to all other groups, religion is regarded as the primary motive and driving force behind murders that are gratuitous, random and premeditated. Moreover, such murders are not single events in the life of an individual, but are committed as frequently as possible. This distinguishes the '*thug*' sharply from the 'evil ascetic' whom we encountered in the cremation ground earlier on.

But the documents relating to these issues are suspect for a variety of reasons.[6] For instance, would people with Muslim names really commit murder for the sake of the Hindu *devī* Bhavānī? This first grain of doubt grows when we read that practically all information about the *thugs* was gained from 'approvers' or, in modern parlance, 'supergrasses' who might well have phrased their information in terms corresponding to the preconceived ideas that they knew their masters had. Finally, no conceptual investigation appears to have been undertaken into whether we are dealing with a social group of criminals who, like most other Indians, also happen to be religious (and furthermore symbolize this link through the pickaxe in the hand of the *devī* and in their rituals), or whether they turned criminal *because* their religious beliefs demanded it of them. Precise answers to these questions cannot be obtained, because such questions were not asked at the time, and because after a systematic eradication campaign over a few decades all *thugs* (and we are talking in terms of no more than hundreds) were reported to have been eliminated. Thus without denying the possibility that something like *thuggee* may have existed, an assumption that 'Hinduism' as such, a communally approved or socially permitted belief, instigated strings of random murders for religious reasons on a large scale, appears untenable.

There is another range of material which might seem relevant to the discussion of overcoming death through violent death. Such a nexus of ideas appears not only in the cremation-ground setting, which has been the point of departure for our present excursion, but also in a far wider segment of popular Hinduism. I am thinking here for example of a process that could be called '*devī*-fication'. In the villages, innumerable *devīs* are worshipped whose stories deal with the theme of death and transcending death in some form. These *devīs* used to be human women and suffered, from no fault of their own, a violent death (this might include suicide). In consequence, they turned into superhuman beings (*devīs*), settled near the place where the violence occurred, and were then venerated by people.

Closely linked with this, at least on one level, is the idea of *suttee* (from Sanskrit *satī*, originally 'loyal, faithful woman'). This is another topic that was very prominent in the minds of the missionaries of the nineteenth century. The general idea is that a truly 'faithful' wife should throw herself into the flames of the funeral pyre of her dead husband. All over India we find *satī* stones, at which *devī*-fied *satīs* are venerated. It is difficult to assess the frequency of this terrible practice, but given the almost total absence of literary references to it for the pre-colonial period, it cannot have been widespread; rules of the 'Vedic life' for the higher castes tend to disapprove of it. An incident of the now illegal *suttee* was reported some years back in Rajasthan;[7] it has triggered off a mass movement of veneration of the *devī*-fied woman, along with all the paraphernalia of commercial and political exploitation.

In popular debate, the issue is confused further when unrelated mythological material or other practices are included in it. One of the best-known myths referred to in this context involves the figure of Satī, wife of the *deva* Śiva, who cast herself into the flames of her father's sacrificial fire in order to avenge an insult to her husband. While this act certainly proves her to be a *satī*, a 'faithful and loyal wife', it cannot be regarded as the mythical archetype of *suttee*. For the fire here is sacrificial, and Śiva her husband stays alive. Similarly, another well-known story is that of Sāvitrī who followed her dead husband into the underworld ruled over by the *deva* Yama and pleaded with him for her husband's life. But again, nothing is said here about her committing *suttee*. In vernacular literature, both in Tamil and in Sinhalese, we find the figure of Kaṇṇaki. The story, as told in the Tamil epic *Cilappatikāram*,[8] is briefly as follows. Her husband Kōvalaṉ had squandered away their wealth on a prostitute, and, totally destitute, the couple wandered through South India. When they arrived in Madurai, Kōvalaṉ was wrongly accused of theft and executed. When Kaṇṇaki heard of this, she tore off one of her breasts and cast it upon the city. By the power of her *satī*-hood it burnt up the whole town. Later she turned into a *devī*, and her cult – in which she is usually called Pattiṉi (from the Sanskrit *patnī*, '[faithful] wife') – used to be widespread in Tamil Nadu, Kerala, and Sri Lanka.[9] Further complications arise, when a custom called *johar* is included in the discussion. This practice takes us to Rajasthan with its Rajput war-lords. When a given fort was besieged and it became clear that the forces of the enemy were about to conquer it, the men would make a last, suicidal sortie while the women, in order to avoid falling into the hands of the enemy, would commit suicide by throwing themselves into the flames of a fire. Thus 'faithful' to their husbands, they avoided being forced to accept new masters.

All these different examples have certain features in common. They involve 'heroic' women who, as victims of aggression and violence, prove their 'faithfulness', or their moral fortitude generally, and thereby gain religious merit and some form of 'immortality' by becoming '*devī*-fied'. By suffering death themselves in this manner they overcome death as it were. Moreover, anybody responsible for forcing the woman beyond the frontiers of life – the most important of all boundaries – commits a forbidden act and will be punished in some gruesome hell or by becoming one of those bloodthirsty demons that have to haunt the cremation grounds in search of their nourishment.

When we compare these ideas with the material introduced at the beginning of this chapter involving bloody and murderous practices performed in cremation grounds, it becomes clear that the earlier material deals with the reversal of the situation sketched just now. (Given that we possess so little reliable information on the *thugs*, it is best to keep this topic out of our further discussion.) In the most extreme example, the murderous sorcerer aims at some form of immortality, of *deva*-fication, for himself by making another person his victim. Similarly, though far less drastically, the old woman in our first story has acquired demonic powers for herself, instead of becoming the victim of a demon's ravenous appetite. The dangerous and forbidden are being used for the increase of personal powers and towards the transcendence of death.

So what is going on here? How can such a reversal be achieved? A belief that it *can* be achieved is clearly suggested by the nightmarish quality of the literature dealing with such a possibility. Here Indian culture imagines its own Frankensteins and Dr Nos. But unlike the latter, their Indian counterparts have actually articulated some of their own perceptions, or at least Indian culture has preserved material that allows us to analyse such perceptions. This means at the same time that there exists a real basis in Indian culture which has triggered off the nightmares expressed in literature, a reality to be sought among ascetics who have broken with all rules of normal society and specifically choose the realm of death, the cremation ground, as their abode, or among people who remain within ordinary society but secretly go out to the same places to 'taste the forbidden fruits'. Fortunately for us, when we follow them (metaphorically speaking) we need not concern ourselves any more with the most extreme of all forbidden aspects in man's life, that of murder, and can turn now to somewhat less horrific topics, although none of them are exactly palatable. One does not have to invoke Victorian prejudices here, for on one level sensitivity is not a culture-specific phenomenon. Up to now, we have been looking at examples in which the powers to be acquired are at the same time personified and located in the outside world. But now it is necessary to make an important conceptual move into other areas where such powers are far more amorphous or directly seen as a potentiality of the person or the body itself. In less abstract language, we can turn from murder to sex, and we shall soon see in what sense the theme of the 'forbidden' continues here.

At this point it is no longer useful to avoid employing a word which over the past two decades has gained enormous popularity and is threatening to usurp conceptual power over a vast and disconnected range of Indian religious phenomena. It is the word 'Tantra'. In its concrete sense it denotes quite innocuously a particular genre of religious texts (parallel, say, to the Upaniṣads or Purāṇas). From this word, most modern Indian languages derive another word, *tāntrika*, to denote a person who practises what the Tantras expound. As long as we restrict ourselves to very well-defined local contexts, there still is no problem, because it is possible to identify ritual professionals in relation to specific forms of religion. For example, in Kerala the whole system of temple-worship is based on a collection of works known, quite logically, as the 'Kerala-Tantra'. Since, unlike the Upaniṣads, such Tantras do not enter into lengthy and lofty philosophical discussions, and unlike the Purāṇas do not tell us interesting myths, instead consist of an enormous number of pages on *mantras* and accompanying ritual acts, it is perhaps not surprising that practically nothing has been translated and very little has been studied. One thing, however, seems clear beyond all doubt, merely from looking at the little information that is available, and that is that, like the Upaniṣads and Purāṇas, the range of material contained in such Tantras is great and varied. So, just as nobody in his right senses would talk about 'Upaniṣadism' or 'Purāṇism' in order to denote a coherent system of ideas contained in all the Upaniṣads or in all the Purāṇas, one would assume that nobody would dream of talking about 'Tantrism'. Unfortunately, this word *has* been coined, and has acquired a very wide currency. Theoretically, the adjective 'tantric' could be used with reference to any random aspect of any one Tantra, but again its common usage in current English is generic, corresponding to the global 'Tantrism' as the noun from which it is derived.

One of the more recent proponents of this Tantrism/tantric fallacy was Ajit Mookerjee. As an art-critic and collector he applied the terms to group together visual material from a great many totally different religious traditions, on the basis of certain common stylistic or thematic features.[10] Thus, at the most, 'tantric art' exists as an aesthetic (but not traditional) entity. It was the art historian Philip Rawson, perhaps more than anybody else in popular contemporary British writing, who has been involved in the creation of the 'Tantrism' mythology. For he sets himself the task of preaching to the non-erotic West the secrets of the *Tantric Cult of Ecstasy*, of Tantrism as a coherent system of beliefs and practices.[11] It may all be very valuable in its own right as a corrective to Western cultural prejudices, but it is a mere figment of the imagination as far as the Indian religious material is concerned. Just how imaginative Rawson can be may be illustrated from two examples which I use in an *argumentum ad hominem*. In one of his books he reproduces the painting of a man playing a flute, surrounded by cows, and a girl swimming across a river towards the man. Rawson's comment is: 'On the bank of the river a prince sits playing the flute; its melody is reminiscent of the charming sound of the cowherd Krishna's flute. The cows in the background are also reinforcing the association.'[12] He obviously has no idea of what the picture is about; 'a prince' is a vague guess, and the reference to Kṛṣṇa serves to cover up his ignorance. Unfortunately for Rawson, the reproduction carries in clear and very legible letters the names of the man and the girl: they are Rañjhā and Hīr, the hero and heroine of a famous Panjabi folk-epic (in which Rañjhā was certainly not a prince). Furthermore, he has reproduced a set of miniatures all depicting various positions of love-making. In one of them, the couple is shown riding on a camel. This is what Rawson has to say about it:

> The couple make love as they ride a camel. The theme of intercourse while riding fascinated artists of the East. The important point is the characteristic motion of the animal, as we imagine it, contributing a special kinetic suggestion to the image.[13]

But from the equally legible writing above the picture it becomes clear that we are dealing here with ingeniously imaginative illustrations of various *āsanas*, positions during love-making, in our case not the 'missionary', but the 'camel position'. Another miniature clearly describes a couple as being involved in the 'tortoise position', but without actually showing a tortoise. Does this mean that the artist missed the chance of adding 'a special kinetic suggestion', perhaps by depicting Indians making love on tortoises?

Such erotic images are generally presented in the wider context of 'Tantrism' as the cult of uninhibited sexual pleasures. Here it is 'the five Ms' in particular that have appealed to the popular imagination, and for this reason we can make them the starting point for an exploration of the kind of material found in Tantras and relevant to the present chapter.

Once again we have to go at night to the cremation ground. A man and a woman are having a midnight orgy. This starts with their consuming alcohol; then they eat some fish, followed by a meat course. At least according to the more informed interpretations, the next item is a dish of beans. Once the meal is over, sexual intercourse takes place. The woman is not the man's wife, and comes from a very low caste. The act itself may not involve ejaculation. Since the five crucial items all begin in Sanskrit with the letter M, the ritual is known as the *pañca-makāra*, 'the five Ms' (*mada*, *matsya*, *māṃsa*, *mudrā*, *maithuna*). Before commenting further on it, let me ease the burden that this rather dicey material may constitute for you, by referring you to a Western piece of imaginative exploration of it.

'Ginny, I have been looking for you for months. I thought I'd have to go south to find a woman tuned to my frequency, but here you are. Will you be my shakti?'

'Pardon me?' I was immensely flattered that he thought we were 'tuned to the same frequency.'

'Are you interested in uniting with me in the holy sacrament of maithuna?'

'I'm sorry?'

'Maithuna. Ritual coition.'

'Far out,' I said grinning. I'd never been propositioned in such an exotic fashion.

I leave out the description of the next four weeks during which he trains her for the grand event. When the time for it has arrived, after sunset, we find our two tantric explorers seated in a cemetery, in front of them, an improvised altar, with two candles and a bottle of Southern Comfort – the *mada*.

Hawk tapped the bottle with his finger and said 'phat'. He joined his thumb and ring fingers and gestured towards the bottle saying, 'Namah.'

A little later we hear:

Hawk refilled our glasses. We took a chunk of chicken ... intoned 'om' six times, and ate it, again washing it down with Southern Comfort ... We sat with closed eyes meditating on our upcoming union. Then we tossed off another glass of Southern Comfort saying, 'Kulakundalini.'

Once again I leave out subsequent events, since I do not want to spoil the fun of reading the book; but I cannot resist quoting the final words of our hero, about four hours later: 'Oh Christ,' he wailed, 'I fell asleep! Jesus, I blew it.'[14] So what went wrong here? I don't want to labour the obvious (too much *mada* and therefore no *maithuna*). Instead let me concentrate on what I regard as the central feature, central also in the popular misrepresentation of 'Tantrism'. In the society Alther describes (in her novel *Kinflicks*), drinking a bottle of Southern Comfort, eating fish and meat, and then taking your girlfriend to bed are perfectly normal and acceptable activities. Similarly, traditional India, in its villages, has regarded the drinking of alcohol, the eating of meat and fish, and the consumption of stimuli of various kinds as perfectly normal. But what about weird sex, you may ask? From all accounts it appears that sexual licentiousness was normal at least on certain occasions, such as the annual festival of Holi.

The crux of the matter lies in what one could very vaguely describe as 'middle-class mentality', in other words, the value-system of the higher castes. These were alienated and cut off from the rural scene, not necessarily by being urbanized but by virtue of the mental boundaries that separated them from the lower castes. A total commitment to their own value-system (which did not allow for alcohol, meat, fish, supposed aphrodisiacs and non-marital, low-caste intercourse) was, in fact, one of the strongest factors in the maintenance of such boundaries. From this angle, those activities were vulgar, reprehensible, and thus 'forbidden'.

But we require one further step, before the five Ms and similar material begins to make sense. For so far we have no more than two sharply distinct and demarcated value-systems, totally at odds with each other, and separated by strong boundary walls. What we require is the emergence of a particular subculture which attempts to move into the area of the first (low-caste) system from the realm of its own, high-caste system, and that precisely because it represented to them another example of the realm of the forbidden, comparable to the murder discussed previously.

Initially we may be tempted to associate such practices, on the basis of the term 'subculture', with phenomena in our own culture such as the Hell's Angels or the Cosa Nostra or Timothy Leary and his LSD cult. But such a correlation misses the point to a large extent. For the *tāntrika* remains in basic agreement with the values of his own social milieu, however much he may appear to be breaking them. An example from Spain may lead us at least part of the way towards a better understanding of what is meant here. Gypsies, who after all are a social group from north-western India, have been living there for at least the past five hundred years. On the whole treated as outcastes and evil criminals, they maintained a separate social identity and culture. Precisely because of that, they exerted a strong appeal on the Spanish imagination. This appears in the literature as early as the seventeenth century. So, for example, the famous Cervantes wrote a short story, called the *Gypsy Girl*.[15] Here a man of good family falls madly in love with a gypsy girl he saw at a fair. A scandal is inevitable, society looks upon him as having fallen for the Devil, and he becomes an outcast when he is made to join the gypsy troupe as proof of his serious intentions with regards to the girl. A twentieth-century author might get away with this, but Cervantes would not have done in his time. So we are told that, unlike the other girls in the troupe, our heroine had been obstinately preserving her virtue and honour – that the gypsies have had a code of honour and an obsession about a girl's virtue and faithfulness even greater than that of classical Spanish society is clearly unknown to our author. Thus our fallen nobleman is in love with a pure flower. But a gypsy? No, for it turns out in the end that the girl is of equally noble birth as he and had been kidnapped by the gypsies. So all ends well for the two lovers.

Given this perception of the gypsies in the Spanish awareness, it will not surprise us to find that, in connection with the one thing the *gitanos* became world-famous for, flamenco music, an alternative aesthetic was produced. The highest level of perfection in making 'European' music is called '*ángel*', while the peak of artistic performance in flamenco style is called *duende*, 'demon'. Gypsies worship '*un devil*', which is literally and etymologically 'the *deva*', or 'God', but which is naturally seen by the outsider as 'the devil' (derived from Greek *diábolos*).

Boundaries and contrasts as strong and pronounced as in our Indian example seem involved here. Yet from the late eighteenth century onwards, we witness the emergence of a subculture, a '*demi-monde*' in a more literal sense, called the *afición*. Attracted by flamenco culture (and its – presumably unfulfilled – erotic attraction), more-or-less respectable members of Spanish society and flamenco artists met socially; attempts were made to learn the gypsy language, and a weird hybrid poetry in the style of the *gitanos* and with many presumed gypsy words, was even produced. Middle-class people yielded to the attraction of the erotic, exotic and forbidden, and moved into its realm to enrich themselves, at least aesthetically, but without questioning the fundamental social divide or the evaluative basis for it. It is here that I see the parallel.

Thus the ritual of the five Ms (and everything else that could be listed here) may be interpreted as an attempt by people, for whom the ritual was not part of normal life and was 'forbidden' by very powerful social pressures, to employ it for the acquisition of superhuman powers precisely because it represented a taboo area. Each item turns into a ritually controlled breaking of taboos. Moreover, that we are dealing here with 'acquisition of powers' is evinced from the inner rationale of the five, as presented to us. The first M is seen as reducing the inhibitions of the participants; the second and third as providing a stimulus to the body (the link between eating meat or fish and rousing sexual passion is almost an Indian axiom). Significantly, *mudrā* as the fourth is perceived as a further aphrodisiac, and naturally the fifth is the final culmination and release of this variously heightened arousal process. But, particularly in cases where ejaculation is prevented, the intention of the ritual manifests itself as clearly non-erotic. This applies equally to cases in which the shedding of semen does occur, as we shall see below. In other words, sexuality in its most dynamic (and forbidden) form is transformed into a 'religious' force; it is redirected towards less physical and non-sexual elements located within the personality-structure of the practitioner. Changes of a relatively lasting nature are achieved that bring man closer to the mastery of his destiny. Just as the evil sorcerer aims at overcoming death through killing, man transforms himself from a slave of the passions to a master over the passions. This is an intentionally abstract formulation, because the precise definition of this varies enormously with different groups and traditions.

There are a number of points raised here that deserve further attention. But initially let me extend the list of items that may be perceived to be 'forbidden'. I mentioned previously that all kinds of bodily excretions are regarded as highly powerful and dangerous substances (and thus to be avoided under normal circumstances) – none more so than blood, which is most immediately connected with life and death. When a particular Tantra (the *Caṇḍamahāroṣaṇa*)[16] suggests that the practitioner should eat the excrements and drink the urine of his female partner, only the most morbid imagination can construe this as an example of the pursuit of sexual pleasures. Instead it demonstrates in a most striking (and revolting) manner what is meant here by breaking taboos fenced off through a mainstream value system and by 'heroically' overcoming inhibitions.

Along far less grossly physical lines appears another kind of the 'forbidden'. As we shall see in Part two, there exist religious systems which centre around a God-figure comparable to what we mean by the term: a being qualitatively different from all other forms of life in the universe and therefore demanding human adoration and submission. If somebody from within the premisses of such a belief system performs 'tantric' rituals that are perceived as a means of gaining control over, and absorbing the powers associated with, such a God, he is clearly breaking another taboo.

All our examples involve the individual in pursuit of the increase of his personal power and of mastering his destiny. They also involve contact with physical substances such as blood or alcohol and physical acts such as killing or sexual intercourse. Thus, logically, when we talk here about 'absorption' of powers into the individual, we are at least partially talking about the body. This in turn asks for some kind of physiological model which describes the processes mentioned here. Some way back I introduced the concept of a representational system through which space, time and matter are mirrored and reorganized and thus manipulated. The human body is one such system.

We find endless speculation in our texts about the human body's correlation with the outside world, including cosmology. After all, according to Indian belief the body is made up of the various physical elements earth, water, fire, etc., and these elements constitute at the same time the bodies of all other beings and the material world. Then there is a comparable pulse in both: breathing, growth and the movement from birth to death are paralleled by the cosmic cycles of day and night, creation and dissolution. And probably not totally unconnected with this is that the structure of the universe can be imagined in terms of the man or woman metaphor. On the basis of such initial correlations, our texts (which are mainly Tantras and related material) developed over one and a half millennia an incredibly abstruse and diversified range of physiological models spelling out the details of such correspondences. In spite of all the divergence, it seems possible to isolate one complex of relatively coherent ideas, used fairly ubiquitously, about such a structure, an inner cosmology as it were. Many of the symbols encountered in the previous chapters can be applied micro-cosmically. Corresponding to the very limited power ordinary man possesses in relation to a threatening and infinitely more powerful environment, the normal state of affairs is one of diffusion and separation. Corresponding to the heroic drive into the realms beyond the boundaries, in the present case this diffuse inner energy (let us call it energy A, located at the base of the spine, the *kuṇḍalinī* of *Kinflicks*) is redirected, focused and stimulated to move upwards. Just as, externally, this would aim at acquiring *vidyās*, absorbing the powers of the mightiest of *devas*, etc., internally this aims at coming in contact with a different energy (let us call it energy B) located at the top of the head. Different energy-fields (*cakras*) have to be passed through, which correspond to the different boundaries found in the external world. When energies A and B are brought to unite and fuse, total control and mastery has been achieved. Nomenclature is a nightmare here, but I have no intention of being frightened by it – I shall simply ignore it. That the energy fields are called *cakras* is perhaps worth mentioning, because it might allow for the association with the *cakravartī*, 'the ruler of a domain'. That the energy channels, through which A moves towards B, are called *nāḍīs*, needs to be mentioned only because one meaning of the word is 'vein'. Yet to search during autopsy for such *nāḍīs*, whether understood literally as veins or slightly modified, as nerves, misses the ontology of the Indian model.

But how do you push energy A upwards in the direction of B? Of overriding importance is the element of reversal and redirection achieved through previously activated forces. Energy A is normally diffuse, because it is directed towards the external world. In its most concrete form this is illustrated by the sexual drive and by ejaculation. Thus the redirection necessitates a withdrawal from the world of the senses and desire into the *nāḍīs*. As far as the mechanics of this redirection are concerned, our esoteric subcultures have piled up a vast store of means. Breath-control, self-induced sensory deprivation, concentration exercises, recitation of *mantras*, ritual acts (and that includes the five Ms), invoking external beings into one's own body, placing oneself inside magic diagrams are examples of such means.

All this, however, remains on the periphery of the type of religion we are exploring in this chapter. Thus the crucial question to ask here is how it becomes possible to come into contact with substances and forces that, by common consent, are understood to be dangerous and destructive. It is clearly necessary to wear the right kind of armour and wield the right kind of arms in order to survive such a heroic exposure to the forces of destruction. To say that such armour and weapons are *mantras*, *yantras*, abstract gestures of the hands and sacrifices seems to add nothing new. And indeed there have been various attempts, even by more respectable scholars, to define the 'tantric' by simply listing the same features. Given that all of them also occur in perfectly innocuous and mainstream religious contexts, such a definition merely compounds the confusion surrounding the whole area of 'Tantrism'.[17] What is really important here is the fact that a subculture, an esoteric and originally secret tradition, possesses *particular mantras*, *particular yantras*, etc. which are *exclusive* to it and which alone, it believes, allow for the kind of dominance over destructive forces that we have heard about. Thus once again it emerges clearly that it is neither murder nor sex nor the breaking of any other taboo that is pursued for its own sake. What is pursued is the control over one's own destiny, in the belief that certain specifically esoteric means allow for the control of otherwise destructive forces like death or the rule of the passions.

This now leads us to the question of how this goal is perceived. Given the vast amount of literature available, the long history of its production, and the rather amorphous nature of the esoteric traditions themselves, it will not surprise us to find that somewhere or other just about every conception of human fulfilment is proposed as the goal. To select here those formulations which fit best into our present context may not be quite as arbitrary as it appears, for I have the suspicion that we are dealing here with ideas rather original to, and typical of, our 'tantric' material. That means that complete transcendentality – of the kind introduced in the following chapter – is not envisaged as the final aim, but as a complete dominance of the world and of the forces that desire to control the individual. The potential splendours of the world are not left behind, but are subsumed under a novel kind of universal rulership. Using a similar kind of suspicion, it appears to me that instead of *vidyās*, terms like *siddhis* or *ṛddhis* are more frequently used or more typical of this tradition; in content, however, they overlap for the most part. (If it were possible to draw such lines of demarcation, the terms would suggest a conceptual distinction in India between the more innocuous and the more destructive aspects of 'science', given the correlation suggested in the previous chapter.) A very common list of eight *siddhis* refers to the following: (1) to shrink to the size of an atom; (2) to encompass any space and traverse any distance; (3) to turn weightless; (4) to penetrate any material object; (5) to exert an irresistible will; (6) total control over one's person; (7) total power over the laws of nature; (8) to obtain all objects of desire. Ultimately this stands for total freedom and power within one's physical existence, and is often styled 'immortality'. What the external world has to offer is absorbed into the person and allows, after internal transformation, for a new type of person who is in total control of space, time and matter. Such a person may be styled a *siddha* or a *nātha*, perfected master.[18] He may not be of the world any more, but he is still in the world to enjoy its riches. In the various Indian languages, a considerable amount of literature has been produced which describes the lives of many specific *siddhas* (literally 'perfected ones' – individuals who have mastered all the siddhis) and *nāthas*, 'masters'.[19] Wonderful stories can be found there, but unfortunately they fall outside the scope of the present discussion. Instead, we have to continue with more abstract matters, and that means a look at the social position of such *siddhas* and of the esoteric craft they practised.

Let us initially return to the question of in what sense precisely and to what extent the pursuit of *siddhis* falls under the heading of the forbidden fruit. In three respects such a label can be applied to our present material. First, there is the most obvious case, when features like the five Ms figure as part of his ritual practices. The only point that deserves to be stressed here is the fact that such practices would tend to be kept extremely secret. But in the case of some *siddhas*, e.g. the Tamil *cittar*,[20] a further antinomian element can be found. This now involves a conscious external rejection of social values, breaking of caste barriers, etc. On the basis of the internal belief-system, the external value-system is questioned. Instead of esoteric practices in the sense of our definition, we are now dealing with a public, socially expressed rejection of mainstream attitudes. This is an extremely important distinction, for in popular literature these two phenomena tend to get mixed up. And another distinction must be introduced here, between an actual physical execution of 'tantric' rites of the kind mentioned above and a ritual system that, by substituting innocuous items and abstract gestures for raw physical substances such as blood and gross physical acts such as sexual intercourse, transforms itself into a socially acceptable affair and thus does not need to keep itself secret any more. This latter distinction is well known and is made by means of the terms 'left hand' and 'right hand' – predictably 'left' refers to the secret and physical 'tantric' rites. 'Right-hand Tantra' ceases to be a topic appropriate to the present discussion. It has become 'domesticated' (to use an expression by Sanderson)[21] and therefore can be included in the range of material discussed in the previous chapter.

Secondly, the appearance of *siddhis* or *ṛddhis* is also acknowledged in many further traditions of meditational exercises – traditions about which we shall hear in the next chapter. To the extent that those traditions can be interpreted as reflecting the mainstream of Indian religion, and not, as in our present case, an esoteric subculture, their evaluation is important. For here the *siddhis* (or *ṛddhis* or *abhijñās*, or whatever they may be called) are evaluated as meaningless, but potentially distracting, side-effects of meditation and are rejected as useless. To aim now at precisely these supernatural faculties and to define the goal of the exercise in terms of them is clearly antinomian with reference to mainstream opinion. Yet that in itself hardly matters, for one man's *siddhi* is another man's *mokṣa*. So, thirdly, we have an internal antinomianism. The writings of the *siddhas*, *nāthas*, etc. are filled with scorn, contempt and disgust for woman.[22] She symbolizes to him the wastage of energies into the external world which he attempts to block. The diffusion of man's energies in ordinary life has for this *siddha* its archetype or metaphor in the sexual urge. Because of this, woman represents the forbidden – literally and metaphorically. In view of the logic previously demonstrated, it need not now surprise us that our aspiring *siddha* draws on this forbidden fruit, makes use of it *because* it is forbidden. But what may surprise us is the extent to which the potentials of the body have been experimented with and the results applied to the preservation and redirection of such precious energies. To me none of the techniques developed is more weird and wonderful than the *vajroli* (of unknown etymology). This is an exercise of certain muscles, described to us with all the physiological details we might desire, which achieves the absorption of energies *from* a woman, instead of wasting them into her. By consciously controlling certain muscles which normally function involuntarily, and thereby creating a special suction effect, the *yogī* can recover his semen after ejaculation, together with the vaginal fluid of the woman. Such a man, the *Yogatattva-Upaniṣad*[23] tells us, has reached the peak of all esoteric powers! This may be, but it is clearly one of the rocks upon which our popular understanding of Tantrism as a cult of desire is smashed into a thousand pieces.

What about popular Indian opinion? No society can accept a challenge to its innate value-system. But then the *siddha* in most cases does not do so; in fact, his entire system would collapse if the forbidden ceased to be forbidden, and this must be one reason why these esoteric subcultures could survive in India for more than a thousand years. On the other hand, a sorcerer murdering innocent victims is clearly a different matter. Whether or not he agrees with the rest of society that murdering is forbidden, he could hardly expect public approval for his nightly ceremonies in the cremation ground. Whatever the truth about the *thugs* may be, the fact that concerted British persecution of *thuggee* appeared successful indicates public support. Had this practice had any deep-rooted approval, any law passed against it would have had the same effect as the laws passed at present in India against large dowries, excessive land-ownership, bribery, etc.

This could not be said to leave the more innocuous aspects of the *siddha*'s pursuits untouched. But it is ridicule more than fear or condemnation that we find here. How do you make some blockhead produce a definition of a farce? You might try the following. First you act the part of a yogic *siddha*. Choose as a setting for your little play a lovely garden, and let a luscious courtesan arrive. Let your blockhead disciple see her and fall for her. Assuming that a messenger of death arrives and kills the poor girl, you can then, as *siddha*, reveal your powers by entering the corpse and continuing your lessons, sure of keeping his attention firmly fixed on you. But then it might happen that the said messenger of death has made a mistake, that he returns with the girl's life and, finding her body already occupied, chooses to put her life back into the lifeless body of the *siddha*. Imagine the stern voice of his master emerging from the girl's body, her cooing and seductive voice uttered by an old, emaciated ascetic's form, and your blockhead might well exclaim, as indeed he does in the Sanskrit play *Bhagavad-ajjukīya*,[24] 'What a farce this is!'

Society may be laughing at the *siddha*, but the *siddha* will be content in his personal conviction that his heroism lets him achieve powers far superior to those of ordinary people. His secret tradition, which is not available to them, furnishes him with the armour that makes it possible for him to enter into realms ordinary people would be far too frightened of. Protected by special *mantras*, rituals and so on that have been communicated to him via esoteric channels, he can plunge himself into acts contrary to what society permits, acts that will reward him far more than the morality propagated by society. For example, subjugating oneself in veneration to a *deva* is socially encouraged and will yield certain religious rewards. To stand up against the same *deva* and refuse to yield to his demands will, under normal circumstances, destroy the challenger (and on this, society and the *tāntrika* are in perfect agreement). But the aspiring *siddha*'s circumstances are not normal: his secret knowledge lets him not only challenge the *deva* and survive, but also subdue the *deva*, absorb his powers into himself and thereby multiply the rewards that devotion offers to people who remain under the *deva*'s control. He can experience within himself that he has transcended death and all other forces that enslave man, including sexual desires. He has gained 'immortality' and has become a 'new man'.

To the extent that people are aware of what goes on in his mind, they detect not just the potential of arrogance and pride in his attitude, but also the threat of destruction and of their own death. Thus they react by deriding him, or by imagining in stories other heroes who go out into the cremation ground and kill the evil sorcerer. He is certainly not a popular figure!

So what accounts for the great popularity that 'Tantrism' has gained in the Western perception? Part of the reason will simply be that the latter distorts the Indian material and is attracted to something which objectively does not exist. One such distortion could be the belief that the 'tantric' tradition has preserved all kinds of tricks which could enhance one's sexual performance. Another misconception might approach it as an exotic variety of pornography (a topic to which I shall return presently). Or, again, a synthesis is imagined here between two realms that in our actual society are kept separate – religion and sexuality. I say 'actual society' because it would be difficult to claim that our current social *mores* are derived from a Christian teaching about marriage as a sacrament that imbues sexuality with a religious dimension. Or, finally, there are features in our material that can be associated with the general fashion for self-improvement (starting with health-food and jogging, and culminating in all kinds of new religious movements that offer increased personal power). But in a sense we could say that what 'Tantrism' symbolizes in the popular literature – quite irrespective of what it actually is on the Indian side – can itself be correlated, as one of its relatively harmless varieties, with the 'dangerous' areas into which the *tāntrika* immerses himself. This means that 'Tantrism' is perceived as the means of entry into a religious fulfilment far beyond the potentials of established religion.

Be that as it may, one final question has to be looked at: is 'Tantrism' (or 'Tantric art') pornography? Such a question certainly comes easily to our minds, but it is rather more difficult to answer. There is the problem of how to define 'pornography'. Were we to watch on television any panel discussion dealing with this topic, it would soon become clear that each member of the panel uses the term in quite a distinct sense. But were we to adopt a random definition of pornography, such as 'pornography wants to incite sexual urges', it would not be difficult to find Indian art intended to do just that. Yet such art is likely to have nothing to do with the Tantras (whatever Mookerjee or Rawson may claim to the contrary). Thus all we can really say in the present context is that sexuality is a very pronounced taboo area and that the *siddha* or *tāntrika* uses it, for that same reason, in order to transcend it and gain the personal satisfaction of being slave to neither the sexual urges nor to the taboos or obsessions associated with them. Like murder or sacrificing blood to demons, the sexual component of his ritual is fundamentally accidental and not pursued for its own sake. As the *Treatise on the Purification of Mind* says: 'Just as a washerman removes the grime from a garment by means of grime, so the wise man renders himself free of impurity by means of impurity itself.'[25]

The tree from which Eve picked the fateful forbidden fruit was supposed to be that of 'knowledge'. Yet Christianity has tended to change the symbolism and interpret it in terms of sexuality. This liberated 'knowledge' in all its aspects from being associated with the dangerous and forbidden, to the extent that prominent Christians and Christian theologians can condone or even advocate the production of atomic bombs, while they emphatically condemn 'pornography'. In the light of the material discussed here we may conclude that Indian culture – ordinary society as much as the *tāntrika* – has acknowledged a whole range of dangerous, 'forbidden' territories, which include sexuality as much as killing and murder. The focus on sexual matters in Western writings on 'Tantrism' would appear to be much more a reflection of our own obsessions and taboos than of the actual spread of ideas found in the Tantras themselves.

The *siddha*, the *nātha*, the *tāntrika*, or the (esoteric) *yogī* aims at gaining mastery over the world. Crossing space by the power of thought, transforming his body at will or entering into other bodies, looking into the past and the future – these are expressions of his exhilarating spiritual freedom over space, time and matter. To him this is the climax of what the spiritual hero can achieve – but another type of religion writes off everything said here as limited, external and earth-bound. True transcendentality, this new voice of critique says, requires a different kind of hero, a spiritual giant who has no need for external rituals and substances to enrich himself, does not require 'grime to purify himself', and who interiorizes his conquest of the universe by unleashing the powers found within himself.

CHAPTER 8

Unleashing the powers of the self

Imagine a beautiful palace, filled with all possible luxuries and comforts. Somewhere inside, on a soft couch, a prince is reclining. Many beautiful girls are ready to fulfil any desire his fancy might design. High walls protect the idyllic scene against the intrusion of the normal world of man, with its ugliness, suffering and violence. And this pleasurable imprisonment is intended to influence the prince's destiny, for he is endowed with the thirty-two characteristics of a 'superman'. Aware of the ambivalence this implies about his future, his father the king has tried to push the prince in the direction of becoming a *cakravartī*, a universal ruler, away from its alternative, that of a Jina, a 'spiritual conqueror and victor'. Since our prince is quite happy inside his golden cage, the Buddhas abiding in other universes are forced to gather together and resort to a means of impelling him into the outside world. As the girls begin to play on their musical instruments, the melodies turn into words, words about the transience of all pleasures and about a mission that awaits the prince beyond the walls of his palace:

> 'The objects of desire always contain danger and strife;
> they are like the edge of a sword, like a leaf smeared with poison.
> They must be avoided, as if they were pots filled with excreta.
> The objects of desire are like a blazing pit of fire;
> like quicksand or the blade of a razor covered in honey.
> The objects of desire last but a moment
> and are false like a conjurer's trick.
> They are as real as a bubble or foam on water.'

And a refrain tells the prince what to do: 'Now is the time, the opportunity for you to step out from here!'[1] Thus driven by the magical songs, our prince sets out to explore the world beyond the protective walls of his palace, and he finds disease, old age and death. These experiences make him give up everything that has so far filled his life: his family, palace, social status and luxuries. In the dark of the night he leaves the palace and sets out to find liberation from the suffering of being alive in a world that is filled with pleasures that are but misery. The name of the prince was Siddhārtha, later to become known as the Buddha, the 'Enlightened One'.

But we could equally well have gone to another palace, where another prince, called Vardhamāna, has been kept sheltered from the world of transience and suffering. This Vardhamāna similarly sets out and eventually becomes known as the Mahāvīra, the 'Great Hero', the twenty-fourth and last *tīrthaṅkara*.[2]

These are two legendary accounts of events that led to the formation of two of the great religious systems of ancient India: Buddhism and Jainism. Naturally it is in the interest of each religion to demonstrate that their founder achieved something unique. In the case of the Buddhist version, we are told that Siddhārtha first studied with two brahmin *yoga* teachers. But very quickly he reached the levels of meditational awareness they had on offer, and realized that he was still very far away from the task he had set himself – to find a means of going beyond disease, old age and death. He then turned to another means, which bears remarkable similarity to what prince Vardhamāna was engaged in: the systematic cultivation of self-imposed tortures and physical deprivations (*tapas*). But after some years, Siddhārtha found himself close to death but still far from his goal. So he abandoned his *tapas*, to take up a far more moderate activity: meditation. And with a deceptive ease he soon reached the peak of insight: he achieved his enlightenment. During the first watch of the night he succeeded in surveying the endlessly long chain of existences that led finally to his own existence as Siddhārtha. In the second watch of the night he gained insight into the general laws that govern the destiny of all living beings: transmigration and *karma*. Finally, in the third watch of the night, he perceived the truth which would then be communicated to mankind as the Buddhist teaching. Along with this insight, the awareness arose in him that he had stepped beyond disease, old age and death and that there would be no further return for him into the realm of suffering. What he had set out to do had been achieved: his liberation from *saṃsāra* had been achieved.

On the surface this looks as if Siddhārtha tried Hindu *yoga* and then Jain *tapas*, but succeeded through a uniquely Buddhist method. Clearly such an interpretation was intentionally built into the legend, to demonstrate that Buddhism is quite unique and distinct from these two other systems. Before pursuing this further, let us cast a brief glance at the Jain side of the story.

Prince Vardhamāna's parents had been lay-followers in a religious community that derived from a Pārśva. When Vardhamāna stepped out of his palace in pursuit of liberation, he first joined a group of ascetics belonging to the same Pārśva community. But after a while he abandoned their company which was far too lax for his liking. On his own he roamed through the country for many years, wearing no clothes, enduring incredible hardships, insults and persecutions, and imposing equally incredible penances, fasts, etc. on himself. Then one day he achieved what he had set out to achieve, liberation from *saṃsāra*. So here again we are presented with an initial experiment (living as a Pārśvaite ascetic) that was felt to be a failure, and a success that was the outcome of something uniquely 'Jain'.[3]

On the other hand, this feature of 'uniqueness' is complemented by a second concern, that of demonstrating that Siddhārtha and Vardhamāna did not discover or invent something totally novel. What they unearthed is shown to be a primordial truth which, by their time, had been completely forgotten. Moreover, stronger connecting links with that past are established. The very first time the being who was to become Siddhārtha conceived of the intention to become an enlightened one was many aeons ago, in front of the previous *tathāgata*, Dīpaṅkara. Similarly, Vardhamāna's soul is traced back in the Jain world-history to the very first *tīrthaṅkara*, Ṛṣabha, whose grandson Marīci was then the embodiment of the soul that found its final body as Vardhamāna. So the overall intention here is to emphasize uniqueness and novelty in relation to the contemporary scene, but continuity in respect to the history of that same truth.

Things are, however, more complicated than this. For from the outsider's point of view this postulated uniqueness reveals itself as a relatively minor variation on a general theme. This 'theme' is one of the greatest and most famous Indian cultural constructs, and it is into this realm that both Siddhārtha and Vardhamāna move when they abandon their homes. What I am talking about here is a pre-Buddhist and pre-

Jain tradition of renouncers, a tradition that evinces a strikingly similar lifestyle, religious preoccupation and view of the world, and shares a stock vocabulary. Both Jain and Buddhist accounts of the lives of their founders have preserved traces of the prior existence of such a renouncer tradition.

According to some accounts, when Siddhārtha went out to explore the world of ordinary men beyond the palace walls, he not only met two men and a corpse, illustrating disease, old age and death respectively, but, during a fourth outing, he also saw a mendicant. This sight pointed him in the direction that his own quest was to take. But this also means that the path, in the form of homeless, religious mendicancy, had already been laid out. In the case of Vardhamāna we have already heard about the Pārśvaite ascetics whom he initially joined. It is, however, unnecessary to pursue such allusions, for we also possess independent testimonies to assure us of the existence of this renouncer-tradition. It is fairly certain that well before the sixth or fifth century BC – the likely period of Siddhārtha and Vardhamāna – such a tradition existed. Jainism and Buddhism thus reveal themselves as particular manifestations within the wider frame, and against the background, of this tradition. To explore it further, to delineate the common ground and sketch some of the differences and variations on the underlying theme, and to relate it as a further type of religious enterprise to the observations made in the previous chapters – this is the main intention of the following pages.

First of all, we may ask what precisely constitutes this cultural construct of the renouncer tradition. Buddhism and Jainism are two obvious illustrations. But then we also know about less famous groups within the tradition, like the followers of Maskarī Gośālīputra. The followers of Pārśva can be ignored, because Jainism looks back at Pārśva as its penultimate *tīrthaṅkara* and presents the Mahāvīra, the last *tīrthaṅkara* of our present age, as the reformer of the Pārśvaite group. Moreover, the peculiarities of this branch of renouncers are rather obscured by the mist of prehistory. But we can extend the range of the tradition by including forms of *yoga*, and even by drawing into it the teachings of the early Upaniṣads, mystical scriptures in the Vedic tradition from the eighth or even ninth century BC onwards – although in this case we have to be very careful not to blur certain important differences.

The old sources refer to members of this tradition through a variety of names. So we hear about the *parivrājaka*, 'who steps out of ordinary life into the realm of homelessness'; about the *śramaṇa*, 'the wanderer'; the *bhikṣu*, 'who lives by religious alms'; and the *saṃnyāsī*, 'who has put down all burdens of worldly life'. As time went on, a certain specialization of these terms took place: *saṃnyāsī* became associated with Hinduism, *bhikṣu* with Buddhism, *śramaṇa* with Jainism, but on the whole I shall ignore this distinction and talk, for instance, about the '*śramaṇa* movement' merely as a synonym for 'renouncer tradition'.

Some of these names already point at the demarcation lines of this tradition. Ordinary life, represented by home, possessions, family, profession, social status, etc. is abandoned in favour of its opposite: a homeless, poor, celibate existence, supported by alms and empty of the signs that mark people's status. So these are the boundaries our present type of hero crosses, and this is the particular realm he enters. Again we notice a systematic reversal of factors found in the realm of ordinary life, possession versus poverty, married life and sex versus celibacy, etc. But clearly this reversal does not involve the breaking of taboos and the committing of forbidden acts. I shall return to this shared lifestyle and its underlying rationale presently.

Let us first pause and survey the steps our exploration has taken so far. The second and third chapters introduced us to a vision of the world which not only knows of oceans of milk but also, now metaphorically speaking, of a terrifying ocean of earthly existence (*saṃsāra*) in which death is not the end but merely the transition from one embodiment to the next. This is a world in which the inexorable laws of *karma* govern types of embodiment and produce automatic retribution for good and bad deeds. Such a vision of the world was initially presented as a yardstick, as the most complex superstructure against which we could measure certain types of religion. Now we have reached the point at which we can fuse both lines of our approach, for it is the renouncer tradition which has both decisively contributed to the formulation of this conception of the world, including the regular reoccurrence of important men (*buddhas*, *tīrthaṅkaras*, etc.), and has given rise to those men themselves and their teachings. Our circle can be closed at this point. That means that we know already how, at least in essence, a Siddhārtha or a Vardhamāna viewed the world. Against such a background we can now survey how their religion seeks to 'conquer' it.

The most convenient way of structuring this survey is by utilizing a schema of exposition which the Buddhists present to us as the 'Four Noble Truths'. Let me make clear at the outset that I am not intending an exegesis of this schema in terms of Buddhist thought; rather, I am using it to organize a wider range of material. The fact that material from non-Buddhist branches of the renouncer tradition can easily be accommodated in it is, I think, a most convincing proof of the assumed coherence of that tradition.

The schema of the Four Noble Truths imitates medical procedure in its four steps. The first step investigates whether the patient is really ill, the second then finds out the cause of that illness. Step three is psychologically the most crucial, but contains no more than a decision: can the patient be cured? Finally, step four involves the writing out of the prescription for the appropriate medicine. Accordingly, the first noble truth makes the statement that man is not fooling himself if he looks upon the negative aspects of existence as defining the very nature of life. To be alive means to suffer. To be born means inevitably to fall ill, to grow old, and to die. To live means to search for happiness but never find it, since even the most exquisite pleasures not only come to an end but are also accompanied by the awareness that they cannot last. At the same time, we are surrounded by beings that seek to harm us, and are ready to inflict violence upon us, just as we react against this by counteracting violence with further violence.

If suffering is the overriding characteristic of all beings living in the universe, what is its cause? The second noble truth calls it, rather metaphorically, 'thirst'. This we may paraphrase as: the compulsion to reach out into the external world, grasp objects in it, and draw them into us for the sake of enriching ourselves. At the same time, there is the 'thirst' for personal survival or personal comfort, which may express itself as aggression and violence directed against what is perceived to threaten them. Thus 'thirst' includes hatred and revulsion and murderous instincts. Such a paraphrase now allows us to bring Jain, Buddhist and 'Hindu' ideas together. To the Jains, any act, but particularly acts of desire and of aggression, force subtle matter into man's soul. This matter (called *karma*) fuses with the soul itself, and the resulting synthesis is to various degrees deficient in respect of the pure nature of the soul. Unlimited vision and knowledge, power and bliss get weakened, potentially to levels on which little is left that would allow for the recognition of the original. This influx of subtle matter is called *āsrava*. Now the same two words, *karma* and *āsrava*, are used by the Buddhists, but with a somewhat different meaning. *Āsrava* here paraphrases 'thirst' as that which causes suffering, and is split up into three, closely related, concepts. There is craving or desire, there is ignorance and, linking these two, mistaken notions about I and mine – about the desiring subject, the desired object, and what the former could gain through the latter. Again, in the earliest Upaniṣads, we find desire and ignorance mentioned as the features that account for the acquisition of *karma*. This is envisaged again as something semi-physical which gets soaked, as it were, into a subtle body which, at the disappearance of the visible, gross body, generates, according to its kind and type, the appropriate next gross body in which the soul remains imprisoned. With the Buddhists, the same process of *karma* generating the next body in the chain of *saṃsāra* is depicted in far less 'material' terms, as a sequence of causes and inevitable effects, as conditioning factors. Thus suffering reveals itself here as continuous, without regard for the boundaries that demarcate an individual being's life-span. Suffering implies transmigration, and thereby applies to all living beings in the universe, from the most rarefied *devas* in the highest heavens down to the most wretched denizen of the lowest of hells.

I think it is clear that we are dealing here with a coherent set of ideas which are developed on the basis of a shared terminology. What may be a bit confusing at first sight is the fact that the variations and different emphases imply, at the same time, different meanings of the shared terms. Before we pursue these rather abstract matters further, I think it is time to listen to a Jain story which, in the inimitable manner of these Indian story tellers, illustrates the nexus of ideas mentioned so far.

Once upon a time, a king called Dvipāyana went with his entire retinue into a park, seeking amusement. There he saw a mango tree in blossom. He plucked one cluster of flowers and put it behind his ear as an ornament. Eventually he returned to the spot where he had seen the tree: but now there was nothing left of it. Puzzled, he asked his courtiers what had happened to it. They told him: 'Your majesty! When the retinue saw what you had done, they all imitated you by cutting down every bit of that tree to put behind their ears.' When the king heard this, he reflected: 'Everything in the world appears to be prone to destruction at any moment. Just like the mango tree, people, one's wealth and life will vanish.' He became filled with detachment and, handing over his kingship to his son, became a Jain monk.

So far so good. On his wanderings he came to a town, where a king ruled who kept the company of a dancing girl Lovely-Body. The chief queen could hardly contain her rage, and so one day she bribed the barber who then cut into one of the girl's toes and infected it with something like gangrene. The disintegrating toe began to fill with pus and to give off a bad odour, and this cured the king of his passion for her. She was thrown out of the palace, and our ascetic Dvipāyana met her in the quarter of the prostitutes, where he had gone on his alms-round. Meanwhile Lovely-Body had covered her diseased toe with a golden thimble. Our ascetic could not resist her charms and, by blackmailing the local king, he obtained her from him as his mistress. Years passed. One day a present arrived from the court: a toe-ornament. When Dvipāyana went to put it on her foot, he found out her secret. In disgust he left her, to resume his asceticism. But his concentration did not last for long, because soon her beauty came back to his mind. ('What does one toe matter...?') His teacher fathomed his thoughts and took him to the cremation ground. There he showed him Lovely-Body's corpse, left to decompose there, since she had committed suicide.[4]

We have here an illustration of how the transience of all worldly phenomena is demonstrated by our renouncers, and to what extent they are prepared to go in this. Even the most attractive object of desire lacks an inner lasting core, a permanent substrate, an essence (*sāra* or *ātman*). At the same time human folly is demonstrated: the mistaken belief that any gain could be made for oneself from such objects of desire. It is this folly or ignorance, that expresses itself in the craving for empty and transient things, which is seen as the root-cause of *saṃsāra* and suffering. But ignorance and desire can appear with reference to the subject alone. Here man grasps at his own identity and survival, and protects them through inflicting acts of violence on anyone who threatens them.

All this may appear rather depressing and negationist. But, at least at this point, our renouncer tradition turns very cheerful and optimistic indeed: the suffering can be cured. Each of the various branches proposes a programme that is understood as this cure.

When we cast a closer look at these programmes, we discover a striking similarity between them, not just in the terminology employed, but also in the underlying structure. Needless to add, there are also significant differences. Very generally speaking, the analysis of life as suffering caused by desires and ignorance suggests that the cure will entail two complementary aspects: an ethical or ascetic side that deals with the desires directly, and a mental or meditational side that takes care of the ignorance factor. Classical *yoga* and the Buddhist path agree very closely on this dual aspect, while the Jain emphasis is still rather one-sided on the ascetic practices of *tapas*. It is probably no accident that the Buddhists have the noble eight-fold path, and Patañjali, the *yoga* of the eight components. Anyway, it all starts, wherever we look, with the necessity to make a definite and far-reaching commitment to the path chosen. When properly and fully done (which means, not in the tentative manner of lay-followers), this commitment involves crossing the boundary between ordinary life and the realm of the *śramaṇas*, etc. Given the analysis of desire and ignorance as applied to ordinary life, it need not surprise us to find at the starting point of the spiritual quest the rejection of home, family, possession, power and status, and the cultivation of their opposites. There is general consensus here as to what must be rejected, and what cultivated: total celibacy to overcome sexual passions, total poverty to overcome any clinging to material possessions, total avoidance of doing harm to any living being to get rid of violence, avoidance of alcohol as a prime cause of aggression, lust, and also mental delusion. Truthfulness and not boasting about one's supernatural faculties are further elements here, designed to eliminate more subtle forms of status-seeking and aggression. But more is involved here than a mere external reversal. In more abstract language we could say that man's drive into the external world, expressing itself as sexual urges, as lust for power and status and as violence, is here deprived of its potential objects and, moreover, is redirected towards the self (used here purely as a reflexive pronoun). This we can see in the 'violence' of Jain *tapas*. It is not just the outside world that is allowed to inflict violence on one's self, but great care is also taken to add to it by such things as severe fasts and exposure to intense heat and intense cold. The Jains have an easy explanation for this: these hardships are like a fire that burns up the *karma* mixed up with the soul. As the true nature of the soul is total vision, knowledge, power and bliss, this is automatically realized in proportion to the amount of *karma* thus burnt up.

To the Jains, such afflictions that the ascetic has to endure are not accidental and random, but derive from violence committed in a previous existence, or even earlier on in the same life. So they tell us, for example, about a prince who had performed a mighty deed in battle and had been rewarded by his father with the 'freedom of the town'. He was allowed to do whatever his fancy suggested to him. So he roamed around without any restraint, like a rutting elephant uncontrolled by the mahout's hook. Then he saw the extremely attractive wife of a merchant, and seduced her. Every day he went to sleep with her, right in front of the merchant. The latter was filled with rage, yet he was unable to do anything about it. Time passed, and our lecherous prince converted to Jainism and became an ascetic. He tortured his body with gruesome, fierce and powerful *tapas*. He stayed on a mountain-side, lying on a corpse as his bed. When the merchant heard of this, he had sharp iron spikes made, went to where the ascetic was lying, and, stretching him out over that corpse like a deerskin, hammered the spikes into all his limbs. Suffering indescribable agonies, the ascetic died. So far the story has demonstrated the logical connection between suffering inflicted and pain endured. But then it adds that the ascetic forgave the merchant his cruelty and accepted his fate with equanimity. In this way he could 'internalize' the violence, make use of it as the fire that burns up accumulated *karma*, and as a consequence was reborn in one of the higher heavens.[5]

There is, however, still the need to prevent further karmic matter from entering into the soul, and the means used here correspond more to what *yoga* and the Buddhists are primarily interested in. A strict control of the senses, preventing the indiscriminate absorption of sense data (which would keep the mind distracted or add further *karma* to the soul), is common to all three branches. This is one aspect of the renouncers' religion where some empirical research has actually been carried out, normally under the label of 'sensory deprivation'. When placed in an artificially induced situation of this kind, after a few minutes the subject of the experiment begins to suffer intense hallucinations and panic. These are not unknown to our Indian meditators and may even be personified as, for example, the figure of Māra (who bears a somewhat strange relation with the popular Indian god of love). Another important feature is a striving towards heightened awareness of all one's thoughts, words, and deeds – known as *smṛti*, 'watchfulness'.

Then contemplation proper sets in, quite possibly starting off with a rational reflection and analysis of concrete objects of human experience. But the way such exercises are designed suggests that more than a rational understanding is aimed at: they are meant to break old habits, set up almost instinctive new attitudes, and bring a deeper insight to bear on the external drive. A great variety of such exercises were developed. Let me illustrate this with one example, taken from the Buddhist schema known as 'the four applications of mindfulness'. The whole is divided into four parts, beginning with the body and, via the emotions and thoughts, ending with all possible objects of human perception. A typical meditation on the body could be this:

First imagine a beautiful and attractive woman. Then contemplate this: this body is nothing but hair, nails, teeth, dust, dirt, skin, flesh, bones, sinews, veins, kidneys, heart, spleen, lungs, entrails, stomach, belly, liver, excrement, tears, sweat, mucus, marrow, oil, fat, bile, phlegm, pus, blood, brain, urine. After examining these things, one must realize that even fools would not get attracted to it.[6]

Similarly a heightened awareness is cultivated internally, with reference to one's own nature. Concentration exercises perfect the faculty of the mind to hold on to any given mental object for increasingly long periods, which goes hand in hand with a deeper level of penetration. The culmination of all this is reached when a total insight into the nature of reality is achieved, when everything extraneous to one's self is eliminated, and the fetters of space, time and matter are cast off.[7]

In one sense, the themes discussed in previous chapters are continued here. Heroic beings – thus appropriately styled *jinas*, 'victors', and *vīras* (as in Mahāvīra, 'the great hero') – who possess the potential of becoming *cakravartīs* if they so desire, expose themselves to dangers and violence, to the taboos and forbidden realms of human existence, by leaving behind the safe havens that ordinary life in society offers them. Aggression, murder and sexuality are still the objects of their 'attack'. But the direction of it has drastically changed, for essentially all these factors mentioned so far are internalized and located within the person. Thus from the male ascetic's point of view it is not woman and her alluring sexual attractions that are dangerous, but a craving for pleasure and a misconception of true happiness that demand the hero's aggressive attention within himself. Such an emphasis implies a social critique. It discards the other types of religion which we have discussed previously as limited, far too external, and basically misdirected. These religions cannot possibly offer the total freedom that victory over the self can achieve. That is why we have found such vitriolic attacks in Jain stories on practices like animal or human sacrifice or on the belief that by pacifying the odd *rākṣasa* or by indulging in murderous rituals in the cremation ground anything important could be achieved. Mainstream Buddhism is in perfect agreement with this attitude and evaluation.

What is the nature of this total freedom that the *śramaṇa* (etc.) can gain? Let me initially quote three passages from three strands in the renouncer tradition to illustrate this culmination of the spiritual path. The first comes from the hagiography of the Mahāvīra.

Living thus he with equanimity bore, endured, sustained, and suffered all calamities arising from divine powers, man, and animals, with undisturbed and unafflicted mind, watchful of all his thoughts, words and deeds.

After twelve years, in the second month of summer, when the shadow had turned towards the east, in a field outside a town near an old temple, not far from a *sal* tree, in a squatting position with joined heels, exposing himself to the heat of the sun, in deep concentration, he reached *nirvāṇa*, the complete and full, the unobstructed, unimpeded, infinite and supreme knowledge.[8]

The second passage comes from one of the oldest Upaniṣads.

'This great state of being, infinite, limitless, consists of nothing but consciousness. When the liberated one has departed, there is no more awareness.'

'By saying this, you have indeed bewildered me, by saying: "there is no more awareness".'

'Certainly I am not saying anything bewildering. For where there appears duality, there one smells another, there one sees another, there one hears another, there one speaks to another, there one thinks of another, there one is aware of another. But where verily everything has become the Self, then by what and whom could one smell, see, hear, speak to, think about or be aware of?'[9]

Finally, let me quote from a passage that is found in many places in the Buddhist scriptures and that describes the culmination of Buddhist meditation, the 'enlightenment'.

Now when his mind has become concentrated, purified, cleansed, stainless, free from disturbances, agile, effective, firm and immovable, he directs it to the perception of the destruction of the *āsravas*.

In the thus liberated mind arises the knowledge of his liberation: rebirth has been destroyed, there will be no return into this world. Thus he realizes.[10]

As an overall characterization I would venture to say that the culmination of the spiritual paths, as described here, involves a transcendental experience. The self is experienced as having moved beyond the confines of space, time and matter, into a realm of liberation from *saṃsāra* and suffering. Moreover, some kind of 'altered state of consciousness' is implied, in which the normal boundaries of subject and object have been eliminated. An upsurge of power is experienced, in that the soul's innate power is unleashed (the first example), the ultimate power of the universe realized (*brahman*, in the second example), and total victory over suffering, or contingent reality, achieved (in the last case). For the first and third heroes, the term *jina*, 'conqueror', is used, and the first is also known as Mahāvīra, the 'Great Hero'. Aggressiveness is fully overcome, not just controlled as in our protective systems, nor just used ritually, as with the *siddhas*, etc. Thereby the external drive is totally redirected towards the potentials of the self, and yet a control over the universe is achieved that is exhaustive. There is no need to be surprised when legends then tell us that the *devas* of heaven, the *nāgas*, *gandharvas*, *vidyādharas* and *yakṣas* come to venerate the Jina, that he can move at will into the underworlds and hells or into the heavens, or to the island of Laṅkā, to preach to gods, devils and demons. Powers have been realized that far outshine the *ṛddhis* and *siddhis*, which are discarded here as troublesome side-effects of meditation. But ultimately this is a power that allows one to transcend the world represented by the World-Woman. The Jains, in their typically literal way, see this as moving right up to the very top of the universe. With others, specific localization of liberation is no longer attempted.

To some this particular exercise of attempting a survey of the renouncer tradition as one coherent type of religion in ancient India might appear daring or foolish. Furthermore, I am not closing the case by pointing out that we have thereby been able to achieve a coherent and logically consistent description of it, or that the symbolism analysed in previous chapters finds its neat logical culmination here. Some justification must indeed be given.

So let me start with a straightforward case. Looking at the renouncer tradition in this way has certain advantages and a certain usefulness, for instance, as far as our understanding of Buddhism is concerned – the only strand of the tradition that has really attracted serious and widespread attention. It is useful, because it avoids misunderstandings of the following kind. For example, we are told by one author that the Buddha's enlightenment was no more than 'a humanistic discovery', 'an intellectual penetration into the nature of the human situation', a discovery 'based on analytical reasoning'.[11] Whilst all this could still be defended in some form as merely vague and imprecise language, statements such as the following (by the same author, Trevor Ling) make it clear what he is really up to. 'It is evident that the original Buddhist goal, *nirvāṇa*, was the restoration of healthy conditions of life *here and now*, rather than in some remote and transcendent realm beyond this life ... Individualism is the disease for which a cure is needed.'[12]

There are two points worth noting here. First, in one stroke everything I have said so far about a 'transcendental' experience is wiped off the slate. Secondly, the link with the suffering of *saṃsāra* is cut. Unfortunately, Ling is not unique with respect to these two points. Other authors have dealt with Buddhist teaching in the same way, as if it had nothing to do with belief in transmigration or with the pursuit of liberation from it. Socio-political and economic developments in north-east India during the sixth and fifth centuries BC, which moreover are described in a suspiciously modern terminology of 'urbanization' and 'individualism', are made the primary stimuli for the very nature of Buddhist teaching.

However, there is one feature in Buddhist teaching that must account for the possibility of such widespread misunderstanding as to its religious context and motivation. This is the Buddhists' refusal to talk ontology. However much one may dread this, we cannot now avoid turning to one of the hairiest issues in the discussion of the Indian religions, the so-called Buddhist doctrine of no-self. The need for such a discussion is already clear from the way that the whole argument presented so far depends on a clarification of this 'self', from which the power to transcend the world is unleashed. What on earth have I been talking about, if the Buddhists reject the idea of a self? Unfortunately this discussion will be very complex and cumbersome. However, I have already given an indication of how I ultimately propose to settle the issue: by including the Buddhist version under the heading of 'transcendental' experience and by reformulating the issue as 'refusal to talk ontology'. Let me begin with an easy first step.

'Suppose a man is wounded by an arrow, and his friends and relatives bring him to a doctor. Suppose the man should say then: "I will not let this arrow be taken out until I know who shot me; whether he belongs to the class of warriors or to that of priests; what his name and his family are; whether he is tall, short, or of medium height; which was the kind of bow he used to shoot this arrow at me." That man would die without ever finding out about any of these things.'[13]

This metaphor appears in the context of a refusal by the Buddha to discuss all kinds of metaphysical questions, including the nature of a soul and the ontology of the liberated after death. In concluding his justification of not discussing such matters, the Buddha is alleged to have said: 'So why have I explained the four noble truths? Because they are conducive to full realization, to *nirvāṇa*.'[14] This sounds straightforward, down-to-earth and very practical. But there is more to it than might appear at first sight.

A second aspect of the problem can be derived from the following passage: it might not be possible to grasp the nature of the liberated because of the deficiencies of human language.

'If a fire were burning in front of you, would you know that it was?'

'Yes.'

'And would you know the cause of its burning? '

'Yes. Say it has a supply of grass and sticks.'

'And would you know if it were extinguished?'

'Yes.'

'Would you then know the direction it had gone to from here, east, west, north, south?'

'No, such a question does not apply.'[15]

This metaphor is now applied to the nature of the liberated: 'in the same way that form, emotion, or any other empirically identifiable aspect of a person by which it can be defined has been got rid of, cut off at the root.' So far so good. But while we normally accuse the Buddha of having said too little, here suddenly a lot of unnecessary verbiage, of 'noise' seems to appear. However, what tends to be forgotten in the conventional exegesis of this passage is the fact that 'fire' is regarded as one of the cosmic elements. Thus the point of the metaphor is not at all to suggest annihilation, but to suggest a transformation from one form of being – concrete, empirically identifiable in terms of space, time and matter (in front, duration of its burning, grass and sticks as material fuel) – to another. This other form of being cannot any more be located in our space–time–matter continuum. In that state, the passage continues, 'he [the liberated one] is deep, immeasurable, unfathomable, as is the great ocean'.[16] This is the dilemma: a statement about the nature of liberation is made (comparable to the cosmic fire, to the unfathomable ocean) which implies that it cannot be grasped through human language. Yet this statement not only uses language, it also suggests a direction.

Yet there are two further aspects that have to be added to the two we have listed so far. The third point is again a very concrete and pragmatic one: by refusing to talk ontology, Buddhism avoids the ideological pitfalls of another strand in the *śramaṇa* tradition, pitfalls which it consciously and systematically attacks. This is the way in which the Upaniṣads have presented *brahman*, or better, in which contemporary society utilized this teaching for directly ideological reasons. So far I have ignored this aspect of the concept of *brahman* (and *ātman* can be a synonym for it). What the Upaniṣads tell us is that *brahman* is not just the state of liberation (and to that extent there is no problem in treating it in the context of the renouncer tradition as done so far). It is also a cosmological principle, that one power or reality which gave rise to all phenomena in the world of our experience. Even this is not yet totally at odds with at least some forms of Buddhist teaching. However, Buddhism, and other strands of the renouncer tradition, do fundamentally disagree with a further meaning of the term – in fact the oldest, most emotionally loaded and directly ideological one. This is *brahman* as a universal power contained in and expressed by a specific scriptural corpus, the Vedas, acquired by those who perpetuate these scriptures and who derive their very name from it, the brahmins, and operating through a ritual system performed by brahmins and accompanied by recitations of the Vedas. What makes the whole so obnoxious to the Buddhists, Jains, etc. is not even this assumption of a particular religious system, but the views about human nature and attitudes towards concrete human beings it implies. For not only does it assume no more than a tiny group of hereditary religious professionals, but the whole is restricted to certain members of society – a rough guess would be ten or fifteen per cent at the most. The rest of society is seen as unworthy of access to this religious system. Buddhists and Jains (and possibly some early representatives of the Upaniṣadic tradition) regard this as one of the most obnoxious 'boundary systems', as a 'safe haven' maintained at the cost of oppression and exploitation. By denying now the existence of such a *brahman*, or its pendant in the individual, an *ātman*, the whole basis for this ideology is rejected.

One last comment is necessary in this context, which explains, at the same time, the fourth aspect of the Buddhist refusal to talk ontology. Once again the usefulness of looking at the whole renouncer tradition as one frame of reference is clearly revealed. Buddhism distances itself quite consciously from two extreme positions, which are normally styled 'eternalism' and 'nihilism'. The first is easy: it rejects ideas like those of the Jains concerning an individual, autonomous, inner core (or soul, or self) in man. But so do the Upaniṣads, because there also the *ātman* after liberation merges into something much larger, *brahman*, in which, as we saw, normal ego awareness is cancelled. But nihilism, materialism and other forms of soul loss are more difficult issues. Let me approach them from four different angles.

At its crudest, according to the negative evaluation of the *śramaṇas*, materialism consists in regarding the body and life as one unit and rejecting the existence of anything other than this temporary phenomenon. A classical set of illustrations, accompanied by scientific experiments, can be found in a variety of renouncer texts. The following version comes from the story of Yaśodhara.[17]

A king's henchman meets a Jain ascetic and has an argument with him about the existence of a soul – something that survives a person's death. He reports on the following three experiments he performed. First he threw a robber into a vessel which he made completely air-tight with lac. The robber died, and yet no soul escaped. Then he weighed a criminal on a balance, before and after killing him – the weight remained the same. Thirdly, he cut up another criminal, but, however, small he made the pieces, no soul could be detected. How does our sage get out of this? In the first instance, he suggests to put a man with a conch into that vessel: anybody outside would be able to hear the notes of the instrument blown. With reference to the weighing machine, he points out that a leather bag would also show the same weight, whether pumped up with air or empty. In his third counter-example the ascetic suggests that, however, much one might cut up a kindling-stick, the fire latent in it cannot possibly be discovered. Now it is important to keep in mind that Buddhism distances itself from this form of materialism or nihilism.

Well within the social confines of the *śramaṇa* movement, we find another, more subtle kind of nihilism, that of the Ājīvikas. As the name implies, they deny the existence of a *jīva*, or soul, in any form. Since they figure as the pet enemies of both the Buddhists and the Jains, and since moreover no authentic document of their teachings has survived, it is difficult to specify this much further. They certainly adopted the ascetic lifestyle of the renouncers, and may have believed in some form of determinism or fatalism. But again, this position is violently attacked by the Buddhists and Jains.

Just for the record, one could mention – seemingly without any connection with the renouncer tradition, the philosophy of the *Dice-Man.* In this novel by Luke Rhinehart about a weird psychiatrist called Luke Rhinehart, the hero decides to let his life become controlled totally by the cast of a die. So every day he sets up six alternatives, and executes the one chosen by the die. I cannot resist quoting the last few sentences of our hero:

> One day when Luke was being chased by two FBI men with .45s he came to a cliff and leapt off, just catching the roof to a wild vine twenty yards below the ridge and dangling there. Looking down, he saw fifty feet below six policemen with machineguns, mace, tear gas canisters and two armored cars. Just above him he saw two mice, one white and one black, beginning to gnaw away at the vine to which he clung. Suddenly he saw just in front of him a cluster of luscious ripe strawberries. 'Ah,' he said, 'a new option.'[18]

But in fact this is the old metaphor of the man in the well, meant to illustrate the impossible situation a being finds itself in when living in *saṃsāra* and hunting for fleeting pleasures, which is frequently used in Hindu and Jaina literature. In the case of the dice-man, soul loss occurs because the individual gives up responsibility for his actions and lets chance rule over his destiny. In spite of the Indian origin of the metaphor quoted, nothing could be further removed from the *anātman* doctrine of the Buddhists or, for that matter, from Jain teaching itself. The whole emphasis of the spiritual discipline is to make man more aware of what he is doing and thus more responsible for his actions.

Finally, a fourth avenue into the problem of 'no-soul' might seemingly be found in cults of possession. I. M. Lewis (in his book *Ecstatic Religion*)[19] has dealt with possession and 'soul loss' as closely related manifestations or interpretations of one and the same phenomenon. The rural forms of the religion that is concerned with 'safe havens' makes ample use of possession. But just as the renouncers reject the idea that beings who, according to popular belief (including their own), can take possession of a man, have anything to do with his destiny, they are opposed to any form of suspension of man's own responsibilities and awareness of what he is doing.

After all this abstract talk, I will resort to everyday language for a while. What we are really asking here is how much of the baby must we pour out along with the bath water. The baby obviously stands for any conceivable notion of soul, self, identity, continuity, or ultimate being, and bath water, equally obviously, for the ignorance concerning that which is transient. If we don't go far enough, we mix up the specific Buddhist variety within the renouncer tradition with, say, the Jains, or the teaching of the Upaniṣads. If we go too far, we lose the whole baby and end up in a position of nihilism, materialism, or some other form of soul loss unacceptable to the Buddhists, because a personal responsibility for man's actions would thereby be eliminated. Just to be able to formulate the problem in this manner suggests to me, once again, the usefulness of looking at the renouncer tradition generally as a frame of reference. And, instead of surveying the large literature dealing with the problem of the Buddhist *anātman* that has built up over the past hundred years or so, let me paraphrase the opinion of somebody who, we might assume, knows something about babies. This is queen Śrīmālā. This devout Buddhist lady tells us, speaking in front of the Buddha who is said to have nodded in approval, that certain Buddhists are so preoccupied with pouring the bath water out, that they fail to see the baby. They are totally preoccupied with not regarding the impermanent as permanent, suffering as pleasure, the non-self as self, and the impure as pure. So they cannot see what is indeed permanent, pleasure, self and pure. And what may that be? It is the cessation of suffering, the nature of a Buddha, a reality that is without beginning, unmade, free from death, calm, eternal, inconceivable. At the same time, it is the germ of Buddhahood that lies within ourselves – the exhilarating freedom which is accessible to us through the path they have taught.[20] I think that, in the light of all this, we are justified in including Buddhism under our general heading, as one aspect of a mental culture that aims at a transcendental experience. Whether we go as far as the queen in giving this an ontological basis is a question which does not affect our central discussion. It is sufficient to state that Buddhism knows of an experience called 'enlightenment' in which space, time and matter are transcended and which is achieved through a heightened awareness and personal responsibility for all one's actions. Whatever else one might want to say about *anātman*, the absence of a self, the person's lack of an inner, autonomous and lasting core, or about the possible location of that experience, need not concern us at this point. At the same time, the teaching of *anātman* is a unique feature of Buddhism, while the latter shares with Jainism its analysis of all possible objects of a person's 'thirst' as similarly lacking in a lasting core. The Upaniṣads, on the other hand, firmly hold the belief that all being, man as much as the world, is real to the extent that it is grounded in *brahman*.

It might be tempting to argue now that the Buddhist emphasis on *anātman* is simply a device to distance itself from other contemporary forms of thought and to define its own unique position within the renouncer movement as a whole. But if my characterization of the Buddhist attitude as a refusal to talk ontology or metaphysics is correct, Buddhism would then not simply be one species of a common genus. For such an attitude is qualitatively different from those found with the other renouncers who do talk ontology. One could go even further and suggest that this has been intentional. Chronology is no obstacle here, for the Buddha's teaching occurred a century or two after the earliest Upaniṣads and Pārśva. In this case, Buddhism would present itself as a meta-system that can accommodate the spiritual concerns of the other renouncers without getting side-tracked into developing its own metaphysics.

This is not the right moment to get involved in a detailed analysis of Upaniṣadic, yogic and Jain metaphysical speculation. These are matters that are more appropriately discussed in the context of Wisdom. Instead, let us remain with Power and cast a final glance back over the material we have been accumulating.

Previously I introduced the concept of representational systems in which our space–time–matter continuum is broken down and reorganized. So far we have had occasion to look at two such systems in greater detail: language and the human body. The spiritual path of the renouncers has led us now to another mirror of reality, the human mind. The fact that, in our minds, space, time and matter are contained in a representational form does not require further comment. However, what is worth looking at is the assumption that seems to be running right through our material, that manipulation of the system has a direct effect on the reality symbolized by it. For example, we found previously that by knowing the right *mantra*, one can manipulate the *deva* signified by it. There is a comparable assumption: experiencing a transcendence of space, time and matter is culturally defined and perceived as really achieving it. This 'really' here is obviously my concession to Western parlance. That means, however, that an identity, or at least a causal link between the 'psychological' and the 'ontological' (and 'cosmological'), is assumed. Such terminology is dreadfully inadequate, but I cannot do better here. In the case of Jainism, such a problem does not really arise yet, since, given its ontological premisses, the psychology follows logically. If karmic matter is removed from the soul (*jīva*), the latter gets so light that it can zoom right up to the top of the universe. There lie liberation and transcendence, and there the *jīva* realizes the full potential – which includes complete power – of its true nature. But in the Upaniṣads, where liberating perception along with the transcendental experience is located in a 'self' (*ātman*), such a problem does arise. Time and again we hear that he who knows *brahman* gains control over the world and his destiny. While knowledge is obviously an internal, 'psychological' entity, destiny includes externals such as the destruction of *karma* and the prevention of further embodiments. When we come to Buddhism, the emphasis on the self-authenticating experience of enlightenment does not let the problem come to the surface. For all I know this may be a fifth factor in the Buddhist hesitation to comment on ontological issues. (The implications of all this will emerge in Part three.)[21]

We have reached here the culmination of everything explored so far. We started off with the picture of a vast and variegated, and in many ways terrifying, universe. Surrounded by threatening beings of all kinds, man tries to secure a tiny space in all this by surrounding himself with protective boundaries. But then we met the heroes, of various types and inclinations, who were ready to step beyond these boundaries and conquer for themselves a wider realm. As the realm increased, and the range of beings and powers conquered and acquired widened, we noticed at the same time an increasing trend towards reversing the direction of the heroic drive and bringing it to bear on the inner world of the hero himself. Thus there are two complementary movements that we have been tracing: from the most gross and physical, or external, expression of religion (such as the offering of a piece of meat dripping with blood to a demon) to the most subtle, immaterial and internal (i. e. meditation), and from the small segment of the world occupied by a safe haven to the totality of being. While with the Jains a last vestige of external violence and physical aggression is left in the form of self-imposed tortures and possibly fasting to death, with the Buddhists death is overcome by anticipating it purely internally. Thirst, as grasping at personal identity and survival, is vanquished by letting the person disintegrate meditationally into its transient components. Mind or self, or whatever one wants to call it, emerged as the ultimate control mechanism of man's destiny, a destiny that is realized, in both senses of the word, through a transcendental experience. We noticed a progressive breaking down of boundaries by our heroes, a progressive move away from the safe havens of ordinary mortals, until we reach the point where the ultimate boundary is confronted by them – personal identity. Whether in the Upaniṣadic teaching about man's essence, his *ātman*, being identical with something infinitely greater – *brahman* – or in the Buddhist teaching of *anātman*, the demolition of this last boundary is clearly indicated. By breaking through this final frontier, the hero has established a safe haven that has as its boundaries nothing less grandiose than the boundaries of the universe or of reality itself. Survival and security, the first aspects of the definition of culture proposed at the very beginning of our exploration, and the background to our concept of Power, have found here their most subtle expression.

We have come to the man who has achieved everything that he had to do. But where can we go from a realm that lies beyond space, time and matter? Don't worry: I am not suggesting getting swallowed up in a black hole or, like Dr Who, passing into another universe of antimatter. For a number of reasons it is still possible to explore the Indian religions further. So let us now descend from the top of the universe into the relatively uncharted realm of Love – a new colour in the picture painted so far.

PART TWO

Love: the rhythms of the interior world

CHAPTER 9

The missing colour

Towards the end of the nineteenth century *The Times* carried a review of Edwin Arnold's verse translations of Indian Poetry. There we could read: 'Nothing could be more graceful and delicate than the shades by which Krishna is portrayed in the gradual process of being weaned by the love of "Beautiful Radha, jasmine-bosomed Radha", from the allurements of the forest nymphs, in whom the five senses are typified.'[1] And the *Standard* comments on the same book: 'The poem abounds with imagery of Eastern luxuriousness and sensuousness; the air seems laden with the spicy odours of the tropics.'[2]

In 1925 the Polish composer Karol Szymanowski completed his opera *King Roger*, set in the Sicily of the twelfth century. This setting is not arbitrary in terms of the composer's own interests, for here at the court of Palermo he could find a meeting of Europe and the East, of Christian and Arab culture, which mirrored his own musical pursuits. In the opera, a strange and bewitching young man turns up at the royal court and greets the king with the following words: 'I greet you well, and in the great name of love!' When the king asks him where he comes from he replies: 'I come from smiling southern stars. Far are the lands whither my steps have led me. I offered my prayer for you in white Benares; and here I bring you greeting from the lotus of Indra. My image in the waters of Ganges would greet you too.'[3] Since the libretto is in the symbolist tradition, it requires some decoding. The strange man is the god Dionysus in disguise who with his alluring powers threatens the Apollonian values of the court. Dionysian ideals are derived from the banks of the Ganges!

Very little in the previous chapters has prepared us for such a perception of India. We have heard about violent and bloody means of protecting a human environment against threatening forces, about extraordinary ritual and physiological means of eradicating sexual passions, and about the cultivation of inner, mental strength. If anything, we have encountered in the serene freedom of a Buddha the Apollonian ideal – but not an Eastern sensuousness or the heady drinks of Dionysus. Moreover, I think it could be argued that our own unreflected perceptions of India are not 'laden with the spicy odours of the tropics'. Did Arnold and Szymanowski get it wrong, or did they know something which for one reason or another has been pushed out of our consciousness? I shall argue in favour of the latter alternative.

Queen Roxana cannot resist the temptation of the youth and joins the crowd of the intoxicated Maenads that follow him; King Roger resists, but emerges a different person – a man in whom the Apollonian and the Dionysian have found synthesis and balance. This partial rejection of the Dionysian ideal still tells us very little – no more than that we are dealing here with an age-old Occidental preoccupation. Arnold's case is more revealing. For he does not translate the whole text of Jayadeva's *Gītagovinda.* Where the original reaches its climax, Arnold tells us in a footnote: 'part of [this canto] is here perforce omitted, along with the whole of the last one'.[4] What sort of forces are at work here to explain the mysterious 'perforce'? Obviously we have to find out what happens in these untranslated portions of the poem – they describe Rādhā making love to Kṛṣṇa by sitting astride him. This was obviously too spicy for contemporary Victorian sentiments. Kṛṣṇa's dalliance with the other milkmaids in the forest could still be allegorized as indulging himself in the pleasures of the five senses, and his 'true' love for Rādhā as the weaning from their allurement. But the stark literalism of the final part of the poem put insurmountable obstacles into the path of further allegorization and thus had to be ignored.

Many further examples of such bowdlerization could be mentioned here and could be used to plot the continuation of the same attitude into much more modern times. Thus one could mention Miss Horner's incomplete translation of Buddhist monastic rules. Where they begin to speak in a no-nonsense, straightforward manner about the outer fringes of sexuality, thereby demarcating in a precise way what for the monk constitutes the range of forbidden sexual activities, Miss Horner leaves the Pālī original untranslated. To justify herself, she argues that the rules were written for primitive people who needed such detailed and bizarre information, while modern man knows what is meant by 'sexual infringements' and does not require such unsavoury marginalities.[5]

But my point here is not to make fun of such instances of timidity. No scholar works in a vacuum and he cannot always ignore the social constraints imposed on him by his own culture. Moreover, it would be unwise and unfair to expect him necessarily to be a hero who has the courage to move into 'forbidden' zones. What such illustrations are meant to hint at are certain factors that have a direct bearing on the grand programme outlined in our very first chapter. Such factors occur on different levels and in different contexts, and we shall need a number of steps to unravel this rather complex issue even on a superficial level.

First of all, we must acknowledge a certain affinity between the material discussed in Part one, on the religious pursuit of power, and the kind of values we might describe as 'puritanical' or 'Victorian'. In both cases, the world is perceived as a dangerous, challenging or 'evil' place and a heroic struggle to gain control over it is advocated by means of hardiness, a particular brutality directed towards the emotions, and overcoming the temptations of the flesh. There is no scope here for the imagination, poetry and love of a more romantic or sexual kind – merely honest hard work. Thus right at the heart of the Indian religious traditions, it would seem, lies the justification for rejecting a range of material that falls short of the high moral demands made in the traditions of Power.

However, such a convergence of attitudes (and I have done little more here than caricaturize them) reveals itself as not just the result of some outsider's armchair comparison of two cultures, but – and this is the second point – in some sense brought about through direct social and ideological contact. Victorian Britain was, after all, physically and intellectually present in the India of the nineteenth century. Directly exposed to Victorian values, a fair proportion of more anglicized Indians interiorized these and – this is the crucial part – employed them in the conceptualization of their own religious heritage. Given the affinity of certain aspects of that heritage with the values sketched above, this did not actually involve a major change of heart. But it did create further mental blocks as far as other aspects of that same heritage were concerned. This way of evaluating the past was in turn taken over by the interested Westerner and directly affected how Western scholarship then looked at India. When in more recent years, for instance, the discipline of religious studies set itself up as the communicator of knowledge about 'the other religions', a further purification took place which left little intact of the many weird and wonderful things that may hide behind the label of Love and of the spicy luxuriousness of the East.

This may all be very interesting to the specialist, somebody might object, but what we can learn from it, apart from having to watch out for certain academic biases? So let me come to my third point, which does not concern itself with avoiding distortions or one-sided evaluations of our area of study, but takes us to another level altogether: whether or not we ought to indulge ourselves in the kind of exploration undertaken here. For currently we are being told to jump on our bikes and look for the good old values of the Victorian age. It is the funk – the same stern voice of order and hard work is telling us – of the swinging sixties that has been responsible for all the miseries of our present-day society. This doubtlessly well-intended advice raises a number of problems for our present exploration. I am not thinking here so much of the fact that the swinging sixties were closely connected with an outburst of interest in Indian religions and things Eastern generally, for instance under the banner of Tantrism the cult of ecstasy. Nor am I unduly worried here by the Victorian attitude towards India and the Indian religions. The problem lies in the 'return' movement advocated, back to something in the past. Obviously from the point of view of the moral cyclist this is a false perception of his intentions. The values advocated – he will reply – are not part of a past, bygone age, but possess universal and timeless relevance. For all I know this may actually be true. But by its very nature such an absolutist view cannot now allow for exploration, for the desire of new discoveries, for the play of the imagination, and for the personal freedom implied in all this. Moreover, it may well be possible to postulate a convergence between what such an attitude implies and the kind of values that are advocated through it. This means that the good old Victorian values themselves are perceived to include such a rejection of the imagination and personal freedom. Thus, generally speaking, the kind of exploration undertaken here becomes, by its very nature, an object of neo-Victorian resentment. On this level, I prefer to abandon the discussion and simply hope that the present enterprise proves itself valuable in its own right.

But such a pragmatic solution does not eliminate the problem on another level. Factually, there is so much more to explore than we have done so far, and one of the uncharted territories is that of Love. It does not require much imagination to figure out what sort of things are hidden behind this relatively innocuous term. Just as our term Power contained violence, aggression and adventurousness, it is not difficult to suspect that Love also covers up for sex, eroticism, lust and passion. Thus, for example, it will include the goddess Rādhā, 'jasmine-bosomed Rādhā', making love on top of the god Kṛṣṇa, which brings me back to the very beginning of these reflections. But what initially may have appeared as no more than the amusing inhibitions of a long-past age, has revealed itself as actual in more than one sense.

For us it implies that the move from Power to Love means to swim against the stream in a three-fold manner: against Indian self-presentation, against a popularly promulgated image of the Indian religions, and against the ethos that once again, after the funk of the swinging sixties, pervades much of the contemporary silent majority. A *tour de force* (or a *tour de France*?) appears necessary, which indeed requires the 'heroism' of which we heard so much in previous chapters. But having committed ourselves to a full and honest exploration of the Indian religious traditions under the triple title of Power, Love and Wisdom, this is the route to take, however perverse it may seem to some. Let me assure the faint-hearted that all this sounds much more terrifying than it will turn out to be. After all, the exploration of Love will lead us also to the discovery of true monotheism in India, of a religion with a definite 'God' at its centre. Now why such a feature should remain problematic to the Victorian (and neo-Victorian) sensibilities is a question to which I shall return presently. But for the moment let us forget about psychological barriers and power politics and turn to a novel territory for the sake of a comparative excursion.

This allows me to introduce a figure of empathetic scholarship whose name deserves mention in any such comparative enterprise: Père Charles de Foucauld. He lived for many years in one of the most inhospitable landscapes on this earth, the Sahara, among the notorious and almost mythical 'blue men', the Tuareg, allegedly some of the most violent people on earth. His study of their language not only resulted in four hefty tomes of a dictionary,[6] but – and this is where a surprise awaits us – also in two even heftier volumes of poetry.[7] With inexhaustible care and meticulousness he has collected, annotated and translated (on three levels of literalness) the oral literature which is, to a considerable extent, erotic poetry. But it would be platitudinous simply to exploit for our discussion the fact that the same corpus also contains many poems on warfare and heroism. The correlation between love and power can be established on a far deeper level and in a far more interesting manner. Two main events appear to fill the lives of the Tuareg male: the *rezzou* and the *ăhâl*. The first is what made the Tuareg notorious: setting out on a raid to plunder and kill – often in revenge for similar raids suffered. About the second, *ăhâl*, Father de Foucauld himself writes:

[The word] '*ăhâl*' denotes 'galant meeting (meeting of young men and young women, who have come together to entertain each other)'. In principle, only the young girls, the young women and the men still young and unmarried or whose wives are far away, take part in it. Sometimes young couples also go there together, but more as spectators than as active participants. Old men never go there. Older women attend it quite frequently, but as spectators or as presidents. The real active participants of the *ăhâl* are the men and women who practise the *asri*, 'freedom of manners', in other words unmarried women and unmarried men, or men whose wives are absent, both of an age to be courted or to court respectively. When some such people are living in a camp, they meet every evening at nightfall, either in the open air at some distance from the camp, or in the tent of an unmarried woman, or in a special tent erected by the parents expressly for the *ăhâl*. As the women and men arrive they sit down together, facing each other. One chats, one jokes. If there is a girl who can play the violin, she plays it, and the men accompany her with a refrain. Often the men recite or sing poems [many of which Père de Foucauld collected in his corpus]. This is one part of the *ăhâl*, and for some participants, that is all: nice, clean entertainment (*divertissement decent*). For others, the *ăhâl* is mixed with *asri*, 'freedom of manners'. They engage in very free contact, between man and woman, and make assignments for the rest of the night ... Sometimes the young men travel more than two hundred kilometres to spend a few days as visitors in a camp where a pleasant *ăhâl* is going on ... During an *ăhâl* the men and women gathered together may elect a chairlady (*presidente*), with or without the assistance of a male president, but never a president alone. Her function consists in settling the quarrels that may, jokingly, arise during an *ăhâl*.[8]

Father de Foucauld adds: 'The *ăhâl* accompanied by *asri*, and the *asri* with all it implies, though prohibited by Islam, is universally accepted and permitted in the Ăhaggar.'[9]

His *Poésies touarèges* includes both male and female voices, but here I want to look briefly at the verses composed by the men. When we collect from the poetry the statements and images relevant to these two activities, an amazing parallelism emerges. I refrain from quoting actual passages here, because it is really the accumulation and gradual build-up of many such fragments that yield the picture I am interested in here. There are the details of how the man dresses himself up for the two occasions, how he relates to and involves his camel in it, the psychological build-up for it and the inner feelings about it, the rules of a code of honour regulating both types of event, phraseology – these and similar features reveal that the *rezzou* and the *ăhâl* are perceived as complementary sides of one and the same coin. Both offer the chance for the display of manly virtues and victory, but also for defeat and death which, naturally in the case of the *ăhâl*, means the debilitating glance of love cast upon the man. What we can see here, then, is a similarity of two forms of behaviour, both visually and externally, and in terms of their inner psychology and emotive associations. *Rezzou* and *ăhâl* complement each other as the two modes of male expression, of their pursuit of power and love.

We shall have an opportunity to return briefly to this entrancing poetry and the blue men of the Sahara. For here, too, exist the kind of ideological problems which were mentioned at the beginning of the chapter. But in accordance with the motto 'What is somebody's camel is somebody else's cattle', we may now move over to India, more specifically to its extreme south and to the earliest phase of its documented history. Here we find the Tamils, an indigenous people who were still relatively unaffected by religious and cultural events set in motion by the Āryans who, already one and half millennia previously, had entered the extreme north-west of the peninsula. Again, almost all we know about them for these centuries around the AD watershed derives from a corpus of poetry, usually called '*caṅkam* literature'. In Part one we had the opportunity to learn about one aspect of this poetry: where it depicted 'heroism'.[10] We saw, how in a highly conventionalized manner, the natural environment – trees, flowers, animals, landscapes, and so on – were correlated to typical heroic situations, such as cattle raiding, attacking a neighbouring chieftain's fort, and defending one's own position or possession. All these genres together are styled '*puṟam*', which simply means, 'the outside'. Logically, there exists a complementary category of 'the inside' (or *akam*). This is love poetry. While man (naturally women are included here – *puṟam* has a lot to say about 'heroic women') displays and realizes himself through his deeds of bravery in the outside world and in public, within his heart and his emotions, in his inside (thus *akam*), he encounters another level of reality, love. Also in this category of poems we find the same structural principle of associating types of the natural environment with fundamental love situations. Even some of the symbolically used flowers are the same in either context. This is the overarching feature of both *puṟam* and *akam* and, we could almost say, the defining characteristic of *caṅkam* literature itself.

Whether approached as *ăhâl* and *rezzou* or as *akam* and *puṟam*, such a complementarity or parallelity of human behaviour and attitudes invites further discussion and, in fact, suggests a number of different directions for it. Given that our overall conceptual framework of Power and Love contains a whole variety of specific concepts, it would be easy to construct from individual facets a whole range of utterly confusing and conflicting conclusions. Thus, for example, it might be tempting to interpret the pursuit of 'love' as an extension, or in fact merely one component of, the pursuit of power, by isolating from Love the element of male sexual aggressiveness. We would not have to go far to find perfect substantiations of such a nexus – no further than our advertisements in which 'the wife' or 'the girlfriend' is no more than another item in the list of status symbols like the car, the penthouse, the whisky, and the Armani suit. There is no need to refer to the host of novels and films that depict the power struggles of people supposedly 'in love' with each other.

On the other hand, one could look into the famous epic literature of the world, where time and again passionate love is the primary cause of aggression and violence. Remaining in India, we could look at the story of Rāma and his wife Sītā told in the *Rāmāyaṇa*. When an ogre saw the beautiful princess, he fell madly in love with her and abducted her to his fort on the island of Laṅkā. Rāma then gathered a mighty army together and, fighting bloody battles, recovered his wife and destroyed the ogre's island stronghold. The abduction itself was preceded by another act of violence due to love: initially the ogre's sister had seen Rāma, had made amorous advances to him in her infatuation, and had her nose and ears cut off by the enraged Rāma. And it was love too that created the setting for these violent events: Rāma was exiled into the forest (where the ogress saw him and from where Sītā was abducted) because his father yielded to the request of one of his queens. The same theme appears as the basis for the devastating war fought between two sets of grandchildren from different queens of the same king which is narrated in the epic *Mahābhārata*. A more immediate cause of the bloodshed that was to follow was the attempt by one faction to humiliate the other by publicly pulling the clothes off one of their wives. And victory came to the side of the insulted only because Ambā in her previous life had been rejected by all the men to whom she had offered her love, had sworn revenge and become reborn – in order to change her sex into that of a man – and then killed Bhīṣma whose presence had rendered invincible the side of the offenders.

Thus it appears quite legitimate to reduce in individual instances certain aspects of Love to Power, and in other instances to subsume aspects of Power under Love. But such an ambivalence shows that, as global terms, our Power and Love ought to be maintained as independent concepts. This is the conclusion I derive from the Tuareg and Tamil poetries. In view of the psychological barrier we are trying to cross (and I hope enough has been said so far to prevent the impression that our present discussion is merely a rhetorical problem), I see here the justification for accepting Love as a genuine autonomous area of investigation. Nevertheless, it might be objected that, instead of a reduction of one component to the other, parallelity or complementarity could be interpreted as suggesting that both terms, Love and Power, can be subsumed under one, third, term; that if they are but different sides of one and the same coin, then the 'coin' itself would be here the overriding third. But hints to the effect that we are dealing with real autonomy here and not with two elements that are dependent on a third can be found in the *caṅkam* tradition itself. For there we find a distinctive formal difference expressed between the two complementary genres of *akam* and *puṟam*. Through heroism a man 'makes a name' for himself among people. Thus, necessarily, a hero must be named. On the other hand, love is perceived here as something 'intimate' and personal (in our sense of the word). Thus *akam* poetry is anonymous. However much we may suspect in a particular poem the existence of highly individual persons expressing their love, all we hear about are a stereotyped lover and beloved or wife. The significance of this distinction will be explored at a later stage, and the next chapter will look in detail at further aspects of the *akam* tradition. But in the present context I merely want to derive from such a formal distinction a support for the assumption of an autonomy of Power and Love. Let this assumption be the armour under whose protection we can venture into Love's territory, to search for the face of Dionysus reflected in the waters of the Ganges.

Now it cannot be said that we shall be taken totally by surprise by what we will find here. For time and again in previous chapters we had to struggle to keep at bay and to ward off a most stubborn intruder – eroticism. From the very beginning, when I endeavoured to establish a methodology from the two novels of Canetti and García Márquez, the sexual drive in man presented itself as troublesome. It had been written into the destiny of the Buendía dynasty that love would bring about its ruin after 'a hundred years of solitude'. And the archetype of the pure intellect, Professor Peter Kien – student of Oriental languages and religions – goes up in flames with his books in an '*auto-da-fé*' brought about by his quasi-gnostic aversion to women and sex. This could be constructed as a warning to us to be more balanced and mature in our own exploration of the mysteries of the East! Then we found that the ancient travellers to imaginary worlds had an uncanny tendency to encounter beautiful girls, rather than such profitable commodities as the spices that our own explorers searched for. Even such seemingly safe topics as transmigration and non-violence inadvertently revealed erotic features. Thus Gandhi the fighter for non-violence is inseparable from the Gandhi who steeled his will against the temptations of the flesh, very much in the manner of the early Tristan, and that without the help of a sword. The long chain of rebirths suffered by King Yaśodhara, though set in motion nominally by an act of violence, was filled with bizarre sexual relationships. When I explored how the Indian imagination manipulated the mastery over the space–time–matter continuum, a remarkable interest in love and passion showed itself, and the pursuit of power in the form of the so-called tantric traditions involved erotic symbols and acts. And even at the very end, when we were dealing with the ideal 'world-conquerors' – the Buddhas and Jinas and other giants of Indian religious history – we found a remarkable complementarity between unlimited and, alternatively, radically rejected, sexual conquests. A Buddha or a Mahāvīra had the potential to become a *cakravartī*, a universal emperor to whom all the pleasures of this world would have been available. Moreover, these spiritual giants came into the world for a purpose: to reveal to suffering mankind the medicine of their teaching; thus compassion is here hinted at as another expression of Love. Such a reading of the material discussed in Part one suggests that we may have been leaving one central colour out of the picture. Whatever else could be inferred from all this, it seems clear that such features of Love are more than merely accidental aspects of the Indian traditions. For that reason alone it is a subject to which we ought to pay greater attention and add the missing colour. Incidentally, our own colour psychology (which I assume would associate the erotic with bright red) differs from that of Indian culture where the colour black is centrally associated with Love. But let us now turn away from the level of generality and abstract language and look at some concrete details.

Indian culture knows of a 'god of love' – the *deva* Kāma. By now it is clear to us that such a statement does not actually offer much scope for any religious capital to be made of it. Although *deva* is conventionally translated as 'god', this does not mean much in religious terms. But to introduce Kāma here offers us a first opportunity to study how, in symbolic terms, Indian culture has treated the theme of the antagonism of asceticism and love. Kāma-*deva* is certainly very different from the chubby cherubic figure of Renaissance art: he wields all kinds of weapons and is surrounded by a mighty army. His favourite weapon is the bow, made of sugar-cane and strung with a string made up of humming bees. The arrows are flowers. He also has a wife called Rati – a word usually denoting sexual delight. Let us cast a brief glance over his various adventures and roles in Indian literature. Time and again he is presented as suffering some fatal defeat in his battles with heroic ascetics. We are already familiar with a Jain allegorical poem [11] in which the Mahāvīra defends the honour of his bride Siddhi, 'Perfection'. But much better known among his adventures are the stunning defeat he suffered at the hands of the Buddha and his being burnt to ashes by Śiva. The latter event gave rise to another popular name of Kāma: 'he without body'. With the Buddhists, his name Māra is most common. Here we are told that the Buddha repulsed all the terrifying and entrancing phantasmagoria Māra had conjured up. This episode is usually styled 'the temptation of the Buddha' in Western literature. This suggestion of a biblical parallel is developed further by some writers who attempt to correlate Māra with personified evil or the Devil. This is a fatal equation! It assumes a fundamental dichotomy of reality in terms of absolute good and absolute evil, which is totally alien to the Indian traditions. And as we shall see presently, Indian culture itself remains ambivalent about Kāma.

But let us turn to the second episode mentioned.[12] This involves the god Śiva, so renowned for his unswerving asceticism that a demon could venture to make his death dependent on Śiva's breaking his ascetic practices and procreating a son. An almost certain guarantee of immortality! Umā, the Himalaya mountain's daughter, is willing to tempt the ascetic into procreating a son with her, and Kāma with his army is sent out to prepare the ground for this attempt at seduction. Unhappy Kāma! When Śiva notices what he is planning, he simply opens the third eye on his forehead, emits a beam of fire and burns him to ashes. In the wailing of widowed Rati we can hear the song of triumph of the ascetic ideal.

Yet this is not the end of the story. Umā has set her heart and mind on becoming Śiva's wife, and thereby freeing the world from the demon. So now she herself goes into action and, by playing the ascetic's own game, she manages to win him over. But what happened to poor bodiless Kāma? Mythology[13] tells us that he found a new body, as splendid and attractive as before, by being born as son of Kṛṣṇa and Rukmiṇī, and was called on earth Pradyumna. Literature tells us about the existence of temples dedicated to Pradyumna, often – rather logically – in the quarters of, and devoutly visited by, courtesans.[14] And then the poets tell us, in ever-new variations of the theme, that whenever a man is struck by love for a woman, Kāma, as it were, has entered her and has used her body as his weapons (the eyebrows are the bow, the dark pupils of the eyes the bees, her glances the arrows, and so forth). And whenever a woman falls in love with a man, it is as if Kāma has manifested himself in bodily form before her. What about the ascetic Śiva? In his case the theme of love's and Kāma's victory over him may be expressed, in rather extreme examples, as a word-play. Śiva by himself is '*śava*' (corpse), and artists may well depict him as such, lying prostrate on a pyre in a cremation ground. But the presence of the goddess (Umā, or more frequently in these cases, the rather terrifying black goddess Kālī) brings him to life as she stirs up his passions for her. She may then be depicted sitting astride him and making love to him.

Even the Jains, so well known for their 'puritanical' values, could not resist the temptations Kāma represented. To their system of sixty-three grand men – the religious giants and mighty emperors who fill the history of one cosmic cycle – they added at a later date another set, that of the twenty-four *kāmadevas*, 'the most beautiful persons that ever lived'[15] (in the words of a modern Jain scholar). One of these is Snake-Prince whom we met acquiring all kinds of wonderful treasures in the underworld, and another Vasudeva, the father of Kṛṣṇa, who figures as the amorous hero in the Jain versions of the *Grand Story.*[16]

So what has happened to the heroic and ascetic ideals described under the heading of Power? On the basis of the examples offered so far it might perhaps still be possible to say that nothing has really happened. It might be argued that all I have said here about Kāma and his role in the Indian imagination is pure metaphor. Nevertheless, the re-emergence of *eros* depicted in myth and in the similes of the poets does reflect a reality in the religious history of India. Our examples actually represent some points along the line drawn by the swinging movements of a pendulum. Just as the burning to ashes of Kāma has a real basis in the ascetic ideals of India, the life found by the *śava* Śiva in the love of the goddess does correspond to another real basis in Indian religion. Love is the autonomous second half of the pendulum's swing, and the following chapters will explore this subject in greater detail.

But let us first look at some further general matters before getting involved in those details. Above all, my term 'Love' seems to require some clarification. It is clear from the way in which I have used 'Power' in Part one that 'Love' is a verbal umbrella under which I want to gather together a wider range of phenomena. That such phenomena are indeed related to each other, in spite of what the ordinary usage of the English language might suggest in certain cases, will obviously have to be demonstrated. There are very practical advantages in this usage of the word 'Love' which is intentionally loose and in which the specifics are gathered together almost by free association. Were we to start off by projecting our own conceptual distinctions on the Indian material, we might well miss out on important aspects. That means, it could be the case that sexuality, *eros*, passion, love, compassion, *agape* and devotion (terms so carefully distinguished in our own culture) constitute a kind of continuum in India. To break this up into separate components would mean to destroy one of the most remarkable insights we could gain from the Indian traditions: that religion can manifest itself through such a continuum, instead of restricting itself to its last part. And indeed, even on the basis of the examples found in the present chapter, it will be possible to suggest that Indian religious culture does not use our conceptual distinctions in the same way, and that it can include under 'Love' the whole, or most of, the range of features mentioned above.

If Love is an autonomous aspect of Indian religions and if the fire of asceticism does not universally burn to ashes the stirrings of the heart, this autonomy needs some explanation. But as long as we do not assume that one religious system dominated the minds of all Indians – and, given the size of the country and the enormous social differentiation in it, that would be a very hazardous assumption – there is no problem here. It should be easy enough to realize, therefore, that not everyone shared, or actually was able to share, the heroic ideals of Power. Many remained totally unaware of them, being bypassed by the channels through which these ideals were promulgated in society. Others reacted quite consciously against them, and yet others showed that they were not unduly worried by such ideals and simply ignored them. All these people drew on other cultural traditions in their understanding of man, the universe, and human destiny and gave shape to types of religion very different from those that we have heard about so far. A variety of different cultural constructs that have Love as their central concern were produced by these groups. Here culture pursues comfort and pleasure, rather than survival and security.

Here are some facets of these religious cultures. Love reveals itself as a power latent in the human heart. It awaits external stimuli to trigger off its powers and build up enormous tensions, and does not rest until in ecstasy these tensions have found relief. Such stimuli may be an attractive person of the other sex, a beautiful song, an original turn of phrase or image in a poem, or God. At the same time, the world, the environment in which man lives, is perceived not as threatening and terrifying, but as fascinating and as pervaded by a pulse that seems to correspond to man's own heart-beat. This cosmic pulse may then take on more concrete form, e.g. as God. New challenges lie here – to expose oneself to these powers latent in the heart and in the universe and to respond to them – and new kinds of heroes have accepted them. The experiences cultivated here take the person outside himself, not to master and control, but to be overpowered and to become submissive. The rule of anonymity that governs *akam* or Tamil love poetry could well be connected with this: the individual, identifiable by his name, transcends himself in love. This is the famous freedom that love is supposed to grant according to our own understanding, too; but how would this relate to the freedom, the transcendence, which the hero in the religious traditions of Power gains? This is obviously one of the most important questions we shall have to try to answer.

I have more than once used the term 'God' here. Perhaps it might have been easier to introduce the discussion of the missing colour by talking about theistic religion. Indeed, superficially, Indian theism appears a much more familiar territory to us (although, somewhat surprisingly perhaps, the average textbooks have relatively little to say about it). After the exploration of austere asceticism, where man is totally in charge of his destiny, to hear about God and grace comes as a great relief. But a closer look reveals that this is not really the case. Indian theism may not be drawing on the religions of Power, but neither does it draw on those rarefied emotions which we would assume Love to denote in such a religious context. It draws fully and squarely on 'Love' in all the different senses I have indicated above. So it ends up looking even more foreign and strange than the religious pursuits discussed in Part one. We expect a red (the colour of love), and are given a black instead. Not only is black the colour associated with Kāma, but also two of the major God figures we shall hear about are 'black', not just by their complexion, but also by their very names: Kṛṣṇa and Kālī. In this connection I ought to mention that my term 'God' is generic, covering – like 'man' – both genders: that means, God and Goddess, God as man and as woman. Probably because Indian theism is something theoretically so much closer to home, but in spite of that looks so totally alien, it has been ignored by many an observer and has been treated with contempt by others. A quote from the Abbé Dubois may convey some idea of this.

> We find in the Hindu books a mere tissue of contradictions relating to the three main divinities, and the absurd details which are related in connexion with each are even more inconsistent. The point on which they agree to a certain extent is that which relates to the excesses and abominable amours of them.[17]

It is not difficult to relate the Abbé's assessment to the Victorian value system. But possibly we may be dealing here with an even deeper and far wider phenomenon. To give some indication of how such a wider context could be envisaged, I want to return to the Tuareg, the blue men of the Sahara.

We saw how, formally and psychologically, *rezzou* and *ăhâl* are complementary phenomena. The Tuareg are officially Muslim, and indeed their poetry is pervaded by words and concepts derived from Islam. If one constructs a table of poetic themes, under the headings of *rezzou* and *ăhâl*, and plots such Islamic references on to this structure, it appears that Islam relates positively to just about every aspect of the two complementary activities, except where the poet speaks of the love that powerfully and violently shakes his heart. Here are some examples. It is Allah's will when the men are defeated by their enemies;[18] it is He who may decide that they can have their revenge, 'their faces soaked with the blood of their enemies'.[19] He it is who is thanked when the enemies flee and when a man makes a name for himself through bravery.[20] Who survives in a battle and 'who in future will not continue to speak in this world'[21] is predestined by Allah. A beautiful woman may be said to have 'no equal among all of Adam's children',[22] to be 'like an angel in heaven' and to be 'fashioned by His own hands',[23] with 'perfectly proportioned body'.[24] But when a man loses his strength so that he has to lean on his spear, when he falls powerless to the ground[25] and it is as if the woman has cast burning coals at him that set his heart on fire[26] – then Allah is invoked merely as a witness to his agony and trusted as the one who has predestined whether the man will survive or die.[27] But Allah is not invoked as the primary cause of man's passion. Something of the non-semitic religion of the Berber seems to have preserved itself here, which Islam, as a typical semitic religion, cannot accept. Thus it is not surprising when Père de Foucauld tells us that the *ăhâl* with its *asri*, 'freedom of manners' is forbidden by Islam.

But the particular combination of the concept of God (or Goddess) with eroticism is not our only difficulty. It is easy to look at rituals, study ethics, and observe ascetic practices. It is also relatively easy to gain comprehension of another culture's philosophies and theologies. But to understand its attitudes towards love is predictably much more difficult. Where are the sources we could study? Fortunately for our purposes, Indian culture itself has reflected on many facets of Love in a variety of ways. Poetry is one such area in which these reflections have been recorded. Naturally this creates its own complications and problems, for poetry is one of the most difficult cultural constructs to interpret. Yet I hope to show that it can be done and that interesting insights are in store for us here. For more than in any ritual, any form of religious behaviour or theological treatise, something personal is expressed in it. Poetry allows us, better than any other cultural construct, to look into a person's mind and heart (and may, in the process, tell us more about the personal significance of other, more external cultural constructs, say the temple or the myths told in the Purāṇas).

The religions of Love confront us moreover not only with poetry in a technical sense, but also with 'poetry' in a more metaphorical usage of the word. Here we are dealing with the emotions, the language of the heart, the play of the imagination and human warmth, and not with cold logic or purely cerebral or physical matters. Neither sort of poetry has been very popular with interpreters of the Indian religions. But to ignore it, or consciously to destroy it, means to leave out a primary colour in our picture and to miss out on Love as an autonomous religious reality. For example, lovely stories are told about the god Kṛṣṇa and his love affairs with the milkmaids. Yet in the average textbooks used by students, as in a lot of more modern Indian writing, these often very erotic stories are reduced to 'signifying the longing of the soul for God'. We had an example of this allegorizing at the beginning of this chapter. But I am convinced that the authors of these stories and poems about Kṛṣṇa's love-making were quite capable of speaking directly about the soul and God, had they wished to do so. Thus there must be something here which is irreducible to anything else: the sensuousness of this poetry remains an essential ingredient of the religious reality conveyed by it.

A second example will illustrate this with even greater force. At the same time, it allows us to draw together a number of other features that we have met in the course of the previous pages. When we hear in one Indian theology that the goddess Lakṣmī, beloved of god Viṣṇu, is the '*puruṣakāra*' of all grace to mankind, a translation of the Sanskrit word as 'mediator' seems to settle the issue. But it is a strange word, for which the dictionaries offer as a literal meaning something like 'manly act, heroism', and by extension, 'someone performing a manly act, displaying heroism'. How can the goddess mediating grace be a manly act? As soon as we look at the 'poetry' involved here, the whole begins to make perfect sense. Secular literature on love knows of a particular mode of love-making in which the lover and the beloved exchange roles (naturally in the sense defined by that literature itself). A reversal takes place, to the great enjoyment and satisfaction of both partners. The girl is said to act 'the male part' – as Rādhā did in the last canto of the *Indian Song of Songs* which Arnold left untranslated or as Kālī does when giving life to the '*śava*' (corpse) of Śiva. Somehow this finds resonance in the theological statement just mentioned. Viṣṇu and Lakṣmī relate to mankind in the following way. He represents stern authority and justice which punish the sinner; she on the other hand symbolizes compassion and forgiveness. Given the psychology of the relationship between god and goddess, under normal circumstances the austere justice of Viṣṇu would dominate, and man's fate would be sealed. But within the divine love-life a reversal of roles takes place, Lakṣmī acts as man and gains control, and the outcome is man's salvation. This exegesis (which, I must confess, is my own and for which I am not drawing on Indian originals) has, I hope, made it clear how much 'poetry' (and I am using the word in both senses) can be an essential element even of abstract theology. At the same time, some initial illustration of what a religion of Love can look like has been given.

Let me conclude this introductory chapter by providing a brief map for the following chapters. It was easy enough to employ the conception of the real world as the map of our exploration of the religions of Power. But which route can we devise to lead us through the realms of Love? We might initially be tempted to employ, in similar manner, the map that *akam* poetry has laid out for the interior landscape of love: with its mountains, forests, deserts, coastal and agricultural tracts and their associated amorous situations. With some imagination, one or two of these landscapes could be seen to reflect metaphorically certain types of the religious. But when it comes to the poetry that is set in the agricultural region and deals with the quarrels between husband and wife over his love for a prostitute, it seems wise not to hunt for such external props and to abandon the project.[28] So instead, I shall follow a non-symbolic route.

Having just attempted to defend the necessity of taking 'poetry' seriously, it seems obvious to start here with the analysis of traditions of Indian love poetry. Then it seems fair to listen in greater detail to what the representatives of ascetic religion have to say about the subject and what analysis of love they put forward. Since they do not, as I have tried to indicate above, exhaust the subject, we can turn to such interpretations of love which perceive a transcendental dimension in it, envisage it on a cosmic scale, and give shape to it as God or Goddess. While with us sex, *eros*, *caritas*, *agape*, or *amor Dei* are like stages of a rocket, each being cast off as the rocket moves higher up, the Indian journey towards transcendence carries everything loyally along! Up to this point we appear to be repeating the movement of Part one, from the most ephemeral and narrow to the most transcendental and universal. However, there is also a counter-movement to be explored: the divine taking on physical form on earth, thereby challenging man and asking for a life that is totally structured in accordance with the divine demands. And finally we have to address ourselves to a question stated earlier: the man who plunges himself into the world of the senses and lets himself be carried off by its pulse to freedom – how does he relate to the *yogī* whose whole spiritual career builds up on the rejection of such a plunge? To what extent can compassion modify the ascetic ideal? These are complex movements: man's spiritual path from the world of the senses to transcendence, God's descent from heaven down to earth, and man's continued commitment to the world. But let us trace these movements in a leisurely manner, and begin with a fairly romantic walk through the landscape of the heart.

CHAPTER 10

The landscape of the heart

Once upon a time, King Shehriyaar decided to visit his brother in faraway Samarkand. When he had travelled for a few hours, he remembered that he had left something in his palace and returned speedily. To his great shock he surprised his queen dallying with a black slave. He killed both and arrived at his brother's in a state of great depression. But by accident he witnessed there his brother's queen indulging in a far more outrageous orgy, and his happiness was restored. Eventually he confessed to his brother the reason for his changed mood, and in disgust they both rode off – only to meet a demon who had been cuckolded innumerable times by the girl he kept captive. Their spirits revived, they returned to their respective palaces. Shehriyaar made sure that no further humiliation of this kind could happen to him. Every day he married a virgin, spent the night with her, and had her killed the next morning. After a while no virgins were left in the town, and his *wazir* was forced to supply his own daughter, Shehrezaad. She was as clever as she was chaste and beautiful. And so she began to tell a story which daybreak interrupted; since the king was eager to hear the end of it, he spared her for one day. Naturally, a second story followed during the second night, to be similarly interrupted. With the threat of execution hanging over her, she kept on telling stories, spreading out the whole gamut of human adventures and relationships before the king; and after *One Thousand and One Nights*, he had become so attached to her that he spared her life, having learnt something about the complexities of the human heart.[1]

The threat of gruesome death also gave rise to another collection of stories. In AD 1348 the Black Death was decimating the populace of Florence in Italy.

In the early spring of that year, the plague began, in a terrifying and extraordinary manner, to make its disastrous effects apparent. It did not take the form it had assumed in the East, where if anyone bled from the nose it was an obvious portent of death. On the contrary, its earliest symptom, in men and women alike, was the appearance of certain swellings in the groin or the armpit, some of which were egg-shaped whilst others were roughly the size of the common apple.[2]

One day, when people were dying around them by the thousands, seven women were praying in church; then the most spirited among them suggested that they move out into the countryside, in an attempt to save their lives. When three dashing men turned up, the party was complete, and off they went to a pleasant country estate. And while the danger of the plague was lurking on all sides, they told each other stories in which the mysteries of the human heart were revealed, for *Ten Days*. This is the frame for Giovanni Boccaccio's *Decameron*. Not all these mysteries were to his readers' liking (just as in the book itself there is a lot of blushing and giggling going on), and thus in the *Author's Epilogue* he comments: 'Like all other things in this world, stories, whatever their nature, may be harmful or useful, depending on the listener.'[3]

Both books have been with us for quite a while. In harmless retellings, many a story of the *Arabian Nights* has been a favourite since our childhood (like 'Ali Baba and the forty thieves'). Others, like most of the *Decameron*, we have carried with us with great unease – the first complete translation of the *Decameron* in English was as recent as 1972.[4] It seems to require a liminal situation, such as the threat of death (and the pilgrimage of the *Canterbury Tales* could be included here, since pilgrimage is another form of the liminal situation) to bring out those aspects of our hearts which normally we prefer to keep hidden under the cloak of 'public propriety'. In matters of love and passion, only powerful external forces seem to produce honesty.

Naturally I have another reason for referring to the stories that were collected during a thousand and one nights and over ten days: many of these have been shown to come from India. The East had more to offer than just the plague! Already the frame-story of the *Nights* reveals itself as the synthesis of three Indian stories.[5] It would thus appear that in India we do not require a situation of liminality for these depths of the heart to be explored. Here we find a culturally accepted and shared mode of exploring the ramifications of love and passion in a manner rather alien to us. I don't want to romanticize the issue straight away, but it is interesting to note that classical Indian culture and religion define as respectable an area of talk about love that would surprise the unforewarned Western reader. I do mean surprise here, and not shock. The faint-hearted may rest assured that I shall obey, in what follows, the rules of propriety the Indians themselves valued very highly. Anyway, however tenuous the links may seem, European literature has been connected to the erotic literature of India, without knowing it. So it is time to turn to the Indian material and gather some impressions of what has been going on there. Although not immediately obvious, the selection of facets will be governed by their relevance to the Indian religions.

Of fundamental importance to our exploration of how the Indians listened to the pulse in their heart and in the natural environment surrounding them are two traditions of love poetry. Possibly not unconnected, we find one such tradition emerging sometime close to the transition from BC to AD in the central regions of India, south of the Vindhya mountains (today Maharashtra and Andhra Pradesh). Culturally this was frontier country during that period, which allowed for the cultivation of a novel type of sensitivity. It is significant that a formalized vernacular (a Prakrit dialect), and not the hieratic Sanskrit language, is used as the medium of expression. This poetry appears in the form of couplets that are very short, with no more than thirty or so syllables, and the idea is clearly to compress as much suggestiveness as possible into these tiny pen-pictures. The same King Hāla, whom we followed into the underworld and saw fighting with *rākṣasas*,[6] is associated with the compilation of an anthology, supposedly consisting of seven hundred stanzas and thus logically called the *Sattasaī* (*Seven Hundred*). There are a number of problems connected with the nature and history of this text into which I need not enter here. There are about a thousand poems extant in various recensions, many of them expressing the spirit of a later and different age.[7]

The second, roughly contemporary poetic tradition is that of *akam* poetry of the extreme south in the Tamil language, which has been mentioned previously. More than two thousand poems have been handed down to us, in various anthologies; the smallest poems have only four or five lines, but the longer ones can be quite complex edifices of a hundred or more lines. In each, a considerable amount of space is given to descriptions of nature with which love is intimately connected. The full Tamil name for these love poems is *akattiṇai*, which means 'realm of the inside' or the 'landscape of the heart'.[8]

Both these traditions had a far-reaching and varied influence on the Indian imagination during the following centuries. The *akattiṇai* structured Tamil literature for a long time after the flourishing period of the *caṅkam*. But far more important for our purposes is the fact that when, some centuries later (say around AD 600), the Tamils developed a devotional poetry, *akam* provided the source of inspiration, and this poetry was then spread all over India.

Hāla's poetry was soon taken up, in somewhat expanded form, by the Sanskrit literati who cultivated the *kāvya* genre. Some poets stand out in this very large corpus through their individuality; Amaru, Bhartṛhari, Dharmakīrti and Govardhana may be mentioned here, since their names will reappear at later stages. Thousands of 'well-spoken stanzas' (*subhāṣitas*) were produced, which many anthologies have preserved for us. Alongside developed increasingly complex and detailed poetics. It is from here that another type of religious poetry derived its form and inspiration.

Incidentally, India developed many further such poetic traditions, in different vernacular languages. Thus, for example, in Maharashtra we find the *lāvṇī*, a highly rustic and erotic genre dating from the sixteenth century onwards, which, in its own way, combined the religious with matters of love. These *lāvṇyā* were sung by dancing girls and served to entertain, and arouse new vigour in, the brave Maratha soldiers after their return from the battlefield, where they had been fighting first the Muslims and then the British.

The story dealing with love and the passions has certainly been a most productive genre in India, but cannot easily be summed up through specific names or through particular traditions. India never quite managed to make the transition from one medium, oral narration of a story, to attractive literary prose. More than anybody else, the Jains have preserved for us a vast store of such stories, used by them for didactic purposes. It is in that connection that I shall return to these stories. However, one collection cannot be passed over in even the shortest survey of Indian love stories: the *Seventy Tales of the Parrot* (*Śukasaptati*). This work has its own history, not only in India through its many vernacular adaptations, but also as it travelled further west. To students of Persian it is known under the name of *Ṭūṭī-nāmah*, the *Book of the Parrot*. It is presented to us as a moral tale (to be dealt with in that context) about a clever parrot who prevented a wife from committing adultery during the seventy nights her husband was away on some business.

The poetry just mentioned is closely related to these love stories; in some cases, Hāla's pithy stanzas offer us in a nutshell an episode treated at much greater length in the *Tales of the Parrot*, like the girl who pretended to be bitten by a scorpion in order to have a chance to be with her lover, the local doctor.[9]

Finally, in my account of the primary sources at our disposal on the Indian imagination concerning love must be mentioned the most boring of all the world's notorious books, the *Kāmasūtras* (and other works in the same genre of scholastic treatises on love-making). Poetry and story are highly imaginative, original and often full of charming realistic touches; the present genre is armchair advice and sets quite unrealistic norms. What is, however, interesting here is that, as has been convincingly shown,[10] the actual model for the *Kāmasūtras* was not the world of love, but that of power – the handbook on ruthless Machiavellian statescraft called *Arthaśāstra* (attributed to Kauṭilya, both by name and legend one of the shrewdest and most crooked politologists of ancient India). If you have problems with such a statement – a treatise on love-making modelling itself on Machiavellian politics – you may compare what is said in the former on the art of seducing other men's wives with what the latter teaches on how to undermine a rival king's authority and how to conquer his country! But whether boring or not, ruthless or wise, the *Kāmasūtras* (and similar treatises) belonged to the standard syllabus of a budding poet or writer and thus influenced the way in which he expressed himself on the topic of love. This is what I am fundamentally talking about: concrete culturally evolved and accepted modes of talking about love, eros and human sexuality. Let us now look at some of the details.

Akam poetry is structured according to five types of landscape, and it is the mountains to which the anthologies normally take us first. Imagine a millet field guarded by a few young girls against the voracious appetite of parrots. Suddenly a young hunter turns up, looks at the girls (and one in particular), and is pierced at first sight by the arrow of love. He strikes up a conversation with them: Have they seen an elephant passing by? or, Are they really human beings and not damsels from a supernatural realm? Sooner or later, our hunter has a chance to meet his love privately in the bushes, and the waterfalls symbolize the impetuosity of young love.

Now it may happen that the secret meetings have to be stopped because the lover has to be away for a while, the chances of being detected at night in the girl's house are too great, or the girl is simply getting fed up with waiting for him to propose. Whatever the reason, she falls ill, or better, shows all the symptoms of illness.[11] She becomes emaciated, her bangles are now too wide for her thin wrists and fall off, and her healthy black complexion turns a sickly golden-yellow. Her people are getting worried and decide to organize a dance of possession during which the priest, in a state of trance, can reveal what kind of demon has occupied the girl and what remedy should be used against it. Now her heart fills with fear that the priest will discover the true reason: that her illness is that of love. Among all the different solutions that the poems may come up with, none is more original than the following. While the women are still busy with their chanting – their throats getting sore and their tongues suffering fatigue – and while the priest is sweating and doing wild things in his state of possession, the girl's lover actually arrives, sneaks into her room like a young tiger and gives her the only medicine that can cure her. 'I laughed, until my sides split!' the poetess tells us, recollecting the incident.[12]

In these poems, the natural environment is seen as parallel to the human. Not only do the mountains and everything associated with them symbolize the basic amorous situation of premarital love between young people, but individual features (like the waterfall in my example) are also employed by the poets to add specific details, of characterization, psychology, or incidents. But of greater interest is the perception of man's natural environment implied in this poetry. Being homologous to man, it ceases to be threatening and dangerous. Where the timid ritualistic religion we studied in Part one would try to defend, placate and sacrifice substitutes, our poetry can laugh at it all. Love tells the girl what is wrong with her, and with her lover she finds the cure which no rituals could ever produce.

From the mountains we descend into the realm of the forests where cowherds graze their cattle and where the white jasmine is in flower. The poetic 'hero' and 'heroine' are now apart: a military campaign may have taken him to some distant country, or the need to make money has forced their temporary separation. It is now their memories of each other and their longing for reunion that fills the poems. The playing of the flute by a herdsman, or the tinkling of the bell around a bull's neck, suggestive of the beast's mating with a cow – such features turn the wife's waiting into agony. When the first signs of the rainy season are written on to the sky by the dark clouds, the tension reaches its climax. For all travellers are expected to return before the onset of the rains. And indeed many a poem takes us to the man, frantically shouting at his charioteer to hurry up and get him home as soon as possible. When we move to the region along the coast, things are not so simple any more. Just as the vicious shark, caught in the net of the fishermen, struggles, bites and more often than not succeeds in tearing the net and in escaping, a lover does not always remain faithful. Now it is the agony of the girl hoping for the return of her lover that we hear about. The passions, as they burst forth from her heart, take on a note of despair, and this despair turns to venomous anger, when they actually meet and quarrel.

Then we have the agricultural region, the quasi-urban environment. Man finds himself here at a crossroad: one path leading to his loyal wife, and the other to the quarter of the prostitutes. It may be that it is the latter which leads him to true love and fulfilment. But our poems also let the wife win or, sometimes at least, carry off the palm of victory in the match of insults she heaps upon her husband's mistress ('you horse that many a man has ridden!'[13] and other such pleasantries). The fifth landscape is that of the desert, the least well defined and specific. The harsher side of reality catches up here with even the most romantic lover, as he painfully walks past dried-up trees with vultures perched on their dead branches and past the skeletons of oxen from long-lost caravans. What seemed an easy option to a young couple, when their relations did not consent to their marriage – to elope together to some distant place – the merciless sun is now literally turning into a crucible of their love.

This is a sketch, drawn with a few and often random brush-strokes, of the landscape of love, as *akam* poetry has designed it. The range is actually wider, and I shall return to it further on; but for the time being we can restrict ourselves to the five regions which are envisaged as 'normal' and as representing the way a respectable member of society expresses love. Many facets found here strike me as very 'modern'. I am thinking not so much of the carefree manner of accepting physical love between youngsters (if that can be called modern). What is worth noting, above all, is the degree of honesty revealed by the range of psychological situations and of impulses lurking in the human soul, of how much is accepted as being the normal course of events in matters of human love. But it is time now to say a few words about Hāla and his kind of poetry.

In the *Seven Hundred* we do not find a system or formal structure comparable to the five regions and, except for late poems in which the categories of Sanskrit poetics are expressly stated, the reader himself has to reconstruct the context in which a stanza is placed. This makes it rather more difficult to decide, for instance, whether a quarrel is taking place between young, innocent lovers, husband and wife, or prostitute and customer. But there is enough evidence to suggest that all three possibilities are explored in Hāla's corpus, and thus we can state that the range of situations, external and psychological, is very similar indeed to that of *akam* poetry. The world upon which the poetry reflects and from which it derives its raw material is also similar. On the one hand, it is still in close touch with rural life, but on the other hand, we are obviously not dealing with 'peasant poetry'. Just as 'ploughman' is unlikely to be a king's name, the real ploughman is unlikely to have produced poems of the kind found in Hāla's *Seven Hundred*. For both *akam* and Hāla we must assume a more urbanized élite which could encompass in their poems both their own environment and that of their more rural and rustic neighbours. That he dealt with 'rustic' subjects in a non-rustic manner has been Hāla's praise in later Indian literary criticism.[14] While we cannot detect traces of a correlation between types of landscape and of love in Hāla, the natural environment in general is very important in the poems. Particular species of tree and bush may acquire a suggestive symbolism by virtue of the fact that their long drooping branches make an ideal tryst for lovers; species of flowers suggest different kinds of girls (thus the *ketakī*, apparently very fragrant but covered in thorns, symbolizes a beautiful but prickly girl). Descriptions of love-making are as delicately put as in *akam*, and as frequently found as there. Poems on *viraha*, the agonies of lovers separated, are quite numerous, but of all situations, that of quarrel, disagreement, unfaithfulness, and sulking is by far the most common. Greater emphasis is given to the sort of things that make Indian love-poetry initially so inaccessible to us. I shall deal with them at a later stage. Let me first extricate from this general picture I have given of *akam* and the *Sattasaī* some points relevant to our exploration.

One of the first things the uninitiated reader of this poetry will notice is the unexpectedly large number of descriptions of nature found in it. The functional reason for this has already been mentioned earlier. But, naturally, a particular view of the world provides the background for this formal poetic function. The careful and meticulous study of nature, which alone could yield the differentiated and minute correlation between it and the human heart, derives from an interest in, and an affinity with, the natural environment. Stanzas from Hāla illustrate such an affinity in a more obvious manner. We hear a lot about animals such as monkeys, elephants, and deer. Though greedy to eat it, a monkey does not dare to touch a fruit of the rose-apple tree: it reminds him of a bee that once stung him.[15] A captive elephant loses his appetite even for juicy stalks of the lotus, because he remembers his beloved in the forest,[16] and, 'fettered by love', an elephant cow runs frantically around a pool, stretching out her trunk to help the male to extricate himself from the quagmire into which he is sinking.[17] Struck by a hunter's arrow, a female deer twists her body in the pangs of death to cast a last glance at her mate.[18] These and many similar poems make it clear that our poets impose human emotions on certain animals of their natural environment; love is perceived as a continuum that stretches beyond man into the world of beasts. Before evaluating this further, it is wise to strengthen our case by looking at a second poetic approach to reality via love. We have a fairly good idea of those people whom both *akam* and Hāla regarded as respectable. From the fact that other social groups are expressly named and treated as sources of amusement, we can infer that 'respectable people' are not included among them. Thus groups like cow- and goatherds, milkmaids and deformed people belong to the realm of the vulgar in terms of *akam*,[19] and in the eyes of Hāla's poets, 'vulgar' people include peasants, hunters living in the forest, wrestlers and tribesmen. Yet they are shown to behave, in matters of love, just like respectable people, capable of both deep passion and loftier feelings such as sadness at the death of a beloved. A number of *akam* poems tell us about the love-life of the cowherds out in the forests. Girls are apparently offered by their fathers as brides to the winners in bull-baiting contests. Yet the poems are at pains to point out that an individual winner has actually had a relationship with the respective girl long before the contest. And I cannot refrain from mentioning another poem in which a hunchback and a dwarf are pondering on how to make love.[20] There is certainly humour here, but also an honest sympathy.

That such an attitude to low- and outcaste people is not commonplace becomes clear if we look at the way later medieval literature has viewed the tribesmen living in the jungles. There they are depicted as savages, bloodthirsty and cruel, practising abominable religious cults and living like animals. Naturally the Jains reserve rebirth among them for more severe infringements of the ethical code. A new age, with a new culture and isolationist view of society reveals itself here. Thinking in terms of 'castes' and of transmigration has replaced the far wider, all-inclusive and empathetic perception of *akam* or Hāla. I think it needs no special pleading to see in this awareness of a wider social context the causal factors behind the emergence of this kind of poetry, in which a close attention to reality mingles with a sophisticated form and psychology. Incidentally I may mention here that such a fertile constellation occurred again, towards the close of the twelfth century AD in rural Bengal. Far from merely imitating Hāla in Sanskrit, the poet Govardhana succeeded in creating a unique type of poetry on the basis of the same two ingredients: a sharp eye for what goes on in ordinary, rural life and a complex, sophisticated artistic form.

I pointed out, when initially discussing *saṃsāra* and rebirth, that the belief in transmigration carried an important implication: the acceptance of the 'animal side' in all of us.[21] Thus the question could be asked whether what I have said here about the poetic entrance into the realms of the animals and inferior social groups has anything to do with this. Historically, I think they are totally unrelated and, in terms of content, are the exact opposites of each other. What Hāla and *akam* suggest is that all aspects of love between the poles of physical desire and deep attachment elevate the beasts and the people at the fringes of society to an almost human or almost respectable level. *Kāma* is seen as a universal phenomenon that pervades all forms of life and as a 'civilizing' influence. But what about the violence that lurks in all of us and can drag us down to the level of the animal? This is an important question I shall take up presently.

But first there is another point to explore. If love is something that pervades the realm of living beings, how far can this realm be extended, and where are its boundaries? On this point again Hāla and *akam* show remarkably similar attitudes. In Hāla we find three poems, inconspicuously mingling with hundreds of others of similar content, in which the proper name Kṛṣṇa appears.[22] Other contemporary sources make it clear to us that we are dealing here with a figure who later turned into one of the most important God-figures of Hinduism. What is worth keeping in mind for the moment is the extent to which this god mingles totally unobtrusively with the other rustic lovers in Hāla's anthology. Let me illustrate this with one example.

> 'Kṛṣṇa! When you remove
> with the breath of your mouth
> a particle of dust from Rādhikā's eye,
> you blow away at the same time
> the pride of those other milkmaids!'[23]

Rādhikā or Rādhā was Kṛṣṇa's favourite among the milkmaids, and the special attention he paid to her ruined the other girls' hopes of winning his love.

Turning now to *akam*, traditional poetics tells us that each of the five landscapes can also be alluded to by means of the name of a god. But when looking at genuinely old examples, it turns out that only two such gods really figure in the poems: Murukaṉ and Māyōṉ. The first abides in the mountains and is thus associated with unencumbered and youthful love-making, as we saw above. Logically, a later poem tells us about a couple, long after marriage and in a state of profound disharmony, who make a pilgrimage to one of the major shrines of Murukaṉ and pray to him for the restoration of their earlier harmonious bliss.[24] Māyōṉ is linked with the forests, the jasmine and the waiting of a wife for the return of her husband. Now what is said about Māyōṉ reveals that his identity is that of the Kṛṣṇa just mentioned. In fact both names mean the same thing, 'a man of black complexion'. I shall have to show in a later chapter how Māyōṉ, like Murukaṉ, can be perceived to grant what he symbolizes in terms of *akam* conventions. For the present it will suffice to note how the episodes told about the girls of the cowherds who long for his presence, fit neatly into the landscape envisaged. This now means that when we try to delineate the region encompassed by love, according to Hāla and the ancient Tamil poets, we must include the realms of at least two god-figures, Murukaṉ and Māyōṉ/Kṛṣṇa. Not only is it important to find such figures in the landscape of the heart; of equal importance are the particular emotive associations, such as the connection of 'love in separation' with Māyōṉ/Kṛṣṇa. In the *lāvṇyā* of Maharashtra, incidentally, it is in Kṛṣṇa's naughty flirtations with the milkmaids that the rather down-to-earth erotic adventures of dancing girls can extend themselves into myth and religion.

After all this talk about 'love' in poetry, I am sure that, in the minds of many, something like the following question has arisen: what is the relationship between this poetry and real life, between how people act in the imagination of the poets and in the confines of society? However important such a question would be in the context of a literary critique of Indian poetry, here is not the place to answer it fully and in detail. Yet, in view of the fact that the poetic conception of the landscape of the heart was transposed on to the realm of the divine and from there radiated back into human life – the real life of devotion – consideration must be given here to this nexus. For the early material in Hāla and in the Tamil anthologies, we have to face the following methodological difficulties. Since all we know about those societies is told to us by the poems themselves, we have no immediate means of telling the difference between the real and the imagined. For the later period, when the Sanskrit *kāvya* has been developed, things are somewhat clearer. I shall try to explore the situation by ignoring here such differences in the nature of our sources and shall present a very generalized picture. It should be clear from the outset that we cannot expect poetry to mirror society. And when I have spoken about 'honesty', I meant this in relation to potentials of the human heart and their poetic – which is public – expression and exploration.

Let me begin with fairly straightforward cases, that is, where the poetry expressly deals with antinomian behaviour. I mentioned earlier that the five segments of the *akattiṇai* are regarded as delimiting the range of normal, respectable human expressions of love. But *caṅkam* literature is more honest, for it acknowledges the existence of two further landscapes, while disapproving of them. The first (called *kaikkiḷai*) may involve an adult man falling passionately in love with a girl who, at closer inspection, turns out to be far too young for this kind of approach. Half-jokingly he tells her off for flaunting herself provocatively.[25] More important is the other genre, significantly called 'the landscape of excess' (*perun-tiṇai*). Here the passions have grown so strong and love so unbearable, that social propriety and decorum are abandoned. In the case of a girl it means that, instead of waiting passively for her man, she decides to go actively out and search for him. A rather remarkable feature can be detected here: some of the outspoken poems of this kind were actually composed by real women.[26] The man who finds himself in this situation indulges in a formalized act of public blood-letting, and complains about his love's, or her relatives', cruelty in not granting fulfilment to his desires.[27] In Hāla, and then in innumerable Sanskrit poems and stories, we have the figure of the 'unfaithful' or 'wanton woman' (*asatī*). Boccaccio took in many of these stories, to the considerable consternation of the respectable ladies listening to them. In some cases, he could not ascribe such break of decorum to a Christian heroine, and a Muslim princess has to stand in for her.[28] The *asatī* rejects the constraints that society imposes on love by trying to enforce unmitigated fidelity on the woman. A vast amount of interest is shown by our poets and writers in the subject, in the subtleties of suggesting a secret rendezvous, in the shrewd avoidance of threatening disaster, and in the power-games the detection of such secrets can give rise to in an extended family. Humour is an intrinsic ingredient in all this. At least poetically, woman appears here in a most emancipated manner, and the poets love it!

There are two points we can extract from all this. Poetry can imaginatively and emotively explore subjects and situations it regards, by its own confession, antinomian in real life. Secondly, it thereby offers, if only by substitution and mere representation, the realization of personal freedom over and above the constraints of real life. It requires an avant-garde poet to write poetry about commuting, being a secretary and typing away at the word-processor, being an insurance broker, a machine-operator in a factory or, for that matter, writing a book. The nitty-gritty of ordinary life does not have the power to impel the imagination and fly out in search of personal freedom and fulfilment. Precisely because social constraints cause the ennui of everyday life, the potentially antinomian, if only imagined in poetry, can symbolize that freedom. If we accept this interpretation, it will not surprise us when we find theistic mystics infusing their devotion with precisely these poetic types of antinomianism and freedom, particularly as envisaged through the *asatī*. Similarly unsurprising is the resistance of neo-Victorianism with its hard-work ethics to poetry.

The time has come to turn to what some might regard as the less savoury aspects of Indian love-poetry. A famous quote has it that Indians cannot make love without scratching and biting.[29] The *Kāma-sūtras* in their typically clinical manner (no pun intended) provide us with the details of where and how and when. They also tell us about a king who used some kind of scissors for the purpose and thereby 'accidentally' reduced the number of his queens by one.[30] An element of violence and male aggression seems to emerge here which, together with the profuse sweating and the standing on end of the body-hairs as the symptoms of physical arousal, make up the nightmare repertoire of anybody trying to translate Sanskrit love-poetry. It is necessary to understand various other things in this connection. The girl seems to regard the marks of his nails and the wounds inflicted by his teeth with an inordinate amount of affection and pride. When the mother of a newly-wed girl infers from certain gestures of her daughter the presence of such sweet traces, she is, equally inordinately by our standards, elated: things are fine between them![31] We have to be careful with all this; let us remind ourselves of what has been said already about poetry in relation to reality. Moreover, let us accept this further aspect of the Indian male poet's honesty, that he does not cover up in his imaginings that element of violence which is contained in love-making. But something else must serve us here as a further qualifying factor. When we listen long enough to the voices of males dreaming about matters of love, as they become audible in these poems, a very different aspect emerges. Were I asked to identify that area in the male dream most intensely desired by our poets, I would have no hesitation to refer to what the scholastics call *puruṣāyita*. I have referred to it in previous pages;[32] in ordinary English we could call it the reversed missionary position. The psychology that expresses itself here is one of relished role-reversal, the girl losing her inhibitions and offering the man a side of her soul that was covered up till then through social conventions. It is an act of trust and self-revelation, and cherished as an expression of true love. In other words, psychologically a male dream emerges here which tries to transcend precisely the aggression associated conventionally with man, by becoming submissive to the woman. In that connection ought to be mentioned a related theme, that of pacification. Conventionally, men are not only unfaithful, but also so stupid as to leave detectable traces of their misdemeanour. In these poems this is not our famous blonde hair on the suit or lipstick on the collar of his shirt, but the remnants of the other woman's saffron powder, or her name uttered by mistake. Often all hell's fury breaks loose, if we can believe the poems, and the man is expected to fall at his wife's feet, touching them with his head, and it may well get him a few kicks in the process. Given the very great amount of poems about this situation, it is clearly something our poets felt attracted to exploring in their imagination. Whether Govardhana speaks with any more general authority, when he claims that a man has come to know the full pleasure of love only when he has been kicked on the head and beaten by his enraged mistress,[33] is a different matter which I shall not discuss here. What I shall look at in the following chapters, when we make our inroad into the landscape of the gods, is how even such aspects as those mentioned just now have their immediate and very specific religious relevance.

The overall question as to the relationship between this poetry and real life is still with us. What happened to Hāla's conception of a world pervaded by love? Sanskrit poets picked it up and developed it further, at least in terms of formal sophistication. In terms of content, we witness a reduction in the themes treated, an increasingly high degree of stereotyped descriptions, and a steady move away from any recognizable natural environment. Woven into these trends is the work of the scholastics, classifying and categorizing with meticulous tedium. The landscape of the heart expressed here has turned into a pure dream-world. Jealousy among co-wives, passionate desire for a young girl in a often-married man, dealings with expensive courtesans, emancipated girls hurrying through dark woods to meet their lovers – where in real life could this be found, except among the wealthiest and in the harems of the courts? From the point of view of most of the poets and their audiences, these were stereotyped dreams and possessed only the most tenuous links with reality. My point here is not to detract from the attraction of this poetry in its own right, but to emphasize that we need have no doubt that the Indian reader was aware of the dream quality of this literature. It is very unlikely that the average male who had enough Sanskrit to read it would dream of moulding his life according to the rules that governed the interactions of the poetic lovers. Thus we are back to my earlier point: Indian literature about love is primarily the exploration of the landscapes of the heart, which means it is psychological and aesthetic. But precisely because of this, it acts as an alternative mode of envisaging the world in which man lives. The interest shown in the antinomian behaviour of poetic 'heroes' highlights this function further: the dreams make free. On the other hand, it must not be ignored that from such an imaginative exploration of the powers of the heart a feedback on the interaction of real people, say an ordinary husband and wife, must have occurred.

A further point can be made here. Given that the medieval Indians saw the actors in the landscape of the heart – as formulated in the literature of love – not as somewhat idealized and rarefied versions of themselves, but as autonomous beings whose ontological status was purely psychological and aesthetic, it became possible for them to expand this inner geography. So far we noticed such an expansion in the cases of Māyōṉ/Kṛṣṇa and Murukaṉ – both rustic gods, easily accommodated in the world of the *akattiṇai* and of Hāla. But with the transformation of Hāla's poetry into that of Sanskrit court *kāvya*, it became possible to encompass gods and goddesses in their heavenly palaces and courts. Myth could now be envisaged as a comparable landscape of the imagination, and its actors could be depicted in terms of the lovers of poetry. This is precisely what happened in India, and this is the reason why the study of seemingly non-religious subjects like love-poetry is essential for an understanding of Indian theism.

Now there are two ways of looking at this approximation of myth to poetry. On the one hand, divine action becomes comprehensible to the human heart, because it is structured according to the laws of poetic action with which man is familiar. Moreover, the honesty implied in the imaginative exploration of the heart acquires divine, religious archetypes. The inner freedom that is gained through the move into the alternative world of the imagination is given an ontologically real dimension, in myth. But there is another way of looking at this. A considerable amount of self-critical humour pervades the poetry of love, a humour that breaks through the tedious stereotyping of later heroes and heroines. Any projection of this on to the realm of myth would necessarily reduce the status of the gods, by turning them into figures of amusement. Thus when it is said in a poem[34] that Śiva, lying at the feet of Pārvatī to pacify her, receiving many a kick from her, is busy holding on to the moon and the river Ganges that customarily rest on his head, to prevent them from tumbling down due to the commotion caused to his head by her kicking feet – when we hear all this, we cannot doubt that in this case Śiva enjoys an extremely low religious status. Now this may well be the intention of the poet himself and he may well be using it for some other serious religious purposes. It is a topic to which we have to return at a later stage when discussing the difference between a *deva* and God.

Let us step back now and cast a final glance over the material discussed in the present chapter. I have, time and again, used words like 'honesty' and 'freedom' to characterize basic qualities in the landscape of the heart – in the way that India has analysed and imaginatively explored love and sexuality. To avoid any misunderstandings here, let me emphasize that I am not talking directly about society, real people and their attitudes, but about a culturally developed type of discourse. That may reduce the value of this kind of honesty and freedom somewhat but, at least to the extent that the imagination is culturally shared and socially acceptable, we are dealing here with more than a private fantasy world. A further reduction in its value may be seen in the fact that very few female voices can be identified in this discourse. Women appear prominently as one of its topics, as items in the imaginary landscape of the heart. Yet a careful study of *akam* poetry (where the names of the authors are known and poetesses can therefore be identified) will, I am convinced, unearth far more female reflection on love and sexuality than has been done so far.[35] Finally, we have practically no biographical information on most of the poets whose poetry has been mentioned. Much of the poetry is anonymous anyway, and most of what is told about famous poets in much later texts is pure myth and legend. It is only when we can look at the religious usage of this material and encounter forms of devotional 'autobiographies' that individual personalities come into sharper focus.

Now what precisely is it that makes this poetry 'honest' and provides it with a 'modern' flavour, in spite of the limitations mentioned just now? For example, we could speak of an honesty of range – the range of man–woman relationships reflected upon. Not only does our poetry explore the sensuous attractions of a young girl or the appeal of a handsome man, or present us with a love of a couple that integrates sexuality (to the extent of describing the various 'positions' they may use), romantic emotions, and a curiosity about the partner's deeper feelings – it also acknowledges the instability of affection, unfaithfulness, and major frictions and disagreements, and it is prepared to consider the pros and cons of visits to brothels, of more permanent liaisons with courtesans (who may be highly educated and cultured ladies) and of polygamy. It allows for rebellious female voices to be heard. If we recollect that until quite recently the typical Hollywood film avoided just about every facet listed here, except for idealized romanticism, or if we remind ourselves when it was that the earnestness of a D. H. Lawrence, the introspection of a James Joyce and the exuberance of a Henry Miller (to name a random sample here) introduced an element of honesty into all this, we may appreciate better the achievements of this poetry of nearly two thousand years ago.

We could also refer to an honesty of time-scale that prefers to take a long-term view instead of pretending, for a very limited period, that everything is wonderful. In fact, India has been blamed for not having produced any true love-story. The romantic image of total, ultimate love implied in this typically non-Indian critique may often be connected with a morbid fascination for death: look at Romeo and Juliet, or the box-office hit called *Love Story*. This links us with the Muslim world, where most of the famous love stories (like Laila and Majnun) end with the tragic death of the lovers. And let us recollect the theme of death at the very beginning of this chapter which surrounded (and made possible?) the telling of rather erotic love stories. But why do we need death as a kind of *Deus ex machina*? What would have happened to Romeo and Juliet's ultimate love after twenty years of marriage? The long-term view of *akam* poetry spreads out a range of possibilities that have been mentioned above under the heading of honesty of range! Alternatively, if it is not death that limits the time-scale, there is the other type of Hollywood romance. Not only is this once again purified stuff, with all traces of man's physical being removed, but it also cunningly stops when the 'happy ever after' begins. Thus it is honesty not just about oneself, about the drives lurking in one's soul, but also about the course that most people's lives take.

But this honesty implies freedom. In its most concrete form such freedom occurs in relation to what we would call the repression of certain basic human facets and the frustration caused by an irreconcilable contrast between socially enforced or encouraged stereotypes and the actual variety of human potentials. But in our context a different aspect of this freedom is central: since the honesty of love encompasses even the gods, we can anticipate that some forms of religion enhance, not repress, the freedom experienced in love.

What I have been trying to offer in the present chapter is an introduction into an unfamiliar world. An introduction is like the first pages in a language course, a drill necessary to obtain mastery of the language. Much of what I have said may have appeared a self-fulfilling exercise that seems to be spreading out interesting and amusing features of no further value in the perusal of Indian religions. Let me assure you that this is not the case. Everything said here will reveal itself as essential for the comprehension of theistic India. The pointers I have set up in that direction will, I hope, have given some indication of it. It is, however, not yet possible for us to make this move into the realm of theism. In the poetic anthologies and other traditions, further aspects of the analysis of love can be found. So I shall have to turn from the rather carefree landscape of the heart investigated so far to much more troublesome items: the deadly weapons of Māra.

CHAPTER 11

The deadly weapons of Māra

Murders in the meadow

Shortly before dying, the daughter of a local landlord confessed to an extraordinary tale of crimes. She had been found by neighbours, lying in a state of shock, between the corpses of her own mother and brother. She was still holding the blood-smeared iron pestle in her hands which apparently caused the death of both. Fingerprints however showed that the mother had initially beaten the boy to death with it. Then the woman and the girl struggled, and the girl, grabbing the weapon, killed her mother. It appears that the son had tried to reprimand his mother about an affair she was openly carrying on with a farm hand. The boy had just slaughtered the latter with an axe, in revenge for his having killed his father some months earlier, at the instigation of his mother. After these sensational revelations, the girl passed away.

Well, you may have guessed that this is not a quote from one of the gutter presses, but a somewhat altered Jain story.[1] It is meant to illustrate what can happen when someone becomes addicted to the pleasures that the sense of touch can offer – which in our example is illustrated by what the farm hand granted to his mistress. This is a far cry from the frequently rather idyllic material we heard about in the previous chapter. There I spoke of honesty and freedom as characteristic of poetry exploring the human heart, and when more violent aspects are touched upon, they tend to be treated in a highly stylized manner. Above all, male aggression is balanced through various forms of imaginatively developed role-reversal. But in this little story we find nothing of the kind. The violence which resulted in a whole string of murders remains unmitigated, and from the world of poetic imagination we are brutally dragged down to 'real life'. At least my rephrasing of the story as a newspaper cutting shows that real events could have been referred to. From an environment pervaded by a love that seems to civilize even the beasts we have once again moved into realms of dangerous threats and destructive forces – the potentially fatal 'beast within ourselves', the powers of sexuality. Love appears to possess chameleon-like qualities, and in the present chapter I would like to trace some of the more sombre among the different shades of colour it can take on. Or in terms of a different imagery we could speak, instead of colours, of a variety of voices that discuss the nature of love. To this discussion both the poet and the storyteller, the learned 'academic' and the ascetic have contributed, and while some opinions expressed remain adamantly opposed to others, we can also detect some readiness for compromise in other opinions. Not all the topics will be new to us, and some of the arguments have been mentioned previously in different contexts. But here the potentially deadly aspects of love will provide the central theme.

A convenient starting-point can be found among the poets who have developed the 'landscape of the heart'. I characterized as 'honest' the two traditions of poetry which were produced by the Tamils in the extreme south of India and which were collected in Hāla's anthology from further north. One of the central areas in which this honesty expresses itself is in the realization that the matters of the heart are extremely fickle and unreliable. And, indeed, such reflections are frequently found, for example, in Hāla.

The course of a love-affair is as crooked as the filaments on a cucumber.[2]

Once a relationship has broken down, to patch it up is as insipid as boiled water that has cooled down.[3]

From not seeing each other, love disappears; from too much seeing each other, it also disappears. Also through the gossip of people it disappears; in fact, it disappears just like that, without any reason.[4]

Love is something that can vanish in a moment, that disappears as soon as it is seen, like a treasure found in a dream.[5]

All this is said in the context of mutual love, at some early stage at least. But that in itself is not the general rule; more often, love is but one-sided, as these two female voices tell us:

'You love her who can't stand you. And though I know this, I can't get rid of my damned love for you.'[6]

'And whatever the mind may paint with the brush of hope on the canvas of the heart, that fate, like a naughty child, secretly wipes off, laughing.'[7]

Thus love is a transient affair even in the best of circumstances, and otherwise causes frustration, unfulfilled desires and disharmony. Like fate itself, it lies outside human control and behaves in a random manner. But to know this is one thing, to act accordingly is quite another. Past experience is no remedy against future mistakes:

'O my heart! Like a piece of wood you drift away with the smallest current, and get stuck in ever so many places. One day they will burn you!'[8]

Love can be like an addiction, and it can be dangerous. 'Love is like a poison that infests the whole body', a girl complains in Hāla,[9] and another one is comforted by a more experienced friend: 'Why do you cry? Love is like a vicious poison that no one is able to block!'[10]

This deadly aspect of love is personified in Māra, 'the killer', which is basically another name for the 'god of love' Kāma. Appropriately, when he appeared before the Buddha to force him into giving up his quest for liberation from suffering, disease, old age and death, not only did he conjure up the most lascivious girls, but also the most terrifying and deadly demonic creatures. In Indian poetry, we find innumerable metaphors and similes involving Māra's deadly weapons. A whole arsenal is piled up here: a girl's glances are his arrows, her eyebrows his bow, and so forth. Usually he wins. In the words of the poet Govardhana:

When Śiva was touching Umā's foot with his head, her leg appeared as the victory column of Kāma who conquers all, including Śiva.[11]

Mythology may tell us that the staunch ascetic Śiva burnt the god of love to ashes. But the passionate attachment he has for Umā makes him accept even this most humiliating of all situations: to lie grovelling at her feet, risking being kicked by them, and begging for forgiveness. This is mighty Kāma's victory! But it is also a symbol of man's slavery, of his imprisonment in the futile pursuits of his addictive passions. But let us move from poetry to poetics.

When the scholastics in their armchairs began to reflect on the course of love, they evolved the following schema. In fact, there are two classes of scholastic, the poeticians (who know about love from poetry) and the eroticians (who know about it from treatises such as the *Kāmasūtras*), and their respective schemata differ somewhat. But there is no need to enter into such fine detail here.[12] The starting point is that a person has been struck by one of Māra's deadly weapons. The longer the desire thus created remains unfulfilled, the further this person will move along the ten stages of 'love in separation'. Initially, there is a fairly innocuous desire to see the beloved person. Then there is a concentration of thinking on the one topic: the mind becomes filled with him/her. Physical symptoms now begin to appear: paleness, erratic behaviour, emaciation. On the sixth rung of the ladder, a general withdrawal of the senses from the outside world sets in; this is followed by a loss of all sense of shame and social propriety. Mental confusion, dissociation and depression arise from this. Now the person is obviously ill. Protracted periods of loss of consciousness set in, and finally, as stage number ten, there is death. Thus, quite literally, the weapons that Kāma has used are deadly. Given that the description of death is a rather inauspicious topic in Indian literature, we don't actually hear much about people dying of love. But we hear a lot about the belief in it, which then in turn usually makes even the most adamant relent. This is due, at least partly, to another belief: to be personally involved in the death of another person will give rise to very bad *karma*. Thus the mention of someone approaching stage ten appears to work wonders and makes the most virtuous woman change her mind and softens the heart of the most obstinate man. So the poems and stories tell us. But from the same kind of sources it follows that we are dealing with a vicious circle: love is transient and fickle, and the heart is ever prone to be hit by new arrows: it starts all over again.

How can this vicious circle be broken? How can man gain victory over Kāma and his deadly arrows, how can he find a firm ground in the transience of his emotions, and prevent the addiction that love produces? The various ascetic traditions of India, Jainism, Buddhism and Hindu teaching on *vairāgya* (passionlessness) have a lot to say about this and, in fact, developed a highly technical discourse in the process. But let me begin this topic with two stories. To illustrate the drifting of the heart on the currents of the passions and the degree of addiction possible, regardless of the price that has to be paid, the Jains have a famous, and rather extreme, story.

Once there was a beautiful queen who had a lover. The king's absences, when fighting mighty wars, allowed them to meet and dally in the palace. But one day the king returned unexpectedly and the lover had nowhere to hide – except for jumping into the privy. Yet even when he had spent many a day submerged there in the foul liquid, his passion for the queen remained unabated – so that at the very next opportunity he returned to the same palace, taking the same chances.[13]

The other story focuses in similarly drastic manner, on the object of desire.

Once upon a time, in the town of Benares, lived a royal priest who had a beautiful daughter; her father was extremely fond of her. When she reached womanhood, it was as if fate had created a Mārī [a murderous *devī*, a kind of female version of Māra] for the crowds of young men. Now the priest was very pious, and had constructed a special hostel for religious mendicants whom he offered food and shelter there. One day a young and handsome mendicant, a devotee of Viṣṇu, arrived and began to live in the hostel. Impressed by his devotion, the priest entrusted his daughter to him for religious instruction: 'like a bowl of yoghurt is given to a cat for safe-keeping'. The inevitable happened, and the two began a passionate affair. Now the rainy season came to an end, but the lovers could not bear to separate [for he ought to have set out on his alms-wandering], and so both eloped together. The priest was distraught by this turn of events and went to the king to complain. The latter sent his soldiers out who caught up with the couple and dragged them back to Benares. For violating a virgin girl, the mendicant was put to death and left to rot in the cremation ground. The girl kept on going there, decorated the corpse with garments, ointments and jewellery, and took *pān* from her own mouth and put it into his. Eventually she was found out in these strange nightly rituals, and the king had the corpse cremated. Again that girl, still blind with love, went to where the ashes were, sprinkled fragrant substances on them, decorated them with flowers and, weeping, cast herself on to them. Her father found her in that state in the morning, and he had the ashes scattered into the river. But the girl jumped after them and tried to clasp the ashes which the water was carrying off.[14]

And the narrator of this story adds: 'what pleasure could she get from embracing the waves mixed with his ashes?'[15]

I mentioned previously that Boccaccio in his *Decameron* retells stories of ultimately Indian origin. I think it is not difficult to see in his story of Lisabetta[16] an example of this. Lisabetta was the orphaned daughter of a rich merchant. Lorenzo was employed by Lisabetta's three brothers to assist in their business, and he had an affair with the unmarried Lisabetta. One of the brothers found out about it, and all three killed him secretly. One night Lisabetta had a vision of Lorenzo, who told her about his fate and revealed where his corpse was buried. Indeed she found it there, when she dug the earth. She severed the head from the shoulders, and back home, she buried it in a pot, growing basil on top – her tears watering the plants. Every day she performed morbid rituals with the basil pot, until her brothers found out about it. Initially they just took the pot away, to put an end to such silly behaviour. But when she kept on asking for it, they investigated it, found the head and hid it. The girl searched for it everywhere without success, and ultimately died of a broken heart.

When we compare the two stories, we notice some interesting differences. The brothers, without the controlling influence of a father, are presented here as secretly, without public approval, committing a criminal act, and the girl's mad behaviour is rationalized through the ghost who speaks to her in the dream. But more interesting is the context in which the story is presented. The whole of the *Decameron*'s *Fourth Day* is filled with stories about tragic love, like the one about Lisabetta. But the *Third Day* tells us about people who, through their own effort, recover an object deeply desired, and the *Fifth Day* about lovers who survived misfortunes and attained a state of happiness. Thus stories like that of Lisabetta serve as the sad interval between far happier matters. In fact, that is precisely the purpose for which the 'king' of the *Fourth Day* has chosen this subject. The sadness generated is intended to soften the heart of a lady in the gathering who has so far rejected his advances.[17]

We find nothing of this relativizing context in the case of the Jain story: an essential statement is made here about the nature of love. The crucial point made here is not so much the potential madness brought about (in the subject, namely the girl) by her infatuation, as the very nature of the desired object. What may appear initially as a solid, lasting entity (the lover), is revealed to be no more than a temporary position on a scale that stretches from live human being to corpse to ashes. When properly analysed, the passions aim at no real object. The transition from lover to rotting corpse and to ashes and water demonstrates, on the one hand, the transience of the object of desire, but at the same time highlights in a most striking manner the autonomy of desire which does not decrease in proportion to the degree of evanescence of the lover. The girl's passions remain unabated, regardless of what transformations he is undergoing. In order, therefore, to escape from the vicious circle mentioned earlier, it is necessary to separate the real object of desire from the image that passion projects on to it, and – that is the conclusion drawn from this –

to reject both. It is not in the nature of love to be transient, murderous, and an addiction, but it becomes so in our deluded perception of it. The love the poets may be complaining about is an imperfect affair, but this type of analysis wants to show that it is fundamentally a mistake.

The story itself is found narrated in various Jain texts, and it does express typically Jain ideas. But in one version, a Buddhist origin is hinted at. For there the narrator adds: 'The Buddha has taught that there exists not a single permanent substance; everything is empty, in every respect.'[18] These are resonances of a technical discourse which was developed in the various renouncer traditions. Let us now look at some of the details. Since early Buddhism is particularly articulate in this respect, I shall begin with its analysis. The Buddha is supposed to have presented the essentials of his teaching in the form of the Four Noble Truths. The first of these makes a fundamental statement about human existence: it is the truth of suffering – *duḥkha.* Initially it might seem that under this heading all the more negative aspects of life are gathered together. 'Birth is suffering' – one could think here of the pains of childbirth, or of the painfulness of transmigration. 'Old age is suffering', and so are disease and death. However, it becomes clear that more than just the negative sides of life are included in this truth, when we look at a second explanation of what is meant by this 'suffering'. 'Contact with what one does not love is suffering, and not to be with what one loves is suffering; every wish unfulfilled is suffering.' This now makes it clear that 'suffering' is intended as a statement about the essence of human existence: among all wishes left unfulfilled is the foremost, that of wanting to be together for ever with what one loves. The occurrence of pleasure and happiness are not denied, but what is emphasized is that such happiness, by not being permanent and by being surrounded by unhappiness, is relative and actually is 'suffering' on a deeper level of analysis. In the transient nature of love and happiness an illustration is seen of the very nature of human existence.

Incidentally, this learned discourse has been picked up in Hāla's anthology, where we read: 'To be separated from whom/what one loves, and to see someone/something unpleasant – these two are profound suffering.'[19] And much further afield similar resonances can be found, as in the following little poem:

Even to my enemies
God may not send

these black sufferings of death
which he has sent me.[20]

From the context it is clear that it is love that has caused this deadly suffering. To reveal that the ditty is actually a flamenco stanza sung by the gypsies of southern Spain may still not explain much. But the original has for 'suffering' a word from the ultimately Indian language of the *gitanos*: *duca*. Neither is it difficult to recognize our *duḥkha* in the word, nor *kāma* in the gypsy word for love, *cam*. But from such an unexpected diffusion of ideas about the deadly suffering love causes we must return to the original argument.

So life is basically a stream of suffering that carries as its flotsam and jetsam moments of happiness. The next question that has to be looked at by anybody who wants to do something about this situation is obviously, what it is that brings about such a situation? The Buddha's answer is: 'thirst'. That means, carrying on with my metaphor for a minute: we have such a craving for the flotsam and jetsam that in our thirst we try to drink up the whole stream that carries it. Initially it might seem to us that what is being suggested is simply to stop desiring that the moments of happiness should be everlasting. But such an interpretation ignores a far more fundamental problem which arises from the perception of life in Buddhism and many other strands of the renouncer tradition. We are not talking just about one life, but about transmigration, about a potentially infinite number of lives filled with 'suffering'. Thus it is not adjustment to the stream that is advocated, but a radical escape from it. The term 'thirst' explains not just our unhappiness but, on a far deeper level, how transmigration itself comes about.

Speaking in purely empirical terms, there is very little in our experience that would give us a clue as to the rationale of our being. But we possess one minimal area of observation that is available to all of us prior to any theorizing: that is, our passionate desires. They provide the link between the two mysteries that surround our lives: birth and death, filling in the space in between. Moreover, they are causally connected with those same mysteries. Passionately we hold on to being alive and defend ourselves against threats through violence and inflicting death on others. Equally passionately we throw ourselves into the matters of love and thereby cause birth and bring forth new life. In itself, this empirically given fact is open to a variety of interpretations and practical conclusions. But given the belief in transmigration, and that as something fundamentally undesirable, any attempt to escape from it has to eliminate these passionate desires. It is not difficult to see that the analysis of 'thirst' is intended to do precisely that. On the one hand 'thirst' is accepted as the mechanism behind *saṃsāra*, and, on the other, is demonstrated to be folly. The object desired in 'thirst' is envisaged as lasting happiness, but in reality what is achieved is permanent unhappiness, an endless revolution from birth to death and rebirth. Thus a nexus is established here between 'desire' and 'ignorance'. 'Thirst' thus includes both our passions and a basic misunderstanding about ourselves and what these passions may gain us.

Early Buddhism tried to spell this out in greater detail, through its notoriously difficult teaching on 'conditioned origination'. This schema wants to establish a nexus of conditions without, it seems to me, wanting to get involved in any particular philosophical theory of causality. Instead of getting side-tracked into discussing such highly abstract and controversial matters as the question of whether an effect is already found in its cause(s) or whether cause and effect are separate entities, in a typically pragmatic manner it points at a situation that is obvious to common sense. To paraphrase the intention, we could say that it is sufficient to realize that the occurrence of smoke is inevitably 'conditioned' by the presence of fire. If we don't like the smoke, because it makes us cough or makes our eyes water, the most sensible way of getting rid of it is by pouring water on the fire. This is all we need to know and we can leave it to the philosophers, who are not bothered by the smoke, to sort out what precisely the relationship between fire and smoke is, to what extent some aspect of fire (the cause) actually enters into the smoke (the effect), and whether or not smoke is a transformation of the fire, or a new kind of entity. The smoke of our example corresponds, in Buddhist teaching, to the occurrence of birth along with all its concomitants of suffering. And where is the fire without which we find no smoke? Initially, we could point to conception: the moment when the male sperm fertilizes the female egg in the mother's womb. Technically this is referred to rather confusingly, by the term *vijñāna* – a word that normally means 'consciousness'. But traces of a more archaic meaning of the term have been detected in early Buddhist writing, according to which we could translate it as 'life principle' or indeed 'conception'.[21] But Buddhism is not interested in birth-control; instead, it repeats the analysis and searches for increasingly basic 'conditions'. So we are now given *saṃskāra*, another highly complex and also confusing term. A whole cluster of ideas is compressed into it. Thus conception is not a random affair, but something consciously wanted: it involves the will. Again the acts of the will are not arbitrary, but derive from deep-rooted character traits and mental attitudes (an area where past *karma* plays a considerable role). But even this can be shown still to be smoke: expressions of the will are in turn conditioned by ignorance. In our concrete example we can interpret it as that particular clouding of the mind which is found in people passionately in love, as the delusion that has been so dramatically illustrated previously in the story of the girl chasing after the ashes of her lover. In her 'ignorance' of what her lover 'really was' she constructed a mental world filled with expectations of pleasure and personal fulfilment which bore no relationship to the real events. Her ignorance tried to grasp at a solid object, which in fact was progressively revealed to be 'empty'.

I hope that what I have presented so far is acceptable as a very narrow and personal, but legitimate interpretation of some aspects of the schema of the 'conditioned origination'. The sexual model behind it would in that case be quite apparent, and the schema can be regarded as a legitimate topic in the exploration of love and human sexuality. But let us remind ourselves of the ultimate purpose of the schema. The eradication of this ignorance, the insights into the nature of the beloved person and into the mechanisms within oneself that construct the image of 'a beloved person', is intended as the water poured over the fire, to put an end to the smoke of further rebirth.

Although I am presenting such ideas here in typically Buddhist terminology, in essence the other renouncer traditions would not find it difficult to accept all this. The same can be said for many of the finer details of the analysis of desire and ignorance, details that are encapsulated in other aspects of the schema of the 'conditioned origination' and also in the Buddhist teaching of five 'components of grasping'. According to these, man's corporeal existence implies his being in contact with the outside world, by means of the senses located in the body. These senses pick up data, which however do not remain neutral. They are turned into emotive bits of information about our environment, according to which we not only construe an image of it, but also relate through our volition to it: passionately craving for what we perceive as pleasurable. This is a very drastic identification of the root of *saṃsāra*: the sensuous information we take in about our world, along with its sensual dimension. Jainism and other, 'Hindu', expressions of the renouncer tradition stop more or less here. But Buddhism carries on with its analysis in an even more ruthless manner.

For both its teaching of 'conditioned origination' and of 'the five components of the person' carry the argument way beyond the dangers lurking in our senses. The very nature of the person is questioned. Empirically it is reduced to five, equally transient, components and to the processes holding these together and occurring between them. In terms of transmigration, a sequence of conditions is postulated which eliminates the need of talking about any permanent entity that courses through *saṃsāra*. All this is implied in the idea of *anātman*, 'no-self' or 'lacking in an inner, autonomous and lasting individual core' – a concept we have discussed at length in a previous chapter.[22] So what all this leads up to in the end is the claim that the very subject of passionate desire has been dissolved. 'Ignorance' consists in a delusion of an autonomous core in ourselves, in an 'I'. By extension, any lover or beloved acquires being only through the same delusion. This is the most radical way of analysing love imaginable! The denial of a loving self subsumes the realization that the relationship between lover and beloved may be transient (our poetry) and that the object of one's love is transient (our Jain story about the girl chasing after her lover's ashes).

Someone familiar with the far more abstract way in which this Buddhist teaching (particularly of the 'conditioned origination') is normally presented, may find my concrete paraphrase in terms of love and sexuality somewhat puzzling. So let me back it up with an illustration from an ancient Indian Buddhist source. From Pālī sources (preserved in Sri Lanka) we are used to a fundamental antagonism between the Buddha and his treacherous disciple Devadatta. But when we look into the *Mahāvastu*, a life-story of the Buddha from a different Indian school (the Mahāsāṅghikas), we find the whole structured rather differently.[23] The primary antagonist is Māra, and not only in the Buddha's last earthly existence, but right through his many previous lives. Thus a number of Jātakas, stories told about a past existence of he who was to become the Buddha, appear here shaped in such a way that the antagonism to Māra and his deadly weapons of love is emphasized. This includes a variety of stories narrated here about the past deeds of she who was to become Siddhārtha's wife (in the Pālī tradition they have nothing to do with the lady). By abandoning her at the moment of his renunciation, he puts an end to a struggle that had occupied him in many past existences and that had been one aspect of his continuous fight with Māra. Resisting Māra's temptations symbolizes the final victory. I think it needs no explicit commentary to recognize, in such a popular conception of the Buddha's antagonism to Māra since primordial times, the concretization of ideas which I have been attempting to extricate from the more abstract teaching. Though not as blatantly obvious as in a large number of Jain stories, the central preoccupation with the passions and love can therefore also be inferred for earlier Buddhist teaching from India.

Let us briefly turn to the Jains and the way they deal with matters of love.[24] There is no need to survey the whole system of their teaching about it. Most of what has been said earlier applies here also. They agree with the Buddhists that the concrete, empirical person does not possess an 'essence' (which they tend to call *sāra*) and that man is therefore transient. The major difference lies in the acceptance of a permanent, autonomous core in each living being, a 'soul' (*jīva*). This allows them to explain the pernicious role of the senses in a most concrete and substantialist manner. Any action, including those of the senses perceiving the world, lets a subtle matter (called *karma*) enter the soul, making it heavy, clouding its faculties and keeping it down in *saṃsāra*. Moreover, such matter stimulates further action, and the more 'violent' or 'passionate' this is, the more new *karma* enters. All this *karma* now conditions a variety of aspects of further rebirths. I extract from these those aspects which might be of interest in the present discussion. (As in the Buddhist teaching mentioned previously, *karma* also plays an important role in the formation of mental attitudes and character traits.) Thus one's basic psychological make-up in relation to sexuality is determined: whether one is reborn as a man, a woman or a hermaphrodite; as a lustful, virile, potent or impotent person. Moreover, certain sexual proclivities are fixed (such as an incestuous desire), as are situational aspects (such as getting married, or being rejected by all men). Even the peculiar affection someone might have for a particular animal is explained by reference to past interaction with the soul of the beast, in whatever body it may then have been. Particularly nasty things happen to those who insult Jain ascetics, as is shown by the illustration below.[25]

There is a learned brahmin, who has two sons. One day the three see a couple of Jain monks, and they heap the most obscene ridicule upon them. The monks do nothing, for *karma* will take its automatic course. The father is reborn as a beautiful prostitute, and the twins she reluctantly gives birth to are the reborn sons. She abandons the boy and girl soon after their birth, finding them repulsive. They are rescued and brought up separately, to be married with each other. As if this was not enough, during a business trip the man consorts with the said prostitute and desires her so much that he remains with her. His wife (and sister) becomes depressed at this rejection and consults a Jain ascetic who, due to his supernormal knowledge, is able to tell her the whole story of their previous lives. In due course, the husband and the prostitute are also informed about their true relationship and their past offences, and everyone repents. They accept the Jain faith which they had ridiculed in the past – a ridicule for which they were punished through their incestuous relationships.

How is all this abstract analysis applied to the realities of life? It goes without saying that any serious application cannot possibly be envisaged in the context of ordinary married life. The essential ideals are asceticism and renunciation. When we now consider how in ancient India these communities of renouncers formulated disciplinary rules, it is obvious that the avoidance of all sexuality and of all forms of violence are the central norm. When we look at the Jains, we reach the most archaic layer and find a most surprising and unexpected connection between love and violence. For they believed that any sexual intercourse involved the killing of innumerable minute animals living in a woman's vagina! But the ideals of the renouncers affected wider areas of society. For these ascetics established lay-communities, into which they infused a somewhat diluted version of their own disciplinary code. Meditational exercises were designed that had a wider popular appeal and inculcated typical attitudes to matters of love and sex (like the 'four applications of mindfulness' or reflections on the 'objects of desire' among the Buddhists, which we met with in a previous chapter).[26]

On the Jain side we find an incredible work, which unrestrainedly takes the bull of seductive love-poetry straight by the horns. This is a collection of poems (by Amitagati) which, in its title *Assembly of milk-like well-spoken verses* (*Subhāṣita-sandoha*), conjures up romantic images by alluding to anthologies of love-poetry of similar names. And, indeed, many of the themes dealt with in other such anthologies are also found here – but treated in a very different manner. For example, the heading 'investigating the qualities of women' might evoke expressions of delight at some particularly attractive female form. But this is what Amitagati offers us:

> It is better to throw oneself
> into a blazing fire
> or to jump into the sea
> infested with sharks and crocodiles
> or run into battle
> where mighty soldiers hurl all kinds of weapons
> – better to do this
> than to indulge in sex with a woman,
> for that would generate hundreds of rebirths
> and endless suffering.[27]

Well, I leave it to the reader's imagination to figure out what other nice things are said about the female body, and about other topics like eating meat, drinking alcohol, and consorting with prostitutes who 'pass on with their bodies hundreds of impure substances'.[28] In a sense we have here the culmination of my previous observations: Amitagati has moved right into the heart of the Indian cultural exploration of love, Sanskrit love-poetry, and by using its form he applies the ruthless Jain critique to its subject-matter.

But the Jains are better known for their storytelling. It is here where they apply the theoretical teaching to the concrete realities of the religious life. I would like to demonstrate this with the help of two examples. The first is one of the great pan-Indian literary constructs, which the Jains (but also the Buddhists and Hindus) have made use of. The second is a story of great popularity, but found only in Jain literature. Both stories have been discussed and partially summarized in previous chapters,[29] and thus we can here concentrate on those features that have a direct bearing on the matters of love and sexuality. I am talking here about the *Grand Story* (*Bṛhatkathā*) and the story of Fame-Bearer (Yaśodhara).

Let us begin with the *Grand Story* or, as one might be tempted to translate the title, 'The Great Male Dream'. As previously pointed out, we are not dealing here with an actual literary work, but with a vast bulk of literature in different languages and by different authors which shows a common range of themes and a common basic plot. It is to this common plot that I shall in general restrict myself here.

At the beginning, we have a prince who has grown up in rather unusual circumstances (in a forest hermitage, among lepers, in a cremation ground with untouchables, or in an underground realm of the *nāgas*). Thus he has acquired particular skills and powers but, above all, women find him extremely attractive. In most cases he appears happy to enjoy his fortunes in a passive way, and thus it requires again some unusual event to push him out into the wide world (like a palace intrigue against his mother, the complaint of decent citizens to the king about his driving their wives crazy with passion, or being abducted by a *vidyādhara*). Now a string of adventures begins, each ending with our hero falling in love with a girl and making love to her. He may win her in a competition (by defeating her at playing the lute), or by unknowingly fulfilling a prophecy ('he will be your husband who falls down from the sky'), or as a reward for some help given (for example, curing someone of bad breath or of frigidity), or by being tricked (by a *vidyādhara* princess assuming the form of one of his earlier conquests, for example), or as an 'extra bonus' (because a girl has inseparable friends who insist on getting married to him too). Eventually, that is, when the number of conquests has reached five hundred and one, or five hundred and seven, or seven hundred and seven – usually about twenty-five are described in any detail – his roaming through the world comes to an end and he settles down to rule the earth as a mighty emperor. Messengers are sent into every quarter to fetch his many wives and bring them to his palace.

Woven into all this is the world of the *vidyādharas*, those beings who live in a realm of their own, can fly through the air, change their bodily appearance at will and, naturally, are renowned for their supernatural sexual prowess. Many a *vidyādhara* princess is included in the catalogue of our hero's conquests, and often he also becomes ruler over the *vidyādhara* kingdoms. What more could a man dream of?

By far the largest number of literary works dealing with this story are Jain, though the theme itself is not their creation. On the whole, they apply their critique in a delicate manner and not, as in the case of the *Assembly of milk-like well-spoken verses* (*Subhāṣitasandoha*), with crude brutality. The *Grand Story* offers an ideal illustration of the fickleness of human emotions and passions: as soon as our hero's cravings have found fulfilment through the love of one girl whom he desperately desired a few days ago, some new infatuation hits him. The way in which he is presented to be drifting from one girl to the next is psychologically very interesting: the powers of his passions are actually the powers of his fate and destiny that activate him. No real fulfilment lies in all this, and each satisfied desire gives rise to new, unsatisfied ones. What about the eventual climax, the grand imperial rule he achieves? At this point our Jain authors introduce death: what may appear as the ultimate fulfilment of man's dreams is as fickle and transient as the passions that make up its individual images.[30] Sooner or later in every Jain version, the hero has to encounter death and face his own mortality, and, pulling his hair out, he turns Jain ascetic.

The theme itself is well known to us, for instance from the story of Don Juan, but its evaluation is totally different. The original creator of the Don Juan figure, Tirso de Molina (his real name was Gabriel Téllez, 1584-1648)[31] was a Spanish monk who, like his Jain counterparts, obviously wanted to demonstrate the fundamental 'unfulfillability' of male passion. But Don Juan's punishment is meted out by the ghost of one of his mistress's fathers whom he had murdered. And what lies at the heart of de Molina's criticism is the fact that Don Juan persisted in depriving one girl after another of her honour, promising marriage in exchange. Thus appropriately his drama comes to a happy ending, when a number of honourable gentlemen decide to accept in holy matrimony the girls previously dishonoured by Don Juan. The Jain authors had no such social and religious framework to fall back on in their critique: their hero always does the honourable thing and marries the girl. So not sin, but delusion provides the key idea for their evaluation.

I mentioned earlier that the Buddhists also use this material. Their version (told in the commentary on the *Dhammapada*)[32] is rather archaic and lacks the embellishments of later medieval sources. Here the hero marries a more modest number of queens, three in fact. One of these becomes a Buddhist, and another hates Buddhism. Previously she had tried to seduce the Buddha, but was rejected by him – thus her hatred. After an unsuccessful attempt to persuade the king to kill his favourite (the Buddhist queen), she succeeds in burning her rival to death. When the king finds out about it, half-demented from grief over the loss of his favourite, he has her tortured to death in a most gruesome manner. Unfortunately, the framework that the commentary provides for this powerful tale about the deadly weapons of passion is rather feeble: all it draws from it is the morale that caution is a useful virtue.

After this relatively tranquil material, we must turn to an extraordinarily powerful and gruesome story which is exclusive to the Jains. The story of Yaśodhara previously served us as an example to illustrate the consequences (in terms of excruciatingly painful rebirths) of even a symbolic act of killing. But the story is pervaded by references to lust, passion and perversion, and it is this aspect which makes it relevant to our present discussion.

As the reader will remember, a king is passionately in love with his wife. But one night, when he cannot fall asleep and is lying quietly so as not to awaken her, he notices her suddenly rise from the bed and disappear. Curious, he follows her from a distance. This takes him into the stables where he sees her being whipped by an ugly and deformed *mahout*, who then makes love to her – to her apparent delight. The king's only reaction is to become deeply depressed and yet, in a sense, that is enough to justify the punishment meted out to him in his subsequent rebirths. For the depression reveals that his attachment is still there, highlighting the degree of delusion love can cause. It is this delusion which all the agonies of his next lives gradually eradicate.

By an unusual deviation from normal Jain story patterns, in his subsequent rebirths the king is time and again brought together with his mother, while his unfaithful queen is almost totally ignored. But this situation can easily be explained. For it was his mother who enticed him to perform a symbolic animal sacrifice, in order to cure his depression. Thus in an ingenious way the choice of the wrong means of overcoming sexual attachment (the direct cause of the depression) is linked here with violence and killing. From this we can logically derive the violent, but also the sexual nature of the relationships between these two, mother and son, in subsequent animal rebirths. I cannot detect any suggestion in the different versions of the story that the theme of sexuality – for instance, when the son, reborn as a billy-goat, mounts his mother, now also a goat and indeed the goat that gave birth to him – derives from some further, unconscious element in the mother–son relationship. For all I know, we are dealing here with another example of the nexus between deriding Jain monks and incest (in some lost version, did a monk try to prevent the queen from performing the symbolic sacrifice and was derided by her?)

Be that as it may, after a number of extremely bizarre, violent and painful lives as animals, mother and son are reborn as a couple of fighting-cocks. This, naturally very violent, existence comes to a violent end when the king's own son, during love-making in a park pavilion, hears their crowing and shows off to the queen by aiming an arrow merely at the sound. The queen conceives – the souls of the two animals her husband has just killed enter her womb. They are born as twins, a boy and a girl. Once again human, they do not miss this rare chance to escape from the woes of earthly existence and become Jain novices. From a sage they hear all about their past lives.

Now comes the final dramatic climax. Wandering through the country, they are captured by the soldiers of a king who wants to sacrifice them to a particularly bloodthirsty goddess. When the executor's sword is already threatening, they manage to convert the king and the goddess to the Jain religion. But there is more hidden here than the obvious logical connection with the animal sacrifice the king (as Yaśodhara) had initially performed. The purpose of the gruesome human sacrifice for the goddess was, as an evil ascetic had promised the king, his acquisition of the faculty to fly. Now hidden behind this is the belief in acquiring the powers of a *vidyādhara*, renowned for his sexual prowess on a scale far superior to any human being. It is almost as if the king wanted to realize for himself what he might have read about in the *Bṛhatkathā*! But as far as the (reborn) Yaśodhara is concerned, we can conclude our interpretation as follows. He paid off his final debt for having been attached sexually to his queen by suffering the agonies of facing execution for the sake of somebody else's deluded pursuit of sexual gratification.

We seem to have ended up in a cul-de-sac: what is left of love and lust, after this devastating critique put forward by our renouncers? Everything seems to have been vivisected, cut up and dissolved in the acid of ruthless analysis and its application to life and cultural constructs dealing with the matters of the heart. And as far as this type of discourse is concerned, I doubt that it is possible to argue with it, at least in terms of its own references. But what we can do is to step back and survey the scene as it has now evolved, including the material discussed in the previous chapter. Obviously we are dealing with more than just abstract systems of thought: what we have here are culture-historical processes. Looking at it from this point of view, we can, in the form of a simile, think of a lake into which, at different times and in different places, two stones are thrown. Both trigger off concentric circles of increasing radius of waves and ripples which, at a certain stage, will begin to interact with each other. When we unravel the simile, the two stones turn into the two perceptions of love (and everything else that I have included under that heading) as expressed by the renouncers and the poets respectively. But the one was formulated in northern India, from about 800 BC onwards, and the other in southern India, from perhaps 100 BC onwards. Both were powerful influences, the first consciously inculcated into society, and the second more instinctively pursued. Having attempted to present them in their individual pristine form, we may now look at the question of what happens after these two spreading circles of waves have met: neither succeeds in cancelling out the other. Some examples of this 'interface' have been given earlier: Hāla knows of the teaching on 'suffering' (*duḥkha*), and Amitagati adopts the form and topics of Sanskrit anthologies of love-poetry. Obviously the results of this interaction were far more variegated and numerous. So let me briefly illustrate some of this here.

We saw how the renouncers set out to spread their teaching into wider areas of society by gathering lay-communities around themselves. Given the fact that the life of a layman could only be regarded as second-best (in comparison with that of the ascetic), it need not surprise us that teaching began to concentrate on a second-best spiritual goal: that of acquiring merits (which, strictly speaking, allows for such rebirths as are more conducive to the obtainment of the ultimate, best goal). Moreover, ritual means of acquiring such merits evolved: fasts, all kinds of vows, worship of images of the Jinas, etc. A vast literature especially on these matters was produced, and some surprises are in store for us in it.

Not all the Jain versions of the *Bṛhatkathā* and the secondary stories they derived from it are structured in the way I indicated earlier on. In many cases, the same plot (the hero making hundreds of conquests of beautiful girls) is employed to demonstrate what wonderful results derive from the merits acquired – in some past existence of the hero – by performing a particular vow (or *vrata*).[33] The description can be quite glowing and enthusiastic; one Tamil work (the *Cīvakacintāmaṇi*) has in fact been regarded as 'pornography' by more puritanical members of Tamil Nadu society.[34] Religion can be fun, at least in a future life, when enough merit has been accumulated – that's the message here.

From the pen of the Buddhist Āryaśūra (third or fourth century AD) we have the *The Jewellery-Box Filled with Well-Spoken Verses* (*Subhāṣita-ratna-karaṇḍaka*). This is what he promises to anybody who makes generous donations to the monks:

> That one gains women
> whose beautiful eyes can compete
> with the immaculate petals of the blue lotus,
> whose loins and buttocks are caressed
> by golden zones and red garments,
> who have firm, large breasts and lively eyebrows,
> – that one can gain them as dedicated servants,
> is the result of the merits arising from donations
> that break open the gates of meanness.[35]

The same rewards, lovingly spelled out in many of the poems, are promised also for meritorious rituals performed in front of statues of the Buddha, and so on.

Let us recollect what the Jain *Assembly of milk-like well-spoken verses* (*Subhāṣita-sandoha*) had to say about the qualities of woman. I cannot say whether it was a joker or a complete fool, but someone inserted into that chapter a string of twelve stanzas of very different content.[36] They do not, like the rest of the collection, dwell on her body as an abode of all kinds of impure liquids, oozing out of the various apertures. Instead, they promise in a future life the most alluring ladies and all the pleasures of the senses they have to offer to the man who in this life piously accumulates religious merit!

Obviously we find many further, but less extreme, examples of the interaction between the two culture-historical trends. So we have the Buddhist abbot Vidyākara who compiled one of the most charming anthologies of Sanskrit love lyrics,[37] or the Buddhist philosopher Dharmakīrti who proved the truth of the Buddhist doctrine of the absence of a creator god in the following ingenious manner.

> Had the creator seen her –
> this beautiful girl with deer-like eyes
> and a face golden like saffron –
> he would never have let her go away from him.
> Or had he closed his eyes,
> he could never have created her.

From all this we can infer:
the Buddhist teaching must be true
that the world is uncreated.[38]

But perhaps the most famous of all examples I could give here to illustrate the interaction of our two trends is the poetry of Bhartṛhari. In him we find a torn personality expressing itself because both the values of the renouncers and the entranced raptures of the poets have been interiorized by him, without fusing into some kind of synthesis. Thus he says:

The pleasures of sense may be trivial
and bitter in the end;
they may be despised as abodes of evil;
and yet, even the supreme power of men
whose thoughts are fixed on truth
falls sway to that mysterious power
throbbing in our hearts.[39]

Is there any way in which that 'mysterious power throbbing in the heart' can be guided into a direction that might carry love beyond the fleeting moments of its transient and destructive nature?

CHAPTER 12

Beyond the fleeting moment

The poets may agree with the renouncers that love is a fickle, transient and even potentially destructive affair. The renouncers may agree with the rest of the populace that not everybody is immediately ready to accept their ruthless, cerebral rejection of the passions lurking in the human heart, and therefore consent to some compromise. Desire and ignorance may be the root cause of continued rebirth, but religious merits and their appropriate rewards can at least add some pleasure to it. All this sounds very much like an entertaining, but ultimately inconsequential panel discussion. 'Interesting, but so what?' we may want to comment at the end of it. However, we are not dealing here with media entertainment, but with different cultural traditions and their drastically different value-systems which – and this is the crucial point – may well meet in one and the same individual and turn him into their battlefield. In our own parlance, we could speak of a possible neurosis, if this individual does not resolve such conflicts of values, or of repression, if one side is merely pushed, unresolved, into the dark recesses of the subconscious. A poet like Bhartṛhari speaks of an agonizing contest between the mind and the heart.[1]

Most chairpersons of panel discussions are too busy to raise questions of 'truth', if only in order to prevent libellous accusations or physical violence between the different members of the panel. They are happy enough if they can find some compromise formulation of the issues at stake. Something similar happened in India. There, without doubt in response to the kind of Buddhist and Jain ideas about desire (and also to more implicit suggestions found in the Upaniṣads and some *yoga* schools), an interesting compromise was formulated in the area of the 'Vedic tradition'. Here, in what is sometimes regarded as the 'Hindu mainstream', the course of a human life is divided into various stages (called *āśramas*). Each one is reserved for the pursuit of specific goals which are legitimate then and only then. There is first the period of study, characterized by the pursuit of knowledge and total celibacy. In fact, the idea of total sexual abstention during the years in 'school and college' is so strong, that the name of this phase, *brahmacarya*, became the word for 'celibacy' generally.

The second phase is that of the married householder. Three pursuits (styled *puruṣārthas*, 'man's ends') are now legitimate, and in fact enjoined: of making money, of sexual pleasures (appropriately called *kāma* and at least nominally taught in the *Kāmasūtras*), and of religious merits. We saw in the last chapter what kind of attractive pleasures are promised as the reward for such pious deeds. Moreover, the more wealth someone accumulates, the greater the number of wives he can acquire and the more frequent the number of his visits to the more sophisticated courtesans. So, in the final analysis, what these three goals come down to is the pursuit of sexual pleasures, both in this and in the next world. This interpretation is not my own: there are many texts, serious and satirical, that clearly spell out this primacy of *kāma* among the three.[2]

Eventually the time arrives to say farewell to the pleasures of the flesh – at least until the merits produce their fruit in a future existence – and withdraw to higher things. Ultimately this means to turn renouncer (*saṃnyāsī*) and pursue the goal the 'renouncer tradition' has put up: the pursuit of liberation from the cycle of transmigration.

This is an interesting and humane synthesis of our two culture-historical trends. In a pragmatic manner the ideal of the renouncers is linked with that of love, by integrating both into the structure of a patterned life. But there are problems here. Thus the pursuit of *kāma* is fundamentally justified through the need for children which, in turn, arises from ideas about a miserable after-life which becomes bearable only through the regular rites performed by one's children. These are archaic ideas, belonging to a view of the world superseded by later conceptions of cosmology, and contradicting what the renouncer tradition then had to say about final liberation. Moreover, it is a theoretical construction put forward by the scholastics. We have no idea how many people actually structured their lives according to this teaching about the four stages in a life and the four legitimate pursuits of pious deeds, wealth, sex and liberation. In a less stylized form, this is obviously how most people lead their lives, and precisely why the renouncers have put forward their critique. Given their analysis of human existence and their emphasis on the urgency of striving towards liberation, a compromise of this kind makes no sense, particularly when it includes insurances for an improved future existence within the same *saṃsāra* (sons feeding you or luscious ladies granting you sexual pleasures as the reward for pious deeds). Thus we are back at square one. More precisely, we have come back to the primary relationship between a desiring subject and a desired object.

Now in a different world, the 'intellectual' would start where the rounding-off comments of a discussion panel's chairperson stop. Although even to him ultimate truth may remain equally elusive, there are a number of useful jobs he could nevertheless undertake and various further questions he could ask. Different people may use the same word when discussing an issue, but are they really talking about the same thing – does the word 'love' or 'passion' necessarily mean the same to the poet and the renouncer? Does a high degree of sophistication and articulateness inevitably have to win over a less cerebral understanding – the Buddhist teaching of 'conditioned origination' over a stanza found in Hāla? Or finally, do the members that happen to be present exhaust the potential of the subject?

I do not want to put myself into the position of such an 'intellectual' here. But something like the kind of job just indicated ought to be undertaken. Thus, for example, we ought to become aware of the fact that the tradition of love-poetry arose hundreds of years after the formulation of a theory about *saṃsāra* and *mokṣa* and therefore we cannot expect to find in the latter an adequate interpretation of the former. At the same time, we cannot expect an immediate production of a highly sophisticated theory of love-poetry that can stand up to the renouncers' critique. Or, to mention another example, we ought to draw a clearer distinction between real life and poetry. Rather uncritically, in spite of some initial warning signs, we have continued to use a simplistic formula: subject–desire–object. But to be precise, we certainly ought to rewrite this as:

(poetic) subject–desire–object
(real) subject–desire–object.

This now allows us to ask questions concerning the relationship between the two, which in spite of their seeming parallelity may well relate in much more complex ways to each other (as we shall see presently).

Moreover, even as far as a desiring relation in real life is concerned (not to mention an 'imaginary' poetic relation), most or all variables are dissolved through the renouncers' critique into transient, non-substantial and illusory phenomena. But it is clear what effect it would have on the formula, *if a non-transient, substantial, truly autonomous object of human desire could be found.* Is it possible to differentiate various kinds of objects, some of which, at least, would justify human love towards them because they are not transient? To pursue this question will be the main task of the present chapter. But let us remain for a moment with our formula, to unravel some further possibilities. What would be the consequences, if the relationship became reversed – if the subject of love actually finds itself as the object, the recipient of love? Or again, does desire or love necessarily dissolve when both the subject and the object are analysed as *anātman*, as lacking an autonomous core (as Buddhism teaches), or could even the Buddhists find a meaningful role for it?

What initially looked like a simple disagreement over the significance of love and desire has rather rapidly and unexpectedly turned into a highly complex affair with many new parameters. However, I have no intention of carrying on playing some kind of abstract arithmetical game here, by trying to spell out in a systematic manner the various combinations and permutations that our formula would allow for. Instead I shall treat it like a ball of wool, pull at various ends, unroll different strands and hope that by the end of Part two most of the loose ends thus unravelled will have been tied up. As far as the present chapter is concerned, our subject matter has already been indicated. We shall be looking at two or three pointers in the direction of 'transcendentality', at some modes in which human love is carried beyond the fleeting moment of unmitigated transience. Although the concept of 'God' will occupy here most of our attention, we ought to remain aware of the other possibilities that our formula has suggested.

Poetry about a sexually attractive woman, that praises the largeness of her breasts by pitying the slender waist for having to support such a heavy load; poetry about bouncing necklaces and hair wildly flowing as a woman, all inhibitions overcome, makes love astride a man; or poetry about the envy felt by co-wives at discovering the marks of their common husband's nails on the thigh of the youngest wife – this kind of enterprise would necessarily be condemned by the renouncers as one of the lethal stimuli that heighten sexual passions in anyone reading or listening to it. But this would be a naive, literalist critique, for it does not do justice to the general potential of our poetry. Whether we look at Hāla, or the Tamil *akattiṇai*, or later Sanskrit poems, the relative proportion of poems on actual 'love-in-union' is extremely small. A much larger relative number of poems deals with 'love-in-separation'. Now one could offer a frivolous explanation for this: anybody busy with the matters of love has no time or energy to write poems. But I think there is more involved here. We have already found it said that every wish fulfilled generates further wishes, most of which cannot be fulfilled; that every wish unfulfilled is suffering. Now the extraordinary feature of love-poetry is to render such strings of unfulfilled desires into something meaningful, positive and pleasurable. When we hear about a girl unable to find sleep, shutting out the rays of the moon as 'burning hot', and tossing about in a feverish condition on her bed, or when we hear about a man telling his travelling companion how wonderful it will be when he finally sees her again, standing by the gate of their town and looking out for his return, two things happen to us. First, whatever memories or present feelings of such painful matters are stored in our own hearts, flow into a non-subjective universal which the poem conjures up. Secondly, from this experience of the poem a warmth flows back into our hearts: if it is a good poem, we derive considerable delight and happiness from it. It is as if the endless chain of unfulfilled or unfulfilling desires, when itself made the object of poetic exploration, can yield happiness. A catharsis occurs in us which is brought about by poetically, artistically depicted desires. The boundaries of one's ordinary self seem to break down and we appear to be drawn into some transpersonal reality. Momentary individual instances of love or desire become sublimated in some timeless, non-transient entity. Thus, far from merely duplicating on the plane of poetry a desiring subject, the poem as a whole acts in a special way upon the reader or listener and transforms his own passions. In that sense, love acquires a transcendental dimension, and all our passions become pointers to some universal and non-transitory reality. Illusion would then lie in our confusion as to the appropriate manner in which we ought to relate to this universal *kāma*. What kind of religious significance such an entity could possess is another question which can only be answered in a later chapter. But for the present, let us turn to a second illustration of love being lifted beyond the fleeting moment.

Once again the *Grand Story* (*Bṛhatkathā*) offers us some interesting material. Two Jain versions, and the three 'Hindu' adaptations we have in Sanskrit, offer us more than just a string of amorous adventures for our hero. At a certain point, something special happens to the hero, as far as the Jain examples are concerned: he experiences a love that, as he himself confesses, is different from the incidents of infatuation he has so far experienced. He meets a girl and develops an attachment to her which is qualitatively different from all his other attachments (and logically this puts an end to his pursuit of girls).[3] Now the Jains can write this off by simply stating that this was due to his meeting, in a new body, the soul of his wife from a previous life. But in the Hindu versions,[4] the theme is used to provide an overarching structure to the whole narrative. At the very beginning we find our hero in loving union with his beloved, usually called Love-Casket (Madanamañcukā). His whole adventure trip is brought about only because she is abducted, and right through his many conquests runs the theme of his search for the one, true beloved. Logically, reunion with her marks the culmination of his quest.

Incidentally something comparable happened to Don Juan (at least in the literary history of the motif). The romantic dramatist Zorrilla,[5] in 1844, lets him encounter the one true love through which he repents of all his sins and finds salvation (a fate also granted to Dr Faustus by Goethe just twelve years previously, in 1832).[6] Thus even on the level of empirical analysis, the ways in which we relate to objects of desire are variegated and certain particular objects may well have a 'purifying' effect on that relationship itself. The poet Govardhana states something similar when he says:

> 'The other girls are like a string of geese drifting by on the lake of my heart, but you are firmly embedded in it like a lotus plant.'[7]

The same applies when he compares true love to the seemingly still vessel in the centre of the potter's wheel and his many fleeting affairs to the other pots that are flung off by the rapid revolution of the wheel,[8] or to the one god abiding in many statues – the other girls.[9]

In one particular case, we are able to trace the development of a famous Indian story about 'true love'. Originally this story (mentioned previously) was a secondary episode in the *Bṛhatkathā*.[10] When its hero had won the heart of yet another girl, Gandharvadattā, during a lute contest, her guardian, Cārudatta, told him how the girl had come into his care. Cārudatta was a merchant's son who had set out on an adventure trip to make his fortune. The need for such a risky journey had arisen in the following way. His mother incurred her husband's wrath through arranging Cārudatta's marriage without consulting him. Moreover, the mother also had to suffer the insults of the girl's relatives when Cārudatta showed no interest in consummating the marriage. Cursed by her husband and let down by her son, she contrived to have Cārudatta taken to a prostitute, to learn about women and waste his father's money. When totally destitute, he had to set out on the said adventure trip (in the course of which Gandharvadattā was entrusted to him), to return successfully and make up with his wife.

As told so far, the story could hardly be used for a romantic Hollywood screenplay. However, two later dramatists[11] developed from it plays that provide an increasingly more 'refined' and romantic version. The courtesan is now 'secretly' in love with an 'impoverished' Cārudatta (nothing is said about how he became poor), attracted by his noble qualities. She shows herself generous to his little son, whose clay-cart she fills with jewellery, and Cārudatta helps her nobly when a crude member of the royal family molests her. All ends well with Cārudatta marrying the courtesan and his first wife agreeing to it. Thus what started off as a story about a visit to a brothel that backfired, has now become a rather sentimental tale about an 'everlasting' love that overcomes all tribulations.

What these different examples illustrate is an awareness of some kind of qualitative difference between various 'objects of human desire'. The courtesan remains faithful to Cārudatta in spite of his poverty, although many rich and powerful men desire her. In spite of the many other girls the hero of the *Grand Story* wins, Love-Casket remains his true favourite. Whatever affairs the man in Govardhana's poem may indulge in, like the same god in many statues he always finds something of his one and only true love in them. But so what? All this may introduce a certain amount of sophistication, by allowing for at least some empirically accessible differentiation of types of objects of desire. But does this really point at anything more significant?

Our line of argument appears to become increasingly mysterious. So perhaps we ought to make a detour and look at an illustration from closer to home of what has been going on here. Southern France, with neighbouring regions on the Mediterranean coast, witnessed the development of a particular culture of love-poetry by the troubadours who lived between 1100 and 1300. Now it is possible to construct for this culture a chain of logical progression (I am not claiming that this is an 'objective', literary-historical, trend on a global scale). At the (logical) beginning, we find poetry expressing a down-to-earth delight in furtive, adulterous love and straightforward sexual pleasures. But, as William IX, Count of Poitou, puts it (very much in line with Bhartṛhari's complaint about the conflict between mind and heart), 'every day it has struck me that whatever I desired failed to give me happiness; and that, knowing this, I yet do many things about which my heart tells me: all is nothingness'.[12] Thus on the basis of this aversion to the 'coarse', a refined 'courtly love' is built, involving a total commitment to love by way of 'serving' a noble lady, usually from a distance, it would seem. Love becomes 'impersonalized' – not just anonymous, but also deprived of a concrete object. We can see this in Jaufré Rudel de Blaye's poem on 'distant love' (*amor de lonh*). As one critic says:

> The nature of th[is] 'distant love' has been interpreted in extremely divergent ways, ranging from the most literal and biographical to the most abstract, symbolising and mystical. If anything at all is certain, it is that the poet has succeeded in giving form to a mystery, the mystery of a love which is known and experienced only as the end of an unending aspiration, and which is made perceptible only in the self-engendered and utterly isolated reality of the love-song itself ... Critics have variously felt able to identify the poet's distant love with, to mention but a few, the Countess of Tripoli, the Virgin Mary, Jerusalem, or a mystical experience of the divine.[13]

With Guiraut Riquier we reach the final phase of courtly love (1289).

> In times passed I often felt the need to sing about love, but did not know it. What I called 'love' then was but my own folly. But now love has me love a lady such that I cannot honour her enough, hold her in awe or cherish her as she ought to be.[14]

In the final line he says: 'I pray that my lady so maintain her lovers that each one may thereby attain his desire.' Although this seemingly promiscuous lady is not named, critics find it easy to identify her with the Virgin Mary.

We have even less of an exegetical problem with a poem that Ramón Llull wrote on the basis of his own troubadour experiences, and included in his novel *Blanquerna* (*c.* 1284): 'To you Lady Virgin Holy Mary I hand over my will that wants to love you so strongly that without you it cannot desire or love anything else.' In what more dramatic way could the intrusion of a transcendental object of desire into the transient world of human passion be illustrated, than by having a zealous monk push open the door of a low-life tavern and have him sing this poem to the drunkards and harlots, as Llull does in his novel![15]

The momentum of this line of logical progression makes it appear that things were easy for a post-troubadour like Ramón Llull. All he had to do was break open the doors of worldly lust and sing in honour of the Virgin Mary. It may also suggest that the diffuse material we have discussed so far will lead us, by some inbuilt and necessary teleology, to Indian theism. But already Jaufré Rudel de Blaye's 'distant love' suggests a more chameleon-like nature of love, something that takes us once again into closer proximity to what we have been looking at so far on the Indian side. On the other hand, however complex the Indian situation may be, we do find comparable developments here. To give concrete and personal shape to a non-transient, transcendental object of desire (corresponding to God or the Virgin Mary) was indeed one possibility that evolved. But precisely because it is one among various developments of our initial formula, we must be on our guard not simply to say that unfulfilled human longings aim at a divine object for their fulfilment. But for the time being I shall stick to the familiar and concrete: the kind of object of desire we call 'God'. Since this is a topic which has been excluded from our exploration so far, it will be necessary to introduce it in a detailed manner. But love-poetry will never remain absent for long, and thus our detour will be relatively minor.

The key concept for the study of Indian theism is that of '*deva*', or so it would appear. Etymologically related to the Latin *deus* and the Greek *theós*, it provides the most immediate and obvious door of access for any student of the Indian religions. Two histories unfold from this: the history of the concept of *deva* and how it developed, on the one hand, and what Western scholarship has made of all this, on the other. To the uncritical outsider, this is the situation: a large number of *devas* floating through the imaginary world of Indian religions, like bees buzzing around a hive. This then produced the concept of 'poly-theism': a religion in which we find many such entities which we call in the singular, 'god'. More than this, particularly in the case of the Vedic *devas*, correlations between an individual member of that category and a natural phenomenon (say thunderstorm, fire, sun, etc.) seem to exist. This gave rise to a rather rash conclusion that 'theism' can be explained as the 'deification of particularly striking phenomena in nature'. More recently, anthropologists studying *devas* found in folk-religion have suggested that in many cases we can still trace the 'origin' of such figures. Thus we hear of 'deified' heroes, or '*devī*-fied' women who suffered a violent death. At least factually the anthropologists are more accurate than those students of the Vedas. But conceptually it would be a fatal mistake to see in this the 'origin' of theism or even of religion. Whether the concept *deva* is applied to an aspect of nature or to the memory of some special human being, it presupposes the very existence of the concept itself prior to this application. To try and pursue this further back would take us beyond the boundaries of recorded Indian religious history. The documents allow us to study how the concept of *deva* was used and applied, but not how it came about.

In the present context, it is not necessary to look at further such details. Instead let me offer here merely a non-historical, systematic survey. We have not only a large number of *devas*, but in fact a variety of groups or categories. This latter point is not normally emphasized in literature dealing with Indian theism. The first group consist of the Vedic *devas*; a thousand or so of these have been counted in the Vedas, and most are male. The second category is made up of *devas* who come to the fore in epic literature (in the sense of Purāṇas and the *Mahābhārata*); I shall refer to them as 'purāṇic' *devas*, and more will be said on the Purāṇas presently. Female figures are now more prominent. Into a third group we can put *devas* mentioned in yet another genre of literary works, the Tantras. *Devīs*, the feminine of *devas*, are here quite important. In other words, these three groups are individually identified through different genres of religious literature – Vedas, Epics/Purāṇas and Tantras – and follow consecutively in their literary documentation one after the other at intervals of, very roughly speaking, one thousand years (thus: 1500 BC, 500 BC and AD 500). In some sense, no tradition gets totally superseded and instead we have to envisage parallel lines. All this applies to so-called 'classical' material, but besides we must list another group of *devas* who belong to local, regional, folk, vernacular, tribal (or however one wants to label them) milieux. In most cases, the documentation available is fragmentary and not very old. Yet there is enough evidence available to show that in itself we are dealing with an ancient phenomenon which, moreover, interacted with the first three traditions of *devas*. Thus from a certain point onwards, we must imagine four different strands running concurrently – and, to a considerable extent, interactively – through the Indian religious scene, each one with its specific sets of *devas*.

But what are we dealing with here? Nothing much as yet, for the word *deva* may denote hardly more than some superhuman being, comparable to the *nāga*, *vidyādhara*, and *rākṣasa* of previous chapters. *Devas* do indeed live in realms far superior to the world of the humans, full of splendour and luxury and pleasure, and such realms, above the world of man, could well be called 'heavens'. In religious terms, the worship we witness being offered to such *devas* may correspond to no more than the veneration of a Christian saint (minus all the ethical overtones that would carry), and often could be compared to 'magic' (again, minus all the ethical overtones). And in fact, many such religious aspects have already been discussed under the heading of Power. But as we noticed there, from the point of view of the renouncers the status of these *devas* is only quantitatively higher than that of human beings, for the heavens with all their *devas* are included in the cycle of transmigration. Only total 'liberation' allows for a truly qualitative leap into the transcendent. So why mention the *devas* here at all? The reason for this is simply that not everything has been said that can be said about them. This brings me to the tricky theme of 'monotheism' in India.

The *devas* may not be very important in a religious sense. But it happened that, against the background of purāṇic *devas*, India evolved in addition the concept of 'God' – a personal being outside space, time and matter, eternal and autonomous, omnipotent and omniscient, and responsible for the way things are and for man's ultimate fulfilment. In order to avoid confusion, I shall refer to such a being exclusively as Bhagavān (masculine) or Bhagavatī (feminine). That a modern-day *guru* chose to refer to himself as 'Bhagwan' is unfortunate and adds unnecessary complexity to an issue that is complex enough. Thus let me repeat: when henceforth I use the words Bhagavān and Bhagavatī, they are intended to denote 'God' (male or female), and *deva* is rendered as 'god'.

We know of the existence of such a concept from the direct testimony of Indian religious literature, where we find the definition I have just given. Thus it is not an extrapolation, nor a secondary interpretation of the Indian material. What now is the relationship of such a Bhagavān with the *devas*? We may well find texts which use the word '*deva*' when they are talking about a figure to which my definition of Bhagavān applies. Moreover, very often, when such a Bhagavān is given concrete characteristics, a personality, and an 'image', many features known from *deva* figures reappear. These connections between the *devas* and Bhagavān are interesting and important, and we shall return to them in due course. But conceptually they obscure a vital difference. It is not possible to argue that the concept of Bhagavān was produced by developing the concept of *deva* further. Indian monotheism cannot be derived from so-called polytheism. Even if we translate *deva* with 'god', the jump from the lower case to the capital is qualitative. One of the greatest disservices to an honest struggle with the nature of human religiosity has been the pretence that the two (*deva*/Bhagavān) are the same, are similar, or a straight continuum. As in all good science, it is important to acknowledge holes, blanks, jumps and discontinuities which existing theories cannot explain. The origin of Indian monotheism is one such case. Bhagavān is like the queen bee in a beehive; or, in terms of another simile, the *devas* are not the fossils out of which a palaeontologist can reconstruct the evolution of Bhagavān. All we can do is accept the fact that suddenly in the history of the Indian religions we are faced with the documented appearance of the concept 'Bhagavān'.

This is still not the end of our difficulties, and some further misconceptions have to be attacked. Since nothing is ever easy and simple in India, it is necessary to establish a whole catalogue of such Bhagavān figures. But doesn't this automatically change the mono- back to polytheism? It does not. For such a catalogue does not make up one religious system, but belongs merely to the outside observer who needs a metasystem to make sense of the complexities of India. In other words, such a list of Bhagavāns and Bhagavatīs is comparable to a directory of the various monotheistic religions we find in India. The mistake anybody makes who lumps all the different Bhagavān figures together and calls that polytheism is similar to the foolish theory some Martian might produce about Britain being polytheistic, because God, Jahweh and Allah are all worshipped in that one country.

There still remains one last popular misconception to be got rid of once and for all: this is the idea that Hindus believe in three main gods. These are supposed to be Brahmā, Viṣṇu and Śiva (the *trimūrti*), who somehow manage to run the world by consensus and as a team, looking after creation, preservation and destruction, respectively. Once again this myth is used to show that Hinduism is polytheistic, and once again this is utter nonsense. In all instances known to me in Indian texts where we hear of these three *devas*, we also hear about the one who, or that, transcends them. Frequently it is actually Bhagavān who creates the three to perform their respective tasks; or it may be some other ultimate being.

What is essential to keep in mind from all this is the following. It is quite legitimate, and in fact essential, to talk of Indian monotheism, which can neither be subsumed historically under the belief in *devas*, nor typologically transcended in a polytheism (the 'Hindu Trinity'). This Indian monotheism in turn manifests itself as a variety of different systems, with the appearance of a whole range of Bhagavān/Bhagavatī figures. One thing ought perhaps to be said which exonerates the exponents of the various theories I have attacked. When I talk of systems here, they do not always show the same degree of absoluteness as with us. Thus a particular monotheistic system around one particular Bhagavān will not necessarily have the same rigid linguistic, social, political, cultural and historical boundaries that separate for instance Islam, Judaism and Christianity in Britain today. I say 'not necessarily': thus we do have instances of fairly obvious boundaries around some such systems, and it is with the help of these that we can identify the less obvious ones. Thus we could add forms of devotional and institutional monotheism to our list, besides the systematic theological ones. With us such things hardly exist, or are not supposed to exist, since the way a religious system has established itself in society is far more rigid and uniform. Our monotheistic religion wants to be a total system, and makes totalitarian claims over every aspect of man's life. In India, it was quite possible for an individual or a group of individuals to make up their own (say devotional) monotheism, while they continued to belong to other systems that as such fall into a different typological category of religion (say institutionally or theologically).

The purpose of this little exercise has been to isolate within the general realm of the *devas* the concept of Bhagavān/Bhagavatī as autonomous. Once the conceptual autonomy has been established in principle, we can start looking at new issues. What about the documentation of monotheism, and the application of the concept Bhagavān to specific God-figures? Are they equally autonomous with regard to the *devas*? Unfortunately, they are not, for the most part. In more concrete terms this means that the literature specializing in telling us about the *devas* provides us also with the documentation on Bhagavān. So, while it is possible to distinguish at least three groups of different *devas* on the basis of purely literary criteria (Vedic, purāṇic, tantric), no such separate literary genre exists for Bhagavān. It is primarily the Purāṇas (and the epic *Mahābhārata*) that contain our relevant material. Similarly, and possibly directly connected with this, when it comes to giving concrete form to the abstract concept of Bhagavān – in terms of iconography, characterization, 'personality' and individual identity – the *devas* of the Purāṇas (and of folk-religion) provide most of the details. This now also means that for all practical purposes we can forget about the Vedic and tantric *devas* in our present discussion.

Let us pursue the issue of documentation a bit further and look at three seminal works which stand at the respective beginnings of three monotheistic developments. This does not exhaust the subject, and we could have included the *Mahābhārata* or early purāṇic passages here which all tell us about Viṣṇu as Bhagavān, but textually this is very complex material. Moreover, I am sure that there are other such seminal monotheistic works awaiting our discovery in the enormous mass of texts that we have. First and foremost, there is the famous *Bhagavad-gītā* '[the treatise] sung by Bhagavān'; then there is the *Śvetāśvatara-Upaniṣad* (named after an otherwise unknown sage); and finally there is the *Devī-māhātmya*, the 'glorification of the Goddess'.[16] The dates of the first two may well fall somewhere during the last few centuries BC, and the third may belong to the middle of the first millennium AD. They offer us the earliest documentation (known to us so far) of the following figures: Kṛṣṇa (the 'Bhagavān' in the very title of the *Bhagavad-gītā*), Śiva and the Goddess or Bhagavatī. Each work stands apart from its context, on purely textual grounds: the *Bhagavadgītā* and the *Devīmāhātmya* are interpolations, and the Upaniṣad differs markedly from all other early representatives of the genre. Thus my assumption of the autonomy of the concept of Bhagavān finds here, obviously not a proof, but at least some textual backing. Moreover, each of the three texts attempts, in its own way, some linkage of its Bhagavān figure with the Vedas and Vedic *devas*. But these are learned references back to something which is perceived as adding authority and prestige to the respective Bhagavān figures, and not the reflection of historical developments in a forward direction (from the Vedic *devas* to these Bhagavān figures).

At this stage I do not want to digress and spread out the monotheistic theologies developed in the three works. Let it be sufficient for the time being to say that 'Bhagavān/Bhagavatī' are theologically comparable to our God. Here Hindu traditions, at least, have established one personal object of human desire and love that is non-transient. (It would confuse the present discussion too much were we to pay attention also to an impersonal alternative.) This love for Bhagavān or Bhagavatī is generally called *bhakti*, a word that in ordinary contexts can denote the love of a couple for each other (including sexual love) or the loyalty of a soldier for his king. Theoretically it would have been possible for such monotheistic religions to choose a separate course of history and, for example, produce an independent and new type of religious literature (as indeed the Jains and the Buddhists did). Instead, our three seminal works of monotheism attached themselves to existing literatures and their genres (the Vedic Upaniṣads, the *Mahābhārata* tradition and the Purāṇas). This is merely the first instance where we can observe such a choice. Thus to label monotheism 'sectarian', as is conventionally done, is highly misleading, since it suggests a conscious decision to split from a 'mainstream' tradition, instead of, as we can observe here and in further instances, the readiness to associate oneself with such a 'mainstream'.

For all practical purposes, only the Purāṇas – another grand Indian cultural construct – need concern us here. The word '*purāṇa*' may be translated as 'account of past history' and originally that is precisely what it was. All over northern India, in an area roughly defined by the rivers Ganges and Jumna, sometime during the last millennium BC, Ārya kingdoms had established themselves. Politically autonomous, they nevertheless maintained the awareness of a common history, culture and origin, and the various dynasties intermarried. Public record offices had not yet been invented, and other means of storing important information were used. Bards employed at the royal courts served this role, remembering which king married whose daughter and which of his sons was the legitimate heir to the throne. But, obviously, mighty warriors needed more – such as accounts of the glorious deeds of their ancestors. And what was this common bond of Āryaness that held the various dynasties together? How had these royal lineages come into existence? Once you are looking at such questions, there is no need to stop half-way. How did the world come about, who was the first man, and how did the Āryas derive from him? It is this kind of thing that the bards would talk about, naturally in some form of stylized and stereotyped manner, though certainly without a written archetype. Some stories about the past became so popular that they turned into separate repertoire pieces (such as the account of a particularly devastating war which involved practically all Āryan kings, on either side of the battle front, or a more fairy-tale-like story about a prince exiled in a forest who lost his wife and then went to Laṅkā to fight the kidnapping demon and get her back).

These independent repertoire pieces turned into the two great epics of India, the *Mahābhārata* and the *Rāmāyaṇa*. But the masterfile was preserved alongside and developed by different bards in various directions. Then, at some unknown stage, versions of the masterfile were written down, and these make up the cores of what we have today as the various Purāṇas (for instance, the *Mārkaṇḍeya-Purāṇa*, *Viṣṇu-Purāṇa*, *Bhāgavata-Purāṇa*, etc.) If this happened in a rather random and arbitrary manner, the way in which these 'masterfile cores' were expanded was very much more random and arbitrary (including, as an extreme case of randomness, the mixing up of manuscript leaves belonging to different texts). All kinds of secondary material was added, such as accounts of statescraft, the construction of forts, the different kinds of precious stones, and so on. More important for our purposes were the additions of religious material. Obviously right from the beginning religious matters, such as the origin of the world, had been included. This now offered a tempting slot for anybody who had more to say about a Bhagavān figure. Moreover, lots of *devas* were popularly known and worshipped in that society, many of which had no direct link with the Vedic pantheon. This material was added as well, leading to the second set of *devas*, the 'purāṇic' ones. Thirdly, at a certain stage people lost interest in the very long and rather tedious lists of genealogies and instead concentrated on the expansion of stories, now of a decidedly religious nature, connected with a few specific figures found in these lists. These figures are, above all, Kṛṣṇa and Rāma, whose popularity obviously stems from their roles in the *Mahābhārata* and *Rāmāyaṇa* respectively. All this goes on as a free-for-all literary process, and it is not difficult to imagine how amorphous the texts which have come down to us became. It is really only towards the end of the first millennium AD that attempts began to be made, by individual Purāṇas, to streamline the whole and produce more unified works – 'unified' meaning here logically, theologically and structurally consistent.[17]

Once again I must digress and point out a common misconception about the Purāṇas. The popular religious studies books simply define the whole genre as the 'storehouses of Indian mythology', and accordingly individual scholars have treated any and every story found in any Purāṇa as a 'myth' and as more or less interchangeable with any other version of the same 'myth'. Given the compositional history of our texts, all kinds of material was included which a more careful literary analysis would reveal to belong to such varied genres as 'short story', ' novel', 'anecdote', 'folk-tale', 'fairy-tale', 'religious satire', 'polemical writing', or even 'dirty joke', apart from the more obvious genres of historically perceived narratives of what certain *deva* figures did on earth in the past. Clearly we can't lump all this together as making up 'the' mythology of an individual *deva*. Furthermore, it should have become clear by now how *deva* and Bhagavān material is indiscriminately thrown together in our texts, but that any serious religious evaluation of any given 'myth' must begin by trying to figure out its positional value in a given religious system.

Let us briefly look at one example. In a monotheistic system that has Śiva as its Bhagavān, it is perfectly permissible to state the following. Once upon a time, the *devas* Viṣṇu and Brahmā saw an enormous column rising up to the heavens. They attempted to measure it, by going respectively up and down its length; but they failed to discover its ends. The column was, actually, Śiva's *liṅga* (for non-Sanskritists, his penis). Viṣṇu's (and Brahmā's) failure is obviously meant to put them firmly in a very inferior place (as minor *devas*) and to show that only Śiva is Bhagavān.[18] However, from the point of view of a system in which Viṣṇu is the Bhagavān, such a story is no more than vicious sectarian propaganda. Appropriately, 'myths' will be told which make it clear that Śiva is just a minor *deva* (for example, by telling how Śiva, ostracized for having cut off Brahmā's fifth head and holding the skull in his hand as a sign of his crime, came to Viṣṇu and begged him for help).[19] If we wanted a parallel, we could refer to the fact that both Islam and Christianity know of Jesus (Isa). But nobody in their right minds would make indiscriminate use of what both religions have to say about him. In theory, nobody will disagree that this is a sensible methodology, but that does not mean that for every case we still have the information about the individual system within which a 'myth' (or a poem or a statue, for that matter) must be interpreted. (Where such information is built into a purāṇic narrative and when it is then ignored by the analyst because it spoils the story, no such excuses are acceptable.)

Thus our main sources for Bhagavān are the Purāṇas. But they carry that information completely wrapped up with a vast amount of material on the *devas* who are specific to the genre. Given the nature of these sources, it makes little sense to ask what characteristics of a given Bhagavān figure are 'original', and what is a secondary derivation from a purāṇic *deva* figure. On whatever level of abstract, monotheistic theology we find Śiva, he is still in possession of his cosmic-sized *liṅga*, and Viṣṇu never loses his four arms. These characteristics may be given a highly abstract interpretation, but in themselves they are clearly essential to define Bhagavān as Śiva or as Viṣṇu. Similarly, however abstract a theology might be developed around Bhagavatī or however much she might imitate the deeds of male gods in fighting demons, she will always remain a woman and feminine. This is a second instance of a choice by monotheistic traditions not to be sectarian, but to be part of the mainstream. For theoretically they could have preferred to separate their individual Bhagavān or Bhagavatī figure from any association with related *devas*, by introducing new external characteristics. Such a continuity between a black-complexioned *deva* Kṛṣṇa and an equally black Bhagavān Kṛṣṇa does not mean that at least in some cases we cannot trace the projection of the Bhagavān concept on to specific purāṇic (heroic or *deva*) figures. From a certain date onwards, the purāṇic masterfile started to list two heroic princes, Kṛṣṇa and Rāma. But we also see how our sources develop them into *deva* figures, and how, ultimately, each one turns into Bhagavān. One example may illustrate this.

This offers me the opportunity to say something briefly about the role of the fourth group of *devas* I listed earlier: the gods of folk religion. When expanding the hero Kṛṣṇa into a *deva*, the purāṇic tradition actually drew on a source that we must identify as 'folk religious' or 'tribal'.[20] The way that the prince Kṛṣṇa figures in the bulk of the *Mahābhārata* epic created, at a certain stage of his rising popularity, the need to say something about his childhood and youth – a blank in the epic account. Thus the gap was filled with an adaptation of a local religious tradition of cowherds from the vicinity of the town Mathurā. This tradition knew about a boy-*deva* who displayed miraculous powers by protecting the community against all kinds of dangers and also displayed miraculous handsomeness by having all girls and women fall in love with him. His final achievement was the conquest of the town Mathurā. The story told about an exchange of two babies, one born in the royal lineage of Mathurā and one in the family of the chieftain of the cowherds not only accounts for the strange environment in which the prince Kṛṣṇa grew up, but also suggests the joint where the old and the new material was welded together. Thus a heroic prince Kṛṣṇa fuses with a folk *deva*, and in turn this synthesis is associated with the Bhagavān figure Kṛṣṇa whose theology the *Bhagavadgītā* spells out. A lot more will have to be said about Kṛṣṇa at later stages.

We seem to have moved a long way away from the matters of love. Actually, we have just about come back to them. Clearly it was relatively easy to move through the songs of the troubadours and obtain the Virgin Mary (or God for that matter) as the ultimate, transcendental object of human love. All this talk about *devas*, Bhagavān and Bhagavatī, Purāṇas and mythology has been so much more complicated and confusing. But unfortunately it simply is not possible to talk about 'the God of the Hindus', however much certain popularist writers on the subject may want to do so. In fact I ought to apologize to the specialists in the field for having simplified these matters, perhaps beyond their endurance. Anyway, let us return to the point of departure of this excursion into the history and complexities of the Hindu concepts of God, namely the matters of the heart, love and the search for a non-transient object of human desire. From here we can move in a fairly obvious direction, by looking at how such an 'object' actually behaves – at this stage not yet in relation to us, the loving subjects, but as an independent, autonomous reality.

Whether *deva* or Bhagavān, we are not dealing with lonely individuals who may be looking down from some elevated realm upon the follies of human passion with contempt or compassion. They have their own loving partners, and often the set-up is polygamous. Thus Viṣṇu in most cases has as his queens Lakṣmī/Śrī, the so-called goddess of fortune and prosperity, and Bhū who is 'Earth'. Śiva is married to Pārvatī, but that does not prevent him from being quite promiscuous with other ladies, a bit like the Greek Zeus. Kṛṣṇa often has his Rādhā, Rāma invariably his Sītā, and Skanda his Dēvayāṉai and Vaḷḷi. Were we to explain the relative superiority of the respective male *deva* in such a set-up as a reflection of the role of woman in real Indian life, we might be able to explain why the Goddess stays unmarried in those contexts in which she plays a major religious role in her own right.[21] Anyway, what is important here is the fact that almost all purāṇic *devas* have a love-life. Equally important is the fact mentioned previously that, when monotheistic systems draw on the Purāṇas to concretize the abstract category 'Bhagavān', they do not eliminate this aspect. Thus also within the nature of the personal absolute a relational dimension is envisaged which refers to the female partner (say Lakṣmī) as its object.

In terms of our initial formula, the love-life of the *devas* and of Bhagavān duplicates once again (as that of the poetic lovers did previously) the relationship between a desiring subject and its object. A third realm, that of divine love, can be added to those of the 'real life' and of poetry, and it is identical in structure to the other two. Now an interesting question arises. Given this structural similarity, how did the Indian traditions deal with it? Did they choose a Semitic kind of stark separation of human and divine love and treat both in formally totally distinct genres of literature (like 'secular love-poems' versus 'religious poetry'), or did it decide to use the potentials offered by the traditions of love-poetry, like Hāla, the *akattiṇai* and the Sanskrit *kāvya*? On the whole, the latter path was chosen. The traditions of love-poetry were indeed applied to the depiction of the divine love-life. As the *devas* were envisaged as lovers, India felt it to be the most economic thing to apply existing poetic forms and conventions to them, instead of creating new means of expression, and no formal distinction was maintained between poetry about human and about divine lovers. The important implication of this is that hereby the relation between desired object and desiring subject is transposed on to a plane of reality which – given the way it is defined – cannot now be written off as transitory or as mere poetic imagination. Love is taken here beyond the fleeting moment into eternity. Whatever it may mean precisely to say that the *devas* are religious figures, they are not transcendental beings, and they relate to mankind as potential donors of a prosperity and happiness that will remain transitory. But when we come to Bhagavān or Bhagavatī, even the most severe critique of the transience of all empirical phenomena cannot be applied. For Bhagavān is defined as eternal and outside the constraints of space, time and matter. That, for example, the Jains or the Buddhists would regard the belief in such a Bhagavān itself as pure illusion, is a totally separate issue. Such central contents of religious belief, backed up with a logically consistent theology and defended through philosophical argument, cannot be got rid of that easily, as we know from our own Western religious history.

All this would still be rather insignificant, however interesting it may appear in itself, were it not for another dimension to all this. Man is not just the observer of a divine love-life which possesses non-transient reality. His existence is intrinsically connected with Bhagavān, who accounts for man's very being and for his ultimate fulfilment. This now allows for a number of interesting interrelated questions. Does the love-life of Bhagavān in any way affect the *bhakti* relationship between himself and his devotee? Or are the two regarded as separate and fundamentally different relationships? Given the fact that the divine love-life can be described in terms of love-poetry, does this have any bearing on man's *bhakti*, devotion, in terms of the transcendentalizing function of poetry (which was discussed at the beginning of this chapter)?

It is clear that what we have achieved in this chapter is no more than to catalogue a number of important building-blocks and to establish a number of suggestions as to ways in which these blocks could be used to construct various kinds of edifice. The concrete details will be explored in the next chapter. But first let me offer a foretaste in one concrete example.

I mentioned earlier that the account of Kṛṣṇa's childhood and youth was derived from a folk-religious tradition. We have no independent testimony of this, and thus we must rely on the earliest version of the adapted form the story took. This is the *Harivaṃśa*, an appendix to the *Mahābhārata*, perhaps written in the second or third century AD. Here now is one little episode in the account of his youth. Kṛṣṇa, attractive beyond all normal human standards, has infatuated all the girls of the cowherds. They regularly meet in the forest for fun and games, and also have wonderful rolls in the hay (after all, this takes place in the cowpens!). But obviously such delights are not possible all the time, since Kṛṣṇa has various jobs to do during the day. Thus the girls have to spend painful hours longing for his return.

> These women sang with a sweetness brought about by their emotions. With Kṛṣṇa as object of their affection, they became happy.
>
> Their bodies smeared with cowdung and mud, some girls ran after him in great delight, as elephant cows run after the bull, and had their fun.
>
> Others, with laughing faces, 'drank' Kṛṣṇa through eyes that desire had made wide open, and could not get enough.
>
> Yet other girls of the cowherds, eager for sexual pleasures, became 'thirsty' when seeing his face, and then 'drank' it, when, during the night, they had occasion to make love.[22]

In this extract, we find a number of concepts and ideas that are already familiar to us. Obviously the author wanted to spell out quite consciously and explicitly that Kṛṣṇa, as a divine object of desire, completely alters the whole intellectual edifice that the Jains and Buddhists had erected. (The senses perceive objects which cause 'thirst' – passionate desire and craving – and this in turn is the cause of fundamental suffering.) By feeding the eyes with the sight of Kṛṣṇa's beauty and 'drinking' his face, an intense lust arises in the heart. But since this 'thirst' is directed towards a 'drink of immortality', a transcendental object of desire, it yields happiness (*sukha*, the opposite to the Buddhist *duḥkha*). Thus, in a Bhagavān such as Kṛṣṇa, India found a non-transitory and transcendental reality for the human passions and for the poetic imagination, far beyond the fleeting moment emphasized by the renouncers. But as this realm includes the world, man and God, love turns into a cosmic reality.

CHAPTER 13

Cosmic desire

From one point of view, the world is a frightening place. A cholera *devī* may become restless in her shrine, since people have stopped offering her the worship she was accustomed to, and may spread herself out all over the villages. Wild tribesmen may be lying in wait in the forest to ambush a traveller and offer him in human sacrifice. The glance of an untouchable may ruin a complex ritual, so that the ancestors, left without food, may return as hungry ghosts into the world of man. The bite of an irate cobra may put a tragic end to the hopes of a full, rich and long life for an innocent child. Passions, unsuspectedly hibernating for many years, may suddenly burst out of the recesses of the heart and create havoc and murder.

And yet, seen from a different point of view, the world is a lovely place. A warmth and beauty pervades it that allows for a feeling of comfort and homeliness. The different categories of beings, including the tribesmen and the untouchables, the animals and *devas* (like Murukan̲ or Kṛṣṇa/Māyōn̲), all appear to share in one and the same grand experience of love. Whatever imperfections this love may possess in real life, poetry about it has the power to transform them and give rise to a profound aesthetic happiness. Although the human heart may frequently be fickle and infatuation can rapidly turn into ennui or even revulsion, it is also capable of a lasting and deep loyalty and attachment. And in all the transitoriness of earthly happiness and in all the sufferings of human existence, there is the one solid rock of Bhagavān or Bhagavatī who makes the world what it is and looks after man.

It is relatively easy to construct a coherent description of the world as a terrifying realm, governed by the laws of aggression, greed, passion and delusion. But what has been said so far about the world as a love-filled place adds up to little more than fragmentary inklings and tentative suggestions. Is there any coherence in this? Particularly, what has a Bhagavān to do with love-poetry to which we seem to be paying a disproportionate amount of attention? So let us take up the suggestions made towards the end of the previous chapter, in order to address ourselves to such questions in detail.

To say that empirically 'love' somehow points at a transcendental dimension, by coupling the experience of unfulfilment on the worldly plane with an unabated drive towards further satisfaction, is one thing. To say that the divine is therefore the appropriate object of human desire, is another thing. But it would be rash to infer from this a causal link between the two: that the realization of the unfulfillability of human love generated the concept of the divine. 'God' and 'Goddess' make their appearance in Indian culture all of a sudden, without us being able to trace a development or a logical progression or any kind of causal nexus. In terms of a simile I used earlier on, theism can be compared to a further stone thrown into the lake of Indian culture. While the waves stimulated thereby have to hit those made by the renouncer tradition in full frontal attack, a much more harmonious interaction, one of intimate complementarity, with those of the traditions of love, also took place.

My choice of 'God' as the first example of a non-transitory aspect of our formula has been motivated by the well-known didactic principle of introducing the more difficult and unfamiliar by means of the familiar and less complex. But that does not mean that when we hear about Bhagavān our familiar concept of 'God' could exhaust the significance of the former. An initial, quite striking, fact must be that Bhagavān may appear as a male figure – and that is familiar ground – or as a female Goddess. Now this implies another puzzling fact: we are dealing with a whole string of monotheistic systems, and in any genuine catalogue of such systems, various Bhagavāns and Bhagavatīs will be found. Moreover, the inner nature of the divine tends to be envisaged as relational. Obviously this is also the case with the Christian Trinity. But here the relational model is unique and, one could venture to claim, not directly paralleled in a primary human relationship: Father–Son, and the Holy Spirit as the Love between them. With Bhagavān, the model for the relationship is that of the love between husband and wife, or lover and beloved. Thus there is a 'love-life' of the Indian gods, which theoretically allows for a description in terms of the traditions of love-poetry. Further important differences in the Judaeo-Christian and Indian conception of 'God' will become apparent at later stages (for example, the fact that the divine in India is envisaged not only as the instrumental, but also as the material cause of the world; or that Bhagavān is not primarily a stimulus of human action in history and society, but can be, more appropriately, compared to a poem to be enjoyed by man).

The *devas* and *devīs*, Bhagavāns and Bhagavatīs, have a love-life. Now it is easily conceivable that, in the cultural expression of this, some distinction from the current traditions of love-poetry could have been established, either in terms of form or of content and structure. However, this is not what happened and, given the initial presence of figures like Kṛṣṇa and Murukaṉ in the landscape of the heart, this comes perhaps as less of a surprise to us. This now means that both in terms of form and content, man, *deva* and Bhagavān are depicted in the same kind of love-poetry. Let us look at five specific examples.

Anybody in traditional India who wanted to write a book, even on such unpoetic subjects as mathematics, linguistics, love-making or statescraft, would begin his enterprise with a little prayer. Similarly, no drama could be enacted, unless a string of prayers had been recited. A highly stereotyped form evolved for these prayers, usually ending in 'may ... protect you' or 'victorious be ...'. In a poem it is not only a god or goddess who 'protect' or 'gain victory'; these terms could also be applied to a minute facet, like the reflection from a toe nail or the gesture of a hand or a smile, associated with the respective god. But the constraints of the form are complemented by incredibly creative and imaginative explorations of the content. Derived in the most informal way from the 'myths' told in the Purāṇas (and let us not forget that such myths themselves were constantly created and added to these same Purāṇas), our poets made up their own miniature picture of divine reality. Not only were such prayers then collected in classical anthologies, but later poets had the tendency to produce whole collections themselves, or write whole poems in this form. Thus, for example, the poet Govardhana (*c.* AD 1175) introduces his work with a string of twenty-nine such prayers; I shall use a few of his poems here to illustrate the genre.

Six different *deva* figures are addressed and, besides, we find eight prayers in honour of various *devīs*. For Śiva, the poet focuses, for instance, on that particular mythical moment when the ascetic, after burning the *deva* of love to ashes and then having been seduced by Umā, is marrying her. By virtue of his asceticism, Śiva's body is smeared with ashes. But as he holds Umā's hand during the wedding ceremony he becomes sexually aroused – something the Indian poet can always tell from the hair on the body standing on end, all the more so here, when the black hair contrasts sharply with the white of the ashes covering the skin. With his raw material laid out like this, the poet can now infuse the situation with an imaginative, unique explanation.

Victorious be Śiva's body,
smeared with ashes:
at the touch of Umā's hand
its hairs stand on end,
as if from it were sprouting
new Kāmas
– though nothing but ashes was left of him! [1]

By glorifying this body of Śiva, the poet implies that humanity has found in it a new bliss-giving personification of love.

In another poem,[2] the focus is on Śiva's and Umā's love-making, more precisely, when they have reversed roles and she is 'acting the male part' astride him. Now in order to understand what Govardhana makes of this situation, it is necessary to know, first, that a beautiful woman's face is always synonymous with a lotus-flower in this poetry; secondly, that one very popular iconographic type of the *deva* Viṣṇu shows him reclining, a lotus-flower growing out of his navel. Given the position of Umā, the poet can now imagine a lotus flower (her face) hovering over Śiva's chest, with Umā's body suggesting the stalk that links the flower to Śiva's lower region. But that is not enough. Govardhana eulogizes Umā's face for turning, as it were, Śiva into Viṣṇu or, better, imbuing him with characteristics typical of Viṣṇu. Furthermore, a reference to Brahmā, who is supposed to take his birth in that same lotus growing from Viṣṇu's navel, is clearly implied. Thus the poet states that due to Umā's presence all three gods of the *trimūrti* – Brahmā, Viṣṇu and Śiva – become unified in one body. I could go even further and extrapolate a theological statement from this: the Goddess is supreme, the three male gods fused to lie supine under her and to serve for her pleasures. It could be argued that such a theological interpretation is rather too extreme as far as Govardhana is concerned. But later on we shall encounter material where such a theology is expressed in all seriousness and without any poetic conceit. It is possible that already Govardhana was somehow influenced by it. Here is the poem:

Victorious be the face
  of the Mountain's Daughter Umā:
as she makes love astride Śiva,
  it makes it look
as if he too had a lotus
  growing from his navel!

The last poem[3] in the series of introductory prayers admonishes the reader to bow down in devotion to the god of love and to beautiful women. While we may accept the first object of devotion, the second one requires explanation, and Govardhana knows it. So he goes on to say: 'for they are joined in mutually beneficial work'. That means, one cannot be thought of without the other. Why? He who lost his body, when Śiva burnt him to ashes, acquires through the women's physique new bodies. They, on the other hand, supposedly the weaker sex, acquire a full arsenal of weapons from him. Love on the plane of divinity and in real human life are inextricably interwoven.

These three examples from Govardhana – chosen here either because they do not require an inordinate amount of mythological background information or because they keep the degree of embarrassment for both author and reader at a bearable low – may suffice to illustrate a genre of literature of which we possess thousands of examples. It is here where, in the most obvious manner, the interaction between theism and love-poetry can be demonstrated. But let me now turn to a few examples of more-or-less famous literary works which are conceived of on a far larger scale than the self-contained four-line poems of the introductory prayers.

Conveniently, we can begin by looking once again at Jayadeva's *Gītagovinda*,[4] which was written in Bengal towards the close of the twelfth century AD. It could be classified as a libretto for a musical dance-play. Relatively few stanzas provide us with the narrative of the action – the plot. The bulk of the work consists of lyrical songs, in different *rāgas*. The main actors are Kṛṣṇa, his favourite beloved Rādhā, and a number of milkmaids. The setting is romantic: the forests and meadows during the season of spring, with flowers everywhere. Rādhā is intensely jealous, because promiscuous Kṛṣṇa is chasing after other milkmaids. Her friends tell her tales about his amours, and she curses her bad luck for being in love with such an unfaithful playboy. Memories of past bliss mingle with her intense anger. But also Kṛṣṇa recollects her love, and broods. Through the reports of various go-betweens not just we, but also Rādhā and Kṛṣṇa, learn about the agonies they experience because of their love-in-separation. But eventually he manages to break her anger, and the lovers unite, and Rādhā shows that she has now a lover totally devoted to her by adopting the *viparīta* position, sitting astride him (the event Arnold 'perforce' had to leave untranslated).[5] Naturally, prayers provide the frame for the poem. In the very first stanza Jayadeva eulogizes the love-play of Kṛṣṇa and Rādhā, and at the end he prays that Kṛṣṇa's deeds may confer prosperity and happiness to all of us. But to what extent we are dealing with a religious poem is a question that has vexed many a critic. Jayadeva does not help us: in stanza three he simply encourages anybody whose mind finds delight in recollecting Kṛṣṇa's deeds, or who is curious about the arts of love, to listen to his poem. Make of it what you like – this seems to be the message which we shall later return to.

From Kṛṣṇa we turn to Śiva, and from Jayadeva to the most famous of all Indian poets, Kālidāsa (fifth century AD). His *Kumārasambhava* opens with a description of the Himalaya mountain, on top of which Śiva, the greatest of all ascetics, is engrossed in asceticism. We also hear about the mountain's daughter, Pārvatī or Umā. She was the reborn Satī who had immolated herself in the fire of her father's sacrifice, and was destined to become Śiva's wife. We then hear about the ravings of the demon Tāraka, whom the gods had promised to die only by the hands of Śiva's son – a very unlikely possibility. So the gods now scheme to have Śiva fall in love with Pārvatī and procreate this son. Kāma is sent to weaken the determination of Śiva's asceticism, but is burnt to ashes. Umā approaches Śiva directly, imitating his severe penances. Now he begins to take an interest in her, variously tests her love and resolution, and then confesses his own love for her. Arrangements for the marriage are made: the wedding takes place and their love-making is described, with all the themes that were available, at this relatively early date, to a poet in that tradition. This is probably as far as the genuine poem by Kālidāsa goes, although the last canto (8) has been looked upon even in India with some embarrassment and hesitation.[6] In it we hear about Śiva's and Umā's love-life, beginning with the wedding night and his gentle seduction of her. We hear how she slowly overcomes her shyness and inexperience and begins to develop a liking for intercourse that can match his. We hear about the inevitable nailmarks and about bitten lips, about drunken frolicking and eyes red from lack of sleep, and we are told that even a hundred seasons passed like a single night and still both did not get satiated with the pleasures of making love. Many manuscripts leave this canto out, and a number of ancient Indian critics objected to the depiction of such physical delights of their Bhagavān Śiva. Yet even a staunch Victorian author like Keith (who wrote, in 1920, one of the best-known histories of Sanskrit literature)[7] had to confess:

> Canto viii describes, according to the principles of the *Kāmaśāstras*, the joys of the wedded pair; doubtless such frankness is abhorrent to western taste, but the doubt of its genuineness which have been expressed are clearly groundless … nor in poetic skill is it in the least inferior to Kālidāsa's [other] work.

Some later poet seems to have added nine further cantos, which spell out the birth of a son and his killing the demon. But, as conceived of by Kālidāsa, the *Kumārasambhava* is fundamentally a love-poem, the demon offering no more than the pretext for it. It is a love-poem in more than one sense of the word because, as we saw, it is also about love personified, and about the victory of love over asceticism. At least seen within the context of the genre of stories about demons troubling the gods, Śiva is presented as superior to all other *devas*. But that does not make him absolute: see how 'love' or Pārvatī ultimately carry off the laurels of victory even over Śiva.

From Kālidāsa I want to move to a relatively unknown work, the Tamil *Kantapurāṇam* (by Kacciyappa Civācāriyar, fifteenth century AD).[8] Not only will this allow me to introduce another important god-figure, Skanda/Murukaṉ. We also have here an example of an interesting extension of the processes discussed so far. The projection of love-poetry on to the world of the *devas* did not just involve the purāṇic gods, and not just the poetic tradition using Sanskrit. With Murukaṉ we are dealing with a *deva* in my fourth category, the gods of the folk or tribal traditions. Moreover, the *Kantapurāṇam* not only uses the Tamil language, but employs also the typically Tamil love-poetic tradition of the *akattiṇai*. This is the story as found in the last section of the work (canto 24).

Once upon a time there was a hunter, Nampi, who lived in the forest at the foot of a South-Indian mountain. He had a number of sons, but no daughter – a fact that caused him considerable unhappiness. One day he found a baby girl who had been abandoned and he adopted her as his daughter, calling her Vaḷḷi. When she had grown up and had become an attractive girl, she was sent to guard the millet fields against the birds of the forest. The *deva* Murukaṉ heard about her beauty, and in the disguise of a hunter went to her field. He had just begun to chat her up, when Nampi and other hunters arrived; quickly he hid himself by taking on the form of a *vēṅkai* tree. The hunters were worried by the sudden presence of the tree, but were prevented from cutting it down by Vaḷḷi. After a while, Murukaṉ was able to continue his amorous conversation with the girl, offering to marry her. Yet again they were disturbed by the return of the hunters. Then, unknown to the girl, Murukaṉ returned in the guise of an ascetic and asked the hunters to have Vaḷḷi show him a particular mountain stream for his ablutions. Once he got there, he tried to seduce the girl, but was angrily rejected by her. After this test, he revealed himself to her and now they agreed on their marriage, consummating it in advance. A period of love-in-separation set in, since Vaḷḷi could not meet again with Murukaṉ. The symptoms of her suffering made her mother suspect that she was ill, and through a rite of possession it was found out that the *deva* Murukaṉ had caused the illness. Offerings for him were made, to make him leave the girl – but naturally he had possessed the girl in a very different sense and form! Then one night, Murukaṉ arrived and Vaḷḷi eloped with him. A whole band of hunters pursued them and actually managed to catch up with the couple. When they shot arrows at Murukaṉ, the cock which is his symbol crowed, and all pursuers fell down dead, so that the couple could continue their journey. Reprimanded by a sage, Murukaṉ turned back, brought the dead back to life and revealed his true form to them. They worshipped him, and then had the wedding celebrated on a lavish scale. Murukaṉ and Vaḷḷi then left for their palace on mountain Taṇikai.

The whole story is pervaded by themes that are typical of the old Tamil love-poetry (girls guarding the millet field, a hunter chatting them up, dance of possession, elopement, and many more). But obviously the *akattiṇai* – the interior landscape – is no longer the realm of poetic imagination, but that of religious myth. Incidentally, Tamil and Sanskrit/purāṇic mythology were welded together by turning Murukaṉ into precisely that son of Śiva and Pārvatī we heard about in Kālidāsa's poem. This fusion also finds expression in the fact that Vaḷḷi is Murukan̲'s second wife. Thus in our present story, the couple return after spending a while in Taṇikai to Kantakiri, where Vaḷḷi is met by Dēvayān̲ai, his first and upper-class brahmin wife, who is glad to have found such a nice companion.

Let me conclude this first section of our exploration by looking at another Sanskrit poem, Bāṇa's *Caṇḍī-śatakam* (seventh century).[9] This is a collection of roughly one hundred (thus the *śatakam*) self-contained stanzas, all in honour of Caṇḍī. But who is this Caṇḍī? To explain this means to unravel the complexities of the poem. First of all, Caṇḍī is one of the names of the Goddess. From among the various myths narrated in the *Devīmāhātmya* (a work mentioned previously as one of the seminal works of Indian monotheism),[10] Bāṇa chooses one single episode. When a particular demon who had taken on the form of a gigantic buffalo (thus his name, Mahiṣa) was creating havoc in the universe and the gods were at a loss as to how to deal with him, the Goddess manifested herself and managed to kill the demonic beast in battle. Merely alluding every now and then to the rest of the story, Bāṇa focuses on the moment when Caṇḍī pressed her foot down on Mahiṣa's head and killed him.

Using all the techniques available to the *kāvya* style of Sanskrit poetry, the poet expands this central image in various directions. Through puns and many poetic conceits the scale of events is suggested (Mahiṣa was truly cosmic in size, but in comparison with the Goddess he is puny); the male gods are firmly put down in their place, as even punier and more ignorant creatures (they mistake the dead carcass of the animal for the Himalaya mountain and begin to climb up its flank); the single act of the Goddess contains all the beneficial deeds done by other gods (her stretching her body when pulling the string of her bow is described in such an ambiguous manner that a string of puns describe all kinds of grand myths associated with Viṣṇu and Śiva); and though the myth is full of violence, spurting blood and horrific appearances of the Goddess, by means of the same techniques Caṇḍī is presented as extremely beautiful, attractive and desirable. Now to touch with one's head the foot of a deity is generally regarded as a religious act of devotion and as yielding religious rewards. Bāṇa applies this to his central image: to be put to death through the pressure of Caṇḍī's foot actually constituted the demon's salvation.

But there is one further dimension contained in all this. 'Caṇḍī' is also a technical term in Sanskrit love-poetry and poetics, denoting a 'fierce' woman, namely the beloved in a state of rage at some unfaithfulness of her lover. Poetically, the lover's only chance of appeasing her lies in prostrating himself at her feet. Bāṇa built enough clues into his poem to tell us that he himself is envisaging himself in such a situation. Lying prostrate before Caṇḍī, he is confessing his sins and ready to accept the punishment her foot might mete out – which will constitute his salvation, as it mythically does for Buffalo. It is needless to add that Bāṇa did not miss such a chance to use this symbolism for his rendering of the myth: Mahiṣa is, as it were, lying prostrate before the Goddess, begging for her grace and forgiveness, which she grants him along with his death.

Here now we have seen five illustrations of how love-poetry could be applied to the love-life of the gods. I hope I have given enough material to illustrate the range and the variety of style, technique and content. It is obviously difficult material, and I am not thinking here so much in terms of the unfamiliarity of such an approach to the divine for anybody used to the Judaeo-Christian tradition – it is already difficult within the Indian context. For what are we dealing with here? A considerable amount of ink has been spent by scholars on discussing whether this is religious or secular, and, if religious, in what sense. Let us first get rid of one of those irritating myths that is perpetuated by a whole branch of writing on India. These writers tell us that traditional India did not know the distinction between the secular and the divine, the sacred and the profane. In romantic and precious language they tell us that every object, gesture, act and thought was imbued with the sacred. This is obviously the origin of the great fallacy of the 'mystical' India. There is no doubt whatsoever in my mind that classical India was completely capable of distinguishing the sacred from the profane and the secular from the religious. These concepts must be accepted as operative in Indian society. But what did not happen was an external, objective compartmentalization of the realms corresponding to these concepts. I think we need no better illustration or more convincing proof for this statement than Jayadeva. 'Kṛṣṇa may not mean anything to you in religious terms, or he may be your Bhagavān; what I am doing is making a lovely poem about Kṛṣṇa. This work of mine may fill you with a transcendental bliss (since it is about your Bhagavān) or satisfy your curiosity about the matters of love (because it is about the vagaries of the emotions of lovers), or confer upon you divine blessings (because my poem involves *devas*). I don't care – the choice is yours!'

Incidentally, we find something comparable from Bāṇa. Legend tells us that he composed the *Caṇḍīśatakam* when his own mistress was '*caṇḍī*', in a state of rage. Thus the poem could be regarded as a prayer directly addressed to the Goddess to help him pacify his mistress, and/or as a love-letter indirectly begging his mistress to forgive him. Thus, here also the 'secular' is inextricably linked with the 'religious'. All this is inevitable from the premises that no formal distinction is drawn between the depiction of human and of divine love, and between the material connected with the *devas* and Bhagavān and Bhagavatī. Considering how difficult it has been for Christian poets to draw on the *Song of Songs* even for religious purposes – not to speak of secular ones – the Indian attitude is rather remarkable. In India, we find a whole civilization pervaded with this kind of material. While the purāṇic myths provide the raw material of the stories (and we must imagine many a granny passing the knowledge of it down the generations, as ours used to pass on the fairy tales of the brothers Grimm, etc.), the poets elevated it on to a most sophisticated plane of Indian culture, to be spread because of the fame of the poets.

We have previously noted the power of poetry to 'transcendentalize' the painful and fleeting moments of love and also its happy hours.[11] By projecting the techniques and conventions of love-poetry on to the love-life of the *devas* and Bhagavān, this seemingly amorphous aesthetic transpersonalization can thereby acquire an objective ground of being. Bhagavān is not merely man's (non-transient) object of desire, but in the love-life between Bhagavān and his goddess(es) man's love itself becomes universalized. At the same time, from the poetically structured world of the gods, some mysterious force flows forth which in the heart of the sensitive 'reader' reveals itself as love and beauty. In this context it makes perfect sense to pray for the victory of this beauty and for the protection that this love can provide. Here now we have another kind of hero: the man who opens himself to the stimuli that a wonderful world offers to his senses, who lets his heart resonate with the pulse of love that pervades the world, and who becomes submissive to and totally dominated by some higher power. Already Bāṇa illustrated this point. We can imagine him lying prostrate at the feet of his violent and beautiful Goddess and awaiting her grace.

So far we have treated as more-or-less interchangeable the *akattiṇai*, the interior landscape developed in the ancient Tamil poetry of South India, and the *kāvya*, the poetic conventions of Sanskrit love-poetry which ultimately go back to Hāla. Indeed, it would not be difficult to imagine a Kālidāsa depicting Umā's love-sickness by describing a ritual of possession arranged by her mother to ascertain the cause of her illness. Similarly the *Kantapurāṇam* might have included Murukaṉ's 'biting and scratching' of Vaḷḷi when describing their love-making. It simply so happens that the dance of possession and the marks left by nails and teeth are exclusive to two specific poetic traditions. However, besides this basic comparability which only culture-historical factors have kept separate and distinct, the *akattiṇai* was developed in a unique direction to which we can turn now.

Something extraordinary
    I have witnessed today!
When I told her
    'Is it not customary
    – you who are like Kṛṣṇa's heaven!
    to go away on some business
    to faraway places
    in order to make money?'
her carp-like eyes
    big like the palm of the hand
produced strings of white pearls
    that turned into gold
– enough to buy the whole world.[12]

In a lotus with tinkling earrings
two dashing carps
– kept apart by a creeper –
darted about and cast spear-like glances at me.
All who saw this happen
that day
when they stirred me up
    like the ocean with its nectar
    was agitated
    when churned by Viṣṇu's hand,
will not blame me.[13]

The literal meaning of these two poems is not difficult to unravel. In both cases, the husband or lover is speaking and reference is made to the woman's or girl's carp-like eyes (a conventional metaphor). In the first poem, the husband is about to leave on a longer journey; separation of the couple is imminent. While he tries to justify his decision, she breaks out in tears. As these tears run down her cheeks, their initially white colour changes into golden, because her dark skin has lost its lustre and has become 'pale' at the thought of his long absence. This manifestation of her love moves him, and metaphorically speaking the woman here and now offers him all the wealth he is planning to acquire in some foreign land. In the second poem, the man tells us how the girl's amorous glances went straight into his heart and created a turmoil there which he compares to the agitation of the milk ocean when the gods churned it. People may find his infatuation excessive and silly, but had they seen how she looked at him, they would understand.

On this level the poems read like amorous miniatures that are vaguely structured according to the *akattiṇai* conventions. We are given facets of a world pervaded by love, the resonances of which we pick up in our, the readers', hearts. It is an imperfect love, with strands of pain and suffering woven into it. Lovers have to spend long periods without each other, and to fall in love is like being hit by a spear in the heart. But instead of transcending these darker tones merely by poetically transforming them into an aesthetic experience for us, these poems explicitly refer us to another level – a level unknown to older *caṅkam* poetry. It establishes a tenuous link with another, perfect and lasting world: the world of Kṛṣṇa or Viṣṇu which is transcendence, eternity and pure, unadulterated love. The formal means of establishing this link is, in both poems, the metaphor.[14] In the first, the girl is lovingly addressed as resembling Kṛṣṇa's heaven, and in the second, the comparison is between the turbulent mind and the ocean, when it was churned by Viṣṇu. These similes hint at a similitude of human and divine love, in spite of their obvious differences. Like the beauty of a poem, the world of Viṣṇu does not know of the imperfections of earthly love. He is the solid rock in the middle of all the turmoil in the human heart.

These two poems are taken from a collection (called *Tiruviruttam*) of a hundred such stanzas, written in Tamil by a Caṭakōpaṉ, around the eighth or ninth century AD. Now this poet is better known as Namm-Āḻvār, 'Our Saint', and he belongs to a group of (nominally) twelve Āḻvārs who lived in the Tamil country during the second half of the first millennium AD and produced a large corpus of religious poetry. Stating in poetic terms a monotheistic belief, they deride other gods and forms of religion as aiming at useless goals. Man's salvation can only be achieved through the grace of Māyōṉ – a Bhagavān figure that fuses aspects of the Kṛṣṇa of the *Bhagavadgītā*, the *Harivaṃśa*, and the Viṣṇu of the Purāṇas. Their love is so intense that they throw themselves into the full range of sensuous and sensual beauty Māyōṉ religion displays, and they express their desire to unite with their God totally. At a certain stage in the historical development of this religion, the imagery and conventions of the older, secular Tamil love-poetry begin to be employed in the expression of this intensely passionate love. Let us recall that from those olden days, when that Tamil love-poetry (the *akattiṇai*) was cultivated, Māyōṉ had been associated with love-in-separation. Somehow, this old emotive association carried on. Nammāḻvār was possibly the first to experiment with such poetic possibilities which the two examples just quoted illustrate.

In the same region, during the same period, we have a parallel movement that focuses on Śiva as its Bhagavān, its monotheistic God. These poet-saints are called Nāyaṉārs, the 'leaders'. Among them it was Māṇikkavācakar, 'whose words are like rubies', who produced a collection of poems very similar in form and structure to Nammāḻvār's *Tiruviruttam*. This *Tirukkōvaiyār* systematically collects all conventional themes and formalized episodes from the old *akattiṇai* and, in four hundred such amorous miniatures, makes the world of human love transparent for Śiva's grace.[15] But let us return to the Āḻvārs.

We have seen how the simile establishes a tenuous link between man and God. (Nammāḻvār and Māṇikkavācakar also use other, more indirect or oblique stylistic means – note the reference to Viṣṇu's churning of the ocean.) This may be an extremely sophisticated way of utilizing a poetic tradition for religious expression; but it could hardly enjoy a wider, more popular appeal. Thus we witness the emergence of the song, accompanied by music (and possibly dance). Nammāḻvār and other Āḻvārs composed poems for them in which a new kind of poetic landscape is presented. The autonomy of the *akattiṇai* is to some extent eroded here: instead of a man–woman relationship that, through similes (or other means), hints at Māyō<u>n</u>, we find here the focus on the 'girl' directly in love with Māyō<u>n</u>. She is still the heroine of *caṅkam* poetry, and she lives in the same kind of poetic landscape as her archetype did. But the lover is now Māyō<u>n</u>, frequently linked directly with a particular South Indian temple. This girl, passionately in love with Kṛṣṇa, is in most cases depicted as suffering unbearable agony because of his absence. The girl may speak directly (to herself, to her natural environment, or to her friend and confidante), or it may be the girl's mother lamenting about the miserable condition – either the girl's or her own – or we may hear about the girl from one of her friends.[16]

A lot of nonsense has been talked about this and similar poetry, naively applying an allegorical interpretation to it: the girl is merely the soul of the mystic, suffering the dark night of the soul as the purification before final and total union with the divine. Such an interpretation fails to see that these poems are autonomous artistic creations. In the physicality of the love depicted between the girl and Kṛṣṇa her lover, the poet expresses his own sensuous, sensual existence as a person of flesh and blood and conveys this to his listeners. Moreover, he tells us quite explicitly that the poem as a whole is meant to convey the grace of Kṛṣṇa and an experience of his. Poetry dealing with 'separation', as developed in the *akattiṇai* and as depicted here with the whole gamut of its paraphernalia, is meant to be an appropriate mode in which a contingent human being can realize the divine. Relishing the songs, and cultivating within oneself the sentiments of love-in-separation, produces a state of ecstasy which combines the symptoms of utter pain and suffering with the feeling of ultimate happiness and fulfilment. More than an aesthetic experience, these love songs convey Māyō<u>n</u>'s beauty and grace.[17]

Towards the later stage of the Āḻvār tradition, we notice another interesting development. Almost imperceptibly at first, the girl and the landscape in which she suffers change into the mythical milkmaid and the forests near Mathurā. Thus from the poetic realm of reality we move to the mythical one. Now the daughters and wives of the cowherds are depicted as suffering intense pain at Kṛṣṇa's absence, with all the accessories that the conventional *akattiṇai* has to offer. The forest turns into a landscape of jasmine, one of the pointers in the old poetry towards separation. Thus we end up with a situation that we have encountered already in the *Kantapurāṇam*: the projection of *akattiṇai* conventions on myth. But in the course of these complex literary developments in the South, something quite major has happened. Love of Bhagavān had been known for a long time, in fact from the times of the *Bhagavadgītā* and the *Śvetāśvatara-Upaniṣad* onwards. But with the Āḻvārs (and we could mention the Nāyaṉārs here as well) this *bhakti*, this devotion, acquired a completely new character due to the impact of Tamil love-poetry. Moreover, it did not remain isolated in a small cultural niche of the South. This ecstatic *bhakti*, along with its typical depiction of 'love in separation' (in the mythical landscape with Kṛṣṇa and the milkmaids) was incorporated into a Sanskrit text which was produced in South India around AD 900. This is the extremely famous and influential *Bhāgavata-Purāṇa*.[18] Through this text, Āḻvār *bhakti* was made known to other parts of India, and Tamil religious *akattiṇai* could begin to interact with the conventions of Sanskrit love-poetry.

But nobody wrote the theology that was implied in the religion of the Āḻvārs and in their poetic creations. Indeed, as we shall see presently, theologians appropriated the Āḻvārs, incorporating them into their own institutional heritage and drawing on them for their own theological purposes. But that is a far cry from spelling out, in theological terms, what their religion was about, or from accepting that religion itself. Enormous ideological pressures of various kinds had to be overcome before a theology could be created that was directly congruous with the kind of religion we have been discussing. One of the better-known examples of this theology, and perhaps its most all-embracing expression, is connected with the name of Caitanya. It is to this system that I shall turn now.

Caitanya lived in Bengal during the first part of the sixteenth century. After a conversion experience, this formerly non-religious man became an ardent devotee of Kṛṣṇa, abandoning the life of a householder and dedicating all his time and energies to singing and relishing poetry and songs on Kṛṣṇa's love-life with Rādhā and the milkmaids. He would plunge himself into the emotions of this poetry to such a degree that he would enter a state of trance (in other religious contexts one could speak of 'possession'). The symptoms are also well documented from other forms of ecstatic religion: sweating, shivering and uncontrolled movement of the muscles, strange noises, weeping and dissociation. In many ways this comes close to what the beloved of poetry, in her state of separation, displays. However, while externally such poetically formulated symptoms of 'separation' appear re-enacted (and Caitanya tended to favour poems on separation), internally these states of trance were experienced by him as ecstasy and some kind of ultimate bliss.

He gathered a number of disciples around himself,[19] among whom Rūpa Gosvāmī and his nephew Jīva Gosvāmī deserve to be mentioned here. At the religious centre of this community we find the *kīrtan*, communal recitation and singing of Kṛṣṇa poetry. The literary sources used for it are interesting. There is the *Bhāgavata-Purāṇa* (and thus, indirectly, Āḻvār religion finds here a new expression) and also the *Gītagovinda* of Jayadeva. Caitanya had no problem with the ambivalence of this poem: to him it was a central scripture about his Bhagavān Kṛṣṇa. He goes further than this: even 'secular' poems on Kṛṣṇa, or even poetry just on a lover and a beloved, are perceived by him in the same way. But Rūpa Gosvāmī was a gifted poet himself, and through his creativity the poetic repertoire of the community was greatly expanded. Moreover, Rūpa had studied the learned treatises on poetics, and thus could provide the theoretical details of religious aesthetics without which the theology that was integral to Caitanya's religious life could be created. It was Jīva Gosvāmī who formulated such a theological edifice.[20] His task was to provide some theological framework within which the recitation of poetry (religious or secular), the agonies of separation depicted in it, the states of ecstatic 'soul-loss' displayed by Caitanya as a consequence of reading it, and the bliss this experience contained (according to Caitanya's own testimony) could acquire a religious, metaphysical significance. Or in other words, a theory was required that could combine the aesthetic and psychological with the cosmological and ontological, the mythical with the poetic and the 'real'. Obviously such a theology was not created by Jīva *ex nihilo*; many of the building-blocks for it had been produced over many previous centuries. But since I am not aiming at a history of Indian theology, I shall ignore those aspects here. Let us simply look at the finished product.

From an absolute point of view, reality and Bhagavān are one: autonomous, undifferentiated and eternal. But from a different point of view, there is obviously the universe with all its multiple forms and beings. This is seen as a differentiation within the nature of Bhagavān itself (the idea being that no autonomous second real could be conceived in view of Bhagavān's status as one and only true being). Thus a relational dimension within Kṛṣṇa is introduced, and naturally this is depicted in concrete terms as the relationship between Kṛṣṇa and Rādhā. Their union and their separation thus correspond, cosmologically speaking, to the ultimate unity of all being and to the differentiation of the universe. Moreover, this relational aspect of the divine is also given a psychological dimension: Kṛṣṇa and Rādhā grant to, and receive from, each other transcendental bliss. This allows for the incorporation of the aesthetics of the movement. I previously referred to the power of a poem to trigger off aesthetic experiences. The poem itself may be about the agonies of lovers in the state of separation. But, if properly constructed and appropriately received by the reader, it is not that same emotion of suffering that is conveyed, but an essentially blissful experience which takes the individual beyond himself. All this the theoreticians of classical poetry had observed and reflected upon. Their theory calls the experience itself *rasa*, literally 'flavour' or 'taste'. Rūpa and Jīva Gosvāmī applied this concept to their theology. The emotion contained in the poem is identified with the cosmic love of Rādhā and Kṛṣṇa. When absorbed by the perceptive devotee, it turns not just into an aesthetic experience, but in fact also into a religious one. Not just poetically, but also ontologically he is drawn into the mysteries of Kṛṣṇa's and Rādhā's love. The bliss he experiences during his states of ecstasy is part of that bliss that Rādhā and Kṛṣṇa grant each other. By constantly meditating on the love-mysteries of Bhagavān and his beloved, and by identifying himself with the attendants of the two, man loses his separate existence, overcomes the separation from the divine and, by being absorbed into the relational dynamics within the divine nature, he finds his salvation. Appropriately this is called *bhakti-rasa*: devotion to Bhagavān which involves the realization within oneself of the emotions that exist between Rādhā and Kṛṣṇa, within the divine archetype.

This is a very brief sketch of the aesthetic theology which Caitanya's disciples constructed. In terms of our formula 'relationship between desiring subject and desired object' we find here that the relationship itself is absorbed into the 'object's' own relational nature (love between Rādhā and Kṛṣṇa), and the subject is drawn into the 'object' (Bhagavān's nature). This system of thought represents an ingenious synthesis of monotheism and love-poetry: both these cultural traditions have found here a harmonious union, as a total conception of cosmic desire. But belonging to the sixteenth century as it does, it is late in terms of the theological history of India. We have many earlier theological edifices which no discussion of 'cosmic love' must ignore, however brief. The difference here is that desire, passion and love are built into such systems without much or any recourse to the traditions of love-poetry. But there cannot be any doubt, as we shall see presently, that such edifices fall squarely under the heading of 'Love'. I have chosen my illustrations from three examples, which – however random – ought to give some idea of the variety and the scale of what we are dealing with here.

The earliest systematic theology known to us from India is that of Rāmānuja, a South Indian who lived during the eleventh to twelfth centuries AD. Bhagavān here is Viṣṇu, and his consorts are Lakṣmī, Bhūmi, etc. The relational dimension in the divine is seen as love, which moreover flows over into the whole cosmos. I showed in the opening chapter of Part two how the stern authority of Viṣṇu in his own, abstract nature becomes transformed through the 'manly deeds' of Lakṣmī, as a result of which the universe is pervaded by compassion and grace. Bhagavān appeals to man to accept his grace and thus find salvation, through the display of his beauty, naturally along with that of Lakṣmī. Fundamentally all that is required of man is for him to hand himself over to the dynamics of this cosmic love. He has to abandon his illusory ideas of independence and the false belief in his own powers, and must accept the fact that his is but a *śeṣa*, a totally dependent entity which does not even exist without Viṣṇu wanting it.

Another interesting idea is developed by Rāmānuja. He envisages the relationship between Bhagavān and the cosmos with all its material and animate objects and beings as comparable to the relationship between a soul and a body. The cosmos is God's body. Incidentally, this conception is also expressed in late-medieval Indian paintings for Kṛṣṇa and the Goddess,[21] and, moreover, has also a parallel in recent Christian theological thought.[22] To the extent that the divine is differentiated into two '*personae*', namely as Viṣṇu and Lakṣmī, the cosmos, too, contains their loving communion. It is not difficult to see that we are dealing here with one of the building-blocks that were put together to construct Caitanya's system half a millennium later.

Theoretically, Rāmānuja's movement incorporated the Āḻvārs. Indeed, they were regarded as earlier teachers in the lineage of his system, and very lengthy commentaries were written on their poetry. But for some reason – and this could well have included a certain puritanical attitude – the whole was allegorized and theologized and the erotic, ecstatic and aesthetic dimensions of their devotion was pushed underground. Even so, the traditions of love-poetry do make their occasional appearance here also. A later theologian, Vedāntadeśika (thirteenth/fourteenth century) produced an interesting hybrid work.[23] This poem is written in the vernacular used by Hāla for his love-lyrics, and is put into the mouth of a 'girl' – an ingenious synthesis of the two traditions, *akam* and Hāla. The content? A summary of Rāmānuja's theology. Also in his, and other poets', Tamil writings the old *akattiṇai* symbolism finds expression time and again.[24]

The Tamil South also developed (from the fourteenth century onwards) a system in which Śiva is the Bhagavān, namely the Śaiva-Siddhānta. Again the cosmos is perceived as pervaded by Śiva's grace – his *śakti* of salvation. Conceptually interesting is the explanation of man's situation. In his 'natural' state, man is under the power of *āṇavam*. That means he has encapsulated himself, is cut off from Śiva's cosmic grace, and lives within the cocoon of his mistaken autonomy and autarky. But when he breaks open the walls of his splendid isolation, at which Śiva's grace is knocking from outside, he finds salvation: a most intimate communion with Śiva. Here again love-poetry is ignored in structuring this religious system of thought, although the Nāyaṉārs, the group of Śiva-worshipping poets who were contemporaries of the Āḻvārs, had laid down the potential basis for it.

Let me conclude by looking at a theology in which God is woman – a theology of Bhagavatī. As the source for this I use a late-medieval Purāṇa, the *Devī-Bhāgavatam.*[25] As the title itself suggests, this is a rewritten version of the *Bhāgavata-Purāṇa* that I mentioned earlier, organizing its teaching around the figure of Bhagavatī. Actually, very few new myths are told about the Goddess or the *devas*, but the old ones are told in a novel manner. In each and every case the Goddess reveals herself as the real 'heroine'. Whatever the male *devas* may be achieving, they can do so only because Bhagavatī is working through them. In a number of important respects, the personality of this Bhagavatī differs from that of the Bhagavān figures we have been looking at so far. A more consequential and ruthless attitude is expressed here. If Bhagavān or Bhagavatī are truly the absolute, and everything in the cosmos depends on him or her for its being and mode of operation, then the problem of evil has to be tackled. Our present text deals with it in the following way.

First of all, it accepts from the renouncer tradition its analysis of 'thirst', of desire and the human passions as the root evil behind the suffering of transmigration. In the Purāṇa the whole cosmos is envisaged as pervaded by and, in fact, operating due to, egotistical desire, lust, craving for power and pleasure. This is the extremely pessimistic part of the Purāṇa's teaching. Now for the optimistic part: if desire is the central power in the universe, then this is most centrally and apparently where the Goddess expresses herself, as Bhagavatī. What is left for suffering man to do? First of all, he can learn to acknowledge the presence of Bhagavatī in every manifestation of desire. But secondly, he has to do more. Our text now suggests that obviously the cosmos is the expression of Bhagavatī, but by that very fact is also a cover around her true, absolute nature. This necessarily lies beyond all the violence and desires of the universe, and this it is where man has to advance to. The cosmos is, as it were, a veil that covers up Bhagavatī's nature; by breaking through it, one breaks away from the desires and violence of the world into a realm of utter calm and bliss.

Why it should be that the Goddess manifests her ultimately peaceful and calm nature in desire is a mystery beyond the potentials of human reasoning. Appropriately, Bāṇa lay prostrate at the feet of Caṇḍī, ready for the violent kicks as much as waiting for her grace. It is particularly in the figure of Bhagavatī that Indian monotheism acknowledges the existence of the rougher sides of life. To a considerable extent this has to do with the social position of different Bhagavān and Bhagavatī figures. If an extremely sweeping generalization were allowed, I would venture to say that certainly Bhagavān figures like Kṛṣṇa, Viṣṇu, or Śiva belong to a relatively high social milieu. Bhagavatī, on the other hand, draws on folk and regional traditions in lower social milieux. Here the concrete experiences of a rough and often cruel life appear incorporated into the nature of the Goddess. Far from being a 'mother' or the 'Whore of Babylon', she is a strong person who resists the amorous advances of, and the implied subjugation to, any male. In her all the evils, cruelty and violence of the world fuse with all its love and beauty.

What we have been looking at in the present chapter has been one aspect of Indian monotheism: its imaginative and theoretical foundations. 'Love', in a variety of aspects, has been the central concept around which whole theological edifices were constructed. To a considerable extent, the traditions of love-poetry provided the concrete material through which this cosmic desire was envisaged. But even where such a link between 'God' or 'Goddess' and erotic poetry was more tenuous or altogether absent, Bhagavān's or Bhagavatī's love for man, his or her compassion, work for man's salvation. Whether man is exhorted to break through the illusory walls of his independence or to realize that his very existence derives from Bhagavān's grace, whether he is encouraged to open his heart to the poetry of cosmic love and receive the *rasa* of its passions, or is asked to accept behind all the greed and desire of the world the peaceful love of Bhagavatī – in all these instances it is total passivity, powerlessness, and not an active pursuit of power which these types of religion are demanding. Here, in a total submission to, and subjugation under, a divine love, culminates man's drive towards a non-transitory lasting basis of his desire – a drive which is clearly the direct opposite of the religions of power. Happiness and freedom are discovered in total obedience and servitude. Bhagavān (or Bhagavatī) is in absolute control over man's destiny. This destiny is placed close to man; all he has to do is open himself up for it. But how is this divine love made available? By placing it close to man, by infusing it into his heart, Bhagavān and Bhagavatī are prepared to expose themselves to the humiliations and sufferings of this world, to the extent even of choosing to enter into stone, to abide permanently in the world of man.

CHAPTER 14
Love abiding in stone

In one of his provocative aphorisms, Canetti says: 'Human beings can only be saved by other human beings; therefore God dresses up as man.' [1] The types of religion we are exploring at present, namely Indian theism and monotheism, certainly share his sentiment. But when we look at the range of forms this 'dressing up as man' may take, a number of surprises are in store for us. The love that is perceived to pervade the cosmos, to constitute the relational dimension within the divine, and to possess there its transcendental foundation does not stay abstract and impersonal. The divine has to im-personate and in-carnate itself to communicate to man its nature and its loving intentions. In terms of our formula of subject–desire–object, the previous pages have already shown to what extent this abstract 'object' itself is a loving subject, internally and in relation to man. From such a transcendental subject flows forth beauty and grace, but also power and even aggression (I am thinking here particularly of the Goddess), which aims at subjugating man. However, this is still a one-sided description. Logically we can ask, how can man know of such a transcendental reality which is at the same time the object of his desire and the subject of his salvation? Our traditions agree that pure logic, speculation, or inference alone cannot tell us about Bhagavān. It is only because he chooses to reveal himself that our logic can complete the drive in our hearts that aims at a non-transitory object of our desires. But in the process of revealing himself (and the masculine here, as much as elsewhere, includes the feminine) the all-powerful absolute humiliates himself, gives up his position of absolute power. Not only does he reveal himself, but he also chooses to turn himself into an object of human care and affection. In fact, we shall see that a whole range of such 'objects' are known to a variety of religious traditions.

Yet the paradox remains: even in the most humble form of material embodiment, Bhagavān's active desire for man's well-being and salvation remains intact. The title of the chapter, 'love abiding in stone', hints at this paradox, for one of the major types of divine manifestation is the temple image. Bhagavān wants to be available as an actively saving grace, in a form that is as permanent and as solid as the rock out of which the image has been made. Revelation, incarnation, concrete objects of human veneration and their saving activities – these are the subjects of the present chapter.

To speak of 'manifestations of the divine' also means that as soon as Bhagavān or Bhagavatī takes on human form they leave the realm of eternity or, as it is usually called, of 'myth' and enter into that of history. And it is in history that we have to look for the 'origins' of the concept of 'incarnation'.

There are two historical events on which the Indian and the Western scholar will agree: the historicity of the Buddha and the Mahāvīra, the 'founders' of Buddhism and Jainism respectively. These were true human beings – however gifted and endowed with extraordinary qualities they may have been. Their followers regarded them as having achieved fundamental insights into the very nature of human existence and into the appropriate manner of transcending the 'suffering' that characterizes this existence. Two important features deserve our attention, as far as the subsequent interpretation of these Jinas is concerned. On the one hand, neither tradition transcendentalized the status of such a Jina by regarding his *persona* as divine, and his historical existence as the incarnation of 'God'. Neither Jainism nor Buddhism developed a concept of a transcendental being even vaguely comparable to the Hindu Bhagavān. Yet it was unavoidable that the truth their Jinas perceived had to be envisaged as something outside themselves or, in other words, as latent in the universe and available since time immemorial. But it is not something that had been kept hidden in the realm of the divine and only now was revealed in the person of a Jina. An important decision had to be made, as to whether the Jinas were the very first in the history of the cosmos to perceive it, or not. Both movements chose the latter alternative (for whatever reasons – humility, generosity of heart, or the scale on which cosmic history was envisaged). As we have previously seen,[2] a whole string of previous Jinas was stretched out into the past, multiplying the two

Jina figures of the Buddha Siddhartha and the Mahāvīra Vardhamāna. While the Jains established a system of twenty-four such figures, the Buddhists simply mentioned an indefinite number, listing a variety of individuals. Thus truth is always available, but it needs to be picked up time and again in the course of cosmic history and actualized.

When we now turn to the Hindu side of things, the impressions we gathered in previous chapters should forewarn us that 'truth' may not necessarily have the same ethical connotations here. Anyway, I referred previously to the *Bhagavadgītā* as one of the seminal works in the history of Indian monotheism.[3] Here we find Kṛṣṇa who reveals himself – both through the theology he delivers and through a vision of himself in his cosmic form – as Bhagavān to the warrior Arjuna. His present physical form (as prince Kṛṣṇa) he explains in the following manner. As Bhagavān, he is active in the universe, creating it, maintaining it, and dissolving it at the end of a cosmic cycle. But he is active also in a more specific sense: 'whenever the law of righteousness withers away, I take on physical form, for the protection of the righteous and the punishment of evil-doers'.[4] And he explains this by saying: 'Unborn I am, changeless is my self. Yet by my creative energy I come to be in time. [Thus] many a birth have I passed through.'[5] Truth is now seen as an eternal, transcendental entity, which through the 'in-carnations' of Kṛṣṇa is time and again brought into time and enforced there.

Do the Indian traditions have anything to say about those previous incarnations of Kṛṣṇa, similar to what the Buddhists and Jains have to say about the past Jinas? The answer is both no, and yes, due to a textual difficulty. The *Bhagavadgītā* was included in that vast mass and mess of the *Mahābhārata*. Unfortunately (as far as neat logical consistency is concerned), the bulk of this epic has as its Bhagavān figure Viṣṇu, and not Kṛṣṇa. Now such a contrast was obviously noticed, and eventually the following solution evolved. Bhagavān is Viṣṇu, and Kṛṣṇa is his incarnation. A technical concept was developed to describe their relationship in more precise terms: the concept of '*avatāra*'. This denotes Viṣṇu's 'descent' into the world of man, his incarnation, but not as due to the laws of rebirth and *karma*, or as due to a curse by a sage, but entirely as the result of Viṣṇu's free will. However, this technical terminology was only developed some centuries after the composition of the *Bhagavadgītā* and, though highly influential, it by no means found the approval or acknowledgement of everybody to whom Kṛṣṇa was, and remained, the Bhagavān. This is unfortunately not realized in the popular books on Hinduism: with unremitting tedium it is there repeated that – globally, including naturally the *Bhagavadgītā* itself – Kṛṣṇa is Viṣṇu's *avatāra.*

Be that as it may, systems in which Viṣṇu was the Bhagavān found this a convenient way of appropriating the Bhagavān-figure Kṛṣṇa. But they did not stop there. Both from the renouncers and the *Gītā*, many past appearances were known, and that idea was adopted by them. Further *avatāra* figures emerged. This could be done in a threefold manner. First, there were other such God or Bhagavān figures which could be similarly appropriated. There is some evidence to suggest that the cosmic Boar and the cosmic Tortoise may well have had such an independent origin, since the stories told about them seem to derive from fully fledged and self-contained creation myths. Secondly, the concept could be applied to figures which were originally heroes or, at the most, minor *devas*. I am thinking here of Rāma, whose 'deification' from heroic origins is still clearly traceable. Also the Dwarf may be mentioned in this context, because his story of recovering the cosmos from demonic occupation had been told, in rather different form, about a minor Ṛg-Vedic *deva.* Thirdly, some figures could well have been made up, to complete the system, once a more structured approach to the *avatāras* of Viṣṇu had become popular.

The outcome of all this was that after a few centuries of uninhibited exploration of the potentials of the *avatāra* concept, a pattern of ten emerged as widely popular. But since nothing in India has ever been a rigid norm, even in cases where a group of ten *avatāras* was acknowledged, the list of these still varied. Nevertheless, the rationale of the pattern is clear. Viṣṇu reveals himself at ten different points during a cosmic cycle. The first appearance he makes in the form of a Fish, to save the first man, Manu, from drowning during the deluge. Then, as the Tortoise, he dives to the bottom of the ocean to support the mountain with the help of which the 'nectar', the drink of immortality, was produced. Earth is lifted out of the ocean by the Boar, and the Man–Lion (see Plate 11) rids the world of an evil demon. The Dwarf repeats this, taking on cosmic size when recovering the world in three steps. The progression from ocean to dry land and earth, and from animal to human being, is clear here. The fish is obviously purely an

Plate 11. Viṣṇu as Man–Lion in Tirukkuṟaiyalūr, near Tirunakari, Tamil Nadu

animal of the water; with the turtle/tortoise we move partially over to the dry land, and with the boar a connection with water is still maintained, since this animal loves to wallow in the mud. From animal we move over to human being, first in a combined human–animal, and secondly in a deformed human shape. The second half of the pattern is made up of fully human figures. Among these Kṛṣṇa, Rāma and the Buddha may be mentioned. As number ten we have the figure of Kalki, and he – unlike the other nine who all appeared in the past – is still to come in the future. More precisely, Kalki signals, and in fact brings about, the end of our cosmic cycle. Thus he is by no means a Messianic or millennial figure of religious expectation and longing. The system has simply created a figure that in terms of its function corresponds to Śiva's role in other religious traditions: to destroy the world.

Let us look at certain features of this pattern in greater detail. The occurrence of the Buddha in it may have been noted with some surprise. He is not found in all the lists of ten *avatāras* and, when he does appear, the story told about him is not always a positive one. We may hear that Viṣṇu appeared in this form to teach humanity about non-violence (which fundamentally is understood as ritualistic non-violence: not to kill animals in sacrifice); but we may also find that he decided once for all to separate the sheep from the goats, which means, the truly religious and orthodox people from the latently heterodox and atheists (naturally, here, the Buddhists). Certainly, on the positive side an attempt is made to incorporate or appropriate a religious tradition which possessed its autonomous existence. Worshippers of Viṣṇu tried to draw communities of Buddhists into their movement; to what extent they succeeded is now impossible to tell. Certainly in Nepal, where even today Buddhists and Hindus live side by side, the idea of the Buddha being an *avatāra* of Viṣṇu allows the Hindus to define their position in relation to the Buddhists.[6] But it is clear that others felt no such positive affinity towards the followers of the Buddha. They either kept silent, by not having the Buddha in their lists of the *avatāras*, or explicitly rejected them by providing a negative rationale for this *avatāra* (namely, to bring the heterodox out into the open).

In the hagiography of the South Indian Viṣṇuite saint Parakāla, who is one of the twelve Āḻvārs mentioned previously, these issues take on concrete shape. The saint is universally lauded for stealing a golden Buddha statue from the temple in Nāgapaṭṭiṉam, melting it down, and using the gold to build various shrines in Śrīraṅgam, an important centre of Viṣṇu worship in the south. Only one of the many accounts of the legend that were produced among the Śrīvaiṣṇavas (followers of Rāmānuja) indicates the awareness of a moral problem. In this one text we are told that the Cōḻa king reprimanded Parakāla for this theft, referring to the Buddha as an *avatāra* of Viṣṇu.[7] But obviously Parakāla succeeded here in producing theological arguments against such an interpretation, taking a staunchly anti-Buddhist line. One other account goes so far in the opposite direction as to have Parakāla desecrate the Buddha statue by urinating over it.[8] Such accounts are worth keeping in mind when we read about the universal principle of tolerance demonstrated through the list of the ten *avatāras*.

It is actually quite dangerous to approach the *avatāra* concept from the familiar concept of 'incarnation'. An ethical dimension is thereby suggested which is, on the whole, alien to the *avatāra*. No moral example is set, and little concrete ethical teaching is provided by them. Rāma is perhaps the most 'moral' of these ten figures, suggesting something of matrimonial love and faithfulness and also of righteous rule by a king. Kṛṣṇa certainly gives ethical instruction in the *Bhagavadgītā*, but when he is then depicted as indulging in adulterous affairs with the milkmaids, it is clear that no moral example, to be imitated by man, is being held up (nor was it ever perceived to be in this sense). Similarly, the drunkard Balarāma, who on one occasion, in a state of utter inebriation, forced the river Yamunā to alter her course by threatening her with a plough, or Rāma-with-the-Axe, who in a state of rage chopped off the heads of all warriors on earth with his battle-axe (and, in obedience to his father, the head of his mother), cannot be expected to be upheld as moral exemplars. Incidentally, one could wonder whether these two *avatāras*, one with an axe and the other with a plough over his shoulder, are not derived from one and the same earlier figure, the plough being mistaken for an axe. Anyway, what we do find in all these instances is that Viṣṇu is constantly interested in the world, constantly interfering in its course, maintaining the order according to which things and beings ought to be and act. But instead of giving moral preaching, he carries out what could be called 'cosmic repair-work'.

But even if the ethical role of Viṣṇu is underplayed, his 'objective' interference in the events of the world and the cosmos does not exhaust the purpose of his incarnations. For, as we have seen in previous chapters, Bhagavān is also the transcendental basis of love and of poetry (in more than one sense of the word). In other words, behind the many and variegated events narrated about the different *avatāras* is revealed a permanent love: a love that wants the world to become the way we know it, to allow for human beings to live in it; a concern that fights with the demonic forces of darkness; and a self-revelation that, in the love of a Rāma for Sītā, or Kṛṣṇa for the milkmaids, Rādhā and other female figures, demonstrates something of the inner nature of the divine as the loving couple Viṣṇu and Lakṣmī.

The way in which the pattern of the ten *avatāras*, along with its story material, was put together must have been very haphazard and unsystematic. But it served as the raw material for further theological reflection and religious developments. Thus we find, for instance, the following reflection in a purāṇic passage:

> In this world of death, which has no essence, which is full of suffering and extremely transient, resembling the bubbles on water, how could the *avatāras* find delight in entering a womb and a body, defiled by faeces and urine and the cause of nothing but suffering? How could Viṣṇu, the refuge of all men, take on a human body?[9]

The question expresses typical Jain and Buddhist sentiments and concepts, and the answer demonstrates what monotheistic theology made of it: it is an act of love, carried out in free choice, for the sake of the order in the cosmos and the welfare of human beings. That in fact is Bhagavān's greatness, that he can choose to enter into such foul habitats as a human womb.

Thus these *avatāras* are quite definitely envisaged as Viṣṇu's entrances into the constraints of space, time and matter. That means that the stories told about his deeds are perceived to be historical narratives. To call them 'myths', as many a writer has been wont to do, automatically destroys one of their most central features: Bhagavān's presence – his availability – in human time. It is this presence alone which allows for a religious perception and response – in poetry, ritual, meditation and the deeds of daily life. But this now implies also its relativization. Since existence on earth is transient, Bhagavān's appearances in time are limited. Ten may be a large number compared with the single Christian incarnation, but the history of the world and its human beings is measured in terms of billions of years.

None of the *avatāras* remained on earth for longer than the span of an ordinary life. Now this would obviously present no problem, were such appearances solely due to some major repair-work that had to be carried out on the machinery of the cosmos at large. But the religious perception was not content with this alone. A number of individual human beings came into personal contact with the *avatāras* and thereby directly encountered divine love. This is most dramatically and drastically illustrated by the milkmaids who left their husbands to dally with Kṛṣṇa. Obviously such human encounters were interpreted as significant in a basically religious sense. But then another question had to be asked: was such a meeting a random affair? If so, what was its special religious significance? If not, then how could its highly restricted occurrence in space and time be explained? If the primary motive behind the *avatāras* was love, then, it was felt by some, its restriction to ten instances over the whole cosmic history was far too narrow. The concept itself was therefore extended, and applied to another element of the Indian religious scene, the temple image.[10]

The origins in India of the worship at, or of, a visual representation of a *deva* or a *devī* are lost in undocumented prehistory. But it seems safe to locate it in the realm of what I have listed as the fourth category of 'gods': tribal or folk *devas*. Out of the complex interactions between this folk religion, art-historical traditions of sculpturing and the emergence of purāṇic deities, there arose, around the beginning of the first millennium AD, a particular synthesis: the temple image of Bhagavān (variously called *arcā*, *mūrti*, etc.) And it was towards this that the concept of *avatāra* was extended. Thus we get the *arcāvatāra* – the incarnation of Bhagavān in the statue of a temple. Made of solid rock, his availability to man is greatly improved, compared with the transience of a human body. And, since a vast number of such *arcās* were scattered all over India, the limitations of space were also overcome. Bhagavān could thus manifest himself to a very much larger number of people than the *avatāras* were able to do. Nominally at least, every village thus acquired the presence of Bhagavān. Love, though turned into stone, had acquired a far more dynamic role.

We are dealing here with one of the seriously misunderstood areas of Indian religions. Earlier Western observers of the Indian scene called it 'idolatry' – the naive worship of a material object, believing it to be a god. Nowadays even the most orthodox Hindu, rather unwittingly, may use the English word 'idol' to translate *arcā*. If the concept of 'incarnation' is acceptable, an expansion to include temple images should not create any problems. More recently, a strand of literature on India has emphasized the role of the Hindu temple as a symbol of man's drive towards the spiritual. But building temples with heavy stones and making the central statue of Bhagavān of solid granite suggests to me quite the opposite: man's desire for the permanent presence of the divine in this world. That is certainly how the texts interpret it.

Naturally, such an understanding of Bhagavān's presence in the *arcā* triggered off a number of important cultural developments – cultural contexts in which the religious significance of his presence among men was spelled out and made concrete. Among these must be mentioned, first of all, the temple as a religious institution.[11] Already folk religion had provided some of the inspiration. The area around the statue was sacred space, and had to be demarcated as such. The tree that might shelter a village deity was not good enough for Bhagavān: a proper house or palace had to be built for him. What folk religion knew as offerings of pieces of cloth, bits of costume jewellery, libations of water, portions of food, incense and perfumes, turned now into proper and lavishly decorated garments to be draped around the *arcā*, expensive ornaments of gold, rubies and diamonds to be placed on it, elaborate bathing ceremonies with different types of fragrant waters, elaborate meals (some of the best food the hungry traveller through South India can eat is cooked in Viṣṇu temples), and ritual displays of the *arcā*'s beauty through the burning of camphor. Instead of the odd flower plucked at random, a whole flower garden became cultivated to produce elaborate garlands for the image, and permanent lights lit the otherwise unilluminated interior of the shrine.

Such daily rituals involve not just a whole group of properly trained temple priests, but also many other professionals, including the cooks, garland-weavers and accountants. The most common model for the treatment of Bhagavān in his *arcā* is that of the royal palace, and indeed some temples developed such a complexity and scale that any earthly king would be envious of them. Just as in folk religion the worship of a village deity would be accompanied by song, music and dance, in the temples properly trained musicians, singers and dancing girls would perform before Bhagavān. All these activities can be summarized with the word *pūjā*. *Pūjā* also means to wake up Bhagavān with songs in the morning, to put him to rest for his daily siesta, and put him to bed in the evening. Similarly, it means to pay respect to his consort and other companions. But not only does it refer to the daily routines; it also includes the celebration of annual festivals. Like a king, Bhagavān emerges from his palace, carried on the shoulders of his devotees or seated on a chariot pulled by them and, in procession through the village or the town, confers his blessing on it and infatuates the world with his beauty. For this purpose, the statues which are made of rock and often much more than life-size, cannot be used, and another type of image, made of bronze or the five precious metals, is employed.

While describing all this, the religious movement organized by Rāmānuja and generally known as Śrīvaiṣṇavism has been at the back of my mind. This is a monotheistic system, with Viṣṇu, Lakṣmī and Bhū (Earth) as the Deity. The theologians of this tradition derived their ideas about Viṣṇu's love and beauty brought into the world of man partly from the poetry of the Āḻvārs, and partly from two earlier, professional traditions specializing in temple worship (the Pāñcarātra and the Vaikhānasas). Thus we have here an example of a religion of Love imposing itself on a religion that seems to belong more under the heading of Power. However, the Śrīvaiṣṇavism of Rāmānuja is merely one expression of Indian monotheism. Many closely related and similar ideas, along with significant differences, could be explored for the other monotheistic Hindu systems. Thus directly parallel to the Pāñcarātra is the Śaivāgama tradition in South India with Śiva as the Bhagavān. Furthermore, to complete the picture and to confuse the outside observer totally, there are further traditions of temple worship without the concept of Bhagavān or Bhagavatī (e.g. the *Kerala-Tantra*). So let me clarify: what we are looking at in the present context are perceptions of Bhagavān as abiding in the statue of a temple in order to grant to humanity his grace, to appeal through the physical beauty of the image and the ritual to man's emotions, and to stimulate a religious experience. The whole complex of temple ritual is the means by which this beauty is created and communicated, grace is conveyed, and man expresses his veneration and gratitude for the divine presence. It does not mean that in every temple in India this is the theology a priest or a devotee would be professing or be familiar with. Instead, we may well be dealing with a religion of Power, aspects of which have been discussed when looking at the temple as a 'safe haven'.[12]

Let me mention another confusing phenomenon. By no means all temple images follow a classical and unambiguous iconographic canon. We may well find statues that are older than the extant or classical treatises which spell out the details of how precisely to sculpture a Viṣṇu or a Goddess killing the Buffalo demon. Or it may be some obscure religious tradition, now lost and superseded by another, that produced such an unconventional image. This can now give rise not just to intellectual problems of identification, but also to inter-religious controversy concerning the right of ownership of the temple. A well-known example is the famous temple of Tirupati (in Andhra Pradesh).[13] It belongs now to the Śrīvaiṣṇavas, who obviously worship Viṣṇu there. But in the past devotees of Śiva have repeatedly claimed that the statue is actually of their Bhagavān (and thus that they ought to instal their tradition of temple *pūjā*). Just as beauty lies in the eye of the beholder, the identity of a temple image may often lie in the belief of the devotee. This is borne out in particularly notable instances where the image is actually not iconic, revealing itself (when all flowers, garments and ornaments have been removed) as a weird-looking piece of stone or part of the rock of a mountain. I will just mention two out of innumerable examples here. Close to the university of Pune is found the temple of the *devī* Catuḥśṛṅgī. It is built against the rocky side of a hill, and the actual image of the goddess is a protruding piece of rounded rock, with two striking holes in it. We would be tempted to say that 'with a bit of imagination' one could see in this the face of a person, the holes suggesting eyes. Indeed this is the way the image is developed: black and white stones have been inserted into them, and a nose-ring (a typical woman's ornament in Maharashtra) has been fixed to the ridge in between them. But to the devotees, it is not man's imagination that is at work here, but divine revelation. For we are told that the goddess appeared to a particularly devout devotee in a dream and promised him that she would come and live near him. When he went out to search for her the next day, he found her looking at him. Thus he built her a proper home.[14]

I cannot resist quoting from a modern poem by the Maharashtrian Arun Kolatkar, which comments on this phenomenon, tongue-in-cheek, with reference to the temple of Jejurī (not far from Pune).

Are you looking for a god?
I know a good one.
His name is Yeshwant Rao
and he's one of the best.
Look him up
when you are in Jejuri next.

I have known gods
prettier faced
or straighter laced.
And although I am sure they are all to be praised,
they are either too symmetrical
or too theatrical for my taste.

Yeshwant Rao,
mass of basalt,
bright as any post box,
the shape of protoplasm
or a king size lava pie
thrown against the wall,
without an arm, a leg
or even a single head.

Yeshwant Rao.
He's the god you've got to meet.
If you're short of a limb,
Yeshwant Rao will lend you a hand
and get you back on your feet.

Yeshwant Rao
does nothing spectacular.
But if any bones are broken,
you know he'll mend them.
He is merely a kind of bone setter.
The only thing is,
as he himself has no heads, hands and feet,
he happens to understand you a little better.[15]

I don't think these stanzas require much explanation: the shape of the stone, the image perceived in it and the *deva*'s function are all obvious. The only point worth adding is the fact that a large number of wooden replicas of legs and arms are stored next to Yeshwant Rao, left there as tokens of thanks for his healing powers (see Plate 12).

Plate 12. Yeshwant Rao, outside the main temple of Jejurī, Maharashtra

The temple of Jejurī offers a convenient point of departure for some further comments, turning now to matters connected with Śiva. Although the concept of '*avatāra*' was developed in Kṛṣṇa/Viṣṇu contexts, it gained far wider popularity. Iconic representations of Śiva in the temples are much rarer (although the corresponding bronze or precious-metal images from South India are very famous). On the whole he tends to be incarnated in the stone *liṅga* – his phallus (though the majority of Indians are not aware of this 'original' significance). This is a cylindrically shaped stone, set in a stone base that is shaped a bit like the famous Indian mango-leaf motif (and represents Umā's *yoni*, meaning vulva). Moreover, as we shall see presently, Śiva religion developed its own mode of envisaging the communication of grace between man and Śiva. But when it comes to the incorporation or appropriation of autonomous cults with their own divinities, the concept of *avatāra* was felt to be useful also in Śivaite circles. Thus the main deity in the temple of Jejurī is Khaṇḍobā (who, unlike Yeshwant Rao at the outer side of the temple wall, is 'em-bodied' in a strikingly sculptured statue, see Plate 13). Very likely Khaṇḍobā was originally an autonomous *deva*, or possibly even a Bhagavān figure. But secondary iconographic details and subsequent legends about the temple and the events associated with Khaṇḍobā's presence there have turned him increasingly into an *avatāra* of Śiva.[16]

The *Devīmāhātmya* – our seminal text for the religion of the Goddess – still spoke simply of her various appearances. But here again, later works in this religious tradition show less hesitation. They employ the word *avatāra*[17] with reference to the classical myths associated with the same Goddess, and add new events and new *avatāras* to their list. Moreover, such goddesses or *avatāras* of the Goddess are often localized, being perceived as abiding in specific temples. *De facto* we are also here dealing with *arcāvatāras* (although the term itself may not be used).

Generally, the concept of *avatāra* has proved extremely productive in India. Thus the mystic Caitanya is regarded by the members of the movement he founded as an incarnation of Kṛṣṇa or, by some, as the manifestation of Rādhā and Kṛṣṇa in one (so that his mysticism of separation mirrors precisely the love-life of the divine archetype).[18] Naturally, Caitanya, like innumerable other such '*avatāra*-saints', has his own temple statues where he is worshipped with *pūjā*. By now the

Plate 13. Khaṇḍobā in the main shrine of Jejurī, Maharashtra

inflation of its usage has increased so much that even modern politicians can be lauded as *avatāras* of one deity or another.

If the temple is one of the great cultural constructs that India produced around the concept of Bhagavān and his *avatāras*, the literature that develops this theme is another. We have already noticed the important role played by local legend in identifying the image and narrating the god's history in that particular place on earth. Such legends may be produced in the typical manner of unrestrained, jungle-like growth of Indian oral literature. Or they may receive a more developed treatment by literati and become written up as proper 'texts'. And indeed we possess a vast mass of such works – literally thousands – in all the languages of India. These are known as *sthala-purāṇas*, Purāṇas dealing with a particular locality (in most cases, a particular temple). Basically they have two features in common. One is a formal one: they tend to orientate themselves in some way or other towards the classical Purāṇas as their models. The second concerns the content. Thus they may tell us about individuals who are mentioned in the great Purāṇas, or associate themselves with one or more of the *avatāras*. Classical 'myths' may be rewritten as historical events that happened in precisely that place. Thus they attempt to write the religious history of one particular temple or cluster of temples with its/their Bhagavān or Bhagavatī.[19]

Such a history has one obvious starting point: the arrival of Bhagavān in that locality. In South Indian Śaivite works, the reason tends to be located in the nature of the place itself (for example, the *axis mundi* runs through it). In the Vaiṣṇava texts, however, no such determinism interferes with Bhagavān's free decision. Often it is a sage who is performing devout asceticism, with the aim of obtaining Viṣṇu's grace. As a reward for his devotion, Viṣṇu then manifests himself before him and bestows his grace upon him. When asked for a boon, the sage then tends to reply: 'Please abide permanently in this place, in the form in which you have appeared before me.' Viṣṇu grants this request, and (turning into stone, although this is merely implied in the narratives) remains there, available to all as the *arcā*. Note here once again the emphasis on 'permanently'. Since the Indian gods don't travel just like that, but in a proper aerial palace (called *vimāna*), this too comes to stay on earth, conveniently providing Bhagavān with a palace (to be called, appropriately, *vimāna*).

Let me continue by restricting myself to this Śrīvaiṣṇava material (which is less well known than the corresponding Śivaite literature), to illustrate the genre further. Once Viṣṇu has settled in a given place, either his two consorts Lakṣmī and Earth are already with him, or some further events have to be narrated in consequence of which the two Goddesses remain permanently there, too. Not satisfied with this, very often we hear about a local girl, who, passionately in love with Viṣṇu and totally devoted to him, receives the honour of being married by him, to abide there permanently next to him. Historically we might see in this type of story the reflection of social processes. When Śrīvaiṣṇavism expanded its range of influence, it frequently encountered local cults of *devīs*, which, by having these goddesses married to Viṣṇu, could thus be accommodated. Anyway, most Śrīvaiṣṇava temples have a special shrine for this *taiyār*, or local girl (see Plate 14).

Now were we dealing with blocks of stone, this could be the end of the 'history'. But that is obviously not how the Śrīvaiṣṇava would see it: these are *arcāvatāras*, which means that they remain active. In a poetic context we have encountered such an idea already with the Āḻvārs. There the poetic heroine was desperately in love with Viṣṇu who frequently is the Viṣṇu of a particular temple. This sophisticated poetic construction was then developed further in the much more literalist popular imagination. Thus innumerable stories are told about all kinds of events that involved a local *arcā* in some amazing, wonderful, or frightening activity. In one locality, a very pious robber used to dedicate faithfully half of every booty he had plundered to the *arcā*. As a reward for his piety Viṣṇu actually took on his disguise, when the local king was out to catch and kill the robber. Ever since then, the *arcā* is known as the Cora-nātha: the Master of Thieves.[20]

Indeed, every single *arcā* in the South (whether of Viṣṇu, Śiva or Bhagavatī) can be specified by a proper name. This divine nomenclature has produced its own ramifications of fascinating features. Thus the orthodox Śrīvaiṣṇava will not only speak of what, for example, Coranātha has done, but might well tell one to 'go to Coranātha' – puzzling advice, since no map would show such a town. But the initiated knows that the temple of Viṣṇu, the Coranātha, is in the town of Śrīvaikuṇṭham. Moreover, what can be made of a name like Uppiliyappaṉ, the 'Lord without Salt'? Appropriately the food cooked here is without salt, and the legend tells us that Viṣṇu agreed here to a

Plate 14. Taiyār in Tirupputkuḻi, near Kāñcīpuram, Tamil Nadu

marriage contract with Bhūmi's father. Since the girl was far too little to know about the proper amount of salt to be used, she was allowed to cook without salt. All very logical, but what is the origin of the name? In the Āḻvārs we find the learned and abstract attribute of Viṣṇu: *opp' ili* 'without comparison', which popular perception turned into a much more concrete *upp' ili* 'without salt'![21]

In another sthala-purāṇic story, again involving a pious bandit (this time the Āḻvār Parakāla),[22] Viṣṇu takes on the form of a wealthy brahmin bridegroom, to allow himself to be plundered and then to bestow his grace on the robber. This story illustrates another important feature, which I have styled 'secondary transfers'. The earliest version simply states that it was 'Viṣṇu' (which would suggest that it was the heavenly Viṣṇu who for this specific purpose manifested himself on earth). But later versions are more specific: it was Raṅganātha, the *arcā* of Viṣṇu in Śrīraṅgam. When he revealed himself to the robber just outside his home-town, miles away from Śrīraṅgam, the robber requested him to abide permanently in his town. Viṣṇu accepted. Ever since, in the town of Tirunakari, we find Parimaḷa-Raṅganātha, 'the fragrant lord of Śrīraṅgam'. Thus many temples all over India possess *arcās* also of famous Bhagavāns from other temples.

Let us stay in Śrīraṅgam, in order to illustrate one or two other interesting features of this literature. The ordinary visitor to the temple would probably comment, when looking at the *arcā*, that it was another example of the iconographic type 'Viṣṇu reclining in the ocean, on the serpent Śeṣa'. Local tradition is aware of the existence of other, similar such *arcās*. However, it very carefully derives from minor iconographic variations totally different incidents (due to which Viṣṇu came to abide there). In the case of Śrīraṅgam, it is actually Rāma, on his way to Laṅkā in search of his wife Sītā, who laid down here to rest his weary body, was seen by a sage and asked to abide there permanently. This he did – while naturally in another manifestation of his he continued towards the island. This means that, in many cases, the local history links itself with that of the classical models told in the Purāṇas about the *avatāras*. Often this is no more than a locally accepted claim, and a number of different places rival each other as the 'real' place where such and such an event took place.

But something else is interesting here: a very novel understanding of time. We are used to talking of the space–time–matter continuum and to contrasting it with the transcendental realm of eternity. But this is not sufficient for an integral interpretation of our present material. In Ahobilam (see Plate 15),[23] the Man-Lion *avatāra* killed the demon who was threatening the foundations of the cosmos. So far this is another example of classical *avatāra* material being connected with a specific place. But we are told more. The demon's ministers and generals all fled when they witnessed the destruction of their lord. The Man-Lion, while 'remaining permanently' in Ahobilam, raced after them. During his pursuit, he sometimes rested, sometimes waited outside a cave where they were hiding, sometimes chased them up a hill. Time and again a sage, saint or king encountered him and made the stereotyped request for him to abide there permanently. This now means that the whole area from Ahobilam down to Kāñcīpuram is filled with, as it were, frozen frames of a film. Moments of the divine action in time (the pursuit of the demons) were eternalized. The pilgrim to these temples can thus participate in that historical event, which has stayed permanently on earth. As he moves from temple to temple, the whole story unfolds itself for him. While in the case of the classical *avatāras* we could speak of temporalized eternity, here we must speak of eternalized time. This complex understanding of the relationship between time and eternity leads me to another area, outside Śrīvaiṣṇavism.

I mentioned earlier that, right from the beginning, the stories told about Kṛṣṇa's amours with the milkmaids were localized: in the forest near Mathurā.[24] For as yet rather obscure reasons, sometime around the fifteenth century it became a great fashion for religious figures to travel all the way to that locality, search for the sites where the incidents narrated in the Purāṇas had taken place, and settle there permanently. This included the disciples of Caitanya. Theologically, this seems to make little sense. As past events, they could have no relevance, physically, in the present. On the other hand, the *arcāvatāra* seemed to fulfil all requirements of present relevance. But in India theology does not necessarily control and restrict human behaviour; the latter is quite capable of creating its own appropriate theology. This happened, and something like the concept of a grand mega-*arcāvatāra* evolved. This meant, first of all, that the historical deeds of Kṛṣṇa in Vṛndāvana were regarded as manifestations of an eternal reality, literally. Eternally in his heaven, Kṛṣṇa plays with Rādhā and the milkmaids. Secondly, Vṛndā-

Plate 15. Viṣṇu in the cave-shrine of Upper Ahobilam, Andhra Pradesh

vana is that place on earth which is in direct contact with heaven: both join up here. Thus by moving from some other part of the country to Vṛndāvana, still within the confines of space and time, one approaches heaven. By living here and relishing the mysteries that are going on – invisibly to the human eye but eternally to the eyes of faith – one is slowly drawn into them. One is pulled, as it were, upwards in an upside-down funnel, into the eternity of heaven. The trees, stones, rivers, flowers, and the grass of the earthly Vṛndāvana make up a physical 'poem' which yields *bhakti-rasa* to the devotee, providing the force that pulls him into eternity.

Comparable theologies are found in the *sthala-purāṇas* or in the religious literature of a number of famous temples all over India. Examples from Guruvāyūr in Kerala, Tirupati in Andhra Pradesh, Śrīraṅgam in Tamil Nadu, Paṇḍharpur in Maharashtra, and Puri in Orissa are known to me.[25] In each case, the temple is envisaged not only as the centre of the universe, but also as the earthly door linking up directly with heaven. From our view of history, we could say that the earthly *arcāvatāra* was re-eternalized, and that on the basis of the physically manifest temple image a theological image of the eternal god incarnated here was created. That 'originally' (in terms of our understanding of the religious history of India) the *arcā* was no more than one of the innumerable incarnations into stone of Viṣṇu, is forgotten. A new religious universe has emerged, centred around the one *arcā*.

Granite is not the only substance in which a god or God can incarnate him- or herself. Far more fragile and transient media may be chosen, at least outside the Viṣṇu/Kṛṣṇa religions. Let us cast at least a cursory glance over these possibilities; the present scope does not permit me to enter into the details as we have done for sophisticated temple culture connected with Bhagavān or Bhagavatī. For Śiva or for the Goddess, a heap of sand may actually be sufficient to serve as his or her abode for the duration of a single ritual. Temporary images of the Goddess Durgā (particularly in eastern India) or the elephant-headed god Gaṇeśa may be created annually out of a lot of wood, tinsel, silver and gold paper, and plaster of Paris, by different neighbourhoods in competition. The cult of Gaṇeśa is prominent in modern Maharashtra. Since Gaṇeśa loves a particular kind of sweet, this is just the right food to offer to him and then give to the children. Moreover, what better way could there be to symbolize the sweetness of Bhagavān's grace and of his presence on earth! Moreover, during his festival increasingly complex tableaux are produced with the sponsorship of the different sweet-merchants of a town. Whether tableaux of Gaṇeśa, or fragile images of Durgā, these are judged as to their 'artistic' merit, and are then carried to a river or the sea and drowned, after the appropriate rituals have been performed around them – naturally, the incarnated deity has been asked to leave this temporary body before that.

Somewhat less transitory is another kind of incarnational image which is, for example, found among low-caste bards of Rajasthan. This is a long piece of cloth, say 6 metres by 1.5 metres, on which long epic tales (for instance of Pāpūjī) are visually narrated in fine detail. For his performance, the bard unrolls the cloth and hangs it up, to point at the relevant pictures as he recites the story. But more is involved here than merely an epic recital. Iconography places the main hero of the story emphatically into the centre of the picture, depicting him on a scale far larger than any of the other characters. This central image of the hero turns into an icon, to receive *pūjā*, at the conclusion of the story's recital.[26]

Besides images and statues, an altogether different kind of divine manifestation must be mentioned. This is the concept of the *guru*. Originally it seems to have been developed in the circles of Śiva worshippers – possibly in reaction to the concept of the *avatāra* which they must have perceived to be specifically Viṣṇuite. Thus Śiva impersonates himself, as it were, in human beings, here, now and anywhere, to offer a concrete and inter-human opportunity for the reception of the saving teaching and grace. Like the *avatāra* concept, the idea of the *guru* achieved enormous popularity and was adopted by very many different religious groups (including most Vaiṣṇavas). In a very special way, the concept of the *guru* acquired prominence and centrality among the Sikhs who indicate it by their very name: *sikh* means disciple of a *guru* – in this case, Gurū Nānak and his nine successors. That the Sikhs have ten *gurus* cannot be a coincidence – the model of the ten *avatāras* of Viṣṇu must have been in the mind of the tenth, who ordained that the lineage of *gurus* ended with him. The same Sikhs evolved yet another variant of our theme: once the line of their *gurus* had come to an end, the holy book, containing the hymns of many of these *gurus*, acquired the status of a manifestation of the divine truth, comparable in many ways to the *arcāvatāra*. Many rituals performed in honour of this book, reverentially called 'Lord Teacher Book' (*guru-granth-sāheb*), resemble those of the *pūjā* performed in front of the *arcāvatāra*.

In the course of previous chapters, two major regional deities of Maharashtra have been referred to: the goddess Yellammā and the *deva* Khaṇḍobā. We saw how the 'mythical' intrusion of Yellammā into the world of man implied a demand for veneration that seemed innocuous enough (a slice of onion), and an extraordinary act of benevolence (curing the gardener of his boils).[27] In that context it was also mentioned that such an 'almsround' of Yellammā is meant to be the archetype for the real almsrounds undertaken by her special devotees, the *jogtīs* and *jogtīṇs*. Similarly, Khaṇḍobā is associated with the (male) *vāghyā* and the (female) *muraḷī* (see Plates 16/17).[28] On special occasions, they are called into someone's house and perform special religious ceremonies. An interesting feature here is the opening ritual: a long list of Khaṇḍobās in the various temples of Maharashtra and Karnataka is recited, with the request to come and attend the function. Moreover, it is suggested that they all take their temporary abode in the musical instruments that are going to be used. These are interesting further variations on the themes we have been discussing: the divine

Plate 16. *Vāghyā* and *Muraḷī* near Jejurī, Maharashtra

Plate 17. *Vāghyā*, Jejurī, Maharashtra

presence in special human beings (*jogtī*, *vāghyā*, etc.) and in particular material objects (the drum, etc.).

Whether as *avatāra* or *arcāvatāra*, as *guru* or as *guru-granth-saheb*, as *jogtīṇ*, or in a drum, or simply as 'manifestation', India produced a great variety of conceptions of the divine manifesting itself in concrete form to man on earth. In one way or another, each conception stimulated one or many cultural constructs in which its significance was spelled out and realized. But there are some conceptual issues which deserve to be looked at here briefly. They arise because of the interference or intrusion of material that, at least popularly, would be called 'tantric'. In particular, this involves the usage of *mantras*. Even orthodox, classical Śrīvaiṣṇavism employs *mantras* in a ceremony known as *pratiṣṭhā*, the 'consecration' of an *arcā*. This means that what until then had been no more than a stone or a piece of metal (however artistically shaped), is transformed into Viṣṇu's body, is imbued with his divine presence. A comparable idea, styled transubstantiation, is known from Roman Catholic theology. And indeed, the usage of a *mantra* in this context is theologically justified along similar lines. This is not 'magic', gaining control of the deity by reciting its secret formula and forcing it into the material form before one. It is simply one further facet of Viṣṇu's readiness to humiliate himself, to enter into the world of space, time and matter. Of his free will he chose to make himself available, as the *arcā*, by means of this particular ritual and in consequence of the recitation of this particular *mantra*.

Perhaps somewhat more problematic is the custom which can be observed in another ritual of the Śrīvaiṣṇava temple. Here the temple priest, by means of stylized gestures and, naturally, the recitation of *mantras*, draws the deity into his own body. No internal theological reflection on this is known to me, but one could still argue that, even here, transport of divine grace into the priest is due to a free choice by Viṣṇu, as in the case of the *pratiṣṭhā*. Unless we can look into the mind of such a priest and analyse the precise theological attitude found there, the theoretical distinction of a religion of Power and of Love will be impossible to apply to such a concrete instance. In other areas of the 'tantric' tradition, the problems are compounded. For there we do not have a decidedly monotheistic system in the background, against which the practices could be measured. Unless careful conceptual research is carried out in this area, it is very difficult to decide whether theistic terminology and imagery are used metaphorically, literally, or in an altogether new significance. What is clear is that we are dealing with rituals (as always, accompanied by secret *mantras* and gestures) that are presented to us as drawing 'the divine' into the person of the performer. Theoretically it would certainly be possible to link this idea with the types of divine manifestation and embodiment we have been looking at so far. Also theoretically it would thus be possible to list this as another mode of participating personally in the cosmic desire. If we envisaged it as being carried out along the lines of the famous five Ms, or in some other, less startling, mode of sexual intercourse, we could indeed speak here of a fusion of human, earthly and sexual love with the divine archetype. But to decide whether in these traditions we are dealing with the same concept of 'divine', in the sense of 'connected with Bhagavān', or with a different category, requires further study.

Such a 'tantric' approach may or may not be one way in which man expresses his reaction to the presence of Bhagavān here on earth in some material shape. But many other modes of responding to it were developed in India. Sporadically (as in the case of Caitanya or the Āḻvārs), some examples have been touched upon, but primarily from a theoretical perspective. It is now time to look at further, much more concrete, illustrations of the melting of the human heart in front of the divine presence.

CHAPTER 15

The melting of the heart

There was a king called Ravivarman, and at some stage during his reign he decided to abdicate. Padmanābha took over as king, and Ravivarman continued as his minister. There are three points here that deserve to be noted as rather remarkable. First, kings do not normally like to give up the privileges of power. Secondly, the event I am referring to did not take place in the hoary past, but very much in the twentieth century. And thirdly, there is the person of King Padmanābha himself. Now this 'Padmanābha' happens to be Bhagavān Viṣṇu, incarnated in stone in the enormous temple town of Trivandrum in Southern Kerala on the west coast of India. In the previous chapter we looked at how Bhagavān's love for the world expresses itself through innumerable manifestations among people, and how people react to his presence by constructing temples which use the royal court as one of their symbolic models. But in our present example, the symbolic has turned into a very concrete social and political reality: Padmanābha is quite literally the king of the state of Travancore. I shall not enter into the background to this rather amazing event; for all we know, to be the minister of a king who happens to be God was felt to be an ideologically more powerful, and politically more impressive or convincing role for Ravivarman than to be king in his own right. But when looked upon as a religious event, it is perfectly logical. If Bhagavān in the temple is symbolically the king, why not turn the symbol literally into what it denotes? But before this little anecdote is used as yet another weapon to attack the folly of Indian 'idolatry', let us briefly put it in context. In a sense, it is quite a pragmatic, realistic solution to a potentially dangerous ideological conflict: the conflict between religious and political power. When we look at medieval kingship in Kamboja, which draws directly on Indian sources, we appear to find the reverse situation: the king is himself the god, incarnate on earth. (This is the popular theory of the Kambojan 'god-king' which has recently been challenged.)[1] On the whole, classical India kept the roles of god, religious leader and king strictly separate and thereby avoided a potential theocracy in which the *guru* is also the king. The case of the Sikhs, with whom political and religious authority combines in the Guru, stands out for its relative uniqueness. Times have obviously changed: our modern idols are film stars, who to many a fan are like 'gods'; moreover, it has become fashionable for such celluloid divines to become politicians. But then this is something not exclusive to India.

In more general terms, what I would like to explore in this chapter is the way in which human beings react to the divine presence manifest in the confines of human society and life, and how they personally let it enter into their hearts, thereby altering the course and structure of their lives, possibly very radically. So let us look now at a variety of ways in which Bhagavān's or Bhagavatī's presence on earth among people stimulated a reaction, and in which it became operative in relation to actual human life. Thus this is the point where we can most clearly and immediately learn about the nitty-gritty of the life Indian theism and monotheism can give rise to. Since 'the melting of the heart' in front of a 'love abiding in stone' is initially perhaps a bit hard for us to relate to, let me begin with some examples in a much lower key.

Around AD 1400 we find King Śivasiṃha ruling in the north-eastern kingdom of Mithilā. As is appropriate for a king, he has a harem, a fact which nevertheless does not bring to rest his roving eye for pretty girls. He also has a man-of-letters at his court, the learned brahmin Vidyāpati,[2] author of many a treatise in Sanskrit. Then something remarkable happens. Vidyāpati transforms the rustic vernacular of the region, Maithilī, into a language of literature. He begins to compose songs in this language which not only feed into the culture of the court, but also spread into the villages, to be picked up by the common folk. What are the songs about? They are about lovers, particularly the divinely manifested lovers Kṛṣṇa and the milkmaids. But in two very central respects, Vidyāpati's songs differ from other examples of the genre. First, through the figure of Kṛṣṇa or the lover we are made to see King Śivasiṃha (or, we could say, behind the foreground references to Kṛṣṇa we can detect the king in the background). What Kṛṣṇa and the milkmaids did on earth serves as the ordering mechanism according to which the love-life of the harem is depicted and directed. Secondly, although in many ways Vidyāpati draws on the conventions of Sanskrit love-poetry, he introduces a novel feature: his lovers are not the professional experts of Sanskrit poetics, but ordinary human beings, unsure of themselves, scared or embarrassed, hesitant, eager but inexperienced, and needing advice. Something like real individuals can be guessed behind the stereotypes, and the poet is able to give advice, either through the mouth of a milkmaid's confidante, or directly in his own name. All this means that, through the creative and imaginative mediation of Vidyāpati, Kṛṣṇa's amours on earth are turned into the exemplar of a refined psychological education in the complexities of love and making love, not just for the harem – the immediate setting of the songs – but also for the ordinary folk in the villages.

Further East, in Bengal, we have another poet, Caṇḍīdāsa,[3] who may have lived around the same time or somewhat earlier. He too was a brahmin and, though not the first, made a very important contribution to Bengali literature with his songs. Again it is Rādhā and Kṛṣṇa we hear about, but Caṇḍīdāsa emphasizes the painful aspects of illicit love: the waiting, longing, social opprobium and ostracism, and the few moments of happiness in all the suffering of such a love. What makes this poetry so interesting is what folklore, as popular as Caṇḍīdāsa's own songs and often mixed up with them, says about Caṇḍīdāsa's own life. He fell in love with a low-caste washerwoman, Rāmi; not content with carrying on a secret affair, he publicly acknowledged his love and sought to have it acknowledged by his fellow brahmins. Rāmi is his Rādhā, and the songs are the outpourings of his own experiences. Rādhā and Kṛṣṇa are the archetypes for his personal relationship with Rāmi, they are the symbols through which he reflects upon it and expresses it, and in fact his justification. More than the psychological inspiration expressed through Vidyāpati's poetry, Rādhā and Kṛṣṇa have become, as it were, the meaning-system for Caṇḍīdāsa's own life.

What is obviously still missing in these two initial examples is a directly causal link between the divine manifestation and the human life responding to it. So let me turn to the Maharashtra of the seventeenth century. From a young woman known as Bahiṇā-bāī (possibly a nickname, meaning 'older sister') we have something extremely rare in pre-modern India, an autobiography.[4] (Some aspects of it were discussed in the context of 'safe havens'.) At the tender age of six or seven she was married to a relative, a man of about thirty, previously married, and of shady connections. By profession her husband was one of those brahmins who look after ordinary people's 'religious' needs – producing horoscopes, performing rituals for a safe childbirth, for instance. He was a cruel and vicious man who used to beat her regularly. Because of his shady past, the whole family had to flee from their home and lead a wandering life. Here now Bahiṇā discovered what gave her consolation in the tribulations of her life: the beauty of Viṣṇu's temple images and of the songs sung in the temples about the past deeds of Viṣṇu and Kṛṣṇa. This is true religion for her, and not the mechanical, impersonal rituals performed by her father and husband. During that period she met Tukārām (at least from a distance) – now one of Maharashtra's most famous saints and poets, but at that time still a very controversial figure (he belonged to a low caste and was promulgating a classless religion of devotion to Viṣṇu). Already pregnant, she is beaten up by her husband more viciously than ever for displaying publicly her religious inclinations, for being seen in the crowd of *śūdras* gathered around Tukārām. But the experiences of that period lead her not only to the conviction that she has found liberation, but also to the realization that she can write poetry. The divine manifestation of Viṣṇu in the temple, brought to life for her through the person and the songs of Tukārām, not only provided comfort and emotional solace in a most painful life, but unleashed in her the creative potentials which have provided us with her moving poetry.

Perhaps a thousand years before Bahiṇā-bāī, in Tamil Nadu, lived another girl and poetess, called Kōtai ('Flower-Garland').[5] She is the one female saint among the Āḻvārs (see Plate 18), and is commonly known as Āṇṭāḷ, the 'Lady'. A religious autobiography is clearly way beyond the cultural horizon of the period. Nevertheless, I think it is possible to interpret Kōtai's poetry as documenting some religious process of growth and personal development. In her first few poems we find her merged into the anonymous 'we' of young girls playing games and performing rituals. In this 'we', the words of the milkmaids in love with Kṛṣṇa fuse with what stereotyped Tamil folk-songs put into the mouths of girls singing them. Kōtai's environment is, as it were, the world in which Kṛṣṇa lived and where he could be spoken to directly: the local temple is his house – no conceptual distinction is drawn with his 'mythical' house in Vṛndāvana. Then the innocence of early

Plate 18. Various Āḻvār and Ācārya figures in the Uṭaiyavar (Rāmānuja) shrine of the Varadarāja-pperumāḷ temple, Kāñcīpuram, Tamil Nadu

childhood is replaced by the awareness that her own environment is not the realm of myth: Kṛṣṇa has moved away. Kōtai begins to speak as an 'I', as the 'girl' of ancient Tamil love-poetry, and expresses her longing for Kṛṣṇa by talking to the flowers, birds and trees in her garden. Here the adolescent girl experiences the world as pervaded by love, Kṛṣṇa's love, and yet he remains elusive. She entrusts nature with messages to him, and she dreams of him arriving and marrying her. But then she reaches womanhood, becomes aware of herself as a being of flesh and blood, as an individual, and as someone pushed into a socially defined role. Passionately in love with Kṛṣṇa, her whole physical and emotional being desiring him, she refuses to be drawn into an ordinary marriage. She argues with the representatives of society that ask her to conform. She wants marriage with Kṛṣṇa. Desperate in her separation, one of her final poems expresses her frustration in a most dramatic manner. 'I shall tear out these breasts of mine, for they gained nothing from being dedicated to him. I shall cast them on to his chest, to extinguish their fire.'[6] Kōtai alludes here to, and plays with, a famous episode found in a Tamil epic, which has been mentioned previously.[7] The king of Maturai had rashly executed an innocent man, and his wife took revenge by tearing off her breast and casting it upon the town, setting it on fire and destroying the royal palace and the populace. The utter despair that is expressed in Kōtai's poetry over Bhagavān's 'separation' is the trigger for the release in ecstasy realized through the mysticism of separation cultivated by many of the Āḻvārs. (It will be in a different context that the significance of this 'irreducible particularity' will be discussed.)[8]

Already the four examples I have presented so far have brought certain important features into focus. First, from the physical form taken on by divine manifestations follows logically a physical – sensuous and sensual – perception of, and reaction to, it. Secondly, when this is done with any degree of commitment to the religious content of such manifestations, a clash with social values has to occur. Bahiṇā came into conflict, emotionally and socially, with the brahmin establishment generally and in particular with her husband, one of its representatives. Similarly, Caṇḍīdāsa could at least infuse religious significance into his own social dilemma. And Kōtai tells us that it would be like a jackal sniffing at the sacred oblations offered by sages, were a man other than Kṛṣṇa to touch her body.[9]

In the poetry of the Āḻvārs, the senses are presented as taking in the beauty and the love displayed by Bhagavān through his temple images. They convey it to the heart and make it melt. When this emotive response is depicted by means of the 'girl' symbol, the figure of the 'mother' appears who makes all kinds of comments on the state in which the 'girl' finds herself. Such comments show that the 'mother' stands for conventional society. Her daughter has gone mad; she behaves as if she is possessed by some demon; all her own efforts to bring up a nice girl have been ruined; she has no concern for the social respect and name of her family. But the girl argues back. How can you blame me? It was you yourself who kept on taking me, as a little girl, to the temple and pointed out and explained to me his image; it was you who drew me into this manifest beauty which made my heart melt.[10]

The Āḻvārs manipulate another symbol of ancient Tamil love-poetry: the 'landscape of excess' (*peruntiṇai*). I mentioned previously[11] that Tamil poetics had defined five landscapes as representing respectable behaviour between lovers. In addition, it had acknowledged that not everybody followed such refined norms; this it called the 'excessive landscape' of love. What better way to illustrate the fact that passionate devotion to Bhagavān had a tendency to break all social conventions than to move the girl over into this unconventional 'landscape'? Thus it had been the norm (poetically, that is) for the wife or the beloved to wait, and for the lover not to make a public display of his unrequited love. Now the Āḻvārs' 'girl' breaks both norms. Her frustration makes her get up and go out in search of her distant lover and publicly proclaim her love for him, scolding him in front of everybody for his lack of concern. As I said, these are poetic conventions and codes. But behind them lies the clear statement that, once the heart has melted, it may not find rest in the normal pursuits of society. The religion of Love can develop here a freedom which the religions of Power find hard to accept or tolerate.

Northern love-poetry had a different symbol for the woman who breaks social conventions: the *asatī*, the 'unfaithful woman'.[12] And, indeed, we find this theme used in the same devotional context. To the Marathi poet, Tukārām, are ascribed a number of rather rustic songs in which the intensity of the religious response to Bhagavān's manifestation is described through this symbolism. Here is one example, to convey the flavour of this poetry.

My first husband was useless in bed:
that's why I took a lover.
Whether it is day or night,
I must have him by my side.
A moment without him
is time wasted in misery.
My name, family, relations?
– Forget about them!
Tukā says: Only Viṣṇu arouses me.[13]

This is all very well: the freedom to which religion gives rise, depicted poetically through the imagery of the unfaithful woman. But how would this look in the nitty-gritty of daily life? The same Tukārām offers us a rather interesting insight into this. He was married and had children. But being constantly engrossed in thinking of his God, sitting at the feet of his statue, and composing songs and entertaining ordinary folks by singing them did not fill any stomachs. As it happens, he himself allows us to listen in on the daily scenes that were going on in his house between him and his wife. A lot of four-letter words are exchanged, and Tukārām's wife includes the local Viṣṇu in her objects of abuse.

'What could I give you to eat, son?
My husband has become mad.
He has lost all interest in making money.
Cymbals in his hands,
his mouth gaping wide open
and howling away,
he sings in the temple,
next to that damned god.'

Tukā says: 'You bitch!
The pile of what you try to store
will get you nowhere!
You're stupid:
you put a heavy load on your head
and then make vulgar noises,
as if you suffered from constipation!'[14]

We have here a very rare testimony of what the 'melting of the heart' can mean in terms of the actualities of real, gruelling, struggling daily life. Poems about an adulterous wife loving Viṣṇu are one thing, but a real wife clamouring for money to feed the children is quite another thing. The poetry may be extremely romantic, but the real-life context in which it was created and back into which it is infused may be far from romantic.

A further example may illustrate this harsher side of *bhakti* religion. For this we return to Bengal, but this time to the Bengal of the eighteenth century. It was a period of general hardship, punctuated by severe famines and starvation. After five hundred years of Muslim rule and its demoralizing effects on the Hindu mind, yet another foreign power was establishing itself in the country. Rāmprasād Sen, a village boy, grew up in utter poverty, and in his teens became an accounts assistant to a local landlord. But instead of filling the books with numbers, he filled their pages with poems, and it is in these Bengali songs that the miseries of the time and of his own life find moving expression. While Bengal and other parts of India had been familiar for centuries with religious songs in the vernacular about gods like Kṛṣṇa, Śiva, Viṣṇu, or Rāma, Rāmprasād created something completely new: poems addressed to the Goddess. On the surface the symbolism is that of the child addressing his mother. But it is a wailing, unhappy child, and at a closer look, it is hardly a 'mother' at all that is addressed. It is the Goddess of Rāmprasād's village temple: Elokeśī 'she with the wild hair'. Here is an extract from one of the songs.

> Why do you walk about naked?
> Shame, shame on you! You have no shame!
> Clothes and ornaments you do not wear,
> and yet you behave like a princess.
> One foot you have put on your husband.
> Yourself naked, your husband naked,
> you haunt the cremation grounds.
> Instead of your necklace,
> you wear a garland of human heads.
> For once, woman, put on a dress!
>
> Prasād says: Of such an apparition
> even a naked Śiva would get scared![15]

Hardly a cosy and romantic mother-child idyll! In fact, in the image of the Goddess – her skulls, nudity, blood-dripping sword, tongue hanging out, and black body smeared with blood – the entire gruesomeness, cruelty and violence of life takes on concrete form. The poet mocks her, alluding to one of her titles:

Full of compassion –
who would call you 'full of compassion'?
Someone's milk is mixed with sugar-syrup,
but in the state that I am in,
– where are there even rice and vegetables?
Some you gave wealth, servants, elephants,
horses, chariots
– am I nothing to you?[16]

Here is another example:

I know you, I do know
how much compassion you have!
Some at the end of the day have eaten nothing.
Others have a tummy filled with food,
and a chain of gold constrains their waist.
Some move about in a palanquin,
and others have to carry it on their shoulders.[17]

The Goddess causes the world to be what it is, and is thus responsible for all the injustice and cruelty found in it. (We encountered similar ideas in the *Devī-Bhāgavata-Purāṇa*, a work that must have been quite popular in Bengal.)[18] But, however much suffering man may cry out, she remains deaf – is that why her image is made of stone?[19] But, dark as she may be, and as all the dark things of life may be contained in her, Rāmprasād has nowhere else to go. 'And, were she to send me away, I would not leave. I would fall at her feet and die.'[20] 'Prasād is like that: a sucker who, in spite of the kicks he receives, cries out: "Mother!"'[21]

Somehow in all his sufferings, Rāmprasād can find a blind trust and unquestioning confidence in the purposefulness of it all. The Goddess remains an object of love for him, because in the middle of all pain he perceives her own love. Playing on the literal meaning of the Goddess's name Kālī, 'of black complexion', he says:

There are many black things in the world
but that Black one is the greatest marvel!
When put into the heart, it lights it up with brilliance.
Black of complexion, black by name, blacker than black
– yet he who sees her form,
is swallowed up by it
and finds no pleasure in other forms.[22]

Thus there is bliss and fulfilment in the passive acceptance of all of life's negative sides. In suffering as much as in happiness lies

Bhagavatī's grace. But there is also the release of creative power:

> People say: Rāmprasād is mad.
> But I cannot control my tongue,
> and turn my words into poetry.
> Are these words of mine ridiculous?
> I try so hard,
> but people fail to understand me.[23]

Still, things turned out to be not quite so negative as Rāmprasād imagines them here. His songs in honour of the Bhagavatī Kālī Elokeśī soon became immensely popular all over Bengal among the ordinary people. And that's not all. Dozens of further poets over the next hundred and fifty years imitated his songs, and thus Rāmprasād became the founder of a whole new genre of religious poetry.[24] Thus somehow he managed, in describing the tribulations of his own life and those of society around him, and in expressing his total, though desperate, trust in the Goddess, to strike sympathetic strings in other people.

I have offered here six possible ways in which the human heart perceives and receives Bhagavān's or Bhagavatī's manifestations. Since it is precisely the nitty-gritty of ordinary life that we have been interested in as the area in which the response expresses itself, a variety of very specific instances have been referred to. But it is time to abstract from these specifics and look at more general matters.

By now we have become used to the fact that specific features of Indian religious history are always connected with specific cultural constructs. But do we have anything like this in relation to the human responses to divine manifestations spoken about earlier on? In one sense, we do indeed possess such a cultural construct; in fact, this has already been referred to time and again. I am thinking here of the production of religious songs in the various vernaculars. In the cases of Bahiṇā-bāī and of Rāmprasād Sen, the writing of such poetry has been stated explicitly to be an outflow from religious experience. It would also be easy to adduce examples from Tukārām and the Āḻvārs. To the extent that the communal singing of these songs in temples, etc. became formalized, we could indeed speak of two cultural constructs here. The production of millions of *kīrtans*, *abhaṅgs*, *bhajans*, *kritis*, *padas*, or whatever other names refer to the various genres that evolved, would be one, and its ritualized performance, the other. But in a different sense this could also be regarded as the re-socialization of trends that by their natural momentum threatened social values and structures (remember the *asatī* and the *peruntiṇai*, the 'unfaithful woman' and 'excessive passion').

But there are further structures which have to be considered here. The first is the easiest, because it is merely an imitation of something already existing. Tukārām's poetry revealed to us how difficult it was in real life to combine the duties of a father and husband with a total commitment to Bhagavān. While Bahiṇā clearly resolved the dilemma in her own case and could write a series of poems on the virtues of 'the woman totally devoted to her husband' (*pati-vratā*)[25] and advocate this as religiously meaningful, saints like Caitanya and Rāmānuja found this impossible. They turned *saṃnyāsīs* and thus resorted to the renouncer tradition as the appropriate life-style also for the monotheistic devotee. Institutionalized, this turned into the *maṭha*, or 'monastery'.

In some cases, the momentum of *bhakti* pushed much further and generated fully-fledged alternative societies in miniature. Here conventional values were consciously discarded. In particular, this referred to the daily performance of all kinds of rituals without theistic content, and to the restrictive behaviour of the so-called 'caste system' in relation to salvation. The charismatic figure of a *guru*, who succeeded in gathering around himself a sufficient number of, and sufficiently variegated, followers to allow for such an alternative society to emerge, is particularly important here. Thus we may recollect, for twelfth-century Karnataka, the Liṅgayites or Vīra-Śaivites founded by Basavaṇṇa who are, as their names indicate, worshippers of Śiva.[26] For thirteenth-century Maharashtra we have the Mānbhāvs who take their origin from Govindaprabhu and Cakradhar, and who profess an extremely idiosyncratic form of Kṛṣṇaism. In the fifteenth century, a schismatic movement within Rāmānuja's Śrīvaiṣṇavism arose which also produced the most sophisticated and complete theological justification known to me for such an alternative society derived from monotheistic values.[27] Naturally the movement initiated by Caitanya deserves to be mentioned here, as do also those of the Sikhs and of Vallabha – all roughly from the fifteenth or sixteenth centuries. These are obviously examples of cultural constructs on the largest possible scale: complete and closed religious systems.

But let me now turn to another concrete expression of the 'melting of the heart'. This is a feature of the cultural history of India that aroused the horror of earlier Western observers as much as the deadly silence of modern India. Let me refer to it by its conventional label: the institution of the *deva-dāsī*. Officially, this does not exist any more (because an Imperial Law was passed in 1919, the Devdasi Act, which made the institution illegal) and has never existed (as the modern silence wants to claim). But things are not quite so simple. When I was staying in Madras some years back, my innocent scholastic zeal made me try to find surviving *devadāsīs* to interview them about what was going on before the Act was passed. This was a fatal mistake which gave rise to considerable animosity. Thus forewarned, I forgot my scholarliness when I saw in a temple in Goa an actual *devadāsī* officiate during the daily temple rituals. And when in Maharashtra, I decided not to investigate the rumours that the temple of Khaṇḍobā in Jejurī, as also that of Yellammā in Saundatti in neighbouring Karnataka, still provided the home for *muraḷīs* and *jogtīṇs*, two classes of *devadāsīs.* Sensationalist journalism nevertheless made a recent inroad into this area of silence, by reporting that the girls offered to Yellammā nowadays end up in the brothels of Bombay.[28] It is only very recently that more serious scholarship has begun to appear, but this concentrates almost exclusively on the musicology of the *deva-dāsī* tradition and on their ritual functions within the temple.[29]

Clearly we are dealing with a very difficult subject. Now in the light of poetry like Kōtai's and other ancient sources, one could venture to assume the existence of an institution which accepted young girls for temple services. They would be married, either directly to the *arcā*, or to some other symbol, and thus could never become widows. Educated in the temple and trained in the arts (dancing, singing, etc.) and in ritual, they could spend there a life totally dedicated to Bhagavān. Kōtai's poetry would suggest that such a life could be the result of free choice. But if this was ever possible on any significant scale, another mode of recruitment must have been much more prominent: parents dedicating children to a temple, say in fulfilment of a vow or due to economic pressures.

Again we can only guess at what happened at a later stage. Perhaps it was due to the collapse of endowments made to temples which covered the costs of such an institution or due to the frailty of human nature. But these 'servant-girls' of the god turned into prostitutes or kept women. Popular literature from the South India of the sixteenth, seventeenth and eighteenth centuries make this quite clear.[30] And, indeed, even something like a theology was evolved. Bhagavān grants his grace in the form of the *prasāda*, which could be any item used in *pūjā* and imbued with his grace through contact with the *arcā*. What better way of symbolizing love 'abiding in stone' than through the love granted by a *devadāsī*?

But let us not get carried away by useless speculation. There is one further cultural construct associated with the human response to divine manifestations which deserves a closer look. As in all other religions, India has preserved the memory of outstanding individuals who in some stunning or impressive manner responded to the manifest divine grace. A vast literature arose which tells such stories. But though I shall refer to it, for the sake of convenience, as 'hagiography', such stories are not necessarily about 'saints' in the familiar meaning of the word since, as I mentioned already, the concept of '*avatāra*' may well be projected on to 'saints'.

Hagiography comes in all kinds of shapes in India. Sometimes it has grown out of the literary genre of the *sthala-purāṇa* – a natural growth, since very frequently 'saints' were associated with a particular temple. Sometimes it is included in the repertoire of the *bhakti* poetry mentioned here – again a natural location, since often such a poet is aware of his predecessors. Sometimes it is part of an ideological programme: the stories about 'saints' are meant to validate certain claims made by certain institutions. Sometimes hagiographical accounts provide an imaginative and, alas, all too frequently, imaginary biographical background to a given corpus of poetry. Sometimes we notice a real attempt to write a 'critical' biography of a historical person, while at other times, purāṇic thought generates its own characters. And finally, there are the late encyclopaedists who take a delight in just collecting every story about a saint they can find. By now it is clear that once again – inevitably you might say – we are dealing with an extremely bulky literature. So what follows is no more than a very superficial glance at this material, meant to illustrate the possibilities listed just now.

Let me begin by looking once again at the robber Āḻvār Parakāla. The first time we hear about his life is in the *sthala-purāṇa* of his home-town, Tirunakari.[31] It is a story about divine grace and salvation, granted to his soul at the end of a number of rebirths. That he started off in one life as a pious brahmin who faithfully performed his rituals, and ended up, in his fourth rebirth, as a *śūdra* who plundered travellers, including Viṣṇu himself, emphasizes the mysterious workings of grace. It is this plundering of Viṣṇu which not only brought him in direct contact with his salvation, but also gave rise to one of the temples in Tirunakari. The second time we find the story told, it is in a Sanskrit epic[32] which sings the glories of Śrīraṅgam. Parakāla is now one of the many examples of people who totally dedicated all their efforts to adding to the glory of this temple. From the theme 'robber', this text developed a very lengthy account of his setting out to steal the golden statue of the Buddha in Nāgapaṭṭiṉam and of similar exploits. Moreoever, twice he committed murder. First, he cut off the head of his own brother-in-law (whose body got caught inside the opening into the Nāgapaṭṭiṉam temple), to avoid detection. Secondly, when he had run out of money and could not pay the masons who had built various shrines on his behalf in Śrīraṅgam, he drowned them in the Kāveri river, but then comforted their relatives by having the masons reappear and tell them how wonderful it is in heaven.

Then again his story is told[33] in conjunction with those of the other eleven Āḻvārs. All twelve are envisaged as incarnations on earth of Viṣṇu's weapons (compare Plate 19) – Parakāla being that of his bow. Clearly here the emphasis is even less on what he does as a human being. Basically the story now illustrates the workings of Viṣṇu's punishing and protective qualities (symbolized by the weapons) in the world. At the same time, the Āḻvārs are presented here as the precursors of Śrīvaiṣṇava teachers, such as Rāmānuja: a pedigree is established for this religious movement which begins in the protective love of Viṣṇu himself. Moreover, Parakāla was a poet, and all versions tell us something about individual circumstances which gave rise to this or that poem of his. In most cases, however, there is no hint in the poem itself which could have suggested such details.

Another Āḻvār was Kōtai.[34] Now in her story we find that a careful reading of the poetry itself triggered off some biographical speculation. I mentioned earlier that her poetry ends on a note of frustration, and it is here that hagiography sets in. Her stepfather (for she was a foundling) noticed her single-minded devotion to Viṣṇu and decided to arrange the marriage of his girl with him. However, the singular 'him' is wrong. Śrīvaiṣṇavism has a list of one hundred and eight primary *arcās* of Viṣṇu in India (most of them in the South). So her stepfather invites them all to his home and lets Kōtai choose her favourite. Raṅganātha is the lucky one, and their marriage is celebrated in great pomp.

Plate 19. Bronze figure of Sudarśana, Viṣṇu's heavenly servant and 'discus', Varadarāja-pperumāḷ temple, Kāñcipuram, Tamil Nadu

The devotees of Śiva in the South have their own set of saints: nominally sixty-three are listed. Here we encounter a much more 'violent' note. One saint organized the impalement of six thousand Jains who, though heretics in the eyes of the staunch Śivaites, had dared to challenge the saint to a religious debate.[35] Another saint cut his own stomach open with a knife, to avoid contact with a blasphemer. Two saints are responsible for a vain queen having her nose and hand cut off, when she had picked up a sacrificial flower and smelled it. Another saint cuts his own eyes out to offer them to an eyeless Śiva-*liṅga*. Often Śiva himself appears, usually in the guise of a Śaivite mendicant, to test his devotees. On one such occasion a couple is ready to roast their own child, in order to offer it to the mendicant for a meal. Naturally, in most of these cases, Śiva reveals himself in the end and rewards the particular brave act of piety, restoring or reviving whatever got cut off or killed in the process.

I could go on telling you such stories, from all over India and from many different theistic traditions: like the story about Kabīr's wife who was prepared to yield to the amorous demands of a merchant in order to obtain food from him with which to feed mendicants, and about Kabīr himself carrying her on his shoulder through the rain to the merchant for their dalliance,[36] or about Gorā-kumbhār the potter who was so engrossed in meditating on Bhagavān while moulding the clay with his feet that he did not notice his little son getting squashed in the process.[37] I could tell the story of the poet who was so madly in love with a prostitute that he took all kinds of chances crossing a flooded river to be with her, who then taught him that such single-minded devotion deserved only a Bhagavān as its object.[38] Or the story about Tukārām's wife who kept on ranting at Viṣṇu and insulting him until he took pity on her and gave her the things required to run the house.[39]

But by now I think you have gained some idea of the kind of material we are dealing with. It is a genre of religious literature that is still very much alive in modern India. Popular stories are told about miracles worked by saints who lived not long ago or who are still alive. But even as early as AD 1278, a different attitude was possible. Cakradhar, the founder of the Mānbhāv movement, had just died, and Mhāimbhaṭ set out to collect anecdotes and events of his life.[40] Travelling all over Maharashtra, he carefully sorted out the material that was offered to him. He evaluated the trustworthiness of his informants, verified accounts by insisting on more than one informant, and thus attempted to establish something like an authentic biography of Cakradhar. The result might still strike us as rather fantastic. For we hear about Cakradhar feeding a herd of cattle merely by allowing them to look at him, or digging up a dead baby, putting it at its mother's breast and thus bringing it back to life. Nevertheless, the 'scientific' principle Mhāimbhaṭ applies is interesting. The Mānbhāvs generally produced thousands of pages of hagiography about their earlier teachers. The motivation here is to do the second best: at least to recollect their lives, by meditating on the many episodes narrated, since they themselves have passed away and thus cannot be met. And again, such life-stories are not normative, for teachers like Cakradhar and Govindaprabhu were regarded as *avatāras* of Kṛṣṇa.[41]

Hagiography is in fact one of the most popular genres of Indian religious literature, and the material available to the interested scholar is almost unlimited. It is fascinating stuff, and opens up all kinds of possibilities for further exploration. Thus, for instance, one could study the kind of personality envisaged here. Given the very limited number of such stories that I have studied, my tentative suggestion would be that an 'obsessive character' is portrayed in many of these hagiographical accounts: the person 'with a bee in his bonnet', the monomaniac – like the Śaiva saint who used up all his wealth to keep a lamp burning in his local temple, and who then ground his own arm to pulp to burn this instead of oil.[42]

However, before some psychoanalyst goes to town over this, let me at least put forward some signs of caution. It would be terribly easy to assume that what hagiography tells us about an individual's life structured according to the demands made by divine manifestations, is actually intended as a literal, normative prescription or model for others to follow. A saint is a saint, and any decent Christian tries to model his own life accordingly. But in view of the great variety which even Christianity spreads out as the ideal of sanctity, such an attitude would be mistaken. Even the traditional Christian range is far too wide to be taken seriously, *in toto*, by any individual Christian. The range in India is far wider, and thus far less likely to function as the norm for an individual. But this is still not really the point. For what ought to be investigated is really the question of whether such hagiographical accounts are meant to be normative. My feeling is that on the whole they are not. At best we could say that a religious tradition spreads out a spectrum of possibilities, advertising its own values thereby and perhaps also trying to beat a rival tradition at its own game. What any individual, producing such lives of the saints, could really hope for was a raising of consciousness, a slight increase of openness for the divine challenge. After that, there had to be the trust that the same divine manifestation will take over, and dictate or suggest what ought to come next. So, in my reading of this material, realistically speaking all that is being suggested is an increase of awareness, openness, readiness to respond when the divine demands manifest themselves. But, moreover, it is clear that in many cases not even that much was intended. Typical examples are the cases of the Āḻvārs and of the five Kṛṣṇas of the Mānbhāvs. Since they are the incarnations of Viṣṇu's weapons and of

Parameśvara respectively, how could they represent the norm for a Śrīvaiṣṇava's or a Mānbhāv's religious life?

All this may be fine, as long as we are dealing with a situation in which Bhagavān manifests himself in a temple image, or something similar, or in the past. But things do get different when we turn to the demands made by an actual human *guru* here and now. In all the cases where a *guru* appears on the scene, and in particular where such a *guru* is supposed to be Śiva in disguise, our minds would want a set of objective criteria for judgement. Quite logically we would ask whether such a belief does not allow for the proliferation of sham *gurus*, of fraudulent teachers. Neither traditional nor modern India has evolved such a set of criteria by which the genuine *guru* could be distinguished from the fake. In our hagiographical stories, such a possibility is practically never envisaged; it is always the real thing that appears in the most fantastic guises. And no other literary genre went very far in establishing such criteria. Was India unaware of the problem? If that were true, we must assume that people never received a negative feedback from fake teachers. Was it realized that no such objective criteria could be established in principle? Given the nature of the divine and how it was experienced – in particular one could think here of Rāmprasād Sen – a neat set of rules about a 'nice' or 'reasonable' *guru* are clearly out of the question. My own feeling here is that no need for objective criteria was felt. Where the authority for any judgement was located was the individual person's own feeling. Given the massive availability of *gurus* at any time and in any place, most would be ignored or rejected, for purely personal reasons. What mattered ultimately was whether or not one got something out of one's relationship with a *guru*. What he is, or what he feeds into the relationship does not matter, but what I receive from it does. This may strike us as extremely random, but then most of Indian religion is 'random' in this sense. While the stories, at the most, advocated an ideal and tried to inculcate a general attitude or readiness, a solid amount of common sense kept the balance. It could perhaps be argued that it is this common sense which appears sadly lacking in modern Western converts to *guru* cults. Yet it could also be argued that what is sadly lacking is society's readiness to accept that something might – objectively – be meaningful simply by virtue of being – subjectively – perceived to be so. That to me seems to be the Indian idea.

What all this has led up to is basically two points. First of all, people's behaviour is, in most cases, determined by social conventions which logically predate any monotheistic challenge. Secondly, even such a challenge does not normally present itself in ethical, positivistic-legalistic terms, as we have had ample opportunity to realize. We have the famous injunction (by Augustine): *ama et fac quod vis*, 'love, and do what you want'. The divine manifestations we have been looking at can be described as the appeal for this *amare*, the injunction to love. They reveal 'lovable' aspects of Bhagavān or Bhagavatī, however much madness, irrationality, or cruelty may be contained in them. Once this openness for love has been achieved, a freedom of action arises: 'do what you want'. But there are two constraints upon this action implied here. The first is simply that someone in a state of loving just does not do certain things. The second is the considerable pressure of conventional Indian social morality (and I would be inclined to include here a good amount of common sense). It could well be that hagiography feels obliged to spell out unconventional behaviour in such thick colours precisely because these pressures were so strong. The Law is not something a prophet has to proclaim and enforce; it is something already operating in a premonotheistic environment. Monotheism brings love into it, and thus frequently has to appear as the 'law-breaker'.

The time has come to cast a final glance back over the material that we have been discussing under the heading of monotheistic devotion. We started with a general formula: relationship between desiring subject and desired object. So far we have seen that we can insert God or Goddess in the slot 'desired object' and that the relationship is usually styled '*bhakti*'. However, we also notice that the object itself has desires: for man and his salvation. Moreover, we have noticed a considerable fluctuation, both on a purely psychological and on a metaphysical level, in the status of our 'desiring subject'. Sometimes he seems in total control, and sometimes he seems totally subjugated to, or entirely absorbed into, the desired object. Thus we have many instances of divine helplessness. Already the *arcā* is, as some Śrīvaiṣṇava texts put it, dependent on the priest and the devotee.[43] Then we have the monotheistic system created by Vallabha which concentrates on the baby Kṛṣṇa. In South Indian folk-religion we have the figure of Kāttavarāyaṉ who quite consciously organized his earthly life in such a way that he ended up impaled – his many wives and humanity lamenting his cruel fate – and then mysteriously comes back to life, to bless the world.[44] *Bhakti* here is the tender care and motherly love, as it were, given to the *arcā*, the baby Kṛṣṇa or Kāttavarāyan̲, or the lamenting of the latter's misfortunes. At the other end of the spectrum we have the Goddess and various goddesses in the folk traditions. They are powerful ladies, challenging man and demanding his total subjugation. As we saw in the chapter on 'safe havens', Yellammā punished an unwilling gardener with eczema, and Manasā piled misfortune upon Chando, until he finally yielded and worshipped her. This was analysed under the heading of Power, but our material from Bāṇa and from Rāmprasād Sen revealed that here also Love can be present. It is thus clear that, corresponding to the fluctuation of how the divine manifests itself, love as the human response oscillates in a similar manner. We have seen how *bhakti* can unleash the powers of creativity and personal freedom; how it can offer new and meaningful insights into one's life; but also how it can imply a total submission to the divine will which, moreover, may appear as mad, illogical, or cruel. Even so, we found that these are not separate phenomena. Bahiṇā found her creative potential through the total submission to her miserable fate, and so did Rāmprasād. Kōtai's (or for that matter, Caitanya's) freedom and happiness derives from her (and his) intense suffering in separation. Thus submission to sheer unbearable pressures seems to be the mode in which love expresses itself. What is confusing for the outside observer is the coding-system of this expression – whether it is the poetry about Kṛṣṇa's adulterous love or about the lover lying at the feet of his beloved, waiting for her kicks, or about the 'saint' totally enslaved to an obsessive ideal. Love makes free, but only through enforcing submission.

One thing is clear: in all these different variants of our initial formula we are dealing primarily with the relationship between man and his God, or Goddess, as a drive towards some form of transcendentalization of man's love. Yet there remains the divine descent into the world: are there any indications that this changed man's own position and role in the world and in society? Moreover, we must remind ourselves that the purpose of the abstract formula (subject-desire-object) was to allow for the insertion of more than just God (or Goddess). After the present, rather extensive, observations on Hindu monotheism, it seems appropriate to make some comments also on the other possibilities. Either way (and we shall see that this need not be an alternative at all), we shall return to the world.

CHAPTER 16

Return to the world

The Spanish mystic Íñigo de Loyola wrote in a letter of 1551 to a student: 'You should practise looking for the presence of our Lord in all things, in walking, seeing, hearing, tasting, thinking.'[1] This is familiar ground to us: to seek out, as it were, divine love present in the world, and to absorb it through our senses. Now the same author includes in his famous *Spiritual Exercises* a meditation entitled 'in order to obtain love'. There one should meditate 'how God works and acts for my sake in all created things on the face of the earth'. A curious phrase in Latin is added: 'that means how he acts as if he is working'. The whole exercise concludes with a prayer: 'that I may love and serve in everything his divine majesty'.[2]

This now introduces a theme which has not been encountered so far. The divine presence is not just something to be experienced in all its beauty or accepted in all its gruesomeness, sung about and danced to in states of ecstasy, but demands specific action. Indeed, there is a common link between Íñigo and our Indian material: no positivistic Law is spelled out. The individual has to search for his particular call, and his particular mode of reacting to it. In the previous chapter I pointed out how the Indian monotheistic material we looked at possesses such an 'anarchic' quality. With Ignatius – to refer to him by his Latin name – this does not surprise us. After all, he was the founder of the Jesuit order, whose flexibility and adaptability (its critics would call this its craftiness) make it possible, for instance, for a Jesuit to have been a minister in a previous government of Nicaragua. So the difference lies in the kind of response suggested: in our present example it is clearly a commitment to the social, political and economic issues of society. Note also how closely Ignatius links such a commitment with the divine exemplar; in fact he has to remind himself, in Latin, that God is not quite like a committed spiritual activist. This we have heard nothing about in the Indian sources.

In fact, if we could find illustrations of this in India, this would be our 'return to the world'. It would mean that all the talk about the Indian religions being 'world-negating', which is still fashionable among certain sociologists, would have to be modified significantly. The intention of all the types of religion we explored under the heading of Power was to gain control over the external world, and the culmination of this trend has been the transcending of it altogether. Existence in this world, when seen as *saṃsāra* or as *duḥkha*, as the cycle of transmigration or as suffering, could only suggest a total escape from it: renunciation. Our illustrations of Love have so far revealed a far more positive attitude to the world of sense – so positive sometimes that the mystic can proclaim that *saṃsāra* and *mokṣa*, the escape from it, mean nothing to him.[3] For in his ecstasy he experiences total fulfilment, here and now. But what about social issues? This may sound initially as if I am imposing a modern, Western category on our material. But this is not the case. So let me now conclude our exploration of Love by looking at types of religion that suggest a return to the world, down from the transcendental experiences of the renouncers and the lofty states of ecstasy of the monotheistic mystics.

We can begin by still remaining in the realm of Indian monotheism, and by looking at what, in fact, is one of its earliest expressions. This is the *Bhagavadgītā*, one of our seminal works in the history of Indian monotheism. The setting for this text is a battlefield. Two armies are lined up facing each other and ready to exterminate as many members of the opposite side as possible. But one of the princes, surveying the ranks of his enemies, discovers all kinds of well-known faces there: relatives, friends, teachers. He is suddenly struck by the realization of what his entering into battle would actually mean, and he refuses to go ahead and fight. A very modern and relevant 'social issue' this would appear to be, but it was formulated as early as perhaps the second or third century BC. Now the prince I have mentioned – his name is Arjuna – has a charioteer called Kṛṣṇa. It is this Kṛṣṇa who now takes upon himself the task of persuading Arjuna that his moral, personal scruples are nothing to be proud about and that he must go ahead and fight the battle. Clearly this Kṛṣṇa seems to be the villain of the play!

Kṛṣṇa's initial arguments derive from the socially defined role of a *kṣatriya*, a member of the clan of warriors. It is their duty to fight in battle. Born into this class, Arjuna cannot now opt out and pretend to belong to another class. This is conceptualized as the obedience to *dharma*, the nature of things and beings as they ought to be and behave. While we have enough evidence from classical treatises spelling out the *dharma* of kings that such advice could well concern the fighting of wars for the sake of fighting them, Kṛṣṇa at least does emphasize that this is a 'just' war: the leaders of the other side are, objectively speaking, the villains.

Now Arjuna draws on the ideas proposed by the renouncer tradition: the effects of *karma* on further rebirths, the negative role of violent action in this context, and the need for withdrawal from the world. There is a decidedly Buddhist flavour about many of the points he makes. But Kṛṣṇa too knows the teaching of the renouncer tradition. What he now attempts to do is abstract its spirit from its letters. Thus he argues, for example, that the concept of pure actionlessness is nonsense, for even the *yogī* in his meditation is still active.[4] What he proposes instead is action that is carried out for its own sake – or better, for *dharma*'s sake – without any motive of personal gain or any emotive concern for or attachment to, the possible outcome of it. With this attitude, action becomes hallowed as a sacrifice, and the selflessness expressing itself here is equated with the Buddhist idea of overcoming desires and a wrong understanding of 'I' and 'mine',[5] of the nature of the person and of what it could gain. The meditational exercises of *yoga* find a place here as well: they can serve as the mechanics for withdrawing the senses and the emotions from their involvement in the world of sense and as the means to obtain that state of selflessness and lack of desire. Incidentally, the *Gītā*, together with our second seminal text of Indian monotheism, the *Śvetāśvatara-Upaniṣad*, make up our earliest more detailed accounts of the Indian meditation techniques known as *yoga*.[6]

Thus action carried out for its own sake is advocated here as the area in which Buddhist and yogic values find their concrete expression. But what could the authority be for such action? Kṛṣṇa draws heavily on the ideas about *dharma*, a cosmic order and rhythm into which man must join, thus participating in the processes that are going on, cosmically, and thereby ceasing to interfere with it through his personal, individual desires and motives. Actually a detailed account of the mechanical side of these cosmic processes is provided, but there is no need to go into these details here. What is important is that the acting person can, as it were, disassociate himself from the actions themselves; sitting back he can observe them like external events that are no concern of his (precisely what is needed to avoid the accumulation of further *karma*).[7]

But Kṛṣṇa goes further than this. Thus far the need for selfless action has been at the centre of the argument, but now he turns to what Arjuna can actually get out of it. This is an inevitable subject of discussion, in view of what the renouncer tradition had to offer concerning man's ultimate spiritual fulfilment. The *yoga* which allows for the performance of selfless, disinterested action does yield, Kṛṣṇa now claims, precisely that spiritual fulfilment spoken of in the renouncer tradition. The Buddhists may call it *nirvāṇa*, and the Upaniṣads may refer to it as the realization of *brahman*, but now it has become available to the man of action.[8] As he carries out his duty in the world, the *dharma* laid down by tradition, and lets himself be carried by the cosmic processes with which his actions are integrated and harmonized,[9] he moves over into the realm of eternity, obtains total freedom, peace and happiness, beyond space, time and matter.

All very well, but why make such a fuss about action in the world, Arjuna replies. What is so special about the world and the processes going on in it that such a cumbersome attempt at synthesizing *dharma* and *brahman* or *nirvāṇa* should be undertaken?

Well, whatever traditional religious thinking could contribute to the discussion is exhausted at this stage: this is a problem which required a solution outside anything known till then. And when Kṛṣṇa does produce such an answer, it must have been like a bombshell for contemporary religious thought. This is how Kṛṣṇa does it. Initially through seemingly innocuous hints and then through increasingly bold claims, Kṛṣṇa suggests to Arjuna that he is not quite what he appears to be. At a certain point Arjuna loses his patience and asks: 'What do you mean? I know you, you are my friend and companion of many a year and adventure, and born like me of a human mother.'[10] 'That's what you think', is Kṛṣṇa's reply. 'I have existed long before time itself began. Many a birth I have taken on earth.' And then he explains his absolute, eternal nature as encompassing *brahman* and *nirvāṇa*, but also filled with a personal love. This love makes him evolve the world, and time and again appear in it to look after its welfare. *Dharma* is his way of spelling out to ordinary people, in a positivistic manner, what is expected of them; how they can harmonize their actions with the rhythm that pervades the cosmos. Meditation is the means of getting deeper into the spirit of the whole enterprise. And indeed, if this *yoga* is pursued to its final culmination, not just *brahman* or *nirvāṇa* awaits the *yogī*, but Kṛṣṇa himself, as he is in his true nature, and his love.[11]

This is all too much for Arjuna. This kind of religious bombshell leaves him, as it were, suffering from shellshock (an appropriate simile, for we are after all on a battlefield). So Kṛṣṇa resorts to a different means in order to make sense to Arjuna. He grants him the 'divine eye', that is, a visionary experience of what Kṛṣṇa in his cosmic form and role looks like and does. But what Arjuna sees is not the idyllic cowherd boy playing his flute in the forest among the cattle and flirting with the milkmaids.

> Then Arjuna saw a form with many a mouth and eye and countless marvellous aspects. Many indeed were the weapons raised on high.
>
> If the brilliance of a thousand suns should arise in the sky, that might resemble the brilliance of this great God.
>
> Then filled with amazement, his hair standing on end, Arjuna spoke:
>
> 'So do I see you: your mouths flaming fires, burning up this whole universe with your blazing glory. You touch the sky, your mouths wide open: so do I see you and my inmost self is shaken. Lo, all these kings rush blindly into your gaping mouths that with their horrid tusks strike them with terror. Some stick in the gaps between your teeth, their heads to powder ground.'

And Kṛṣṇa replies:

> 'Stand up, win glory, and gain a prosperous kingdom! Long since have these men in truth been slain by me: yours is to be the mere occasion.'[12]

Arjuna is panic-struck, and he cries out: 'I cannot bear it. Please turn back into the Kṛṣṇa I have known prior to all this.' Logically, this is the climax of the teaching of the *Gītā*. The text itself does not structure all this so neatly and logically, so that Zaehner could call the chapters following after the vision of Kṛṣṇa's cosmic form 'one of the biggest anticlimaxes in literature.'[13] But that does not matter. Arjuna does learn his lesson eventually and tells Kṛṣṇa to start the battle by driving his chariot towards the ranks of the enemies. Arjuna has ceased to interfere through his pacifism with the devouring violence of Kṛṣṇa's cosmic role. Arjuna does win, but at the cost of an astronomical number of kings and soldiers being killed on the battlefield.

What we have here, in a nutshell, is a vision of divine love and destructiveness manifesting itself in the world and demanding social, political and historical action from man, because that is the way God himself expresses this love. Arjuna is asked, through loyalty and love towards Kṛṣṇa, to commit himself to the affairs of the world, and he is promised to encounter in this Kṛṣṇa's own love towards him. Love is a mutual affair, and expresses itself through action in society and the world.

In view of what has been said previously about Rāmprasād Sen's or the *Devī-Bhāgavata-Purāṇa*'s conception of the Goddess, such a paraphrase of the *Gītā* in terms of 'love' will not now appear quite so overdone. Monotheism in India hardly ever postulated that God's or the Goddess's nature includes 'goodness' in the sense that this could be abstracted, as its ideal expression, from human 'goodness'. The kind of dualism involving 'evil' which is, however reluctantly, implied in such a conception, is alien to Indian monotheistic thought. Theodicy is an unknown subject in Indian theology. The nature of the divine lies outside human categories, and the world with all its variegated events points *in toto* to this truth. In India the history of the cosmos has, since ancient times, been envisaged as cyclic. So there are constant evolutions and dissolutions of the world – like a pulse. Indian monotheism must attribute the cause of this pulse to God, and that inevitably implies an association of God or the Goddess with destructive events and dissolution. The knowledge of all this is, on the whole, derived from 'revelation' in the various traditions. In this light I would also interpret the chapter of the *Gītā* with its vision of the cosmic Kṛṣṇa. Neither reason nor yogic experiences by themselves can serve as the final authority of monotheistic religion.

What we have been looking at over the previous pages could be described, somewhat simplified, as two movements in opposite directions. The religions of Power took us from the world into a transcendental realm beyond the constraints of space, time and matter. The religions of Love tended to find fulfilment in the world by reacting to a divine love that has descended into it and is offering saving grace within it. According to the reading of the *Gītā* I have been presenting here, both movements are combined. There is the pursuit of the transcendental joined together with the move of love into the world. Moreover, concrete action in society (and it may be as unattractive to us as fighting in a battle) is what motivates the combination and holds it together. But this now implies something very important: a different model of what constitutes 'liberation' or 'salvation' for man.

Man here does indeed realize himself in such a way that space, time and matter do not constrain the nature of the self. Yet this does not take him out of this world, for over and above this 'liberation' – if we are still allowed to use this word here – lies his involvement in the world, and that as an expression of divine love. A two-tier structure of reality is implied in this, and the religious task asked for here is to fuse these by abandoning oneself into the love of Kṛṣṇa which pervades both.

Two interesting questions arise from all this. First: what happened to this extraordinary teaching expounded by the *Gītā*? Secondly, would the *Gītā* be the only Indian scripture to express the complex structure of thought isolated just now? Let me deal briefly with the first question, before turning in greater detail to the second one.

Were the *Gītā* to be marked as an undergraduate essay, most people would give it very low marks for its structure and for the logical development of its argument. In terms of presenting its points, it is a total mess. Possibly as a despairing reaction to this situation, it became fashionable to say that the *Gītā* taught three alternative paths towards liberation. This is a facile solution, and is certainly motivated in part by reinterpretations by Indian authors, both medieval and modern. One of these paths is supposed to be the path of action. This could then be interpreted simply as adherence to conventional social behaviour. Or it was more and more regarded as 'ritual action' as, for example, in Rāmānuja's Śrīvaiṣṇavism. In any case, the text turned increasingly into the great authority that was seen to defend, in religious terms, the social status quo, namely the traditional *dharma*. Obviously, it thereby lost all power to stimulate a more positive and forward-looking social and political commitment.

But perhaps this was a good thing, for the ideological programme implied in Kṛṣṇa's teaching is actually blank. It was easy enough for Kṛṣṇa personally to spell out precisely what it entailed in the specific case of Arjuna. But in the hand of ruthless politicians, it could have played a most dangerous role. Such a potential dilemma was brought to the fore in a striking manner in the early twentieth century. During the struggle for independence from British colonial rule, two important personalities used periods of protracted leisure (they had been imprisoned) to study the *Gītā* and write commentaries on it. While Gandhi made the work his scriptural authority for his philosophy of non-violence and passive resistance to British rule, Tilak interpreted it as advocating the tactics known nowadays as political terrorism. A rather extreme divergence of opinion, derived, after all, from the same text! Or again, it is only during the past century or so that the Indian intelligentsia developed the concept of the *karma-yogī*: the man of action who finds his fulfilment in social commitment. Although this is obviously claimed to derive from the *Gītā*, both the concepts of 'society' and of 'nation' demanding such commitment are clearly derived from English. It is in view of such an ideological blank which could be filled in such a variety of ways, that I have spoken of the advantages of linking the *Gītā* with the status quo.

Incidentally, popular mythical imagination had its own ways of trying to rationalize Kṛṣṇa's concern for the world which expressed itself in such a strange way – having millions of kings and warriors killed. Here now we are told that Earth suffered unbearably from far too heavy a load of generals and soldiers on her back. Viṣṇu promised to help her, turned into the *avatāra* Kṛṣṇa (the story is told in a Viṣṇu-religious context), and organized the devastating battle we have heard about. Now Earth can breathe again: most soldiers, armies and generals have disappeared. Seen in this light, the *Gītā* could make almost cheerful reading.

Let me now turn to the question of whether the basic structure of thinking expressed in the *Gītā* has any parallels. If it is true that the work was written around the third or second century BC, we can indeed point at parallels that would be roughly contemporary. But this is the point at which we shall have to say farewell to the multi-faceted figure of Kṛṣṇa and, in fact, to Indian monotheism. Here we have finally arrived at the non-theistic variants of our formula, the existence of which has been hinted at in previous chapters. Love itself is transcendentalized, as it holds together our desiring subject and desired object, both of which are not transcendental by themselves. As I explained earlier, the reason for such clumsy formulations is simply to emphasize the overall structure within which our present exploration is carried out. For the particular case which we are going to study now, we can rephrase our formula like this: compassion for the suffering world is proposed as a spiritual ideal that overrides, it would seem at a first glance, the quest for individual liberation. It is clear that once again we are dealing with a definite 'return to the world', a commitment to social issues.

Let me start at the beginning, and that means some centuries prior to the *Gītā* and the material that will be discussed presently. This is the India of the sixth or fifth century BC, when presumably the Buddha[14] and the Mahāvīra lived. Both religious founder-figures are reported to have obtained enlightenment and *nirvāṇa* (a term we can use for both Buddhist and Jain sources) and thus completed their spiritual career years before their deaths. The period in between they filled with teaching and recruiting others to the spiritual programme. Compassion with those who lived in the realm of suffering is clearly identified as the rationale behind these activities. This now raised some interesting and important metaphysical questions. Thus it could be asked what precisely the relationship is between spiritual fulfilment and those acts of compassion. Are they just an accidental afterthought, or are they in some sense causally related to the obtainment of *nirvāṇa*, or could it even be thought that the latter were the purpose of the former? Another question was to what extent the realization of something outside space, time and matter was relativized by the following forty or so years of preaching, or to what extent *nirvāṇa* could be regarded as independent of all this. Clearly the precise evaluation of that compassion, the love for suffering humanity, had to depend on the kind of answer given to such questions. The Jains did not make much fuss about all this. The Mahāvīra was one of a group of twenty-four comparable figures who appear in cosmic history, achieve enlightenment, and thereby once again perceive the means for others to find their liberation. Man's task is to follow the programme laid out by the Mahāvīra and his fellow Jinas. But with the Buddhists, a great amount of further attention was paid to the issues. And, in fact, we find that in the great variety of Buddhist traditions current in ancient India most of the alternatives suggested just now were developed.

In many cases, the Buddha's enlightenment was not regarded as a qualitative jump beyond space, time and matter – in other words, as a final realization – but as a penultimate stage which required the *pari-nirvāṇa*, that is physical death, to complete the whole spiritual progress. Inevitably, the Buddha's compassion remains here as something prior to final fulfilment. But in other traditions, the enlightenment is accepted as a final event – all has been done that had to be done. What follows after it becomes then the outflow of that transcendental experience back into the world in the form of Love, or more precisely, compassion. It turns into acts that have a decisive influence on the spiritual life of individuals. Through contact with the Buddha and his teaching individuals encounter compassion, which sends them on to a path that otherwise would not have been available to them.

And we find a third alternative. Here now the aeon-long preparation of the being that was to become the Buddha in his final rebirth is envisaged as motivated by the desire to help suffering humanity. Enlightenment turns here into a necessary, but dependent event – for only by means of this event can the medicine be procured that will effect such help.[15]

By now it may have become apparent that in the last two cases we are actually dealing once again with the same complex structure of thought that was isolated from the *Gītā*. On the one hand, the aim is towards transcendental realization, but on the other hand it is fused with a return to the world which is motivated by love or, more precisely, compassion. But now we have reached the real crux of the matter, and it is here that the ways of Indian Buddhism parted in a very fundamental manner. The crucial question to be asked now is: how special and how unique was the Buddha?

Let us begin with the possibility that the Buddha was indeed a unique figure, belonging, like the Jinas, to an extremely small number of comparable individuals. His appearance in the world was an exceptionally rare event. Again two possible effects of such an evaluation can be noted. In one interpretation this could now mean that the chances for other beings to achieve what the Buddha achieved, in particular enlightenment and *nirvāṇa*, were seen as lying far beyond the horizon of an ordinary person's life-span. Indeed, as more and more generations separated an individual from the time of the Buddha, the scale on which the possibility of achieving *nirvāṇa* was envisaged became larger and larger. And, given the enormity of the task lying ahead of one, all one's energies had to be used to proceed that one little step further on the path that any single life-span offered. Let us call this the attitude of the *śrāvaka* so that we can refer back to it later on.

Yet the uniqueness of the Buddha could be seen in a very different light. If you believe in transmigration and in the laws of *karma*, the retribution of positive and negative deeds (and that over a potentially immeasurable period of time), a definition of 'realism' must differ from what we are used to. Within such a belief-system, it is perfectly 'realistic' to expect that in some rare cases an absolutely enormous store of *puṇya*, that is positive *karma*, can be accumulated over hundreds of past existences. Early Buddhism generally loved to envisage such past existences of the Buddha – when he is known as the Bodhisattva (with a capital B). Often such stories are told at random, to serve as illustrations of various virtues, etc. But sometimes they are put together in a more systematic manner, to demonstrate more directly the steady accumulation of *puṇya*. Obviously this is a handy way to explain why precisely the Buddha was unique: he was the world-record holder in the possession of *puṇya*. Now what would such a person look like? Naturally, he would be endowed with all the thirty-two auspicious characteristics Indian folklore knows of. Naturally, his skills, talents and powers go way beyond that of beings less well endowed with *puṇya*. He can even manipulate the laws that govern the space–time–matter continuum of our world in a way that ordinary mortals could not. In that sense he is *lokottara* – beyond the potentials of ordinary folks. (I mention this technical expression here because, all too rashly, early interpreters of the *Mahāvastu*,[16] a text that belongs to the Lokottara tradition, saw this as meaning 'transcendental' and regarded the form of Buddhism found here as 'Docetic'. In my reading of the text, none of this is necessary: it is not an instance of theism 'rearing its ugly head' in Buddhism, as it has been put in some critical quarters.)

What would all this lead to, if it were placed at the disposal of Love, of compassion? In a straightforward real-life context, the charisma that such a person inevitably beamed out to all who came in contact with him would represent a very powerful initial thrust, propelling a person up the spiritual path. What I am trying to emphasize here is the direct causal link between an individual's religious fulfilment and the Buddha's charisma. It is, in such a case, not a question of the Buddha transferring some objective entity, such as part of his *puṇya*, to somebody else (which is not possible according to early Buddhist teaching). It is simply a case of creating a context that is particularly conducive to the pursuit of enlightenment.

If such an assumption is acceptable, we may proceed one step further. Why restrict the setting up of such a particularly favourable environment to the relatively few years of the Buddha's life and to the relatively few people who came in personal contact with him? Could it not be imagined that the vast store of *puṇya* was used to create a more permanent and more universally accessible context of that kind? Given that ancient India scattered all kinds of realms (which we popularly call 'heavens') very liberally over the space above the earth, it is perhaps not all that difficult to see how the concept of Sukhāvatī came into being. This 'blissful realm' – the meaning of the name – has been created through an enormous store of *puṇya* and is due to the all-embracing love for suffering mankind of a past Buddha called Amitābha or Amitāyu: 'he of unlimited lustre' or 'of unlimited life'. Other names for this realm are the Western Paradise and the Pure Land. As far as the Indian sources that deal with Amitābha and Sukhāvatī are concerned,[17] all they say is that this is one such environment conducive to a relatively easy achievement of *nirvāṇa*, because all causes that on earth make its pursuit so difficult, have been kept away from it. But how can one get there? Easy enough. After all, it is part of the ordinary world, like any other such heaven or underground realm. Thus it is included in the circuit of transmigration. All that is left now is to determine in advance how to make sure that one will be reborn there. Now we know that rebirth is governed by the laws of *karma*, and naturally it needs the right kind of *puṇya*, positive *karma*, to be reborn in the Pure Land. So why not worship Amitābha himself, who after all has had such an enormous store of it? And his worship itself, even according to the most 'orthodox' Buddhist beliefs, generates *puṇya*.

Well, this may not be the Buddhism we are most familiar with, but at least I hope to have shown that it can be derived logically from a central set of ideas with which we are familiar. It is not, in my opinion, the white elephant that popular literature has been chasing under the headings of 'Amitābha-Buddhism', 'Buddhism of Faith' or 'theistic Buddhism'.

In view of the fact that this form of Buddhism has been practised traditionally by the majority of Japanese, it may be permitted to say a few words about the further transformations it underwent while moving to China and then to the Land of the Rising Sun. Clearly the Indian Buddhist environment exerted certain controls on the religion of

Amitābha, which made it possible here to develop it along 'orthodox' lines. Once such controls were removed, things did change in two important respects. First, the pursuit of *nirvāṇa* became replaced by a conception that now saw ultimate spiritual fulfilment in Sukhāvatī itself. The Pure Land turned into heaven, in our sense of the word. Secondly, the figure of Amitābha was transcendentalized to such an extent that his grace alone, received through ritually reciting his name, was the means to enter it.

So far we have looked at trends in earlier Indian Buddhism that looked upon the Buddha as a unique figure. 'Buddha' here could refer to Siddhārtha or to Amitābha. But what were the effects of regarding the Buddha Siddhārtha instead as 'an ordinary human being', of the type we are familiar with? The most obvious and important consequence of such a view was to regard also his achievement, his enlightenment and *nirvāṇa*, as within the potential of ordinary human beings. That means, quite seriously and realistically, that one could set out on the Buddhist path in the expectation of gaining enlightenment within a lifetime. Moreover, this conception was intrinsically linked with the pursuit of compassion. In other words, it draws for its model precisely on that interpretation of the Buddha's life-story mentioned above, which fuses the transcendental achievement of Siddhārtha with that of the conveyance of compassion within this world.[18] By deriving from the Buddha's life a generic structure according to which the individual follower moulds his own life, what must have appeared as a novel ideal to some was set up. The type of ideal Buddhist envisaged here was now called a *bodhisattva* (spelled here with a small b, to indicate its generic character). I have just said that to some it must have appeared as a novel ideal. Clearly if my argument is correct, it is not novel at all, for it follows directly from the kind of life led by the Buddha and from the fact that it can be perceived to be exemplary for all. But historically, it is something that is formulated in conscious confrontation with the *śrāvakas* mentioned previously: the pious monks pursuing their *nirvāṇa* over many lifetimes and regarding the Buddha as a very special being. We must see in this conception of the Buddha the reason why now the *bodhisattva* is put forward as the ideal. For it is in the innumerable stories told about the Bodhisattva and shared by all Buddhists that the virtue of compassion could be demonstrated most easily and uncontroversially.[19] The best way, in my opinion, to envisage the situation is to think of the controversy as comparable to, say, 'revivalism'. It is not a case of yet another so-called sect splitting off from the mythical Buddhist mainstream, nor is it a case of some localized separate development. The advocates of the *bodhisattva* ideal draw on Buddhism generally and cannot be identified as institutionally separate for many centuries. Instead, we hear a lot about internal monastic fighting, expulsion and antagonism. We hear about the 'final age' – another typical revivalist symbol.[20] Thus, from an unidentifiable centre a new revivalist vogue spread over the whole of the Buddhist community, challenging with its understanding of the life and the status of the Buddha the attitudes cherished by the *śrāvakas*. The overriding concern of the controversy centres around compassion. That is what the *śrāvakas* are being attacked for: being so busy pursuing their own liberation from *saṃsāra* that they have no time, energy, or will to express in concrete terms their compassion for suffering humanity. I hope it has become clear from my previous remarks that, given the developments of their belief-system, the *śrāvakas* act with perfect sincerity and logic; but I also hope to have made it clear that such a belief-system is not a necessary one and must be regarded as only one possibility, in itself perfectly logical, of interpreting the role of the Buddha.

The advocates of the *bodhisattva* ideal would present their own case in something like the following manner. The Buddha obtained through his enlightenment the medicine to cure the suffering of earthly existence. This medicine is the Dharma – for all practical purposes, the Buddhist teaching. (Unfortunately, the same word that we encountered in the *Gītā* in the meaning of 'cosmic order' reappears here in a rather different significance.) It was now the duty of every *bodhisattva* to receive this same Dharma, to understand it fully through his own spiritual realization, and to convey it in the spirit of compassion to the suffering world. But in order to convey it efficiently and accurately, he had to cultivate the virtue of 'skilfulness in means'.[21] In some cases, particularly the famous *Lotus Sūtra*, this whole conception produces almost a transcendentalization of the Dharma itself. There it is envisaged on a grand cosmic scale and full of dynamism, conveying itself, as it were, through the mediation of the *bodhisattvas*. It is here that this type of Buddhism and the *Bhagavadgītā* come into the closest proximity. That this goes to the extent of verbal resonances is perhaps no accident.[22] It might be of interest to note in this connection that, once again in Japan, this *Lotus Sūtra* gave rise to an extremely dynamic, not to say aggressive, but certainly socially committed branch of Buddhism, founded by Nichiren. This, in turn, is the historical basis for modern religious movements which still demonstrate the same dynamic commitment and activism, for instance the Soka Gakkai.

I mentioned earlier that there was considerable antagonism between the *śrāvakas* and the followers of the *bodhisattva* ideal. Now it may be asked how that controversy resolved itself. Eventually, it appears, the disagreement ossified and acquired more easily identifiable institutional structures. Probably hundreds of years after the issues originally emerged, the whole discussion settled down by crystallizing as two grand branches of Buddhism, the Mahāyāna and the Hīnayāna. The latter term refers to the religion of the *śrāvakas* and is, at least originally, abusive. Theirs is the 'inferior' spiritual programme, while that of the *bodhisattvas* is 'superior'. Not all the connotations of the term '*yāna*' are clear. But an ancient verse speaks of the *bodhisattva*, all armed, 'mounting it'; and that would suggest a (probably metaphorical) meaning like 'war chariot'.[23] In that case, like Arjuna and Kṛṣṇa, the *bodhisattva* is a warrior who drives out into the world to save beings – Power and Love combine in him. But his armour is that of Wisdom, and this directs our exploration beyond the confines of the present discussion, just as a proper explanation of the Mahāyāna, etc. can only be offered under the same heading of Wisdom. At this stage I would merely like to add a warning against the way in which the situation has been presented traditionally. Take bits and pieces from the whole discussion I have been trying to reconstruct, with all its possible variables and all its logical developments; sprinkle them generously and in a rather random manner over both branches (the Hīnayāna and the Mahāyāna) as they might be envisaged around the second century AD; pick further ingredients from later Indian Buddhist sources and stir them vigorously into the 'Mahāyāna'; then write the latter off as a late ('theistic' or whatever) distortion of 'authentic' or 'orthodox' Buddhism which is supposed to be the 'Hīnayāna'. A recipe for disaster, I would have thought, but, unfortunately, precisely what you can still find in many a book on Buddhism.

Whatever the truth may ultimately turn out to be, 'compassion' is found in many forms of Buddhism as an active, driving force, stimulating a positive commitment to society and history. Obviously in the strictest sense, this 'compassion' can offer no more and no less than the Buddha's Dharma, the spiritual path leading towards *nirvāṇa*. But where we find a more dynamic understanding of this Dharma itself, and where this dynamism is linked to the 'skilfulness in the means' displayed in conveying it, 'compassion' signals then a real 'return to the world'.

To state it in a less abstract manner: the way that Buddhist compassion expressed itself was in the spread of Buddhist teaching all over Asia. Moreover, there is the infusion of Buddhist values into society. Documentation of such a restructuring of society becomes available to us for the first time in the inscriptions of the Emperor Aśoka (third century BC). Here are some examples:

> For all beings the Beloved of the Gods [=Aśoka] desires security, self-control, calm of mind, and gentleness.
>
> In the past kings sought to make the people progress in the Dharma, but they did not progress. And I asked myself how I might uplift them through progress in the Dharma. Thus I decided to have them instructed in it, and to issue ordinances of the Dharma, so that by hearing them the people might conform, advance in the progress of the Dharma, and themselves make great progress.
>
> For that purpose many officials are employed among the people to instruct them in the Dharma and to explain it to them.[24]

All this may sound rather paternalistic to us, and may bring to mind ideas of 'political indoctrination' and so on. But, given the great variety of religions in India and the instability of political units, this never really turns into a 'national' or 'State' religion. However, Aśoka goes on to tell us:

> I have had banyan trees planted on the roads to give shade to man and beast; I have planted mango groves, and I have had ponds dug and shelters erected along the roads.
>
> What I have done has been done that men may conform to the Dharma.
>
> And this progress of the Dharma among men has taken place in two manners, by enforcing conformity to the Dharma, and by exhortation. I have enforced the law against killing certain animals and many others, but the greatest progress of 'righteousness' (Dharma) among men comes from exhortation in favour of noninjury to life and abstention from killing living beings.[25]

This is a good illustration of the kind of things that are included in this Buddhist return to the world. It almost sounds here as if the Dharma is set up as the alternative to the *dharma* of the status quo – as if the Buddhist Dharma wants to replace the Hindu *dharma*, of the *Gītā* for example, by introducing certain more humane features. But we have further examples of such a social commitment from other Asian countries. Thus, for instance, in Japan and in Tibet the Buddhist Dharma was directly involved in the formation of a nation. Not only that. In Tibet both the political and the religious authorities were eventually combined in one person, in the hands of the Dalai Lama. In Japan this almost happened, when the Empress Shōtoku (shortly before her death in AD 770) was ready to abdicate in favour of a monk becoming Japanese emperor, but this was prevented by the interference of the nobility. Anyway, these few examples may have illustrated to what extent and in which sense a positive commitment to society resulted from the Buddhist idea of compassion.

We have now almost reached the end of our journey through the landscape of Love. So let us first cast a glance back over the material discussed in the present chapter. We have encountered examples (both Hindu and Buddhist, both theistic and non-theistic) of a fusion of Power and Love. A concern for the concrete matters of society and human existence initiated a return into the world, from a transcendental state or from the ecstasy of union with God. Either by introducing a transcendental object of love (God/Goddess) or by transcendentalizing the relationship itself between compassionate, contingent subject and cared for, equally contingent object, the problem raised by the renouncers against Love could be resolved. Not that this is the end of all speculative dilemmas; far from it. In fact, it will be the task of the third part, dedicated to Wisdom, to look in greater detail at some of them. But at this stage one dilemma at least, which grows directly out of the kind of ideas explored in the present chapter, may be introduced.

The question is this: to what extent has the commitment to the world, acting in society and fulfilling the demands of *dharma* or the Dharma, anything to do with man's spiritual fulfilment *vis-à-vis* the workings of God? Behind such a question we can sense echoes of a problem we are familiar with: that of grace and human co-operation with it – the 'works' of Christian theology. At least once, to my knowledge, this question is asked in comparable form in India, and a second time in Japanese Buddhism. In India it was in the Śrīvaiṣṇavism of Rāmānuja that the problem was raised. If God – Viṣṇu – is omnipotent and casts his grace upon us, and if human nature is totally dependent on Viṣṇu, how is it conceivable that man could actually work towards his own salvation? The other side then argued that some form of human co-operation with grace must be assumed: otherwise all human beings must be saved, or, if not, then such a random choice would turn God into a tyrant.[26] Naturally, the issue could not be resolved, and eventually produced two strands of Śrīvaiṣṇavism. The antagonism between the two groups is so strong today that a whole set of lawyers makes a living by specializing in court cases over temple ownership, etc. Every movable and immovable being and object in a Śrīvaiṣṇava temple is marked with the respective symbol of the group. This includes not only the temple elephant; it also includes the statues of Viṣṇu and Lakṣmī themselves. More charming is a rather late metaphor for the theological differences. One is the Cat School, and the other the Monkey School. While the cat just grabs the kitten in its mouth and carries it off to safety (grace alone), the baby monkey in a similar situation has to hold on to its mother's neck to be taken away (co-operation with grace). To what extent this view of 'works' still addresses itself to the needs of society, beyond a purely ritualized preoccupation, is another question which cannot be looked at here.

The second, Japanese, example involves Shinran (twelfth century AD), the founder of the most important branch of Japanese Amitābha Buddhism. He started off as a monk, but then saw in the monastic discipline, with its pursuit of virtue and merit, a dangerous arrogance which implied that man thought he could actually work towards his salvation. Thus he broke his vow of celibacy and married, to spend the rest of his life in exile and in very humble circumstances. He regarded one sincere invocation of Amitābha's name as sufficient to ensure rebirth in the Pure Land. Without the restraint that Indian Buddhist sentiment would have exerted on such a concept, the Pure Land could develop here into something like a heaven and Amitābha comes close to being God. However, in this case such a theoretical rejection of all religious 'works' did not prevent an increasing 'return to the world': later generations of Shinran's followers actively participated in exploiting the chaotic political situation in the Japan of the sixteenth century by attacking (in the form of military bands) feudal lords and monasteries of rival sects alike.

After this little excursion, let us return to India and cast a more general glance over the material that the previous pages have explored. It is probably no exaggeration to claim that Love has revealed itself very much as Power's equal, and that it is more than merely one missing colour in our picture. It has manifested itself as imbuing a culture with a high degree of sophisticated eroticism and, perhaps more surprisingly, as the stimulus behind the development of elaborate monotheistic systems with a number of possible Bhagavān or Bhagavatī figures at the centre. Frequently it appears to be drawing man away from the world of everyday affairs and getting him absorbed in the worship of temple images, in the cultivation of *yoga*, in the ecstasy of singing communally religious songs, or in the total submission to a *guru*. Yet we have also noticed a thrust back into the world and into the demands of society formulated as the Hindu *dharma* – a movement that parallels the divine desire of 'work' and manifestation in the world, with all its horrifying and beautiful aspects. Finally, Love in the form of compassion imposed itself on the 'world-negating' trends of the renouncers and redirected their attention back to the world.

These are some of the basic parameters that could be used in the construction of a typology of the Indian religions of Love. It might be tempting to design a scale, parallel to the one we used in the first part on Power, which measures the range or degree of 'reality' (if such a thing could be measured) that is encompassed in *bhakti*. Thus the naughty boy, Kṛṣṇa, at the centre of Vallabhite *bhakti* whose *pūjā* involves a lot of sweets would probably figure relatively low on such a scale. The Goddess Elokeśī of a Rāmprasād, or the Kṛṣṇa of the *Bhagavadgītā*, might well appear towards the top of it. But there are obvious difficulties here for, unlike the map of the universe, Indian culture itself has not evolved such a scale. We find instead – and that only for theistic *bhakti* – a different scale which measures emotive intensity, while laying out a variety of relational models. At the bottom we find the loyalty of a servant, then comes friendship, then somewhere higher up the love of a mother for her child, and the culmination is found in the passionate desire of a beloved for her lover – often symbolized by the love of the *gopīs* for Kṛṣṇa.[27] As far as our non-theistic material is concerned, further scales suggest themselves.

For example, we could try to measure the degree to which 'compassion' is perceived of as grace. While at one end of the spectrum the Buddha is seen as having done no more than laid out the path that each person has to follow himself, at the other end we find quasi-theistic ideas about Amitābha's grace alone achieving man's spiritual fulfilment. But what is probably more important is the realization that happiness and joy can be derived from compassion, love without a transcendental object. The Buddha's Dharma can be envisaged as something loving, compassionate, and pervading the world – to be absorbed and then communicated by the *bodhisattva*, yielding intense pleasure to him – without necessitating a theistic interpretation.

It is a well-known phenomenon that people who have enjoyed unchallenged political power for a number of years, or have fallen 'madly' in love, tend to lose all sense of proportion, reason and reality. Whether blinded by power or love, their vision of the world as it really is gets distorted. It seems logical at this point to ask whether this has any relevance to the material we have discussed under the headings of Power and Love. The various traditions affected by them tell us emphatically that this is not the case. Spiritual giants like the Buddha, the Mahāvīra or the *yogīs* realized, along with their own liberation from the cycle of rebirth, a total understanding of the nature of things. When the *bhakta* loses himself in divine love, he encounters there the inner meaning of all things. Unlike the popularist evangelical or fundamentalist preacher, the *bodhisattva* requires skill in the means through which he conveys his compassion and draws on the 'perfection of wisdom' which shows him what things really are.

But such answers imply various assumptions, presuppositions and, in turn, many further questions. For example, they suggest that somewhere in Indian culture it has been spelled out what 'nature of things' or 'inner meaning of things' means precisely. But is this 'spelling out' done exclusively by the spiritual giants themselves, or are there other cultural realms which they make use of for this purpose, or in opposition to which they establish their own thought? Moreover, how important have such concerns been in Indian culture generally? After all, there is no inner necessity for the spiritual giant or the *bhakta* to get involved in elaborate explanations of this kind. Yet we might suspect that ideas discussed particularly in the present chapter, involving complex and seemingly precarious balancing acts (like a loving absorption into God alongside a commitment to *dharma*, or striving for enlightenment while showing compassion to suffering humanity), suggest more than mere religious activism and emotional indulgence. It suggests a further theme in Indian culture, Wisdom.

PART THREE

Wisdom: commuting within one world

CHAPTER 17

All the valleys filled with corpses

We have noticed some rather strange pointers beyond the realms of Power and Love in the direction of a third, Wisdom. There has been the gruesome battlefield – soon to be covered with the corpses of soldiers and the carcasses of war-elephants – on which Kṛṣṇa, God incarnate, has told prince Arjuna that his ultimate destiny depends on fighting the war in the spirit of total submission and love. Similarly we have heard about the hero who steps on to the 'large chariot' (*mahā-yāna*) in order to drive out into an apparent void, motivated by compassion and protected by the armour of 'perfect wisdom'. Soon we shall hear about Bhartṛhari[1] who had his chariot waiting to take him to the tranquility of meditation, away from the crumpled sheets stained with saffron and squashed flowers that tell the tale of Kāma's frenzied battle. Such pointers towards the wise man evoke in our minds images of peace and silence.

The yonder snow-swaddled summits of the Himalayas were tranquil: at peace.
The pines and poplars were still: their scent, too, asleep.
Came wafting from afar, the hushed murmur of a brook.
The Sage of *All-India* was meditating.
Past midnight, he opened his eyes.
He asked the disciple for some ash and sought rice and water.

Satiated, said the Sage to the disciple, 'Ask what thou wilt, my son. My heart is exceeding glad upon thy humility, thy selfless service. Know, thou hast served me for two years this Thursday. Thou has served me well, dear one. The auspicious moment for rewarding thee has come.'

'O mightiest of all the Sages,' said the disciple, going down on his knees, 'I am ignorant. I have no learning. I beg of thee a boon, liege! Give me, Sire, one instruction, one mighty aphorism, which thou knowest to be the best, the wisest of all the lore which befalls from gods on unworthy humans.' …

'Verily, my son, the aphorism of all the aphorisms, the doctrine of all the doctrines, the rune of all the runes, the Hinduism of all the Hinduism, the *mantra*-supreme, and the reward for thy two years' labour is now uttered as follows: *Abscond from charlatans and deceivers as thou wouldst from venomous snakes*!' ...

That night, the disciple absconded.

Unserved, unriced, said the Sage of *All-India* to himself, 'Verily, I repent! Methinks, the highest wisdom must be withheld from the perfidious.'[2]

G. V. Desani, who is telling us *All about H. Hatterr*, has followed his hero's spiritual quest from *guru* to *guru*. Here the quest (and the book) reaches its climax, for this is the first time that the disciple actually obeyed an instruction.

This may seem a somewhat ominous beginning to our exploration of the realm of Wisdom. Of all the many facets of the Indian religious traditions, 'wisdom' is probably the most obvious and familiar one in our own minds – a facet we would be inclined to approach with all earnestness. Yet, far from taking it seriously (and it is not necessary to read the whole book, this little extract being sufficient for the purpose of conveying its flavour), Desani appears to be making fun of it. Or is he? For all we know, he may well be making fun of our, typically Western, mystique of India – of the above-mentioned earnestness itself. For the actual 'hero' is the disciple who proves himself capable of a good deal of common sense (which is Wisdom at its most practical). When we read this alongside a passage from Gita Mehta's *Karma Cola*, a book very much in the tradition of Desani, the implications become apparent. '"I don't know," says a female German economist from Hamburg ... "But I think they should definitely have a quality control on *gurus*. A lot of my friends have gone mad in India."'[3] No doubt, the disciple enforces his own quality control and thereby unwittingly re-enforces, on a meta-level, the mysterious workings of the wisdom of the East.

Here we are rapidly collecting somewhat unexpected facets of Indian wisdom, and seem to be 'problematizing' the subject beyond all recognition. It appears wise to reduce our pace and reflect on some of the basics, namely the popular Western perception of the 'wisdom of the East'. For a number of decades now, it has symbolized for many people not just some exotic or funny curio, but a source of advice and guidance, an oracle to be consulted about ultimate questions for which the West has ceased to have satisfactory answers. But underlying this is a frequent denial, on a more fundamental level, of occidental modes of reflecting on life. This denial is coupled with a belief in some objective, non-historical and unchanging entity outside any industrial or preindustrial social contexts. The idea of the '*philosophia perennis*' is symptomatic of this approach.[4] This is arcane, primordial 'wisdom', a Tiger Balm for all illnesses, an all-purpose panacea.

By contrast, when we speak of a 'wise move' or a 'wise choice', this implies a knowledge of consequences, a foresight of developments that are predictable on the basis of apparent possibilities – the 'wise' looks into the future and assesses the best possible outcome of the particular move or choice. On the other hand, 'to get wise to' something implies the collection of many experiences over time by observing the relentless repetition of events up to the moment when, finally, all the pieces fall into place and some inner logic or law reveals itself – 'wise' here looks back into the past and realizes where and how mistakes were made. Such idiomatic expressions show 'wisdom' to be joined up with time and with concrete events and facts.

Thus it is not surprising to find the Eastern alternative being looked upon as a wonderful, fascinating idea – an oasis for all those suffering from thirst in the arid desert of occidental historicity and factual empiricism. But alas! The idea reveals itself to be a mirage. It is but a dream, possibly triggered off by the sense of loss felt at the erosion of long-cherished and secure fundamentalist beliefs which a critical investigation of so-called religious certainties have brought about in Western culture. But where lies the authority for claiming that the popularly dreamt-of wisdom of the East is a mirage? It lies in the reading of Eastern thought itself, which is suggested here. By a strange irony, what is perceived to be a-temporal and non-contextual understands itself, in its most critical and sophisticated expression, as a demolition exercise directed against all forms of narrow, fundamentalist or literalist beliefs.

Details of such a demolition exercise will be met with at later stages; for the moment, it seems appropriate to comment on the clause 'in its most critical and sophisticated expression'. This will allow us, at the same time, to say a bit more about what is meant by 'wisdom'. Previously we have traced a continuum of 'power' from its minimal applications (say the keeping at bay of a demon) up to its maximal expression as total control over one's destiny in the universe, and similarly of 'love' from, for example, the reward in the form of big-bosomed and amorous ladies for meritorious deeds up to the harmonizing of all one's inner emotions and drives with the pulse beating in the ground of being. As I hope to show, 'Wisdom' presents a third such continuum. Theoretically we could assume it to run from 'knowing the truth' in a kind of fundamentalist sense (which is meant here as the naive projection of emotions on to a few scraps of knowledge of the world) up to the total insight into the nature of 'reality'. At this point we can see that our 'wisdom' continuum is not quite like the other two. No doubt it concerns itself, once again, with the universe, the beings in it and our own nature. But this must include also what the previous pages have explored under the guidelines of Power and Love. These are now turned into objects of this critical analysis. Yet there is still something else which must be included in the range of what we call 'reality': that very same 'total insight into the nature of reality'. In other words, at this end of the spectrum 'wisdom' transcends itself and turns the other forms of wisdom, lower down in the continuum, into objects of its own reflection. So we could speak of two types of 'wisdom'. The first concerns itself with matters outside itself – it is represented by modes of making sense of the world and of attributing meaning to human experience in it. The second type reflects upon itself. It critically analyses the ways in which we perceive the world and construct models of it which we regard as meaningful. It is these reflecting properties of Wisdom which I have styled 'most sophisticated'.

Now I am aware of the possibility that such an understanding of Wisdom will not be acceptable to the advocates of the 'wisdom of the East'. They might object that the interpretation offered here is far too narrow and limited, because it restricts itself to 'rational' or 'object-bound' aspects of wisdom. This raises such a fundamental question about the nature of the Indian religions and religion itself that it is clearly not possible to deal with it properly in this introductory chapter. Nevertheless, certain presuppositions underlying such a critique deserve to be discussed at this stage; at the same time it offers me the opportunity to introduce the notion of 'modes of making sense' which will accompany us through the following chapters.

The world that we experience around us, and within us, manifests an infinite variety. Each person we meet is different from all others, and the story he could tell us about his life will be unique. The same applies to the animals in our gardens, parks and forests, to their plants, flowers and trees. Each constellation of natural phenomena – what we call landscape – is distinct from all others in the same way that no two hand-knotted carpets or improvisations of a *rāg* could ever be identical. Physical objects occupy their own specific points in a multi-dimensional system of coordinates that measures their characteristics. Also within ourselves we notice a similar variety of emotions and thoughts, impulses and images. However, culture (in the widest sense of the term) introduces structure and order into this amorphous mass of phenomena that make up human experience. This ordering process involves abstraction – gathering together the similar and comparable under the headings of genus and species – and the tracing of recurring patterns and causal relations. Culture introduces the question of meaning and purpose, and provides us with modes of making sense of it all. I don't think it is difficult to see in all this an aspect of wisdom: the ordering of the world and the making sense of it. But it is worth reminding ourselves that 'culture' in real life manifests itself as many different cultures.

Some implications of this view of culture-specific wisdom-enterprises are immediately obvious and need not detain us for long. For example, it is quite common in popular literature on India to use individual and isolated pronouncements and expect them to be immediately 'meaningful', without having to look at the culture-specific process of constructing meaning in which such a pronouncement has emerged. The result is as disastrous as any attempt to translate a Sanskrit poem, word for word, into English. In both cases it is like lifting a fish out of the water that offers it life and freedom. Just as the individual poem tacitly relates to the contexts of the poet's other works, of the poetic theory he follows, and of the general poetic culture in which he operates, any isolated pronouncement of 'Eastern wisdom' has to be seen in the context of the specific system or teaching in which it appears, of the particular concerns of a particular tradition, and of the religious culture generally which suggests modes of ordering and making sense of the world.

But there is another implication here, far less obvious than the previous one. Separate cultures do not simply offer a context within which 'wisdom' is carried out; they also provide different modes of doing so. I am not aware of any attempt to establish a systematic catalogue of such modes in our own culture. But, were we to ask the man in the street 'who makes sense of the world for you?', I am convinced that on a normative level the answers would congregate around the scientist, philosopher and theologian or preacher. By subtler means of investigation, we would probably also encounter the journalist, politician and psychologist, and would hear about pop music and soap opera. We could add to the list the man who carries a sticker with 'Jesus is alive!' on his car window. Anyway I think it has been made clear what I mean by 'modes of making sense' in a general way: certain methods of sorting out a mass of phenomena and imposing a logic upon them which leaves the observer satisfied. 'Yes, that does make sense to me. This is how it is.' Perhaps a concrete example might help here.

> Then Job answered the Lord:
> 'I know that thou canst do all things,
> and that no purpose of thine can be thwarted.
> Therefore I have uttered what I did not understand,
> things too wonderful for me, which I did not know.
> I had heard of thee by the hearing of the ear,
> but now my eye sees thee;
> therefore I despise myself,
> and repent in dust and ashes.'[5]

Job, 'afflicted ... with loathsome sores from the sole of his foot to the crown of his head'[6] had spent thirty-five chapters cursing his fate and arguing with his friends about divine justice. Then, to put a stop to this useless philosophizing and theologizing, 'the Lord answered Job out of the whirlwind'.[7] That this meant more than just further words is clear both from Job's own words and from similar divine manifestations in the whirlwind mentioned by Ezekiel, Nahum and Zechariah.[8] In the light of what Job 'heard' and saw, the paradoxical and disparate fragments of his experience fell into place and everything made sense. Although we are not dealing here with a culturally evolved and shared mode of making sense of the world, since the whirlwind-vision is clearly a unique phenomenon granted by God to Job, the example may be useful in clarifying what is meant by such modes in some general sense.

But what does it mean to say that such modes are culture-specific? Popularly the question is simply ignored and an easy, unambiguous cross-cultural correlation between our own modes and those of another culture is assumed as if they were human universals. Out of the trinity of science, theology and philosophy it tends to be philosophy which is most frequently used as the category under which to approach Indian material. (I am leaving out of the discussion the catch-all notion of 'mysticism' as far too vague.) My contention here is not that it would not be possible in certain circumstances to identify areas of Indian thought which bear sufficient family resemblance with what we would call philosophy. The point I am making concerns the other – perhaps the majority of – circumstances in which philosophy is the wrong category to apply or in which important material is left out of the discussion, because it appears to be blatantly unphilosophical. In the latter case, the confusion may become compounded when, with 'philosophy' as the yardstick, such material is then judged to be 'irrational' or 'illogical', or to belong to a 'primitive' or 'preliterate mind'. (It would be an interesting side-investigation to analyse the dominance of 'philosophy' among the cross-culturally projected categories. I suspect that philosophy functions here not merely as a heuristic tool, but also as a factor of making value-judgements in the context of social prestige and a positive self-image. My impression is that this is implied also in the way in which nineteenth- and twentieth-century India has adopted the category of philosophy – and not, for example, that of theology or religion – in its handling of the religious heritage. However, this is a matter outside the scope of our present reflections.)

Let us continue with the concept of 'modes of making sense'. Given that these are aspects of wisdom and that they are culture-specific, it is thus not sufficient simply to look at philosophy and claim to have exhausted the wisdom aspects of Indian religions. We ought to ask whether we can isolate further modes of making sense of the world, either specific to India or known but unacknowledged in our own culture. It is clear that in trying to answer this question we could easily get involved in an extremely cumbersome and sizeable monograph. I hope I shall be forgiven for restricting myself to offering in the following chapters no more than a very tentative and impressionistic catalogue of such modes. At this stage no more needs to be done than to introduce these categories.

'Philosophy' itself requires few comments: it strives to present a rationally constructed model of the world which consists of clearly defined concepts and their logically coherent relations. 'Theology' is more difficult. We could define it as a type of philosophical analysis which adds 'revelation' to the legitimate range of its objects, over and above empirical facts. This would do justice to much of the Indian material, but excludes the '*theós*', God, as an essential component of revelation. Still more difficult – because far less familiar, or in fact unknown in our own culture – are modes which we can label 'mythical', 'linguistic', 'aesthetic' and 'psychological', all of which have their own sub-categories. The following chapters will provide the concrete details.

It has become clear that the initial objection to an exclusively 'rational' and 'object-bound' investigation of Indian 'wisdom' has certainly pointed us in the right direction. By allowing for culturally defined modes of experiencing the world as meaningful, of which 'philosophy' is only one, I think that, at least in general terms, justice has been done to the objection. Moreover, I would agree that it requires means corresponding to the respective modes in order to 'recreate' transculturally such experience of meaningfulness directly. For example, our 'aesthetic mode' would call for aesthetic means, say a poem or a piece of music. This does not, however, prevent us from trying to speak sensibly, academically, about Indian wisdom and reflecting rationally on it. The introduction of a concept like 'mode of making sense' aims to contribute to precisely such a theoretical framework.

Often the popular mystique of the 'wisdom of the East' appears to be connected with the belief that it is something solid and monolithic. It follows directly from the previous observations that no such monolith can be the object of our exploration. Instead, we shall be looking at processes of making sense of the world and at a variety of modes in which this is done. What all this means in more concrete terms can be illustrated by looking at a seemingly very different objection. Again, the point of the objection is to deny that Indian wisdom is a legitimate object of academic investigation. The reason given in this case is that as a private, individual experience it lies beyond the outsider's range of observation. Strictly speaking, this is a valid argument, and nothing can be done about it. In no way are we in a position to enter the minds of people who have spent thirty years of their lives staring at a white wall, or standing on one leg, or cultivating and sharpening their mental faculties in other, less spectacular ways. What spiritual experiences and achievements they may come up with is, strictly speaking, a totally closed book for us. However, we find that time and again some of these spiritual giants begin to talk – not just about their experiences or insights, but also about what it all means and how others can gain similar insights. This talking objectifies at least something of the private experience, and opens it up as a socially shared phenomenon. But more than this happened in India. These socially shared insights developed their specific cultural expressions and, furthermore, fed into a much more complex and variegated concern of society at large to reflect on the world and to make sense of it. So what we get is a whole array of different types of voices, a continuous discussion on many levels, ever-new suggestions being made and ever-new participants joining in. Now all this does constitute a legitimate area of academic investigation, not only theoretically, but also in practical terms, for the Indians took endless trouble in recording parts of the discussion and rerecording it at a rate faster than the white ants could eat up the manuscripts. It is this kind of discussion that the present chapters want to explore, and which is hinted at by the overall theme of Wisdom.

This talk about wisdom as different modes of making sense of reality, including the reality of religion, and as a 'discussion', may surprise some, among them even those who have no preconceived ideas about the monolithic nature of the Eastern mysteries. Anybody used to Popes and Councils, Synods and Faculties of Theology and 'authorities' in various fields of theological investigation, may well find this kind of seemingly random and disorganized discussion of fundamental human and transcendental issues disturbing. It almost sounds like a committee or television chat show. Indeed there never existed in India a central authority, even for a relatively small religious group, to which issues of controversy could be referred for a final and binding decision. Thus the seeker, if not happy with the religious climate into which he had been born, would have to set out, like H. Hatterr, and try out a series of *gurus*. Such a situation may be regrettable, not only for the German lady, who complained about the lack of quality control, but also for the student, because it makes the study of these religions so much more difficult. It is not that we do not encounter material comparable to our 'revelation'. But, in the absence of a final authoritative institution, the interpretation of what revelation (as much as religious experience) actually means remains part of the Indian pursuit of wisdom, of its cultural concern with making sense.

There was a time when 'wisdom' alone probably summed up the great mysteries India held in store for the West. At that time, somebody might well have wondered why a book on the Indian religions should only in its third part turn to the theme of Wisdom. The relevance of Love and Power would not have been apparent. But times have changed and new trends have emerged. One such trend could be traced under the heading of demythologization.

In my reading of Kipling's *Kim* and Forster's *A Passage to India*, the country appears as a land of mysteries and ultimately incomprehensible differences. Events take place which are inexplicable in terms of logic, and strange forms of knowledge and insights are lurking in the minds of ostensibly ordinary people. Such a mystique of things Indian is still recognizable in later writers, and the indigenous authors among them are fully aware of it. But an element of '*verfremdung*' has crept in as well, a tongue-in-cheek attitude that does not take all this mystification quite seriously any more. The inimitable *All about H. Hatterr* by Desani is a good example. Similarly, some of the novels by R. K. Narayan fall into this category, as do some of the stories of Ruth Praver Jhabvala. Mehta's *Karma Cola* is probably the most biting and thorough example of looking behind the façade of this mystique. A process of demystification has set in: the uncritical following of a *guru* is ridiculed by pointing at the fraudulent character of some and the accidental or random status as *gurus* of others. Spiritual quests, either of modern Indians or of Western enthusiasts, end in disaster and/or a return flight home. The seeker returns, not necessarily a wiser man or woman. But the 'not necessarily' is important here. Criticism may be brought to bear on certain aspects of the Eastern wisdom enterprise, but there is still a lurking sense of being prepared to accept that, at least in some cases, there is truth in it. In the case of Desani, it has always puzzled me to read that the author of *All about H. Hatterr* returned to India after World War II 'where for the next fourteen years he practised yoga and meditation under the guidance of teachers, travelling as far as Japan to get specialized practice'.[9] The book itself appeared in 1948.

Arun Kolatkar's collection of poems, first published in 1974 and called *Jejuri*, is inspired by the temple of the same name not far from Pune that is dedicated to the Maharashtrian folk deity Khaṇḍobā. Here we read lines like

> what is god
> and what is stone
> the dividing line
> if it exists
> is very thin
> at jejuri
> and every other stone
> is god or his cousin
>
> there is no crop
> other than god
> and god is harvested here …
> out of the bad earth
> and the hard rock[10]

or

> a herd of legends
> on a hill slope
> looked up from its grazing…
> a cowbell tinkled
> and the herd of legends
> returned to its grazing.[11]

This strikes me as a rather charming way of demythologizing. However, for some this is not radical enough. In a fictional setting (a bar in Bombay), the documentary film-maker George Miranda's 'new girlfriend, a tall, thin Bengali woman with cropped hair' attacked

> Bhupen Gandhi for having published a volume of poems about his visit to the 'little temple town' of Gagari in the Western Ghats. The poems had been criticized by the Hindu right; one eminent South Indian professor had announced that Bhupen 'had forfeited his right to be called an Indian poet', but in the opinion of the young woman, Swatilekha, Bhupen had been seduced by religion into a dangerous ambiguity. Grey hair flopping earnestly, moon-face shining, Bhupen defended himself. 'I have said that the only crop of Gagari is the stone gods being quarried from the hills. I have spoken of herds of legends, with sacred cowbells tinkling, grazing on the hillsides. These are not ambiguous images.' Swatilekha wasn't convinced. 'These days,' she insisted, 'our positions must be stated with crystal clarity. All metaphors are capable of misinterpretation.'[12]

This is a scene from Salman Rushdie's novel *The Satanic Verses*; the author acknowledges Kolatkar's *Jejuri* as the inspirational source.[13] From the 'crystal clarity' of Swatilekha's position, the mystique of India is demolished down to the bits of stone that seem to grow out of the hills of Maharashtra.

There is a second trend, possibly not unconnected with the above-mentioned demythologization, which has affected our perception of Indian culture. Here we can trace now how eroticism is in the process of subsuming or eroding the role of Wisdom. One striking example is David Lean's film based on Forster's *A Passage to India*. What the novel left ambiguous – Miss Quested's unease in a strange cultural environment – the film overtly eroticizes by explicitly showing her looking at erotic statues. Another example comes from the seemingly innocuous realm of the Hindu temple (also one of the sources for Lean's rendering). While for an Indian publication a title like *Cult of Desire*[14] is sufficient (the book deals with erotic temple sculptures), other books, meant for the Western reader, are given an additional term of mystique: *Tantra: The Indian Cult of Ecstasy*[15] and *Sexual Secrets*[16] (a work that draws heavily on the same tantric material from India and Tibet). But visually most stunning for me were two television programmes. One was called *Sacred Sex* – a documentary on a variety of Occidental groups inspired by 'Tantrism'. The other one, called *Naked Yoga*, showed – incredible though it may sound – nothing but ladies in various yogic postures, including the head-stand, on sandy beaches with nothing on but a few grains of sand. But note: this still has to do with the 'wisdom of the East', for it is still religion (though in its esoteric, yogic and tantric side) which overlays the purely erotic with the mantle of mystique. Even this mantle is removed in more recent explorations of life in India. *India Cabaret* was quite an interesting TV programme on nightclub dancers. But I found a book of photos which carries the innocuous title of *Falkland Road* deeply disturbing.[17] This has nothing to do with navy ships bracing themselves against the storms in the South Atlantic. It is about the notorious street in Bombay where the ladies of the night are housed.

Whether we look at such a trend away from the spiritual to much more down-to-earth matters like sexuality, or survey the process of demythologization and increasing cynicism, we need not hunt far for reasons. Not only has the number of people visiting India increased enormously since the days of Forster and Kipling; our own cultural climate has also changed. And one further obvious reason for the decline in media attention to the travelogues of the seekers of Indian wisdom is the increasing presence of Indian teachers and teachings in the West itself. This has also meant that the searcher of esoteric mysteries who finds this domestication of Indian wisdom too cosy and commonplace has to move to other regions of the globe. Thus another Indian, this time Mexican and very likely fictional, has triggered off quite a cult. I am talking here of Don Juan, whose teachings Castaneda purported to expound.[18] What struck me most while reading Castaneda's books was the extent to which the Indian sorcerer expresses ideas that were popular during the sixties, when they were still going under the title of Buddhism or Zen. There exists, I think, a book comparing the teachings of Don Juan with Mahāyāna Buddhism. I wonder whether this tells us more about Castaneda the writer than Don Juan the *guru*. Or is this a sign of the hardiness of Indian spirituality – that it re-emerges in the mouth of another type of Indian, when cynicism and erotic fascination have quietened it in the mouths of the original ones? However, and perhaps predictably in view of my suspicions, even Don Juan turns in the last book of the series to matters more typically associated with his Spanish namesake, namely sexuality – although this eroticism is still presented within the frame of esoteric religion. Perhaps, after all, Castaneda can also be included in the trend delineated above.

What does all this entail for us in our exploration of the Wisdom of India? Given the fashions sketched so far, it might seem very much out of touch with current trends. But fortunately the situation is more complex. At present, attempts to demonstrate some kind of confluence of Western scientific thought with Eastern wisdom are enjoying considerable popularity. I am thinking here, for example, of *The Tao of Physics* by Fritjof Capra. This immensely popular and influential book appeared in 1975 and carries the subtitle 'An exploration of the parallels between modern physics and Eastern mysticism'. To talk of 'parallels' is quite a drastic move away from the claims made in the nineteenth and early twentieth centuries that West means science and materialism, and East (i.e. India) means poetry and spirituality. This formulation of the contrast between the 'twain that shall never meet' can be interpreted as a defensive self-definition of the Indian intellectual *vis-à-vis* the threats of the combined forces of colonialism and Western culture. Whether it is possible to interpret the more recent claims by a scientist in a similar manner is a more difficult question to answer. At least in the frequently repeated 'the East has already gained the insights Western science is in the process of uncovering' or 'modern science has confirmed most dramatically ...'[19] I sense a similar element of self-justification, a defence *vis-à-vis* internally growing criticisms of our Western scientific enterprise. Yet it is a double-edged sword, if indeed it is wielded here in self-defence. For the Eastern wisdom referred to did not produce atomic weapons and missiles which are capable of filling the valleys with corpses. And even if this difference between Western science and Eastern insights is ignored, one could still ask what the point is of carrying on with scientific research if the results are already available somewhere else. Incidentally, we shall not only hear more (in the next chapter in fact) about the man sawing off the branch on which he is sitting, but shall also have to explore further the question of why, or at least how, it happened that India, in spite of promising starts, did not develop a science in our sense.

Whatever may be the eventual outcome of this trend that now homes in on another aspect of the Wisdom of the East and searches for parallels to scientific insights in Eastern thought, one point is clear and deserves to be highlighted. Such a claim of parallels could not be maintained over hundreds of pages, in this and many other publications of a similar kind, if the materials were not at least logically congruent or contiguous in some sense. Let us assume, for further clarification, that the wisdom of India had as its object something lying beyond the realm of human experience and that it concerned itself, metaphorically speaking, say with the flora and fauna of a star at the fringe of our galaxy. It would then, first, constitute an area of investigation totally separate from those of Love and Power. Secondly, its content could only be either a 'revelation' by some divine being or, more likely in India, an insight gained through meditation by some being who has thereby become 'omniscient'. Whether a revelation or a meditationally gained insight, ordinary mortals will have to accept it in its entirety on trust. Neither would there be anything in their own life-experiences that could mediate some comprehension, nor would it have any applications to their life. The monsters and gigantic palm trees on our hypothetical star may be very exciting and full of strange powers. But the ordinary person is still left with nothing but his terrestrial pine trees and squirrels. By saying now that our Indian wisdom can be contiguous to a critical Western view of the world, we open up its content not just to description and paraphrase, but also to critical investigation. It should become clear in the following chapters to what extent the 'Wisdom' aspects of the Indian religions deal with matters of straight human experience, matters that allow for the impression (if nothing else) that they relate to 'science'.

It cannot be easy to stand at the receiving end of these different trends and fashions. Increasingly interwoven with the rest of the world, Indian culture has begun to take its own critical view of being the object of an occidental mystique. What this looked like, some years back, in concrete terms may be illustrated by the following passage from *Karma Cola*.

> While population control and pop culture raced hand in hand through the Indian countryside, we of the cities and the universities were getting restless too. But just when the accelerator seemed within our reach, the unthinkable happened.
>
> The kings of rock and roll abdicated.
>
> To Ravi Shankar and the Maharishi.
>
> As the sitar wiped out the split-reed sax, and mantras began fouling the crystal clarity of rock and roll lyrics, millions of wild-eyed Americans turned their backs on all that amazing equipment and pointed at us screaming,
>
> 'You guys! You've got it!'
>
> Well, talk about shabby tricks.[20]

This is the second time we have heard about the search for 'crystal clarity' from the mouth of a modern Indian. It is a warning for us not to get mesmerized by the pendulum of fashions swinging to and fro in front of our eyes and trying to lull us into some obscurantist stupor. (It is a different question to what extent we want to regard a radical 'Marxist' position, or rock and roll, as a mode of achieving such 'crystal clarity'.) Anyway, how shall we proceed in our own exploration?

In view of the various remarks made so far on Indian wisdom, it seems wise not to prejudice ourselves from the start. Instead of restricting our attention to some narrow, preconceived idea of it, let us employ once again the free-wheeling associative play which has proved itself useful in the case of Power and Love. So we can begin by looking at Indian culture generally and by gathering together a variety of attitudes towards worldly wisdom and common sense, intelligence and shrewdness, reason and rationality. From this general cultural foundation of Wisdom it seems appropriate to move to more complex matters, such as the application of a comprehensive and systematic analysis to the world in which we live and to ourselves as some of the beings living in that world. Such an analytical approach to the world might well be called proto-scientific. But as we shall see, that does not place it necessarily in opposition to religion. Instead, it is the world-view derived from the experiences of the renouncers that established itself as the grand rival of the analytical enterprise (regardless of whether secular or religious). Thus the contrast is not so much that between reason and faith, but between reason and (self-authenticating religious) experience, with revelation adding complexity to the issue. Now we know that the experiences of a *yogī* or a Buddha contain Power, the control over their destiny. Inevitably this raises questions about the relationship between the external world and the experiencing subject's 'soul' or 'mind'. At this stage Wisdom begins to include itself in its reflections. But it does not stop here. For the whole enterprise of constructing meaningful models of the world and of our experiences of it can be subjected to further analysis and critique. The potential for scepticism, cynicism, and nihilism is certainly latent in such an analysis, but at the same time this may open up new modes of experiencing the world or life as meaningful.

This may provide some idea of the route we shall follow through the realm of Wisdom; but it might be useful to reflect first on our expectations and attitudes. More likely than not, we anticipate to receive objective pieces of knowledge, positive statements about the world and ourselves. This is certainly what the disciple (H. Hatterr) asked for. Yet he received a piece of practical advice, which his shrewdness turned into prompt action. Similarly, we expect to hear about religion as a constructive enterprise ('beliefs in...'), and may well be surprised or even shocked, when it turns out to have destructive qualities. Here is a little anecdote associated with the Chinese Buddhist teacher Ts'ao-shan who lived in the eighth century AD. 'Someone asked: "What is the essential meaning of Buddhism?" The Master said: "[Countless dead bodies] fill all the chasms and valleys."'[21] Without doubt it is material of this kind which has given rise to the mistaken notion of Eastern wisdom being irrational. Yet we can read it on two levels, each of which makes perfect sense. By a more literalist reading, Buddhism is stated to aim at *nirvāṇa* for the whole of humanity. If all people actually achieved it, it would take human beings out of the cycle of rebirth, and nothing but their corpses would be left behind. But, given the conventions of this genre of literature, a more subtle reading suggests itself. The master's answer tells the person asking that it is the wrong kind of question to ask; that 'Buddhism' is not some kind of entity that can be conceptualized and looked at from the outside, but a practical demolition exercise that leaves the valleys filled with corpses. The answer aims at shocking and thereby at destroying deeply ingrained mistaken notions and attitudes.

We do not have to travel to China to find shock used in this way. Centuries earlier we find Indian Buddhists making the claim that *saṃsāra* and *nirvāṇa* are actually the same sort of thing. This must have been perceived as so challenging and so undermining the established modes of religious thinking, that in a different religious climate the Buddhists would have been burnt at the stake without further ado. For what is being claimed here puts an end to the way in which *nirvāṇa* was traditionally envisaged as the goal of achieving liberation from *saṃsāra*, the suffering-filled cycle of transmigration. To strive for *nirvāṇa* is shown to be qualitatively not different from being impelled by desires into further rebirths. Religion itself can acquire an obsessive quality which is counterproductive in relation to the freedom it is supposed to lead to. The psychological effect of such a shocking idea may well correspond to somebody claiming from the pulpit that heaven and hell are the same sort of thing.

Given the presence of such attitudes in classical Indian culture, there is no need to look upon a writer like Desani or even Mehta as someone introducing a 'modern', Western, critique. We shall see in due course, certainly the spirit, if not the letter, of well-established traditions of critical distance, which probe right into the core of the whole Wisdom exercise, carries on in such writers. As far as our expectations are concerned, it should have become clear by now that our exploration of the realm of Wisdom is unlikely to lead us to some grand culmination in the form of 'the ultimate essence of Indian religion'. Instead we may expect to find out something about a very complex and culture-specific enterprise of making, and maintaining, sense of our religious drives.

Thus the answers we may be given could be very different from the kind of questions we ask, and could tell us something about the questions themselves. Yet none of this ought to take us totally by surprise, if we were familiar with a further trend in our own occidental culture. This particular trend is not immediately obvious, because neither does it make overt references to Eastern wisdom nor is it implicitly about it. Instead, we are dealing with a Western cultural phenomenon which only at closer investigation reveals certain influences from Indian thought. I am thinking here primarily of two novelists, but doubtless many further names could be adduced by specialists in the field of modern Western literature. The two writers I am thinking of are the German, Alfred Doeblin, and the American, Thomas Pynchon. John Dos Passos could possibly be added to the list, and Antonioni's film *Blow-Up*. My reason for drawing attention to these names is certainly not academic in the strict sense. But anybody who wants to get some idea of some aspects of the mysterious wisdom of the East in a familiar setting will profitably read and reflect on Doeblin's *Berlin Alexanderplatz*, Pynchon's *V.*, *The Crying of Lot 49* and possibly *Gravity's Rainbow*. Earlier novels by Doeblin make it clear that he had delved into Eastern thought; his verse epic *Manasa* bears this out even by its title. In my highly selective reading of the critical literature on Pynchon, who apparently leads the life of a recluse totally cut off from all contact with the media and academic researchers, I have not encountered any reference to his acquaintance with Indian ideas. Yet his writing carries such a pronouncedly Buddhist flavour that one might assume some direct influence. Yet, as I said, it is not the objective influences that are my concern here, but the confluence of ideas (however they were brought about historically).

In my understanding of all this material, at the forefront stands the problem of how the individual relates to, and interacts with, the forces that shape his life, character and destiny – the world. The uniqueness of the approach lies in the attempt to reveal both the active and passive sides of these forces. An effective way of demonstrating this problem is the collage: a generous scattering of seemingly random extracts from contemporary history: the large-scale political decisions and events. Caught up in this are the life-stories of the heroes of the novels, and yet they remain seemingly unaffected by it. But, far from being able to lead autonomous existences that are entirely under their own control, this material reveals in different ways the mistaken nature of such ambitions. In Doeblin the hero desires to be 'a good man', yet he fails – not because external circumstances directly interfere with this laudable aim, but because of himself. And again, this 'himself' is not a solid substance but his gullible attitude, his openness for ever new impressions, and his allowing himself to be influenced and swayed by them. Pynchon's heroes are seekers obsessed with discovering some profound secret. This may be the identity of a person, as in *V.*, or that of a secret organization (the Trystero system) in *The Crying of Lot 49.* Ever new possibilities emerge in the course of this quest: individuals appear who seem to fulfil all the requirements, but new clues turn up and the quest is pushed into yet another direction. The characters drift along the surface, from one stimulus or clue to the next. Usually it is only in the eyes of the reader that this accumulation of clues reveals itself as totally random. But in one case, one of the characters in *V.* has actually become aware of some of it. Thus, when writing his autobiography, he rejects the idea of a personal continuity and talks instead of Maijstral I, II, etc.[22] In another part of the same novel *V.*, Weissman has been trying to decode the messages that might be contained in atmospheric radio noise. And one day he appears to be succeeding in breaking into the mysteries of the stars: his decoded message reads – in atrocious German – '*Die Welt ist alles was der Fall ist.*' Mondaugen, to whom this is read out, translates it for the reader: 'The world is all that the case is', and adds 'I have heard that somewhere before.'[23] Pynchon does not tell us where that could have been; it is in fact one of Wittgenstein's aphorisms.

Paraphrasing all these different ideas, we could say that in these works the course of an individual through time and his search for meaning on the surface of the world (and it is one of the stylistic peculiarities of the books mentioned here that they require the reader to repeat this search for meaning) are revealed as a random and futile affair. Neither is the individual in control of external events, nor does he even make up a permanent whole, nor do the drives that push him forward actually lead to any goal, conclusion, or fulfilment on that level. The world is all that the case is, the individual cannot pursue any given clues to get out of it, for all signs found on its surface are random. Incidentally, the curious may derive from this a first indication of the meaning of the subtitle for this third part: commuting within one world.

Paraphrased in this manner, these ideas readily show their congruence with *some* typically Indian, particularly Buddhist, thought. The rejection of a permanent, autonomous core in the empirical person, the description of the individual purposelessly drifting through the world of phenomena, impelled as he is by delusions and sense-impressions picked up at random, and the realization that any possible alternative to this rather miserable existence cannot lie altogether outside this same world – these are ideas that could come straight out of a Buddha's mouth.

However, to point out such a confluence of ideas (which in addition have some real historical links with Buddhism) does not mean that by reading Pynchon or Doeblin one could get the whole of Buddhist teaching. We find a cynicism and agnosticism expressed here which is totally alien to genuine Buddhist ideas. For whatever may be said there about the purposelessness of chasing objects of desire on the surface of the world, the theory of the workings of *kamma* represents a pronounced belief in the rationality of the chasing: it is subject to strict and well-defined rules and laws. Nevertheless, even if it may be only part of the picture, some aspects of Indian wisdom have actually been around with us for a while. This is meant as an encouragement to those who, until now, have been frightened of the difficult and alien world of Indian thought. Without knowing it, they may well be more familiar with it than they are aware.

On the other hand, I may be wielding a double-edged sword here. So let me add another word of encouragement to those who are familiar with the material mentioned here only from Fassbinder's deeply depressing film version of *Berlin Alexanderplatz* (which was shown on British television some time ago in serialized form). On the whole, our Indian thinkers refrained from indulging themselves in the profundities of Teutonic angst. Instead they have a fine sense of humour which I hope can, after some initial obstacles, be appreciated. And it is in this spirit that we may now enter into the realm of Wisdom in its most down-to-earth form, namely where it expresses itself as strategic initiatives.

CHAPTER 18

Strategic initiatives

At a time of financial hardship for institutions of higher learning, the following words of the poet Bhartṛhari may offer some comfort:

> He may sleep on bare ground or on a couch,
> Fare on roots or dine on sweet rice,
> Wear rags or heavenly robes;
> When he is rapt in reflection, a sage
> Pays no heed to pain or pleasure.[1]

The comfort lies obviously in the fact that poverty is by no means a necessary adjunct of wisdom! And in fact, depending on what is meant by 'wisdom', it could well be argued that the luxuries of a soft couch, sweet rice and heavenly clothes can actually be acquired by means of wisdom. That certainly is the argument of most of the material I would like to look at in the present chapter. 'Wise' in this case refers, rather humbly, to the man who is clever, shrewd and even ruthless or crafty. Whatever complexities of Wisdom may be in store for us at further stages of our exploration, no such difficulties are attached to the ideas we shall be exploring here. This worldly wisdom possesses a neatly defined home in the wider context and structure of Indian culture. Sandwiched (as *artha*) between *dharma* and *kāma*, 'religion' and 'love', it makes up together with these two the triad of the three ends in a man's life, the three legitimate aims to be pursued during one's active career in the world.[2] As part of the triad, it has infused some of its particular spirit into the other two, and we shall have ample opportunity to see how this has worked. Naturally, it is the relationship between worldly wisdom and religion – in the many different connotations of both terms – which is our main concern.

'Strategic initiatives' alludes to the realm of politics, and thus we may conveniently begin our discussion here. No doubt it is the

Arthaśāstra,[3] attributed to a Kauṭalya or Cāṇakya, which stands in the centre of the ancient Indian discussion of *artha*, political craftiness. The date of this highly influential work is still disputed; suggestions have varied from the third century BC to the first few centuries AD. The overriding task that Kauṭalya has set himself in this *Treatise of Polity* is the maintenance and increase of royal power. Political expansionism is the primary objective. This is the end which justifies every means, and a lengthy catalogue of such means is presented. Different types of torture are meticulously described; we hear of spies in all kinds of disguises (as monks, beggars, jugglers, etc.). Also the *agent provocateur* and propagandist are known. Human weaknesses are analysed in the finest detail, so that the king can exploit them, for instance by bribing those prone to greed. The administrative and economic structure of the kingdom is envisaged as highly centralized and state-controlled.

The *Treatise of Polity* has often been compared to Machiavelli's *Il Principe*. But Max Weber has confessed that the Italian is harmless compared with our Indian author.[4] Doubtlessly he had in mind the utter ruthlessness advocated here, a ruthlessness that does not allow for any clash even with *dharma*, with 'religion' in the most familiar sense of the word. All neighbouring kings are natural enemies, all their neighbours natural allies. Every trick in the book is allowed to reduce these enemies and to increase one's own area of influence. Every human weakness has to be exploited towards this aim. According to Wilhelm, 'it is a consequence of Kauṭalya's sceptical investigation of human nature that his picture of man as a political being is much more differentiated, but also much shadier and more ambivalent, than known in any other branch of Indian literature'.[5]

It is in this context that a methodology is developed concerning the correct application of different strategies. Kauṭalya speaks of the sixfold policy: peace, war, neutrality, sabre-rattling, seeking protection through an alliance, and waging war with one king while making peace with another. A slightly different schema is that of the *upāyas*, 'strategies': sowing dissension among one's enemies, negotiation, bribery and open assault.[6] We shall meet again with this concept of *upāya* in a very different context.

Incidentally it may be mentioned that the practical application of Kauṭalya's principles has been presented to us in one of the best-known Sanskrit dramas. This is *The Minister's Seal* (*Mudrārākṣasa*) by prince Viśākhadatta.[7] The author may have lived during the early fifth century AD at the Gupta court, and his audience may well have picked up from his play allusions to contemporary political events. But the action of the play itself is set almost eight hundred years earlier, at the beginning of the first great Indian dynasty, that of the Mauryas. The plot – like most political intrigues – is far too complex to summarize here. But we may note that the main character is our Kauṭalya, who ruthlessly brings to power the king he is loyal to, by exploiting the one human weakness of another minister. That the weakness should be his unfaltering loyalty shows most dramatically to what extent human beings can be manipulated.

Probably neither the *Arthaśāstra* nor the *Mudrārākṣasa* are historical in the sense of depicting a real historical situation or event. Yet as expressions of a, very sceptical, view of man they must have reflected attitudes prevalent in certain strata of society, just as they infused their flavour into further reflections on worldly wisdom. So (as Wilhelm points out) in Delhi today you can walk on the Kautilya-Marg (or Street), the diplomats' quarter of the same city is called Canakya-puri (Kauṭalya-Town), and Nehru considered Kauṭalya far more important, because far cleverer and more enterprising, than Machiavelli.[8] At the same time, India has remained suspicious. Popularly Kauṭalya is changed to Kauṭilya and thus brought into etymological proximity with *kuṭila*, 'crooked' – an attribute not only omnipresent with the eyebrows of beautiful women, but also proverbial with the bawds and heterae about whom we shall hear presently. In *The Tales of the Ten Princes*,[9] the teachings of this 'Kauṭilya' are mocked. Were a prince to follow all his instructions concerning his daily routine, his life would be so deprived of fun that it seems hardly worth becoming a king; even the life of a monk would have less rules and hardships. The person giving this down-to-earth instruction to the prince and making fun of Kauṭalya's scholasticism, is said in the text to be 'expert in ascertaining others' minds'. But, suspicion or mockery aside, this is obviously a talent required by anyone who wants in earnest to educate unintelligent princes in the art of statescraft. And legend tells us that such a man was Viṣṇuśarmā. Who he was or when he lived – if indeed there ever was such a man – is unknown. But we do have a book allegedly written by him. Faced with the task of getting across the principles of polity to princes whom even their own father has written off as 'utter fools', he used an ingenious device, and thereby created one of India's most famous books. He told stories, particularly about animals, and thereby illustrated five major themes of policy: how to break up friendships, how to win friends, the alternatives of war and peace, the loss of what one has obtained, and the dangers of hasty action. The book that evolved out of the lessons acquired the title *The Five Sections* (*Pañcatantra*).[10]

It would be something of an exaggeration to claim that no book except the Bible has been circulated as widely in the world as the *Pañcatantra.* But it must be true that no other Indian book has influenced world literature in the same way. More than two hundred versions of it are known, in over fifty languages. From a lost Pahlavi version, an Arabic translation was made in *c.* AD 750, under the name *Kalilah wa Dimnah*. From this text derive all early European versions: a Greek by the end of the eleventh century, a Hebrew in the twelfth century, an Old Spanish in *c.* AD 1251, a Latin (*Directorium Vitae Humanae*) of *c.* AD 1270, a German (*Das Buch der Beispiele der alten Weisen*) of the fifteenth century, and an Italian by Doni (1552) from which, in 1570, the first English translation was made under the title *The Morall Philosophie of Doni*.[11]

In some form, many of these timeless stories have been known to us since our childhood – like the story of the tortoise[12] that was being carried away to safety from a dried-up lake by two geese, holding on with his teeth to a stick that the geese held between them. When people saw this apparition, they shouted, seemingly innocently, asking what was going on. The tortoise could not resist commenting, 'What is all this fuss about?' and, naturally, he came crashing down to earth. The moral of the story seems obvious: sometimes silence is better than speaking. Yet that is not what the context in the *Pañcatantra* suggests. The story is included in the section on 'how to break up friendships'. The relevance may not be obvious, but when we read at the end that 'the people, eager for his meat, cut him to pieces with sharp knives as soon as he struck the ground', the whole cynicism of the story reveals itself. The shouting by the people at a strange sight was not at all innocent: it was a clever device, a provocation designed to break up the link – literally and metaphorically – between the geese and the tortoise.

Quite apart from world literature, the *Pañcatantra* has had an enormous influence in India itself. Often under different names (the *Hitopadeśa*, 'Wholesome Teaching', is perhaps the best known of these versions), these and many other stories were retold. Often also, or in fact in the majority of cases, the underlying spirit was changed, and the practical moral turned into moralizing. But not always! One of my favourite stories is about 'the man who impersonated god Viṣṇu'. It is found in some versions of the *Pañcatantra*, under the same heading of breaking-up friendships, has appropriately been included in the *Ocean for all the Rivers of Stories* (*Kathāsaritsāgara*), and not only does Shehrezaad fill one of her thousand and one nights with it, but we also know it from Boccaccio's friar who impersonated the Angel Gabriel.[13]

A young, but very poor, brahmin had the good fortune of being seen by the courtesan Lovely, and she fell so much in love with him that she forgot about all other clients and spent her time with him. [His name Lohajaṅgha, 'Iron-Shank', may well be bowdlerized for Lohajaghana which would let us into the secret behind this strange affair. Delicately put, it means Iron-Loins.] Anyway, Crocodile, the girl's mother and bawd, is extremely unhappy about this turn of events and scolds her severely. 'A decent harlot would rather bed with a dead man than a poor one!', etc. She succeeds in having the brahmin beaten up and thrown out of the house. Deprived of his unearned fortune, he now resorts to his own shrewdness. In some versions, he goes directly to a Greek and buys from him a flying-machine. In others, events are more complicated but lead to a similar outcome: Lohajaṅgha returns into the town riding on a bird – a large kite which he has broken in as his pet. Dressed up in the paraphernalia of the god Viṣṇu – wielding a mace, conch shell and war-discus – he flies to Lovely's terrace. She does not recognize him, and is so totally overwhelmed by this divine attention and made to feel so proud that, even to her mother, she will only talk through a curtain. The bawd comes to know of the nightly visitations and does not want to be left out of things. So Lohajaṅgha promises to lead her straight into heaven. He tells her to appear the next evening with shaven head, smeared in ashes, naked with only a garland of skulls around her neck [thus looking just like Śiva]. In this disguise he will smuggle her into heaven. Indeed he comes and picks her up, but sets her down on top of a pillar. In his real form, he spreads the warning among the people that next morning the Plague-Goddess will fall upon them, unless they pray to Viṣṇu. When the procuress cannot endure her standing position any longer on the pillar and shouts: 'Ah, ah, I am going to fall!' devotional fervour in the town reaches its climax. But in the light of morning, the Goddess is recognized for what she is, and tells her story. The people of the town burst out laughing, and the king offers a high reward to the unknown joker. Lohajaṅgha reveals himself, receives many gifts and is allowed to marry a, by now much humbler, Lovely. [Friar Alberto had no such luck. His angelic disguise was discovered and, dragged back into a cell in his monastery, he was kept under lock and key until the end of his life.]

What is the moral of this story, and what does it yield for our present discussion? First, the versions I summarized bowdlerize probably far more than just the brahmin's name. Here it sounds, at least part of the way, like the typical story of the poor simpleton who makes his fortune due to good luck. More original must be versions, like Boccaccio's, in which the impersonator is initially rejected by the girl. As Monna Lisetta says: 'My charms are not at the service of every Tom, Dick or Harry who happens to fall in love with them.'[14] Thus mother and daughter are in cahoots with each other, and our hero, right from the beginning, displays the shrewdness required to break up friendships, as indeed the conceptual context in the *Pañcatantra* suggests. Secondly, behind the motif of the bawd is hidden a whole branch of literature on worldly wisdom. Not only does this literature spell out in great detail, and as serious warning, the extent of the proverbial bawd's shrewdness, but with great delight it also tells many a tale of exceedingly clever people who could outwit her. That explains the laughter of the whole town. But thirdly, notice what has happened to religion. In three different ways three deities have been mocked and made fun of. There is Viṣṇu, impersonated by our hero; then there is Śiva, most visibly parodied in the appearance of the bawd, and thirdly there is the Goddess whose name is invoked in vain. Yet the town laughs, and Lohajaṅgha is generously rewarded (while Friar Alberto is punished for his blasphemy). Let us note for the moment this puzzling relationship between the religious and the worldly-wise.

From the story we must turn to the small poem. Worldly wisdom in the form of gnomic stanzas and proverbs must have been current in India from time immemorial. Eventually conceptualized as *nīti*, it came to include a wide range of material. Since *nīti* can be synonymous with *artha*, the teaching of how to pursue one's worldly profits is certainly one of the themes encountered here. But other themes are also found: reflections on virtue, different types of people (the good and the evil man), and on the misfortunes of the learned or wise, etc. Classical anthologies of Indian poetry almost invariably have sections on such matters. But besides simple and anonymous stanzas, we also have the sophisticated poets who deal with such matters; among these, none is more famous than Bhartṛhari.

Bhartṛhari was probably the earliest of the great Indian Sanskrit poets to be translated into a European language:[15] into Dutch in 1651, and from there into German in 1663. The original poetry has been collected in three sections. The first carries the title *Nīti*. But it is not abstract moral advice we find here, nor assistance in the pursuit of craftiness. In a fairly unique way, the poet conjures up a very concrete situation with which we can immediately identify. He describes the fate of learning in a world that does not care for it, the pursuit of wisdom in the face of corruption, greed and treachery, and the impotence of knowledge over the fools that may well be wielding the power. Though still clearly adhering to the idea that this should not be the case and that the wise man should be in control of the world and its comforts, there is a definite note of withdrawal and scepticism struck here. People of the world are analysed in all their sordidness and folly – not to be exploited (as in Kauṭalya), but to be despised. Bhartṛhari's style is simple, but as Sanskrit poetry developed, much more complicated means of expression evolved. This may take the form of substantiations (as Ingalls[16] translates *arthāntaranyāsa*). Literally, these are poems in which a second, epigrammatic meaning is drawn out of the primary subject matter. This may be illustrated by the following little poem by Govardhana, who wrote in Eastern India shortly before AD 1200.

> A rich man may have good qualities,
> but they quickly disappear;
> a poor man keeps them.

This is the first half of the stanza – a piece of general though slightly puzzling insight. The second half provides the 'proof' for it through poetic substantiation:

> A full vessel may snap the rope
> that pulls it upwards,
> but not the empty one.[17]

There are various puns here which show us that the fragile rope (*guṇa*) stands for a person's 'virtues' (*guṇas*), and the fullness for 'riches'.

This brief excursion into Sanskrit poetics would be of limited value in our present discussion were it not for one interesting feature. When searching in the realm of human experience for symbols and substantiations that can lend (at least poetical) weight to some truth, our poets do not hesitate to draw also on the world of the gods. Here is one illustration, from the same Govardhana.

> Lakṣmī [=goddess of wealth] like a whore
> gives excessive pleasures,
> but does not care for knowledge.
> Sarasvatī [=goddess of learning] like the wife
> of good family
> will not abandon her husband
> even in many lives to come.[18]

Clearly in the pursuit of gnomic insights the poets know of no respect for 'religious' matters! But let us return to Bhartṛhari. His section on *Nīti* is followed by two further ones, on 'Love' and on 'Resignation'. The second section need not detain us here long. One quote will suffice to illustrate the subject matter:

> How could men of wisdom
> Let their minds' vigor be sapped,
> Be distracted by the ignominies of courting
> At the gates of an evil king's palace,
> Were it not for maids flashing lotus eyes.[19]

Here Bhartṛhari reveals a deeper level of the problem of wisdom in the world. The chain that binds the learned, wise man to the vagaries of the sordid world of power is the passion inspired by women. And to help him get away from it all, there is the ideal conceptualized as *vairāgya*, withdrawal from the realm of passion. Here sometimes quite morbid reflections occur, on the transience of human life and on the futile motives that impel it.

> Birth is scented with death.
> Youth's brilliance is shadowed by old age.
> Contentment is menaced by ambition,
> Calm, by impudent women's amorous looks.[20]

This could be a Buddhist monk talking, but one still struggling to achieve a lasting renunciation. And indeed, I-ching, the seventh-century Chinese pilgrim to India, retells what was probably no more than a legend he had heard. There was a famous philosopher and poet called Bhartṛhari who desired the monastic life, but simply could not give up the affairs of the world. Once he even kept a chariot ready at the monastery's gate, in case he could not resist the temptations of the flesh.[21]

Generally we find in the anthologies ample material which expresses similarly morbid reflections on life's transient aspects. The *Śāntiśatakam*, the *Century of Mental Peace*, which is attributed to Śilhaṇa, offers particularly valued material for the anthologists.[22] Naturally the transience of love and lust is one important theme here. Yet the *sthavira*, the old man, may well appear as a comic figure: his longing for the fulfilment of desires that cannot be fulfilled any more makes him an object of ridicule, particularly on the stage.[23]

Books that combine reflections on worldly wisdom and good conduct, on love and on withdrawal from the world, have emerged in many parts of India at various times. The most famous of these, apart from Bhartṛhari's *Three Centuries*, is the Tamil *Tirukkuṟaḷ*.[24] '*Kuṟaḷ*' is simply a very concise verse-form, and *tiru* is the Sanskrit *Śrī*, 'holy'. Composed way back in the first millennium AD, this work stimulated a whole host of imitations and translations into many other languages. In its three sections we can easily recognize the Hindu *dharma*, *artha* and *kāma*: 'religion', worldly wisdom and love. Yet it has been suggested that its author, the nebulous Vaḷḷu, was in fact a Jain. Quite unlike Bhartṛhari, the *Tirukkuṟaḷ* explores its subject matter without inner tensions and without any suggestion of a torn person. If the final lines that we have would indeed mark the culmination of the whole, what extraordinary acceptance of the world would be expressed here. 'Sulking adds to the joys of making love: the subsequent embrace tastes all the sweeter' – with these words Vaḷḷu's reflections on life conclude.[25]

There is no space to do any further justice to this interesting work. But I would like to refer to a matter connected with Yogi Shuddhananda Bharati's translation of it.[26] This will remind us that 'wisdom' in India is a complex affair, and that the mastery over one type does not automatically imply mastery over others. In the 'Foreword' to the above-mentioned translation it is suggested that *yoga* (confused here with *tapas*) can assist in translating into a foreign language. This is envisaged to work in the following manner.

> The most important pre-requisite to the translator of the Kural is that he should have disciplined himself by performing *tapas*. He must have effaced his own ego and merged himself without reservation in the thought-processes of Valluvar. If the translator could keep his mind long enough in this dedicated condition of reverence, humility and advaita, his sub-conscious would become

a fit medium for receiving Valluvar's genius. In this condition of intensity, the sub-conscious invents appropriate combinations of words and patterns of rhythm which have the power to crystallise the authentic Valluvar in the English language. It is significant that before commencing this translation Suddhananda Bharati took to a month of silence, and after commencing it, he remained in silent communion for two days every week. I consider that this is the first English translation ever made by a yogi who has been in Maha Samadhi for a number of years.[27]

After such an introduction, I must leave it to you to judge the results. Here are three examples:

Those who live by slaying are
Eaters of carrion bizarre!

The careless king whom none reproves
Ruins himself sans harmful foes.

Rushing flood of love sweeps away
The raft of shame and firmness, aye![28]

While it might be unwise to try to use the method of one type of wisdom (in this case *yoga*) for the pursuit of the goal typical of another (knowledge of English and poetry), the analysis of the principles behind shrewd and ruthless action can nevertheless be transferred from politics to matters of love. The *Tirukkuṟaḷ* culminates with a section on *kāma*, passionate love, and Bhartṛhari too does not allow us to forget its presence even in his world-weary reflections on *vairāgya*, 'resignation'. But Kauṭalya triggered off yet other reactions. As we saw earlier, it has been demonstrated rather convincingly that India's most famous textbook on erotics, the *Kāma-sūtras*, was actually modelled on the *Arthaśāstra.*[29] Here we find the same kind of ruthlessness advocated in the seduction of women as, there, in the conquest of neighbouring kingdoms. What this looks like in practice, and at the same time how closely related *kāma* and *artha* can be, is demonstrated in *The Tales of the Ten Princes*. Many of them illustrate all kinds of ruthless tricks and shrewd stratagems, usually in the conquest of small kingdoms. But there is also a story in which the compass is wider.[30]

A certain prince is brought by various misfortunes to the town of the king who had conquered the prince's own kingdom and had imprisoned his father. All this he finds out when by chance he meets his former nurse, now a nun. Through her daughter, who is a chamber-maid of the queen, the nun is more than willing to assist the prince in his schemes. 'For this matter cannot be achieved unless through treachery. And of all deceitful contrivances, women are the source.' Accordingly he instructs the chamber-maid to keep on insinuating to the queen that the king is a loathsome husband, and no match for her. At the same time, she is to find out about all his amorous ways in the harem, even the most secret of them, and tell them to the queen, to make her jealous. When after a few days reports reach him that the queen is now indeed lamenting her miserable marriage, the prince draws a picture of himself and has it sent to the queen, to be presented to her as that of a secret admirer. The queen is more than willing to meet him in an arbour in the palace garden. The prince, resorting to what must be the earliest reference to pole-vaulting in Sanskrit literature, gets there, and after a lot of flattery, he makes love to her. When exhausted, she is initiated into his further plans. She is to approach her husband with the picture, but present it to him as a sample of what he could look like after performing certain religious ceremonies. She should persuade the king to perform these for his rejuvenation. At the same time, all people in the town should be informed about the imminent transformation of the king. The queen has no problem arranging all this, and the priests perform a particular sacrifice, offering a goat and burning a lot of fragrant wood. This produces a lot of smoke, hidden in which the prince appears, pretends to be the queen, draws the secrets of state out of the king, and then cuts him to pieces. Then he shows himself in public and proclaims himself as the rejuvenated king. Everyone extolls the powers of the priestly ritual, and the prince frees his own father and moves into the quarters of the queen.

At one point he shows scruples: 'Could *dharma* be violated by my making use of another man's wife for my scheme?' But he answers himself: 'Not really, because the writers of the learned treatises have allowed this for achieving the two ends in a man's life, *artha* and *kāma*. Moreover, I am doing it to free my father.'[31] And at the very end, our prince's friend comments: 'Though adultery is a dishonest business, here it has achieved abundant riches and virtue: it ended the grief of your father's imprisonment, destroyed a wicked usurper, and allowed you to win a kingdom.'[32] Religion, through its conception of the three legitimate ends, is squarely used as the defence for such ruthless action. Notice that the killing of the king is passed over without any comment whatsoever.

Thus it is clear that the cultivation of shrewdness in pursuit of *artha* and *kāma*, worldly-political profit and love, can potentially give rise to utter lawlessness and thus directly interfere with *dharma*, the religiously founded rules governing society. Let us now look at an example in which this tension is resolved in a most ingenious manner.

Once upon a time there was a rich merchant with a beautiful and faithful wife. Another man had been ogling her for a long time. Finally, when the merchant had departed on a journey, the love-smitten man seemed to be about to be rewarded for all his efforts to seduce her – very much along the lines advocated by the *Artha*- and *Kāma-śāstras.* The lady in question was ready to go out and meet her new lover for the first time. But a last-minute hitch turned up from a rather unexpected quarter. There were two birds in the house, a mynah, looking quite austere with its black feathers, and a parrot, naturally much more colourful. The first took a staunch law-and-order line: 'the family is the centre of society, and you must not indulge in such liberties'. But our lady had no time for this nonsense: she grabbed the mynah by its neck, and only a desperate flight saved the bird from being throttled to death. The parrot was much wiser. Not that he took an 'everything goes' stance – far from it. He too was interested in the status quo of society, but he went about it in a much cleverer and, to us, much more interesting manner. 'Nothing wrong with going out to meet your lover' he said to the woman. 'Go ahead, and good luck to you! But ... well, I am sure you know what to do when something like what happened to so-and-so occurs ...' Curious, the woman stopped in her steps. 'How is that? What happened?' The parrot was more than willing to oblige and began telling a story. But at the critical moment, when the heroine or hero of the story is caught up in a tricky and highly dangerous situation, he stopped. 'How would *you* get out of it?' The woman was baffled, pondered backwards and forwards to find a solution to the dilemma the heroine or hero is caught up in, but failed. By the time the parrot had told her the end of the story, I am sure she had lost the desire to go out and risk similar dangers for which she may not have the quickwitted reactions required. Anyway, the parrot made sure by demanding an assurance that she would stay in the house until morning. These nocturnal happenings repeated themselves seventy times.

Predictably, the majority of the stories deal with unfaithful women who, caught in the act or leaving dangerous evidence, come up with all kinds of wonderful answers and tricks to prevent their husbands from finding out the truth. Many other stories concern rogues who through their quickwittedness make a dishonest profit.[33] Those with no access to the original Sanskrit can read some of these stories as they are told on the *Seventh Day* of the *Decameron.*

When the seventieth night had passed, the husband returned and everything ended well. The parrot managed to save not only his life, but also the honour of his home; the wife had learnt that to be unfaithful you have to be clever, and we the readers have by proxy enjoyed all kinds of dangerous and adulterous situations without ever being in danger ourselves – physically or morally. It is not difficult to predict the title of the book: *The Seventy Stories of the Parrot* (*Śukasaptati*). Once again this is a famous collection of tales that travelled West: into the *Arabian Nights*, the various *Parrot Books* or *Ṭūṭī-nāmehs*, and naturally into Boccaccio. It is mass entertainment at its best and most sophisticated, and totally in the service of the status quo!

To the extent that the moral status quo is a religious concern because it is enshrined in the concept of *dharma*, already the *Śukasaptati* allows us to speak of religion using the theme of shrewdness for its own ends. But before exploring this further, let us cast a glance back over the material discussed so far.

What is perhaps most striking is the cultural flavour contained in the various examples we have looked at. We might even be tempted to call it 'modern', in spite of the fact that some of the sources mentioned take us back in time perhaps one and a half millennia. A critical distance to religious matters characterizes this flavour. Religion may be laughed at, mocked, parodied and abused for very secular purposes. The world of the gods is scrutinized for parallels to very down-to-earth human attitudes and experiences. This distance is supported by a very pragmatic and sometimes cynical attitude towards life and human nature. At least in the stories, people are not expected to be 'good': it is accepted that Mr Average wants to make money and have fun. Moreover, the appropriate skills are encouraged: an intuitive grasp of the crucial factors determining a particular situation, and a spontaneous manipulation of these for one's own profit. In most cases, such factors are not arbitrary or random, but embedded in human weakness, ignorance and credulity. To hold such a view of man does not necessarily imply a critique of religious beliefs. On one level, it may well stimulate a sense of frustration and disgust, and a withdrawal from all worldly concerns (*vairāgya*). Again we see religion at work to accommodate all this in one system and balance it: this is the teaching of the three, mutually dependent, ends of a man's life: *artha*, *kāma* and *dharma*. In most cases, our stories do not simply want to illustrate what *artha* (and *kāma*) actually mean in concrete terms; they also want to demonstrate how, when pursued in isolation, they can lead to social chaos. In that sense, stories about *artha* remain stories about *nīti*, good social behaviour, and thereby belong under the heading of *dharma*. That many of the texts I have referred to have been handed down to us in overtly religious versions bears this out.

On another level, the analysis of human nature which is expressed in our material does not differ fundamentally from what, for example, Buddhism has to say about it. At the root of man's nature lie his greed and his ignorance. Given that such views are culturally spelled out in our material with all their depressing aspects, what the Buddha and others have to say additionally (about the possibility of freedom from all this) becomes therefore 'very good news' – *euángelion*, or Gospel – indeed. Every religion derives practical conclusions from its view of man. In the case of classical India, we have the remarkable situation that such views are essentially the same as those discussed above for secular culture

However, it is by no means the case that 'shrewdness' is merely used as an object of religious reflection. *The Seventy Stories of the Parrot* have given us a first demonstration of how positive use can be made of the theme. A wide range of further possibilities developed in the course of the religious history of India, and the following examples may give some idea of it.

We saw in the section on Love how the conventions of eroticism (as developed in actual love poetry, in the schemas of the poeticians, and in the rather arid scholasticism of the erotic pundits) were reflected in the realm of Hindu mythology, in the love-life of the gods.[34] Can anything similar be said about our present theme, the display of shrewdness and ruthless pursuit of personal ambitions? Indeed it can. It could be illustrated very convincingly from the great epic, the *Mahābhārata*, by demonstrating to what extent Kṛṣṇa – God incarnate – schemes and intrigues and resorts to all kinds of vile tricks to achieve his end: the regaining of a kingdom. Not that it is for himself: the kingdom belongs to his friends. But whilst they are ready to forgo any claim to it, realizing what enormous amount of bloodshed and suffering such a reconquest would entail, Kṛṣṇa has no such worries. His intrigues bring about the final battle, and his friends do gain victory. Details cannot be given here, for this would mean paraphrasing and summarizing the longest epic in the world. Instead, I shall refer to a small facet of another related and very large theme: Kṛṣṇa as the shrewd and ruthless lover. In the fifteenth century, the mystic and Kṛṣṇa devotee, Caitanya, had as one of his primary disciples Rūpa Gosvāmī, a gifted poet, poetician and playwright. *Vidagdha-Mādhava*, or *Crafty Kṛṣṇa*, is one of Rūpa's dramas,[35] and it seems that the learned ascetic himself played one of the roles in it. I cannot summarize the plot of the play here; but the epithet 'crafty' or 'sly' of the title refers to Kṛṣṇa the clever seducer, who in his love for Rādhā, married to a cowherd, manages to outdo the guardian of Rādhā's honour (her mother-in-law) in spite of all the tricks and craftiness of the latter. The literature dealing with Kṛṣṇa's amorous escapades is boundless, and craftiness is displayed in them in abundance.

When celibate ascetics write and perform dramas in which God Kṛṣṇa displays his shrewdness in seducing another man's wife according to the rules of the *Kāmasūtras*, or when the epic *Mahābhārata* depicts the same god as using all the political ruthlessness advocated by Kauṭalya, the remoteness of the past, the abstraction of art and the qualitative difference between a god and human beings all exonerate the rogue. But what on the plane of myth may be perfectly legitimate, to us at least would seem to have no place in real life. Yet when we look, once again. at the life of Parakāla,[36] we are indeed brought down to the plane of real human beings. Not that this chieftain of a little Tamil kingdom, who probably lived in the eighth century AD, is still available to us in his true biography. The poetry he composed offers us very few clues as to his life, his deeds and his personality. But legends about his life are available in many versions, Tamil and Sanskrit. These offer us the picture of a man who was tricked and then became a trickster himself, and all directly in the service of religion.

Parakāla had fallen in love with a pious girl who would only agree to marry him if he converted to her religion (Vaiṣṇavism). But even then conjugal rights were withheld, until he had fed a thousand Viṣṇu devotees every day for a whole year. By that time Parakāla had interiorized Viṣṇu religion to such an extent that he involved himself fanatically in a building campaign on a fantastic scale. In Śrīraṅgam, the centre of South Indian Vaiṣṇavism, he began to construct all kinds of temple buildings. When his money ran out, highway robbery yielded further funds for a while. But then a better solution to his continuing financial problems was suggested to him. Off he went with his companions to Nāgapaṭṭiṉam, to steal a large golden statue from the Buddha temple. At first, no access to the inside of the shrine could be found. So the gang travelled to an island, where they endeared themselves to the architect who had built the temple. Told that the image had been stolen, the poor man got into such a state that he revealed inadvertently how cleverly he thought he had hidden the one passage leading inside. That was all they wanted to know, and they sailed back in the ship of a betel merchant. Jokingly, Parakāla broke into halves one betel nut which the merchant had given him and, seemingly by accident, one half fell into the hold of the ship. The merchant still considered it a joke when Parakāla made him sign a chit promising to return 'half the betel'. But back in Nāgapaṭṭiṉam, Parakāla took him to court and succeeded in obtaining half of the whole load of betel nuts. In the night, they discovered the secret passage and Parakāla's brother-in-law was let down to get the statue. Unfortunately, although the opening was just big enough for the statue to be passed through, the man got stuck. Parakāla did what readers of Herodotus can predict: he cut his head off and took it along, leaving the headless body inside the shrine. Disguised as a mourning party, the robbers then carried the statue on a bier towards Śrīraṅgam. But, through clever detective work, the Buddhists of Nāgapaṭṭiṉam managed to trace him, and challenged him in front of the Cōḻa emperor. Our saint signed another chit promising to return the statue in a year's time. But the Tamil wording of this promise was phrased in such a way that when they returned after a year, he gave them merely the little finger of the Buddha and actually thereby fulfilled the letter, if not the spirit, of his promise. Finally, finding himself once again without money but with the masons demanding their pay, he promised to pay them in a place across the Kāveri river. During the crossing, he had them all drowned. When the relatives complained, he brought the deceased down from heaven, and they reported how wonderful life was there and how richly they had been rewarded in this manner.

There are a number of points that could be mentioned here which would speak against a literalist interpretation. Moreover, this legend occurs in many different versions, and as told here it is not found in the more respectable Sanskrit and Tamil versions.[37] Nevertheless, when one considers that Parakāla is one of the twelve great saints of Śrīvaiṣṇavism and that his statue is venerated in all the temples, one is allowed, I think, to feel some amazement at this inclusion of the theme of the shrewd and ruthless rogue and trickster in hagiography.

Yet this is not an isolated example of worldly wisdom applied to the practice of religion itself. Not only would we find similar stories in the hagiographic material of South Indian Śaivism. But we find the theme also among the Buddhists, though in a rarefied and elevated form. Here it figures under the heading of 'skilfulness in means', and the word used for 'means' is *upāya*, a concept we have encountered in the discussion of the *Arthaśāstra* – there denoting modes of political action: breaking up alliances, etc. With the Mahāyāna Buddhists, who developed the idea of such 'skill in means' along very complex and sophisticated lines,[38] it has far less cynical and depressing associations. In its original conception, *upāya-kauśalya* derives from the following situation. There is, on the one hand, the Buddha's teaching, his Dharma, which contains the medicine for the suffering of the world. There is, on the other hand, the mass of greedy and ignorant people who, precisely because of these qualities, suffer continuously. Then there are the *bodhisattvas*, the people who have received the Dharma and are supposed to communicate it to these suffering masses. 'Skilfulness in means' advocates the particular mode in which this mediation and communication ought to take place. To offer merely a brutal confrontation with the Dharma to the world would have little effect. Instead, all the cleverness, perhaps even shrewdness, man is capable of has to be resorted to. The ground has to be skilfully prepared for the seeds of the Dharma and, equally skilfully, the initial commitment to the path of the Buddha has to be nurtured and brought to maturity. The preacher is replaced by the *kalyāṇa-mitra*, the helpful and clever friend.

But apart from this most practical and literal aspect of 'skilfulness in means', Mahāyāna Buddhism developed the concept further and included itself in it: the concept becomes part of the self-definition of the Mahāyāna. This may be illustrated from the famous *Lotus Sūtra*. The state in which we have the text today reveals that many generations and many Buddhist trends have contributed to it. But it is possible for textual scholarship to reconstruct without too many uncertainties a relatively small 'original' of less than seven hundred stanzas. Its date may well go back into the BC period. The basic point to be made here is very simple. The institutionalized pursuit of *nirvāṇa* – understood here as the eradication of ignorance and desires – is criticized for being far too selfish and yielding a far too limited spiritual result. Not that it is regarded as a deviation from the Buddha's own teaching and is rejected. In fact, it is accepted as an expression of his 'skilfulness in means'.

A number of allegories (literature tends to refer to them as 'parables') are told which illustrate this. Thus we hear about the guide who has to lead a caravan through difficult and large forests. At a certain point the travellers are so exhausted and disheartened that they do not have the will to proceed any further. Skilfully, the guide conjures up a beautiful city, where everyone can relax and recover from the strains. Then, at the right moment, the city vanishes and the guide leads the merchants further to their final destination. This final goal stands here for the goal the Mahāyāna is interested in, while the magic city of rest stands for the limited spiritual achievement of *nirvāṇa*. Naturally, the guide is the Buddha who, by skilfully structuring his teaching and the goals it advocates, reveals his skilfulness in means and thus gradually leads people to the highest perfection of wisdom and compassion.[39]

The other allegories[40] make very similar points. Thus there is the burning house: the children inside are so absorbed in their games that they do not notice the fire. Their father tries to call them out on to the street, but only when he mentions that he has a whole set of wonderful toys do they come out. This would be sufficient to illustrate *upāya-kauśalya* in action. But our text expands the story: the father does actually give them one lovely toy. And the interpretation offered is once again that the promised toys are the more limited forms of Buddhism, and that the real toy is the Mahāyāna. The text does ask the question whether it was permitted for the father to tell such 'lies'. Indeed it was, is the answer, since they were an expression of *upāya-kauśalya.*

Writers have paid particular attention to the allegory of the lost son.[41] Although externally the story resembles the biblical parable of the Prodigal Son, the intention here is totally different: there is no desire to moralize. The son has been away for so long that he has forgotten who he really is. When his father, now a wealthy and powerful man, recognizes the destitute son, by no means does he open his arms immediately and welcome him back. Only by gradually introducing himself to him, giving him employment, and becoming increasingly friendly with him does he prepare the son for the great revelation: that he is his true son. This is explained as follows. Deep down within ourselves, we are all the true sons of the Buddha, capable of the Mahāyāna ideal of perfect enlightenment. But if the Buddha (the 'father' in the allegory) told us this straight away, we would be quite horrified by the prospect. So instead, he designs much less demanding and more limited types of Buddhism, which slowly prepare us for the final part of our spiritual career.

Let us now turn from the Buddhists to the Jains. They, too, are familiar with the theme of shrewdness and cleverness, and have used it in their own, inimitable way. The fool and half-wit is the opposite to the clever and shrewd; thus the depiction of the former may serve to inculcate the qualities of the latter. But in doing so, other motives may enter, such as interreligious rivalry and criticism. This produces the satire.

When passers-by see a fool sawing off the branch on which he is sitting, they warn him that he might get killed. He does fall down, but as fool's luck has it, he remains unharmed. 'I must be dead', he thinks, 'for that is what those people have told me.' So he lies absolutely still, like a corpse. When his friends come and ask him what he is doing, he tells them that he is dead and that they must now cremate him. Promptly they get hold of a bier and carry him towards the cremation ground. People who witness this procession are rather amazed at a corpse giving his friends detailed instructions as to how he wants to be cremated. Only with great effort do they succeed in persuading the 'corpse' and mourners that he is still alive![42]

A silly story perhaps, but also a satire. For the fool and his friends are identified as *bharaṭakas*, a class of Śaiva ascetics. A Jain monk produced thirty-two such tales, mostly set in Gujarat, though written in Sanskrit. In fact, some of the stories deal with language itself. Our ascetics, and also the village *bhaṭṭ* (priest), are ridiculed for their minimal Sanskrit learning. Sanskrit phrases they have learnt with great effort inevitably come out of their mouths as Gujarati obscenities. In the hands of our Jain monk, the pursuit of cleverness has turned into a biting weapon of attack, which breaks through the pretentious façade of semi-educated Hindu mendicants and priests, and their totally ignorant rural devotees. The *Bharaṭaka-Stories* may be amusing in their simplicity. But the Jains have also handled anti-Hindu satire with far greater sophistication. The *Dhūrtākhyāna* (*Tale of the Rogues*)[43] is a splendid example of this.

Once upon a time, a whole host of rogues had gathered together in Ujjain. They were organized in five gangs, each led by an arch-rogue. Four of the leaders are men (and their number includes Mūladeva, the epitome of shrewdness in the kind of literature referred to previously). Then there is the gang of female rogues, led by Khaṇḍapaṇā. Because of the heavy rains, they have to stay idle, and soon hunger asserts itself. They are too lazy to do much about it, but then Mūladeva has the following ingenious idea. Each of the five leaders has to tell a 'tall' story, something completely unbelievable. Naturally their pride will be at stake and they should try to outdo the others. However, there is no prize for the tallest story. Another leader has to prove that such a story could actually be true. So there can only be a loser: the one whose story cannot be verified by the others. And it will be the loser's task to organize food for everybody else. Here now is the brief summary of one of these tall stories.

'In my youth, I was obsessed with the idea of becoming rich, and I practised alchemy. A secret treatise told me about a well in a faraway mountain. I went there, lifted up the rock covering it, which was a hundred miles in diameter, and took out the elixir. Back home, the liquid made me incredibly rich and handsome, and I surrounded myself with all imaginable luxuries and hundreds of dancing girls. But news of my wealth reached robbers who one night came to plunder my house. I resisted and with each shot of my bow I killed seven, eight, or even ten robbers at a time. It needed a hundred of them to cut my head off, and then they cut up my body into small pieces. They stuck the head on a *badarī* tree and went away. This head of mine, sitting comfortably on the tree, with its blood dripping and the earrings dangling, ate the tree's berries. When people saw this, they gathered all the bits and pieces of my body together and joined them, so that I became whole again, my beauty unimpaired.'[44]

An impossible story? Not at all! As in the case of the other, very similar, stories, the next leader carefully analyses each seemingly impossible item (here: lifting such an enormous mountain, the miraculous qualities of an elixir, shooting ten people with one arrow, the survival of a head, and the resuscitation of a person by putting the bits of his body back together). And for each he quotes generously from the Hindu scriptures and abstracts from them 'scientific' principles which all substantiate that such things are indeed possible. Space does not permit me to illustrate this here, and all that I can do is refer to the story of Rāma-with-the-Axe (Paraśurāma) as one of the proofs for the resuscitated head. In total obedience to his irascible father, Paraśurāma cut off the head of his own mother, and then, as a reward for his loyalty, was allowed to put it on again and bring her back to life.

But I think I ought to tell how the contest ended. Khaṇḍapaṇā, who is introduced to us as the author of an *Arthaśāstra*,[45] speaks last. At various points during her narrative she is actually ready to take on the task of securing the food, if the male rogues are prepared to acknowledge her as the greatest rogue of all. Naturally their male pride does not allow this, and they demand that she carry on till the bitter end. In her story she includes an incident where, as a washerwoman, she lost all the clothes entrusted to her – the wind blew them away. And she lost her four servants who were afraid that they would be punished for this loss. Now, Khaṇḍapaṇā says in her tall story, she has come to Ujjain and sees her own servants sitting in front of her (the four leaders of the male rogues) and actually wearing the clothes she has been searching for. Who would have the courage to prove her right in this by confessing to being a washerwoman's servant, a woman in disguise, and to wearing somebody else's soiled clothes? They did not have the courage and thus, by losing the contest, Khaṇḍapaṇā proves herself the shrewdest of all the rogues.

The author Haribhadra, who lived in the eighth century and wrote in Rajasthan, concludes by telling his readers that clearly stories in the Hindu scriptures do not stand up to critical analysis and thus ought to be rejected, in favour of the Mahāvīra's teaching that does make empirical sense. It is obvious that, by having a rogue – the epitome of ruthlessness *à la* Kauṭalya and the *Kāmasūtras* – prove the validity of Hindu myths, extraordinary fun is made of, and insults heaped upon, Hindu beliefs. But given that the *Tale of the Rogues* is written not in Sanskrit, but in Prakrit, which at that time was almost exclusively cultivated by the Jains, we should not overemphasize the 'anti-Hindu' character of the text. It is aimed at a Jain readership, warning them against the temptations of Hindu literature. It is not addressed as open polemic to the Hindus themselves. Nevertheless, the argument put forward here is extremely interesting. Rationality and common sense are brought to bear on religious beliefs and, moreover, something perceived, though not explicitly conceptualized in this form, as the laws of nature is made the final authority. The world of human experience is not like that of the fairy-tale or that of a dream. There are quite specific and well-definable laws operating in it and once these are isolated and understood within an overall systematic framework, human reason can encompass the galaxies and make sense of the universe.

CHAPTER 19

Encompassing the galaxies

You can't extricate from Hindu myths some general principles, or 'laws of nature', and use them to describe the world as we know it. That was the lesson Haribhadra wanted to teach his Jain readers in his Prakrit *Tale of the Rogues*.[1] Instead, something rational and reasonable, like the Mahāvīra's teaching, must be used for that purpose. This seems to introduce a straightforward contrast between myth and science, and offers us the cue to turn away from rogues and ruthless politicians to areas of greater profundity.

Let us first look a bit closer at the material which has been criticized here through the mouths of the various rogues. The *reductio ad absurdum* undertaken by Haribhadra may not do full justice to every aspect of myth. Not that I would want to perpetuate certain romantic views commonly associated with it – myth as the expression of human 'wholeness', as a vision of the cosmos still imbued with the sense of the sacred and 'holy'. This stance has to be discussed separately, and I shall do that presently. But what could a 'non-romantic' view of Hindu mythology be, other than what Haribhadra has already offered? Let us look at some examples, to find out.

Yama, the god of death, was standing at the gates of heaven and interrogating three women. 'What have you done with your life?' he asked the first one. 'I loved one man, but then I married the man my parents chose for me, and I never looked at another man.' 'Let her in through the silver gate!' Yama told his assistant. The second one stated that she only loved the man she had married. She was let in through the golden gate. Then came the third, a dancing girl. 'Lord!', she addressed Yama, 'I have never made a man unhappy. I have given pleasure and fun to so many that I cannot count them.' 'Give her the key to my room!' was the god's instruction to the assistant.

By no stretch of the imagination could this be regarded as a 'scientific' description of reality. That its function is rather different ought to become clear when I reveal the origin of the little myth. It comes from a television documentary on *India Cabaret*, and is told by one of the dancers, in reply to what can be inferred to be a question about possible shame and guilt. A particular range of symbols is drawn on (Yama, heaven, *pāpa*) and out of it is made up, in a particularly witty fashion, an interpretation of human life – a life that is by no means 'whole' or 'holy', but is elevated by it above its sordid base. The mythical reference imbues it with 'meaning' in some form, and that includes dignity.

Here is another example.[2] When the gods had churned the milk ocean, out of it arose Lakṣmī. Seeing her, Viṣṇu fell passionately in love with her, but concealed his feelings. At the same time, Lakṣmī desired Viṣṇu and, in order to obtain him, went to do *tapas* near a certain pond. Whenever her mind got distracted, she forced it to turn back to Viṣṇu. The latter could not constrain his passion for her any more and went near her place of *tapas*. With the help of a messenger, their mutual feelings were revealed to each other, and their wedding could be celebrated.

This may not be a very exciting story, but behind its seemingly simple plot hides a very complex interpretative mechanism. If you went to a Viṣṇu shrine in Tamil Nadu called Tirukkaṇṇamaṅkai, you would find that the 'myth' is meant to be a 'historical' account of a whole range of items which are arranged together in such a way as to make up one coherent, meaningful whole. The pond will be identified as the 'Darśana-puṣkariṇī', so called because Viṣṇu revealed himself (*darśana*) here before Lakṣmī – whose penance naturally imbues it with great power. From her constantly directing her mind back to Viṣṇu she acquires the name Śrī ('to resort to'), and because she aroused great passion in him, she gets the name Ramā ('to make love'). Where he descended in his *vimāna*, his aerial palace, is the actual temple: both Viṣṇu and *vimāna* solidified permanently in the form of stone. And because he showed such great affection towards Lakṣmī, who was devoted to him, he becomes known as Bhaktavatsala, 'affectionate towards his devotees'. Since their marriage was celebrated here, the shrine is called Kṛṣṇa-maṅgalam (Kṛṣṇa = Viṣṇu, *maṅgalam* = wedding).

The name of the pond, shrine and Viṣṇu in that temple are all unique, exclusive to the present place of pilgrimage. Śrī and Ramā are universally known synonyms of Lakṣmī, but even they are provided here with a unique, local explanation. 'Bhaktavatsala' is similarly a universally used attribute of Viṣṇu, but here it is his proper name. To go to Bhaktavatsala in South Indian Vaiṣṇava parlance means to go to the temple of Tirukkaṇṇamaṅkai. *Maṅgalam* or *maṅkai* in Tamil place names signifies that this is a brahmin village, set up through royal endowment, but our story is ignorant of this 'real' historical meaning. The churning of the milk ocean is an ancient and universally known myth; our story draws on it for the religious prestige of this particular locality.

The choice here of a myth about Tirukkaṇṇamaṅkai is more or less random: similar stories are available for many thousands of Indian temples. Moreover, I have selected only a few items that are explained in this particular manner. Often the local mythology deals with hundreds of such features which the visitor can see. And finally, the temple and its various aspects are only one set of themes: instead of a temple, it can be a particular sacrifice, domestic ritual or custom, festival, or social convention. What we are dealing with here is, in fact, a particular pan-Indian mode of 'explaining' things. Underlying it is a curiosity that, astounded by a set of phenomena, wants to understand them, and this in terms not just of isolated bits and pieces of information, but of an overall logical coherence. Narrative is the most popular and easily comprehensible expression of such a coherent frame, and it is on the whole the Purāṇas and the classical epics that furnish the raw material for it. Some of these points deserve to be looked at in greater detail.

First of all, such explanatory stories are not random affairs. They tend to occur in a very specific question/answer situation.[3] Indeed, very frequently the texts actually record for us the questions that trigger off the narrative. Analysts of myths have tended to find this device cumbersome and unnecessary, spoiling a good story. But by eliminating such precise clues as to the significance of a particular narrative, they have left the myths hanging in mid-air. Thus it might appear that Indians did nothing but record, in millions of purāṇic pages, their random dreams.

Secondly, the kind of questions asked deserves a closer look. Again, often it is not merely an amorphous curiosity that expresses itself here, but critical, analytical observation. For example, there are twenty-seven major Viṣṇu temples in South India where the statue belongs to the iconographic type of the god reclining. Critical observations (obviously necessitating a visit to all twenty-seven shrines) and their compilation and comparison reveal that the details differentiate this one posture into eight distinct types, and also that the most common of the eight (*bhujaṅga-śayana*, 'reclining on the serpent') shows many minor variations. By no means are these variations the result of differentiation laid down in the textbooks on temple iconography. On the whole, they must be explained as random variations due, for example, to the sculptor making mistakes or using his own inventiveness. Naturally, there will be twenty-seven myths 'explaining' the variations, in the manner outlined above. But, were we to listen only to any one of them in isolation, we would fail to appreciate how much critical observation lies behind them and how complex the question actually is to which the stories address themselves.

Thirdly, even the answers in the form of a story or myth often reveal considerable ingenuity. What to the collector of variants of a myth appears as no more than a minor change in detail may well represent, in the context of our question/answer situation, an ingenious punch-line. Thus to narrate how Rāma travelled south towards Laṅkā to free his wife Sītā whom the ogre king of that island had abducted, is nothing new. To mention that at one stage he felt very tired and decided to have a rest, lying down in such a way that he was facing Laṅkā, seems to add nothing but perhaps a charming human touch to the story. However, in the myth of Śrīraṅgam it actually identifies the sleeping Viṣṇu as Rāma and 'explains' the position of the face towards the south.

Fourthly, by pointing out the elements of ingenuity and critical observation behind the mythical mode of making sense, I am not suggesting that this is actually a kind of 'proto-scientific' approach. But it is definitely more than random dreaming, or expression of subconscious images, or the mere telling of entertaining stories. At the same time, it is usually less than what a certain school of scholarship – most prominently represented by Mircea Eliade – associates with 'myth': grandiose conceptions of a cosmos in which man is whole and every aspect of reality is holy.[4] The purāṇic material discussed here is far more ambivalent and, on the whole, far less grandiose, while decidedly more rational in its intentions.

Whatever the empirical and critical aspects of this enterprise may be, ultimately it rests on a large set of traditional mythical symbols, and on beliefs. And when it 'makes sense' of a particular facet of reality, it wants to imbue it with a quality that has devotion or whatever as the appropriate response. Moreover, by playing freely with the meaning of words, it contradicts what etymology (e.g. in the case of Śrī) or social history (e.g. in the case of *maṅgalam*) would have to say. Immensely popular, it has, nevertheless, obvious limitations as an explanatory mechanism.

But even within the confines of a given belief system, Indian thinkers can do much better. Let us look at the example of the sound *oṃ*. Whatever its original meaning and etymology ('yes, indeed' has been suggested), since the times of the Upaniṣads this syllable has been surrounded with the greatest mystique and imbued with the greatest sanctity. Lower castes must not utter, not even hear, it, and it is regarded as the quintessence of the religious content of the Vedas. Yet, in spite of this exalted status, it has been subjected to critical analysis. A brief glance at the Śrīvaiṣṇava tradition of South India may illustrate how strong the desire has been to 'make sense' and to explain things rationally, by constructing a coherent frame of interpretation.

Inherited from tradition is the division of *oṃ* into three separate sounds: *a*, *u* and *m*. Once you have three items in India, a projection of other triads upon them is almost inevitable. In our case, it is the three Vedas: 'these three letters have been churned from the Vedas, just as butter is obtained by pouring curds into three vessels and churning them'.[5] This is meant to explain its traditional sanctity, but not yet its rational content. For this the three letters are treated separately, starting with *a*. Not only does the Sanskrit alphabet begin with *a*, but traditional grammar also regards *a* as implied in all following letters. Thus *a* symbolizes beginning, origin and cause, and at the same time the immanent essence in everything derived from that initial cause. Thus *a* stands for Viṣṇu. *U* now is a real word: it appears in Vedic Sanskrit in the meaning of 'only'. Not so easy is the case of *m*. However, in the Sanskrit alphabet it figures as number 25 of the consonants, and in the Sāṃkhya system of philosophy there are twenty-five basic categories, the twenty-fifth being the human soul. So: *m* = the human soul. To complete a meaningful sentence, it is postulated that in *a* a dative is implied. Thus the whole is read as: the human soul is meant for the service of, and totally depends on, Viṣṇu from whom it derives its being. Thus according to Śrīvaiṣṇava interpretation, this is the essential message to be derived from the entire Vedic tradition and summarized in *oṃ*. It is needless to add that this is only the very beginning of the exegesis; in fact the whole theology of Rāmānuja could be read into, or derived from, this one syllable.

The similarities between this and the mythical method of explanation are apparent, but so are, I think, the differences. In the present case, it is not a given system of mythical symbols and the mere logic of a story-plot that are utilized. Empirically available matters of a much more abstract nature are resorted to: the Sanskrit alphabet, the Sāṃkhya teaching, actual texts that use the words *a* and *u*. Let us call it here the 'correlational' mode. Moreover, we may note the particular emphasis here on the need for rationality, even in the case of emotionally highly loaded and doctrinally fixed material.

Like the mythical mode of making sense (think of the Third Reich or the Oedipus complex), this correlational mode is not unknown to us. Much of political rhetoric or advertising derives its convincing appeal from such means. More serious is its occurrence in the field of academia. For instance, many pronouncements made in the social sciences belong to this category. One of my favourite examples of such pseudo-scientific correlationism concerns itself with the striking image of the Hindu goddess Kālī. Blood-dripping tongue sticking out, hands holding a sharp knife, sword and human head, neck adorned with a necklace of little skulls, black body hardly covered in a tiger skin, and standing on the corpse of a man, she would seem to be a haven of Freudian symbols. Accordingly the image has been interpreted as the expression of male fear of the female personified as mother. The blood-thirsty mother demands surrender of one's manhood and feasts on the blood of the murdered father; if one eats the meat offered to the goddess one consumes the father's penis, the symbol of virility. This is then 'explained' by correlating the image to such Indian social conventions connected with one's mother as seclusion during menstruation and late child-weaning.[6] I call this 'pseudo-scientific', because it is totally unfalsifiable (or verifiable). Moreover, important points are ignored in such correlational constructions. This image of Kālī is merely one among hundreds of iconographic types that evolved in Hinduism (and this drastically reduces its significance for a global description of 'Hindu culture'). Secondly, non-Hindus share in the social customs referred to above; yet no statue of a blood-thirsty, castration-demanding Virgin Mary is known to me from any Indian church. Indeed science works with correlations of the kind 'if ... then' to describe and to predict. But the conclusion to be drawn from the present example is obvious: not each and every correlation is meaningful – makes sense or satisfies a more critical mind – however 'convincing' or 'charming' they may strike the less critical. Such correlations only work in a wider, systematic framework of investigation.

One may wonder at the success of this correlational approach in Western writings on India (which may present itself, for instance, under the title of 'structuralism' or 'psychoanalysis'). Part of the explanation must lie in the fact that it is felt to be 'convincing', because it expresses itself in often very charming, readable and attractive books. But probing further we can point at a still fashionable mystique associated with things Indian that sets the standard for what is attractive or convincing. Such a mystique expresses itself in a mythical view of the world in which man has not yet compartmentalized himself, is still aware of the cosmos as a whole, with all its interrelated aspects, and plunges himself through the illusory surface of the world into the ultimate essence of the universe. Naturally the advocates of such a romantic picture ignore the material discussed in the previous chapter, with its sometimes very cynical and pessimistic view (and exploitation) of the weaknesses in human nature, just as they will ignore any 'rational' component of Indian 'myths'. But it is more serious when these blinkers distort the perception of the Indian struggle to interpret the world rationally, systematically, and (quasi-) scientifically – in short, when they distort the way we deal with Indian philosophy.

This is a big subject, and all I can hope to do in the limited space available is to draw attention to what strike me as interesting trends and tensions. But even such a humble aim is not self-apparent. It is not just the romantics who have postulated the total coherence and homogeneity of the Indian tradition (so that every facet can be correlated with any other), thus rejecting the idea of both inner tensions and historicity. Only superficially can the reason for such misunderstandings be identified as the native concept of the six orthodox *darśanas* (with Buddhism and Jainism listed as the two heterodox ones). This list indeed pretends, or at least has been assumed to imply, that the Hindus have at their disposal six different and alternative systems of making sense of the world, which nevertheless all deal with roughly the same raw material. By talking of 'alternatives' and 'same raw material', inner tensions and fundamental differences are covered up, and by speaking of 'systems', all historicity is denied.

But deeper than such problems connected with our heuristic concepts lies another problem. Inadvertently, a significant trend in scholarship got caught up in a circular argument. Attracted to the 'mystical' side of India, that is what it studied, and inevitably its whole view of India became determined by this selective choice. But then it was inferred that mysticism lies at the heart of the Indian modes of making sense of the world. To put it plainly: what I shall be suggesting in the following pages is that India developed a very strong 'empirical', or at least non-mystical, culture of analysing the world (which I shall call the analytical traditions), and that mystical trends could only with great difficulty be integrated into this enterprise.

Already in the previous chapter we encountered a considerable amount of analytical acumen at work in the area of exploring the mechanics of human behaviour and attitudes. A very critical, detailed and differentiated view of human nature was developed under the different headings of '*artha*', '*nīti*', '*vairāgya*' and '*dhūrta*' (the rogue). Essential factors in a given situation are intuitively perceived and manipulated. But naturally, the scope remains limited, and the moments of insight remain isolated. No overall systematic framework is provided for the essentially anecdotal approach. But there are other traditions which developed far more sophisticated methods and expanded their compass to the whole universe with all its galaxies, its heavens and wonderful beings.

Long before we hear anything about mystical experiences, we find the ancient Indians busy trying to understand the world of ordinary experience. The Vedic hymns, and then the Brāhmaṇas, and even many a passage in the early Upaniṣads, allow us, perhaps more than any other documents from other contemporary societies, to look into the minds of people who are in the process of becoming conscious of the world and themselves. Things are noticed and reflected upon which we take totally for granted – for instance, that predictable regularities exist in the world: after the cold of winter will follow the heat of summer. Thus the world reveals itself as an ordered affair, a cosmos. But what is interesting here is the fact that the reason for this order is not located in some divine being. Although the earliest layers of Vedic literature show a considerable preoccupation with beings called *devas*, no such *deva* figure emerges – for a long time to come – as the creator of the world or the one who has instituted and still maintains its regularly recurring events. Instead, when the perceived cosmic rhythm and its laws are conceptualized, it is through an abstract concept (*ṛta*, then *dharma*). Moreover, the *devas* cease to be of great interest. Instead, sacrificial acts are now at the centre of attention, because through these man can not just produce replicas of cosmic events, but can draw also on their inherent power for his own purposes. What is even more fascinating to observe here, more than the decline of the *devas*, is the fact that the literature itself, which expressed such ideas, came to function as 'revelation' in some traditions of a much later period.

Anyway, let me introduce the subject of the analytical traditions by turning to a concrete passage illustrating in a very concise, though somewhat archaic, manner, typical features of this mode of making sense of the world. This passage comes from an ancient account of the origin of the world which is found in one of the oldest Upaniṣads, the *Chāndogya*. 'In the beginning, this [universe] was nothing but being. It thought: "May I become manifold, may I evolve." It emitted heat. That heat thought: "May I become manifold, may I evolve." It emitted water. That water thought: "May I become manifold, may I evolve." It emitted food.'[7] What is the logic behind this puzzling evolutionary sequence? We might be tempted to use our own imagination to make sense of it, thinking of expressions like 'being hot and bothered' which correlates some inner mental state of agitation with the generation of heat. But there is no need for this, since the passage itself adds its own reasoning and empirical 'proof'. The transition from heat to water is explained: 'whenever a person feels pain or sweats, water is generated from that heat'.[8] And of the third transition, from water to food, it says 'whenever it rains, abundant food is brought about'.[9]

Thus, already at this stage, some form of critical reasoning is at work. But the text wants to do more than merely tell us about the first four evolutionary steps of the universe. What it suggests here is a reduction of the totality of human experience to three fundamental principles or elements: heat, water and food. That these are understood as abstract categories becomes clear from the sequel. There we hear that 'being' decided to enter into these three principles with its own self, make each of them threefold, and generate the concrete forms and names of things. This means that each concrete building block of reality possesses – in unequal amounts, we must infer – portions of the three abstract principles. 'That which in fire has a red appearance is the appearance of heat; what white, that of water; what black, that of food. [Thereby] fire ceases to be "fire" which exists [merely] as a word; it is a concretization [of being, in conjunction with heat, etc.] and name. In reality, there are [merely] the three principles.'[10] The same is repeated for the sun, the moon and the lightning; but to make the system complete, one ought also to apply this analysis to a variety of liquid and solid substances.

Anyway, the intention and method are clear: the external world is reduced to a set of primary components which, in various combinations and permutations, make up the concrete objects. But our text does not stop here, for does not man also belong to reality? Thus we hear: 'Food that has been eaten develops in a threefold manner: what is its coarsest component becomes faeces, its medium, flesh, and its most subtle, intelligence.'[11] This is continued for water, with which the breath of life is correlated, and heat (interpreted by the commentators as heated oil, ghee, etc.), which is the substance of speech. And, in order to realize the logic of these correlations empirically, the disciple to whom this teaching is given is told not to eat for fifteen days – at the end of which period his mind has become a total blank. Had he not drunk for some days, we may add, his very breath of life would have left him.

Finally, the analysis is extended to basic human experiences such as sleeping, feeling hungry and thirsty, and dying. The first occurs when the intellect (or conscious mind) comes to rest in the breath of life to which it is tied. Hunger arises when water has absorbed food; thirst, when heat has removed water. Finally death is the last stage of this evolutionary reversal, when heat too is reabsorbed into being, when concrete form and name cease to exist.

In our present discussion we can ignore further aspects of the passage, to return to them at a later stage. What we have looked at illustrates very clearly to what extent rational, systematic thought endeavours to achieve a complete and coherent description of man and the world, and how from a few abstract, primary principles the enormously complex and variegated world of our experience is reconstructed. Moreover, time and again this construction is justified by reference to empirical data.

After this concrete early example, a brief sketch may convey some idea of typical later developments in the analytical tradition. Thus from a very early date (possibly as early as the beginning of the last millennium BC) we find certain people taking a great interest in the structure of the external world, often guided by very practical motives, namely to manipulate it. From this emerged the concept of a space–time–matter continuum. Objects occur in specific places, and have to move physically from one spot to another. They do not remain constant, but change in the course of time. As far as matter is concerned, from early on this is analysed further in terms of four or five basic substances (the idea of a tripartite principle, heat–water–food, never became popular). Out of the combination of various such 'elements', in various quantities, the whole range of observable physical objects is developed. The list includes the standard four: earth, water, fire and wind, with a possible fifth, ether.

However, it was clear that the world consisted of more than just the space–time–matter continuum. Various physical objects showed features that made them very different from such things as rocks. Man was the most obvious one among them: he and, to some extent, animals are in a strange way in contact with the outside world. From this area of reflection, we obtain another stereotyped list: that of the five senses: sight, hearing, taste, smell and touch. Secondly, man and animals constantly absorb physical substances from their environment (eating and drinking), which allow them to function actively while also gradually transforming them (baby to grown-up person, etc.) Moreover, their bodies reveal considerable healing skills, closing smaller wounds on their own account. But above all, man can speak, think and communicate with others about his feelings and thoughts. The early literature I mentioned is particularly fascinating on this point. For we can still witness the intellectual struggles involved in formulating a concept that could describe all these features. 'Speech' is frequently suggested, or 'breath'. An abstract idea of 'fire' is particularly favoured in some texts. The advantages of such a 'fire' concept are numerous: to be alive means bodily warmth; to digest food is similar to cooking; like a torch in the dark of night, the inner fire illuminates the world and allows us to perceive it; put your fingers into your ears, and you can hear a crackling noise. However, eventually, concepts like '*jīva*' (and in some quarters, '*ātman*') emerged to denote all these aspects observed in man and in other living organisms.

All this may not strike students brought up on Einstein as very exciting stuff. But it is sufficient as the basic raw material to produce a system that explains the universe. Space, time, the elements, *jīvas*, and the interaction between *jīva* and body, and between the senses and external objects – this is all that is needed to accommodate the basic facts of human existence in an explanation of the world. And, indeed, this remains the essential structure of much, if not most, of later and more developed Indian thought.

I would like now to illustrate by some examples how these analytical traditions developed further sophistication. Already at an early date, the concept of the 'elements' was felt to be too imprecise. The idea of the 'atom' is introduced – and it has been a hairy academic question whether or not this is historically connected with the Greek concept and, if so, who learnt it from whom. The inconclusive evidence we have would, ever so slightly, suggest that the Indians knew it before the Greeks. Matter is thus cut up into invisibly small particles which, in aggregates of very large numbers, make up physical objects. The idea of the elements is redefined, and atoms of basically four or five different types are assumed. It was tempting to regard the *jīva* too as atomic in nature, but not everybody saw this as useful. Thus, as an alternative, the *jīva* was regarded as of flexible size, determined by the size of the body in which it dwelled.

Perhaps not immediately obvious is the link between this problem and another area of discussion. This concerns, initially at least, the relationship between an object and its attributes. The most archaic view – still preserved in the Sāṃkhya system – cannot quite conceptualize this. It speaks of qualities (*guṇas*) which nevertheless carry the connotation of 'components', in other words, something still substantial or quasi-physical. The idea of the categories raised the discussion to a much higher level of sophistication. The world of phenomena is now divided into various types of the 'real'. Substances become a different sort of thing when compared with their qualities or attributes, and their relationship – the inherence of the latter in the former – in turn is another different kind of reality. So is action. Not only did this innovation allow for a view of reality in which not everything that is real could be lined up like different chairs on one floor. It also allowed for a more advanced discussion of the relationship between the body and the *jīva*. Note that, for example, the Jainas regarded 'action', which generates *karma*, as a form of material substance.

One further point may be made in this context. Already, in the conception of the various categories, or levels, of reality, can be seen the influence of a more critical look at language: substance, qualities and action can be correlated without difficulty to noun, adjective and verb. But it is in this area that the analytical thought of ancient India really excelled. This is not the place to spell it out in detail, but it is easy to show that in more than one way language has influenced the way Indian thought, 'secular' and 'religious', has looked at the world and made sense of it. By the fourth century BC, grammarians had succeeded in establishing a purely formal system of describing the Sanskrit language. By that date, it had ceased to be a spoken, living language. In the manner of breaking down the infinite variety of words to their basic components (roots and morphemes), of distinguishing different types of words (nouns, verbs, etc.), and of isolating the general laws operating on the combination of roots and morphemes – in all this we can, I think, recognize the scientific principle. But more than that. Though India cannot pride itself in having built the first computers, it can claim to have produced the first computer software, almost two and a half millennia ago. I am speaking here of the way that this formalized grammar is actually presented. In four thousand lines (called *sūtras*) of symbolic, formulaic language, variables are defined, functions spelled out, and subroutines inserted. And, moving slowly from the first to the last line, somewhat meandering because of the many 'go to's', subroutines and 'returns', the human brain at the end of it has been programmed to generate any Sanskrit word and any Sanskrit sentence. Man thereby becomes capable of creating a universe, if only of words. No wonder then that Sanskrit, and the Vedas as the literature written in it, were sometimes absolutized, transcendentalized, and conceptualized as the essence of the universe, and words were regarded as the archetypes of material objects.

However, the ingenuity, not just of analysis, but also of organizing its results, was not lost on other analytical traditions. Thus, generally, anybody who tried to explain the world, or a more humble subject like making love, at least tried to present the subject matter in this *sūtra* form (to write it up like computer software). However, like any more complex computer program, this concise and formalized exposition is comprehensible only to the original programmer/thinker. Unless he explains it, by writing in a generous amount of rem(ark)s, *sūtras* are extremely troublesome affairs. The frequent absence of original explanations and commentaries implies, for the historian of Indian thought, an enormous amount of guesswork and uncertainties; for the Indian thinkers it meant enormous latitude of interpretation.

Let me conclude this general survey of the analytical enterprise with another concrete example to illustrate its sophistication and complexity from a period of greatest creativity and liveliness. The example is taken from the school of the Vaiśeṣika in which atomism, the categories, and particular theories of causality and of the laws of mechanics are combined to make up a grand systematic interpretation of the universe.

> Movement is on the whole caused by pushing or hitting, which may have an immediate or a mediate effect. When an object is made to move through pushing [or hitting], it acquires a momentum that lets the movement continue. Either this momentum gradually decreases, or the movement comes to an end, when it encounters resistance, in other words when the moving body hits another object. In the latter case, a reverse push may occur, when the momentum is directed in the opposite direction.[12]

The whole passage is pervaded by technical terms in Sanskrit, each carefully further defined. In isolation it obviously makes little sense, but as a building block in a general theory of mechanics it gains central importance. To what extent this acquires even further relevance in the Vaiśeṣika may be illustrated from one application.

> When one pounds rice in a mortar with a pestle, in order to remove the husks, the following takes place. Under the influence of the soul, a movement is caused in the hand. This movement of the hand is communicated to the pestle held in it and lifts it as high as one wishes. A further impact of the soul causes the falling down of the hand and of the pestle, while a momentum is brought about in the latter. When the pestle hits the bottom of the mortar, this impact

together with the momentum inherent in the pestle cause a movement of the pestle in the opposite direction which also the hand follows. In this instance neither the movement of the hand is caused by the influence of the soul nor the movement of the pestle by the hand; instead, both are brought about through the impact alone.[13]

Here now the relevance of such an analysis is revealed: by ruthlessly expanding its theory of mechanics, of which this treatment of motion is part, to include even the activities of the soul, the Vaiśeṣika lays the basis for its own specific teaching on *karma*. And this brings us to the question of what all this has to do with religion.

In a sense, there is no intrinsic connection at all. Thus the earlier Vaiśeṣika (as reconstructed by Frauwallner) was very likely an intentionally mechanistic system that tried to explain the world of human experience without recourse to 'ultimate' and non-empirical matters. Yet this stark realism became modified (mollified) and covered up by later developments in the tradition that began to pay lip service to religious matters. A Buddhist nevertheless confessed that he would prefer to be reborn as a jackal than to achieve liberation *à la* Vaiśeṣika.[14]

Other teachings were far less subtle and thus much more easily detectable. Unfortunately, the extremes of their position gave rise to such animosity that they did not survive in institutionally formulated expression – if ever they existed in that form. Bits and pieces of *sūtras*, ascribed to them, have come down to us only in the writings of their opponents. And when the best known among these schools is called Lokāyata, 'the worldly system', one could ask whether this is not just what ordinary persons in the world actually believe in, but elevated to the status of a *sūtra*-tradition to allow for respectable abolition. Whether or not we are dealing here with 'professional' and institutionalized philosophy, the ideas mentioned are interesting, because they symbolize the minimal boundary of the Indian mainstream. This was the fence that marked off the area which in any, even the most minimal, sense had to do with religion. It is a rather different affair when a modern Indian Marxist writer (Debiprasad Chattopadhyaya) explores, under the heading of 'Lokāyata', ancient Indian materialism as the 'religion' or philosophy of the masses.[15]

Anyway, one of the famous maxims (which at least in English allows for a nice pun) attributed to the Lokāyatas says: 'earth, water, fire and air are the realities that make up the universe. Spirit derives from them, like the power to intoxicate derives from yeast, etc.'[16] Thus, basically, spirit or mind is regarded as an epiphenomenon of matter, and the existence of a *jīva* as separate entity (*tattva*) denied. By implication, transmigration, as a retributory process for one's actions, and liberation are also denied.

Clearly, even a minimalist religious philosophy like early Jainism depends on the acceptance of a *jīva* as an autonomous, eternal, essentially pure and perfect entity. And it is the Jains who have argued this particular case intensively. Some reference may be made to this, because it will allow us at the same time to meet with something rarely mentioned in the literature of India: the scientific experiment.

The old Jain scriptures know of a king Paesi (who is also known to the Buddhists as Pāyāsi), a ruthless tyrant very much in the image of the *Arthaśāstra*. But, unlike most dictators, he is actually interested in the truth. He has carried out a series of scientific experiments (previously alluded to)[17] in pursuit of this evasive entity, and as a result he is now a staunch materialist. A famous medieval Jain story reports very similar deeds and convictions about a police inspector. I shall follow this version, as it is less well known.[18] The policeman is an untouchable and carries the significant name Caṇḍakarmā, 'Vicious Brute'. One day he meets a Jain monk and asks him what the purpose of all his *tapas* could be. 'Body and soul are one and the same thing,' he tells him, 'there is no separate *jīva*.' And he gives empirical proof: 'Some time back, I threw a robber into a big vessel, put the lid on it and made it completely airtight with lacquer. The fellow died, but I did not see any *jīva* escape.' The Jain monk counters by suggesting that when a man is blowing a conch inside such a cauldron, no sound could be seen leaving it, and yet everyone would hear it. But the policeman has made other experiments, like weighing a criminal before and after executing him and observing no change in his weight, and cutting up another into tiny pieces, without discovering anything called a soul in the corpse. No difference in weight could be detected, were one to put a bag on a scale, regardless of whether it is full of air or empty, replies the monk. And were one to cut up a stick into the smallest bits, one would still discover no fire. It is this last point that floors the policeman, who consequently turns Jain monk.

There must be many reasons why India did not develop the sciences in our sense of the word. It is clear that without scientific experiment, speculation on the nature of the universe and on the natural laws operating in it has to end in a cul-de-sac. And this little story may well throw some light on one or two aspects connected with the latter point. Note the characterization of the experimenter: he is an untouchable and a man of vicious qualities. To carry out his experiments, he has to kill and pollute himself by cutting up corpses. No self-respecting academic, particularly not a purity-conscious brahmin, would dream of doing such things. Moreover, the experimenter is a materialist, totally opposed to any religious ideas. Yet common sense, without resorting to any violence, can disprove his views easily. And behind this lies also the problem of social distance. The people speculating on matters of physics and cosmology would have very little contact with the peasants, artisans, craftsmen and doctors who might well have taught them a thing or two.

Before exploring how in India the proto-scientific and analytical modes of making sense of the world were made use of for the formulation of religious ideas, it is appropriate first to look at a view put forward by a Western scientist nearly a century ago. In a *Letter On the Religions of the British Empire*, addressed to the governing body of the University of Oxford in 1907, Henry Wilde expresses his hope that:

> As from reeking decomposition and frost-bound winter spring forth forms of beauty that ravish the senses, so from the corruption of Eastern creeds [which in the context means all historical religions] will arise a religion worthy of modern civilization, so will its truly learned and devout ministers, casting aside the debasing superstitions inherited from their ignorant forefathers, breathe into the peoples of the earth the living intelligence which brought them into existence.[19]

Sketched out in a few daring strokes is the underlying assumption that the traditional religions are but primitive anticipations, foreshadowings on an evolutionary scale, of the potentials the natural sciences are now in the process of exploring. Science is the fulfilment of religion, not its replacement. It means that science does the job better than religion: miracles were sporadic and random occurrences among primitive people of phenomena that science now offers on a global scale. It also means that science comes closer to an understanding of the religious dimension in the universe. Thus Mr Wilde censures his atheistic colleagues who fail to recognize, for instance behind 'natural selection', the workings of a 'purposive intelligence in the universe'.[20] He correlates the crude incipient scientific explorations of the Greeks to monotheism with its 'animistic and anthropomorphic concept of the creative intelligence' and, at the top of his scale, the modern sciences of his day with pantheism (*inter alia* Brahmanism and the thought of Spinoza) where an 'all-pervading intelligence' is identified 'with the attributes and modes of the infinite substance of the universe itself'.[21] Reality itself consists of six basic categories. Five of these bear striking similarity to the categories known to the analytical Indian traditions: space, time, matter, rest and motion. The sixth is 'substance', a rather nebulous category which carries the religious onus of his whole system.[22] Thus matter is defined as the 'mutable qualities or forms inherent in substance, as the radiant garment of Divine Substance'.[23] Science and what Mr Wilde calls 'natural religion', and advocates as the religion of modernity, are thus united in the one purpose of recognizing the purposive intelligence at work in the universe. Such an abstract and scientific religion will liberate the conventional systems of belief from the 'enslavement of human understanding' and from 'persistent intolerance and persecutions [of the scientific mind]'.[24] On the practical side, Mr Wilde endowed a lectureship, towards the furtherance of his ideals, hoping 'to bring about some kind of unity in the heterogeneous religious elements of the Empire'.[25]

The Jains were not concerned with running an empire that contained many different religions with a 'hostile attitude towards each other'.[26] Yet in their own way they wanted, like Mr Wilde, to demythologize religion on the basis of a (quasi-) scientific view of the world. It is probably accurate to say that Jainism represents the earliest attempt of drawing on this analytical material for the sake of expressing religious beliefs. Religious in this case means: the belief in transmigration and thus in the retribution for one's deeds, and in the soul's essential nature beyond the limitations of space, time and matter. The way early Jainism expresses this shows immediately how initial and archaic the conception still is. The centre of man is his *jīva*, which is not just surrounded or encased by the body, but constitutes together with it one functional unity. Naturally, this psychosomatic entity is involved in all kinds of activities, in thought, word and deed. Thereby very fine, invisible matter called *karma* ('action') enters into the *jīva*. This *karma* not only interferes in various ways with what the *jīva* by itself could do, but it also makes it heavy, literally keeps it down in the universe and generates another body around it after death. Thus the *jīva* by itself is immortal; moreover, if the *karma*-determined psychosomatic unity were broken up, the *jīva* could recover its pure nature and leave the world of change and material imprisonment behind. The fire of *tapas* is the means to achieve this, and literally it may well be a fire, lit during the heat of summer and, like all other kinds of physical pain, capable of burning up *karma*. Slowly the *jīva* can thus extricate itself from all material constraints, from *karma* and from the weight that keeps it down. When all *karma* is burnt up, weightless it ascends to the highest point in the universe, where space, time and matter have ceased to influence it and its innate qualities of infinite bliss, etc. are realized.

It is not difficult to see in this conception the strong influence of early realist and, we could even say, 'literalist' ideas. And, indeed, Jainism maintained its close connection with the analytical tradition during the subsequent centuries when these ideas were given a more systematic expression. There exist five primary categories of the real (*asti-kāyas*); 'time' as a possible sixth created certain conceptual problems. These are space, motion (called strangely '*dharma*') and rest (*adharma*), souls (*jīva*) and matter; they are all eternal. Space is infinite and thus contains within itself the world in which the remaining four, plus time, are found. Matter is atomic in nature, each atom occupying one single point in space. Atoms, by combining into aggregates, make up all physical bodies. When the latter get pervaded by a soul, we are dealing with a living being; when the soul gets disentangled from its material involvement, we obtain liberation. It should be clear from this brief sketch that the religious content of such a system is minimal. It depends primarily on the teaching of the individual soul's eternity and potential non-material autonomy, along with its implications of the workings of *karma* and of *tapas*.

It cannot be my task to trace all further expressions of the analytical tradition and survey all other attempts to graft religious ideas on to it. Instead, I would like to explore some general trends and some crucial problem areas. This can be organized around two or three central ideas: the absence of empirical research, the challenge of self-authenticating religious experiences, and (less centrally than we might expect) the role of revelation.

The analytical enterprise approaches the world from a realistic angle, uses reason, common sense and empirical proof for its explanations, breaks reality down to a number of primary principles, establishes laws that govern the interaction of these principles, and aims at an exhaustive and coherent description of the world or one of its aspects. But, as we know from our own cultural history, to pursue this further than the level of the immediately obvious requires measurements and quantification and, above all, scientific experiments. This did not happen in traditional India, and the schools of thought involved in the enterprise developed instead an increasingly dry, lifeless and purely speculative scholasticism. This must be regarded as one of the reasons why society at large lost interest in it and switched its loyalties to other cultural matters – namely, religion. It is probably not an exaggeration to identify certain developments within the institutionalized pursuit of the analytical enterprise as reactions to such changing fashions and waning popularity. For instance, the Vaiśeṣika begins to include the workings of *karma* in its system, under the significant name of the 'unseen' (*adṛṣṭa*) – an extraordinary concept in a system that set out to be thoroughly realistic and empirical.[27] The Nyāya, which originally shared with the Vaiśeṣika its non-religious cosmology, begins to argue in favour of a creator-god and, in fact, thereby provided later theistic systems with stereotyped arguments for the existence of God.[28]

Religious concerns may blur the outlines of what many an analytical system in India originally, or during its earlier phases, was aiming at. But that does not mean that the general attitude and rational approach simply evaporated in Indian culture. The following pages will demonstrate time and again the enormous influence these had on the whole development of religious thought. Moreover, our knowledge of the cultural history of India is so imperfect that we cannot actually identify cause and effect in what I have referred to as changing fashions. All we can really do is to acknowledge that from a certain time onwards Indian society began to take increasingly seriously the pronouncements of a different group of people – the 'mystics' (that is, the renouncers) with their claims of self-authenticating religious experiences – and that these people, or their followers, themselves became involved in the formulation of systematic, rational accounts of their religion. 'Revelation' need not be mentioned as an independent factor, because as far as we are concerned here the concept applies merely to one set of textual pronouncements (the Upaniṣads) by one group of mystics.

Let us return to the passage, from one of the Upaniṣads, on the origin and the functioning of the world, which I discussed partially above. First of all, nothing has so far been said about the central category, 'being'. From the verses of the *Chāndogya-Upaniṣad* quoted above it is clear that it is the ground from which the three primary principles, and then the whole world of forms and names, arises; that it is capable of some kind of consciousness, intentionality and action; and that it is the final resting place for the person after death. It is not difficult to see the affinity of such a concept with Mr Wilde's category of 'substance', the 'purposive intelligence' operating in the universe. Although in his *Letter* he does not refer explicitly to the Upaniṣads, the supreme position he allocates in his schema to 'Brahmanism' makes it fairly certain that this is his source of inspiration. The passage continues but, were we to read it in isolation, even the verses left undiscussed would add nothing new. Here they are, nevertheless, in the form of a conversation between spiritual teacher and disciple.

> 'Fetch me a fruit from that banyan tree.'
> 'Here it is, sir.'
> 'Split it.'
> 'It has been split, sir.'
> 'What do you see inside?'
> 'These seeds [small] like atoms, sir.'
> 'Now break up one of them.'
> 'It has been split, sir.'
> 'What do you see inside?'
> 'Nothing, sir.'
>
> Then he spoke to him: 'From this atomic entity, which you cannot see, this mighty banyan tree grows. That which is its atomic essence, is the essence of this entire universe. It is the [ultimately] real. It is the "self" (*ātman*). It is you.'[29]

Thus, like the banyan tree, man possesses some inner, invisible essence. He is not a conglomerate of a variety of interacting and delimiting factors, but an organically developed complex manifestation of one, central force. This is called *ātman* or 'self' here, in so far as it centralizes the individual and the universe.

But this text was not read in isolation. It figured alongside many other texts of similar or comparable content in the Upaniṣads, and inevitably the reading of all this material systematized and rendered the disparate ideas more homogeneous. Crucially the abstract 'being' was not left alone and became equated with the (ideologically much more coloured) concept of '*brahman*', found in other innumerable Upaniṣadic passages.

The implications of all this are tremendous. On seemingly empirical grounds (the organic growth of a tree out of an atomically small seed-essence), the totality of the real is derived from one ultimate principle. Both mind and matter, body and soul, are seen as essentially identical with the one, *brahman*. Moreover, and this is where the 'ideological colouring' comes in which interferes even further with the empirical principle of the analytical traditions, the knowledge of this ultimate reality is accessible only through a socially carefully controlled and filtered 'revelation'. However, this construction provided, at the same time, a fertile blueprint for certain forms of self-authenticating religious experiences to construct a systematic account of their enterprise. Given that man's *ātman* was seen here as essentially one with *brahman*, mystics could say that what they experienced was precisely this oneness. That they were, in turn, challenged by other mystics on the grounds of a logic derived from the analytical traditions, and that in the course of time logical flaws in this construction were recognized even system-internally from a similar analytical perspective, makes the study of these developments all the more exciting.

Within the confines of the present chapter, none of this can be dealt with. Instead, let us content ourselves with more manageable implications. These have to do with the enormous usefulness of the concept of *brahman* that was found in the development of system-internal religious ideas. By this I mean the following. As academic disciplines, taught by father to son, and to outsiders for money, analytical traditions of a more limited scope, dealing with special aspects of reality, continued over centuries in a relatively undisturbed manner. Inevitably, they developed not only an aura of primordial antiquity and their own mythologies and legends, but also self-reflections on their significance and meaning. Why should one study over many years, for instance, grammar? This was a question a father had to answer his son, and a teacher society at large. Perhaps inevitably, the direction these self-reflections tended to take was to conceptualize one's discipline as a self-fulfilling exercise. This yielded a cluster of minor religions which we ought to add to our typological catalogue. Thus grammar – and naturally that means Sanskrit grammar

– could be envisaged as the medium through which man could not only encompass the world, but also reach the transcendental and undifferentiated language-archetype, *śabda-brahman*, the underlying essence not just of language, but of the world. Similarly, the execution of the complicated Vedic rituals became regarded as a self-fulfilling act – a mode by which man could transcend the limitations of the world and become one with the source of the Vedas themselves. *Dharma* offered a third possibility: by faithfully obeying all the minute rules laid down in the *Dharma-śāstras* and discussed by the relevant academics, man would find his fulfilment. And even music appears in this context, allowing for the realization of the *nāda-brahman*, the 'note-absolute'.[30] Some of this self-fulfilling transcendentalization was spelled out in great detail in fully-fledged systems like the Mīmāṃsā; some of it can be isolated only from vague suggestions and implicit assumptions. But all four disciplines (and more could be mentioned) are in origin and in intention analytical: social behaviour, grammar, ritual and music; all have enjoyed considerable attention by the intellectuals who have explored their minutest details; and when their cultivation is transcendentalized, we may find no reference to such well-known religious themes as God or 'mysticism'. Instead, their subject matter is presented as a model or blueprint of reality, which is generated from some transcendental source. An ultimate and fulfilling union with this source can be achieved by analytically plunging into its concrete manifestations (language, music, etc.). Wisdom, as an analytical enterprise, experiences itself here as self-fulfilling human activity. Yet how could the exuberance of a grammarian compare with the claims of a mystic? If *brahman*, 'purposive intelligence', inhered in the universe, the mystic's testimony may well be pointing in the direction of an all-pervasive, cosmic mind.

CHAPTER 20

The all-pervasive mind

This self (*ātman*) within my heart is smaller than a grain of rice or of barley or a mustard seed, than a grain of millet or a kernel within a grain of millet. This my self within the heart is greater than the earth, greater than space, greater than the sky, greater than these worlds.

This self within my heart is this *brahman*. 'Passing away from here I shall enter into it' – he who has this conviction will suffer no anxiety.[1]

It is clear that an Upaniṣadic passage such as this does not merely want to make a theoretical point (e.g. that the *ātman* is essentially identical with the *brahman*). Its author desires to express what I have called a 'self-authenticating experience'. Beyond all rational analysis, the experience carries its own validity, 'conviction'. The world is made sense of not by means of mythical images, correlational constructions, or quasi-scientific analysis, but through a different mode. Let us call it, temporarily, 'mystical'.

But what do we mean by 'mystical'? Within the Christian tradition, the word appears to refer to experiences which are granted to a few select and saintly individuals and which simply happen to them. Not so in ancient India. There such experiences are understood to lie within the potential of every human being, provided he knows how to go about it. Let us first look at a passage in which the continuity with other forms of experiencing the world is suggested. 'The self (*ātman*) must be looked at, must be heard about, must be thought about, must be contemplated.'[2] Here a scale of increasingly abstract modes of perception is established, which culminates in 'contemplation' or 'meditation'. The following passage highlights the fundamental difference of the meditationally gained experience itself from all other types of knowledge.

As long as there is anything resembling a differentiation, one smells something external to oneself, sees, hears, speaks about something external to oneself, thinks about and perceives something external to oneself.

But when all of that has become the self (*ātman*), with what could one smell, see, hear, speak about what; with what could one think about what; with what could one perceive what?

With what could one perceive that with which this whole universe is perceived? With what could one perceive the perceiver?[3]

Thus a type of knowledge, and it is indeed called 'wisdom' (*prajñā*), is suggested which transcends the division of perceiving subject and perceived objects: perceiver and perceived have become one, have melted down into the one solid mass of the experience of the self. And we are given a metaphor for this extraordinary wisdom, a metaphor not just for the transcendence of subject and object, but also for its extraordinary blissfulness.

Like a man, who is enveloped in sexual embrace by a woman he loves, is not aware of anything at all that is outside or inside, in the same way he, once he has merged with the self that is wisdom, knows nothing at all of what is outside or inside. That now is his form in which his [external] desires are fulfilled, his passions are his *ātman*, his cravings cease, and in which all unhappiness has come to an end.[4]

Such claims do not simply want to add 'wisdom' (*prajñā*) to a list of modes of making sense of the world. They express an exuberance, an enthusiasm, an overabundance of happiness. To achieve this kind of wisdom does not just tell you something about the world and about human destiny in it: it affects that destiny itself in the most fundamental and exhilarating manner. What kind of defence could the dry analytical enterprise put up against this? Yet the following observations will demonstrate how also in India reason and rationality survived; in fact, how strong its influences remained in Indian culture. But it is worth reminding ourselves that here fundamental decisions were taken culturally which resulted in a picture that is very different from what we are familiar with. Let us assume that we exposed Mr (or Ms) Average on our own streets to the kind of ideas put forward by the exponents of 'wisdom' (*prajñā*), but with all traces of their Indian mystique carefully removed. Personally, I could imagine the following reactions. If our Mr Average were inclined to be polite, he might say that such rarefied mystical experiences may be wonderful and terribly fascinating. But in his heart he is likely to categorize them together with having a good drink and then to discard them as ontologically invalid events. Less politely, he may even compare them to the weird experiences and paranoias reported by people who take speed and ecstasy, uppers and downers, Benzedrines and amphetamines, hash and ganja, pot and crack, or whatever else is pushed on to the market by aggressive salesmen. Yet in India these self-authenticating experiences generated such a strong conviction, that their advocates fought hard to establish a central place for them in Indian culture. However, this fight had to take the form of constructing a meaningful and comprehensive account of what the relevance and effects of such experiences could be.

Before turning to a few interesting details of such accounts, we ought to look at some practical matters. For, besides reporting on wonderful experiences, our mystics also established concrete methods for achieving them. These are the meditational exercises mentioned above. When I refer to them by the well-known term of '*yoga*' for the sake of convenience and simplicity, I may be blurring certain historical and doctrinal differences; but given the structural similarities of early Buddhist accounts of meditation with what follows, this may not be too grave an offence.

We possess a very famous *sūtra*-text, which by its very title suggests that the system spelled out in it wants to be a systematic account of *yoga*. These are the *Yoga-sūtras* attributed to Patañjali. Here we find the classical account of *yoga* exercises. That this should be organized in the form of eight limbs or steps, that the Buddha presented his spiritual programme as the noble eightfold path, and that both paths culminate in *samādhi* is probably no coincidence. One might even venture the claim that the *Yoga-sūtras* adopted it from the Buddha.

The first two steps are of a general ethical and moral nature: to stop doing certain bad things, such as killing people, lying and stealing, and to cultivate positive virtues such as inner contentment. We need not go into the details here, but it is worth keeping in mind that whatever mystical experiences may result from the whole enterprise, they are carefully contained within this moral and ethical framework, which naturally is also maintained during the subsequent stages. This created some misunderstanding during the swinging sixties, when certain criminal 'mystics' like Charles Manson made claims to the effect that they were beyond good and evil. In turn, they were taken rather seriously by writers like Zaehner,[5] who perhaps did not fully realize the implications for a moral constraint on mysticism of these two nitial stages of *yoga.*

Now the actual exercises begin, and the first one concerns *āsana*, posture. This is a theme where the uninformed Westerner is highly prejudiced: innumerable cartoons have depicted the *yogī* seated on his bed of nails, and film makers have dwelt on strange contortions of the limbs or on long stretches of colon emerging from the *yogī*'s anus for cleansing purposes. As far as I am aware, these are late medieval developments. The classical account simply refers to choosing a quiet, pleasant place and a comfortable, relaxed bodily posture. Then a new rhythm is imposed on one's breathing – which, as we all know, affects the way we feel and think. 'Take a deep breath!' is the advice we give people, to put them into a calm mood before surprising them with some shocking news. Withdrawal of the senses follows which, in my understanding, means to use and intensify the filtering mechanisms that we all carry in us. Normally we only see, hear, or feel what is relevant in a given situation and cut out sense data (like the noise of the traffic on the road outside) which are superfluous. This has the effect of making it possible for the mind, now undisturbed by external sense-data, to start collecting itself. It can focus on its objects for increasingly long periods, and thereby penetrate deeper and deeper into their essence. Eventually, the object fills the mind totally – the mind penetrates and pervades it completely. Like a man in the embrace of a woman, subject and object merge into one. This culminates in *samādhi*, the grand and blissful experience of 'gathering together'.

Perhaps imperceptively, our account has reached the point at which a qualitative leap is required. Naturally we want to ask what this *samādhi* is, but any answer to that question will jump from practicalities to metaphysics. As an experience it may be 'self-authenticating', but its significance requires authentication and that means it must resort to rational thought. Let us remind ourselves[6] of the *yogī* who tried to use *yoga* to translate Tamil poetry into English, showing us that *samādhi* does not, in itself, reveal the unknown. Similarly, a man at the moment of sexual climax does not learn thereby to conceptualize 'involuntary muscular spasms' or 'psychosomatic responses'. If any cultural impact of *samādhi* was desired (and the mystics felt strongly impelled to achieve this), it had to be discussed, at least initially, with the discursive tools available in that culture.

The details of this discussion, as it evolved in India, are enormously complex; the scale of suggestions put forward is very wide indeed. All that I can hope to achieve here is to convey some general impressions and mention some typical or interesting examples. As the focus for this I suggest two central problems, the place and the effect of the *samādhi* experience. What precisely is it, within the complex inner structure of man, upon which the meditational exercises work and which they sharpen and perfect? Closely related, though not necessarily identical with this question is another one: where should we locate the *samādhi* experience itself? The second problem seems to be quite distinct. What precisely does the *samādhi* experience achieve, over and above the feeling of intense joy and total freedom? To say that it achieves liberation from all the constraints of *saṃsāra*, of the cycle of rebirth, merely shifts the problem to the question of how this is achieved. However, in practice we find that statements about the results of *samādhi* are linked intrinsically with those on its location. Thus there will be no need for us to deal with the two questions separately.

It would be logical for us to consult Patañjali's *Yoga-sūtras* on how the place and effect of *samādhi* are interpreted. For these *sūtras* cover a far wider ground than merely that of practical meditation exercises; they are the summary of a fully-fledged metaphysical system. But, unfortunately, no ancient commentaries on the *sūtras* that unravel for us their cryptic, formulaic language have survived. Thus, instead of losing ourselves in vague speculations, we can turn to another system, the Sāṃkhya – a philosophical school tradition that has, in fact, also produced the commentaries on the *Yoga-sūtras* that we do have.

According to the Sāṃkhya, the totality of the real falls into two primary categories, matter and souls. Closely resembling (and probably historically derived from) Upaniṣadic passages is the definition of matter (called *prakṛti*). In its abstract, undifferentiated and unmanifest form it is one; everything that is regarded as 'material' in the universe is thus derived from one ultimate principle. An analytical element is nevertheless introduced into this speculative construction by postulating that *prakṛti* itself has three aspects; these are called 'qualities' (*guṇas*), but are in archaic manner envisaged as 'components'. *Prakṛti* evolves into increasingly solid and physical manifestations, which include the five elements (that also make up man's body) and the five sense organs. But also included here are the mind, a person's sense of identity, and *buddhi.* This *buddhi* is frequently translated as 'intellect', but we would do better to describe it as something like 'consciousness', which is only accidentally connected with a sense of 'I'. Thus, rather surprisingly, practically the whole of man's physical and psychological make-up is derived from the material principle. This is, I think, an expression of the analytical spirit that treats man as a psychosomatic unit. But it is not an expression of materialism. For in addition to *prakṛti*, the Sāṃkhya assumes an infinite number of souls (called *puruṣa*), eternal, essentially free and blissful, but accidentally caught up in *saṃsāra*, and thus in the limitations imposed upon it by the 'body' (everything that derives from *prakṛti*).

How does meditation work? Its exercises gradually reduce, and eventually eliminate, the disturbing influences upon the mind of the external world, which are caused through the senses. Mistaken notions about one's identity are removed, and the *buddhi* is developed to its full perceptive faculties. These can be projected upon the nature of *prakṛti* and the soul, and their fundamental difference is revealed. Thereby *prakṛti* loses her hold over 'man' (*puruṣa*), retreats, and the *puruṣa* becomes free from all material constraints, to enjoy his eternity and ultimate bliss.

This is an extraordinarily roundabout construction. Liberating insight and mystical experience are split up by locating them respectively in the *buddhi* and in the *puruṣa.* We can only speculate as to the motives for this. Some may well derive from problems connected with explaining the effect of liberating insight (which we shall turn to presently). To a certain extent, though, we may detect the work of the analytical spirit, having resisted the location of rationally paraphraseable insights ('essential difference between matter and soul') in a purely hypothetical entity (the *puruṣa*) that, unlike the *buddhi,* lay outside its own empirical parameters.

If anything, the situation in Buddhism is even more complicated. At the heart of early Buddhism lies a self-authenticating experience, the Buddha's meditationally gained 'enlightenment'. From it Buddhists derive certain central contents of Indian belief: the fact of transmigration, the law of retribution for one's deeds, and the possibility of overcoming or transcending the suffering that characterizes existence on earth. But early Buddhism denies the usefulness of placing such ideas within a systematic and comprehensive metaphysical framework. Yet that makes it only seemingly 'irrational'. Even if we knew nothing about the existence of the analytical traditions in ancient India, we could not fail to detect a very rational and 'empiricist' note in early Buddhist teaching. This in turn would suggest to what extent contemporary society demanded and relied on these characteristics in a given religious exposition. The degree to which even a self-proclaimed anti-metaphysician like the Buddha rationalized aspects of his teaching contrasts very sharply with the credulity of modern *guru*-seekers. For what is presented to us under the heading of the Four Noble Truths contains complex and far-reaching analyses of human nature, human existence and the spiritual progress towards *nirvāṇa.* A lot that is found here is clearly intended as empirically verifiable insight, like the impermanence of human pleasures, the inevitable outcome of craving in suffering, and the primary responsibility of the senses in stimulating that craving. In fact, the emphasis on a realist and mechanistic analysis of empirical man is so strong that it could be, and indeed has been, mistaken for nihilism, if taken out of context.

I am not actually thinking here of Western interpretations of Buddhism. We do not have to go that far to find attempts at presenting the Buddha's teaching in a systematic manner which move precariously close to nihilism. These are, perhaps rather surprisingly, Buddhist-internal, and by no means the fabrication of inimical Hindus or Jains. I am referring to the Abhidharma, or more precisely, to some Abhidharmas, or to some interpretations of it. It is a subject notorious for its complexity and abstruseness, but some facts are clear and beyond dispute. One or two centuries after the Buddha's life, in certain quarters of the Buddhist community the temptation to systematize the Buddha's teaching in some form was felt to be irresistible. Initially, this may well have been for reasons the Buddha himself would not necessarily have objected to: to teach novices what Buddhism is all about, or to provide detailed outlines to incipient meditators of what they ought to meditate about. Given the empiricist stance the Buddha himself seems to have taken, it was quite natural that for such purposes the analytical traditions were resorted to.

But in these traditions ideas were encountered which went directly against fundamental Buddhist beliefs – so that it became necessary to demonstrate how Buddhism differed from them. Thus we end up with treatises that offer us a systematic, and typically Buddhist, analysis of the world. What is interesting to us in the present context is the fact that the empirical, analytical, or realist traditions were so influential that in some cases they appear to have smothered the mystical content of early Buddhism altogether.

In the world of our experience, nothing lasting can be identified. This applies to *saṃsāra* as much as to the person itself. Nothing but processes are at work here: man constantly receives through his senses data from the outside world, he constantly reacts to them emotionally and mentally, and constantly thoughts flash through his mind that construct such non-empirical notions as that of a 'self' or of some inner, immutable core or 'essence'. Given this fundamental Buddhist emphasis on transience, concepts typical even of the analytical traditions were unacceptable, like the eternity of both matter and individual souls. This had to be rejected as 'essentialist', purely hypothetical thought.

The concept of the 'atom' of other schools appears in the Abhidharma as the '*dharma*' (not to be confused with the Dharma, the Buddha's teaching, nor the Hindu *dharma*, the universal rhythm built into the cosmos, nor the Jain *dharma*, the principle of motion). '*Dharma*' here denotes the smallest bit into which reality can be cut up, and of which there are many different kinds. As far as matter is concerned, it is first differentiated into the traditional elements and then reduced to atomic bits. These are the innumerable earth-*dharmas*, water-*dharmas*, etc. But the Abhidharma generalizes this: the other aspects of man (his emotions, acts of will, thoughts, etc.) are similarly cut up into atomic particles, and thus further kinds of *dharmas* (like *dharmas* of the emotion 'pleasure') are listed. But in the other analytical traditions, this atomism was connected with the assumption that such minute particles by themselves were eternal and autonomous entities. This went totally against the Buddhist teaching of transience. Thus, instead, the Abhidharma resorted to the most radical alternative available: it defined each and every *dharma* as lasting merely one single moment. For thought-*dharmas*, this made immediate sense. But what about material *dharmas*? Our Buddhist systematizers did not shrink from the consequences. What appears as solid matter, they say, is actually no more than an aggregate of innumerable material *dharmas* which are replaced every moment by similar ones.

Another ancient Buddhist concept, conditioned origination, is applied to this in a generalized manner. Here now it means – and I shall not try to summarize what this notoriously difficult concept may have meant in the earliest teaching – that the particular constellation of *dharmas* that make up a person at any given moment is conditioned by the one of the previous moment, and in turn conditions that of the following moment. That means, this conditioning accounts for continuity in time. But there is at least one *dharma* which is not conditioned: *nirvāṇa*. (Others may be space, or the truth of the Buddhist teaching itself.) To be conditioned thus defines the realm of *saṃsāra*. And again, the earliest teaching could be applied here: it is due to desires and ignorance that these transient and conditioned processes are triggered off which make up the continuity of coursing through *saṃsāra*. Naturally also 'desire' and 'ignorance', the *āsravas*, are cut down to the level of *dharmas*: they are the 'glue' that connects one momentary constellation to the next.

This ruthless type of analysis that the Abhidharma pursues is certainly impressive and fascinating, and without difficulty we can see here the analytical method and view of the world at work. But the Abhidharma is running down a steep hill, and not all representatives of this enterprise managed to stop their downward momentum before crashing down the vertical sides of a quarry. The critical boundary, where the sloping line suddenly turns into a vertical one, is obviously reached when it comes to deciding what to do with the one unconditioned *dharma* of *nirvāṇa*. Often the momentum of the movement down the hill could be used to fly off at that critical boundary into the realm that 'is not made and has not become,'[7] that is 'unfathomable and unchartable like the ocean',[8] that can be experienced, but not described in terms of categories like 'is', 'is not', etc. This is the *nirvāṇa* mentioned in the early scriptures and which still appears in later, less ruthlessly analytical, writings (like those of Buddhaghosa in Ceylon).[9] But others on the mainland of India, like Vasubandhu in his *Abhidharmakoṣa*, appear not to have succeeded in this kind of lift-off. By defining the *dharma nirvāṇa* as that factor which cancels out desire- and ignorance-*dharmas*, these Abhidharma traditions exhaust the role of *nirvāṇa* in putting an end to *saṃsāra* – to the continuity in time of *dharma*-aggregates. *Nirvāṇa* has been reduced to the status of a mathematical constant which subtracts the *āsrava* variables from *dharma*-sequences. Some last wild waving of the arms can be observed in the claim that 'all is real' (*sarvāsti*), even the past and what lies beyond the present, which the Sarvāstivāda made; but with the Sautrāntika the bottom is reached: *nirvāṇa* is shattered to pieces as literally 'nothing'. A fatal price to pay for systematic consistency and for adhering to strictly realist principles! By refusing to locate the transcendental experience, which the Buddha may have had and advocated, within a realist system, these Buddhist traditions end up with a minimal religious content. They may be able to explain the workings of the liberating insight which bring *saṃsāra* to an end, but they have also put an end to any kind of understanding of 'enlightenment' as a transcendental, self-authenticating experience of highest bliss and total freedom. All this is a bit like the attempt to explain the 'thrill running down one's spine' (for instance, when listening to an exciting piece of music) or 'raucous laughter' (at a splendid joke) by analysing muscle movements and nerve energies.

The Upaniṣads offered a seemingly much easier and more promising blueprint. As we have seen at the beginning of this chapter, they do not hesitate to locate the grand liberating and exhilarating experience in the *ātman*, the innermost self and centre of the individual person, and then to interpret it as the realization of *brahman*, the innermost centre of the universe. Meditationally to purify the *ātman* means to remove the accidental walls that cut it off from what it fully is. Throw a bottle into a lake and let it sink down, filling itself with the lake's water. Cause the glass to disappear – what sense would it then make to distinguish, and refer with different words to, the water of the lake and the water that had previously been contained in the bottle?

But the material presented in the Upaniṣads is on the whole unsystematic, random, intuitive and extremely diverse. It took almost a thousand years – a fact hardly ever mentioned or emphasized in most books on Indian thought – before any known attempt was made to put the teaching of the earlier Upaniṣads together in some kind of systematic account. These are the *Brahma-* or *Vedānta-sūtras* attributed to Bādarāyaṇa. We can only speculate on why it should have taken such a long time. The overwhelming dominance of the analytical traditions in India was bound to counteract attempts to build a system around Upaniṣadic thinking. The radical Buddhist critique of such non-empirical and unverifiable constructions as that of an *ātman* and a *brahman* could not easily be overcome. When the documentation of such system-building derived from the Upaniṣads becomes available, we can still recognize the struggle and the joints where disparate aspects of *brahman* are linked together.

The concept of '*brahman*' was not new to the Upaniṣads, unlike their teaching about transmigration, liberation and meditation. Texts that are possibly hundreds of years older search, in primarily mythical manner, for the one original reality out of which the world evolved. Initially the imagination of the poets suggested a whole host of different concepts and symbols (like Speech, Primordial Man, Cosmic Pillar, Golden Germ) besides *brahman*. But it was the latter term alone that eventually established itself as standard. There may well have been ideological factors at work in this, for '*brahman*' was a loaded term. It was associated with the idea of a special sacred power which was particularly located in the *brāhmaṇas*, 'brahmins', who knew the Vedas and utilized them to render efficacious the sacrifices performed by them. To conceptualize now the very centre of the universe, from which everything evolved, as '*brahman*', inevitably elevated the status of the brahmins themselves and added to the elitism of the religious system managed by them. This is clearly an important factor in the Buddhist (and Jaina) critique of the concept. But the Upaniṣads inherited and accepted it. They tell us that *brahman* is like the spider that emits the web from within itself, or like the fire that sends out sparks. *Brahman* is like the solid substance gold, and the world is like the many golden objects: ear-rings, wedding-rings, vessels and statues. This means that, causally and materially, *brahman* is the basis of the universe which, as all these images suggest, is thoroughly real. Bādarāyaṇa in his *Brahma-sūtras* begins, logically, with cosmology and immediately identifies *brahman* as that 'due to which the evolution etc. [namely, existence and eventual dissolution] of this [universe occur]'.[10] Although this is another *sūtra*-text without ancient commentary, there are ample indications in the following *sūtras* of a realistic interpretation of this evolution and of this universe. *Brahman* is the material cause of the world.

What entered into the Upaniṣads as a novel idea, that of meditationally achieved transcendental experiences, was integrated, as we have seen above, into the older conception of reality by first locating this experience in man's self, and by then identifying this (individual) *ātman* with the (cosmic) *brahman*. All liberated souls or *ātmans* lose their separateness and individuality in an undifferentiated, single whole. This is envisaged like the flowing of different rivers into the same ocean, thereby losing their distinct names, or like the pollen of many flowers fusing to make the one honey. Superficially, this looks just like the reverse of what was said about *brahman* earlier. But a more critical look reveals that it is not at all the same sort of thing. The world, with all its physical and mental aspects, which evolved out of *brahman*, is a real world, realistically perceived. To say now that the *ātman* can realize a state of being which lies outside the real world and its space, time and matter continuum, and that this state is actually the one core of reality, means to talk about something very different. When both the source of the universe and its innermost, transcendental core are called *brahman*, the concept *brahman* is once again expanded far beyond its previous connotations. The concept is made to do a lot of work, and one might once again suspect that it is ideological work. For, by connecting the liberating and self-authenticating experience with *brahman*, a potentially fatal challenge to the Vedic tradition is avoided. Instead of being latent in everybody, liberation is only possible via the Vedic tradition, for it alone teaches about *brahman* and decides who ought to be taught about it. Whilst the Buddhists and Jains had no time for that kind of convoluted argument, Bādarāyaṇa builds all this into his system. Already in the fourth *sūtra*, he states that *brahman* can only be known from the Vedas. But it is the contrast between *brahman* as material cause of the world and as meditationally accessible transcendence which we have to keep in mind. As far as we can tell, it is left unresolved in Bādarāyaṇa.

This particular contrast is, I think, part of a much wider problem which we can initially envisage as the contrast between action and contemplation. The real world, of the kind looked at by the analytical traditions, is fundamentally a world of action; one has actually to do something about one's liberation. Thus Jainism, on the whole, has retained the archaic *tapas* as its liberating method. Concrete things are done to the soul (like exposing oneself to excruciating pain and hunger), and it is merely as a side-product of such actions that the *jīva* develops complete perception and knowledge. But when we turn to other traditions in which meditation is the method, the emphasis shifts from action to 'knowledge'. In the case of ancient Buddhism, this shift did not immediately give rise to conceptual problems. On the surface, 'suffering' could be analysed as the result of actions performed out of 'desire', the motive behind it. But desire itself could be derived from 'ignorance', a misconception of the nature not just of the desired object, but also of one's own self. This allowed for a mediate connection between meditation (which removes the ignorance) and achieving something in the real world (eradicating suffering). Note, however, how little is retained here of the exuberance of the Buddha's experience of 'enlightenment'. Such exuberance is certainly expressed by the Upaniṣads and the Vedānta that purports to summarize their teachings. *Jñānān mokṣaḥ*,'liberation on account of knowledge',[11] is propagated here as the grand ideal, and *jñāna*, 'knowledge', is definitely more than, and something different from, any paraphraseable knowledge with objective content. It is the realization of *brahman*.

Before exploring this grand programme further, we may want to recollect what we heard about the Sāṃkhya. There we found a paraphraseable knowledge (the fundamental difference between *prakṛti* and *puruṣa*) located in the *buddhi*, itself a manifestation of *prakṛti*, which achieves the liberation of *puruṣa* from *saṃsāra*. So far I have interpreted this convoluted construction as illustrating generally the dilemma caused by combining analytical ideas with those derived from meditation. But there is also a specific problem involved in this. The real world of the analytical traditions is a world of processes, of action. But action generates *karma* and thus perpetuates *saṃsāra*. The Sāṃkhya's *buddhi* acts – if only by analysing, reflecting and realizing. Thus it cannot play a part in the grand achievement of liberation which is attributed to the *puruṣa*, a totally passive entity. Yet in some sense, at least, *puruṣa* must be responsible for his liberation – there is the axiom of free will which the Indian traditions accept unequivocally. A causal link has to be established between achieving something and not doing anything. The following metaphor is supposed to illustrate it.

Imagine a stage, an audience of men, and a dancing girl. The men do nothing; they are sitting there passively and allow the girl to entertain them. As long as the girl perceives that the men are enthralled by her performance, she keeps on dancing. But then comes a point at which the men lose interest, and the girl stops her dance and withdraws behind the curtain. The only really active factor in this scenario is the girl; she corresponds to *prakṛti*, matter. Yet she is affected in her actions by the men – the *puruṣas* –who nevertheless remain passive. The loss of interest perceived by *prakṛti* is transformed into *prakṛti*'s action of withdrawal, which is synonymous with liberation. Free from the enticements of the dancing girl *prakṛti*, the *puruṣa*-men can become free and independent.[12] It is not difficult to see how contrived such a simile is. Clearly it is difficult to conceive of a type of perception or insight, untarnished by *karma*, which is capable of affecting reality without getting involved in any *karma*-generating action!

Nevertheless, the idea of 'liberation due to knowledge' gained enormous popularity in Indian religious discourse. Even Jainism was drawn into this new approach. Thus the Digambara philosopher Kundakunda adopted the idea that it was not some physical action like *tapas* that could give rise to liberation, but the overcoming of ignorance.[13] And based on his suggestions we find medieval Jain texts in the popular Apabhraṃśa language that call themselves unabashedly *Yoga-sāra*, 'The Essence of Yoga', or *Paramātma-prakāśa*, 'The Shining Forth of the Highest *Ātman*'.[14] Neither '*yoga*' nor '*ātman*' are terms known in ancient Jainism.

We could summarize the problems created by the meditational mode of experiencing man and the world, when it comes in contact with the analytical mode, by simply speaking of the contrast between the psychological and the ontological. We can imagine Mr Average telling us that he has heard of people on drugs thinking that they could fly who, jumping out of a window, broke their necks on the pavement far below. I do not think that we can solve the problem. All we can do is recognize the fundamental conviction expressed here that meditationally gained experiences have the power to affect man's physical being, by putting an end to rebirth. But there is something else we can do, and that is to turn now to radically different ways of making sense of the world in the light of the meditationally achieved experiences. Here now the whole approach is turned upside down: instead of presenting the significance of one's experiences within a given, or only partially modified, analytical framework, why not generate one's own coherent system of explanation out of the experience itself? If mind can affect the world, why not postulate that the world itself is fundamentally a 'mental' phenomenon? Why not live up to one's convictions and recreate, not the world itself, but the views held about it. Why not bring out the full implications of an 'all-pervasive mind'?

Some initial thoughts on this puzzling subject can be picked up from the nocturnal streets of Buenos Aires. The Argentinian writer Jorge Luis Borges is well known for his interest in Buddhist ideas. Thus it comes as no surprise to find him wondering, at the beginning of his poem 'Daybreak' (*amanecer*), about the practical consequences 'if things are devoid of substance'. Of similar Buddhist flavour is a second supposition: 'and if the populous city of Buenos Aires / like an army in its complexity, / is no more than a dream'. It might remind us of the folk-song's 'life is but a dream'; however, for Borges, Calderón de la Barca's drama *La vida es sueño* ('Life is a dream') seems a more immediate source of inspiration. On the Buddhist side, we hear time and again that the external world is 'like a mock show, dew drops, or a bubble, a dream, a lightning flash'.[15] Like the Indian thinkers, Borges is aware that the metaphor cannot imply an individual 'dreaming' – each person dreaming his own individual world. Thus he explains: '[a dream that is] produced by many souls in common alchemy'. Thus the city and its life is a communally created entity which requires for its continued existence all the dreams it can get. By this (poetic) logic, 'there is a moment / when its existence is in particular danger / and this is the tremulous moment of dawn'. It is the 'hour in which the persistent dream of life / is in danger of breaking'. Fair enough, we may comment: if life is a dream, the hour of daybreak must symbolize its end, since waking up puts a stop to our dreaming; but what a trite elaboration of the simile! Yet Borges shows, as he himself unpacks the comparison, that more is meant. He characterizes the 'moment of dawn' as the time 'when sleep breaks down the activities of thought' and speaks of the 'dream of life' being 'reduced' at that hour 'to the narrow channel of a few souls still thinking'. This means that, by a nice poetic touch, the metaphorical 'dream' is made to signify its opposite in real life, 'thought'. Thought, communal thinking, is the real cause of the world. We think the objects of our experience which therefore lack substance and independent autonomy. Thus, precisely because they have not succumbed to dream and sleep, Borges can say of 'only a few night-strollers' that they 'preserve / the ashen and vaguely outlined / vision of the streets'; they are the 'few souls still thinking'.[16] Known for 'his habitual nightwandering through the suburbs of Buenos Aires',[17] Borges poetically alludes to ideas which are as puzzling in the context of Western realism as their Indian source of inspiration must have been to anyone brought up in the analytical tradition.

Given the abstract nature of much of the Indian material, it is useful to begin our consideration of the 'cosmic mind' with something concrete, in fact, rather solid and material. This is a relic of the Buddha's body left after the cremation, like a bit of bone or tooth. Lay-Buddhists, particularly, cherished such relics with great love and devotion; they built architectural structures (the *stūpas*) to accommodate them. Incidentally, from the casket with a relic on top of such a *stūpa* we get the word pagoda. This is a Burmese distortion of Sinhalese *dagoba*, which derives from Sanskrit *dhātu-garbha*, the relic casket. Still talking very much about ordinary earthly things, *dhātu-garbha* could also be paraphrased as 'a womb-like container for a bit of the Buddha left after his *parinirvāṇa*'. Now the construction of *stūpas*, the veneration of the *dhātu-garbha*, and the rituals and institutions connected with all this certainly developed in ancient India on a large scale. It may well be possible to speak here of a second milieu[18] in which Buddhism expressed itself as a religion – the first one being obviously the monastery. But it must have been predominantly a lay-Buddhists' affair. For it would be difficult to imagine that monks, engrossed in the pursuit of their Abhidharma analysis and forbidden from participating in this merry-making around the *stūpas*, cared much for what was happening in that milieu. We have, in fact, questions to that effect recorded in the scriptures: what is the use of making all that fuss about a merely physical remnant of a being who has totally passed away from this world and is thus beyond all human access? When this question is countered by another question: 'but then how is the Buddha available to us?' the answer was: 'in his teaching'. Thus the Dharma is that one aspect of the Buddha which is still amongst us. That is his, metaphorically speaking, relic worthy of veneration, his 'body' (*kāya*) which even now pervades the world. And that body is like a diamond: radiant and immutable. It is the indestructable *Dharma-kāya*.[19]

None of this would be very sensational, were it only meant in the metaphorical sense indicated so far. However, it has been suggested that this second Buddhist social milieu was one of the hothouses in which Mahāyāna ideas were developed. More speculative is the suggestion that at least one such Mahāyāna *sūtra* originated in a particular *stūpa* milieu, that of Āndhra in South India. This is the *sūtra* of the noble queen Śrīmālā[20] who, in front of the Buddha and very much with his approval, teaches about the *Garbha* and the *Dharma-kāya*, but in a very different sense indeed. Perhaps I ought to mention that *sūtra* here has nothing to do with our systematic formulae that are so concise as to be incomprehensible without commentary. Mahāyāna *sūtras* are sometimes very long scriptures indeed – the longest one identical in size to the *Mahābhārata*, the world's longest epic. They may present all kinds of other problems, but it is not a problem of too few words!

Whatever the value of these sociological and historical speculations may be, what is certain is that we have a whole range of Mahāyāna *sūtras* that discuss, or centre around, a particular set of ideas.[21] Unfortunately none of them have been preserved in the original Sanskrit, and thus one has to rely on translations from the Tibetan or Chinese translations. The *Āryā-Śrīmālā-sūtra* is best known among these texts, and the only one (re)translated into English. The central concept in the queen's teaching is that of the *Tathāgata-garbha*. The first part of the word creates no problem: it is a synonym of 'Buddha'. But the second member of the compound is more difficult: does it still mean 'womb' or 'container', or is its other meaning of 'seed', or 'germ', used punningly here? But the real problem lies in what is said about this *Tathāgata-garbha*. For we are told that it is the one reality in the universe which can be described as 'eternal' (*nitya*), 'true bliss' (*sukha*), 'existing as an autonomous and unconditioned reality' (*ātman*) and 'splendid' or 'self-luminous' (*śubha*). In case we are still in any doubt as to what this entity could be, the queen identifies it for us with the *Dharma-kāya*.[22] We have clearly moved a long way away from the original meaning of the terms. If it is indeed true that the *stūpa* cult was the home of such ideas, we could say that here the institution responsible for it has reflected on its activities and has transcendentalized its concrete raw material. Traditional concepts are developed in a unique manner and, one sometimes gets the impression, conventional word meanings are imaginatively played with. Thereby *Dharma-kāya* and *Tathāgata-garbha* are made to denote here a transcendental reality which is identified with buddhahood in the abstract. In each of us rests the germ of this Buddhahood and, by purifying our minds, this is developed to its full potential: we become enlightened beings by literally merging into Buddhahood – into the Universal Mind.

These stunning ideas are not yet presented in a systematic manner in queen Śrīmālā's teaching. Similarly, nearly ten other *sūtras* spell out related ideas in an equally unsystematic fashion. It is Sāramati, who may have lived in the third century AD, who attempted to put all this material together in a coherent system. (The text is the *Ratnagotra-vibhāga*, and it is still available in Sanskrit.)[23] Very lavishly he quotes from all the *sūtras* that deal with the *Tathāgata-garbha*, but most of all from the *Śrīmālā-sūtra*. The point that interests us most in the present discussion is that Sāramati includes cosmology in his system.

It is an extraordinary kind of cosmology; until now we have heard nothing of the sort. Given that the *Tathāgata-garbha* is the one reality in the universe, this system does not hesitate to connect it also with the origin of, and the processes we observe in, the universe. Indeed there are the material aspects of reality, but they are derived, through stages of progressive abstraction, from Mind. On the grand scale, pure space generates consecutively air, fire, water and finally earth. In the case of the individual person, first mistaken ideas, then *karma* and mental impurities, and finally their solid result, the five *skandhas* (man's whole psychosomatic make-up) evolve, one by one, out of the innate germ of Buddhahood. Thus incorrect thought is the innermost layer of the film that individually and universally covers up the essentially pure *Tathāgata-garbha*. But these solidified clouds of ignorance contain within them *saṃsāra* and suffering. Knowledge is the means by which this film can be destroyed. Concrete physical reality can be affected by it, because this reality itself is nothing but mental impurity.[24]

Such ideas must have come as a great shock to many Buddhists at the time. To unify all liberating enlightenment experiences (and naturally all the Buddhas known in Buddhist traditions) in one grand cosmic Mind was daring enough. To describe it in terms of an '*ātman*' struck one of the most sensitive spots of Buddhist teaching generally. But to integrate it into a fully-fledged cosmological theory which, moreover, followed principles totally alien to the Abhidharma and the analytical traditions generally (by having mind generate matter as a nebulous, unsubstantial entity) was even less reconcilable with mainstream teaching. To the majority of Buddhists, even the Mahāyānists, this must have appeared, not like the Abhidharma's abortive crash at the bottom of the pit, but like Icarus who soared so high that the sun burnt his wings. All this meant that in this form the *Tathāgata-garbha* tradition could not assert itself, and it vanished from the scene.

But it did leave its mark on other Mahāyāna traditions, which for centuries afterwards attempted in their own ways to explain the world around the self-authenticating experiences of the mind. Clearly such a mind could not be 'individual'. For since ancient Buddhist days there was (apart from the fact that each of us appears to be talking about a very similar world) the fundamental doctrine that the empirical person does not contain an inner centre, a permanent substance. To this the Mahāyāna added a second important task: to realize that the external world and all its objects also lack an essence, an autonomous core. Thus, even if one had been tempted to locate the liberating experience in a transpersonal and discrete entity, all the factors that could have supported this discreteness itself were thereby eliminated.

Nevertheless, ideas encountered in Sāramati reappear and colour the understanding of materiality. In these later trends which I am sketching here, the emphasis shifts more and more to the 'mental' nature of all objects of our experience. But instead of assuming rather naively – as Śrīmālā and Sāramati had done – that matter was the most solid aspect of the *Tathāgata-garbha*'s impurities, a different line is taken. More careful analytical introspection suggested that we don't really ever get that far in our perception of the world. For our minds, in their impure states, are busy 'imagining', constructing mental images which we then project on to the outside world, and then read them back from there, as if they were objective facts. This kind of analysis led to the radical formulation that everything (at least as far as we are concerned) is essentially no more than a mental construction – *prajñapti-mātra*. Popular literature on Buddhism goes so far as to render this 'Mind-Only'.

What today is very rough country indeed – the North-West-Frontier Province of Pakistan which borders Afghanistan – must have been rather different during the fourth century AD. For here, in Peshavar, were born two brothers, Asaṅga and Vasubandhu, who are associated with the construction of the most complicated (and, some will argue, most sophisticated) system Mahāyāna Buddhism has produced. (The latter brother ought to be specified as 'the older', because it seems that the author of the *Abhidharmakoṣa*, also called Vasubandhu, who was mentioned previously, lived almost a century later.) One of the reasons why Asaṅga's and his brother's system is so complex is that they tried to incorporate the whole of the Abhidharma into it. But the *dharmas* here are no longer the smallest solid building blocks of the world; they have been reinterpreted as bits and pieces floating through our consciousness.

Instead of entering now into a discussion of the details of Asaṅga's and Vasubandhu's minute analysis of epistemological matters, it will suffice for our purposes to look at one central concept. This is the *ālaya-vijñāna*, normally translated as 'storehouse consciousness', which lies at the very basis of all mental processes. Pure and undefiled in its essential nature, it gets pervaded by special kinds of smells and fragrances – *vāsanās*, usually translated as 'karmic seeds'. Yet 'karmic smells' would emphasize far better the extent to which Asaṅga wants to avoid any material aspects of it. These heady perfumes work on the mind and make it start 'seeing things', we could say. This is the beginning of the process by which imaginary ideas of a perceiving subject and perceived objects housed in a real world are generated. Naturally, out of these mistaken notions and the attitudes derived from them further fragrances are released, which in turn affect the mind. Having talked about Icarus, we might once again resort to classical mythology and speak here of the Scylla. But there is also the Charybdis, which in Asaṅga's case represents the problem of avoiding the pitfalls of an unabashedly substantialist view of the pure mind. This he tries to achieve by postulating that even the *ālaya-vijñāna* ceases once full enlightenment has been achieved. The highest universal Mind that is left is so ethereal and lacking in an essence or self that nothing really can be said about it. Let us also note, for the time being, how little is actually left in this system of the external world. It has become like a dream, and is indeed compared to it. But, given that it is filled with *saṃsāra* and *duḥkha*, we might as well call it a nightmare.[25]

On the whole, these speculations are not reflected prominently in the Mahāyāna *sūtra* literature, or better, what has been studied of it. But there is at least one exception. In the unlikely setting of a court of ogres on the mythical island of Laṅkā, the *Laṅkāvatāra-sūtra*[26] presents us with the Buddha preaching an extraordinary hotchpotch of ideas. Without any recognizable system or order, bits and pieces of philosophy on the *ālaya-vijñāna*, the *Dharma-kāya* and the *Tathāgata-*

garbha are put together. (Śrīmālā is referred to by name.)[27] Suzuki is probably right when he suggests that we are dealing here with no more than lecture- and reading-notes of a monk who was interested in meditation. But what he jotted down in random fashion and left in a chaotic state acquired the status of a *sūtra*. In fact, the *Laṅkāvatāra-sūtra* was initially the only text that Chinese Ch'an Buddhism (better known in its Japanese expression as 'Zen') cared for.[28] Let us retain for future reference the fact that chaos may appear as the other side of the coin of systematization.

We have not yet exhausted our exploration of ways in which coherent systems were constructed around the concept of the all-pervasive mind. The structure of Sāramati's thought appears to possess a close affinity with ideas that we have encountered in the Upaniṣads. But no hard evidence has been discovered to suggest that we are dealing here with a line of direct, immediate historical influence. Thus instead of losing ourselves in empty speculation, we can turn to another and well-established line of influence, in the opposite direction. We observed previously that Bādarāyaṇa's systematization of Upaniṣadic thought had left the two aspects of *brahman*, as source of a real, material world and as transcendental experience, unresolved. It was now, during the sixth and seventh centuries in South India, that a much more coherent interpretation was brought to bear on the *sūtras*, above all by the famous Śaṅkara. The influence of ideas like the *Tathāgata-garbha*, *Dharma-kāya* and *ālaya-vijñāna* is unmistakable; in Śaṅkara's teacher's teacher, Gauḍapāda, Buddhist terminology is directly used. But Śaṅkara himself is more subtle (and presently we shall look at his motives). By carefully eliminating all terms of Buddhist association and replacing them with words hallowed by Upaniṣadic usage, he constructed a system that looked thoroughly 'orthodox' – Vedic and 'Hindu' – and yet followed very much along the lines of Śrīmālā, Sāramati and Asaṅga. Predictably, the Universal Mind is *brahman*, the only truly real, pure consciousness, and bliss. But no real world evolves out of it. *Avidyā*, 'ignorance' (for which we find later in the history of the Vedānta more commonly *māyā*, 'illusion'), like a film is superimposed on *brahman*, and the self-luminous consciousness, when projected through it, seemingly solidifies as the world with all its beings. The world appears real, like the snake seen on a beach in the evening (and we react to it in the same way that we run away from the snake). But in the light of knowledge and wisdom, as in the light of the next morning, we realize our mistake – the snake turns out to be merely a piece of rope. All this means that the 'mystical' side of the *brahman* concept is made here the overall interpretative principle, and is applied to the cosmological aspects of *brahman*. Thereby a logically coherent system is achieved.

Thus, in spite of a different terminology, the fundamental similarities with the teachings of queen Śrīmālā, Sāramati and also Asaṅga are apparent. But there is one fundamental difference. The *Tathāgata-garbha* is not only present in all of us, but all of us can realize it. All we have to do is become (Mahāyāna) Buddhists. Śaṅkara does not deny that *brahman* too is in all of us as our *ātmans*. But, he insists, it needs the Vedas – which is here the Upaniṣads – to provide us with the fundamental knowledge of, and access to, *brahman*.[29] Vedic and brahmin orthodoxy have once again been saved. The Vedānta, by which name Śaṅkara's system became universally but somewhat confusingly known (strictly speaking, 'Vedānta' denotes no more than the Upaniṣads), was not merely added to the list of philosophical school traditions. It succeeded in becoming the Hindu philosophy *per se*. Occasionally, opponents of Śaṅkara's thought tried to insult him by calling him a crypto-Buddhist; but there cannot be any doubt that, apart from marauding hordes of Muslims, the Vedānta was one of the most important causes of the disappearance of Buddhism from India.

Our Buddhist thinkers' systems developed within existing religious institutions. But in the case of Śaṅkara's Vedānta this may not have been so. Certainly according to legends, Śaṅkara personally set out on a grand tour to conquer, like a mighty emperor, the regions of India. Time and again he succeeded in defeating in debates opponents who challenged his Vedānta teaching. Moreover, the foundation of a variety of monastic traditions is attributed to him, as part of his 'conquest' of India. Certainly such traditions exist today; members can be recognized by their 'surnames', like Pūri, Bhārati, or Caitanya. Various Śaṅkarācāryas represent the central authority in these traditions. Whatever the historical facts may be, it is clear that the success story of the Vedānta as the dominant Hindu philosophy was not merely due to an individual formulating striking ideas and proclaiming them. We must not underestimate the impact of this network of powerful monastic institutions in which the grand theories were applied to the practical, meditational pursuit of *brahman* in society.

Thus ideas remain tied up with matters of this world. Meditationally gained experiences reject the world of the senses as disturbing and irrelevant; any attempt to make cultural sense of them brings it back into play. Ruthless analysis breaks man down to his atomic components, and yet it is as a person that he suffers and enjoys the poetry of being alive. Certainly, the world is not what it appears to be on the surface, whether looked at analytically or meditationally. But how can a balance be struck between these different approaches and their respective insights?

CHAPTER 21

Striking a balance

Once upon a time there ruled six kings over six different kingdoms in India. As fate would have it [which actually means here, as their *karma* was influencing events], they all came to know, in different ways, of a princess called Mallī, the daughter of the king of Mithilā. The chief queen of one of these six kings was performing the Snake Festival on such a lavish scale that the king boasted to one of his ministers that surely he had never seen anything like it anywhere else. Indeed I have, was the answer, at the birthday party of Mallī. Similarly the pride another king took in the grand Bathing Festival he had arranged for his daughter got dampened. A third king asked sea merchants about their adventures, and they told him not just about storms and ogres, foreign lands and dangers, but also about the extraordinary beauty of Mallī. The king of Kāśi heard about her beauty from goldsmiths who, because of their incompetence, had been banished by her father. A painter scheming revenge for his banishment from Mithilā (his skill – to infer the whole person from seeing merely a toe – had not been appreciated by Mallī's father, when he saw her painted in a compromising harem scene) showed her picture to a fifth king. A Śaivite nun, defeated by the Jaina Mallī in an argument over true religion, went and told the sixth king about her beauty. Each king fell passionately in love with the Mallī they had thus heard about and, notwithstanding the fact that their harems were well stocked, they sent messengers to Mithilā to ask for her hand in marriage. Mallī's father was not interested and, rather rudely, turned the request of each king down. War was declared and the six kings joined forces and invaded the kingdom of Mithilā. When there was little hope left of repelling the attackers, Mallī knew what to do.

A secret message was sent to each of the kings promising fulfilment of their demands and calling them into the palace. At twilight, they were taken into the inner part of the palace. They were given six magnificent rooms in a pavilion in the middle of a park. Each of the rooms overlooked a central chamber, the walls of which consisted of intricate lattice work. Through the holes of these walls they caught sight of what they thought was the real Mallī. Actually seeing the object of their desires, which had been kindled by verbal descriptions, made the flame of passion blaze up with full violence in their hearts. After what we may assume to have been a night spent by the kings in sleepless anticipation, Mallī herself appeared – all bathed and beautifully dressed up. She went to a golden statue which was an exact replica of her own form (and for which the kings had mistaken her the previous evening). From its head she pulled out a plug in the shape of a lotus and the whole building was filled with an unbearable stench. Then Mallī explained to the kings, who had their faces covered in their upper garments and their heads turned away, the nature of physical bodies and of the passions roused by them. As a result of all this, they succeeded in breaking through to a higher level of consciousness and in remembering their previous lives.

What was the mystery of the statue? Mallī had it installed in that pavilion (which was specially built for it) a long time ago. After every meal she dropped some bits of food through the opening at the top into its hollow inside. This is how she unravelled the metaphor: 'If bits of delicious food, thrown every day into this beautiful golden statue, produce such a foul transformation of matter, then what sort of transformation will there be for this material body [of mine] which [already now] secretes phlegm, vomit, bile, vaginal fluid, blood and pus, emits foul-smelling breath, and is filled with equally foul-smelling urine and stinking faeces, when it has actually decomposed? Therefore do not get attached to the sexual pleasures human [persons can offer], do not delight in them, do not covet them, do not get deluded by them, do not hold on to them!'[1]

But why did Mallī have the pavilion with the six rooms constructed? Had she anticipated the visit of the kings? Indeed she had, and for the following reason. A certain King Mahābala had six friends with whom he had been brought up and who were very close to him. When, after listening to the sermon of a Jaina monk, he decided to abdicate and take initiation, his friends did the same. They made a pact that they would take upon themselves the same kind of penances and would progress at the same rate. But then Mahābala cheated: he always fasted a bit more than the others. For this he was rewarded by obtaining the (potential) status of a *tīrthaṅkara*, but also punished by having to achieve it, in his next-but-one rebirth, as a woman! The seven friends died, were reborn in heaven, and descended once again into the human world: the former Mahābala as Mallī who, thanks to the extra portion of merit made previously, knew all about their former lives, and the six companions as the six kings. Thus it was a combination of Mallī's designs and the workings of *kamma* that brought about the events told above.

It is worth looking at some of the details in this design of Mallī. For it involves more than a metaphor used for preaching purposes. Initially, it is not difficult to recognize themes we have encountered previously. In a ruthlessly analytical manner, the human person is broken down to its components of blood and flesh, phlegm and pus, etc. The kings are reported to have gained an insight into the nature of things in the light of which the world of the senses fades away to nothingness, as it were. But let us look at the psychology behind it all. There is first a particular mental image that each king builds up merely on the basis of aurally received information; it is enough for them to react to this image with an ardent passion that does not hesitate to use violent plunder and war in order to achieve its objective. Then there is another image, the golden statue, now seen with their own eyes and, after the violence of battle, in a totally different atmosphere (the park, the beautiful pavilion, the calm of the beginning night). Although imperfectly perceived – merely through the holes in the lattice work and in the fading light of day – this image reinforces the reaction of desire and lust. But, at the moment of greatest tension, after the long build-up of day-dreaming, waiting for messengers to report back, going to war, looking at 'Mallī' literally within reach of their outstretched arms, and a sleepless night fantasizing, the mental image is broken apart. First there is the shock of seeing the real girl next to the statue, and then there is the infinitely greater shock caused by the rotten food. Suddenly it says 'click', latent memories are awakened in the kings, they see the world in a different light, and approach it with a new attitude. This is *vairāgya*, a total loss of attachment to the world of the senses, and it results in their becoming ascetics and achieving liberation.

The Jaina canonical text, in which the story of Mallī as told here is found, has a tendency to intellectualize. Thus it feels the need to spell out, by means of the words of Mallī, the 'significance' of the stench. Moreover, it resorts to scholasticism when explaining the effect all this had on the kings.

When those six kings heard that exposition of Mallī, due to the positive transformation [of their *karma*], auspicious application of mind, and the removal of karmic material obstructing it [namely, deeper knowledge] on account of the soul being cleansed of its defilements, memory of their past existences [and other forms of knowledge, like] discrimination, arose in them.[2]

A recourse like this to the complicated Jain theory of the workings of *karma* and its effect on the soul somewhat veils the psychological processes that the theory purports to explain. But hundreds of other Jaina stories allow us to bring these processes into focus without scholastic interference. Essential here is a particular constellation of usually starkly contrasting factors. This can be, as in our example, the striking contrast between the beautiful, 'golden' Mallī and the stench emanating from her statue. Or it could be, as in an even more impressive example,[3] the agony of death suffered by a goat whom a well-meaning son sacrifices for the well-being of his father – who happens to be reborn as that same goat. This triggers off the memory of past lives, according to these stories, but – what is more important – it also generates *vairāgya*.

Our story concludes by telling us that Mallī judged the time ripe to become a Jaina nun, and the six kings, due to their *vairāgya*, eventually became Jaina ascetics who, under the spiritual guidance of Mallī, achieved their liberation. Mallī herself fulfilled her destiny by becoming one of the twenty-four *tīrthaṅkaras* known in Jainism.

On the one hand, there are a number of familiar elements in this story. In the pus and phlegm we can recognize the analytical approach which breaks the material world and the person down to their smallest components. We can recognize in the *vairāgya* of the kings something of the meditational experiences that similarly reject the world of the senses. Now this in itself is interesting: to find here elements combined which we have so far encountered in contrast to each other. But on the other hand, there are also interesting new ideas. The stench of the rotten food may be used as an illustration of Mallī's nature. But it is not an 'essential' statement about her. If she were no more than decomposing matter, the kings would have gone away and simply occupied their minds with other things. Instead, through her guidance (as *tīrthaṅkara*) they obtain liberation. What is presented to us as a statement about the 'real' Mallī merely puts an end to the king's amorous designs on her. It changes their attitude, and both the beautiful Mallī and the stinking statue were required to do this. The liberation resulting from their asceticism required Mallī the *tīrthaṅkara*. All this can be identified as a new mode of making sense of the world which could be called 'attitudinal'. On the theoretical side we notice that a balance is struck between seeing into the sordid and worthless nature of the world of the phenomena with all its false beauty, and relating and reacting to it.

It could now be objected that we are extrapolating something general from material that is presented to us within very specific contexts of large-scale biographical developments of individual persons. This is true. As far as Jainism is concerned, it suggests no 'method' by which such an attitudinal mode could be cultivated. Individuals, over many lives, generate the kind of *karma* which eventually sets up a situation in which the 'sudden' insight can be triggered off. It is nevertheless possible to abstract certain features from this Jaina material and apply these to a wide variety of other materials. I suggest here three such features.

First, from the psychological trigger mechanism illustrated by the story one can derive the idea of the 'click phenomenon' – a variety of discrete elements joined in such a way that together they trigger off a sudden experience. Secondly, there is the feature of 'attitude', a practical way of making sense of the world and relating to it in the light of that sense. Thirdly, we can assume a reflective element, for Indian thinkers were not unaware of the theoretical issues underlying such an attitudinal approach, and brought their own rational analysis to bear on them. For our exploration this means that we have collected here three themes which we can trace in a great variety of materials. That this tracing will follow a meandering line is inevitable, given that such themes may occur both in conjunction with each other and in isolation. But let us turn from the Jainas to the Buddhists and see how they have attacked the problem of striking a balance.

Traditionally, this area of Buddhist culture has been regarded as one of the most difficult aspects of Indian thought. What look like very heavy boulders are rolled into our path: 'perfection of wisdom', 'emptiness', 'Nāgārjuna and his system'. Yet if I understand this material at all correctly, it is not really all that mysterious. I think the alleged difficulties lie in our misunderstanding concerning the nature of the material itself, in our confusion over the precise mode of making sense of the world to which it belongs. We all know what it is like to teach somebody to ride a bicycle. We also know what it would be like to write a thesis about the theory of riding a bicycle, or even about the theory underlying the teaching of how to ride a bicycle. In terms of this metaphor, our material is easily comprehensible, if we regard it as 'teaching to ride a bicycle', out of which arose, eventually, theories of riding it and teaching it. What we are dealing with are skills which are made possible through certain attitudes.

But this is not how the material has been looked at conventionally. Presented under the heading of 'Mahāyāna philosophy', inevitably it has been perceived as constituting, in terms of our metaphor, 'a theory of the world' or even 'a theory about our experience of the world'. Instead, what I am suggesting here is that, at least at the basis or beginning of this Mahāyāna thought, no such complications existed. But before I try to show what riding a bicycle and Buddhist spirituality may have in common, let me give some more factual information on the textual home of such ideas.

It all seems to have started with about forty, often very repetitive, stanzas in some sort of Prakrit.[4] That they must have been produced in some Mahāyāna milieu perhaps as early as the second or first century BC seems fairly certain. That it was in Southern India, in the Āndhra region, is rather more speculative. Who wrote them is naturally totally unknown. These core-stanzas suffered the common fate of other early Mahāyāna material: a large amount of secondary material was added, and then a more elaborate prose version in relatively proper Sanskrit was produced. By the second century AD, the prose text was translated into Chinese, as the *Perfection of Wisdom* (*Prajñā-pāramitā*) *sūtra*. More precisely (since somebody had the patience to count the number of syllables of the Sanskrit original) it became known as the version in eight thousand units (a unit here consists of thirty-two syllables).[5] Such information would make little sense, were it not for the fact that in the course of time many further and larger versions evolved: in eighteen thousand, twenty-five thousand, and finally in a hundred thousand (the size of the *Mahābhārata*). By now the bulk had become rather unwieldy, and the Buddhist monk reading through all this may well have asked himself whether this scriptural study was really the purpose behind the original formulations of ideas. To a very limited extent this problem is catered for, not just in the various *Perfection of Wisdom sūtras*, but in most Mahāyāna *sūtras* generally. They have a tendency, from a certain stage in their historical development onward, to make themselves the object of reflection and praise. Early chapters tend to proclaim ideas, and later chapters proclaim the greatness of the *sūtra* itself, and the merits arising from reading or listening to it. So it is not that a hundred thousand units were reached by merely adding new ideas. Not only is the whole Abhidharma incorporated, but also the self-praise enormously enlarged. Anyway, at some stage yet more versions were produced, which once again attempted to concentrate on the essentials and present the key ideas in more manageable form. Thus we obtain the *Heart-* or *Hṛdaya-sūtra* (of only about twenty or so units), and the particularly famous *Diamond-* or *Vajracchedikā-sūtra* (in a few hundred units).[6] This *Diamond-sūtra* soon replaced the *Laṅkāvatāra-sūtra*, mentioned in Chapter 20,[7] as the central text of Ch'an or Zen. By the inner logic of this development, we end up with a version in one syllable only, 'a'.[8]

The study of all this bulky material is associated with the name of one man, Edward Conze, who spent decades of his life pursuing the 'perfection of wisdom' through all its textual ramifications. The single-mindedness he brought to bear on this pursuit would be the envy of many a Buddhist monk; an almost obsessive exclusivism and Teutonic earnestness suggest the Jain ascetic. However Conze may not, I fear, have approved of the rather light-hearted approach I am about to apply to this material.

But let us return to the beginnings. These can fairly safely be identified as the first two chapters of the *Prajñā-pāramitā-sūtra* in eight thousand units, with the separately handed-down corresponding Prakrit stanzas. The central theme here is the training of the *bodhisattva* in the pursuit of wisdom and compassion. This is a seemingly innocuous theme; read with a capital B for *bodhisattva*, no form of Buddhism would find any problem in it. For this is, according to the enormously popular Jātaka literature of all branches of Buddhism, what the Buddha-to-be did in past existences: perfect himself in the various *pāramis* or virtues of generosity, endurance, etc.[9] Thus, if Sanskrit had capital letters, we would have to use them in this case. On the other hand, lower-case '*bodhisattva*' suggests a generic term, referring globally to all those people who are aiming at the culminating ideal of Mahāyāna Buddhism, and that is precisely what the stanzas are about. They talk about complete enlightenment as a universal ideal which, let us recall, is regarded as lying beyond the *nirvāṇa* of the Hīnayāna. This enlightenment is seen as the perfectly balanced combination of the perfection of wisdom and the perfection of compassion. One of the points of criticism raised against the Hīnayāna is its selfish spiritual pursuit, without compassion for others equally caught up in the realm of suffering.

Still, so far we have not said anything which could not be found in many other Mahāyāna *sūtras* as well. What is new can be introduced by looking at what happens when someone learns to ride a bicycle, or to swim. At an early stage in the learning process, there is a decidedly literalist and particularist attitude at work. We hold on to the handle-bars of the bike anxiously, seeking support, and protection against crashing to the ground. We try to hold on to the water, as if it could save us from sinking. All the while we seek material support, while anxiously reminding ourselves of the specific ideas we have learnt. In spiritual terms, this is called in our text 'holding on to form and ideas', 'settling down in form and thought', 'grasping at form and ideas', or 'apprehending' or 'comprehending them'.[10]

Let us return to our metaphor. After a lot of practice, and that means a lot of water swallowed and lots of bruises, we reach a point where for the first time something 'clicks' and we get it right. But the second we realize that the helping hand holding on to the bike or our stomach has been withdrawn, everything goes wrong again. This is known to our text as the trembling, the fear, the panic and the terror of the *bodhisattva*: suddenly he is reminded that there is nothing to support him, like the swimmer who feels nothing but water beneath him. But, the text continues, in the hands of good friends, the *bodhisattva* overcomes this fear and carries on with his training.[11] Eventually he will succeed: he will 'course' in perfect wisdom. In terms of our metaphor, that is easy enough to comprehend. The perfect cyclist can take his hands off the handle-bar, smoke a cigarette and carry on a conversation with a friend, while merrily pedalling away. In terms of the spiritual goal, it is a bit more difficult to make sense of this. But by paraphrasing slightly what we can observe in the case of the cyclist, I think it is possible to gain some understanding of it. There is freedom and spontaneity: the moment we forget that we have learnt certain actions and that we desire a certain goal, it becomes possible to perform the actions in such a way that we achieve the goal. Initially we felt enslaved to gravity, but now we move through the air or over the water; initially, we constantly thought of swimming or whatever, but now we actually swim, whithout thinking about it. For as long as the *bodhisattva* grasps at the external world and thinks: 'I must see into its true nature', and as long as he grasps at the goal of 'perfection of wisdom'; as long as he grasps at other beings and at the thought 'I must save them', he is caught up in form and thought. But the minute he ceases to hold on to form and thought, not only does he become spontaneously 'wise', but also 'compassionate'.

Some further comments may not be out of place here. First, 'spontaneity'. During the sixties, Zen was widely advocated as the 'religion of spontaneity', and this was understood as a kind of religious free-for-all. Accounts of what actually happened in Zen monasteries appeared much later,[12] but they made it clear how strenuous and painful the actual training was, and how many years went into it. It takes time to acquire a skill. Secondly, 'not to abide in form and thought' has often been mistaken for some form of nihilism, or at least as an extreme type of religious passivity. But it is precisely the person who 'spontaneously' rides a bike who rides it best and achieves something through his action. Similarly here, the *bodhisattva* coursing in the perfection of wisdom and compassion does precisely that: he moves through form and thought and acts compassionately. The classical formulation of this is as follows:

> Here the *bodhisattva* thinks thus: 'countless beings should I lead to salvation, and yet there are none who lead, or should be led, to salvation'. And indeed, however many beings he may lead to salvation, yet there would not be any being whom he could have led to salvation, nor who could have led them.[13]

This is starkly paradoxical language, but with a purpose. What better way of telling somebody to stop grasping at water as if it were branches one could hold on to, than by telling him about the non-solid nature of water and encouraging him to make his mind empty? The themes that we derived from the story of Mallī are not difficult to recognize in all this. Here again is the 'click phenomenon' when suddenly, after a long struggle, the *bodhisattva* ceases to grasp at form and idea and when he begins to approach the world with a new attitude – an attitude that is paradoxical to the logical mind.

Behind all this lies a lot of humour and spiritual humility, but also polemics and even some implicit philosophical reflection. Polemic is the easiest bit to pick up. Mahāyāna *sūtras* generally know of Sāriputra. This disciple of the Buddha serves them as a caricature of an unimaginative, literalist and pedantic follower of the Abhidharma.

Sāriputra is always terribly serious and tries to make up for his very limited intelligence by putting things into neat schemas and by sorting out the *dharmas* involved in them. The line taken in our text is simple: you must realize that even the *dharmas* you keep on talking about are not solid, real things. This was indeed the way the Abhidharma saw the nature of the *dharmas*, as real – for the one moment they existed. In other words, if sufficiently small pincers existed, it would be possible to pick up, for one moment, a matter-*dharma*. For our text, and many related ones, this was a mistaken notion. Instead, they suggested that all *dharmas* are 'empty'. They are like the water that cannot be grasped, like the rainbow that cannot be felt, or like the shape made by a moving torch in the night. In terms of ontology, the realism of the Abhidharma is thereby overcome, and (what our texts are really interested in) in terms of spiritual attitude, a freedom from holding on to or grasping 'form' is achieved. This made it possible not only to eradicate desires and to overcome ignorance (something all forms of Buddhism wanted to do), but also (and this is specific to the Mahāyāna) to relate back to the world with its suffering beings in the spirit of compassion. Thus it is clear that to say that *dharmas* are empty does not deny their existence. Philosophically, which means from the point of view of presenting this paradoxical attitude within a rational framework of explanation, it involves the problem of envisaging the relationship between the surface of the phenomena and their inner essence as irreducible.

But the earlier texts in this tradition of the *Perfection of Wisdom* do not develop such an intellectual framework, for reasons that will become clear presently. Yet they say more than what has been summarized so far. Some remarkable insights are expressed, along with an equally remarkable courage. Not only does the person learning to swim have to realize that water is not a substance he can hold on to; he has also to learn to relax with reference to the idea 'I must swim!' Similarly, our text is prepared to say that '*bodhisattva*', '*nirvāṇa*' and – to top it all – even 'Buddha' or 'Mahāyāna' are equally empty *dharmas*. They, too, must not be grasped, anxiously held on to as if they could provide real support or possessed autonomous being. Even these concepts are nothing but surfaces which the perfection of wisdom breaks through. At this point, our text is not really polemical any more: it makes fun of itself. Consider the following.

Sāriputra: 'When the *bodhisattva* thus trains, which *dharma* does he train in when he trains in the perfection of wisdom?'

The Buddha: 'He does not train in any *dharma* at all. Because the *dharmas* do not exist in such a way as foolish people are accustomed to suppose.' [Note that there may well be a pun here on Dharma and *dharma*! But even the surface ideas expressed here are lost on Sāriputra who merrily keeps asking his questions.]

Sāriputra: 'How then do they exist?'

The Buddha: 'As they do not exist, so they exist.'[14]

It is as if the Buddha wanted to say: 'stop asking such childish questions and start pedalling!' Anyway, these early *Perfection of Wisdom* texts are marvellous debunkers. 'So what?' they reply to even the most sophisticated intellectual system, even when it is proposed in their own midst. It is needless to add that they offer marvellous quotes for the right kind of dinner-party conversation. 'Is that thought which is no thought, something which is?'[15] asks Sāriputra, in one of my own favourites. Such usage of the *Perfection of Wisdom* literature may be shocking to some people who take the whole of Buddhism very seriously, but I have at least one very respectable predecessor (apart from Vimalakīrti whom we shall meet in Chapter 22). Jaroslav Hašek, in his novel about *The Good Soldier Švejk and His Fortunes in the [First] World War* (which was published in 1923), introduces us to the 'occultist cook' who quotes passages from the *Perfection of Wisdom sūtras* in the kitchen, to the great consternation of Švejk and the other soldiers.[16] Thus once, when this 'rarity in the officers' kitchen' had accidentally knocked over all the glasses standing in front of him on the table, he commented: 'There exists the non-being of all phenomena; form is non-being, and non-being is form. Non-being is not different from form. Everything that is form is also non-being.' ['Non-being' here might translate a Czech word denoting 'emptiness'.] After that, he 'wrapped himself in a shroud of silence'.[17]

Hašek, one of the great debunkers in more recent European literature, had a great affinity with the ideas quoted from the *Heart-sūtra*, far more than what the explicit reference to a Buddhist scripture might suggest. For his naive and yet cunning soldier Švejk, who quite innocently drives insane everybody he comes in contact with, breaks through the surface of even the grandest ideas (for example, 'Kaiser', 'dying for the Vaterland', 'Austrian Empire' and 'military efficiency'). In his own ingenious way, Švejk does not grasp at form, nor is he unduly worried by thought. He floats through the events of the war, at the front, without suffering serious harm. Not only that: those who are prepared to accept him for what he is do receive benefits from his good-hearted nature.

It is most regrettable that we know nothing about the social context in which the earliest expressions of perfection of wisdom evolved, nor of the concrete form through which this type of religion expressed itself. I do not want to put too much weight on the fact that in China this teaching was taken up in the Ch'an school. Both the cultural and chronological differences are quite considerable, and by themselves would warn us against trying to reconstruct the earliest milieu on the basis of it. But just from reading the texts, certain points are clear. In spite of the humorous aspects, it must have been a serious affair, both in its training and in its application. As far as the training side is concerned, our texts themselves are part of the process. Even later works to which I shall turn presently, maintain this emphasis: instead of being reflections on the religious path, they make up part of the path itself. They are exercises designed to encourage spontaneity and freedom in relation not just to form, but also to thought. To read them as 'philosophy' would thus mean to misunderstand the type of discourse involved here – most of which would in any case be written off by philosophers as total nonsense.

As far as the application is concerned, it seems worth pointing out that 'compassion' remains at the centre. But what a difference, when we compare this with certain attitudes we are much more familiar with. I am thinking here of the professional do-gooder, the man dedicated to improving the world. Whatever the motives, in his case there is always a residue of unease. For not only do we see time and again how the 'good' is derived from a total conviction of one's own righteousness or at least of one's own knowledge of the truth. We also witness to what extent this do-gooder tries to force others to accept his ideas. And even when personal conviction (which is, after all, a 'holding on to thought') does not play such devious games by forcing others to hold on to the same thoughts, it is quite possible to work through one's own goodness towards fame, respect, power and perhaps the Nobel Prize for Peace. The man who shows compassion in the same way that we cycle or swim is indeed a very different person, and surely it will not be easy to reach such a state. Totally unreflecting, he does what must be done, and does not bother about *nirvāṇa*, or the improvement of the world, or even the status of a saint. He remains in the world of the surface, precisely because he has broken through it. As another early *sūtra* puts it rather drastically:

> Though endowed with defilements [from living in the world], the *bodhisattva* is infinitely more useful than the *śrāvaka*; just like the manure collected from the town serves a useful purpose on the fields, where it is used as fertilizer for the sugar-cane.[18]

Mallī was 'useful' to the kings, irrespective of the analysis she produced of her nature as attractive woman. By his inner attitude of 'not grasping' at the world and at its beings, the *bodhisattva* becomes useful precisely because he remains a human being with all his external imperfections.

The quotation comes from a *sūtra* called the *Ratna-kūṭa*, 'Collection of Jewels'. It was translated into Chinese as early as the (*Eight Thousand*) *Perfection of Wisdom sūtra*, along with an interesting interpolated passage[19] about one of the key concepts we have encountered already, though not yet properly discussed: 'emptiness' (*śūnyatā*). The concept appears together with that of the 'middle path', which by itself once again highlights the fact that we are not simply dealing with an attempt to spell out the ideas discussed so far in a systematic, 'philosophical' manner, but also and, in fact, primarily, with spiritual method and attitude.

The correct attitude towards all *dharmas*, we are told here, is to be aware of their being empty. This emptiness, in turn, is that which lies between two extremes: to be real, existent, and not to exist at all. This is the middle path: to go for the emptiness, and not for either of these extreme views. Once again, all *dharmas* are included here; even 'correct perception' and 'wrong perception' are nothing but two extremes. Emptiness is where there is no thought, no perception and no mind. The same applies to purification and defilement, and – to top it all – emptiness itself. Emptiness is not 'something', and therefore cannot be added from the outside to the phenomena, 'purifying' them. By their very nature, all phenomena and concepts are empty. But woe to the man who now tries to grasp emptiness itself: it is like taking a poisonous medicine (or enema) to cure an illness – if the poison remains in the body, its effects will be more devastating than the original illness.[20] No doubt, something more than just method is at work here. Systematic interpretative thought has begun to deal with it as well, although it attempts to maintain a critical distance to its own enterprise.

This is perhaps even more apparent in another section which is found in a somewhat later *sūtra*, the 'Explication of the Implicit Meaning' (*Sandhinirmocana*).[21] This section carries the significant title: 'the characteristics of ultimate reality' (*paramārtha*). *Paramārtha*, which could also be translated as 'highest truth', is a new word for a concept we are familiar with, 'emptiness'. Five such characteristics are mentioned: inexpressible, non-dual, beyond all logical (or philosophical) discourse, transcending identity and difference, and offering only one flavour. There is no need to provide an elaborate exegesis of all five terms. The third and the fifth directly make fun of the systematizers, the philosophers who 'reflect, measure, examine, enquire', 'dispute, quarrel, insult each other and beat each other up'; who are 'presumptious, caught up in conceit and delusion, and show off to each other with the bits of knowledge they have acquired'.[22] 'Offering only one flavour' means: once emptiness has been perceived with reference to one single piece of reality, one single topic of Buddhist discourse, everything is realized; it cannot be accumulated step by step. At the same time, this 'ultimate truth' transcends all logical argument and discussion.

The remaining three terms imply the following. Traditionally, reality has been divided into conditioned *dharmas* and at least one unconditioned one, *nirvāṇa*. Yet this construction is no more than the work of a magician who conjures up all kinds of weird objects and events by the roadside.[23] From an ultimate point of view, the division ceases: the relationship between the conditioned, namely the surface of things as we perceive it in our unenlightened minds, and the unconditioned, is realized as non-dual. This is further spelled out in the characteristic called 'transcending identity and difference'. Non-dual means not to look at the world as if it consisted of nothing but the surfaces of the things and thoughts, but also not to look at it as if highest reality is something totally different from it. Highest reality is no more than what makes up the content, or the inner nature of things and thoughts. As the *Heart-sūtra* (and the cook in Hašek) says, 'emptiness is form and form is emptiness'.[24]

As stated more than once, this will not satisfy the philosopher; but then it is not meant to. *A-dvaya*, 'non-dual', is the key idea put forward here, and essentially this will remain the position of subsequent thinkers in this tradition. You cannot describe the world in the manner of one logical plane, without damaging religious experiences. But neither can you dissolve it in some grand mystical experience, without damaging other important aspects of religion (like compassion or, in Mallī's case, the need for a teacher). The best you can do is to take a middle path, move freely between both extremes, and call the whole a non-dual relationship. That in other texts the idea of two levels of truths, one relative and one absolute, was developed does not add anything to this: for even the relationship between two such levels would then be defined as non-dual.

All this anonymous writing has fed into a more organized and institutionalized tradition, which is associated with the name of Nāgārjuna, who probably lived around the second century AD, and the school of the Madhyamaka (or Mādhyamika). There are considerable academic problems associated with 'Nāgārjuna', but by placing the one work which can safely be connected with Nāgārjuna, the founder of the Madhyamaka tradition – his *Madhyamaka-kārikās* – into the context of our present exploration, it may be possible to sidestep these. By linking him with the material that advocates a balanced attitude, he ceases to be the spiritual nihilist some scholars (even Buddhist ones) have accused him of being. Thus we could include him in the tradition of spiritual debunkers. But then it is important to point out the differences with the *sūtra* material we have been looking at so far. In Nāgārjuna there is a new element of seriousness at work; systematic thought is indeed brought to bear on the demonstration that everything is empty.

Both its central concept of emptiness and its name, 'Madhyamaka' or 'Mādhyamika', ties the school to our earlier material. As the 'system about the middle ground' or the 'school pursuing a middle course' or the 'method of balancing extremes' (these are all possible free paraphrases of Madhyamaka) it is directly linked with the *Ratna-kūṭa*'s exposition of the middle path. Although, no doubt, one could say that a 'philosophical' school-tradition arose from Nāgārjuna's teaching and fully fledged systems evolved around the concept of emptiness, as one of the predominant trends prevailed the debunking. Critical and systematic analysis is used to demonstrate that no coherent system can make much sense *vis-à-vis* the nature of reality. Thus the practical conclusion to be drawn from this is to steer clear of all speculative extremes and penetrate into the ground that lies between them.[25]

From this general sketch of Nāgārjuna's thought, I would like to select one or two points for further discussion; these are directly connected with our present exploration. We can begin by once again looking at the nature of the *dharmas*. Naturally they are empty, but this is now shown by Nāgārjuna in an interesting and new way. We all know what a TV picture looks like; but now imagine that it consisted of only one colour. Obviously, we would have no picture at all – the whole screen would be just black, or white, or red. It is only through contrasts (white versus black, or red versus blue versus yellow) that a picture is created. The picture is conditioned, Nāgārjuna would say, by colours. However, imagine a world which has only one colour; in that case, we would not even talk of colour. Only when we have at least two colours does it make sense to use the word. Moreover, each individual colour is only there by virtue not of itself, but because of the existence of at least one other colour. Thus again each colour is conditioned and empty, because it exists only by virtue of some other colour. But obviously, Nāgārjuna is not interested in colours or TVs. So, consequently, he extends this analysis to the most abstract level of contrasts possible: that of *saṃsāra* versus *nirvāṇa*. Could we conceive of one without the other? No, Nāgārjuna says, and thus even here one conditions the other and both are therefore empty. Thus there is only one totally undifferentiated and unconditioned reality: emptiness itself, the common ground or the common characteristic of *saṃsāra* and *nirvāṇa*. Naturally, the relationship between *dharmas* and emptiness is an *advaya* one, 'non-dual'. It should be clear from all this how neatly it fits into the context discussed earlier. To me this is not nihilism, but merely a further variation – this time put forward with a fair amount of systematic thought – on the theme of how a *bodhisattva* can move through form and thought and yet be free from it. By jumping into emptiness, he makes the qualitative leap from the surface into the 'essence' – which naturally does not involve any movement at all (since emptiness exists only in the *dharmas*) nor an 'essence' (since all *dharmas* are empty).

I think it is possible to argue that, in a sense, Indian religious culture has reached here its culmination. This is the wisdom that expresses itself as 'commuting within one world', an active spiritual discipline that relates to the world in a spirit of love without seeing in its 'forms', and the 'ideas' about it, anything other than 'emptiness'. But 'culmination' carries perhaps too strong an association of a value judgement, and something like 'central cultural blueprint' might be more appropriate here. Given that, in the previous pages, the philosopher has not been taken too seriously, it is probably fair that he, in turn, may not be very interested in the kind of thinking that expresses itself here (through concepts like *advaya, śūnyatā* and 'middle path'). This is not very important, because what matters here is the method and the attitude, the spiritual approach characterized by both total freedom and commitment. What is suggested here is that religious experience does not lie within the realm available to empirical, analytical investigation and, at the same time, that it does not dissolve the phenomena into nothing. Instead, it breaks through the surface without breaking it to pieces. The cyclist ceases to be aware of what he is doing, and can fully concentrate on the beauties of nature or the dangers of lorries passing him. We can recognize here a structure that influenced not only many other Indian religious systems and movements, but that also lies at the heart of much of Indian culture generally. Because of this, most of the material we shall be looking at in the following pages will fall, directly or indirectly, within this framework.

Having said all this, it seems opportune to add that the various concrete expressions of this underlying structure may fluctuate considerably between an 'attitudinal' emphasis and a more theoretical, speculative one. Given that the general drift of the present chapter has been towards the more theoretical side, I would like to continue here with this kind of material in order to illustrate some of the further ramifications of maintaining a balance. The obvious topic that offers itself as the starting point for this exploration has already been introduced in the previous chapter: Śaṅkara's systematic account of the Vedānta. Our present material can throw further interesting light on it.

Śaṅkara adopted the Buddhist idea of the 'two truths'. Absolute truth he called *paramārtha* (a term used also in the *Sandhinirmocana-sūtra*), and his *vyāvahārika* could be rendered 'relative' or 'functional' or 'pragmatic' truth. The relationship between these two is styled, not quite *advaya*, but near enough, '*advaita*' (a term found in the

Upaniṣads).[26] This would initially suggest that it is not possible to treat either kind of truth independently from the other and that both are joined together as one whole. It also implies that this union does not cancel out the lower or relative truth. So far this is hardly different from what we found in the Mahāyāna *sūtras* and in Nāgārjuna. But, as we have seen in the last chapter, Śaṅkara concretizes the two truths by identifying them with *brahman* and *avidyā* ('ignorance') or *māyā* ('magic illusion'). This *avidyā*, as pragmatic truth, denotes the entire world of human experience, including one's own sense of identity and autonomy. *Brahman*, although it is, as absolute truth, beyond the denotative powers of words and beyond the grasp of rational, philosophical thought, can be hinted at by saying that it is 'pure reality' (and pure consciousness and bliss). Naturally, the concept '*advaita*' applies here too: it defines the relationship between *brahman* and *avidyā*. But, given the way that *brahman* is defined, this represents a considerable shift in the meaning of the term '*advaita*'. *Brahman*, as the truly and uniquely real, can indeed be thought of in isolation from *avidyā*, while *avidyā* depends totally on *brahman*, drawing from it, as it were, whatever relative reality it may possess. (We may want to remind ourselves here that 'empty' denotes a state of being that can neither be described as 'real' nor as 'unreal'.) Thus when applied to *brahman* and *avidyā*, *advaita* describes a dependent relationship which allows the second term merely a 'pragmatic' autonomy, and a hierarchy from the 'real' to the 'not totally unreal' is set up.

Why not simply contrast in this case the real with the unreal? The balance may have come heavily down on the side of *brahman* in Śaṅkara's system, but it remains a question of balance. Just as Mallī the attractive is not totally dissolved into Mallī the evil-smelling one, *avidyā* or *māyā* cannot be nothing. Perhaps the most famous simile in Śaṅkara's Vedānta to illustrate the fallacy of our view of the world is that of the snake and the rope. In the fading light of evening we see something on the beach that looks like a snake and, terrified, we run away. Next morning the object is still there, but we realize that it is merely a rope. But note where the emphasis of the metaphor lies: what we actually do at the sight of the rope.[27] This only makes sense, because there does exist somewhere a real snake, the image of which we project on to the rope and which, in turn, stimulates our fear-motivated behaviour. Again it may not be 'philosophy' in any recognizable sense of the word, but we find here suggestions of the attitudinal mode. Ultimately, what matters is how we react to the world (as relative truth) and to *brahman* (the ultimate truth and absolute being). From this angle, Śaṅkara, for all his systematic thought, remains a commentator on practical spiritual attitudes.

Attention now has to be drawn to a further, fundamental shift of approach that expresses itself in Śaṅkara's thought. By identifying the absolute truth with *brahman*, not only did he tilt the balance in one direction, but he also introduced a basically different mode of making sense of the world. Theoretically one could claim that by searching deep enough in ourselves – our *ātmans* – *brahman* becomes available to all of us and is discovered as a given fact of human nature. But, as we have seen in the previous chapter, this is precisely how Śaṅkara does not want to argue his case. According to him, *brahman* is only knowable (in both senses of the word, empirically and meditationally) through the Vedas. Thereby, apart from restricting its access to a small elite who are allowed to benefit from the Vedas, he erects his whole system on the foundation of 'revelation'. This introduces a new type of discourse which we might want to call (quasi-)theological. It is 'theological' to the extent that here also rational, systematic thought is brought to bear on an analysis of the world which presupposes certain assumptions that are accepted from revelation and not rationally derived. But the qualification 'quasi' is required, because we take it for granted in our own culture that 'theology' is about *theós*, God, as its central content. This is manifestly not the case in Śaṅkara. What appeared in his culture as the god-figures of theistic religions is relegated in his system to the foremost position of *avidyā*, 'ignorance'. The full realization of *brahman* inevitably means to leave all ideas of a personal God behind.

Incidentally, we have here a good illustration of the workings of the *advaita* principle. It is to the world of relative truth that we must ascribe phenomena like the Vedas, Īśvara ('God' who 'creates' the world), Īśvara's incarnations (like Kṛṣṇa) who promulgate the Vedas (as in the *Bhagavad-gītā*) and the *gurus* (who alone can initiate one into the secrets of *brahma*-knowledge). They are clearly not unreal, because they constitute essential features in Śaṅkara's quasi-theology. Given the importance of the *advaita* principle, we need not be surprised to find that Śaṅkara's system is referred to as the Advaita-Vedānta, or frequently simply as the Advaita.

By now some readers might be becoming impatient to ask the following question. After all this talk about analytical and meditational, attitudinal and quasi-theological modes of making sense of the world, when do we finally hear about proper theology, a rational system of thought based on the belief in a personal God? After all, as Part two has made clear, Hinduism at least seems to know a lot about (different kinds of) God. My answer to the question is: partly now, and partly later. My reason for splitting up 'theology' in this manner is this. On the one hand, theology is indeed the rational discussion of contents of belief derived from revelation. In that sense, we can continue our exploration here quite organically by moving from quasi- to proper theological types of discourse. But on the other hand, I understand theology also to be the critical reflection on religious practice. To explore this side will require us to return to our wider framework of discussion, and that takes us beyond the confines of the present chapter.

Surprising though it may sound, all the basic raw material for a theology in the first sense has already been accumulated. Nothing like the drastic shift from emptiness to *brahman* (as found in Śaṅkara) needs to be repeated, because in such a theology God is *brahman*. The convinced monotheist will not be satisfied to find Īśvara, 'God', positioned at the apex of *avidyā* in Śaṅkara. Referring to his own self-authenticating religious experiences, he will point out that his God is very much at the centre of his own spiritual fulfilment. He is the true being, *brahman*, referred to in the Upaniṣads. Once this equation has been established, it is not difficult for most of the conceptual material and the fundamental structures of thought of the Vedānta to be carried straight on from Śaṅkara. It was he who established a respectable Hindu orthodoxy *vis-à-vis* Buddhist and Jaina thought, and most forms of Hindu monotheism derived their own orthodoxy from the same source, the Vedānta. Those who did not, or did so in a much less direct manner, are far less well known and studied, and I shall ignore them in the present discussion.

The early Upaniṣads, by suggesting that 'being', or *brahman*, 'desired' or 'reflected' or 'willed', laid the basis for a later interpretation of *brahman* in theistic terms. Thus from a relatively early date (third century BC?) onwards, we find more complex and systematic monotheistic views of the world – visions at the centre of which is found a personal absolute God. Those I have discussed under the title of 'Love'. But that is not the same as fully-fledged systems that draw on all the available philosophical material to interpret monotheistic devotion within the framework of the universe at large. Conventionally, Rāmānuja is associated with this achievement. He was a South Indian brahmin connected with a monotheistic Vaiṣṇava movement and lived during the eleventh/twelfth centuries AD. Nowadays we have something that could be called a 'Rāmānuja industry'. In the cesspool of all this Indian atheism and monism, he has appeared as an island of the known and familiar to those few Christian theologians who dared to venture into the unknown of the Indian religions. But it is not our concern here to investigate to what extent, if any, such a view is justified. Instead, let us remind ourselves of the current theme – striking a balance – and of the claim just made that the Vedānta determined the kind of theology that was initially developed.

For us (and much of the current Rāmānuja scholarship) to say that *brahman* is identified with God raises far less complex issues than for Rāmānuja to claim that *brahman* is Viṣṇu. His task as a theologian will involve him not just in deriving, from Upaniṣadic passages, features that suggest a 'personal' nature of *brahman*. It is his task to demonstrate, beyond general personal characteristics, that *brahman* is a 'he' and not a 'she', and that he possesses four arms, rather than a third eye on the forehead. In other words, it is necessary to distinguish Viṣṇu from Śiva, and his maleness from the femininity of the Goddess. This necessarily involves a widening of what is regarded as revealed scripture. But this expansion of revelation is a quantitative step, not a qualitative leap as in Śaṅkara. On the other hand, this insistence on attributes (like four arms for Viṣṇu) necessitates a different emphasis when it comes to defining the balance between the absolute and the realm of phenomena. This, Rāmānuja presents under the simile of the body and the soul: *brahman* is the soul, everything else (and that means the universe and all its beings) relates to him like the body. It is not that this psychosomatic imagery wants to restore the balance totally; even here *brahman* remains the one reality that can be thought of in isolation from everything else. But *de facto* *brahman* expresses himself in concrete (called 'differentiated' or *viśiṣṭa*) form. The relationship between Viṣṇu and the world with its embodied souls is also called '*advaita*' here, and it also denotes a relationship of total dependence.

Man is only there because of Viṣṇu, and to realize (again in both senses of the word) this, means to find his ultimate fulfilment. This is not some ultimate transindividual fusion, but an *advaita* relationship of the soul with Viṣṇu. Incidentally we may note here that such ideas offer Rāmānuja the tools to interpret the *Vedānta-sūtras* of Bādarāyaṇa coherently, but in the reverse direction from Śaṅkara. Viṣṇu evolves the world, as a dependent but real 'body' of his and the *ātman* achieves salvation without totally losing himself in Viṣṇu.

As to the means of achieving this salvation, Rāmānuja, like Śaṅkara, anchors it deeply in the Vedic tradition, and thus accepts Vedic exclusivism.[28] Moreover, he cannot but resort to the Upaniṣadic dictum of *jñānān mokṣaḥ*, 'liberation is due to [meditationally gained] knowledge'.[29] By deriving such 'knowledge' from what he styles *bhakti-yoga*, he does not actually substitute devotion for meditation. *Yoga* remains the method, but devotion (*bhakti*) provides it with its goal. In the light of what we know about the religious practice (namely the mysticism of the Tamil Āḻvārs) for which Rāmānuja's Viśiṣṭādvaita claims to provide the theology, this represents a major shift in emphasis. I shall return to this point at a later stage.

Rāmānuja created a blueprint for numerous further theological systems that were developed within Hinduism under the banner of the Vedānta, and in most cases also under that of the Advaita. They all attempt to show, by means of scriptural exegesis, that their God (or Goddess) is the *brahman* of the Upaniṣads, and then to define the precise relationship that exists between *brahman* and the world of human experience, human beings, and the soul in the state of liberation. But all this lies outside the scope of the present exploration. Similarly, space does not permit me to enter into a discussion of theological problems subsequent to the designing of an orthodox Vedic and Hindu theology. Such secondary problems evolved organically from a system-internal discussion and often they can still be presented under our present heading of striking a balance. For instance, Śrīvaiṣṇava theologians after Rāmānuja were intensively involved in the attempt to define the relationship between Viṣṇu's saving grace (as an aspect of the absolute) and man's personal striving for purity, knowledge and salvation. It is probably no accident that subtle forms of compromise (divine grace requires at least a token of human co-operation) were suggested by the theologians predominantly rooted in the Sanskritic

Vedānta, while a more radical position (grace alone can save) was taken by other theologians who concentrated on the Tamil mystics.[30]

On the whole, the material we have been looking at in the present (and in many a previous) chapter is expressed in serious prose. Yet this is not a necessary feature in the way that we make sense of the world. There is a considerable amount of material waiting to be explored, which takes us beyond the confines of prosaic language.

CHAPTER 22

Beyond prosaic words

However 'self-authenticating' a religious experience may be and however much it may want to enclose itself within its own transcendental bliss, for a number of different reasons it cannot totally write off the world of phenomena. This may be, as we have seen, for reasons of social justification and explanation, of providing a rational exposition and of showing itself to be the most reasonable course of action to take. Or it may be that the causal role of the phenomena in the experience is acknowledged. The human body and mental make-up may yield meditationally gained insights, or a particular constellation of phenomena may suddenly trigger them off, or other persons may be required to convey the initial knowledge necessary for entering the path of meditation. Or finally, it may be that the religious experience itself contains a reference to the cosmos and the world: the realization of a universal soul present in all beings, or the stimulus towards compassion for all beings. Whatever the individual case may be, it raises the issue of a balanced attitude, and also of providing the latter with a theoretical basis.

The previous chapter concentrated on such speculative balancing exercises. It explored how this relationship between the phenomena and the insight into some deeper dimension of theirs found conceptual expression as *advaya* (on the Buddhist side) and *advaita* (among the thinkers of the Vedānta tradition). But even then we noticed that the interest was not merely in speculative or philosophical-systematic matters, but was also very much concerned with the practical side of religious method. The *advaita* – whether theistic or non-theistic – obscures this to a certain extent, because it aims overtly at providing a coherent and systematic metaphysical frame for *yoga* as the method. The Buddhist *advaya*, too, can be interpreted on the one hand as a comment on the world, but its connection with method and attitude is much more apparent. By learning to see spontaneously what things really are, by realizing that both 'form' and 'thought' are 'empty', attachment to them is eradicated, and 'coursing' in total freedom through form and thought and, at the same time, through emptiness, becomes possible. As a metaphor for this I introduced the person who has learnt to swim or to ride a bicycle. An alternative metaphor would be the person who can play the piano in such a way that all his attention is focused on the music he is playing, and not on the mechanical and theoretical aspects of playing the piano.

In all this we can see rational thought reflecting on its own limits: objects, words and ideas are perceived to be empty or to be manifestations of ignorance (*avidyā*). Yet in spite of this, we have noticed the construction of theoretical edifices (which naturally use words and ideas) meant to provide this perception with a rational basis. This by no means need be carried out naively (viz. by using the same kind of 'ideas' in the meta-theory which the initial theory identified as 'empty'). Thus for instance Nāgārjuna built very strong 'anti-constructivist' features into his analysis, by trying to show that, given the nature of the *dharmas* as empty, no theory of causality is possible – which would be essential in any coherent philosophical system. For if you cannot demonstrate a causal link between fire and water turning into steam, how can you explain the world philosophically (or scientifically)? 'Neither by itself, nor by something else, nor by a combination of both, nor by anything at all has any *dharma* ever and anywhere been caused', he tells us.[1] But instead of continuing our exploration along these theoretical lines, for instance by trying to unravel the complexities implicit in this quotation, let us move in a different direction, away from speculation. For the pursuit of maintaining a balanced attitude towards the world of empty phenomena or of ignorance has also been developed in altogether different manners – manners that draw the practical conclusions from the limitations of words and ideas by going altogether beyond the prosaic word. We may turn our attention to them (not to abandon theoretical reflections altogether, but to store them for future reference in the background).

It is difficult to imagine how the ideas expressed in the *Perfection of Wisdom sūtras* – like coursing through form and thought while realizing their emptiness – could have had a formalized or institutionalized application. Strictly speaking, 'life' itself could be the only area of application. For 'compassion' relates to all *dharmas* indiscriminately, just as all beings have at their innermost centre an *ātman*, the spark of *brahman*. Unfortunately, very little information on the social context of earlier Indian Mahāyāna (or for that matter, on the Advaita) has come down to us. Most likely, this free coursing through the world as if on a bicycle was, on the whole, carried out between the walls of the monastery (note that tradition also ascribes to Śaṅkara the foundation of monastic institutions). But, at least in one case, we are offered some hints as to how a more radical and socially unrestricted application of perfect wisdom in conjunction with perfect compassion could be envisaged. These hints are found in a Mahāyāna *sūtra* of enormous popularity in Asian countries: the *Teachings of Vimalakīrti.*[2] And this Vimalakīrti is a layman who, perhaps better than all the scholastic treatises on emptiness, communicates what it is all about.

Vimalakīrti is a layman who lives in the town of Vaiśālī. Externally, he lives a totally worldly life, socializing with all kinds of people and frequenting all kinds of dubious places. Without any discrimination, he consorts with the wise, learned and pious, and the gamblers, drunkards and prostitutes of the town. Thus he appears like one of the *dhūrtas*, 'rogues', and moves in the milieu frequented by them. But this commitment to the world and, in fact, its seediest aspects, is on the surface. Within himself, he is totally detached from all this, for he has realized what its nature is: emptiness. And that is precisely why he frequents the world: to express compassion with it and bring the light of the Buddha's teaching into its darkness.[3]

When the Buddha is visiting the town with his disciples, Vimalakīrti pretends to be ill, in order to lure them into his house. Fourteen times the Buddha asks a disciple to go and comfort Vimalakīrti, but each one refuses, for each has his own story of how, sometime in the past, Vimalakīrti has created havoc by everything he has said. Made at that time to feel utter fools, they do not have the courage to expose themselves to further ridicule. In the end, it is only Mañjuśrī who feels brave enough to do the decent thing and visit the sick man.

With a retinue of other disciples, he goes to Vimalakīrti's house, which they find completely empty – no furniture, no curtains, nothing. Naturally that offers Vimalakīrti his first opportunity to confuse everybody by giving a discourse on 'emptiness' itself.[4] Many further funny events and discourses follow. He breaks down their 'substantialist' thinking by proclaiming the 'emptiness' of all Buddhas,[5] and shocks their fastidious minds by merrily accepting a whole bevy of enticing girls sent by Māra to tempt him.[6] He horrifies the naive realist (and monk!) Sāriputra by turning him into a woman, and fools around with the hallowed laws of *karma* by turning a goddess into a respectable man.[7] But the *sūtra* reaches its culmination when Vimalakīrti innocently asks the assembled disciples of the Buddha what is meant by entering into an *advaya* relationship with all phenomena. Thirty-one theories are proclaimed with enormous acumen and subtlety. Then it is Mañjuśrī's turn to speak. 'Good men, you have all spoken well. But all that you have said still implies duality.' And he adds his own theory: 'Shunning all words and not saying anything, not expressing or teaching anything, not pronouncing or denoting anything, that is entering into an *advaya* relationship.' In passing we may notice that Mañjuśrī uses a lot of words, and a lot of rhetoric, to make that point. But then he does something much more naive: he treats the whole affair like a quiz and asks Vimalakīrti to tell them who among the thirty-two speakers got it right. 'But Vimalakīrti remained silent.'[8] The text does not tell us whether Vimalakīrti smiled, or – what seems more in character – grinned.

Were we Sāriputra, we might be tempted to comment that the thirty-two theories about *advaya* progressively suggested an erosion of concepts and words and that this found its culmination in Vimalakīrti's silence. But this would keep the passage enslaved, tied down to one and the same logical plane. It would ignore, for instance, that Vimalakīrti did what even Mañjuśrī merely talked about. Moreover, it would ignore that words and silence are in qualitative opposition, just as – and I have no hesitation to interpret the text like this – the earnestness of the eager disciples stands in contrast to Vimalakīrti's humour. Above all, he wanted to teach something (and one hopes he succeeded at least with some of the disciples in this aim), in spite of Mañjuśrī's 'not teaching anything'.

Once these features are acknowledged, it is not difficult to recognize similarities with the story of Mallī. Both describe a teaching situation, both present the religious communication as working through means other than words or mere ideas. But above all, I think in both cases we are dealing with 'click phenomena'.[9] What can this mean in the present case? The gradual build-up of a whole string of theories, carried out in seriousness, trepidation (because of Vimalakīrti's notorious insults and scorn), and eager expectation (for the reward in the form of Vimalakīrti's approval) culminate in a totally unexpected and, in some sense, shocking (re)solution. What makes our present example complicated is the fact that two features are woven together in the trigger-mechanism of the 'click': silence and humour. By remaining silent, Vimalakīrti cracks a joke – a joke that, unlike most jokes, cannot use words, because it is actually about using words. Provided his joke was understood, he taught something that (by Mañjuśrī's definition) could not be taught through prosaic words.

I would like to extract from all this two themes that deserve to be explored further: humour and silence. Everyday English helps us to make sense of the link between a joke and silence. 'I told him such and such, and that shut him up' will inevitably cause laughter. Provided we understand a joke immediately – and we all know that an explained joke is never funny – we laugh spontaneously. Like the swimmer or cyclist (in my metaphor), we are totally unconscious of what we are doing, and when questioned 'what is funny about that?' we are incapable of explaining it – an expression of silence. But let us now separate the two themes and look first at humour.

Animals don't laugh, and in German an expression exists that highlights this: *tierischer Ernst*. This could be translated roughly as 'beastly seriousness'. Thus by laughing, we realize something of our humanity. In an age of endless lobbies and pressure groups, politically-correct speaking and thinking and a general literalist moralistic climate, it is difficult to realize what actually happens through a joke and through laughter. The literalist holds slavishly on to form and thought: a joke is 'dirty' or 'racist' or 'anti-feminist' or whatever, merely by virtue of referring to some sexual subject matter, or a German, or a woman. Yet provided the joke is good, our laughter caused by it abstracts from all such concrete references. We laugh at the good-ness of the joke itself, not its particular subject matter. And more than this. If the joke is really good, we laugh at ourselves. Laughing does not cancel out the concrete situation we are in, but it allows us to break through the surface, to gain an inner distance and freedom from it. When it says 'click' and we laugh, we experience the world in a new way – we make new sense of it through the mode of humour.

To see this at work in our own culture, we would have to go to the grandmasters of European humour: the Yiddish-speaking Jews of the Central Europe of fifty or a hundred years ago. The 'Joys of Yiddish' advocated today from the States has lost that kind of quality, of making sense of an almost intolerable situation. And the hard realities encompassed through the *advaya* of humour in the original 'Scholem Aleichem' quite literally have dissolved as the *schmalz* running down the roof with its fiddler.

I would like to refer here also to Umberto Eco's novel *The Name of the Rose*, a brilliant who-dunnit kind of book. Its central themes are human nature, the essence of philosophy and religion, the central role of humour in all this, and the message that not only an animal, but also the Devil, does not laugh. In the very last pages of the book our detective-monk concludes: 'there was no plot ... and I discovered it by mistake'.[10] When the novice counters by pointing out that, nevertheless, 'it' was discovered, not just Eco, the professor of semiotics, but also Nāgārjuna could be speaking through the mouth of our detective:

> 'I have never doubted the truth of signs; they are the only things man has with which to orient himself in the world ... There was no plan ... [just] an initial design, and there began a sequence of causes, and concauses, and of causes contradicting one another, which proceeded on their own, creating relations that did not stem from any plan. [Eco obviously knows his Pynchon!] ... The order that our mind imagines is like a net, or like a ladder, built to attain something. But afterward you must throw the ladder away, because you discover that, even if it was useful, it was meaningless.'[11]

And he repeats the same idea in learned Middle High-German, which suggests that the original might be found in a mystic like Meister Eckhart or Tauler. Replace ladder by raft, and the same could be found expressed in not-so-learned Mahāyāna Buddhist Sanskrit. And what has all this to do with humour? 'Perhaps', our detective-philosopher says, 'the mission of those who love mankind is to make people laugh at the truth, *to make truth laugh*, because the only truth lies in learning to free ourselves from insane passion for the truth.'[12] Laughing is the throwing away of the ladder of all prosaic words.

Humour is ubiquitous in Indian religion, and this is perhaps the greatest stumbling-block in its appreciation from a traditional Christian religious point of view. Far too often we find the gods in situations reserved for the Irishman or German in English jokes. And not just the gods: Vimalakīrti has no scruples to show that the Buddha is 'empty'. Now it is clear that a considerable amount of such humorous material occurs in the context of inter-religious polemics or of a critique of religious hypocrisy. This is satire, and Indian dramatists have loved it. Two dramatic genres were developed specially for this purpose: the *bhāṇa* and the *prahasana*. Unfortunately we do not have the scope here to dwell on this most exciting material. All we can do is to take notice of the fact that classical Indian society had enormous latitude in making fun of what it perceived as religious hypocrites and charlatans. The 'pious' brahmin caught in a brothel or the *kāpālika* ascetic seen in a cremation ground in drunken stupor and in the arms of a woman are some such favourite characters and must suffice to illustrate the kind of material I am referring to. What better way to tell people what real religion is all about than to make them laugh at mistaken and distorted expressions of it; no earnest sermon could possibly have the same effect.

But even within a strictly religious context, humour is possible and in fact fairly ubiquitous. One minute example may provide here some idea of what this involves. Even the most serious religious poets, such as Ānandavardhana or Vedāntadeśika (about both of whom more will be said later on), are quite capable of using a particular Sanskrit figure of speech (the *prahelikā*)[13] within their religious poetry. This is a kind of mixture of poetic crossword puzzle and joke. Often it works by suggesting initially a rather vulgar surface meaning, which the resulting shock forces the reader to reconsider. Then a perfectly innocent second meaning can be discovered. Here is a well-known standard example from one of the textbooks of poetics.[14] 'Freely the gods roam about the temple, as drunk as if they had bathed in a lake of liquor.' Instantly we react, rather shocked, by saying that such a rendering cannot possibly be meant here, and try again. A contrived etymology for the word normally denoting 'gods' now yields 'alcoholics', and for 'temple' we can read 'drinking den'. That makes much better sense. Yet the poet still has the last laugh, for 'lake of liquor' in the metaphor could also mean 'heavenly lake'. This is ingenious irreverence, and perfectly permissable in the most serious religious poem. I shall presently comment on the fact that here it is poetry which breaks through the surface and creates an *advaya* situation. Moreover, when we search for the modes in which Indian thinkers have conceptualized humour, we find that, on the whole, it has remained subsumed under the general heading of poetics. But poetry is a theme which will be reserved for the second part of this chapter.

Here is an example (of considerable poetic charm in the original) to illustrate humour in myth or, better, in the behaviour of a god (and to many, of God) incarnated on earth. When Kṛṣṇa, still a boy, was living with the cowherds, not only did he create confusion in the herdsmen's minds through his supernatural strength – a strength that could lift a whole mountain and employ it as a communal umbrella – but he also created consternation in the minds of the girls through his divine handsomeness. So when winter came, they performed a popular ritual associated with that season and that mental anguish. Bathing nude in the cold water of the river, fasting and worshipping the goddess, they prayed that Kṛṣṇa should become their husband. Kṛṣṇa found out about it, and so one morning he sneaked up to the place where the girls were bathing, snatched their clothes and climbed up a tall tree. From there he called out to them: 'If you want your clothes back, you have to step out of the water and come here, and hold your hands folded over your heads.' What could they do but obey, freezing in the cold water and being tickled by the fish?[15]

The laughter that this episode, in the right kind of context, is able to generate, can give rise to an affection and love for Kṛṣṇa that no prosaic treatise could hope to achieve. We can merely speculate that Kṛṣṇa himself wanted to be funny and that, by laughing, the milkmaids found their own affectionate pleasure. But what concerns us here is the relationship between the author of the passage which I have summarized and his readers. He wants to communicate the love of Kṛṣṇa and chooses for that purpose what, in rather cumbersome academic language, could be called the humorous mode of making sense of God and the world. For this he employs, unlike Vimalakīrti, verbal means. But besides silence and words, actions (which after all speak louder than words) can figure as the tools in a comparable teaching situation. To see at work such humorous actions, which are intended to communicate a religious reality, we can turn, for example, to the rough world of the rural, medieval Maharashtra of the thirteenth century.

To say that Guṇḍam Rāūḷ was a monk (*saṃnyāsī*) initiated into one of the traditions allegedly founded by Śaṅkara can hardly convey an idea of the kind of person we are dealing with. To label him a rustic 'saint' who moved from village to village to interact with ordinary folks of the countryside would be rather more appropriate. But basically he evades all such categorization, for his behaviour breaks through all conventions (whether those of a 'monk' or a 'saint' or an ordinary person). 'Guṇḍam Rāūḷ was leaving [the town] by the eastern gate. Near [the temple of] Paraśurāma, to the northeast of it, he farted. "Die, die, you buttocks!" he exclaimed. "Why are you shouting?" With these words he slapped his own bottom, laughing. Then he went away.'[16] This may perhaps not seem very respectful to Paraśurāma, Rāma-with-the-Axe, but Narasiṃha suffered even worse humiliation. Statues of the Man-Lion incarnation of Viṣṇu tend to be terrifying, not just because of the claws that are digging into the demon's chest, but also due to its frightening lion's face. But Guṇḍam Rāūḷ playfully put his hand on such a statue's head and stuck his fingers into its mouth. While presumably tickling its inside, he teased: 'Surely he will bite me now! – No, he doesn't bite. But he will laugh! – No, he doesn't laugh either. At least he will talk! – No, he doesn't even talk!'[17]

Humans fare little better at his hands. One day a lady called Ābāisẽ was fed up with Guṇḍam Rāūḷ coming into her kitchen and messing up her food (to use it as gifts for his devotees). 'She put the widow Sādhẽ on guard.' Promptly Guṇḍam Rāūḷ appeared and began to handle the food. Sādhẽ shouted, to call Ābāisẽ.

> Guṇḍam Rāūḷ said: 'Damn you! Why are you shouting!' He went for her. She tried to escape, but she was so fat that she got caught in the small doorway. Her garment had slipped off. He clasped her breasts in his hands and instantly began to fool around. 'I must cut them off with a knife! Then they must be fried, or ground into spice powder, or made into rice cakes. They would also be nice in a yoghurt dish!'[18]

On another occasion the same Sādhẽ was bathing in the nude, and Guṇḍam Rāūḷ saw her. Instead of doing the decent thing and looking the other way, 'he grabbed a burning faggot from the stove and ran towards her. "Damn you! Get dressed!"' he shouted at her.[19]

Such episodes (and more than three hundred have been lovingly collected by his devotees) reveal Guṇḍam Rāūḷ as more than just an eccentric or 'mad'. In spite of their unique unconventionality, his deeds remain within the framework of our present exploration. For they are means by which he communicates, granted, in very much his own way, religious attitudes and truths. In the case of Paraśurāma and Narasiṃha, this hardly needs elaboration. The two anecdotes involving Sādhẽ conclude by telling us that 'from that day onwards' blouses were distributed to the women and the women 'wore a cloth when they bathed.' Another anecdote explicitly spells out the teaching intentions of Guṇḍam's crazy behaviour. He used to go and visit the stalls of the butchers and, breaking a most powerful brahmin taboo, play around with pieces of meat dripping with blood. One day a brahmin teacher, whose house Rāüḷ frequented, saw what he was doing. Instantly he could imagine what Rāüḷ would do next: he would come to his house and wash his hands in the drinking water. Hastily he returned home to prevent this – and there he saw Guṇḍam already washing his hands. 'In this way he destroyed his misconception,' concludes the anecdote.[20] It is possible to interpret 'misconception' as referring to the brahmin's ideas of purity and pollution. But given that Rāüḷ appeared to have 'flown' to the house – a fact the brahmin commented on by wondering 'is there any place without Rāüḷ?' – the misconception must relate to the very nature of Rāüḷ. This is indeed the way that the Mānbhāv religious movement (which originated from the devotion to Guṇḍam Rāüḷ and two other teachers) perceived it. To these Mānbhāvs, the historical Guṇḍam Rāüḷ (as also, significantly, the mythical Kṛṣṇa) is one of the incarnations of God (called Parameśvara) who, through his peculiar behaviour, communicates the truth about himself to mankind and inculcates the appropriate attitude of devotion.

Let us return to Vimalakīrti, who initially set us off on this exploration of humour as a means of making sense of the world and of communicating the latter. While it may be slightly speculative to interpret his behaviour as a joke, his silence does not allow for any such doubt. But what is it set in relation or opposition to? We could label it scholasticism. Lamotte, the translator of the *Vimalakīrti-sūtra*, has added a very bulky and impressive apparatus to the different theories on *advaya* put forward by the disciples. I wonder whether this display of scholarship was tongue-in-cheek. For, clearly, the text itself makes it abundantly clear what validity is attached to such speculative scholasticism. On the other hand, it is clear that even *advaya* and emptiness had become victims of systematic thinkers, in spite of all the warnings expressed in the literature dealing with 'emptiness'. To grasp 'emptiness' and manipulate it conceptually would be like the poisonous enema remaining in the body, instead of purifying it. Lamotte's references in the footnotes are helpful, in that they show that the author of the *Vimalakīrti-sūtra* did not make up many of the philosophical theories mentioned, but that they actually existed in Buddhist literature at the time. Vimalakīrti's silence makes a very loud comment on this scholasticism. Unfortunately, many a student of Mahāyāna Buddhism has not had the benefit of Vimalakīrti's delightful and infuriating company. So he has had to turn to what looks like the obvious source of insight into the 'mysteries of emptiness', Conze's chapter on 'Emptiness and Nihilism' in his *Buddhist Thought in India*. Alas! More or less immediately he tells us that there are eighteen types of emptiness, and that these 'derive from age-old meditational processes by which the intuition of the Absolute is actually realized'.[21] At the very end, when he has reached emptiness number 18, he concludes with an even more cryptic remark: 'On [this] highest level, an eloquent silence prevails. Words fail, and the spiritual reality communicates directly with itself.'[22]

There may be further hints here of the bizarre potentials of scholasticism; but for us it might be profitable to cast a brief glance at the man with whose name our concept of 'scholasticism' is intrinsically connected. I am referring to one of the most creative minds of medieval Europe, the famous polymath Thomas Aquinas, who wrote a large number of learned tomes. One day towards the end of his life, he made a strange remark. 'Everything I have written suddenly appears to me like meaningless rubbish.' And he meant it, for from then until his death he never again put pencil to paper and thus left his *Summa theologica* unfinished. Incidentally we may observe that we are dealing here with another 'click phenomenon' – note the 'suddenly'. Yet, tragically, this silence of the *doctor angelicus* was not heard, merely his words, and these were increasingly abused for the sake of what we call 'scholasticism'.

'Silence' in the religions of India is a seemingly problematic theme. The naive literalist will use it in his argument against talking about Indian religions altogether. A lot of precious and romantic writing on the East has been developed from this theme, and no doubt has contributed considerably to the mystique of Eastern thought. We hear about the Buddha silently holding up a lotus flower and without words communicating his teaching to a receptive disciple; we hear about a tradition outside all scriptures that derived from this teaching. But it tends to be ignored here that most of this material is found in Ch'an (better known in its Japanese form, Zen). Whether we interpret it as the result of imposing typically Chinese cultural features on to Buddhism, or as a (more conscious) Buddhist legitimation exercise in the absence of an Indian cultural framework, the fact remains that within the Indian context it is an alien, or at least extremely marginal, theme. We have had ample opportunity to observe how deeply Indian culture is interested in making some form of rational sense of self-authenticating religious experiences.

However, even a literalist stance, provided that it is consequential, can reveal the limitations of a simplistic 'cult of Eastern silence'. Were we in a position to consult Vimalakīrti on this, his answer might be something like the following. Obviously, 'silence' is a conditioned phenomenon. Just as it makes sense to speak of the colour white only when there is at least one other colour that is not white, silence exists only by virtue of sound. Thus not just words are conditioned and empty, but also silence. Therefore one cannot absolutize it. In the immediate context of the *sūtra*, it serves to illustrate the emptiness of all words. But in the wider context, silence itself is revealed as relative. Vimalakīrti's commitment to the world expresses itself in actions motivated by compassion, and not in words or in their opposite, silence. Through his 'skill in means' (*upāyakauśalya*), Vimalakīrti can manipulate actions, words and, in this particular case, silence, for a particular purpose. The purpose of his silence is to make the disciples stop talking about *advaya*, and 'do it' instead. I would also imagine that the person who, after perhaps a month-long struggle, is hit by the 'dynamic silence' that is hinted at in the 'sound made by one hand clapping' (this is a famous Ch'an/Zen puzzle, *kōan*) experiences a loud bang.

The romantic writing on 'Eastern silence' deals with more than just silence as a method or as an attitude. A lot has been made of pronouncements in Indian scriptures about the ineffable nature of the absolute. Time and again reference is made to the Upaniṣadic passage which tells us that ultimately all we can say about the *ātman* (in which we realize *brahman*) is *nêti*, *nêti*. With tedious regularity this phrase is mistranslated as 'not thus, not thus'. At least one ought to be accurate in one's mystifications. What the phrase means is that the *ātman* can be described, but only in terms of negative attributes. The phrase itself reads: 'This here is the *ātman* [described as] "not", "not".'[23] In another famous passage, *brahman* is referred to as that 'from which all words, together with the intellect, return, not having reached it'.[24] But if this were all, nobody would know about the Indian religions, there would be no Indian religious literature, and the country would be filled with silent sages. Silence remains a contextually conditioned mode of relating to the world.

At this point I am tempted to enter a little side-street off the main road of European literature and introduce you to the writer Robert Walser. His seemingly idyllic writing is characterized by an extraordinary lack of personal commitment and involvement. Totally oblivious to what literature 'ought to deal with', he aims at complete neutrality and rejects any form of judgement, of values, and of imposing anything of himself on to the subjects he writes about. This could be phrased as passive openness to reality, or as an utter lack of desire and discriminating thought. This is best illustrated in his own words; but, to make things easier, I have chosen some examples in which Walser himself hints more consciously at such a literary programme. The following two extracts are taken from a fictional letter from a painter to a poet.

At present I am living in a small town ... that is situated in the most beautiful and charming landscape which a healthy, lively imagination can visualize. The countryside around it is so beautiful, so green, so inviting and captivating, so lovely and, in its soft loveliness, so entrancing, that it seems one could say that it is fit for the reception of a princess, as it were. I assure you that I am enraptured and that I would wish I could describe to you, at least vaguely accurately, this profound natural rapture, this joy which is as great as it is genuine, in sentences and words.

I paint after nature. I go out into the fresh air, take my fill looking at the divine face of nature, and carry home some deep impression, a projected picture or texture, in order to materialize that idea in my room ... Nature is great in such a mysterious, inexhaustible manner that the moment one enjoys it, one begins to suffer as well. But I remember to remind myself that perhaps nowhere in the world can happiness be found without the admixture of pain – which really means to say simply no more than that I am struggling. Melodies get mixed into the colours which are in the whole expansive nature. Then also our thoughts are added to this. Moreover I would like to ask you to consider that everything is constantly changing, the times of day, morning, afternoon and evening; that already the air is actually something quite strange, peculiar and fluid which flows around all phenomena, provides all materiality with manifold surprising faces, and transforms, bewitches all forms. Now picture a brush and a palette; all the slowness of the tools, of the craftsman's work by means of which the impatiently yearning painter is supposed to capture, captivate as something solid and lasting, transform into radiant, lively pictures which brightly blaze up from the picture-soul, the thousand forms of strange, vague and scattered beauty which often meet the eye only fleetingly – then you will understand the struggle! Alas, why cannot the love that we feel, the joy, the contented charming thought, the yearning, the ardent well-intended wish, or the pure, unadulterated, blissful contemplation be sufficient![25]

Stylistically (and that is typical of all his writing) we note his hesitation to commit himself: strings of near synonyms attempt to capture an idea within, extraordinarily convoluted sentences are used as nets to hold on to fleeting impressions, and constantly adverbial qualifiers soften the impact of statements. When Walser does express a global truth ('all happiness is mixed with pain'), immediately he shrinks back and modifies it by turning it into a bit of personal information. Generally his peculiar style is the means by which he attempts to realize what he puts into the mouth of the painter. He is after a blissful, passive contemplation of reality without the interference of substantial forms and definite ideas – a reality aptly symbolized in its fluidity by the air. Like our Buddhist material, this goes hand in hand with an absence of desire; and what better place to realize this than a brothel? Here now is a passage which is found in a little piece called 'Weakness and strength', in which Walser reports on a (presumably fictional) first visit to such a house of ill repute (which Vimalakīrti also frequented).

A receptionist took me to a group of girls who were not badly made up and I chose one of them. A bottle of champagne was brought; the girl said that this was proper, and I did not object. The perfumed state she was in greatly attracted me to her. She took her clothes off and asked me to do the same; I obeyed her like a child ... I had not gone to the house out of need, but out of a sense of duty; I ordered myself to go, although I had no inclination to do so ... There was no question of satisfaction; she offered me what I did not need, gave me what I did not take; nothing in me demanded anything of her ... I told her 'It is not your fault, but that of my lack of desire which does not let me take any pleasure in possession ...' I was born to be without need.[26]

All this may seem rather far-fetched in an explication of Indian thought. But no less an author than Canetti can say this about Walser.

His deep and instinctive dislike of everything 'elevated', of everything that has status and pretension, makes him an essential poet of our time that suffocates from power ... It is not possible to read him without feeling ashamed about everything that one regarded as important in the external world. Therefore he is his own saint, not a saint by antiquated and empty prescriptions.[27]

In the course of his life (and his writing), Walser's enthusiastic openness for the world changes gradually into pessimism and despair. His earlier expectant passivity is replaced by the realization that there is nothing to wait for. Biographically this is mirrored in Walser's madness due to which he spent the rest of his life in a mental asylum, 'the monastery of modern times',[28] as Canetti calls it, and thereby establishes the logical link between Walser's 'sanctity' and madness. At this point our comparison does, I think, break down. Whatever similarities we may see in the themes of not interfering, not imposing ideas, and not desiring, neither Mahāyāna Buddhism nor the Advaita recommends that kind of monastery. However lovingly the Mānbhāvs may call Guṇḍam Rāūḷ 'mad', they do not mean it in a clinical sense.

'Why cannot blissful contemplation be sufficient?' Obviously life is more than the cultivation of ecstatic rapture at the beauties of nature; there are darker sides which even Walser, however much he may try to ignore them, eventually has to acknowledge, both in his writing and in his own life. But the question was asked in the specific context of artistic expression. Now one could answer that Walser's struggle with words was his way of fighting off madness and of maintaining a balanced attitude, by attempting to keep captive in words a sense of reality that he feels slipping away from him. Yet if we knew nothing about his madness, the question would allow us to focus on a further theme, silence (here Walser's passive receptivity) that stimulates poetic words (his desire to communicate through his writing).

A fine example of how silence generates its own poetic words is found in Gurū Nānak's *Japjī*. Gurū Nānak, the founder of Sikhism, had his roots in the North Indian *sant* tradition which, indeed, emphasized the ineffable nature of the Absolute. Yet, as he tells us in this poem, which is one of the most revered prayers among the Sikhs, while his thoughts are busy stressing that God cannot possibly be described, his tongue is busy bursting out with words about the same. Thus the compulsion to speak is itself a self-authenticating experience. His words cannot speak about God the ineffable, and attempts to do so merely repeat this inability. Yet the urge to speak speaks, as it were, of God. Here is a small sample from the poem.

> Innumerable [your] names, innumerable [your] places;
> inaccessible, inaccessible [your] innumerable worlds –
> to say 'innumerable', is itself nonsensical.
> Yet [your] Name [is produced] by letters,
> [your] praise [is sung] through words;
> with words [we] must write about mystical knowledge,
> with words hymns [about] the depth of [your] qualities;
> [we] must talk about the Word with words.[29]

Similar ideas were expressed by Caṭakōpaṉ (Nammāḻvār), one of the South Indian Tamil saints of the latter part of the first millennium who are known as the Āḻvārs. A whole song of his tells how he falls silent because Viṣṇu/Kṛṣṇa has entered his tongue, making it speak out about God to the world.[30]

Even in less overtly theistic contexts, such an urge to speak stimulated by religious 'silence' can be observed. One example is Bahiṇā Bāī, the seventeenth-century Marathi poetess we have discussed previously. She wrote a moving autobiography (in Marathi verse) about the years when she was a young girl. She had to suffer enormous hardship and physical brutality, particularly at the hands of her husband, but her *bhakti* somehow saw her through that difficult time. Then one day 'all things were forgotten and silence descended ... Duality disappeared in the one and undivided essence in which words lose their sound.'[31] This overwhelming experience, clearly phrased in *advaita* terms, had not at all the effect we would expect. For, contained within that experience, Bahiṇā Bāī felt the urge to speak out: biographically that was the moment when she began to compose poetry. These are a few examples of silence not being empty at all, but impelling the utterance of words. And in all three cases it is the medium of poetry that is resorted to. The time has come, I think, to take a closer look at religious poetry generally.

India produced a whole host of poetic traditions. But for the present exploration I shall focus on only one of them, the *kāvya*. This is primarily a highly learned and complex style cultivated in Sanskrit, but it found imitators in other languages, such as Prakrit, Apabhraṃśa and Tamil. On the one hand, it comes closest to what we would expect from 'poetry' in the sense that we use the word; but on the other hand, it manifests itself also as unrhymed, unmetrical prose. (The reverse is also true: there is a lot of metrical and even rhymed 'poetry' in India which does no more than summarize a lesson in mathematics.) What we are mainly interested in here is one characteristic feature of *kāvya*: its use of a whole host of carefully formulated and conventionalized figures of speech (*alaṅkāras*). But let me introduce the material in a less abstract way.

Fortunately for us, *kāvya* does not just describe the world – in whatever complex and sophisticated terms it likes – but it also describes itself. In other words, the poets build self-reflections into their poetry. Govardhana provides us with striking illustrations of this feature. In perhaps as much as ten per cent of his poems, our poet from twelfth-century Bengal employs a symbolism which one could style, somewhat jokingly, 'hole in the fence'. Often this symbolism appears precisely in this form of wording and literal sense. Thus, a man is reminded of his luck by pointing out how a particular girl looks at him through a hole in the fence surrounding her house.[32] Or we hear that a man is watching a couple through the hole in such a fence: the more she strokes and fans her husband, the happier he becomes. (For those not familiar with such material I may be allowed to explain what is obvious to the connoisseur: she is putting her husband to sleep so that she can receive her lover – the man watching.)[33] In another poem, the nectar of the gods is written off as insipid, when compared with a kiss a man can get from a girl who offers him her lips through a hole in the fence.[34] Besides this literal usage of the symbol – for which I could quote many more instances – Govardhana applies it to all kinds of further situations in which some form of fence, protection, cover, hide, wall, blockage, secret, or surface is pierced and thereby some hidden wonder revealed. But what Govardhana reveals through such symbolism is his own role: he the poet is the prying eye, the peeping Tom as it were, who prods at things and makes small openings and explores what lies behind. Thereby he can debunk, ridicule and establish totally new connections between things, and causalities between events.

The 'ornaments' (*alaṅkāras*), or figures of speech, are the tools he employs for his task. The world is made sense of in a uniquely poetic manner, its surface is broken through, and extraordinary non-dual relationships established. By now I am not talking any more exclusively about Govardhana, but about the *kāvya* poet generally. Things are not really what they appear to be on the surface – that is what such a poet wants to demonstrate. Now obviously the purpose of looking at the style of *kāvya* and at the role of the poet is not to explore the Indian perception of female anatomy or marital (and extra-marital) happiness. So what does it all have to do with religion? My choice of secular, erotic subjects for the initial characterization of *kāvya* was intentional: I wanted to highlight that the Indian *kāvya* poet is not *ex officio* (meaning: by virtue of being Indian) engrossed in *yoga* and seeing everything in some mystical and all-embracing profound vision of oneness. He is very much a craftsman who, in the tradition of his craft, constructs things comparable to tables and chairs. Once this point is realized, we can turn to the application of this craft to religious matters. At that stage, then, *kāvya* (and poetry generally) turns into an 'aesthetic' mode of making sense of the world.

One of the greatest strengths of European literature, modern and sometimes not-so-modern, lies in the fact that the author can draw on a very wide range of first-hand experiences in a great variety of 'walks of life'. This may or may not be the same as saying that he has had the advantage of a 'bohemian' existence. Not many parallels could be found in classical, or indeed modern, Indian literature. But certainly one of the great exceptions to this rule is the poet Bāṇa who lived during the seventh century AD and (eventually at least) settled at the court of Kanauj. Like few others – and some of them will be mentioned presently – he illustrates how *kāvya* can be applied to religious material. For example, take the following situation.

Imagine a path meandering through the forest. A prince is travelling along it, to visit a temple of the Goddess. He passes large trees, and little fields with scarecrows made of straw by the tribesmen living in hamlets nearby. Then from a distance the temple's flag waving in the breeze becomes visible, and soon the company reaches the actual shrine, guarded, as it were, by a large statue of a water-buffalo. They enter the compound, circumambulate the shrine, and do their *pūjā* with the help of an old and infirm priest.

An innocuous little episode, of no great interest to anybody, you might think. However, when the reader has followed Bāṇa in his description of the scene,[35] he may well think that he has been watching a Hammer House of Horror movie. By skilfully applying the techniques of *kāvya*, every smallest detail of the scenario is made transparent, to reveal the terror that lurks behind the innocent surface. At least twenty or thirty times, blood is alluded to, and references are made to animal and human sacrifices. Redness pervades the whole scene: the temple flag, the saffron powder smeared on various objects, flowers, and the setting sun. And time and again this evokes in the poet's mind 'bloody pieces of flesh', 'freshly cut-off limbs of sacrificial animals', and 'rows of human heads hung up'. Appropriately, in the date-palms with their raised fronds, and in the prickly coconuts, can be perceived the terror which expresses itself in human beings by making the hair stand on end – through horripilation.

The total mental image built up in this way is full of tension and conflicting emotions, and is in a sense a poetic *via negativa.* The beauty of the idyllic landscape and of the innocuous little shrine is aesthetically fused with the terrifying aspects of Goddess religion. Thus *bhakti*, the submission and devotion expressed by the prince, is the only answer to such a variegated divine reality.

But Bāṇa can do more, as I hope to show through a few comments on his *Caṇḍīśatakam*.[36] The raw material used here is the myth of the Goddess fighting a bloody battle with the demons and eventually killing their leader, Mahiṣa ('Buffalo'), in an equally bloody duel. But instead of dwelling generally on this violence and bloodshed, Bāṇa focuses on or, we could say, takes a series of close-ups from, one small detail: the Goddess putting her foot on Buffalo's head. Indeed, this is seen also as the fatal act that kills the demon. But at the same time it is presented as an act of salvation: through this physical contact, Buffalo receives her saving grace and achieves liberation. The symbolism infused into this derives from secular love-poetry where in a rather stereotyped fashion the unfaithful lover invariably ends up lying at the feet of his sulking or infuriated beloved, begging for forgiveness. Even when she kicks him, he is delighted, because this indicates an imminent end to her sulks and anger, and reconciliation is at hand. But furthermore, the dual relationship of Goddess and Buffalo, and beloved and lover, is through the means of *kāvya* widened to encompass a universal situation: the relationship between the human devotee and the divine. Through the Buffalo, Bāṇa depicts all human lovers of the Goddess; and the saving grace which her kicking foot symbolizes includes the element of punishment, since as beings in *saṃsāra*, we are all loaded with negative *karma*.

I hope it has become clear that *kāvya* can achieve wonderful things. It does far more than just add elegant sophistication to a statement that could also be made in a much simpler and more comprehensible manner. *Kāvya* is a particular mode of analysing the world, of looking and experiencing its phenomena. And in the hands of religious poets, it turns into an intrinsic element of stimulating religious experience itself. The following examples will illustrate this with all clarity.

Śrīvaiṣṇavism, the movement for which Rāmānuja provided the definite doctrinal foundation, acquired in Veṅkaṭanātha (or Vedāntadeśika, the 'Vedānta Teacher') one of its most outstanding poets. He lived a long life of almost a hundred years (traditionally, AD 1268–1368). Not only did he produce learned philosophical treatises in Sanskrit, which made Dasgupta speak of him as a 'towering figure in Śrīvaiṣṇava philosophy',[37] and write a whole string of theological works in Tamil; but also composed poetry on a large scale. Thus, when he is called a 'lion among poets and philosophers', the term is anything but rhetorical. Besides his two major epics on the lives of Kṛṣṇa and Rāma, a very long drama, and a collection of *subhāṣitas*, his twenty-eight Sanskrit *stotras* appear like small fry indeed. Yet even here, in any one of many of these 'hymns', we find more material than could be discussed appropriately in the present context. So let me merely make a few comments on one of these, the *Dehalīśastuti*.[38]

The setting of this poem is the temple of Kōvalūr, and that offers four immediate and concrete areas of inspiration to the poet. First, there is local mythology which tells how Viṣṇu came to abide in the temple. Secondly, there is pan-Indian mythology connected with Viṣṇu's Vāmana-*avatāra* or Dwarf incarnation. For it is Vāmana who eternalized himself in this place. Thirdly, there is the temple statue and the temple ritual generally. Fourthly, we have local hagiography dealing with the lives of the three earliest Āḻvārs. The techniques of the *kāvya* allow Veṅkaṭanātha to fuse all four areas, to make them interpret one another and to build up one coherent vision of divine grace pervading the cosmos. This then also allows him personal entrance, both as a devotee and as a poet.

Local legend tells us that one rainy night three devotees took shelter under the porch of a house in Kōvalūr. These were the three earliest Āḻvārs, who until then had neither met nor composed any poetry. There was just enough space for them to stand, but then they felt the presence of a fourth person who began to squeeze them. Thus made aware of Viṣṇu being amongst them, they all burst out in song. The poet sees in the squeezing a metaphorical production of sugar-cane juice (the Āḻvārs' poetry conveying divine grace, sweetness and beauty), imagines in Viṣṇu's expansion of his body a replica of Vāmana's expansion to cosmic size (an act of salvation for the whole cosmos), and in the god allowing himself to be squeezed he reads a sign of humility which calls out for poetic comment and song – his own incompetent poem.

Hectic movement is expressed through the organization of the poem: from the remote (like the Ganges in northern India) to the close at hand (the Peṇṇai river in front of the temple, which is seen as superior in sanctity to the Ganges); from the the past (the Vāmana *avatāra* and the Āḻvār anecdote) to the present (the availability of grace in the temple); from heaven to earth and from earth to heaven (Vāmana's descent and rise, the descent of the Ganges, the path towards heaven opened for the Āḻvārs and the poet himself). Such dynamic movement is infused with a coherent symbolism of 'liquidity': there are endless puns on *rasa* as 'juice', 'pleasure', 'beauty', and 'divine grace'. Like two amorous lovers, Viṣṇu and Lakṣmī are splashing water at each other, but the billowing ocean is the cosmos, the history of divine grace the dynamic movement. And salvation is obtained by letting oneself be carried away by the waves of the divine *līlā*, 'play' or 'game', of beauty. Like the man who has learnt to swim, the devotee 'hands himself over' to the beauty of grace. It is the poet who in his own way attempts through his poem to convey some of that beauty and to draw others into it.

Being a theologian and poet, Veṅkaṭeśa offers us a fairly unique chance to compare what he does or has to say in either capacity. This is not the place to explore the details. But it can be shown without much difficulty that a certain discontinuity exists between the theology expounded by the theologian Veṅkaṭanātha, and the theology that could be extricated through literary criticism from his poetry. The Vedānta simply has not yet developed the conceptual tools to envisage devotion (styled *prapatti*, lit. 'taking refuge') as an act of handing oneself over to a divine *līlā* which has very pronounced aesthetic characteristics. It may not be too contrived to compare Vimalakīrti's silence with Veṅkaṭeśa's speaking as a poet: both illustrate the limitations of a purely conceptual, systematic account of religion. And both complement this by action: moving through the world with compassion in case of the *bodhisattva*, and composing poetry in that of the Vedānta-teacher. From the silence of listening in to the *līlā* of Viṣṇu and Lakṣmī, a creative act and new words emerge.

At this point we can return to the Goddess and cast a brief glance over another religious poem in which the nexus of ideas explored so far is even more apparent. This is the *Devīśatakam* attributed to the ninth-century Kashmiri poetician, Ānandavardhana.[39] The poem is a prayer addressed to the Goddess, and a song in her praise; that is all that can be said about the plot. Mythical episodes, such as her killing of Buffalo are known, but merely alluded to and not spelled out in any narrative manner. Her nature is characterized as encompassing all aspects of reality and as fusing all its diverse and opposing aspects. Thus she is the seat of both liberation and worldly comforts; she is both *prakṛti* and *brahman*, both horrific and most enchanting. As Absolute, she is responsible both for our minds being clouded in ignorance and for mental clarity and the knowledge that yields liberation. She is pure wisdom.

So far things are still relatively easy. That the Goddess should appear here as the *coincidentia oppositorum* is nothing novel, because this is a general feature in Devī religion. That a 'not – not' silence is hinted at is natural in view of the Upaniṣadic passages dealing with this theme. And that *kāvya* is an ideal medium of expressing all this has become apparent from what was said earlier on about its potentials.

Some additional complications arise from the way Ānandavardhana applies the *kāvya* techniques. With relentless vigour each and every aspect of *kāvya* is demonstrated, every figure of speech utilized, and not a single statement made which does not contain at least one further hidden meaning. All the time, language is cut up in different ways and made to express different (and naturally contradictory) things. What is said when read forward is modified by what emerges when the same stanza is read backwards. One stanza may say six or ten different things when read in six or ten different languages. Meaning is produced out of the most minimalist poem – the one that uses a single consonant, and language is forced into all kinds of complex visual patterns. To allow a two-line stanza to be read following the pattern of a 'cow urinating' (*gomūtrika*) – taking a syllable alternatively from the top and the bottom line – is nothing compared with the 'great discus', which from the syllables on its spokes builds up new stanzas.

But all this could be written off as verbal gimmickry, were it not for one important fact: the Goddess herself is stated to be 'speech' and 'wisdom'. This now throws totally new light on this verbal firework called *Devīśatakam*. For it means that through the poem the Goddess expresses herself, in all her manifold and contradictory aspects. The poetic constraints of, for example, making a poem out of one single consonant, symbolize, and in a sense are, the limitations of the human mind in *saṃsāra*. To be able to manipulate language to the extent done here corresponds directly to the freedom of the liberated mind that can swim on the waves of divine speech and wisdom.

But even this is not yet the end. The poem is a prayer for protection. It would not be too far-fetched to envisage a court situation in which the poet is personally threatened by the intrigues of his rivals, or in which preparations are made by the king for a war; *kāvya* generally was perceived as a means of creating stability in an unstable political situation. To ask the Goddess, who is Speech, for assistance implies that language itself can have a stabilizing or protective effect. And, indeed, most of the visual patterns into which language is forced are weapons or associated with warfare: battle-drums, arrows, bows, swords, and the battle-discus which, unlike the Olympic variety, has lots of little knives attached to its edge. By shaping language into these 'weapons', by overcoming the constraints involved in this, the poet thus becomes the vehicle for divine grace and protection in a very concrete context. Reciting the poem actualizes Speech, the saving and protecting Goddess.

By looking at all these concrete examples, we seem to have moved rather far away from the learned framework of discussion that we were developing previously. But this is only seemingly the case. Modes of making sense, *advaya* or *advaita* situations, click phenomena, rational reflection on maintaining a balance – these and other academic notions will resurface when we look closer at the realm into which we have been drawn: that of the irreducible particulars in which lie beauty, ecstasy and suffering.

CHAPTER 23

Irreducible particulars

In the early 1980s, travellers on the M4 motorway into London, just before coming into Chiswick, could study a remarkable phenomenon. On the left is a row of terraced houses with slate-covered roofs, and on one of them was written, in large white capital letters: THE ROOF. I have no idea what the real significance of it could have been; for all I know, it might have advertised a punk-band. But the dozens of times it jolted me out of my morning drowsiness set my own train of thought in motion – which, naturally, is directly relevant to what we have been discussing. The universe is filled with things or phenomena which we, in our everyday lives, perceive merely as an amorphous collection, and not in their individuality. When philosophizing, we abstract even further and speculate on the genus or species, and not the individual object. We speak of 'the human soul', 'the nature of aesthetic experience', or 'the world of phenomena', but not of 'the soul of Mr Smith', etc. It is perhaps with reference to such generalizations that Canetti produced the biting aphorism: 'Most philosophers have too limited a vision of the variety of human customs and potentials.'[1] THE ROOF can serve us as a reminder that, in spite of the existence of a set of millions and millions of very similar objects called 'roofs', the individual roof cannot be totally subsumed under the universality of the set. While in previous chapters we have been generally exploring the relationship between the world of phenomena and a universal such as 'emptiness' or 'enlightenment' or *brahman*, certainly some of the material discussed in Chapter 22 suggests that we might pay closer attention to the particularity of those phenomena. Only that particular statue of Mallī assisted the kings in their insight. Humour only works when the unexpected – and that means, the particular or unique – gets involved. To Veṇkaṭanātha the whole economy of Viṣṇu's grace becomes only meaningful in relation to himself, and that in the one concrete and particular temple of Kōvalūr. Ānandavardhana squeezes, as it were, Speech into the very concrete shape of weapons and impossibly difficult verbal configurations. Gurū Nānak felt impelled to use concrete words to speak of the Word. Particularity thus appears as a theme worth exploring further. The basic questions we can ask, in the light of our previous observations, could be the following. Why does Indian culture express such an extraordinary ambivalence to the phenomena of ordinary life? How have humour and poetry (which manifestly involve the particular) been interpreted? Are there further modes in which religion draws in a positive manner on the concrete world of everyday experience? And, finally, how does monotheistic Hinduism relate to all this?

Yet the relevance of such big questions may not be immediately obvious from our starting-point, which will strike many as rather trite. Not much profit seems to lie in speculating on THE ROOF, as opposed to 'roof' in general. But the perception of 'triteness' in such an approach is actually, as I hope to show, already part of a carefully constructed defence mechanism, a fence we have erected to protect ourselves against a potentially devastating influx of 'particulars'. For the innocuous word 'particular' covers up a whole scale of graded phenomena. Our generalizations filter out aspects of uniqueness which under normal circumstances we could not actually cope with, were we forced to face them. I am obviously no longer thinking of roofs, but of other kinds, or 'lower' levels, of particularity.

A few words of explanation derived from familiar territory may be useful. So let me indicate, from material we all know, the nexus of ideas we are going to explore for India. Let us look briefly at the way we use words like 'vulgar', 'common', 'obscene' and 'dirty'. In most commonly used expressions involving any of these words, they denote far more than, or actually something different from, the literal meaning. A 'dirty' old man is not somebody who could do with a bath. 'Don't be common (or vulgar)' usually implies: don't be individual – make your behaviour conform to the standard we have established, i.e. which is 'common' to us, to distinguish ourselves from the *vulgus*, 'ordinary' people. 'That's obscene!' may well refer to something that is totally unexpected or ugly or out of the ordinary.

Thus, what we see here is a whole range of associations that carry aesthetic, moral, social, or even ideological, and above all, religious overtones. In social terms, a particular group of people, 'the élite', distances itself from 'the masses'. On the surface it looks like individuality standing in contrast to the general ('the masses'). But underneath, the opposite is the case. To be 'vulgar' really implies to stick out as individual in a crowd of conformists – through dress, accent, speech, or behaviour. The man wearing a purple suit at a funeral is 'vulgar' because he sticks out in a group of mourners clad in black. In religious terms, a 'pure' person implies not just a 'clean' person ('cleanliness is next to godliness'); and not just a morally perfect being. It implies some sort of ethereal entity: without 'impure' thoughts (in other words, interest in anything sexual) and physicality generally.

I hope that by now it has become clear to what extent 'particularity' actually implies the unacceptable face of being human. There are layers and layers of covers that hide our individuality, and clothes are just one kind. No wonder that nakedness, sexuality, and all types of instinctive behaviour are censored, for in these we are most unique, individual and particular. In general terms, there is nothing uniquely Western or Indian about all this. Whether conceptualized (on the Indian side) as *saṃsāra*, or as suffering based on 'thirst', or whether analysed by anthropologists as purity and pollution, or as the fear of anything that exclusively belongs to one person (like his saliva), the underlying rationale is the same. The more man gets caught up in the particularity of space, time and matter, and that means, the more he becomes an individual, the greater the religious ambivalence, concern, aversion and censure become.

With these thoughts in mind we can now continue our discussion of Indian attitudes towards the particular. There is no need to worry: after all, I have spoken of a scale, and the truly 'obscene' makes up no more than the extreme pole of that scale. On the whole, we shall be able to restrict ourselves to reasonably respectable subjects.

A convenient starting point is poetry, or better, poetic conventions and techniques. Since the particular is essential in poetry, it offers very concrete illustrations of the filtering processes that keep certain levels of particularity at bay in Indian culture. In spite of everything that has been said about *kāvya* so far, a closer look at it reveals that it does not really open up the whole range of phenomena in the world of ordinary human experience. For there are various constraints at work. Carefully laid down rules specify what kind of subject-matter is actually permissible. Marital unfaithfulness and the sexual act are permitted themes, but there must not be any reference to what we would call the 'clinical' side of things. A spade is never called a 'spade' here. While in the oldest poets of this genre (in particular Hāla) social constraints are still absent, with the later Sanskrit *kāvya* poets, a very idealized 'hero' and 'heroine' emerge. These are refined people belonging to the leisure classes of an urban and court environment. For Hāla it was still possible to explore in the sexual behaviour of peasants, wrestlers, hunters and brigands their basic humanity. This provides his poetry with a particular charm and liveliness. Govardhana has preserved some of it, but note that he has to present it as an imitation of Hāla.

In the *caṅkam* poetry of ancient Tamil Nadu we can see similar constraints at work. Since the poetic theory that was systematically derived from the poetry by the Tamils themselves is known to us, it is also easy for us to trace these constraints here. We can see how, quite consciously, all kinds of subject matter and social class are filtered out from what is permitted to appear in the five landscapes of (respectable) love.[2] Moreover, the poetic theory lays down a further rule which makes explicit what I have said earlier on. While it is permitted to mention individual names and to identify particular individuals in the context of 'external matters' (*puṟam*), which here means primarily wars, cattle-raids and battles, the treatment of 'internal matters' (*akam*) must involve the anonymity of all persons. Thus, while a man makes a name for himself – we could say, realizes his social individuality – through heroism in battle, as lover he loses himself into a stereotype. Breaking the rule means to become notorious, like the poetess Nakkaṇṇai. Three love poems[3] are attributed to her which were not permitted to figure in an *akam* anthology, and were thus included in the collection of *puṟam* poems. These are not outrageous poems by any standard. In a very refined manner she confesses her attraction to the muscular arms and chest of a wrestler. But she breaks the rule by naming her lover: a Cōḻa prince who appears to have wrestled in the spare time he had from fighting battles. An element of particularity is made socially apparent which, according to *caṅkam* taste, should have remained restricted to the privacy of the home.

Ancient Tamil literature has also preserved a most extraordinary collection of one hundred and fifty poems, the *Kalittokai*. The only conventional rule it observes is that of the anonymity of lovers. But in every other respect, it goes its own ways to such an extent that we might well see in it a conscious mockery of *caṅkam* sentiments. Not only does it present us with situations that are totally unacceptable by previous poetic standards, like a man chatting up a girl who, at a closer look, turns out to be far too young.[4] It also delves into the depths of Tamil society by offering poetic explorations of the love-life of cowherds and goatherds which involves dangerous bullfights, and it contains a long poem on a hunchback woman and a midget figuring out how to make love to each other, in spite of the obvious physiological difficulties![5] It is most unfortunate that the wider context of the *Kalittokai* is totally unknown to us. It seems to have been composed around AD 500, when the south had begun to react strongly against the religious and cultural dominance of the Buddhists and Jains. For all I know, such an exploration of *kāma* in all aspects of life and on the most 'vulgar' level was directed against the Jain and Buddhist aversion to 'particularity'. There is certainly a pronounced Hindu flavour in the work (to the extent that the poems make mythical allusions), although obviously its basic character is secular. What we can say, however, is that the collection illustrates an attitude towards the world which shows affinities with religious material, of a slightly later date, to which we shall turn presently.

So far we have looked at how native Indian poetic theory (both for *kāvya* and *caṅkam* literature) lays down rules concerning the permitted range of particulars. Now we saw in the previous chapter how *kāvya* 'breaks through the surface' of things, revealing all kinds of hidden secrets; how it builds up its own complex structures of symbolism and presents reality in all its variegated and contradictory aspects. But the method that we used to unravel all this was our own; it was not another aspect of the native poetic theory. It is true that *kāvya* contains self-reflections, and that such a method was derived from these clues – it is thus not arbitrary. But it is worth emphasizing that our analysis does not correspond to how native poetics investigate the nature of poetry.[6] The direction taken there is different from the one we have taken thus far. Naturally this will make us curious about the indigenous theory. So let us now turn our attention in the direction of classical Sanskrit poetics. This is a subject that will allow us (both *en route* to it and once we have got there) to string together quite a variety of loose ends and, perhaps even more surprisingly, acquaint us with religious ecstasy.

I would like to start by introducing two anthologies of Sanskrit *kāvya* poetry. Since material from it will be referred to in three different contexts, it may not be superfluous to give some details about them. Both were compiled in Bengal, and they share a fair amount of common poetry. Both have flowery and, rather unfortunately, lengthy titles. The older of the two, of the early eleventh century AD (when Bengal was ruled by the Buddhist Pālas), was compiled in the tranquil surroundings of a Buddhist monastery; it is called the *Treasury of the Precious Stones That Are Artfully Composed Poems* (*Subhāṣitaratnakoṣa*). The second was put together at the Hindu Sena court around AD 1200 and is entitled the *Well-Composed Verses That Are Nectar for the Ears* (*Saduktikarṇāmṛta*).[7]

The first 'precious stone' selected here is usually ascribed to the name of Amaru (whether as actual poet, or as compiler of a collection of very similar verses by various poets, need not concern us).[8] I have chosen it not merely for its charm, but also as a convenient symbol of the aesthetic process as envisaged in native theory.

> I had run out of devices;
> as a final resort
> I lay prostrate at her feet.
> Her fine face rested on her hand.
> Then suddenly I received
> the news of her impending favours:
> a tear
> that had been kept back
> in the thick lashes of her eyes
> all of a sudden broke loose
> and splashed on to her breast.[9]

Amaru, here and elsewhere, aims at 'catching the fleeting moment'. Quite unique or 'particular' situations are envisaged, and the momentary interaction of a number of concrete factors triggers off a particular experience – both in at least one participant of the situation itself, and in us as the readers. The particular, unpredictable and unique event of the tear falling and splashing relieves the tension and the anger and produces a solution in a stereotyped situation of dilemma. Moreover, this ingenious poetic device of the 'tear splashing' makes us smile and enjoy the poem. But, as we shall see presently, both the events depicted in the poem and the poetic technique employed, when lifted on to an abstract level of theory, offer us a handy symbol of native aesthetics.

There is obviously nothing religious in this poem. However, it may be interesting to mention as an aside that Indian folklore has added to the figure of Amaru a particular twist, which does introduce a religious element. Once the great Śaṅkara, philosopher, ascetic and advocate of Advaita-Vedānta, was challenged: 'how can you write off the entire realm of the phenomena as illusion, if you yourself never have experienced them where they are most particular – in sexuality and love?' Śaṅkara accepted the challenge, and through the power of his *yoga* left his real body, to enter that of another person, Amaru, in order to experience all aspects of love and making love. Some recensions include the following poem, in which he wonders:

Am I Amaru, the suffering lover,
Or Śaṅkara working undercover? [10]

This is a very charming illustration of the contrast between what a poet like Amaru, who is out to catch the fleeting, unique moment of particularity, and a philosopher like Śaṅkara, who aims at transcending all phenomena, are doing. As far as the popular conception of Śaṅkara is concerned, he learnt nothing new from exposing himself to the particulars. However, we can find some suggestions that the Buddhists of medieval North India got more out of the particularity of the world. For this we have to return to the two anthologies mentioned earlier.

Ingalls, the translator of, and commentator on, the *Subhāṣita-ratnakoṣa*, identified a particular genre of poetry which is exclusive to these two anthologies. [11] This genre is represented by a few dozen poems of a strikingly realistic character. Sanskrit poetics have no place or patience for this type of poetry; they write it off as 'mere pictures' (*citra*), which could almost be translated as 'kitsch'. Purely descriptive passages are, in their own right, of no relevance to the refined Sanskrit or, for that matter, *caṅkam* poet, even though in both traditions they are used for metaphorical or allegorical purposes. Thus, when we find such poetry gathered together in these two anthologies, some explanation for this very striking fact is required. Ingalls has done his best to collect the facts known about this material. We seem to be dealing here with a particular group of poets – and a Yogeśvara is foremost amongst them – who lived in Bengal during the ninth and tenth centuries. Those were the days of the Pāla dynasty, and the Pālas were Buddhists. But, clearly, even the Hindu Senas were aware and proud of this local poetic heritage, and thus more of this poetry was included in the *Saduktikarṇāmṛta.* But what motive did local poets during the Pāla dynasty of Bengal have to develop a totally unique genre of realistic poetry? That has remained the mystery. The solution I shall suggest here is highly speculative, since it is based literally on *one* word.

Two groups of poems can be distinguished (although they cut across the individual poets): rather merry descriptions of all kinds of animals, of scenes of nature and of children playing; and, on the other hand, poems on poverty, suffering and old age. It is the latter group I restrict myself to, though it might be possible to accommodate even the first one in the explanation I suggest here. Here is one example dealing with poverty; it is found in the Sena anthology.

> Her emaciated body is propped up
> by nothing but indifference;
> her garment is in tatters;
> tears have washed clean her face.
> Asked for food by her children
> whose eyes and bellies
> are deep-set from hunger,
> the miserable woman
> would like to make last
> the one handful of grains
> for a hundred days.[12]

This is quite extraordinary material, as far as Sanskrit *kāvya* is concerned. And dozens of similar examples could be quoted. We are clearly delving here into aspects of the particular which conventional *kāvya* must avoid, since the persons it depicts are all idealized types that move in a perfect world of beauty and luxury.

The following example (by Yogeśvara, the most important poet in the group discussed here) might contain the clue for an explanation of this amazing genre of poetry. Its subject matter is

> villages in the morning
> where old men are sitting close together
> along the walls sheltered from the wind

> – beards brown from the clouds of smoke
> the cowdung fires send out–
> and crave for the warmth of sun.[13]

But the poem begins with, and thus heavily emphasizes, the words: '(such villages) give rise to anxiety [or, consternation]' (*udvegaṃ janayanti*). This *udvega* might provide us with the clue: for its synonym *saṃvega* is already used in Pali to denote a particular religious 'shock'. The Jains could have described the effect of Mallī's opening of the statue as *saṃvega*. A constellation of very particular elements produces what, in my terminology, would be a 'click phenomenon'. Suddenly, precisely because the world has been looked at in some of its most particular aspects, it reveals its inner dimension. And if it is true that through *udvega* the poet has revealed his motive, then we could say that here a special poetic culture was created, inspired by Buddhist ideas and ideals, which aims at generating such 'shocks' by offering a minute and very particular description of reality.

But this described reality need not always be 'unpleasant' (the conventional Buddhist themes of old age, disease and death) on the surface. Often we find a humorous note, as in the description of a traveller in worn-out clothes who, at the mere thought of the straw that some kind farmer might offer him to sleep on, falls asleep.[14] Anyway, this type of poetry would be a unique way of demonstrating how, through paying attention precisely to the irreducible particulars of reality, we can be jolted out of our mundane perception of it. If my interpretation is correct, we would be dealing here with a combination of the attitudinal and aesthetic modes in a typically Buddhist expression. This may be a highly speculative interpretation of this particular material; but, generally speaking, it is anchored solidly in Indian theories of language and poetry.

The very nature of meaningful human language contains a 'click phenomenon'. When we speak, we produce a sequence of sounds. Yet, suddenly, out of such a sequence of extremely short-lived, transient and discrete phenomena, something else 'bursts forth': it says *sphuṭ* or 'click' and the meaning of the sentence flashes through our mind. Indian grammarians and philosophers have discussed this particular phenomenon – the theory of *sphoṭa* – in great detail. What is interesting for us in all this is the fact that Indian thought conceptualized the sudden emergence of a mental phenomenon on the basis of a sequence of transient and individually meaningless particulars which precede the event itself. (This is the kind of symbolic interpretation which we could abstract from Amaru's poem on the tear splashing on to the woman's breast.) However, when we turn to the poeticians, we find them using a different terminology. The reasons for this difference may be that these intellectual traditions developed in isolation from each other; they may be professional rivalry. But irrespective of this, I think it is possible to recognize a related structure of thought here.

Ānandavardhana, whose *Hundred Stanzas on the Goddess* (*Devīśatakam*) I discussed briefly in the previous chapter, also plays an important role here. He wrote a treatise called *The Mirror of Resonance* (*Dhvanyāloka*) which had far-reaching influences on poetics and poetry, even though it was later interpreted in a rather one-sided manner. His suggestion is that language is capable of fulfilling various functions. In a sentence like 'this table is brown', it conveys meaning by the literal denotation of words. But when we refer to a man by saying 'he is an old ass', we don't use the literal meaning, because quite clearly we are not mistakenly categorizing a particular human being as a 'donkey'. But beyond this second, metaphorical, usage of language, we can make up a phrase like 'by the towers of London city'. Here a whole complex not just of ideas, but also of emotions is evoked. Any reader of the recent British press has already stored up all kinds of ideas in his mind concerning 'the City' and the kind of things that are going on there. By adding the phrase 'by the towers of ...' those kind of things are correlated to the biblical phrase 'by the towers of Babylon' and to all the sort of things that went on there. Thus language can evoke associations, and that is called 'resonance' (*dhvani*).

Ānandavardhana proceeds by analysing what precisely is 'resounded'. But since later theoreticians focused on only one aspect, we need not list here the wider spectrum suggested by him. The one idea that was picked up was fused with ideas developed in the context of the Indian theory of drama. This is the evocation or 'resonance' of *rasa*. The word itself can mean a host of different things, like the 'flavour' of a dish, the 'juice' of a fruit, or the 'emotion' of joy. Let me translate it here as 'aesthetic experience'.[15]

A poem, according to the theory we are exploring here, contains a carefully selected set of elements (such as a particular feature or gesture of a person, a flower, hints at the specific situation, etc.) Between them, these elements enclose a particular emotion (*bhāva*); in Amaru's poem mentioned above this could be identified as affection, regret and anger. Since they are carefully selected and put together (the element of poetic skill), these particulars of the poem, in interaction with each other, trigger off a particular experience in the listener: *rasa*. It is thus 'aesthetic rapture', but it remains tinged with the flavour of the original 'emotion' (*bhāva*) enclosed in the poem itself. For example – and this is a wonderful lesson for all puritanical literalists and do-gooders – if we happened to surprise two people involved in the act of making love, or if such an act were actually performed on stage, we would burst out laughing – so an Indian text says.[16] For in real life this is an extremely funny and unusual thing to do. It is a ludicrous act, when witnessed from the outside. On the other hand, the good poet can carefully choose such features from the total situation that, when we listen to his poem, trigger off an aesthetic experience with a decidedly erotic flavour. Thus the poet succeeds in rousing within us something comparable to the emotions that compelled the lover and his beloved to indulge in an act which, on the surface, looks quite ludicrous. Chords of a common humanity are struck, the resonance of which is our sharing the inner joy and fulfilment experienced by the lovers.

Incidentally, this is the method by which humour itself was conceptualized in classical India. A careful selection of elements making up a situation that encloses some funny incident can trigger off in us an aesthetic experience flavoured with the *rasa* of humour. What in real life might simply be silly, ridiculous, insulting, or rude can poetically be transformed into joyful sympathy and humorous compassion.

It is not difficult to see that the aesthetic experience of *rasa* is another illustration of a 'click phenomenon'. A sequence of elements, namely the words of a poem, pass through our minds, and suddenly the whole begins to fit together and conjures up an experience which, as such, cannot be conveyed by the literal meanings of the words. But it is not an automatic and mechanical process. For the poeticians mention two important conditions that regulate the spontaneous experience of *rasa*. One concerns the poet and his art. He must possess the particular skills and the imagination which alone will allow him to combine the various poetic components in such a manner that, through their interaction, *bhāva* not only appears in the poem, but can also be successfully communicated to the reader as *rasa*. The second condition concerns the reader or listener. However good and artfully put together a poem may be, it would be totally wasted on someone who had not received training in the art of appreciation. Thus, on the one hand, the experience of *rasa* is spontaneous. When, traditionally, people at an Indian concert suddenly burst out '*wah*! *wah*!', this is the external sign of the inner 'click' experience. That it is a laboriously gained spontaneity can be seen in cases where things go wrong, like when, at the instigation of an up-and-coming musician, an inexperienced person keeps on shouting '*wah*! *wah*!' at the wrong moments (as I witnessed more than once at concerts in Bombay).

This peculiar relationship between spontaneity and gradual learning of the art of being spontaneous is something which has already been encountered in a different context, namely in Buddhism. There it has been, time and again, an issue of considerable importance and controversy: to what extent must or can we prepare ourselves through various forms of 'training' for the enlightenment experience, and to what extent is such an experience a spontaneous phenomenon, since already innate in us? As far as the *rasa* theory is concerned, the situation is clear. However much poetry the boor listened to, he would never experience *rasa*.

So far we have discussed three components: reality itself, the poem that draws on it, and the 'connoisseur' (*sahṛdaya* or *rasika*) who experiences *rasa*. But at this point we can look at a fourth component, that of religion. We are perhaps not quite prepared for this, since in traditional Western culture a strict dividing line is drawn between artistic and religious experiences. Whether one likes Mozart, Beethoven, or Bartók is a matter of individual 'taste', but going to church or to the synagogue or the mosque is not open to discussion. In spite of the much proclaimed 'tolerance' of the Indian religions, the latter is not really the case here either. Thus by bringing religion into a discussion of Indian aesthetics I want to highlight the affinities that were realized here, both practically and theoretically, and that does include monotheism.

First of all, the very nature of the aesthetic rapture, as analysed so far, allows us to point at intrinsic similarities with religious experience. When we read the right kind of poem about a lover, not only do we abstract from the individual lover depicted, but we also transcend, in our *rasa* experience, our normal self-awareness. It is almost as if we merge in a universal experience of love that has cancelled out our own name and particularity. Such an approach is found, for instance, in the Kashmiri tradition of Abhinavagupta.[17] Secondly, there have been attempts to add to the classical set of eight *bhāvas* and their corresponding *rasas* a ninth one, that of *śānti*, the 'peace' achieved through religion. Thus here, instead of seeing in any kind of aesthetic experience a religious potential, a distinction is made between secular and religious aesthetics, and between a worldly poem or drama and a 'pious' one. From the set of particulars available to the poet, a small subset of overtly religious elements is selected. As before, the artfully constructed poem (for example about the simple and peaceful life of ascetics in the forest) will then trigger off an experience of 'religious peace' in the reader or listener. But somehow this approach did not much appeal to Indian sentiments. On the whole, this kind of distinction between a secular and religious poetic raw material was avoided. Thirdly, a religious component could be added by envisaging the hero of the poem as a divine being. Thus, as far as the *bhāva* and *rasa* of love are concerned, Kṛṣṇa offered ample opportunity here. Moreover, we have works in which Kṛṣṇa is dealt with poetically in the context of all eight or nine *rasas* which, by virtue of the divine hero, become tinged with a religious component.[18] But in a sense, this introduces once again a 'literalist' element, by distinguishing a secular from a religious *rasa* experience, at least as far as the lover is concerned.

These rather lengthy remarks on Indian poetic theory could hardly be justified were it not for the fact that such a theory, in a very much more direct manner, played an essential role in the formulation of a theology. Unlike other theologies that we have looked at so far (like that of Rāmānuja), it does not attempt to present (and thereby legitimate) religious beliefs in the rather unyielding mould of the Vedānta. Instead, it tries to provide a rational and systematic account of (certain types of) religious experience. At this point I can introduce a further mode: that of ecstasy.

Let me begin by illustrating the concrete basis of this theology by looking first at some of the external symptoms of what is called 'ecstasy'.

He ran off with the speed of wind, then suddenly he stood still like a pillar, paralysed and unable to move. His hair stood on end all over his body, and he was sweating profusely. Unable to speak, his throat could only emit gurgling sounds. His eyes were filled with tears, his body had turned white like a conch-shell and was shaken by spasms. Shivering and trembling, he collapsed on the ground.

Or again: 'Paralysed and then shaking, sweating and turning pallid, he wept and uttered indistinct sounds. His hair stood on end, he laughed, wept, danced about and sang. He jumped up and ran about, only to collapse and lose consciousness the next moment.'[19] These are descriptions of the mysticism of Caitanya who lived in Bengal and died in AD 1533.

Before commenting on this striking and puzzling behaviour, let me point out how directly all this is linked with our previous observations. For these reactions are the consequence of Caitanya's reciting poetry. In the second case this is explicitly stated and the poem is actually quoted: 'How could I pass these wretched nights, O Kṛṣṇa! without seeing you?' (This is a stanza from the *Kṛṣṇakarṇāmṛta*, a collection of erotic poems on Kṛṣṇa, of South Indian origin.) Hagiography on Caitanya is quite detailed, and thus we have a good knowledge of the kind of poetry that he loved to recite and that triggered off these ecstatic symptoms. The *Bhāgavata-purāṇa* is very important here (and more will be said about this important work presently), as are other overtly religious works like the *Kṛṣṇakarṇāmṛta.* Famous works like the *Gītagovinda*, the Bengali poetry of Caṇḍīdāsa and the Maithilī poems by Vidyāpati – all favourites of Caitanya – may deal with Kṛṣṇa. But, at least for the scholar, they are not overtly religious. But then poems are mentioned in the hagiography of Caitanya which we also find in the two anthologies mentioned above (the *Subhāṣitaratnakoṣa* and the *Saduktikarṇāmṛta*). Although we cannot be sure about the precise wording in which Caitanya knew them, in the anthologies, at least, these poems are definitely not about Kṛṣṇa. There they involve ordinary human lovers (as defined by Sanskrit poetics).[20] We have good reason to believe that Caitanya could read a whole range of erotic poetry, religious and secular, but that he perceived it inevitably as being about Kṛṣṇa.

Still in connection with the poetry, I would like to draw attention to two points that deserve to be discussed in more general terms at a later stage in our exploration. Usually, the poems that trigger off Caitanya's ecstatic behaviour are about 'separation' (*viraha*). When directly dealing with Kṛṣṇa, it means that the poems almost always talk about Rādhā, or some other milkmaid, and her sufferings and agonies caused by Kṛṣṇa's absence or unfaithfulness. Conventionally this is a poetic situation which allows for the depiction of maximum erotic arousal and longing. Now a lot of nonsense has been written on this theme, nonsense inspired by a naive literalist understanding of what is expressed here in the poetry. Because the poem is about 'separation', simplistically it is concluded that therefore, in religious terms, the 'soul' expresses its longing for union with the 'absent' or 'remote' divine. We shall see presently how misleading such an interpretation is. But let me briefly mention the second important point. When Caitanya exclaims 'O Kṛṣṇa! how can I spend these wretched nights without you?', in poetic terms he is making use of a conceit, for he is placing himself in the position of one of the mythical milkmaids. We may say that this is inevitable, since Kṛṣṇa is, after all, a male, and any mystic thus has to relate to him as if he were a female. But there is more to this, as we shall see below.

At present I want to return to the ecstatic behaviour shown by Caitanya. In isolation, it would be very difficult for us to make much sense of this, other than to suspect some mental disorder. However, what we find here is not really an isolated phenomenon. Already the *Bhāgavata-purāṇa*, Caitanya's favourite text, not only describes the *gopīs*, the milkmaids of Kṛṣṇa mythology, as behaving in a very similar manner; it also mentions the same symptoms frequently in connection with the ideal *bhakta*. This by itself is sufficient to suggest that behind the tears and the sweating, the uncontrolled bodily movements and pallor, the indistinct gurgling noises, the collapsing on the ground and the loss of consciousness, some generic type of *bhakti* behaviour is revealed. In other words, Caitanya does no more than what is, at least in our texts, perceived to be a general human potential.[21]

And, indeed, examples can be quoted from all over the world; a good amount of this material has been collected in I. M. Lewis' *Ecstatic Religion*.[22] This does not mean that the global context of interpretation suggested by Lewis exhausts what can be said about our Indian material. In a number of ways, the Indian cult of Kṛṣṇa ecstasy shows quite unique features. One of the most striking ones is probably the trigger mechanism of ecstasy. In most of the cases documented in Lewis, the trigger is some form of music, or prolonged rhythmic sequence of sound or recitation. Now, indeed, such features are found also with Caitanya and other figures. When I have said that he recited the poetry, we must imagine this to take place in a communal setting, accompanied by singing, dancing and music – the *kīrtan*. In the Western world we could go to some pentecostal churches, or watch the Hare Krishna, in order to get some impressions of what is talked about here.

However, from the point of view of the devotees themselves, these external and mechanical features are irrelevant: it is the poetry, the *rasa*, that is regarded as central. In other words, the whole is conceptualized in a unique way. The most apparent indication of this lies in the fact that ecstatic Kṛṣṇaism refuses to use a model almost universally employed in other types of ecstatic religion: that of possession. Thus, for example, in West Indian voodoo, which in turn is a transplant of traditional West African religion, the ecstatic experience is directly explained by reference to one or another deity entering the devotee, filling him and taking over a number of his faculties, such as his speech. Also in India we find many examples of this type of explanation of ecstatic behaviour. But the sources are provided to us predominantly by the anthropologist who concerns himself with rural and village religion. Or we hear about it in vernacular literature that describes the same kind of rustic milieu.[23] In other words, cults of possession are, on the whole, associated with low-caste people and unrefined types of religion.

Ecstatic Kṛṣṇaism, right from the beginnings of its documented history, has operated on a much higher social *niveau*. Indeed, in the earliest sources we find explicit reference to this: on the surface it might look as if the *bhakta* is possessed, but in reality it is the expression of a refined love towards an equally refined deity who has nothing to do with the vulgar cults of peasants.[24] This naturally makes it all the more challenging for anybody who wants to explain Kṛṣṇa ecstasy in systematic theological terms. Thus, structurally at least, it could be argued that the choice of 'separation' poetry is intentional. It is meant to highlight that we are not dealing with 'possession', which poetry on the union of lovers might all too easily suggest. However, there are a number of historical factors that have contributed to this choice, as I shall show presently. Furthermore, the theme of 'separation' must, under no circumstances, obscure one central feature: it is presented to us as stimulating an ecstasy in the true sense of the word, as a totally fulfilling experience, meaningful in an ultimate religious sense. The cultivation of the sentiment of *viraha* acts as the trigger mechanism for an ecstatic experience. Just like the participants in a voodoo ritual, Caitanya speaks about the utter and ultimate bliss experienced. Moreover, such bliss can, in theological terms, only be explained as a direct experience of Kṛṣṇa.

The attentive reader may by now be able to pick up the clues on how all this can be formulated in a systematic philosophical or theological account. Obviously, I am talking about *advaita* and about *rasa.* Caitanya himself did not compose any theological treatises, but he had a number of talented disciples who provided the metaphysical framework for the religious movement initiated by him; Rūpa Gosvāmī and his nephew Jīva Gosvāmī deserve particular mention in this connection. The *Vedānta-sūtras* are nominally acknowledged as the basis for their theology. But unlike Śaṅkara or Rāmānuja (or many other theologians), these writers did not produce a commentary on the *sūtras*. Instead, they regarded the *Bhāgavata-purāṇa* as the final and definitive interpretation of the Vedānta. This allowed them to reflect theologically on issues that had to do directly with Caitanya's mysticism. Here are some characteristic features of their thought.[25]

Brahman is Kṛṣṇa, and everything else in the universe relates to him in an *advaita* manner. Ultimately he is the one reality, and yet in an indescribable manner this 'one' appears differentiated. But an interesting feature is added to this. Kṛṣṇa himself, in his very nature, is one and yet differentiated: he stands in an *advaita* relation to his 'powers' (*śaktis*), which are personified as Rādhā, and so on. In a sense Kṛṣṇa (whose essence is bliss) and Rādhā (the *śakti* of conveying bliss) are one. Yet like, for example, the rose and its fragrance, they are distinct. As eternal lovers, by virtue of their mutual love, they are thus both separate and one. To the extent that this 'separateness' is an obstacle to their total oneness, it can be described as 'separation' (*viraha*). This is an extraordinary extension of conventional, abstract ideas, for it opens the system to the whole range of poetic materials we have met with previously.

This is extended to Kṛṣṇa's *advaita* relation to the world. To the extent that creation (and that includes man) is 'separate', one can speak also of 'separation'. Built into the world is a sense of yearning, of longing. But this is where man's religious chance lies. If he opens himself, like a sensitive 'connoisseur', to this sense of yearning and 'separation' and cultivates it within his heart, *rasa* is triggered off within him. But it is more than merely an 'aesthetic' experience: it is religious ecstasy (thus called *bhakti-rasa*). Given that Kṛṣṇa is defined as 'bliss', and the seat of *rasa*, this ecstasy can now be presented as the working of Kṛṣṇa's 'bliss-giving power', Rādhā, who through the *bhakti-rasa* experience lets the devotee realize his oneness with Kṛṣṇa. The ecstasy triggered off by the cultivation of 'separation' is the *ātman*'s realization of *brahman* and man's entrance into the nature of the absolute. By 'particularizing' himself as the *śaktis*, souls and the universe, Kṛṣṇa sets up, like a skilful poet, the various components which in the receptive devotee, as in a trained reader of poetry, combine to trigger off the *bhakti-rasa* through which man transcends himself.

Casting a critical glance over these ideas, we can see that 'poetry', strictly speaking, appears here in a metaphorical or symbolic sense. Theoretically, it would be possible to envisage all kinds of modes of 'cultivating the sense of yearning built into the world'. For instance, the sight of old men leaning against the walls of ramshackle huts and seeking the warmth of the winter sun could well be envisaged in such a context. But, given the practice of Caitanya and the theoretical background of *rasa* speculation, it seems almost inevitable that poetry is more than metaphor or symbol in Caitanya's tradition. It is the concrete means of achieving *bhakti-rasa*.

Among Caitanya's followers were a number of gifted poets, both in the Sanskrit *kāvya* tradition and in that of the vernacular Bengali *kīrtan*. Rūpa Gosvāmī, in particular, concerned himself with the practical development of a poetic culture. He put together an anthology of Sanskrit poems (drawing heavily on the anthologies from Bengal mentioned above), wrote his own new poems and dramas, and composed two treatises which spell out in minute detail all the rules an aspiring poet in the Caitanya tradition ought to follow. It goes without saying that practically all this poetic activity concerns itself with Kṛṣṇa and his amours with the milkmaids. So it seems that we have come a long way since beginning our exploration of the 'particular', in fact all the way from THE ROOF in Chiswick to the idyllic forest where lovelorn milkmaids pour their hearts out to the flowers. But we have not yet exhausted what can be said about poetry and ecstasy. By leaving Bengal and going to South India, we can add new aspects to our current theme, while at the same time finding out more about the history of Kṛṣṇa ecstasy and the background to Caitanyaite thought and practice.

The obvious starting point is a scripture which has been alluded to previously in a number of instances, namely the *Bhāgavata-purāṇa.*[26] Except perhaps for the *Bhagavadgītā*, I doubt that any other work has enjoyed comparable popularity in the whole of India or exerted a similar influence on the Hindu religious life. There is good reason to assume that it is primarily the work of one, though unknown, author, a South Indian, familiar with Tamil, who lived during the later ninth or early tenth century. In terms of theological stance, the work belongs to the Advaita. With Śaṅkara it shares his illusionism: *brahman* is the sole reality, everything else is like an illusion. But *brahman* here is a named reality: it is Kṛṣṇa. This gives rise to quite extraordinary statements. For instance, when it has been narrated how Kṛṣṇa in his passion kisses the girls, and scratches them and makes them cry, the text adds that all this in reality is no more than a boy seeing himself reflected in a puddle of water and making funny faces at himself.[27] (Incidentally, Guṇḍam Rāüḷ is also reported to have done the same on numerous occasions.)[28] This divine playfulness is the stimulus of devotion (*bhakti*), which the work strongly advocates. The milkmaids in their all-absorbing passion for Kṛṣṇa are the highest symbol and exemplar of it. A lot of ink has been spilled on the 'philosophy' of the *Bhāgavata-purāṇa.* As a poetic text of Kṛṣṇa-Advaita advocating a philosophical illusionism alongside *bhakti*, it certainly does present a remarkable challenge for any kind of systematic exegesis. But these problems need not concern us here. Behind the synthesizing tendency of the work (for which further illustrations will be given) we can recognize the desire to present a particular type of religion in terms as orthodox as possible. Thus, for the outline of its plot it uses the very respectable *Viṣṇu-purāṇa*, but rewrites it in a language that is consciously made to sound like the archaic Vedic. All this may explain some aspects of the text's popularity. But I think it was other aspects that were more directly responsible for the enormous influence the *Bhāgavata-purāṇa* has had on Hinduism. These are poetry and ecstasy.

The text is not interested primarily in theory, but in practice or religious method. It is in this sense not about something, but acts as the stimulus of experience. There is a lot in the *Bhāgavata-purāṇa* which is not new and which is documented fully in other works (like the *Viṣṇu-purāṇa*). Thus by plotting, as it were, the text on to that other material, it becomes possible to isolate precisely those aspects which are unique and new. Most remarkable (particularly in Book ten which deals with Kṛṣṇa) are long passages for which there are no parallels in the earlier Purāṇas; Kṛṣṇa's snatching the milkmaids' clothes is one example.[29] Often these sections are written in a highly poetic and lyrical style, and may take the form of songs. In the manner of Sanskrit love-poetry, the passions and the agonies which Kṛṣṇa has caused in the girls' hearts are described. Passionate love-play, as much as laments over Kṛṣṇa's absence, are treated in powerful poetic language. Moreover, when the milkmaids break down under the strain of their love-in-separation, they duplicate in their tears and sweating, their frantic dancing and speaking nonsense, their swooning and acting as if they were Kṛṣṇa, the *bhakti*-behaviour generally advocated in other parts of the text. They anticipate Caitanya. This is the element of ecstasy, which not only does the poetry describe and the text comment on, but which is also directly stimulated in the reader or listener.

Fortunately, we are in the rare position of still being able to identify the source of inspiration for the novel features of poetry and ecstasy in extant material. But for this we have to leave the realm of Sanskrit and turn to the old vernacular of South India, Tamil. During the sixth century AD, this region of the country witnessed the emergence not just of a large number of temples dedicated to Śiva and Viṣṇu, but also of popular religious cultures. A string of poets, both on the Vaiṣṇava and on the Śaiva side, created a genre of religious songs in the vernacular Tamil. The poets who have sung in honour of Viṣṇu/Kṛṣṇa are called the Āḻvārs; at the most two among the twelve can be definitely identified as brahmins. And it is from these Āḻvārs that the *Bhāgavata-purāṇa* derived its inspiration for what is truly novel and unique in the text. Thus we can trace, for instance, the episode of 'snatching of the clothes' back to a considerable number of references in their songs. Moreover, we can trace the custom of girls bathing during winter as part of a ritual in honour of the goddess, even further back to ancient Tamil religion.[30] Besides, a pronounced eroticism and love for poetry pervades the songs of the Āḻvārs; the kind of *bhakti* they cultivated is very much like the ecstatic type illustrated by Caitanya and in the *Bhāgavata-purāṇa*. By inserting numerous translations and paraphrases of specific passages found in Āḻvār poetry, the *Bhāgavata-purāṇa* has transposed both the letter and the spirit of Āḻvār *bhakti* and poetry into the medium of Sanskrit.[31] By drawing on what, in the eyes of respectable mainstream Hinduism, must appear as low and vulgar (however much the Āḻvārs themselves may emphasize that theirs is not a village cult of 'possession') – Tamil, non-brahmins, ecstatic *bhakti*, erotic poetry – the text could infuse the Vedānta and Advaita with a concrete and immensely lively religious spirit.

At this point it may perhaps be appropriate to ask ourselves how all this relates to our theme of 'irreducible particulars'. We can look at it from two angles: the 'ecstatic individual' and the range of particular phenomena (as found in real life, or mediated through poetry). Let us begin with Caitanya. His ecstatic behaviour is commented on (according to his hagiography), from an outsider's point of view, in a significant manner. He is called *vātula* (in Sanskrit) or *bāül* (in Bengali) which, *inter alia* means, 'mad'. The same accusation of being 'possessed' and 'mad', the Āḻvārs tell us themselves, was made against them.[32] Guṇḍam Rāüḷ is called 'mad'.[33] Now 'madness' is clearly an extreme form of personal particularity, since it implies that one's behaviour and view of the world is unique to oneself and not in conformity with the rest of society. Although we must not interpret these characterizations of the Indian saints literally, at least in a metaphorical sense we can still say that ecstatic *bhakti* is a mode of realizing one's uniqueness and particularity.

Poetry inevitably concerns itself with the particular. As the poeticians point out, there would be no purpose in merely speaking of 'a girl that is beautiful'. Only by focusing on a particular girl, on a particular feature or situation, can something of her attractiveness actually be communicated to the reader. Similarly, Rādhā's and Kṛṣṇa's love could not possibly yield *bhakti-rasa*, were it to express itself merely in the abstract. It is the particular sly glance Kṛṣṇa may cast at a milkmaid, while he is half hiding his face and yet moving his long locks out of the way, it is concrete situations like this that can trigger off, like the tear suddenly falling and splashing on the woman's breast, *rasa* in the devotee. Moreover, as we have noticed, the explicit mention of Kṛṣṇa is not even essential here. Caitanya and Rūpa could read poetry on an unnamed particular lover in a similar manner.

But we must not ignore the various constraints that work on Caitanyaite poetry which impose severe restrictions on the range of the particulars dealt with. Given the erotic nature of the poetic raw material, it is perhaps not surprising that these devotees want to control this through a pronounced puritanism in other respects (for instance, by not looking at or touching any real woman). The choice of poetry itself as the arena of experiencing *rasa* implies all the restrictions found with the *kāvya* generally and mentioned earlier: highly idealized, cultured and upper-caste lovers, restraint in the use of language, and stereotyped genres. Rūpa's poetry, which is in Sanskrit, bears all this out quite clearly: there is nothing here of the rustic vitality of a Govardhana and nothing of the realism of a Yogeśvara and, above all, nothing of the vulgarity of the *Kalittokai*. Moreover, the degree of scholasticism which expresses itself in endless lists of items and their sub- and sub-sub-varieties, runs counter to a more realistic and multifarious exploration of the world which is found in other types of poetry, including even certain forms of *kāvya*.

When turning to the Āḻvārs, we need not repeat various features that are similar to those already pointed out for the Caitanyaite movement. Instead, I would like to highlight certain interesting differences. Once again it is the sweating and swooning we find here, once again it is separation that is explored through poetic conceits, and once again it is Kṛṣṇa and the milkmaids that figure prominently here. But, in addition, there is the concrete setting of Āḻvār religion. This is the temple with its divine presence. Quite consciously and explicitly, the appeal of the statue in which the temple-god has incarnated himself, and of the flowers, incense, camphor, etc. that are offered to him, are perceived as aesthetic. This allows the Āḻvārs to plunge themselves, without restraint, into a highly sensuous and sensual world of tangible human experience – and, I may be allowed to paraphrase, of particulars. Along with mythology (particularly the myths of Kṛṣṇa's amours), the whole acquires a pronounced erotic flavour. Stimulated by this, an intense passion develops which cries out for fulfilment. By drawing heavily on the earlier secular *caṅkam* poetry, many of the Āḻvārs express this passion through love poems. From the association of Kṛṣṇa with 'separation' in *caṅkam* poetry, these poems deal, on the whole, with 'love-in-separation'. But the lover is usually named: Kṛṣṇa/Viṣṇu; the beloved is an anonymous female 'I'. Initially it looks as if the poet tried to locate Kṛṣṇa's presence in the total content of such a love-poem. But in the course of time, the figure of the girl becomes increasingly transparent a mask for the Āḻvār's own self. In the case of Āṇṭāḷ (=Kōtai), the one woman among the Āḻvārs, this poetic conceit ceases altogether. What is so striking here is the extent to which the religious passion remains something that has to do with the whole human being, the person of flesh and blood.[34] It is the senses that stimulate it, and somehow the senses want their fulfilment. Thus Āṇṭāḷ is very strongly aware of her physical being. She tells us frankly about the burning in her breast due to the intense, but unfulfilled passion she experiences. In one striking stanza she threatens to tear off her breast if Kṛṣṇa does not grant her his favours, to extinguish the fire in it.[35] But on this level, fulfilment is obviously not possible. But indirectly, the very pursuit of frustrated passions in song, dance and constant meditation, produces a climax and relief in ecstasy. The unbearable tension itself triggers off the ecstatic and thus fulfilling experience. Moreover, the Āḻvārs continued another feature of *caṅkam* love poetry: the listening in to nature. Thus it is not only the temple and myth that act as stimuli for the passions, but also nature itself. The incessant billowing of the ocean, the romantic cooing of birds and the bell sounding in the night around the neck of the bull, busy mating somewhere in the stables – these and other natural features resound in the poets' hearts and give rise to the agony of 'separation'. However, this recourse to nature strikes me as highly formalized; it is probably little more than a studied continuation of *caṅkam* themes. I would hesitate to call it 'nature mysticism'.

By now we have gathered together quite a variety of 'particulars'. But it is clear that they do not span the whole of any imaginary scale, or cover all levels, of particularity. With Caitanya and Rūpa, it was a highly idealized mythical world, described moreover within the confines of Sanskrit *kāvya*. The Āḻvārs are much more down-to-earth and do not hesitate to identify those parts of the body where passion is experienced; yet the sensuous and sensual stimuli are, on the whole, restricted to 'religious' matters like *pūjā* and Kṛṣṇa mythology. The Pāla poets went further by considering subjects normally taboo in *kāvya*, like old people, peasants and the vicissitudes of poverty. Unfortunately, for the *Kalittokai* no definite religious intention or context can be identified. And the 'undercover' Śaṅkara, roaming as Amaru through the harems to gather sexual experience, learnt nothing he did not know already. Does all this now mean that we have identified the boundary of irreducible particulars which can be accommodated in a religious context? It does not, as I shall try to show very briefly.

Once again we can start from the *Bhāgavata-purāṇa.* Sometime during the medieval period (perhaps thirteenth or fourteenth century AD) and possibly in Benares, a pious brahmin composed a treatise which he called the *Devī-Bhāgavata-purāṇa.*[36] Clearly imitating the *Bhāgavata-purāṇa,* he nevertheless replaced Kṛṣṇa with the Goddess (Devī). Devī religion generally tends to be down-to-earth, since socially it draws, on the whole, on lower strata of society, and thus theologically its scope of 'reality' is much wider. This we find illustrated here in a most striking manner. Mainstream *bhakti* religion tends to focus on aspects in man that are relatively elevated, or in other words, where we are at our best. This Purāṇa now takes a reverse course. We are at our worst, our basest, in our instincts and desires; in our delusion and greed. Here we reveal ourselves in our most particular side: good behaviour teaches us to conform and not to show our anger or our lust. But this is the amazing paradox: it is also precisely here that we reveal our true universality, because – and the Purāṇa takes great pains to demonstrate this from every conceivable angle – even the gods, and not just all human beings, are governed by greed, hatred and ignorance. Instead of simply writing all this off as typical of *brahman* and locating transcendentality in a *brahman* that has nothing to do with these most basic facts of life, the Purāṇa turns the situation upside-down, as it were, and transcendentalizes this very basis of human, animal and divine nature. It is precisely here, in the realm of the most particular, that we can experience the ground of all being, and that is the Goddess. Naturally, everything normally said about *brahman* is also said about her: she is pure bliss, consciousness, ultimate reality, and wisdom and liberation. But how should religion express itself on the basis of this extraordinary conception? Here the text is extremely orthodox and craves for conventional respectability. It is *bhakti* to the Goddess that is advocated, in a straightforward sense. In fact, time and again the Purāṇa takes a very polemical attitude with regard to the religious practices advocated in the Tantras. They are not Vedic and orthodox, and involve indulgence in all kinds of vile acts; but true religion consists in the total submission to the all-pervasive Goddess.

When we turn to the Tantras themselves, indeed we find here that the particulars are accepted not just in mythological or theoretical-theological terms, but also very much in practical terms. Given that we all feel a culturally conditioned horror of the particular, especially towards the lower end of the scale, we are not really free. We repress certain 'base' instincts, but thereby allow for potential explosions of precisely these aspects in us. Instead, the Tantras suggest, it is much wiser to try to eradicate the cause of this repression, the horror we feel in front of the obscene, dirty, vulgar, common and ugly. Such an eradication is possible only if we learn to cope with such elements, learn to come in touch with them without becoming affected by them. Thus, in some controlled environment, the Tantras suggest, we must become exposed to these aspects of reality and train ourselves to cope with them. Thus it is not just a question of resisting the temptations of what is attractive and beautiful, but also a question of overcoming one's revulsion of what is ugly and unattractive. As texts like the *Caṇḍamahāroṣaṇa-tantra*[37] make clear without any ambiguity, the whole scale of particulars is envisaged here, including the eating of excrements and the drinking of urine. And not one's own – that would be respectable (at least in the case of urine), as some recent Indian politicians have publicly advocated – but that of someone else. Naturally, these texts do not use concepts like repression. Instead, we find matters conceptualized for instance in the following way. 'Just as a thorn may be removed by a thorn, so those who know how remove passion by means of passion itself. Just as a washerman removes the grime from a garment by means of grime, so the wise man renders himself free of impurity by means of impurity itself.'[38]

Clearly, we are dealing here with the particulars at their most irreducible, according to the nexus of ideas initially suggested. But, equally clearly, we are dealing with matters that potentially run counter to human social interaction as we know it: the cosmos turns into chaos. Surely, someone might well say after this long discussion of ecstasy and 'madness', of trying to locate religious sense in beauty as much as in ugliness, in spite of all the wonderful theories that were produced around all this, there must also be some common sense reacting and commenting on it. Why are we not looking at the man who keeps his 'head in the world'?

CHAPTER 24

The head in the world

Let us accompany an imaginary tourist on a trip to India. Almost inevitably, after the heat and the noise, the next major challenge for him will be the slums. For many this is such an obstacle that it ruins the whole trip. But let us assume that our traveller succeeds in breaking through this powerful veil and realizes that he is actually looking at a monument to industrial 'progress' of very recent origin. It then becomes possible to look behind the veil and explore facets of the India that these pages have been talking about. For in no immediate sense do the slums throw light on traditional Indian culture, nor are they an integral aspect of it. Go to Rio de Janeiro, Bogotá, Lagos, or Manila and spot the difference! But what lies behind the veil? Visually most obvious are an endless variety of shrines and temples, which are often extremely complex architectural structures that might approximate the size of a small town. At least in medieval India, Buddhist monasteries may also have looked very similar. Still on the visual side, our tourist is bound to encounter a marriage ceremony, a popular festival, or domestic rites; he may be so lucky as to be able to witness the daily or seasonal rituals performed in a temple. The enormous scale and attention to minute detail of these rituals are bound to stun him. It would be even more surprising for him, were he to find out that the objects of such intense ritual veneration include figures like Gandhi, the goddess Naurthā[1] and, in Buddhist days, the goddess Prajñāpāramitā.[2] We know this latter 'goddess' from a different context, for *prajñā-pāramitā* means 'perfection of wisdom'. Naurthā is the personification of 'the nine nights' (*nava-rātrī*), a festival celebrated in honour of the Hindu Goddess. A very strong tendency to concretize is clearly at work here.

It will take our tourist a while to go beyond the visual and become aware of something that impressed the earlier European visitors to India so much that they coined a word for it which we still use: the 'caste system'. (The native category is *varṇa*, lit. 'colour'.) This is a complex social order which involves hundreds of linguistically, culturally, and professionally differentiated groups of people who also seem to have their own religions. Once aware of it, it is not necessary for our traveller to know any of the languages and their complex hierarchies of personal pronouns; merely by observing body language, he is able to assess the social relationship between two individuals.

In addition to these immediately observable forms, there are all kinds of further, less tactile, formal structures that the hypothetical tourist could look at, were he to persevere for a bit longer. Here are just some possible examples. There is the concern for a universal and thus necessarily structured, ordered language: *saṃskṛta* (note that even the official modern Hindi consists of little more than learned Sanskrit words), which transcends the vicissitudes of the many vernaculars. Then we have the endless production of lengthy religious books: sacred scriptures – Vedas, Epics and Purāṇas, Buddhist *sūtras*, Jaina canonical and post-canonical works, the Tantras and many others – besides learned treatises and popular poetry. It would take a gigantic building to store all this material. Or we could mention that the thought of the individual philosopher or theologian, as much as the outpourings of most religious poets, appears subsumed in complex 'traditions', socially distinct movements. (For parallels we could think of how Thomas Aquinas became 'subsumed' in scholasticism, or Karl Marx in Marxism.) However, these three examples belong to what may be called an elitist and pan-Indian level of culture. Yet also on the levels of less exalted and more regional or provincial cultures, very similar trends have been pursued, often in direct imitation of the elitist models.

What is the purpose of this little flight of fancy? Fairly obviously, it reveals to what extent the abstract material explored in the previous pages possesses its concrete face – an incredible richness and staggering variety of formal religious expressions. Theoretically we may have prepared ourselves for this by reflecting on irreducible particulars. But it is still worth our while to dwell on this, as it were, visual or material side of the Indian religions. There are some interesting implications in it which deserve to be brought out fully. These concern the inner mechanics of that fascinating variety itself, the dynamic tensions contained in it.

Surveying all these many expressions of formalized religion, our tourist may well form the idea in his mind that here he is in a country that is dragged down and held away from any historical progress by the enormously powerful force called 'the past'. Some scholars have even gone so far as to claim that there is no history in India at all. For them the whole of Indian culture is one static unity out of which they can then, equally naively, take any and every bit for their 'structuralist' analysis. Yet it requires little effort to see how feebly India has, in fact, held on to the past. 'Classical' music, when performed by a good artist, is actually created that very moment, on the basis of abstract principles stored in the memory, which themselves can be shown to have had a history. Unless manuscripts are copied out regularly, the ravenous hunger of the white ants will condemn even the most profound philosophical thought or the most moving poem to oblivion. Walking through a town one can see the most breath-taking temple or palace crumbling away at every corner; even the scholar would find it impossible to mention dates for, or associate specific buildings and places with, most of the famous names in Indian culture. Surely this illustrates everything but a 'holding on to the past'.

On the other hand, this must not make us blind to other facets. It must be one of the most remarkable achievements of human memory to have preserved over a period of more than three thousand years the Vedas, material that in print would fill many hundreds of pages, accurately down to the last syllable. Many a temple statue is sculptured out of the most difficult and hardest material, granite, in order to let the god or goddess literally 'abide in it eternally'; not a few of them are older than fifteen hundred years. With the ascetic practices of a Jaina monk we may be transposed back into the past by as much as two thousand years or more. No doubt these are examples of areas where the past is still available to us today.

Finally, and we are approaching now the problem area of our discussion, we can identify a strange combination of both attitudes towards the past. Given that value is indeed attached to certain aspects of the past, and that much of it is irrevocably lost in the dust of ruins and palm-leaves and in the air that carried the merely spoken word, it becomes possible to make unverifiable claims about the past. This may, for example, concern 'what the Buddha taught', or deal with the 'true Āryan life', or 'what Hinduism is', and often carries then not just doctrinal, but also ideological implications. Because lost, the past can be manipulated in an obnoxious and oppressive manner. Because of the absence of material that could document the element of historical change in a tradition or an institution, it becomes possible to mistake the current situation for what has always been so, and to reinforce the status quo.

From such reflections we can abstract a progression from concretization to formalism to ossification in religion. Not only does it express itself in concrete terms, but it also creates increasingly solid and rigid structures, that are given further support by reference to the past or even 'eternity'. Much of the material we discussed in the previous chapters suffered this fate: even the most daring conceptions of human religious freedom became dragged down to the level of institutional and ritual formalism. But we need little more than common sense to realize that such a progression towards ossification alone can hardly explain the enormous range and variety of religious attitudes and opinions, experiences and practices that the previous chapters have explored. So what was it that allowed for the proliferation of ever-new forms and counteracted the trends towards ossification? The answer to such a question is bound to be complex. So let us begin with the more concrete element in it (antinomianism), before eventually turning to Indian attitudes towards chaos.

All too rashly our literature on India assumes that the whole staggering complexity of its religious structures has been interiorized by more or less every member of Indian society at large, or at least of each tradition or religious movement. Certainly, in the majority of indological books we hear nothing about how the ordinary person may have perceived it, or about internal critiques. Also the anthropologist, more often than not, tends to be too busy constructing grand belief systems, that are assumed to be valid for the whole 'tribe', on the basis of information provided by a very small number of informants. Internal disagreements and negative assessments are hardly picked up. Yet it is clear that the construction of extremely elaborate formal expressions of religion and their tendency towards ossification found their critics. Thus time and again reactions set in which did what no scholar is allowed to do: criticize aspects of this formalization process. It will be the task of the social historian to deal with those reactions that had an economic, political, or social motive. After all, somebody in society had to do the dirty work of generating the profit which could be used for the construction of a temple or the patronage of a learned philosopher; he may well have had his own opinions about a temple or philosophy. Here we must assume, or at least pretend, that it is possible to isolate a purely religious motive behind such criticisms.

Time and again in the course of the history of Indian religion, individuals and groups of people arose who entered into an open, public attack of formalized and formalistic religion. Immediately we will think of the Buddha, or Vimalakīrti, or the *Perfection of Wisdom* literature. However, these are examples of a learned critique that is capable of (and willing) rationally to defend its premisses. But we also find a whole host of other figures who expressed their attack on lifeless, ossified religion on a very much more popular level and with cruder, though not less effective, tools. Even when I suggest that we have here another mode of making sense of the world and religion, the 'common-sensical' mode (which we can envisage expressing itself with the exclamation 'so what?', accompanied by a shrug of the shoulder), I do not want to separate it too sharply from Vimalakīrti, etc. More than just affinity in attitude and ideas holds both groups together, for it can be argued that historically much of the learned critique filtered down to these popular levels. The following examples will make clear to what extent we can nevertheless speak of a different flavour. It is also important to remember that the individual critics make up a 'group' only by virtue of *my* putting them together here. Unlike say 'Mahāyāna Buddhism' or 'Mānbhāvs', there exists no native category for them.

We are dealing here with people (mostly men, but also some women), usually of humble background, who were prepared to speak out in public and challenge the religious establishment both in word and in deed. Because they openly break fundamental religious taboos, we may call them 'antinomian'. One central feature found in more or less every representative of the group I have put together is the critique of a religion that has exhausted itself in its external forms and has thus lost its inner life and dynamism. Depending on what external aspect is focused on, this critique can be phrased in many different ways. With reference to the temple and its worship of stone images, which is perceived as a purely mechanical affair, we could speak of 'petrification' of religion, of its becoming lifeless 'stone'. A live alternative is then advocated, in the cultivation of the inner religious life and the pursuit of internal moral purity. With regards to sacred, cultured language and scriptures, the attack might concern the death of the spirit behind all the letters. In an intentionally antagonistic and provocative way, the vernacular is used, more often than not in its dialect or spoken forms and not as cultivated by the more learned poets. The rules through which society has regulated access to the elitist forms of religion are challenged, for instance by making fun of brahmins and their pretences and hypocrisies, or by intentionally resorting to obscenities to break through the veil of social propriety. External signs of religious allegiance are consciously discarded, like the wearing of the sacred thread, and schismatic divisions are written off as based merely on externals. And finally, learned attempts at systematizing the religious teaching, be it philosophy or theology, are countered by an emphasis on the theme of 'madness', or through the production of nonsense verses.

There exists a considerable overlap between different members of our list, as far as such themes are concerned, and it would be tedious were I to illustrate for each individual the whole range. But before providing such illustrations, let me make two general points. First of all, however radical such an attack on the dangers inherent in religious formal expression may be, the latter cannot totally be discarded. In their own ways, our poets generate new forms, even if they initially do so merely in order to communicate to others their warning of externalized religion. Secondly, in each case the anarchic and antinomian attack derives from some inner centre of certainty. But interestingly enough, such inner self-authenticating religious experiences draw on a whole range of types of religion (meditational, theistic, etc.) Moreover, towards the chronologically later part of our list, the influence makes itself increasingly felt of a religion about which nothing has been said in the course of this book, namely Islam, particularly in its less normative form of Sufism. But let me now give some concrete illustrations of this material, beginning with relatively unknown examples.

Towards the close of the first millennium AD, Apabhraṃśa served as a *lingua franca* over a large part of northern and central India. It was a linguistic medium that allowed for much closer contact with the grass-roots of Indian culture than did Sanskrit. The Jains cultivated it to tell their rather earthy stories. Some of the Tantras still contain Apabhraṃśa poems which originally may well have been rather obscene folk-ditties. Given this character of the language, it is perhaps not surprising to find that both Buddhists and Jains also employed it to express antinomian ideas of the kind introduced here.

Thus, on the Buddhist side we find the rather nebulous figure of Saraha, classified as one of the *Siddhas*. The key idea in his poetry is that of *sahaja*, the inner, self-authenticating religious experience which is 'innate' in all of us and bursts forth 'spontaneously', once the obstacles of formal religion have been removed. He does not hesitate to provide a specific list of such formal religions: brahmin-controlled Vedic religion and *yoga*, Jainism (whose naked ascetics are mocked: 'if from absence of hair liberation could be achieved, then the loins of a young girl would be liberated'),[3] Hīnayāna, Mahāyāna, and even forms of meditationally orientated tantric Buddhism. By abandoning all formal constraints and leading a most ordinary life, and by merely 'holding on to the *sahaja*', 'its true nature' 'will shine forth in one moment, as supreme bliss'.[4]

On the Jaina side we find the poetry of the even more nebulous figure of Yogīndu, and an anonymous collection of very similar, and sometimes identical poems (called *Pāhuḍadohakosu*). The antinomian challenge takes, for instance, the rather typical following form:

> You are not white, you are not black;
> No colour (*varṇa*) at all you have;
> Know that to be your definition (*varṇa*).[5]

That this play on *varṇa* is indeed meant to express an attack on 'caste' and social hierarchies is made clear in the following stanzas:

> Know these to be your specifications:
> 'I am not a fine brahmin, nor a *vaiśya*;
> not a *kṣatriya* am I, nor what is even lower.'
>
> Do not think any of the following:
> 'I am young, I am old;
> I am a hero, I am a scholar;
> I am a Digambara, I am a Śvetāmbara.'
> Instead consider your inner self (*ātman*)
> to be liberation (*brahman*)![6]

Among other things, the last stanza attacks a sectarian division among Jaina monks (some wear a robe, Śvetāmbara, and others go naked, Digambara). The last two lines are antinomian in the sense that they use terms that are alien to Jaina philosophy. Directing its attack in a different direction, the same *Pāhuḍadohakosu* says:

> Don't break off the leaves of the bel tree,
> nor carry fruits in your hand:
> to Śiva, for whose sake you do this,
> ascend right here.[7]

This stanza contains a pun on Śiva, the god, and *śivam*, ultimate liberation, to be found in the soul and not in external rituals directed to a temple image. Thus:

> In the temples – are stones;
> in the sacred bathing places – is water;
> in all the books – are lots of stories;
> but how will you cleanse your mind
> that is dirty from the dirt of evil deeds?[8]

With similar sarcasm, the *Yogasāra* states:

> O fool! God is not in the temple,
> nor in stone nor in plaster nor in pictures!
> God is in the temple that is your body.
> True religion does not arise from recitation,
> nor can you gain it from masses of books;
> it does not happen by entering a monastery,
> nor from pulling out your hair.[9]

And finally in the words of the *Paramappapayāsu* (which also contains many of the stanzas quoted already):

> Just as the crystal is pure by nature,
> so is your inner self (*ātman*).
> Do not regard it as impure, in your delusion,
> when you look at your body that is impure![10]

I do not think that it will be necessary to add a lengthy exegesis of these stanzas. In the light of what has been said before, their meaning should be clear. In the temple, pilgrimage to sacred bathing places, study of sacred books, *pūjā* offered to Śiva, and social stratification of brahmins, etc. we recognize immediately aspects of formal and ordered religion. Other features are aimed more directly at a Jainism that is perceived here as rather ossified: lay veneration of Jinas in temples, schismatic division of Śvetāmbara and Digambara, concentration on external, physical acts of penance, and the monastic life. What is advocated instead is a concentration on man's inner core – to call this *ātman* and *brahman* is itself antinomian in terms of Jain philosophy.

From roughly the same time onwards, we also find in the extreme south of India, in the Tamil country, individuals who proclaim comparable ideas. On the one hand, a tenuous link is established with Saraha and the other *siddhas* (lit. 'the perfected ones') of Buddhist legend, in that these individuals have been referred to as *cittar* – the Tamil version of Sanskrit '*siddhas*'.[11] On the other hand, we do find an element of theism here, which links these Tamil *Cittar* more closely with other antinomianists that will be mentioned presently. Perhaps the earliest and most important *Cittar* is Civavākkiyār (possibly ninth/tenth century AD). He rebelled against brahmanism and the scriptural authority of the Vedas, against temple worship and the social stratification dominated by the brahmins. Sectarian divisions like Vaiṣṇava and Śaiva are irrelevant to him, and he does not hesitate to resort to obscenities to make his point. All the features except for the last have already been illustrated; here, then, is an example of social critique via obscenity:

> What does it mean – a pariah woman?
> What is it – a brahmin woman?
> Is there any difference in flesh, skin or bones?
> Do you feel any difference when you sleep
> with a pariah or a brahmin woman?[12]

At a slightly later date, in the neighbouring Karnataka, we find a whole host of religious poets who express antinomian ideas in the vernacular Kannaḍa, and who also draw on a vague form of Śaivite monotheism. Most outstanding among them is Basavaṇṇa (AD 1106-68). Here are two samples of his poetry.

> See-saw watermills bow their heads.
> So what?
> Do they get to be devotees
> to the Master? ...
> Parrots recite.
> So what?
> Can they read the Lord?

In a brahmin house
where they feed the fire
as a god
when the fire goes wild
and burns the house
they splash on it
the water of the gutter
and the dust of the street ...
These men then forget their worship
and scold their fire! [13]

I don't think these stanzas require a commentary: they make fun, in a rather striking way, not just of external religion, but also of the hypocrisy lurking behind it. When property is threatened, even the filthiest water will do to extinguish the 'sacred' fire!

Almost at the same time, in the neighbouring region of Maharashtra, we find a very similar antinomian trend. Of a pronounced anti-brahmanism and anti-Vedism, the Mahānubhāvas (Mānbhāvs) developed their own strictly ascetic religion, by drawing vaguely on some form of Kṛṣṇaism. Towards the close of the thirteenth century, they had developed a sizeable literature in the vernacular Marathi. Their antinomian attitude towards temple worship has survived up to the present day and expresses itself in their stunning lack of objection to the taking of photos in their temples. But their general attitude to formalized religion is most strikingly illustrated in their literature on the divine 'madness' of Guṇḍam Rāūḷ, whom we met in a previous chapter. He broke just about every convention of social decorum and every taboo governing the interaction of castes, even, as we have seen, breaking wind near the temple of Paraśurāma.[14]

Next in our rapid and very selective list we may mention, for the Hindi/Panjabi region of northern India, the *Sants*. Again, as in the case of the *Cittar*, we are dealing here primarily with a disparate set of individual poets who, in spite of the absence of any kind of institutional continuity, nevertheless reveal sufficient common characteristics to justify their common label. The best known *Sants* are Kabīr (fourteenth century) and Gurū Nānak (fifteenth century), the founder of the Sikh religion. Practically all typical features of this North Indian variety of antinomianism have already been mentioned, and there is no need to repeat them here. It is, however, interesting to note that the emphasis is less on some innate transcendental dimension in man and more on the all-pervasive availability of divine grace communicated by a *guru*. But another typical feature of these *Sants* is the presence of terms, concepts and sentiments which ultimately derive from (Sufi) Islam. Thus it is striking to find that the Absolute – beyond all human characterization or description – is indiscriminately referred to as Rām, Hari, Allah, Khudā, etc. And, indeed, antinomianism is widened here to accommodate also such fundamental religious divisions. One quote from Kabīr may illustrate this.

> The Hindu died crying: 'Rām!'
> the Mussulman crying: 'Khudā!'
> *Kabīr*, that one will live
> who keeps away from both![15]

Travelling further east, we come to Bengal. I mentioned earlier that Caitanya was actually called '*bāül*', mad.[16] At a later period we find the beginnings of an actual religious movement – unconnected with Kṛṣṇaism it seems – that carried this name: the Bāüls.[17] They still exist today, and their haunting songs have been recorded on disc. In their recruitment, no distinction is made between Hindus (of whatever kind) and Muslims, or between men and women, and in their songs they advocate the cultivation of the inner man and the rejection of all external forms of religion.

Many more examples could be referred to from other parts of India, like the female antinomian mystic Lal Dĕd of Kashmir (fourteenth century), who apparently walked about naked, claiming that there were no real men in front of whom she ought to feel ashamed.[18] Or we could return to a region mentioned already, Tamil Nadu, where – perhaps somewhat surprisingly – in the austere and highly orthopractical Śrīvaiṣṇavism of Rāmānuja, from the thirteenth to fifteenth centuries, attempts were made to create an open religious society solely on the basis of *bhakti* by rejecting external, socially divisive forms of orthopraxy.[19]

Further examples could be cited, but there is no need for us to attempt an exhaustive list of such colourful rebellious figures. The material we have surveyed is sufficient to illustrate the characteristics of this common-sensical mode. What is particularly important to note is the fact that it is not just another mode in our catalogue. With its antinomian inclinations it sets itself frequently in direct opposition to other modes. It creates an anti-structure and thereby introduces a dynamic element into religious history. By advocating an inner 'live' religion for the individual, at the same time it functions as one of the important driving forces behind the impressive variety of religious expression, which was the starting point of our reflections.

One feature of this antinomianism deserves special attention, and that is language. By using the vernacular language of their region and their time, the various poets we have mentioned can obviously communicate their religious ideals far more effectively than can a learned treatise in Sanskrit. But there is more involved here than mere expediency: it is part of the anti-structure itself. For religion breaks here the monopoly traditionally associated with Sanskrit. Even more happens here. By expressing itself in a vernacular language, religion challenges pan-Indian culture. The Buddha and the Mahāvīra also resorted to the vernaculars of their days (the Prakrits) for similar reasons; but eventually Buddhism and Jainism expressed themselves in Sanskrit and in Sanskrit culture. But in the more recent examples we have been looking at, the vernaculars do succeed in moulding new regional cultures. The Apabhraṃśa material to which I have drawn attention lays the foundation for this development, both linguistically and in terms of religious ideas. It is only due to the relative lack of political organization, the relative strength of pan-Indian structures, and the inseparable interpenetration of many traditions in any one region that these developments did not result in the formation of actual 'nations states', as a comparable turn to the vernaculars and to the irreducible particularity of the religious individual achieved at roughly the same time in Europe.

But whatever the case may be, we must not forget that such a random list of antinomian figures can merely highlight features that, in less obvious form, are contained in many types of religion discussed previously. For example, the vernacular poets whose primary concern it is to express a monotheistic devotion frequently show antinomian attitudes. But it is also useful to keep in mind subsequent developments here. In most cases, highly structured religious organizations arose from the antinomian teaching: the Mānbhāvs, the Liṅgayites, the Teṉkalai, the Sikhs, the Kabīr-panthīs, the Bāüls, etc. These, in turn, developed their own temples, sacred scriptures, theologies, hagiographies, social stratification, external signs and forms of worship. Yet such developments do not invalidate the decisive impulses of the critique that the individual poets/saints initially fed into the Indian religious scene.

It is, however, clear that even the widest possible list of antinomian attitudes (including all kinds of Buddhism, Caitanya's and Guṇḍam Rāūḷ's 'madness', etc.) can only be one factor in the dynamics of Indian religious culture that produced such an impressive array of formal expressions. In order to make better sense of this situation, we have to penetrate deeper into its mechanics. This we can do by exploring Indian attitudes towards 'chaos'.

The previous chapters have already provided us with a fair amount of raw material that we can utilize for this exploration. Thus it will not be difficult to see in variety a manifestation of 'particularity' (just as in its opposite, total uniformity or homogeneity, the 'universal' expresses itself). But as we have seen, particularity has an inbuilt tendency towards chaos. General de Gaulle is reported to have complained: 'how can one rule a nation that has hundreds of cheeses?' But what about a country with hundreds of religions? This is certainly how we have to envisage this situation up to relatively recent times (to be precise, until the colonial powers began to play 'Hindus' against 'Muslims' – a game that was then merrily continued by the Indian politicians of the independence movement and of post-independence India).[20] Our variety reveals itself here clearly as chaos from a political point of view. But how was this chaos envisaged from a religious and cultural angle?

Let us first cast a glance over some material discussed previously, to seek out potentials for chaos. When looking at the *Devī-Bhāgavata-purāṇa*[21] and certain aspects of the Tantras,[22] we had to draw the conclusion that the inner momentum of the approach advocated there could potentially dissolve the conventional social, moral and religious order. That ignorance and greed, lust and passion, pride and self-delusion are universal characteristics of human nature, is not in itself a new idea. That animals and gods and demons can be included may strike us as somewhat strange, at least as far as the gods are concerned. But even according to popular Hindu mythology – not to speak of how the Buddhists and Jains saw matters – most *devas* behave in a rather human, and often all-too-human, manner. Conventionally, this assessment of the human situation places it in radical opposition to a totally different reality which is completely untouched by such defilements (e.g. *brahman*, or the *Tathāgata-garbha*, or a God like Viṣṇu or Śiva). This is the contrast between the particulars and the universal. The disadvantages of such a model of thought emerge, for instance, in the case of a radical monotheism. For how could we accommodate in such a model God's omnipotence, or in terms of Indian theological language, the fact that everything which exists depends on God's will? The religion of the Goddess was prepared to face the issue by suggesting a radical departure from conventional thinking. Not only does the divine nature of the Goddess express itself in the sublime universality that is undefiled by the particulars (she is *brahman*). It also expresses itself, as another form of universality, on the level of the lowest common denominator: within the passions and delusions that cause *saṃsāra* and thus human particularity. In religious terms, such texts in the Devī tradition by no means advocate a merry cultivation of our worst instincts and drives. What they advocate is to acknowledge even there a divine presence, and humbly to submit oneself to this factually given and irreducible level of reality. In other words, they warn us not to pretend that the whole could be subsumed in some higher-order system, and tell us to learn to accept that the chaos caused by the passions and by delusion is an integral part of the mysterious cosmic order set up by the Goddess. Chaos itself is provided with a religious dimension.

There are certain strands in the amorphous tantric traditions which, in general terms, illustrate a very similar approach. Naturally, the monotheistic aspects are absent here and, instead of focusing on the universality of human passions and delusions, they emphasize their all-pervasive power. Moreover, they spell out in greater detail the nature of the filtering system which conventionally blocks our access to the lower levels of the particulars. They point out that, precisely because these are kept at bay, they terrify us and prevent us from becoming free. What is advocated here in religious terms is to learn to widen the filter and ultimately to remove it, because thereby we learn to accept the lower levels of particularity and actually eradicate the fear that enslaves us. Given that the filtering mechanism mentioned here derives from established culture and social consensus, the potential for chaos becomes apparent once again.

The particulars, especially on their lowest levels, act counter to what we regard as order. Order of whatever kind – social, intellectual, religious – necessitates the conformity of many particulars, which obviously thereby lose something of their individuality. Thus for any scientific law to work, it is necessary that each and every member of a given species of particulars behaves in identical manner. All stones will increase their speed of falling down from a roof in a predictable manner. It is clear that any emphasis on particularity implies a move away from total order, or scientific predictability, or social conformity, and that means a move in the direction of chaos.

Mainstream Goddess religion has avoided an open social confrontation by counterbalancing its theological conception through advocating conventional *bhakti* behaviour. In some segments of tantric material, open confrontation is avoided by keeping the whole consciously a secret. Moreover (as I have been trying to show in Part one), the actual value-system of conventional society is maintained here; breaking a taboo will only yield additional power if the nature of the taboo itself is left intact.[23] Alternatively, it may become 'domesticated' – socially acceptable. The way in which this can be achieved is predictable from the nexus of ideas explored so far. The lower levels of particulars are replaced by higher-order systems. The real and particular human head, that in the most extreme case of tantric esoteric practices might have to be cut off, gets replaced by a coconut – and *any* coconut will do. The generic or universal, by replacing the particular, ceases to challenge the accepted social and conceptual orders. Camembert turns into 'cheese'.

The antinomian saints and movements challenge the established order in a very much more direct and open manner, as we have seen. But in their own way they avoid total chaos and anarchy by succeeding in communicating their own ideas and values to others (something we might be tempted to derive from their 'common sense'). Moreover, however strongly they may attack all kinds of formalized expressions of religion, they do not challenge religion itself. Note their emphasis on inner purity, openness to the ineffable Word, or internal liberation.

Behind all this material with its implicit tendencies towards chaos we can thus detect counterbalancing factors that introduce an element of order. At this point we can widen our own horizon and, instead of looking at specific examples, try to survey the whole picture. This is none other than the religious culture of traditional India, which has presented itself to us with such impressive variety. Are there any more overt cultural features that deal with the themes of chaos and order? It would indeed be surprising, if Indian culture had been completely oblivious to the chaotic potentials of its own variety. Here are some examples which, to me, illustrate some typical reactions.

Variety implies alternatives, and the 'is' gets replaced by the 'may be'. This is precisely what we find systematically developed by medieval Jaina thinkers.[24] Their primary aim in this may have been to devise a means of dealing with philosophical opponents, but the wider applications are apparent. I am talking here about the *syād-vāda*, 'the doctrine of may be'.[25] A formula of seven possibilities was set up, on the basis of simpler constructions found already in Jaina canonical writings. Any given proposition could now be broken down into these seven possible aspects. For example, 'this man is a father'. We can easily imagine a Jain monk reacting to such a statement with a shrug of the shoulders. 'That may be so. But it may also not be so. For that same man is a son. And while he is a man, he is not a woman. Yet this man may well have been a woman in a past existence. Thus in a sense this man–woman, father–son makes up a being which is clearly beyond description (*avyaktavya*).' And so on. Thus what is denied here is the possibility to come up with categorical statements about reality, since reality itself is varied and reveals different aspects. It is easy to imagine what kind of wonderful stories the Jains themselves could have produced on the basis of the *syād-vāda*. Unfortunately, none are known to me and I am not sure whether the Jain storytellers ever exploited it.

If the irreducible particulars cannot be subsumed in some higher-order universal, they may be contained at least in a purely formal manner. On various occasions, the Sanskrit *kāvya* has been mentioned. Even in its most expanded form as the 'grand *kāvya*' (*mahākāvya*), which may consist of as many as fifty cantos and thousands of stanzas, it offers no more than a fragmented view of reality. In fact, it is fragmented to such an extent that each stanza is left in isolation, as a self-contained entity. Only the common metre or a vague thematic continuity may hold a number of such stanzas together. Less well known are a number of Tamil poetic genres in which, similarly, reality is left fragmented or, we could say, accepted in its irreducible particularity. One such type is the *Antāti* (from Sanskrit *anta*, 'end' and *ādi*, 'beginning') where the sound of the last two syllables of a stanza is repeated at the beginning of the subsequent one, and thus a formal link is established between otherwise isolated verses.

But much more complicated and interesting is the *Kalampakam*,[26] another Tamil genre. Often the *antāti* feature is used, but besides, a whole range of traditional smaller poetic genres are brought together here. That this is done in a relatively random manner reveals itself when we compare different *Kalampakams* with each other. Finally, also in terms of subject matter, we notice a similar 'concoction' (part of the meaning of *kalampakam*). Thus different and often weird types of people are expected to be dealt with. Most of these poems are religious, dedicated to a particular temple. In concrete terms, all this would look like the following. Purely reflective stanzas are interspersed by sensuous descriptions of the god's strong arms; stereotyped situations found in genres of love poetry are adapted, such as addressing a longing message to a cloud or a *koyil* bird, lamenting at the sound of the ocean during the night, and so forth. Then again, a stanza may be set in the frame (and style) of a children's game, like sitting on a swing and singing a song. Finally, time and again the poet intersperses stanzas describing a rough soldier, or a fortune-telling tribal woman, or a low-caste bard, or herdsmen in the forest, or a girl dancing a sword dance. What makes this type of poetic exploration of divine grace, perceivable in the random particulars of the world, so exciting is the fact that it works on two levels. Not only does it draw on a whole array of poetic genres and their cultural and social associations; but it also uses random samples taken directly from a highly varied and colourful differentiation of society.

The figure of Parakāla, the Āḻvār who constructed buildings in Śrīraṅgam with funds raised through highway robbery and the theft of a Buddha image, has already been referred to a number of times. When we survey his hagiography which is available in various works, we find that so many different personality traits and so many personal characteristics have been developed here that the sum total is far greater than life. Appropriately, one hagiographic work has meticulously collected all stories and episodes told about Parakāla from a wide range of sources. Thus the trickster and cheat is set alongside the robber and murderer, the pious devotee and zealous fanatic next to the poet and theologian. Different metres emphasize the different characterizations, and the whole is held together really only through the formal device of the *Seven Hundred* (*sapta-śatī*), a genre hallowed since the time of the *Bhagavadgītā*, which consists of seven hundred stanzas,[27] and famous since Hāla's *Seven Hundred.*

From these few, mainly literary, examples we can extrapolate a general principle of containing chaos in purely formal order. This principle can be recognized on the grand scale of social structure. I am not referring to the traditional theory of the four *varṇas* of society, nor to the much-maligned caste system as such. Neither theory does full justice to the actual social realities, to their regional variety or their flexibility. For example, as the social historians have begun to discover (much to the chagrin of the anthropologists), 'caste' itself is very much more fluid in a historical context than is popularly assumed.[28] But even without looking at the finer details, it is possible to point out for traditional Indian society a rather rigidly compartmentalized structure, consisting of a large number of such compartments. The important point here is that this is a purely formal structure that contains 'chaos' in the form of a latitude of varied human behaviour and cultural and religious expression that is actually quite staggering.

The same repeats itself on the smaller scale of individual groups. There is a formal containment, expressing itself as well-defined 'orthopraxy' or standard behaviour, which allows for a similar latitude of religious beliefs and personal practices. This is the element of chaos, and by now it must have become clear to what extent 'meaning' or religion can be constructed individually here. At any one point, there is a whole host of traditional religious raw material available, out of which, in ever-new combinations and proportions, new syntheses can be constructed. And wherever such a new construction proves successful or attractive, it gets added to the store of raw material for subsequent generations. The possibility for this arises from the absence of any central doctrinal authority, even within relatively small groups. The reasons for this continuous construction enterprise are many. They may be random (the kind of raw material one happens to be familiar with), or simply the universally human delight in creativity. They may be quite rational and resulting from a critical assessment of system-internal unresolved issues, or they may lie in the perception of 'meaninglessness' in purely formal expressions of religion. They may derive from the desire to incorporate what has become fashionable, or they may draw on prestigious material to legitimate what is close to one's own heart. The result is an extremely rich and varied manifestation of the religious. But there is a price to be paid, and this is (group-internal) social conformity. While the latitude on a purely doctrinal or typological level is enormous, how one actually behaves in society is an infinitely tighter-controlled affair, and this not necessarily through religion, but through social consensus. Here are the rough edges of our dynamism, mollified only to the extent that antinomianism, time and again, tried to break through this social conformity. All this should make it immediately apparent what little sense there would be in hunting for one overall social system or structure behind the Indian religions.

It is one thing to wax eloquent about the sheer beauty of this incredibly rich and varied scene we have been exploring, about the latitude and the flexibility of it. It is quite another thing to reflect on the tensions underlying the dynamics and its rough edges. Indeed, it is probably true that there were no religious wars in traditional India, and no Inquisition of the kind we know. But there are, nevertheless, critical points of tolerance. Antinomian movements found it relatively easy to recruit from, and offer access to their religion to, a wider segment of society. But when, for instance, in Basavaṇṇa's movement a brahmin girl married a *śūdra*, this went beyond the level of tolerance and the orthodoxy/praxy reacted violently by dragging all persons involved to their painful death.[29] In South India we find a number of legends and historical incidents that show that the monotheistic Śaivites, through the political powers of the day (the Cōḻas), were quite capable of violent action, such as putting Jains to death through impalement, and blinding Vaiṣṇavas who refused to accept Śiva's supremacy.[30] And we find illustrations of another reaction: antinomian groups actually resorting to armed struggle to defend their independence and lives, like the Liṅgayites, the Sikhs, and marauding bands of ascetics like the Dādū-panthīs in Rajasthan.[31]

Thus internal strife and violence are not unknown, but could be contained within Indian culture. But as far as external threats and attacks are concerned, the Indians would appear a sorry lot if we measured them against great conquerors like the Muslims or Spaniards or Napoleon. At this point the Indian religions reveal that flexibility and latitude also imply a lack of concerted, regimented political and military action. Endless waves of invaders, from the time of the Greeks to that of the British, could sweep over the country and gain control over many parts. General de Gaulle appears to be right. You cannot govern, and use for efficient defensive military action, people who like hundreds of cheeses or follow hundreds of religions. Even so, it could also be argued that, precisely because of this lack of political and military usefulness, the Indian religions could survive and flourish, because, flexible as they were, they could accommodate themselves time and again to the new conditions that confronted them. Without doubt, the case of Buddhism will be mentioned as a counter-example. But given that the Jains, who were very much in the same situation as the Buddhists and suffered equally under the brutality of the Muslims, did survive and continue to flourish after AD 1200 up to the present day, one may well have to search for other reasons as to why Buddhism disappeared from India at that time.

But the fact that the vast array of Indian religions was not harnessed, for political purposes, in some meta-structure (like the 'Hinduism' of more modern times) and was left merely formally contained within a social framework, does not mean that no attempts were made to set up other kinds of meta-structures. It would be surprising, indeed, if traditional India had not been tempted to bring some internal order into all this bubbling and apparently amorphous dynamism of religious proliferation. Already in the case of earliest Buddhism, in its refusal to talk about 'man' or '*saṃsāra*' with reference to a soul or self, we could possibly see an attempt at synthesis. Statements were made about human destiny on such an abstract level that a whole host of specific teachings (like that of the Jainas), which involved many different and contradictory 'soul' or 'self' concepts, could be accommodated within them. A second example, that of Śaṅkara, is far less speculative. His Advaita is a meta-system which subsumes under its attributeless *brahman* a potentially very large range of theistic religions, with their different concepts of God, who naturally possesses attributes. His system also incorporates fundamental Buddhist ideas, but more by subterfuge than by open acknowledgement. Moreover, as I pointed out previously,[32] his is not merely an intellectual exercise, but implies also an ideological stance. Many further examples could be mentioned in which attempts were made to synthesize and subsume under some new umbrella system a variety of disparate religious traditions and attitudes, although perhaps none on the same scale of generality as Śaṅkara's. One could think of Rāmānuja who suggested a meta-system within which the popular and vernacular *bhakti* religion of the Āḻvārs could be accommodated alongside the Sanskritic Vedānta. Or we could refer back to the *Bhāgavata-purāṇa*, a work that (perhaps more formally than systematically) synthesizes a wide range of material. However, such learned and intellectual attempts at creating a religious meta-structure never succeeded fully in their intentions. Like the antinomians, they all ended up as no more than further varieties of the religious in the wider framework of Indian culture.

Was all this abstract and seemingly roundabout talking of structures, anti-structures, and meta-structures, of particulars and universals, of form and formalism, and of chaos, order and syntheses really necessary (quite apart from bringing in French cheeses and politics)? Would it not have been sufficient simply to mention the antinomians, introduce their 'common-sensical' mode of making sense, add it to our list and complete our catalogue and, as it happens, our entire exploration? Well, I am sure one can argue about the form all this has taken, but I regard something like it to be an absolutely essential exercise. For surely we want more than a mere catalogue. If there is anything at all striking and fascinating in the landscape of the apparently wild jungles through which our exploration has taken us, we must allow further *dramatis personae* to enter – ourselves. This raises our discussion to yet a further meta-level. It raises questions of assessment and evaluation (though I shall keep value-judgements out of it), and this not just in the isolation of our own thoughts, but also by relating them to the 'native' assessments. In simpler language this means: what do we make of the material we have been looking at, what do we do with it, and is there anything in it that gives us advice in this matter?

In order to develop these ideas in a concrete way, I shall turn to the symbol of the 'head in the world'. This takes us back to our very first chapter,[33] where I suggested some initial methodological reflections on the basis of Canetti's novel *Auto da Fé*. For the 'hero', if we can call him that, is an indologist very much involved in the study of Indian religions. That the novel ends with the scholar setting fire to himself and all his books suggested that he had approached his task in not quite the right way. There are three parts, each one focusing on a different character. 'Head without world' looks at Professor Peter Kien who lives totally in his own, increasingly chaotic, world of the imagination and breaks down under the intrusion of another person. Then there is Fischerle, a greedy and obsessive cripple who is familiar with all the tricks of a 'world without head'. Finally, 'world in the head' focuses on Peter's brother George, a psychoanalyst, who uses his skills of empathy, by trying to place himself into another person's mind and heart, to bring order back into chaotic lives. At the end, the lives of all three end in failure and disaster. But Canetti hints at a solution that might have been possible, if in each of the three persons characteristics of the other two had existed. That would be the ideal scholar, as much as the ideal human being. Perhaps wisely, he did not develop such an ideal character; but the logic of the three headings suggests that the 'head in the world' would be appropriate for it.

When we let these and similar associations play through our minds, it is possible to accommodate not just the 'antinomians' under this heading of the 'head in the world', but much of the Indian wisdom material generally, thus offering a convenient way of summarizing it. Contrary to the popular myth of the total transcendentality of Indian 'wisdom', it has revealed itself to us very much as an attempt to make sense of the world, by realizing its meaningfulness. From the most obvious level of sorting out and manipulating small facets of everyday life (comparable to Fischerle), the spectrum runs to the universe with its cosmic laws. Another spectrum runs from grand theories about the mental nature of reality to the level of the minutiae of the perceptive mental processes. Beyond purely cerebral constructions and theories, 'click phenomena' offer additional ways of relating to the world. Few of the modes in which this is carried out succeed in 'shutting the world' out altogether; on the whole, new kinds of contacts with the world are established after the liberating insight. Whether such insights are located in a transcendental ground of being (like *brahman*), or in a personal God or Goddess, or identified as the realization that no such essence or ground exists, the phenomena (our particulars) remain irreducible. While aiming at systematic comprehension, this 'wisdom' can nevertheless accommodate chaos. By applying the metaphor of 'commuting within one world' to it, the mysterious *advaya* or *advaita* relationship between the liberating realization and the phenomena, or the head and the world, is alluded to.

But we should not let all these metaphors cloud our own heads and make us forget that we are dealing with very practical matters. The case of Professor Peter Kien is a warning that has been hanging over our whole exploration. He failed to 'commute within one world' and to become a 'head in the world' and burnt himself and all his books instead. Does the present book deserve the same fate? It is not up to me to answer this question. Let me comment, instead, on how the challenge of the 'real' world of Indian religious culture with all its ramifications and all its variety has been faced up to in this exploration.

Power, love and wisdom are, I believe, human universals. These have been projected on to the Indian material in such a way that the widest range of associations my own imagination is capable of can encompass the widest range of relevant material. The material caught in this way has revealed itself as anything but static, monolithic, or arbitrary. Instead, we have found trends and tensions, movements and opposing poles, which I have endeavoured to trace. Thus, time and again, we could see 'escapist' trends operating, away from this world of misery and suffering, and then again, counter-trends back into the world. Moreover, we have witnessed a variety of suggestions as to how these two could be kept together and the tension between them resolved. And 'world' in this context is never merely an abstract, for, consciously or only from the vantage point of the scholar, it also involves concrete society with its complex stratification. We traced a tension between a religious trend to do something about one's destiny and a counter-trend to stop interfering with what there is already, latent and potential in all of us. A catalogue of modes of making sense was established, which in turn was overlaid by the tension between creating order and acknowledging irreducible particularity and chaos, which it implies. There appears to be an inner logic at work, some kind of rhythm that guided us in our movement through the landscape we explored. Since this took us merrily across most of the well-established boundaries of conventional '-isms', this may well raise some eyebrows in Western academic circles. But if it can be shown that the conventional categories of Comparative Religion or Religious Studies (or even indology) do not work, I see no reason to force the material into their Procrustean bed.

Now it is important to realize that this exploration does not duplicate anything that was ever done (or possibly could have been done) in traditional India. I have made no value-judgemental distinctions between the socially high and low (say, brahmin versus untouchable), the orthodox (in the eyes of some, say Advaitins) and the heterodox (in this case, anything from Rāmānuja to Buddhism and tribal religions), or the doctrinal (e.g. Śiva is superior to Viṣṇu), or different kinds of regional cultures. This is bound to raise eyebrows in India. Nevertheless, what appears to have emerged is a genuine Indian discourse that itself cuts across these barriers, while some inner logic unites it. Religion has revealed itself not as an entity comparable to a clockwork, but to a lengthy and unresolved human discussion, from which participants are constantly dropping out, and into which new ones are constantly entering. (The metaphors are derived from Winch, who used them in the slightly different context of the social sciences.)[34] But this means that instead of being able to pontificate about what 'the Hindu' or 'the Buddhist' believes, or about some inner 'essence' (say Advaita) of Indian religious thought, I am left with a fascinating landscape, but no grand system. No doubt one could try to 'systematize' (and regiment) the material in one's own way, but at this point not only Canetti's burning books, but also the acknowledged tendencies towards chaos within the Indian material raise their fingers of serious reprimand. For it would mean to impose another kind of ossification. I may have spoken of inner logical developments; but the chaos resulting from this inevitable variety is not even 'logical' in that sense. No inner logic had to lead to the elimination of Buddhism as one of the more articulate speakers in the discussion, no inner logic suggested the arrival of (Sufi) Islam, or the intrusion of Western ideas at an even later stage.

All this means that a meticulous textual scholar might discover that the individual chapters of this book are held together by the *Antāti* feature mentioned earlier, and also that something of the nature of a *Kalampakam* is discernible in the background. These are meant to be hints – hints that I have made no attempt to create here a grand meta-meta-system of the Indian religions. In the light of everything that has been said, it should be clear why such an attempt would be undesirable and would actually violate the nature of the material itself. Given that our material could be compared to records of a long discussion, what I have been trying to do could perhaps best be described as listening in to it, and attempting to take the minutes – and trying to contain the chaos in a merely formal manner. To what extent all this agrees with the ideal of the 'head in the world' is for someone else to judge. Anyway, at this point the 'I' can once again leave the stage and 'we' can proceed to a further stage of reflection. In other words, how can we make any 'common sense' of the total picture?

There are further loose ends left over from the very first chapter (like general rules or definitions of variables that a *sūtra* text or a computer program has to return to time and again). Thus we may remember the Buendía dynasty,[35] members of which attempted over a period of a *Hundred Years of Solitude* to decipher a Sanskrit manuscript which contained the secrets of their destiny. This was, at the same time, my metaphor for the 'oracle' in the form of Eastern wisdom that we in the West have been trying to consult for more than a century. Having completed our own exploration of the Indian religions, we may be interested in finding out what happened to the last Buendía; for we might find an answer there to our own very natural question: what we ought to make of it all. Well, the moment the last of the Buendías fully deciphered the manuscript, the history of the dynasty itself came to an end: the world collapsed around him and he died, thereby fulfilling his destiny. The decipherment added nothing to the history, it simply signified its conclusions. Ominous ideas, we might think. But given that our own understanding of Indian religions is far from perfect, there is no need to worry in such a literalist sense. Nevertheless, with a bit of imagination we could read into this the following: the journey itself is the purpose, and the chaos experienced is the message.

If it is true that the landscape explored by us as a whole makes up the 'oracle', we cannot derive from it paraphrasable answers to specific questions. Instead, by its variety and its merely formally contained chaos, it challenges us, on a higher level of discourse, to become conscious of our own attitudes towards order and chaos and variety. Now in a world where most people would not dream of travelling to Albania or Mali, Bourkina Fasso or South Yemen, unless there were Hiltons and fish-and-chips there and people who spoke English, our journey through the strange landscape of the Indian religions may well have been arduous and disconcerting. But to be told at the end of it all that a sense of 'chaos' would be the most appropriate souvenir to take home – that surely must be a bad joke. That is the moment when it seems best to follow the example of Mr Hatterr's absconding disciple. But where could we abscond to? Naturally there would be our own home environment of cosy familiarity; or the exotic dream world tourist brochures may promise. But in neither case would we face up to the challenges of 'the world' – either by restricting ourselves to a minute part of it, or by escaping into a dream that lies outside 'all that the case is'. However, I have no intention of turning into a preacher or *guru*.

By a curious coincidence, the concept of 'chaos' has recently become popular in the media. So let me make it clear that I am not using the term in that special sense here. For, as far as I understand it, this scientific chaos allows itself to be defined in terms of a mathematical formula, and nothing of the sort is intended here for the Indian religions. Even so, there is a poetic attraction in the phrase 'a butterfly in Peking' (which, by this scientific theory of chaos can, with the flapping of its wings, affect the weather in England). By this logic one might be tempted to speak of 'a *guru* in the Himalayas' who by a similarly 'chaotic' chain of events can fundamentally alter the face of much of Indian religion – or even of our own self-awareness.

This is not meant to be frivolous. I am not denying thereby that in the chaotic jungle of Indian culture somehow the question of ultimate truth has become irrelevant. If it is somewhere out there, who but an omniscient being can actually identify it? But given that Indian culture has acknowledged many 'omniscient ones', who proclaimed a whole host of different 'absolute' truths, we as the observers can do little more than remember the brutal phrase *Die Welt ist alles was der Fall ist* (the world is all that the case is).[36] This does not mean, as we have surely realized by now, that this 'world' has to be a cold and meaningless place. When the vicissitudes of cultural history time and again relativized absolute truth claims (by balancing a ruthless pursuit of asceticism with the world of the emotions, and pure emotionalism and single-minded renunciation with a concern for rationality), not only did it prevent religious wars and persecutions, but it made the world a much more cheerful place than a corner-shop where everything is neatly arranged on shelves and money the ultimate truth. Mahārājas utterly ruthless in their pursuit of pleasure and expansion of their territory; ascetics brutal to themselves to the extent of suicide through starvation; celibate mystics fainting in erotic ecstasy; thinkers analysing the world, the mechanics of human perception and thinking itself, down to the last atom and the last vestige of ignorance; poets imposing the most rigid rationality on the outrageously irrational, emotional and erotic – this is the contained chaos. Here we find the abstract message we might want to take home from the jungles of Indian religions, and not just some discrete, specific 'spiritual' items (like 'Kṛṣṇa is God') that can safely be tucked away in the innocuous niche conventionally called 'the religious'.

Let me conclude by quoting once again from Mr Hatterr. Appropriately, it is the very last sentence of the book and, equally appropriately perhaps, it is in German: '*Mach's nach, aber mach's besser*'. The book translates this as 'carry on boys [and girls], and continue like hell',[37] but a more correct translation would be: 'do what I have done, but make sure you do it better!' Do what better? you may ask. Naturally, consulting the oracle once again.

Notes

Full bibliographical details are given at the first occurrence only; subsequent references are given in abbreviated form by pointing back to the relevant note; e.g. (Ch. 5, n. 7) means, for full details of the work mentioned, see note 7 of chapter 5. Unless explicitly stated, all translations are my own.

1 CONSULTING THE ORACLE ONCE AGAIN

1 Gabriel García Márquez, *One Hundred Years of Solitude*, translated from the Spanish by G. Rabassa, Pan Books, London, 1978, e.g. p. 24.
2 Ibid., p. 332.
3 Ibid., p. 154.
4 Elias Canetti, *Auto da Fé*, translated from the German by C. Wedgwood, Penguin Books, Harmondsworth, 1965, reprinted 1973, p. 12.
5 Ibid., p. 18.
6 Ibid., p. 20.
7 Ibid., p. 21.
8 Ibid., p. 22.
9 Ibid., p. 15.
10 Ibid., p. 490.
11 The title of the first of the three parts of the novel.
12 Ibid., pp. 484–93.
13 Ibid., p. 66.
14 Ibid., pp. 269–77.
15 Ibid., p. 486.
16 Ibid., p. 286.
17 Ibid., p. 377. For the German see E. Canetti, *Die Blendung*, Fischer Bücherei, Frankfurt am Main, 1965, p. 299.
18 These are actually individual sentences taken consecutively from the passage, ibid., pp. 445–8.
19 Individual sentences taken from ibid., p. 490. The German original (see note 17 above), p. 354, has '*Heimatlosigkeit*' (homelessness) which is more appropriate in the context of the Buddha's life than 'wilderness' with its biblical allusions.

20 Ibid., p. 490.
21 *Viśvaguṇādarśa-campū*, by Veṅkaṭādhvari-kavi, [edited, and] with a Tamil translation, by R. Saroja, The Hind Press, Madras, 1968, from Nos 366 and 367 (pp. 116f).
22 Ibid., p. 117, from No. 368.
23 Ibid., pp. 117f, from Nos 369 and 370.
24 Ibid., p. 117, in No. 370. For a complete French translation of the work see: *La Viśvaguṇādarśacampū de Veṅkaṭādhvarin*, introduction, translation and notes by M.-C. Porcher, Pondicherry, 1972 (Publications de l'Institut Français d'Indologie, No. 48). The verses referred to above are found on p. 89, numbered here 261[b]–4. Porcher retains the singular of the original (*vastv adbhutam*), but given that she herself hesitates to identify such 'un objet étonnant', e.g. with the Fort St George (pp. 9f), and that the commentator ignores the expression (p. 186), I have preferred to use the plural (as in the Tamil translation).
25 Compare P. Winch, *The Idea of a Social Science*, London, 1977 (1st edn, 1958), p. 183.

2 OCEANS OF MILK AND TREACLE

Details on Indian cosmology can be found in the following works: W. Kirfel, *Die Kosmographie der Inder, nach den Quellen dargestellt*, Kurt Schroeder Verlag, Bonn and Leipzig, 1920 (a reprographic reprint, much reduced in size, was published in Hildesheim by Georg Olms Verlagsbuchhandlung in 1967); W. Kirfel, *Das Purāṇa vom Weltgebäude (Bhuvanavinyāsa) – Die kosmographischen Traktate der Purāṇa's – Versuch einer Textgeschichte*, Bonn (Selbstverlag des Orientalischen Seminars der Universität = Bonner Orientalische Studien, Neue Serie, Band 1), 1954; C. Caillat and Ravi Kumar, *The Jaina Cosmology*, published by Ravi Kumar, Basle/Paris, 1981; R. F. Gombrich, 'Ancient Indian cosmology', in: *Ancient Cosmologies*, edited by C. Blacker and M. Loewe, George Allen and Unwin, London, 1975, pp. 110–42; R. Kloetzli, *Buddhist Cosmology*, Motilal Banarsidass, Delhi, 1983.

1 Mrs Sinclair Stevenson, *The Heart of Jainism*, Oxford University Press, London, 1915, reprinted New Delhi, 1970.
2 Ibid., p. 298.
3 See below, pp. 292, 476f.
4 See below, pp. 49, 52, 56.
5 *Bhāgavata-purāṇa* V, 16, 11–25. A handy edition of the text only is Kashi Sanskrit Series, vol. 255, Chaukhambha Sanskrit Sansthan, Varanasi, 1987. G. V. Tagare's English translation (in five volumes, Motilal Banarsidass, Delhi, 1976–1979, Ancient Indian Tradition and Mythology Series) is far superior to the translations by M. N. Dutt and J. M. Sanyal.
6 *Bhāgavata-purāṇa* (see previous note) V, 17, 15; IX, 1, 13–42.
7 Ibid., V, 17, 1–9; cf. IX, 9, 1–15.

8 *Līlāvaī – a Romantic Kāvya in Māhārāṣṭrī Prakrit of Koūhala*, edited (with a Sanskrit *vṛtti* of a Jaina author) by A. N. Upadhye, Bharatiya Vidya Bhavan, Bombay, 1966 (Singhi Jain Series, vol. 31), from vv. 1013–41.
9 Ibid., vv. 1056–61.
10 *Nāyakumāra-cariü of Puṣpadanta, An Apabhraṃśa work of the 10th century*, edited by Hiralal Jain, Karanja, 1933 (Balatkara Gana Jain Publication Society, Devendrakirti Jain Series, vol. 1): V, 10, 20f; 11, 14f; 12, 1–13; 13, 1–7; VI, 1, 1–4.
11 Ibid., VI, 1–7; the concluding verse is: VI, 7, 9b–10.
12 *Bhāgavata-purāṇa* (see note 5 above) V, 26. A variation on this chapter is VIII, 21–3 of the *Devī-Bhāgavata-purāṇa*, edited by Ramtej Pandey, Chaukhamba Vidyabhavan, Varanasi, 1986 (Pracya-vidya Series). A complete English translation by Svami Vijnanananda (alias Hari Prasanna Chatterji) was originally published as vol. 26 (in two parts) of the Sacred Books of the Hindus Series, Allahabad, 1921–3, reprinted New York, 1973. See IX, 32–7 for an independent passage on the hells.
13 *Bhāgavata-purāṇa* (see note 5 above) V, 26, 26. 'Saliva' merely on the basis of the name itself, *lālā-bhakṣa*.
14 Ibid., v. 36.
15 *Muni Śrīcandra's Kaha-kosu, An Apabhraṃśa text of the 11th century*, edited by H. L. Jain, Ahmedabad, 1969 (Prakrit Text Society, Prakrit Text Society Series, No. 13): *sandhi* 45, 12, 8 – 13, 11 (p. 454); *tatta-loha-paḍimā* in line 10. The *Kahakosu* appears to be derived from Hariṣeṇa's *Bṛhat-Kathākośa*, edited by A. N. Upadhye, Bharatiya Vidya Bhavan, Bombay, 1943 (Singhi Jain Series, vol. 17). Here the story is told (much more enigmatically) in story 128, vv. 124–36 (p. 301).
16 See *Bhāgavata-purāṇa* (note 5 above), V, 26, 20 and Manu (see note 17 below) XI, 104.
17 *Mānava-Dharma-śāstra*, XI, 91. An English translation is found in the Sacred Books of the East Series, edited by F. M. Müller, vol. 25, *The Laws of Manu*, translated by G. Bühler, Clarendon Press, Oxford, 1886 (and various reprints). Compare *Bhāgavata-purāṇa* V, 26, 29.
18 *Śrī-Govardhanācārya-viracitā Āryā-Saptaśatī*, edited with Ananta-paṇḍita's Sanskrit commentary by Pandit Durga-prasad, Kasinath Pandurang Parab and Vasudev Laxman Sastri Pansikar, 3rd revised edn, Bombay (Kāvyamālā, vol. 1), 1934. Text with Hindi commentary and Hindi translation by Pandit Ramakant Tripathi, Chowkhamba Vidyabhawan, Varanasi, 1965, Sanskrit Series, vol. 127. The verse is No. 511.
19 See M.-T. de Mallmann, *Introduction à l'étude d'Avalokiteçvara*, Paris, 1948 (Annales du Musée Guimet, Bibliothèque d'études, vol. 57). The *Kāraṇḍavyūha-sūtra* (summarized by de Mallmann, pp. 39–47; Sanskrit text edited originally by Samasrami, Calcutta, 1873; re-edited by P. L. Vaidya in vol. I of his '*Mahāyānasūtrasaṅgraha*', pp. 258–308, Buddhist Sanskrit Texts, Mithila Institute, Darbhanga, 1961) expresses an

extraordinary version of a late Buddhist cosmology. Not only is the Bodhisattva Avalokiteśvara given cosmic proportions, but in each pore at the root of his hairs a whole universe can be found. See p. 288 (l. 14) to p. 303 (l. 9) in Vaidya's edition, = II, 2.

20 See E. Frauwallner, *Geschichte der indischen Philosophie*, vol. I, Otto Müller Verlag, Salzburg, 1953, pp. 51f.

3 NAVIGATING THE SEA OF EARTHLY EXISTENCE

1 On Mallī see pp. 456–9.

2 The Jains appear to be using the word *tīrtha* in its general sense (which is also attested in ordinary Sanskrit) of '[correct] passage (e.g. through a river or through life)', and thus 'spiritual path, advice' or 'religious teaching'. *Tīrthaṅkara* is thus a person who initiates the correct religion. Even with the Buddhists, this meaning is still implied in expressions like *añña-titthiya* (Pālī) or *para-tīrthika* (Sanskrit), 'belonging to another religion'; but the simple *titthiya* or *tīrthaka* then specialized in meaning to denote a 'heretic'.

3 These three are: Śānti, Kunthu, Ara. A brief summary of the lives of these sixty-three great persons can be found in H. von Glasenapp, *Der Jainismus – eine indische Erlösungsreligion, nach den Quellen dargestellt*, Alf Häger Verlag, Berlin, 1925, pp. 247–60. Many more details are provided by P. L. Vaidya in his summaries of the content of *The Mahāpurāṇa or Tisaṭṭhimahāpurisaguṇālaṅkāra, a Jaina Epic in Apabhraṃśa of the tenth century of Puṣpadanta*, 3 vols, Bombay, 1937, 1940 and 1941 (Manikchand Digambara Jaina Granthamala, Nos 37, 41 and 42). One version (the *Triṣaṣṭiśalākapuruṣacaritra* in Sanskrit by the Śvetāmbara Hemacandra of the twelfth century) has been fully translated into English by Helen M. Johnson: *The Lives of Sixty-Three Illustrious Persons*, 6 vols, Oriental Institute, Baroda, 1962.

4 See Padmanabh S. Jaini, *The Jaina Path of Purification*, University of California, Berkeley, 1979 (also Indian edition, Motilal Banarsidass, Delhi, 1979), p. 10, with sources and further literature in notes 16ff.

5 The story of Brahmadatta is told e.g. in H. Jacobi, *Ausgewählte Erzählungen in Māhārāṣṭrī, zur Einführung in das Studium des Prakrit*, S. Hirzel Verlag, Leipzig, 1886, as No. 1 (Brahmadatta's gruesome end: pp. 19f). Compare J. J. Meyer, *Hindu [sic] Tales – An English Translation of Jacobi's Ausgewählte Erzählungen*, Luzac, London, 1909, pp. 3–62. See also *Bṛhat-Kathākośa* (Ch. 2, n. 15), stories 35 and 52, to which correspond in *Kahakosu* (Ch. 2, n. 15) *sandhi* 9, 4–8 and *sandhi* 11, 10–12.

6 P. S. Jaini (see note 4 above), pp. 288–95, discussing Jinasena's account.

7 W. Kirfel, *Das Purāṇa-pañcalakṣaṇa – Versuch einer Textgeschichte*, Kurt Schroeder Verlag, Bonn, 1927.

8 The material is discussed in detail in F. Hardy, *Viraha-bhakti – The Early*

History of Kṛṣṇa Devotion in South India, Oxford University Press, New Delhi, 1983, (Oxford University South Asian Studies Series), pp. 86–90.

9 See P. S. Jaini (note 4 above), pp. 285–306.

10 See Cēkiḻār's *Periya-purāṇam*, 2746–52 (pp. 261f). A 'condensed English version' was produced by G. Vanmikanathan, Sri Ramakrishna Math, Madras, 1985 (to which the page numbers provided here refer).

11 *Bhāgavata-purāṇa* (see Ch. 2, n. 5), V, 1–5; cf. P. S. Jaini, 'Jina Ṛṣabha as an avatāra of Viṣṇu', *Bulletin of the School of Oriental and African Studies* 40, pp. 321–37.

12 See W. Kirfel, *Das Purāṇa vom Weltgebäude* (Ch. 2, introduction), pp. 7*–10*.

13 Edited by E. Senart in three volumes, Paris, 1882–97. For a complete English translation see *The Mahāvastu*, translated from the Buddhist Sanskrit (in three volumes) by J. J. Jones, Luzac, London, 1949, 1952 and 1956 (Sacred Books of the Buddhists, vols 16, 18 and 19). The origin of the world (called *rāja-vaṃśa*) is treated in vol. I (in Jones' translation), pp. 285–301; the different hells and universes, ibid., pp. 6–28; 46–52; the many Buddhas, ibid., pp. 39–46.

14 The story is told in the famous *Devī-māhātmya* (also called *Durgā-saptaśatī*), included in the *Mārkaṇḍeya-purāṇa* (as chapters 81 to 93). A complete translation of the Purāṇa was produced by F. E. Pargiter, Royal Asiatic Society of Bengal, Calcutta, 1888–1904 (Bibliotheca Indica, Nos 700 … 1104). There are many separate editions and English translations of the *Devī-māhātmya*, e.g. by Swami Jagadisvarananda, Sri Ramakrishna Math, Madras, 1969.

15 Elias Canetti, *Aufzeichnungen 1942–1948*, Deutscher Taschenbuch Verlag, Munich, 1965, p. 49; most of this material is also included in: Elias Canetti, *Die Provinz des Menschen – Aufzeichnungen 1942–1972*, Fischer Taschenbuch Verlag, Frankfurt am Main, 1976. Page numbers in brackets refer to this second collection, (p. 40).

16 See H. von Glasenapp, *Die Lehre vom Karman in der Philosophie der Jainas (nach den Karmagranthas dargestellt)*, O. Harrassowitz, Leipzig, 1915, particularly pp. 21–35. This book was translated into English by G. Barry Gifford (edited by Hiralal R. Kapadia), B. V. J. Panalal Charity Fund, Bombay, 1942 (see particularly pp. 5–20).

17 The story is summarized here as told by Hariṣeṇa in his *Bṛhat-Kathākośa* (Ch. 2, n. 15), No. 73; the *Kahakosu* does not narrate the story. A complete English translation of this Sanskrit version, with notes on other versions, can be found in: *The Clever Adulteress and Other Stories – A Treasury of Jain Literature*, edited by P. Granoff, Mosaic Press, Oakville/New York, 1990, pp. 118–39.

18 William S. Burroughs, *Cities of the Red Night*, John Calder, London, 1981 (also available in Picador).

19 See *The Sunday Times Magazine* of 12 July, 1981, pp. 8–21, which had an article by Ian Wilson, 'The myths of reincarnation', derived from his

book *Mind out of Time?* (Gollancz). *The Reader's Digest* of September 1981 had an article by M. A. O'Roark (condensed from McCall's (March 1981) on 'More Evidence for Life after Death' (pp. 59–62)), which surveys work by Moody, Ring, Schoonmaker, Sabom and Stevenson.

20 I am referring here to the work of Jane Goodall (known to me only from her television and radio presentations).

4 SAFE HAVENS

1 *Līlāvaī* (see Ch. 2, n. 8), vv. 1163–85. In v. 1182, a second, punning, meaning is hidden: 'they created (with those sparks in the sky) their own version of the *kṛttikā* constellation' (which is perceived by the Indians as a knife).

2 Ibid., vv. 1192–7. Verse 1194 contains another pun, on 'soldier' and 'wing', which alludes to the myth of Indra's cutting the wings of the Vindhya mountains.

3 Dilip Chitre, *Travelling in a Cage*, Clearing House, Bombay, 1980, p. 18.

4 Adil Jussawalla, *New Writing in India*, Penguin Books, Harmondsworth, 1974, p. 33 (introduction).

5 *Periyâḻvār-Tirumoḻi* II, 8 (contained in the Tamil *Nālāyira-divya-prabandham* of the Āḻvārs).

6 I photographed this in 1982, outside the village of Matappattu near Villupuram, on the main road from Madras to Trichi.

7 Two Marathi books, both edited by R. C. Dhere, deal with the mythology of the temple of Jejurī: Śrīdhar-svāmī Nājhrekar, *Śrī-Malhārī-māhātmya*, Varda Buks, Pune, 1975; Gangādhar-kavi, *Śrī-Mārtaṇḍa-vijaya*, Varda Buks, Pune, 1975. See also G.-D. Sontheimer, *Birobā, Mhaskobā und Khaṇḍobā: Ursprung, Geschichte und Umwelt von pastoralen Gottheiten in Mahārāṣṭra*, Franz Steiner Verlag, Wiesbaden, 1976 (Schriftenreihe des Südasien-Instituts der Universität Heidelberg, vol. 21), Index *sub* Khaṇḍobā.

8 The story is narrated, in Apabhraṃśa, in Śrīcandra's *Kahakosu* (see Ch. 2, n. 15), *sandhi* 25, 1, 5 to 10, 7 (pp. 267–72). The passages translated here are: 25, 3, 1–3; 5, 6b–11; 6, 3f; 6, 9b – 8, 4a. Hariṣeṇa's briefer Sanskrit version is story No. 64, of *Bṛhat-Kathākośa* (see Ch. 2, n. 15).

9 The story of Manasā is told in a special genre of Bengali literature, the *Manasā-maṅgal*. This whole genre is systematically surveyed by W. L. Smith, *The One-Eyed Goddess*, Almquist and Wiksell International, Stockholm, 1980 (Acta Universitatis Stockholmiensis, Stockholm Oriental Studies, vol. 12). A number of versions are also mentioned in D. C. Sen, *History of Bengali Language and Literature*, Calcutta, 2nd edn, 1954, pp. 229–64. The latter half of Ketaka-dāsa's poem has been translated by E. C. Dimock in his *The Thief of Love – Bengali Tales from Court and Village*, University of Chicago Press, Chicago/London, 1963, pp. 197–294. See also P. K. Maity, *Historical Studies in the Cult of the*

Goddess Manasā, Punthi Pustak, Calcutta, 1966; E. C. Dimock, 'The goddess of snakes in medieval Bengali literature', part I, *History of Religions* 1961, pp. 307–21; part II (with A. K. Ramanujan), *History of Religions* 1964, pp. 300–22.

10 *Ek hotā rājā*, edited by Sarojinī Bābar, Mahārāṣṭra rājya loka-sāhitya mālā, Pune, 1965. Part I, pp. 77–93 'Yallammā-devīcī gāṇī', No. 1 (pp. 77ff).

11 Ibid., No. 7 (pp. 83–6).

12 Ibid., No. 7, vv. 6f.

13 Ibid., No. 7, v. 13.

14 Ibid., No. 4 (pp. 81f).

15 Ibid., No. 4, v. 1; cf. Sontheimer (see note 7 above), p. 43.

16 See R. C. Dhere, *Marāṭhī lokasaṃskṛtīce upāsak*, Saṃskṛti-paricay-mālā, Jñānrāj Prakāśan (date and place of publication unknown), pp. 106–14.

17 Manu's *Dharmaśāstra* (see Ch. 2, n. 17), III, 5–19.

18 Ibid., III, 150–82; 237–50.

19 L. A. Babb, *The Divine Hierarchy – Popular Hinduism in Central India*, Columbia University Press, New York/London, 1975, p. 70 (all three quotations).

20 Ibid., p. 71.

21 On Yāmunācārya's defence of the orthodoxy of the Pāñcarātra tradition, see J. A. B. van Buitenen, 'On the archaism of the Bhāgavata Purāṇa', in: *Kṛṣṇa – Myths, Rites, and Attitudes*, edited by M. Singer, University of Chicago Press, Chicago/London, 1966, pp. 26–32.

22 J. M. Freeman, *Untouchable – An Indian Life History*, George Allen and Unwin, London, 1979.

23 Ibid., pp. 362ff; 372; 377.

24 F. F. Conlon, *A Caste in a Changing World – The Chitrapur Saraswat Brahmans 1700–1935*, University of California Press, Berkeley, 1977.

25 See, for instance The Right Rev. Henry Whitehead, *The Village Gods of South India*, Association Press, Calcutta, and Oxford University Press, London (2nd edn), 1921 (The Religious Life of India), p. 46: 'There is no idea of praise and thanksgiving, no expression of gratitude or love, no desire for any spiritual or moral blessings.'

26 See my 'The Tamil Veda of a *śūdra* saint – the Śrīvaiṣṇava interpretation of Nammāḻvār', in: *Contributions to South Asian Studies*, edited by Gopal Krishna, Oxford University Press, Delhi, vol. I, 1979, pp. 29–87.

27 See W. L. Smith (note 9 above), pp. 65 (with his note 5), 131f (with his note 10).

28 Ibid., pp. 139–46.

29 See Sontheimer (note 7 above), pp. 54f.

30 I am indebted to John Smith, Cambridge, for this information. His book on Pāpūjī's epic and paintings has now finally been published: *The Epic of Pāpūjī – A Study, Transcription and Translation*, Cambridge University Press, Cambridge, 1991 (University of Cambridge Oriental Publications, vol. 44).

5 VIOLENCE, AGGRESSION AND HEROISM

1 Abbé J. A. Dubois, *Hindu Manners, Customs and Ceremonies*, translated from the author's later French MS. by H. K. Beauchamp, Clarendon Press, Oxford (3rd edn), 1906, pp. 50f. (Dubois lived in South India between 1792 and 1823; see p. vii.)
2 See above, pp. 47–63 *passim*.
3 See K. R. van Kooij, *Worship of the Goddess according to the Kālikāpurāṇa*, Part I (translation of chapters 54–69), E. J. Brill, Leiden, 1972; p. 1 refers to W. C. Blaquiere's translation of 1799 of the 'chapter on [human] blood'. For a complete edition of the Sanskrit text see *The Kālikāpurāṇam*, edited by Biśwanārāyaṇ Śāstrī, Benares, 1972 (Chowkhamba Sanskrit Series, Jayakrishnadas Granthamālā, vol. 5); here the chapter on sacrifice (which is not found in the van Kooij translation) is numbered 67.
4 The Rev. B. H. Badley, *The Mela at Tulsipur – Glimpses of Missionary Life and Work in India. A Book for Children*, The Religious Tract Society, London [no date, *c.* 1875?], p. 133.
5 Federico García Lorca, *Poeta en Nueva York*, in: '*Obras completas*', edited by Arturo del Hoyo, Aguilar, Madrid, vol. I, 1980 (21st edn, 1st: 1954), pp. 517f.
6 See *Tempeltücher für die Muttergöttinnen in Indien – Zeremonien, Herstellung und Ikonographie gemalter und gedruckter Stoffbilder aus Gujarat*, by E. Fischer, J. Jain and H. Shah, Museum Rietberg, Zürich, 1982, p. 57.
7 The story is told in Svayaṃbhū's Apabhraṃśa epic *Paümacariu* (edited by H. C. Bhayani in three volumes, Bombay, vol. I, 1953; vol. II, 1953; vol. III, 1960; Singhī Jain Granthamālā, vols 34–36), *sandhi* 35, 4–15.
8 *Buddhist legends, translated from the original Pali text of the Dhammapada commentary* by E. W. Burlingame, Luzac, for the Pali Text Society, London, 1969 (Harvard Oriental Series, vol. 28), pp. 79ff.
9 See my article on 'The Śrīvaiṣṇava hagiography of Parakāla [=Tirumaṅkai Āḻvār]', in: *Indian Narrative Literature*, edited by C. Shackle and R. Snell, Harrassowitz, Wiesbaden, 1992, pp. 81–116.
10 *Periya-purāṇam*, see above, Ch. 3, n. 10.
11 See my 'The diary of an unknown Indian girl', *Religion* 10, 1980, pp. 165–82.
12 The story is told, for example, in Anantācārya's *Prapannāmṛta* (edited by Rāmanārāyaṇācārya, published by the Somani Trust, Benares, 1967), chapter 49 (pp. 102f). Compare K. A. Nilakanta Sastri, *A History of South India*, Oxford University Press, London (3rd edn), 1966, p. 430.
13 Vidyākara's *Subhāṣitaratnakoṣa*, edited by D. D. Kosambi and V. V. Gokhale, Harvard University Press, Cambridge, MA, 1957 (Harvard Oriental Series, vol. 42), p. xlv.

14 Ibid., p. l.
15 Ibid., p. 1, note 14.
16 Jussawalla (Ch. 4, n. 4), p. 17 (introduction).
17 A. Duff, *India and Indian Missions: Including Sketches of the Gigantic System of Hinduism Both in Theory and Practice*, Edinburgh (2nd edn), 1840, quoted in: ' *The Faiths of the World – A Dictionary of All Religions and Religious Sects, Their Doctrines, Rites, Ceremonies and Customs*', by The Rev. J. Gardner, A. Fullarton, London and Edinburgh, [no date, *c.* 1855], vol. I, pp. 499f, on the 'charak pujah' (*cakra-pūjā*).
18 For a fuller discussion of *akam* poetry see below, pp. 214–24.
19 The *Tolkāppiyam* (edited by T. C. Pālacuntaram Piḷḷai, South India Saiva Siddhanta Publishing Co., Tirunelveli, 1967) lists these themes in its second chapter of Part III (*Poruḷatikāram*), *sūtras* 1002–37. The longer list is found in Aiyaṉāritaṉār's *Puṟapporuḷ-veṇpāmālai*; see K. Kailasapathy, *Tamil Heroic Poetry*, Clarendon Press, Oxford, 1968, pp. 194ff.
20 English translations of a number of *puṟam* poems can be found in: A. K. Ramanujan, *Poems of Love and War, from the Eight Anthologies and the Ten Long Poems of Classical Tamil*, Columbia University Press, New York, 1985; G. L. Hart, *Poets of the Tamil Anthologies – Ancient Poems of Love and War*, Princeton University Press, Princeton, 1979, pp. 139–209.
21 *Vīr-satsaī* (in Mārvāṛī) by Sūryamalla Miśraṇ (*c.* AD 1850) of Būndī, edited by Patrām Gauṛ 'Vishad', Bangal Hindi Mandal, Calcutta, 1965, No. 18.
22 The best edition of the Prakrit text of the *Sattasaī* remains *Das Saptaçatakam des Hāla*, critically edited by A. Weber, Brockhaus, Leipzig, 1881 (Abhandlungen für die Kunde des Morgenlandes, vol. 7, No. 4). All verse numbers refer to this edition. The first 370 poems (differently numbered) had previously been edited by Weber (same place and publisher, 1870, same series, vol. 5, No. 3); where relevant, the numbers are given in square brackets. The poem referred to here is 173 [175]; cf. also 632 and 742.
23 *Saduktikarṇāmṛta* of Śrīdharadāsa, edited by S. C. Banerji, Firma Mukhopadhyay, Calcutta, 1965; the majority of poems in Section III (Nos 1371–1640, on *cāṭu*, 'flattery'), and also Nos 2086–2110, deal with heroic themes.
24 Jayavallabha's *Vajjālaggam*, edited by M. V. Patwardhan (with English translation), Prakrit Text Society, Ahmedabad, 1969 (Prakrit Text Society Series, vol. 14), Nos 173, 166, 178, 177.
25 *Saduktikarṇāmṛta* (see note 23 above), No. 1585 (by Umāpatidhara). A whole set of poems, 1581–1600, deals with similar themes of destruction and humiliation. Compare D. H. Ingalls, *An Anthology of Sanskrit Court Poetry* (being a translation of Vidyākara's *Subhāṣitaratnakoṣa*, see note 13 above), Harvard University Press, Cambridge, MA, 1965 (Harvard Oriental Series, vol. 44), pp. 372f (section 4).

26 Harieva's *Mayaṇaparājaya-cariü*, edited by Hiralal Jain (with Hindi translation), Bhāratīy Jñānpīṭh, Kāśī, 1962 (Jñānpīṭh Mūrtidevī Jain Granthmālā, Apabhraṃś granthāṅk 5).

27 The *Gaüḍavaho* of Vākpati, edited by Sankar Pandurang Pandit and N. B. Utgikar, Bhandarkar Oriental Research Institute, Pune (2nd edn), 1927, (Bombay Sanskrit and Prakrit Series, vol. 34), pp. 84–100. A more recent edition by N. G. Suru, Prakrit Text Society, Ahmedabad, 1975 (Prakrit Text Series, vol. 18), includes a rather free English translation (pp. 32–7).

28 *Kaliṅkattupparaṇi*, edited by P. Paḻaṉivēl Piḷḷai, Caivacittānta nūṟpatippu kkaḻakam, Madras, 1971 (1st edn, 1950). Compare K. Zvelebil, *Tamil Literature*, O. Harrassowitz, Wiesbaden, 1974, pp. 207–12.

29 Vedāntadeśika's *Yatirāja-saptatī* (e.g. in '*Vedāntadeśika-stotramālā*', Śrī-Vaikuṇṭhanātha-devasthānam, Calcutta, 1970, pp. 184–95), from vv. 3, 12, 21, 35. The following works have all been edited and published (Granthamala Office, Kancipuram) by K. P. B. Aṇṇaṅkarācāriyār: Maṇavāḷa mā muṉi's *Ārttippirapantam* in '*Śrīmad-Varavaramunīndra-Granthamālā*', vol. I (1966, individual pagination), from stanza 29; Tiruvaraṅkatt' Amutaṉār's *iRāmānuca-nūṟṟ'antāti*, e.g. in '*Iyaṟpā*' (1959, individual pagination), from stanzas 26, 33, 52, 77; Āndhrapūrṇa's *Rāmānujāṣṭottaraśatanāma-stotram* in '*Stotramālā*', 1969, pp. 77f, from v. 14; the *Dhāṭī-pañcakam* (attributed for instance to Śrīvatsacihnamiśra) ibid., pp. 76f.

30 This is the *Śūraṅgamasamādhi-sūtra* (see É. Lamotte, *La Concentration de la Marche Héroïque*, Brussels, 1965).

31 *(Prajñāpāramitā-)Ratnaguṇasaṃcayagāthāḥ*, edited by A. Yuyama, Cambridge University Press, Cambridge, 1976, I, 18 (p. 13).

32 W. H. McLeod, *The Evolution of the Sikh Community* (five essays), Clarendon Press, Oxford, 1976, p. 4.

33 See, for example, W. G. Orr, *A Sixteenth-Century Indian mystic*, Lutterworth Press, London/Redhill, 1947, pp. 199–208, on the Nāgās of the Dādū-panth.

34 See A. K. Ramanujan, *Speaking of Śiva*, Penguin Books, Harmondsworth, 1973, pp. 63f.

6 MANIPULATING SPACE, TIME AND MATTER

1 Luis Vaz de Camões, *The Lusiads*, translated by W. C. Atkinson, Penguin Books, Harmondsworth, 1952, pp. 128ff.

2 See above, pp. 31ff, 67f.

3 Muni Kanakāmara's *Karakaṇḍa-cariü*, edited by Hiralal Jain, Bhāratīy Jñānpīṭh prakāśan, Delhi, 1964 (Mūrtidevī Jain Granthmālā: Apabhraṃś granthāṅk 4); also contains an English translation. This is a reprint of the original edition, Karanja, 1934 (Ambādās Chaware Digambar Jain granthmālā, vol. 4).

4 See above, p. 105.

5 Told for instance in *Kathāsaritsāgara* II, 9f, Tawney, vol. I, pp. 94–121 (for bibliographical details, see note 13 below); *Dhammapada* commentary (Ch. 5, n. 8), p. 249.

6 Told about prince Vajrakumāra in the *Kahakosu* (Ch. 2, n. 15), *sandhi* 4, 1–9, with a parallel in the *Bṛhat-Kathākośa* (Ch. 2, n. 15), story 12 (where the prince is called Vairakumāra).

7 Ratnaśekhara-sūri's *Sirisirivālakaha*, edited by N. G. Suru. Only Part II (published by the editor, Pune, 1933), containing vv. 378–757 of the Prakrit text, with English translation, and a summary of the remaining portions of the poem, was available to me.

8 Told about prince Hariṣeṇa in the *Kahakosu* (Ch. 2, n. 15), *sandhi* 8, 1–5, with a parallel in the *Bṛhat-Kathākośa* (Ch. 2, n. 15), story 33.

9 *Nāyakumāra-cariū* (Ch. 2, n. 10), from *sandhis* 2 to 6.

10 Dhanapāla's *Bhavissayatta-kaha*, edited by C. D. Dalal and P. D. Gune, Oriental Institute, Baroda, (1st edn, 1923), 1967 (Gaekwad's Oriental Series, reprints, No. 20). This edition is based on a better manuscript than the one used by H. Jacobi in his edition of 1918 (*Bhavisatta Kaha von Dhaṇavāla: Eine Jaina Legende in Apabhraṃśa*, Munich, Abhandlungen der Königlich Bayerischen Akademie der Wissenschaften, Philosophisch-philologische und historische Klasse, vol. 29, Part 4).

11 The story summarized here follows the version found in the *Kahakosu* (Ch. 2, n. 15), *sandhis* 35, 9 to 36, 14. For other versions see the *Bṛhatkathāślokasaṅgraha* (18, 1–702) and *Vasudevahiṇḍī* (142–54), summarized in Jain pp. 260–308 (for bibliographical details see note 13 below).

12 Told for instance in Haribhadra's *Āvaśyaka-Ṭīkā* (II, 8, 2ff) and Maladhāri-Devaprabha's *Mṛgāvatīcaritra*; see J. Hertel, *Jinakīrti's 'Geschichte von Pāla und Gopāla'*, B. G. Teubner, Leipzig, 1917, pp. 98–105 and pp. 105–23, respectively.

13 The three Sanskrit versions are: Somadeva's *Kathāsaritsāgara*, Kṣemendra's *Bṛhatkathāmañjarī* and Budhasvāmī's *Bṛhatkathāśloka-saṅgraha* (edited and translated (into English) by R. P. Poddar and Neelima Sinha, Tara Printing Works, Varanasi, 1986 (Prācyabhāratī Series No. 21)). For an English translation of Somadeva see: *The Ocean of Story – C. H. Tawney's translation of Somadeva's Kathā Sarit Sāgara (or Ocean of Streams of Story)*, edited and with introduction … by N. M. Penzer, 10 vols, 2nd edn, 1923, Indian reprint (Motilal Banarsidass, Delhi), 1968. A Pālī version is found in the *Dhammapada* commentary (on vv. 21–3) and has been translated by Burlingame (Ch. 5, n. 8), pp. 247–93. In Prakrit we have the *Vasudevahiṇḍī* which is (partially) translated by Jagdishchandra Jain: *The Vasudevahiṇḍī – an Authentic Jain Version of the Bṛhatkathā*, L. D. Institute of Indology, Ahmedabad, 1977. Two slightly differing versions exist in Tamil: *Peruṅkatai* and *Utayaṉakumāra-kāviyam* (both works have been edited, with his own commentaries, by P. V. Cōmacuntaraṉ and were published (the first in two volumes) by The

South India Saiva Siddhanta Works Publishing Society, Tirunelveli, 1970 and 1964, respectively.) No translation of either is known to me. Finally, and to my knowledge as yet ignored in the literature on the *Bṛhatkathā*, is a version in Apabhraṃśa, the *Karakaṇḍa-cariü* (see note 3 above). On the one hand, this work incorporates a brief summary of the *Bṛhatkathā* explicitly identified as such, in *sandhi* 6. On the other hand, the whole work clearly derives its plot and many of its themes from the same source. A synopsis of part of all this material, and of further secondary sources, can be found in Niti Adaval, *The Story of King Udayana as Gleaned from Sanskrit, Pali and Prakrit Sources*, Benares, 1970 (Chowkhamba Sanskrit Studies, vol. 74).

14 See *Kathāsaritsāgara* I, 1–8, Tawney, vol. I, pp. 1–91 (for details see note 13 above).

15 V. Raghavan (*Bhoja's Śṛṅgāraprakāśa*, Punarvasu, Madras, 1963, pp. 846–57) has attempted to identify a poetic fragment as being in Paiśācī and from the original *Bṛhatkathā*, but his argument is not convincing.

16 See, for example, L. Alsdorf, *Harivaṃśapurāṇa*, Hamburg, 1936 (Alt- und Neu-Indische Studien, No. 5), pp. 121f: 'the origin of the *Bṛhatkathā* must be pushed backwards to at least the first, more likely the second, if not even to an earlier, century BC'.

17 Best known are Bhāsa's *Pratijñā-Yaugandharāyaṇa* and *Svapna-Vāsavadattā* (and his *Dāridra-Cārudatta*, from which the *Mṛcchakaṭikā*, see p. 258 below, was derived), and Harṣa's *Ratnāvalī* and *Priyadarśikā*.

18 See, for example, *Bṛhatkathāślokasaṅgraha* (see note 13 above) 5, 199, 250ff, 261.

19 D. R. Hill, *The Book of Knowledge of Ingenious Mechanical Devices (Kitāb fi ma'rifat al-ḥiyal al-handasiyya) by Ibn al-Razzāz al-Jazarī*, Reidel, Dordrecht, 1974; see also R. Ettinghausen, Arab Painting, Skira, Geneva, 1962 (Treasures of Asia), pp. 93–6. Compare D. R. Hill, *Muḥammad ibn Mūsā ibn Shākir: The Book of Ingenious Devices (Kitāb al-ḥiyal)*, Reidel, Dordrecht, 1979.

20 The first frame is typical of the Sanskrit versions, particularly the *Bṛhatkathāślokasaṅgraha* (see note 13 above), *sargas* 1–4. The second is found in the *Karakaṇḍacariü* (see note 3 above), VI, 1. The third occurs in the *Vasudevahiṇḍī* (see note 13 above), 110 (J. Jain, pp. 185f).

21 Lee Siegel's *Net of Magic – Wonders and Deceptions in India*, University of Chicago Press, Chicago–London, 1991, deals with Indian magic in our sense of the word. However, it does not cast light on the question of whether we are dealing here with mass hypnosis.

22 *Sandhinirmocana-sūtra* (I, 4), translated from the French of É. Lamotte, *Saṃdhinirmocana Sūtra – L'Explication des Mystères*, Louvain/Paris, 1935, pp. 170f.

23 See *Obeah*, a short story by Seepersad Naipaul (father of V. S. Naipaul) included in: '*The Adventures of Gurudeva and Other Stories*', A. Deutsch, London, 1976, pp. 162–71.

24 Rudradāsa's *Candralekhā*, a (*saṭṭaka* style) drama in Prakrit probably from Kerala, of *c*. AD 1650, edited by A. N. Upadhye, Bombay, 1967 (Bharatiya Vidya Bhavan Series, vol. 6), pp. 43f (of text).

25 Ratnaśekhara-sūri's *Sirisirivālakaha* (see note 7 above), vv. 388–412, deal with the overpowering of the blood-thirsty goddess.

26 Muni Kanakāmara's *Karakaṇḍa-cariü* (see note 3 above), from *sandhi* 7, 12f.

27 Even Agehananda Bharati (*The Tantric Tradition*, Rider, London, 1965, p. 102) speaks, in an otherwise highly idiosyncratic chapter, about their 'verifiability'.

7 ENTERING FORBIDDEN REALMS

1 This is at least how Goethe, in his *Faust*, treats the theme.

2 Quoted from H. Leivick (=Leivick Halper), *The Golem*, in: '*The Dybbuk and Other Great Yiddish Plays*', translated by J. C. Landis, Bantam Books, New York, 1966, p. 226.

3 Quoted from E. P. Maten, *Budhasvāmin's Bṛhatkathāślokasaṃgraha – A Literary Study of an Ancient Indian Narrative*, E. J. Brill, Leiden, 1973 (Orientalia Rheno-Traiectina, vol. 18), p. 105; cf. J. Jain, *Vasudevahiṇḍī* (Ch. 6, n. 13), pp. 317f. The passage is 20, 29–35; 92–100.

4 Act 5. For a recent English translation of the *Mālatī-Mādhava* see M. Coulson, *Three Sanskrit Plays*, Penguin Books, Harmondsworth, 1981; cf. M. Coulson, *Mālatīmādhava: A Critical Edition*, Oxford University Press, Delhi, 1989.

5 The *Vetāla-pañcaviṃśati* is included in the *Kathāsaritsāgara* (see Ch. 6, n. 13) 12, 75–99 (and thus in Tawney's translation, vols VI, pp. 164–221, and VII, pp. 1–125). For different versions of the narrative frame story and the various recensions see H. Uhle, *Vetalapantschavinsati*, Rütten und Loening, Munich, 1924 (Meisterwerke orientalischer Literaturen, vol. 9), pp. vii–xix.

6 One of the major sources for the 'mythology of *thuggee*' is P. Meadows Taylor's *Confessions of a Thug* (first published 1839), which in spite of its title is actually a novel. The book has recently been reissued, with a new and highly perceptive preface by N. Mirsky (Oxford University Press, Oxford, 1986).

7 The incident took place on 4 September 1987 and was commented on by *Time* magazine on 28 September. See also Julia Leslie, 'Suttee or satī: victim or victor?', *Bulletin of the Center for the Study of World Religions*, 14, 2, Harvard University, 1987/88, pp. 5–23. The only actual report of *satī* in classical literature known to me is found in Narendra and Paraśurāma's collection of anecdotes in Old Marathi called *Smṛtisthaḷa*, of *c*. AD 1308 (edited by V. N. Despande, Vhinas Prakāśan, Pune (2nd edn, 1960), additional anecdote No. 141, p. 123; cf. Nos 149f, pp. 50f). What makes the incident particularly terrifying is the fact that the queen

Kāmāīsā (widow of king Rāmdevrāv) was unwilling to commit suttee, but was forced to do so by the son, Sīṅgāṇā, of another queen.

8 The text of the Tamil epic *Cilappatikāram* was edited by U. V. Cāminātaiyar (Madras, 1920) and, along with various commentaries, by N. M. Vēṅkaṭacāmi Nāṭṭār (Saiva Siddhanta Publishing Society, Tirunelveli/ Madras, 1942). For English translations see V. Ramachandra Dikshitar, *The Lay of the Anklet*, Oxford University Press, Madras, 1939, and R. Parthasarathy, *The Cilappatikāram of Iḷaṅkō Aṭikaḷ – An Epic of South India*, Columbia University Press, New York, 1993 (Translations from the Asian Classics).

9 Gananath Obeyesekere deals mainly with Sri Lanka in *The Cult of the Goddess Pattini*, University of Chicago Press, Chicago/London, 1984.

10 See, for example, A. Mookerjee, *Tantra Art – Its Philosophy and Physics*, Ravi Kumar, Basel/Paris/New Delhi, 1967.

11 P. Rawson, *Tantra – The Indian Cult of Ecstasy*, Thames and Hudson, London, 1979.

12 P. Rawson, *Erotic Art of India*, Thames and Hudson, London, 1977, plate 39.

13 Ibid., plate 32.

14 Lisa Alther, *Kinflicks*, Penguin Books, Harmondsworth, 1977, pp. 499, 534f, 538.

15 Miguel de Cervantes, '*Novelas ejemplares*', edited by J. B. Avalle-Arce, Clásicos Castalia, Madrid, vol. I, 1982, pp. 71–158: *La gitanilla*.

16 *Caṇḍamahāroṣaṇa-tantra*, chapters 1–8 critically edited (and translated into English) by C. S. George, American Oriental Society, New Haven, 1974 (American Oriental Series, vol. 56), VI, 43f (p. 68) VII, 1–22 (pp. 78f).

17 See, for instance, T. Goudriaan, in: *Hindu Tantrism*, by S. Gupta, D. J. Hoens and T. Goudriaan, E. J. Brill, Leiden/Cologne, 1979 (Handbuch der Orientalistik, Zweite Abteilung, vierter Band, zweiter Abschnitt), pp. 7–9, whose catalogue of constituents of Tantrism exhausts most of Hinduism itself.

18 Indian parlance reveals the close link between this form of spiritual pursuit and the seemingly purely mythological figures of the *vidyādharas*. Here is an example taken from a Buddhist context. Speaking about the *siddhas*, Snellgrove quotes Tārānātha: 'no one knew that they were practising the secret *mantras*, until they actually became possessed of magical powers (*vidyādhara*). But when they had these powers, travelling in the sky or becoming invisible ... '. D. L. Snellgrove, *The Hevajra Tantra*, Part I, Oxford University Press, London, 1959, p. 11. Cf. note 23 below.

19 For instance, in Marathi we have the *Śrī-Nav-nāth-bhakti-sār*, Śrī-Gajānan buk depo prakāśan, Pune/Bombay (no date, *c.* 1975). On the *nāthas/siddhas* in Bengal see, for example, S. Das Gupta, *Obscure Religious Cults*, Firmal K. L. Mukhopadhyay, Calcutta (3rd edn), 1969, pp. 191–210.

20 For a collection of the poems of the Tamil Cittar see, for example, *Cittar periya ñāṉakkōvai*, edited by A. Rāmanātaṉ, Madras, 1959; samples have been translated into English by K. Zvelebil, *The Poets of the Power*, Rider, London, 1973.
21 A. Sanderson, in: S. Sutherland *et alii* (eds), *The World's Religions*, Routledge, London, 1988, p. 700.
22 Examples can be found in Zvelebil (see note 20 above), e.g. pp. 90–107.
23 *Yogatattva-Upaniṣad*, Nos 126f, in: '*Yoga-Upaniṣadaḥ*', edited by A. Mahadeva Sastri, Adyar Library, Madras, 1920. By calling such a 'perfected' man a *khecarin* (= *vidyādhara*), this text also exemplifies the inner connection between *vidyādhara* mythology and yogic practice (see note 18 above).
24 *Bhagavadajjukīyam*, attributed to Baudhāyana (edited by A. R. Bannerjea Sastri, *Journal of the Bihar and Orissa Research Society*, March/June, 1924). An English translation of the play was published by J. A. B. van Buitenen in the journal *Mahfil*, 1971, pp. 149–66 under the title 'The hermit and the harlot'; the play was translated as early as 1932 into Italian by Belloni-Filippi, as 'L'asceta trasmutato in etèra' (reprinted in M. Vallauri, *Teatro Indiano*, Milano, 1959, pp. 506–26).
25 *Cittaviśuddhi-prakaraṇa*, quoted from E. Conze, (ed.), *Buddhist Texts through the Ages*, Bruno Cassirer, Oxford, 1954, p. 221 (translation by D. Snellgrove).

8 UNLEASHING THE POWERS OF THE SELF

1 *Lalitavistara*, from XIII, 75–8. The editions of Rajendra Lal Mitra (Bibliotheca Indica, Calcutta, 1877) and S. Lefmann (2 vols, Halle, 1902 and 1908) were re-edited by P. L. Vaidya, Mithila Institute, Darbhanga, 1968 (Buddhist Sanskrit Texts).
2 The life-story of the founder of Jainism can be found in the *Ācāraṃga-sūtra*, Book II, Part 3, chapter 15, and in the *Kalpa-sūtra*, 'Life of the Mahāvīra'; for English translations see *Jaina Sūtras*, translated from Prakrit by H. Jacobi, Part I, Clarendon Press, Oxford, 1884, and various reprints (Sacred Books of the East, vol. 22), pp. 189–202 and 217–70.
3 Ibid., p. 194; cf. Jacobi (Introduction to Part II, vol. 45, London, 1895) pp. xx–xxiii.
4 The story of Dvīpāyana is summarized from Śrīcandra's *Kahakosu* (Ch. 2, n. 15), *sandhi* 33, 6.3–16.12 (pp. 336–41); Hariṣeṇa's *Bṛhat-Kathākośa* (Ch. 2, n. 15), story 81, is a Sanskrit parallel.
5 See note 4 above. Two very similar stories are told in the *Kahakosu* about prince Gayakumāra (*sandhi* 47, 1, p. 473) and prince Lakuca (*sandhi* 11, 5f, pp. 128f). The Sanskrit parallels in the *Bṛhat-Kathākośa* are Nos 128 and 50.
6 The passage is inspired by the first of the four *smṛtyupasthānas*, 'application of mindfulness to the body'. Material on this is also quoted,

from various Mahāyāna *sūtras*, in chapter 13 of Śāntideva's *Śikṣāsamuccaya* (re-edited by P. L. Vaidya, Mithila Institute, Darbhanga, 1961, Buddhist Sanskrit Texts).

7 See E. Frauwallner (Ch. 2, n. 20), pp. 432–7.

8 Derived from *Ācāraṃga-sūtra* (see note 2 above), II, 15, 24f (in Jacobi's translation, p. 201).

9 From *Bṛhadāraṇyaka-Upaniṣad* II, 4, 12ff (cf. *The Principal Upaniṣads*, edited and translated by S. Radhakrishnan, George Allen and Unwin, London, 1953, pp. 200f).

10 This passage concludes a longer text on the path towards enlightenment and liberation which is appended to a number of the Buddha's 'sermons', for example, to *Dīghanikāya* 2 (*Sāmaññaphala-suttanta*, edited by T. W. Rhys Davids, Pali Text Society, vol. I, London, 1908, pp. 83f; translated by T. W. Rhys Davids, *Dialogues of the Buddha*, Part I, London, (1st edn, 1899), 1956 (Sacred Books of the Buddhists, vol. 2), No. 2, 97 (pp. 92f)) and *Majjhimanikāya* 4 (*Bhayabheravasuttanta*, edited by V. Trenckner, Pali Text Society, vol. I, London, 1888, p. 23; translated by I. B. Horner, *The Collection of Middle Length Sayings*, vol. I, London, 1954 (Pali Text Society Translation Series), p. 29); *Majjhimanikāya* 51 (*Kandarakasutta* (edition vol. I, pp. 348f; translation vol. II (1957), pp. 13)). Compare Frauwallner (Ch. 2, n. 20) pp. 162; 169f and his *Die Philosophie des Buddhismus*, Akademie-Verlag, Berlin (3rd edn), 1969 (Philosophische Studientexte, vol. 2), pp. 14–18 (where the translation is from *Majjhimanikāya* 51).

11 Trevor Ling, *The Buddha – Buddhist Civilization in India and Ceylon*, Temple Smith, London, 1973 (Makers of New Worlds Series), pp. 107, 109.

12 Ibid., p. 112 (author's italics).

13 From the *Cūḷa-Māluṅkyasutta*, *Majjhimanikāya* No. 63 (see note 10 above), Trenckner's edition, vol. I, pp. 429f; Horner's translation, vol. II, pp. 99f.

14 Ibid., vol. I, p. 431; vol. II, p. 101.

15 From the *Aggi-Vacchagottasutta*, *Majjhimanikāya* No. 72 (see note 10 above), Trenckner's edition, vol. I, p. 487; Horner's translation, vol. II, pp. 165f. Cf. Frauwallner 1969 (see towards end of note 10 above), pp. 23f and Conze (Ch. 7, n. 25), p. 106.

16 Ibid., vol. I, p. 487; vol. II, p. 166.

17 I follow Hariṣeṇa's condensed narration of the story of Yaśodhara in his *Bṛhat-Kathākośa* (Ch. 2, n. 15), story 73, vv. 131–59. A translation is included in my article on Yaśodhara (Ch. 3, n. 17). A similar passage is found in Haribhadra's *Samarāiccakaha* (edited by H. Jacobi, Calcutta, 1926 (Bibliotheca Indica, No. 169), pp. 172ff). For further parallels see note 31 of my article (Ch. 3, n. 17).

18 L. Rhinehart, *The Dice Man*, Panther (Granada Publishing), London, 1972, p. 431.

19 I. M. Lewis, *Ecstatic Religion – An Anthropological Study of Spirit Possession and Shamanism*, Penguin Books, Harmondsworth, 1971 (Pelican Anthropology Library).

20 An English translation of the Chinese translation by Bodhiruci included in the *Mahā-ratnakūṭa-sūtra* can be found in G. C. C. Chang (ed.), *A Treasury of Mahāyāna Sūtras*, Pennsylvania State University Press, University Park/London, 1983 (Institute for Advanced Studies of World Religions Series, No. 19), pp. 363–86: 'The True Lion's Roar of Queen Śrīmālā'; for the discussion summarized here see pp. 379f. Another, composite, translation, into somewhat idiosyncratic English, based on various versions in Chinese and Tibetan, was produced by A. and H. Wayman, *The Lion's Roar of Queen Śrīmālā – A Buddhist Scripture on the Tathāgatagarbha Theory*, Columbia University Press, New York, 1974 (pp. 101ff).

21 See below, pp. 433–51.

9 THE MISSING COLOUR

1 Edwin Arnold, *Indian Poetry – containing 'The Indian Song of Songs', from the Sanskrit of the Gīta Govinda of Jayadeva* ... Kegan Paul, Trench, Trübner, London (7th edn), 1895. Appended to the translations is an (unpaginated) catalogue of Trübner's Oriental Series (in which the book is included) where, on the ninth page, extracts from the reviews are quoted.

2 Ibid.

3 Karol Szymanowski, *King Roger or The Shepherd*, Opera in three acts; the quotation is from the libretto, p. 6 (English version by G. Dunn), included in the AUR 5061/2, Polskie Nagrania recording, 1977.

4 See note 1 above, p. 96. For complete translations of the *Gītagovinda* see, for example, L. Siegel, *Sacred and Profane Dimensions of Love in Indian Traditions, as Exemplified in the Gītagovinda of Jayadeva*, Oxford University Press, Delhi, 1978, pp. 233–86, and B. S. Miller, *Gītagovinda of Jayadeva – Love Song of the Dark Lord*, Motilal Banarsidass, Delhi, 1984 (both include the Sanskrit text).

5 Sacred Books of the Buddhists, vol. 10: *The Book of the Discipline (Vinaya-piṭaka)*, translated by I. B. Horner, Luzac, for the Pali Text Society, vol. I, London, 1949, pp. xxxvif.

6 Le Père Charles de Foucauld, *Dictionnaire Touareg–Français (dialecte de L'Ăhaggar)*, 2028 pp. of facsimile (edited by A. Basset), 4 vols (Imprimerie Nationale de France), 1951–2.

7 *Poésies Touarègues (Dialecte de L'Ăhaggar)*, recueillies par Le P. de Foucauld (edited by A. Basset), vol. I (658 pp., poems Nos 1 to 352), Éditions Ernest Leroux, Paris, 1925; vol. II (461 pp., poems Nos 353 to 575), Librairie Ernest Leroux, Paris, 1930.

8 *Poésies*, pp. viif; cf. pp. 559–64 (in vol. II) of his *Dictionnaire*.

9 *Poésies*, p. viii.
10 See above, pp. 111f.
11 See above, p. 116.
12 Kālidāsa's *Kumārasambhava* was edited and translated into English as early as *c.* AD 1835 by H. H. Wilson (text and translation reprinted by Indological Book House, Varanasi, 1966).
13 See, for example, L. Alsdorf (Ch. 6, n. 16), pp. 109–16.
14 See, for example, Śyāmilaka's *bhāṇa Pādatāḍitaka* (critically edited by G. Schokker, The Hague, 1966 (Indo-Iranian Monographs, vol. 9)), 62, 2.
15 Hiralal Jain (see Ch. 2, n. 10), p. xxi.
16 On Nāgakumāra, see above, pp. 33f, 126f and on Vasudeva, pp. 133, 143.
17 Dubois (Ch. 5, n. 1), p. 543. I have replaced *Trimurti* by 'three main divinities'.
18 See note 7 above, *Poésies*, e.g. Nos 42, 53, 124, 168, 400, 405, 566.
19 Ibid., e.g. No. 42; cf. 125.
20 Ibid., e.g. Nos 54, 75f.
21 Ibid., No. 77.
22 Ibid., No. 142.
23 Ibid., No. 215.
24 Ibid., No. 219.
25 Ibid., No. 169.
26 Ibid., No. 142.
27 Ibid., e.g. Nos 366, 541, 573.
28 The allegorization of the *caṅkam*-derived poetry of the Āḻvārs and the Nāyaṉārs has its roots in medieval Tamil literature. Nammāḻvār's poetry is allegorized in the *Ācāryahṛdayam* (cf. J. S. M. Hooper, *The Hymns of the Āḻvārs*, Calcutta/London, 1929, pp. 61–88), and Māṇikkavācakar's *Tirukkōvaiyār*, in the later commentaries. For a very brief discussion of such allegorization, see *Indian Ritual and Its Exegesis* (Ch. 10, n. 11 below), pp. 144–7.

10 THE LANDSCAPE OF THE HEART

1 E. Littmann, *Die Erzählungen aus den tausendundein Nächten*, vollständige deutsche Ausgabe, 6 vols, Insel Verlag, Wiesbaden, 1953, vol. I, pp. 19–32.
2 Giovanni Boccaccio, *The Decameron*, translated by G. H. McWilliam, Penguin Books, Harmondsworth, 1972, p. 50.
3 Ibid., p. 830.
4 Ibid., p. 34 (translator's introduction).
5 In the story of Yaśodhara (which is discussed above, pp. 58ff, and below, pp. 244–8), the king witnessed his queen making love to a black stableman; collections of tales like the *Daśakumāracarita* (see below, pp. 391, 398f) tell us about excessively possessive husbands who nevertheless get cuckolded; the device of telling interrupted stories is used in the *Śukasaptati* (see note 9 below).

6 See above, pp. 67f.

7 Although by now a sizeable corpus of Hāla studies has evolved, no critical and complete translation is known to me. Weber's works (see Ch. 5, n. 22) remain essential, at least as far as the text itself is concerned; his German translations are often incorrect.

8 Unlike Hāla, Tamil *akam* literature has enjoyed the attention of many a scholar and translator. The works by Ramanujan and Hart (mentioned in Ch. 5, n. 20) contain much *akam* material. The *akam* anthology *Kuṟuntokai* was completely translated by M. Shanmugam Pillai and David Ludden, Koodal Publishers, Madurai, 1976, and partially by A. K. Ramanujan, *The Interior Landscape*, Peter Owen, London, 1970. See also V. S. Manickam, *The Tamil Concept of Love*, Saiva Siddhanta Works Publishing Society, Tirunelveli/Madras, 1962.

9 On the *Śukasaptati*, see below, pp. 400ff; for bibliography see Ch. 18, n. 33. Hāla's (see Ch. 5, n. 22) poem is 237 [241], and the direct correspondence is with story No. 60 of the Marathi recension; No. 63 of the Sanskrit recension is more remote. Also, poems 297 [300], 301 [305] and 159 [160] reappear as full stories in *Śukasaptati* recensions, as Nos 7, 8 and 13 (in Morgenroth's numbering).

10 According to F. Wilhelm, in: *Indien*, edited by A. T. Embree and F. Wilhelm, Fischer Bücherei, Frankfurt am Main, 1967 (Fischer Weltgeschichte, vol. XVII), pp. 131ff.

11 For material on the *veṟi* see my 'From the illness of love to social hermeneutics: three Tamil customs, with some reflections on method and meaning', in: *Indian Ritual and Its Exegesis*, edited by R. F. Gombrich, Oxford University Press, Delhi, 1988 (Oxford University Papers on India, vol. II, part 1), pp. 116–25.

12 Ibid., p. 121, from *Akanāṉūṟu* 22.

13 Such poems are found in the *Kalittokai* (edited by P. V. Cōmacuntaraṉ with his own and Naccinārkkiṉiyar's commentaries, South India Saiva Siddhanta Works Publishing Society, Tirunelveli, 1969, No. 1377), section containing the *Marutakkali*; the comparison with the horse is made in poem 96; 97 compares the prostitute to an elephant.

14 See, for example, Bāṇa, in the introduction to his *Harṣacarita*.

15 Hāla (Ch. 5, n. 22), 532.

16 Ibid., 383.

17 Ibid., 454.

18 Ibid., 595.

19 See my article 'From the illness of love' (note 11 above), pp. 129–32.

20 Poem 94 of the *Kalittokai*; an English translation can be found in Ramanujan, *Poems of Love and War* (see Ch. 5, n. 20), pp. 209ff.

21 See above, p. 65.

22 Hāla (Ch. 5, n. 22), 89 [86], 112 [115] and 114 [117].

23 Ibid., 89 [86]. The three poems are discussed in my *Viraha-bhakti* (Ch. 3, n. 8), pp. 56–61.

24 The poem is No. 8 in the (late) *caṅkam* anthology *Paripāṭal* (critically edited and translated into French by F. Gros, Pondicherry, 1968 (Publications de l'Institut Français d'Indologie, vol. 35)). It is briefly discussed in my *Viraha-bhakti* (Ch. 3, n. 8), pp. 213–16.

25 Poem 58 in the *Kalittokai*, translated in my article 'From the illness of love' (note 11 above), p. 162.

26 Particularly striking is the poetry of Auvai(yār); see my *Viraha-bhakti* (Ch. 3, n. 8), pp. 147, 336 (note 107).

27 For references and discussion see my *Viraha-bhakti* (Ch. 3, n. 8), pp. 395–8, and 'From the illness of love' (note 11 above), pp. 122–5, etc.

28 See for instance the seventh story of the Second Day (pp. 169–91) and the tenth story of the Third Day (pp. 314–19) of the *Decameron* (note 2 above).

29 The *locus classicus* for this is chapters 4 and 5 of Part II in the famous (and infamous) *Kāmasūtras* of Vātsyāyana. Sir Richard Burton and F. F. Arbuthnot produced a translation in English as early as 1883 ('Cosmopoli: for the Kama Shastra Society of London and Benares, and for private circulation only'). Something of a classic, this translation has been re-edited by W. G. Archer, George Allen and Unwin, London, 1963, and by J. Muirhead-Gould, with an introduction by Dom Moraes, Panther Books, London, 1963.

30 Mentioned in chapter 7 of Part II of the *Kāmasūtras*. Another king killed a prostitute with a 'wedge', and a third blinded a dancing-girl with a 'piercing instrument'. Vātsyāyana refers to these instances explicitly to censure the practices as barbarous.

31 Hāla (Ch. 5, n. 22), 508. Compare Govardhana (Ch. 2, n. 18) No. 375 (where the mother is happy seeing her daughter sleep until late in the morning).

32 See above, p. 210; see also pp. 277ff.

33 Govardhana (Ch. 2, n. 18), No. 188.

34 *Vajjālaggam* (Ch. 5, n. 24), No. 606.

35 See note 26 above. In the *Subhāṣitaratnakoṣa* (Ch. 5, ns. 13, 25), the poetess Vidyā 'writes with nostalgia ... of love unhampered by matrimony' (Ingalls, p. 252), in poems 808 and 809. A verse (815) that is anonymous here (and in the *Saduktikarṇāmṛta* (Ch. 5, n. 23), No. 533), but attributed elsewhere to the poetess Śīlābhaṭṭārikā, laments the aridity that has entered her marriage. These are daring confessions! See also p. 505 below.

11 THE DEADLY WEAPONS OF MĀRA

1 This is a summary of Śrīcandra's *Kahakosu* (see Ch. 2, n. 15) *sandhi* 44, 1ff (pp. 438f); story No. 117 in Hariṣeṇa's *Bṛhat-Kathākośa* (see Ch. 2, n. 15) is a parallel in Sanskrit.

2 Hāla's *Sattasaī* (Ch. 5, n. 22), from 10 [10].

3 Ibid., from 53 [53].
4 Ibid., 81 [80]; cf. 236 [240] and *Vajjālaggam* (Ch. 5, n. 24) 347.
5 Ibid., from 423.
6 Ibid., from 511.
7 Ibid., 658.
8 Ibid., from 105 [106].
9 Ibid., from 114 [111].
10 Ibid., from 517.
11 Govardhana (Ch. 2, n. 18), No. 18 (introduction).
12 The details can be found in R. Schmidt, *Beiträge zur indischen Erotik – Das Liebesleben des Sanskritvolkes*, Leipzig, 1902, pp. 124–31.
13 The story is told in the *Vasudevahiṇḍī* 9, 4 to 10, 11 (J. Jain (Ch. 6, n. 13), pp. 561–4) and in Haribhadra's *Samarāiccakaha* (Ch. 8, n. 17), pp. cxif, 740, 12 to 743, 11.
14 Summarized from *Kahakosu* (see note 1 above), *sandhis* 10, 9, 4 to 12, 14 (pp. 121ff); contained in No. 46 of the *Bṛhat-Kathākośa* (vv. 112–48, pp. 69f).
15 *Kahakosu*, *sandhi* 10, 12, line 11.
16 *Decameron* (Ch. 10, n. 2), fifth story of the Fourth Day (pp. 366–70).
17 Ibid., p. 320.
18 See note 14 above: *Bṛhat-Kathākośa* No. 46, vv. 146 (p. 70).
19 Hāla (Ch. 5, n. 22), from 24.
20 Antonio Machado Álvarez, *Cantes flamencos*, Espasa-Calpe Argentina, Buenos Aires/Mexico, 1947 (Colección Austral 745), p. 53: '*estas duquitas negritas e muerte.*'
21 See E. Frauwallner (Ch. 2, n. 20), pp. 197–205.
22 See above, pp. 181–9.
23 See Bhikkhu Telwatte Rahula, *A Critical Study of the Mahāvastu*, Motilal Banarsidass, Delhi, 1978, pp. 99–114.
24 See above, p. 116.
25 The story is summarized from Śrīcandra's *Kahakosu* (see note 1 above), *sandhi* 51, 9, 4 to 16, 12 (pp. 517–20); in the *Bṛhat-Kathākośa*, No. 150.
26 See above, pp. 168, 178.
27 Amitagati's *Subhāṣitasandoha* (of *c.* AD 995), Sanskrit text edited and translated into German by R. Schmidt, *Zeitschrift der deutschen morgenländischen Gesellschaft*, vols 59 and 61 (1905 and 1907); also available bound together, with continuous pagination (page numbers placed here in parentheses), Leipzig, 1908. The poem translated here is No. 118 (VI, 16), p. 304 (p. 40).
28 Ibid., XXIV, 4.17. On the topics referred to generally, see VI, 13–25, pp. 303–8 (pp. 39–44); chapters XXf, pp. 112–26 (pp. 156–70); chapter XXIV, pp. 298–305 (pp. 182–9).
29 See above, pp. 129–33 and pp. 58ff.
30 See also below, pp. 456–9.
31 Tirso de Molina, *(El vergonzoso en palacio y) El burlador de Sevilla (y*

convidado de piedra), Espasa-Calpe, Madrid, 1939 (6th edn, 1961), (Colección Austral 73), pp. 149–244.

32 See Ch. 5, n. 8 and Ch. 6, n. 13.

33 Thus Nāgakumāra, 'Snake-Prince', in the *Nāyakumāracariü* (Ch. 2, n. 10), *sandhis* I, 12; IX, 16f; Śrīpāla in the *Sirisirivālakaha* (see Ch. 6, n. 7), e.g. vv. 560–74.

34 Thus C. and H. Jesudasan, in their *History of Tamil Literature* (Calcutta, 1961, p. 148), speak of the epic's 'terribly dangerous stimulation to the senses' and recommend that it should be banned for young people.

35 H. Zimmermann, *Die Subhāṣita-ratna-karaṇḍaka-kathā (dem Āryaśūra zugeschrieben)*, Harrassowitz, Wiesbaden, 1975 (Freiburger Beiträge zur Indologie, vol. 8), poem 24 (p. 55f).

36 See note 27 above; VI, 1–12, pp. 299–303 (pp. 35–9).

37 This is the *Subhāṣitaratnakoṣa* (see Ch. 5, n. 13).

38 Ibid., No. 440.

39 *Bhartrihari – Poems*, translated by B. Stoler Miller (with the transliterated Sanskrit text), Columbia University Press, New York and London, 1967, No. 83, p. 65.

12 BEYOND THE FLEETING MOMENT

1 See above, p. 251.

2 A wide variety of sources are discussed in my *Viraha-bhakti* (Ch. 3, n. 8) pp. 388–402.

3 This happened to Nāgakumāra, 'Snake-Prince', when he fell in love with Lakṣmīmati: see *Nāyakumāracariü* (Ch. 2, n. 10), IX, 15–20. Given the incomplete state in which the *Vasudevahiṇḍī* has been transmitted, it is more speculative to infer a similar theme for this work; pp. 367–70 (translated Jain, pp. 548–56) mention that Vasudeva married Devakī, who became the mother of Kṛṣṇa (the primary reason why Vasudeva is famous at all). However, this much is certain: with Devakī and the procreation of Kṛṣṇa, Vasudeva's hundred years of exile have come to an end; Kṛṣṇa, Devakī's son, symbolizes the fulfilment of a hundred years of searching.

4 That is, the three Sanskrit versions (see Ch. 6, n. 13).

5 José Zorrilla, *Don Juan Tenorio*, edited by Aniano Peña, Cátedra, Madrid, 1983.

6 The crucial passage, '*Alles Weibliche* ... ' has become universally famous because of Mahler's eighth symphony.

7 Govardhana (Ch. 2, n. 18), No. 132.

8 Ibid., No. 318.

9 Ibid., No. 43 (cf. 82, where the other women are compared to bees, while his true love is like the deity for the lotus of his mind).

10 See above, pp. 127f.

11 Bhāsa's *Cārudattam* (edited by C. R. Devadhar, '*Plays Ascribed to Bhāsa*', Oriental Book Agency, Poona, 1962, pp. 191–248); Śūdraka's

Mṛcchakaṭikam (edited by N. B. Godbole, Bombay, 1867). The latter play has been the favourite of translators; thus we have A. W. Ryder's translation (*The Little Clay Cart* (Harvard Oriental Series, vol. 9, Cambridge, MA, 1905), J. A. B. van Buitenen's translation ('*Two Plays of Ancient India*', Columbia University Press, New York and London, 1968, pp. 47–180); R. P. Oliver's translation (*Mṛcchakaṭikā: The Little Clay Cart*, Greenwood Press, London, 1975).

12 1*Anthology of Troubadour Lyric Poetry*, edited and translated by A. R. Press, Edinburgh University Press, Edinburgh, 1971 (Edinburgh Bilingual Library, vol. 3), p. 18

13 Ibid., p. 28.

14 Ibid., p. 318.

15 The episode is narrated in chapter 76 of Ramón Llull's novel *Blanquerna* (vol. IX of '*Obres originals de Ramon Llull*', edited by Galmès-Ferrá, Mallorca, 1914, pp. 271–6.) The song is also published separately in *Poesies*, edited by R. d'Alòs-Moner, Barcino, Barcelona (2nd edn), 1928 (Els Nostres Classics, A/3), pp. 25f. For an English translation, see *Blanquerna – A Thirteenth-Century Romance*, translated from the Catalan of Ramón Llull by E. Allison Peers, Jarrolds Publishers, London, [1925]; the song is found on p. 300. In fairness to the author of the original, it should be mentioned that the same singer sits down and buys everybody a drink, and at a later stage organizes a riot against cheating merchants!

16 The first two texts are so well known that there is no need to provide bibliographical details; on the *Devī-māhātmya* see Ch. 3, n. 14.

17 I have attempted to comment on the thematic developments of the Purāṇas in *The World's Religions* (Ch. 7, n. 21), pp. 604–9. Further aspects of the Purāṇas are explored in my article 'Information and Transformation: Two Faces of the Purāṇas', in: *Purāṇa Perennis – Reciprocity and Transformation in Hindu and Jaina Texts*, edited by W. Doniger, State University of New York Press, Albany, 1993, pp. 159–82.

18 References to this myth can be found in W. Doniger O'Flaherty, *Asceticism and Eroticism in the Mythology of Śiva*, Oxford University Press, London, 1973, pp. 32, 319, and under 'theme 5cd', p. 375).

19 Among the Āḻvārs, this is one of the most frequent references to Śiva; for the myth itself (told from a Śaivite point of view) of Śiva's beheading of Brahmā, see O'Flaherty (note 18 above), pp. 30, 319, and 380 (theme 38a).

20 On materials concerning the *Harivaṃśa* and its background, see my *Viraha-bhakti* (Ch. 3, n. 8), pp. 67–73.

21 See, for example, D. Shulman, *Tamil Temple Myths – Sacrifice and Divine Marriage in the South Indian Śaiva Tradition*, Princeton University Press, Princeton, 1980, pp. 144–211.

22 See note 20 above, pp. 72–7.

13 COSMIC DESIRE

1 Govardhana (Ch. 2, n. 18), No. 1 (introduction).
2 Ibid., No. 19 (introduction).
3 Ibid., No. 29 (introduction).
4 See above, p. 194.
5 See above, p. 194.
6 *Kumārasambhava* (Ch. 9, n. 12), VIII (particularly vv. 1–25; 78–89). For cantos IX to XVII see ibid., pp. 110–96.
7 A. B. Keith, *A History of Sanskrit Literature*, Oxford University Press, London, 1920 (Preface dated 1928), and various reprints, p. 89.
8 Chapter 24 (of Book VI, Takkaṉ) is summarized by R. Dessigane and P. Z. Pattabiramin, *Le Légende de Skanda*, Institut Français d'Indologie, Pondicherry, 1967 (Publications de l'Institut Français d'Indologie, No. 31), pp. 221–6.
9 An edition and a – rather stilted – translation of the *Caṇḍīśatakam* is included in G. P. Quackenbos, *The Sanskrit Poems of Mayūra*, Columbia University Indo-Iranian Series, New York, 1917, pp. 245–357.
10 See above, pp. 265f.
11 See above, pp. 256, 272.
12 Nammāḻvār's *Tiruviruttam* (included in the Tamil *Nālāyira-divya-prabandham* of the Āḻvārs), v. 11.
13 Ibid., No. 57.
14 I have discussed the *Tiruviruttam* in my *Viraha-bhakti* (Ch. 3, n. 8), pp. 315–24; see p. 362 on Nammāḻvār's use of metaphor.
15 Unlike Māṇikkavācakar's *Tiruvācakam* (which is well studied and has become well known due to a number of translations, for example, as early as 1900 into English by G. U. Pope, Clarendon Press, Oxford, and, most recently, by G. E. Yocum, *Hymns to the Dancing Śiva*, Heritage Publishers, Delhi, 1982) little attention has been paid to his *Tirukkōvaiyār*. The text has been edited by P. V. Cōmacuntaraṉ, with various relatively recent commentaries, for the South India Saiva Siddhanta Works Publishing Society (No. 1391), Tirunelveli, 1970. F. Gros' French translation of this highly complex work will, I hope, be published in the not too distant future.
16 The analysis of this 'girl symbolism' is the main concern of Part four (pp. 239–480) of my *Viraha-bhakti* (Ch. 3, n. 8); in particular, pp. 447–50 discuss a down-to-earth self-awareness in the Āḻvārs. Selected translations can be found in A. K. Ramanujan, *Hymns for the Drowning – Poems for Viṣṇu by Nammāḻvār*, Princeton University Press, Princeton, 1981.
17 See my *Viraha-bhakti* (Ch. 3, n. 8), pp. 354–60; 385ff; 406–13; 444f; 457–60.
18 This important work will be discussed below, pp. 293; 515–25
19 On Caitanya and his disciples see, for example, S. K. De, *Early History of the Vaiṣṇava Faith and Movement in Bengal*, Firma K. L. Mukhopadhyay,

Calcutta (2nd edn), 1961. On Rūpa see ibid., pp. 170–224; 658–72. Rūpa's *Padyāvalī* was edited by S. K. De in 1934 (Dacca University Oriental Publications Series, vol. 3, Dacca).

20 On Jīva see De, '*Early History*' (note 19 above), pp. 254–421.

21 See Figure 2 in ch. 2 above, and cf. Rawson (Ch. 7, n. 11), plate 48 (Kṛṣṇa) and p. 101, No. 16.

22 Grace M. Jantzen, *God's World, God's Body*, Darton, Longman and Todd, London, 1984.

23 The *Acyuta-śatakam*, included in the '*Stotramālā*' (Ch. 5, n. 29), pp. 115–49.

24 By Vedāntadeśika we have, for instance, the *Mummaṇikkōvai*, which is included in '*Śrī-Tēcikappirapantam*' (e.g. edited by V. N. Śrī-Rāmatēcikācāriyar, Madras, 1950, pp. 75–8). Piḷḷai Perumāḷ Aiyaṅkār composed eight such *prabandhams*, devotional poems pervaded by the 'girl symbolism'. His *Aṣṭa-Prabandham* was edited by Kōpālakiruṣṇamācāriyar in two volumes, Madras, 1966 and 1971 (various reprints).

25 See Ch. 2, n. 12 above, and pp. 333, 351, 525 below.

14 LOVE ABIDING IN STONE

1 Canetti (Ch. 3, n. 15), p. 41 (p. 51).

2 See above, pp. 47ff.

3 See above, pp. 265f.

4 *Bhagavadgītā* (edited and translated by R. C. Zaehner, Clarendon Press, Oxford, 1969), from IV, 7f.

5 Ibid., from IV, 6 and 5 (translation derived from Zaehner).

6 See D. Gellner, 'Buddhism and Hinduism in the Nepal Valley', pp. 739–55 (particularly p. 753) in: *The World's Religions* (Ch. 7, n. 21).

7 See Garuḍavāhana-paṇḍita's *Divyasūricarita*, one of the earliest accounts of Parakāla's story (edited by K. P. Aṇṇaṅkarācāriyar and A. M. Śrīnivāsācāriyar, in Telugu characters, Kāñcīpuram, 1953; and by T. A. Sampath Kumārācārya and K. K. A. Vēṅkaṭacāri, in Devanagari characters, Ananthacharya Research Institute, Bombay, [1978]), canto XIV, 80–7. See also Ch. 5, n. 9.

8 See *Prapannāmṛta* (Ch. 5, n. 12), 100, 69.

9 *Brahma-purāṇa* (Ānandāśrama Sanskrit Series, No. 28, Pune, 1895) 179, 7f, 63f.

10 See *Divyasūricarita* (note 7 above), I, 72–83.

11 For example, see my article 'Ideology and cultural contexts of the Śrīvaiṣṇava temple', *The Indian Economic and Social History Review* 14 (1977), Delhi, pp. 119–51.

12 See above, pp. 78–84.

13 At the time when Rāmānuja attempted to establish Śrīvaiṣṇava control over the Veṅkaṭam temple, his identification of the statue as Viṣṇu was (unsuccessfully) challenged by the Śivaites; references in the Āḻvārs seem

to suggest that they interpreted the image as a combined Hari–Hara statue. See for instance P. Sitapati, *Sri Venkateswara – The Lord of the Seven Hills*, Bharatiya Vidya Bhavan, Bombay, 1972, pp. 20–9. For a different problem of identifying a temple statue that occurs in Tirumāl-iruñcōlai, near Maturai, see Gros (Ch. 10, n. 24), pp. lviff.

14 Told in Śrīkānt Govaṇḍe, *Śrī Devī kathā* (in Marathi), Anmol Prakashan, Pune, 1979, pp. 27ff.

15 A selection of stanzas from Arun Kolatkar, *Jejuri*, Pras Prakashan, Bombay (2nd edn), 1978, pp. 45f.

16 See above, Ch. 4, n. 7.

17 Thus, for example, in a Marathi translation of the *Devī-māhātmya* (Kṣīrsāgar aṇi Kampani, Pune, 1977), p. 169 (16, 7).

18 See S. K. De, *Early History* (Ch. 13, n. 19), pp. 424, 435, 444f; also S. K. De, 'Caitanya-worship as a cult', *Indian Culture* 1, pp. 173–89, and reprinted, pp. 128–42, in *Bengal's Contribution to Sanskrit Literature and Studies in Bengal Vaiṣṇavism*, Indian Studies: Past and Present, K. L. Mukhopadhyaya, Calcutta, 1960.

19 Discussions of sthala-purāṇic material can be found in Shulman (Ch. 12, n. 21) and, more briefly, in my articles mentioned in note 11 above, and Ch. 12, n. 17.

20 For sources and discussions see D. D. Shulman, *The King and the Clown in South Indian Myth and Poetry*, Princeton University Press, Princeton, 1985, pp. 345f, 353, 364, and Hardy (note 11 above), pp. 147ff.

21 See Nammāḻvār's *Tiruvāymoḻi* VI, 3, 9 (where the precise phrase is *oppar ill appaṉ* 'the lord whom no one can rival').

22 See above, pp. 105f.

23 *Ahobila-māhātmyam*, edited (in Grantha characters) by Cakravartī Śrīnivāsācārya, Kumbhakonam, 1912; *Kāñcī-māhātmyam*, edited (in Devanagari) by P. B. Anantācārya, Conjeevaram, 1907 (Śāstramuktāvalī No. 26); see, on the latter work, M.-C. Porcher, 'La représentation de l'espace sacré dans le *Kāñcīmāhātmya*', *Puruṣārtha* 8, École des Hautes Études en Sciences Sociales, Paris, 1985, pp. 23–50.

24 On the localization of *bhakti* see my article '*Viraha* in relation to concrete space and time', in: *Bhakti in Current Research 1979–1982*, edited by M. Thiel-Horstmann, D. Reimer, Berlin, 1983, pp. 143–8.

25 Apart from the *māhātmyams* of Śrīraṅgam and Veṅkaṭam, which are available in various editions and translations, reference may be made here to the following works: Melpatur Narayana Bhattatiri's Sanskrit *Nārāyaṇīyam* (translated into English by Ram Varmha, Trivandrum, 1978); K. R. Vaidyanathan, *Sri Krishna – The Lord of Guruvayur*, Bharatiya Vidya Bhavan, Bombay (3rd edn), 1981; J. Rösel, *Der Palast des Herrn der Welt – Entstehungsgeschichte und Organisation der indischen Tempel-und Pilgerstadt Puri*, Weltforum Verlag, Munich/London, 1980, pp. 215–300. On Paṇḍharpūr see pp. 149ff of my article mentioned in note 24 above; see also Sitapati, note 13 above.

26 With thanks to John Smith (see Ch. 4, n. 30).
27 See above, p. 87.
28 On the *vāghyās* and *muraḷīs* generally see Dhere (Ch. 4, n. 16), pp. 47–68 and, on their songs, S. Bābar (Ch. 4, n. 10), Part III, pp. 25–48.

15 THE MELTING OF THE HEART

1 H. Kulke, *The Devarāja cult*, Data papers No. 108, South East Asia program, Department of Asian Studies, Cornell University, Ithaca, New York, January 1978. This is a revised version in English of 'Der Devarāja-Kult', *Saeculum* 25, 1 (1974), pp. 24–55.
2 See W. G. Archer's introduction (pp. 11–32) in *Love Songs of Vidyapati*, translated by D. Bhattacharya, George Allen and Unwin, London, 1963. His poetry was edited and translated by Subhadra Jha, *Songs of Vidyāpati*, Benares, 1954.
3 See D. Bhattacharya, *Love Songs of Chandidas – The Rebel Poet-Priest of Bengal*, George Allen and Unwin, London, 1967, and cf. D. C. Sen, *History of Bengali Language and Literature*, Calcutta University Press, Calcutta (2nd edn), 1954, pp. 119–34.
4 See above, pp. 106f and my article mentioned in Ch. 5, n. 11. Her poetry was edited and translated by J. Abbott, *Bahiṇā Bāī*, Pune, 1929 (The Poet-Saints of Maharashtra, vol. V); S. A. Jāvḍekar produced a critical edition, *Sant Baheṇābāīcā gāthā*, Konṭinenṭal prakāśan, Pune, 1979.
5 On Āṇṭāḷ see my *Viraha-bhakti* (Ch. 3, n. 8), pp. 414–29.
6 Ibid., p. 425; *Nācciyār-Tirumoḻi* XIII, 8.
7 On the *Cilappatikāram* see above, p. 151 and Ch. 7, n. 8.
8 See below, pp. 523f.
9 See note 5 above: p. 418, *Nācciyār-Tirumoḻi* I, 5 .
10 See my *Viraha-bhakti* (Ch. 3, n. 8), pp. 333–6; 350.
11 See above, pp. 219–21.
12 See above, pp. 224f.
13 Viṣṇubuvā Jogmahārāj, *Sârtha Śrī Tukārāmācī gāthā*, Pune (3rd edn), 1964, *abhaṅg* 3397. Similar poems are 3396 and 3398–3420.
14 Ibid., *abhaṅg* 3488. Similar poems are 3484–7 and 3489–91.
15 No. 28. For this and the following translations I have used the text edited (and translated into French) by M. Lupsa, *Chants à Kālī de Rāmprasād*, Pondicherry, 1967 (Publications de l'Institut Français d'Indologie, No. 30). Rather outdated are the translations of Rāmprasād's poetry found in: *Bengali Religious Lyrics, Śākta*, selected and translated by E. J. Thompson and A. M. Spencer, Association Press, Calcutta, and Oxford University Press, London, 1923 (Heritage of India Series), pp. 31–71. This book also contains poetry by later imitators of Rāmprasād (pp. 72–87). See also D. C. Sen (note 3 above), pp. 597–606; J. Sinha, *Rāma Prasād's Devotional Songs*, Calcutta, 1966; and, for a recent selection of English translations, L. Nathan and C. Seely, *Grace and Mercy in her*

Wild Hair – Selected Poems to the Mother Goddess by Rāmprasād Sen, Great Eastern, Boulder, 1982.

16 In Lupsa (note 15 above), No. 35.
17 Ibid., No. 50.
18 See below, pp. 351, 525, 539.
19 Ibid., No. 79; cf. No. 55.
20 Ibid., No. 18.
21 Ibid., No. 79.
22 Ibid., from No. 84.
23 Ibid., from No. 81.
24 On these later poets see Sen and Spencer (both in note 15 above).
25 See note 4 above: *abhaṅgs* 467–73 in Abbott, 440–5 in Jāvḍekar (cf. pp. 92ff of her introduction).
26 See above, pp. 120f.
27 The central works here are the *Ācāryahṛdayam* with Maṇavāḷa mā mu_n_i's commentary. A brief sketch of these can be found in my article on Nammāḻvār (Ch. 4, n. 26), pp. 50–4; I am preparing a full monograph on this and related material, dealing with the monotheistic challenge of orthodoxy and orthopraxy in Śrīvaiṣṇavism.
28 See P. M. Gaede, 'Yellamma-Kult: Sie geben alles für die Göttin', *Geo* 9, (September 1984), Hamburg, pp. 84–102; T. McGirk, 'Saved from prostitution in a Hindu temple', *The Independent* (6 February 1991); P. Hillmore, 'For Sale – India's child brides', *Observer Magazine* (26 January 1992), particularly pp. 34ff.
29 See in particular Frederique Appfel Marglin, *Wives of the God-King – The rituals of the Devadāsīs of Puri*, Oxford University Press, Delhi, 1985; Saskia C. Kersenboom, *Nityasumaṅgalī – Towards the Semiosis of the Devadāsī Tradition of South India*, Proefschrift, University of Utrecht, 1984.
30 For a brief survey of such South Indian, Vaiṣṇava, *bhāṇas* see my article on the Śrīvaiṣṇava temple (Ch. 14, n. 11 above), pp. 138–41.
31 The *Bilvāraṇyakṣetra-māhātmyam*, discussed in my two articles on the Purāṇas (Ch. 12, n. 17 above) and Parakāla (Ch. 5, n. 9).
32 The *Divyasūricarita* (Ch. 14, n. 7 above) VII, 29–79; VIII, 1–66; XIII, 87–122; XIV, 1–103.
33 In the Te_n_kalai *Guruparamparāprabhāvam* (by Pi_n_p' Aḻakiya Perumāḷ Jīyar, edited by S. Kiruṣṇasvāmi Ayyaṅkār, Tirucci, 1968, pp. 57–73) and Vaṭakalai *Guruparamparāprabhāvam* (by the third Brahmatantra-svatantra-svāmī, edited by K. Śrīnivāsācāriyar, Ti Liṭṭil Pḷavar Kampe_n_i, Madras, 1968, pp. 39–43) and in the *Prapannāmṛta* (Ch. 5, n. 12) chapters 26–31).
34 Popularly known as Āṇṭāḷ; see note 5 above.
35 See above, pp. 105f and Ch. 3, n. 10. The other saints are: Ēyarkō_n_ Kalikkāma_n_ (pp. 107–13), Ceruttuṇai and Kaḻarciṅka_n_ (pp. 500f), Kaṇṇappa_n_ (pp. 520–31), and Ci_r_uttoṇṭa_n_ (pp. 354–64).

36 The story is told in, for example, *Śrī-Nāmdev-rāyācī sârth gāthā* (edited by P. S. Subandh, Pune, 1962, vol. VI), *abhaṅg* 37, 1–42, pp. 14–17.
37 Ibid., *abhaṅgs* 44–7, pp. 42–6.
38 Told about Tulsīdās (see Siegel, Ch. 9, n. 4 above, p. 224) and about Līlāśuka (=Vilvamaṅgala) in the commentary by Gopālabhaṭṭa on the *Kṛṣṇakarṇāmṛta*, edited by S. K. De, University of Dacca, 1938 (Dacca University Oriental Publication Series, No. 5), pp. lxxxvf.
39 Told in Mahipati's *Bhaktalīlāmṛta*, Ch. 34, 64–74 (pp. 186f in J. Abbott's translation, Pune, 1930, The Poet-Saints of Maharashtra, vol. VII); cf. ibid. Ch. 33, 67–119, pp. 169–73, on Viṭhala bringing her child back to life.
40 See *Smṛtisthaḷa* (Ch. 7, n. 7 above), Nos 140–2. The passage is also found, with English translation, in S. G. Tulpule, *An Old Marathi Reader*, Venus Prakashan, Pune, 1960, pp. 112f.
41 On Govindaprabhu (= Guṇḍam Rāüḷ), see below, pp. 486ff.
42 *Periya-purāṇam* (Ch. 3, n. 10 above), Mūrti (pp. 469f); cf. the story of Kaliyaṉ who cut into his own throat to keep the lamps burning (pp. 465–8).
43 That by displaying himself as the *arcāvatāras* he would lose his own independence and would have to rely for his 'comforts', etc. on the temple priests is emphasized in the Vaṭakalai *Guruparampāraprabhāvam* (see note 33 above), p. 5. Compare Ch. 14, n. 7.
44 See David Shulman's article on Kāttavarāyaṉ, in: *Criminal Gods and Demon Devotees – Essays on the Guardians of Popular Hinduism*, edited by Alf Hiltebeitel, State University of New York Press, Albany, 1989.

16 RETURN TO THE WORLD

1 Translated from Stierli and quoted from my *Viraha-bhakti* (Ch. 3, n. 8), pp. 572f.
2 Translated from *Exercitia spiritualia Sancti Ignatii de Loyola* and quoted from my *Viraha-bhakti* (Ch. 3, n. 8), pp. 572f.
3 For material in the poetry of the Āḻvārs see my *Viraha-bhakti* (Ch. 3, n. 8), pp. 448ff; in Sanskrit we have the *Mukundamālā* by Kulaśekhara (who is frequently, but probably wrongly, identified with the Āḻvār of that name) which is pervaded by the same disregard for *mokṣa*.
4 See *Bhagavadgītā* III, 3–9 and IV, 14–23.
5 See ibid., e.g. II, 71.
6 See ibid., II, 58–68. Compare *Śvetāśvatara-Upaniṣad* II, 8–15.
7 Ibid., III, 28; V, 9. Compare IX, 4–10 on Kṛṣṇa working through *prakṛti*.
8 See ibid., II, 72 and V, 18–28.
9 See ibid., III, 15f.
10 See ibid., IV, 4 for Arjuna's question, and 5–9 on Kṛṣṇa's answer, in which he speaks of his many births on earth.
11 See ibid., XVIII, 54–8.

12 See ibid., XI, from vv. 10, 12, 14, 19, 24, 27 and 33; the individual sentences are derived from R. C. Zaehner's translation (Ch. 14, n. 4 above), pp. 305–11, with minor modifications.
13 Zaehner (Ch. 14, n. 4), p. 321.
14 R. Gombrich has recently argued in favour of *c.* 404 BC as the date of the Buddha's death, in a paper to be published.
15 See *Lalitavistara* (Ch. 8, n. 1), chapter 13, vv. 1–8; 22f; 36; 69–92; 131.
16 See above, Ch. 3, n. 13. For a detailed discussion of the work see Bhikkhu Telwatte Rahula (Ch. 11, n. 23), where its doctrinal proximity to the Theravāda is emphasized.
17 This is basically the *Sukhāvatīvyūha-sūtra,* which exists both in a long and a brief version. The Sanskrit text has been re-edited by P. L. Vaidya in his '*Mahāyānasūtrasaṅgraha*' (Ch. 2, n. 19), No. 16 (pp. 221–53) and No. 17 (brief version, pp. 254–7). Another edition is A. Ashikaga, Kyoto, 1965. English translations: by M. Müller in *Buddhist Mahāyāna Texts* (pp. 1–72 and 89–103), Clarendon Press, Oxford, 1894 and various reprints (Sacred Books of the East, vol. 49); *A Treasury of Mahāyāna Sūtras*, edited by G. C. C. Chang, (Ch. 8, n. 20), pp. 339–60 (from Bodhiruci's Chinese translation).
18 That the Buddha's life-story was the model is made explicit in the *Lotus Sūtra* II, vv. 112–29. The Sanskrit text of the *Saddharmapuṇḍarīka-sūtra* has been re-edited by P. L. Vaidya, Mithila Institute, Darbhanga, 1960 (Buddhist Sanskrit Texts, vol. VI); so far no critical edition has been produced, and, for an English translation from the Sanskrit, one still has to rely on H. Kern, *Saddharmapuṇḍarīka or The Lotus of the True Law*, Clarendon Press, Oxford, 1894 and various reprints (Sacred Books of the East, vol. 21). For English translations of the Chinese see B. Kato *et alii*, *Myōhō-Renge-Kyō – The Sūtra of the Lotus Flower of the Wonderful Law*, Risshō Kōsei-kai, Tokyo, 1971, and L. Hurvitz, *Scripture of the Lotus Blossom of the Fine Dharma*, Columbia University Press, New York, 1976. See also M. Pye, *Skilful Means – A Concept in Mahāyāna Buddhism*, Duckworth, London, 1978, pp. 18–83; 168–82.
19 One may compare the survey of many Jātaka stories in chapter 13 of the *Lalitavistara* (see above, note 15) with that found in the first part of the *Rāṣṭrapālaparipṛcchā-sūtra* (re-edited by P. L. Vaidya, '*Mahāyānasūtrasaṅgraha*' (Ch. 2, n. 19) as No. 12 (pp. 120–64); translated into English by J. Ensink, *The Question of Raṣṭrapāla*, Zwolle, 1952, pp. 1–59), vv. 112–65. Each of these stories is meant to illustrate a particular *pārami(tā)*, 'perfection', which in the Mahāyāna defines a *bodhisattva*.
20 For instance in the *Rāṣṭrapālaparipṛcchā* (see previous note), I, vv. 201, 206, etc. (where the phrase 'final age' occurs); see the whole passage I, 170–216 (pp. 28–32 in Ensink) on the decadence of the final age.
21 On *upāya-kauśalya*, 'skill in means', see Pye's book mentioned in note 18 above. The expression 'skilful means' does not directly translate the Sanskrit, but the Chinese rendering of the term in Kumārajīva.

22 Such similarities have been noticed by H. Kern in his translation of the *Lotus Sūtra* (see note 18 above). Compare e.g. *Bhagavadgītā* II, 50 on 'skill in works'.

23 See above, Ch. 5, n. 31.

24 Quoted from W. de Bary (ed.), *The Buddhist Tradition*, Vintage Books, New York, 1972, pp. 52f (this paperback edition incorporates material from *Sources of Indian Tradition*, Columbia University Press, New York, 1958). My Dharma replaces here 'righteousness' in the original.

25 Ibid., pp. 53f.

26 Śrīvaiṣṇava literature on this discussion is extensive; reference may be made here only to the two most renowned exponents, Vedāntadeśika and Piḷḷai Lokācārya. The former argues in favour of co-operation in his *Rahasyatrayasāram* (edited by U. V. Narasimmācāriyar, Madras, 1920), chapters 9 and 23ff; the latter in favour of regarding Viṣṇu as the sole means towards liberation, for instance in his *Śrīvacanabhūṣaṇam* (edited, with Maṇavāḷa mā muṉi's commentary, by K. P. Aṇṇaṅkarācāriyar, in '*Śrīmad-Varavara-munīndra-granthamālā*' (see Ch. 5, n. 29), vol. I (1966, pp. 50–5), I, Nos 54–65.

27 This structure is developed in great detail by Rūpa Gosvāmī in his *Bhaktirasāmṛtasindhu* and *Ujjvalanīlamaṇi*; cf. S. K. De, 1961 (Ch. 13, n. 19), pp. 170–224.

17 ALL THE VALLEYS FILLED WITH CORPSES

1 See below, pp. 389, 394–8.

2 G. V. Desani, *All about H. Hatterr*, Penguin Books, Harmondsworth, 1982 (originally published by Aldor, 1948), pp. 251f.

3 Gita Mehta, *Karma Cola*, Jonathan Cape, London, 1980 (also as Fontana paperback, and, only in India, as Macmillan paperback), p. 18.

4 As associated with the names of A. Huxley, A. Coomaraswamy, F. Schuon, R. Guénon, etc. Even E. Conze sometimes points in this direction; see his *Buddhist Thought in India*, George Allen and Unwin, London, 1962, pp. 17–26.

5 Job 42, vv. 1–6; quoted from *The New Oxford Annotated Bible*, Oxford University Press, New York, 1977, pp. 654f.

6 Ibid. 2, v. 7 (p. 614).

7 Ibid. 38, v. 1 (p. 650).

8 Ezekiel 1, v. 4; Nahum 1, v. 3; Zechariah 9, v. 14.

9 Desani (see note 2 above), p. i.

10 Kolatkar (Ch. 14, n. 15) pp. 23; 28.

11 Ibid., p. 49.

12 Salman Rushdie, *The Satanic Verses*, Viking (Penguin Books), London, 1988, pp. 536f.

13 Ibid. p. [549], Acknowledgements.

14 Kanwar Lal, *The Cult of Desire*, Asia Press, Delhi, 1966: 'The sale of

this book is restricted to members of the medical and legal professions, and to scholars and research students of Indology, Psychology and Social Sciences.' (p. ii)

15 See Ch. 7, n. 11.

16 N. Douglas and P. Slinger, *Sexual Secrets – The Alchemy of Ecstasy*, Hutchinson, London, 1979.

17 M. E. Mark, *Falkland Road – Prostitutes of Bombay*, Thames and Hudson, London, 1981.

18 Carlos Castaneda, *The Teachings of Don Juan – A Yaqui Way of Knowledge*; *A Separate Reality*; *Journey to Ixtlan – The Lessons of Don Juan*; *Tales of Power*; *The Second Ring of Power*; for the first volume, my Penguin edition (Harmondsworth, 1970, 1973, 1974, 1976 and 1979) mentions as publishers the University of California Press, 1968; for the subsequent volumes, no publishers are mentioned, only the years of the first American edition: 1971, 1972, 1974 and 1977.

19 See F. Capra, *The Tao of Physic – An Exploration of the Parallels Between Modern Physics and Eastern Mysticism*, Flamingo Paperback, London (2nd revised edn), 1983, in particular pp. 177; 335–40.

20 See note 3 above: p. 6.

21 Quoted from de Bary, *The Buddhist Tradition* (Ch. 16, n. 24), p. 238.

22 Thomas Pynchon, *V.*, Picador (Pan Books), London, 1975, pp. 306f.

23 Ibid., p. 278.

18 STRATEGIC INITIATIVES

1 See Ch. 11, n. 39: No. 21, pp. 18f.

2 See above, p. 253.

3 An early English translation was made by R. Shamasastry, Mysore Printing and Publishing House, Mysore (8th edn), 1967 (1st edn, 1915).

4 As quoted in Wilhelm (Ch. 10, n. 10) p. 78.

5 Ibid., p. 71.

6 The six-fold policy is briefly discussed in *Arthaśāstra* (note 3 above), Book VII, chapter 1 (pp. 295–8 in Shamasastry), and elaborated upon in the remaining chapters of the Book. The four *upāyas* are mentioned, e.g. in Book II, chapter 10 (pp. 75f).

7 Two modern English translations may be mentioned here: by van Buitenen 1968 (Ch. 12, n. 11) and Coulson 1981 (Ch. 7, n. 4).

8 See Wilhelm (Ch. 10, n. 10), pp. 78f.

9 Daṇḍin's *Daśakumāracarita*, edited and translated by V. Satakopan, Sastrulu and Sons, Madras, 1963. Cāṇakya's (=Kauṭalya's) instructions are derided in the eighth *ucchvāsa* of the main work (prince Viśruta's story) by Vihārabhadra (pp. 232–7 of the Sanskrit text). For Vihāra-bhadra's characterization, see p. 232.

10 F. Edgerton's substantial research in the *Pañcatantra* literature resulted in a composite edition of the reconstructed Sanskrit text and its English

translation (*Pañcatantra* Reconstructed, 2 vols, American Oriental Society, New Haven, 1924). Edgerton's *The Panchatantra – An edition for the general reader*, was published by George Allen and Unwin, London, 1965. The *Arthaśāstra* (see note 3 above) is quoted verbatim (1965, p. 11); a brief summary of Edgerton's research in the translation history of the *Pañcatantra* can be found on pp. 11–20. A version of the *Pañcatantra* is included in the *Kathāsaritsāgara* (Ch. 6, n. 13), of which an English translation can be found in Tawney (Ch. 6, n. 13), vol. V, pp. 41–139. Pages 232–43 of the same volume have a detailed '*Genealogical Table*', of different recensions and translations, of the *Pañcatantra* by F. Edgerton.

11 For details see Edgerton, in Tawney (Ch. 6, n. 13), vol. V, pp. 232–43.

12 See Edgerton 1965 (note 10 above), pp. 61f; Tawney (Ch. 6, n. 13), vol. V, pp. 55f.

13 *Kathāsaritsāgara* (Ch. 6, n. 13), Book II, chapter 12; Tawney (Ch. 6, n. 13), vol. I, pp. 139–49; partially translated into English also by van Buitenen, *Tales of Ancient India*, University of Chicago Press, Chicago/London, 1959; also as Bantham Classics, New York, 1961, pp. 68–74. For versions in other works see Tawney, vol. I, pp. 145–8, various footnotes. To these may be added *Kathāratnākara*, story 128 (translated into German by J. Hertel, *Das Märchenmeer – Eine Sammlung indischer Erzählungen von Hemavijaya*, vol. II, Georg Müller, Munich, 1920).

14 See Ch. 10, n. 2, second story of the Fourth Day, p. 345.

15 See Ch. 11, n. 39, p. 154.

16 See Ingalls, 1965 (Ch. 5, n. 25), p. 363.

17 Govardhana (Ch. 2, n. 18), No. 194.

18 Ibid., No. 678; cf. 609.

19 See Ch. 11, n. 39, from No. 97, pp. 74f.

20 Ibid., from No. 197, pp. 144f.

21 Ibid., p. xvi.

22 For instance in the *Saduktikarṇāmṛta* (Ch. 5, n. 23), among the hundred poems from 2259 to 2359 which deal with themes like old age, resignation, disgust with the world, inner peace, withdrawal from the world, etc., a third is also found in the *Śāntiśatakam* (edited by J. Vidyāsāgara, '*Kāvyasaṅgraha*', vol. III, Calcutta, 1888).

23 For instance in the *Subhāṣitaratnakoṣa* (Ch. 5, notes 13 and 25), No. 1526.

24 See Zvelebil (Ch. 5, n. 28) pp. 119–23, with note 24 on p. 122 on translations (as early as AD 1730 into Latin); also K. Zvelebil, *Tamil Literature*, E. J. Brill, Leiden, 1975, pp. 123–7, with note 99 on p. 127 on translations. For a detailed study and French translation of the third part, on *kāma*, see F. Gros, *Le Livre de l'Amour de Tiruvaḷḷuvar*, Gallimard, Paris, 1992 (Connaissance de l'Orient).

25 Poem 1330.

26 Yogi Shuddhananda Bharati, *Thirukkural Couplets with Clear Prose Rendering (in English)*, South India Saiva Siddhanta Works Publishing Society (no. 1352), Tirunelveli/Madras, 1971.
27 Ibid., from the *Foreword* by S. Maharajan, pp. 9f; the use of the word *tapas*, instead of *yoga*, is rather confusing in the quotation.
28 The three poems quoted here are 329, 448 and 1134.
29 See Wilhelm (Ch. 10, n. 10), pp. 131ff.
30 *Daśakumāracarita* (see note 9 above), pp. 128–53 of the text: the third *ucchvāsa* of the main work (prince Upaharavarman's story); translated also by van Buitenen (note 13 above), pp. 190–201.
31 *Daśakumāracarita* (see note 9 above), p. 139 of the text.
32 Ibid., p. 153.
33 The work appears in two recensions; the Sanskrit text of both of these was edited by R. Schmidt (*Zeitschrift der deutschen morgenländischen Gesellschaft*, 1893) who also edited and translated the Marathi version (*Zeitschrift der deutschen morgenländischen Gesellschaft*, 1897) and translated the longer version (Stuttgart, 1899). For another, composite, German translation see *Śukasaptati – Das indische Papageienbuch, aus dem Sanskrit übersetzt* by W. Morgenroth, E. Diederichs Verlag, Cologne, 1986 (Diederichs Gelbe Reihe, vol. 66). A brief survey of translations of the work into other languages can be found in Morgenroth, pp. 244ff.
34 See above, pp. 276–84.
35 For an English translation see D. M. Wulff, *Drama as a Mode of Religious Realization – The Vidagdhamādhava of Rūpa Gosvāmī*, Scholars Press, Chico, CA, 1984.
36 See above, pp. 105f, 301f, 337f.
37 These episodes are found in the *Prapannāmṛta* where they appear to be translations of material found only in some manuscripts of the Teṉkalai *Guruparamparāprabhāvam* (Ch. 15, n. 33).
38 See Pye's study of the concept, on the basis of Chinese translations of various Mahāyāna *sūtras* (Ch. 16, ns. 18 and 21).
39 *Lotus Sūtra*, chapter 7, prose Kern pp. 180–3, vv. 92–109.
40 Ibid., chapter 3, prose Kern pp. 70–82, vv. 39–149.
41 Ibid., chapter 4, prose Kern pp. 99–108; vv. 1–36.
42 See *Bharaṭakadvātriṃśikā – The Thirty-Two Bharaṭaka Stories*, critically edited by J. Hertel, Leipzig, 1921 (Forschungsinstitut für Indogermanistik, Indische Abteilung, No. 2), story 25 (pp. 39f). Hertel translated the stories into German in: *Zwei indische Narrenbücher*, H. Haessel Verlag, Leipzig, 1922, pp. 19–104 (Indische Erzähler, vol. 5); our story is on pp. 83–6.
43 The Prakrit text of Haribhadra's *Dhūrtākhyāna* was edited by Śrī-Jinavijaya-muni, Bharatiya Vidya Bhavan, Bombay, 1944.
44 Ibid., Elāṣāḍha's story (No. 3), condensed, pp. 12ff.
45 Ibid., Khaṇḍapaṇā's story (no. 5), v. 1, p. 24.

19 ENCOMPASSING THE GALAXIES

1 See above, pp. 407ff.
2 The *Śrī-Bhaktavatsala-māhātmyam (Śrī-Kṛṣṇamaṅgala-kṣetram)* was edited, in Devanagari, by E. Śrīnivāsa-Rāghava, in 1940 (publisher and place of publication unknown.)
3 See my article on the Purāṇas (Ch. 12, n. 17).
4 For a critique of the Eliadian approach see T. Alliband, 'Lobe das Primitive – verfluche das Moderne! Eliade als Protagonist einer prämodernen Reinheit', in: *Sehnsucht nach dem Ursprung – Zu Mircea Eliade*, edited by H. P. Duerr, Syndikat, Frankfurt am Main, 1983, pp. 59–70; cf. in the same volume Agehananda Bharati, 'Mircea Eliade – Privilegierte Information und anthropologische Aporien', pp. 32–58.
5 Śrīvaiṣṇava literature dealing with the three *rahasyams* (the three central *mantras*) is vast; see K. K. A. Venkatachari, *The Maṇipravāḷa Literature of the Śrīvaiṣṇava Ācāryas*, Ananthacharya Research Institute, Bombay, 1978, pp. 95–166. The quotation is *sūtra* 33 in Piḷḷai Lokācārya's *Mumukṣuppaṭi*, edited by K. P. B. Aṇṇaṅkarācāriyar (see '*Śrīmad-Varavara-munindra-granthamālā*', vol. I, 1966 (Ch. 5, n. 29)).
6 See P. Spratt, *Hindu Culture and Personality*, Manaktalas, Bombay, 1966, pp. 2, 228–35, 248, 261; G. M. Carstairs, *The Twice-Born*, Hogarth Press, London, 1968, pp. 159, 166; R. Lannoy, *The Speaking Tree*, Oxford University Press, London, 1971, pp. 106f. Less extreme is S. Kakar, *The Inner World – A Psycho-analytic Study of Childhood and Society in India*, Oxford University Press, Delhi, 1978, pp. 103–12.
7 *Chāndogya-Upaniṣad*, VI, 2, 1.3.4.
8 Ibid., v. 3.
9 Ibid., v. 4.
10 Ibid., VI, 4, 1.
11 Ibid., VI, 5, 1.
12 See E. Frauwallner, *Geschichte der indischen Philosophie*, vol. II, O. Müller Verlag, Salzburg, 1956, p. 86.
13 Ibid., p. 240. The source paraphrased here is Praśastapāda's *Padārtha-dharmasaṅgraha.*
14 Ibid., p. 105, with note 142 (where also Hindu versions of this critique are mentioned).
15 *Lokāyata – A Study in Ancient Indian Materialism*, People's Publishing House, New Delhi, 1959 (3rd edn, 1973).
16 Quoted, for instance, in the *Pramāṇatiraṭṭu* to the *Īṭu*, introduction, vol. I, pp. 31 ('*Pakavatviṣayam*', edited by Kōpālakiruṣṇamācāriyar, Triplicane, 1925–30). Cf. Frauwallner (note 12 above), p. 303 with other sources in his note 388.
17 See p. 184 above and cf. Frauwallner (note 12 above), pp. 297–300, with sources in his note 381.

18 The story of Yaśodhara; see Ch. 8, note 17.
19 The full title of this letter, of twelve printed pages, is: *Letter On the Religions of the British Empire, and the Endowment of a Lectureship in Natural and Comparative Religion at the University of Oxford. From Henry Wilde, D.Sc., DCL, FRS*. The quote is the concluding paragraph on p. 10.
20 Ibid., p. 4.
21 Ibid., p. 11 (Table I, Nos 1 and 5).
22 Ibid., pp. 7f.
23 Ibid., p. 7.
24 Ibid., pp. 9 and 3.
25 Ibid., pp. 2 and 10.
26 Ibid., p. 2 (No. 3).
27 On the 'unseen' see Frauwallner (note 12 above), pp. 92–5.
28 See, for example, M. Hiriyanna, *Outlines of Indian Philosophy*, George Allen and Unwin, London, 1932 (6th impression, 1967), pp. 241ff, with references to sources.
29 *Chāndogya-Upaniṣad*, VI, 12, 1–3.
30 V. Raghavan extricated from the vast output of the South Indian composer Tyāgarāja (*c.* 1759–1847) his reflections on '*nāda yoga*' and 'music itself as *mokṣa*' in: *The Spiritual Heritage of Tyāgarāja* (text and English translations by C. Ramanujachari), An introductory thesis by V. Raghavan, Sri Ramakrishna Math, Madras (2nd edn), 1966, pp. 42–64 and 509–517 (the culminating sequence of songs, according to Raghavan's schema).

20 THE ALL-PERVASIVE MIND

1 *Chāndogya-Upaniṣad*, from III, 14, 3f.
2 *Bṛhadāraṇyaka-Upaniṣad*, from II, 4, 5.
3 Ibid., II, 4, 14; cf. IV, 5, 15. *Prajñā* appears e.g. IV, 5, 13.
4 Ibid., from IV, 3, 21.
5 R. C. Zaehner, *Our Savage God*, Collins, London, 1974, passim.
6 See above, pp. 397f.
7 *Udāna* (edited by P. Steinthal, Pali Text Society, London, 1885), No. 80f.
8 Cf. Conze (Ch. 7, n. 25), p. 106 and related materials listed above, Ch. 8, n. 15.
9 See, for example, Buddhaghosa's *Visuddhimagga* (edited by H. C. Warren and D. Kosambi, Harvard Oriental Series, vol. 41, Harvard University Press, Cambridge, MA, 1950), pp. 507–9. This passage (which quotes from *Udāna* No. 80, see note 7 above), is translated as No. 99 in Conze (Ch. 7, n. 25), pp. 100ff.
10 *Sūtra* I, 1, 2.
11 Mentioned, for example, by Śaṅkara in his *Brahmasūtrabhāṣya* on *sūtra* II, 1, 14.

12 See Īśvarakṛṣṇa's *Sāṃkhya-kārikās* 59–66.

13 On Kundakunda see, for example, Frauwallner, vol. II (Ch. 19, n. 12) pp. 254ff; 286–90. He wrote in Prakrit, and little text-critical work has been done on the treatises associated with his name. Moreover, available translations of his main works (*Paṃcatthiyasaṃgaho*, *Pavayaṇasāro* and *Samayasāro*) are dependent on the medieval commentators, particularly Amṛtacandra, whose interpretation is often questionable. Most attention has been paid to the *Pravacanasāra* (*Pavayaṇasāro*) which was edited, with Amṛtacandra's and Jayasena's commentaries, and translated into English, by A. N. Upadhye, Bombay (2nd edn), 1935 (Śrī Rāyachandra Jaina Śāstramālā [vol. 9]); B. Faddegon (Cambridge University Press, 1935, Jain Literature Society Series, vol. 1) translated both the text and Amṛtacandra's commentary. For a recent, detailed discussion of this work and of the *Samayasāro*, see W. J. Johnson, 'The Problem of Bondage in Selected Early Jaina Texts', D. Phil. thesis, University of Oxford, 1990.

14 On Yogīndu's works see below, Ch. 24, n. 9.

15 For example, in the *Diamond Sūtra* (*Vajracchedikā*), 32 (quoted from E. Conze, *Buddhist Wisdom Books*, George Allen and Unwin, London, 1958 (2nd edn, 1975), p. 68); *Lalitavistara* (Ch. 8, n. 1) chapter 13, vv. 95–8.

16 The poem is quoted from J. M. Cohen, *Jorge Luis Borges*, Oliver and Boyd Edinburgh, 1973 (Modern Writers' Series), p. 21. The complete original can be found, for example, in: Jorge Luis Borges, *Obra poética (1923–1969)*, EMECÉ Editores, Buenos Aires (9th edn), 1972, pp. 46ff.

17 Cohen (see note 16 above), p. 21.

18 Hirakawa Akira, 'The rise of Mahāyāna and its relationship to the *Stūpa*', *Memoirs of the Research Department of the Toyo Bunko* 22, Tokyo, 1963.

19 See for instance *Samādhirāja-sūtra*, chapter 22 (*Tathāgata-kāya*), pp. 296–304 of N. Dutt's edition, *Gilgit Manuscripts*, vol. II, part II, Calcutta, 1953.

20 See above p. 186, and Ch. 8, n. 20 for bibliographical details. Wayman suggests, in his introduction, that this *sūtra* might have been composed in Āndhra.

21 The *Ratnagotravibhāga*, attributed to Sāramati, is a lengthy treatise on the *Tathāgatagarbha* theory. It quotes extensively from the *Āryā-Śrīmālā-sūtra* and from a number of other *sūtras* that deal with the idea. The Sanskrit text was edited by E. H. Johnston, Patna, 1950 (*Journal of the Bihar Research Society* 36, Part I), and translated by J. Takasaki, *A Study on the Ratnagotravibhāga (Uttaratantra) – being a Treatise on the Tathāgatagarbha Theory of Mahāyāna Buddhism*, Istituto Italiano per il medio ed estremo Oriente, Rome, 1966 (Serie Orientale Roma, vol. 33). On the *sūtras* quoted by Sāramati see Takasaki, pp. 32–40. See also E. Frauwallner, *Philosophie des Buddhismus* (Ch. 8, n. 10), pp. 255–64.

22 See for page references Ch. 8, n. 20 above.

23 See note 21 above.

24 *Ratnagotravibhāga*, '*śloka-grantha*' (Takasaki, note 21 above, pp. 18f; 393ff), 5–22.

25 A useful collection of (German) translations from Asaṅga and Vasubandhu, with extensive comments, can be found in Frauwallner, *Philosophie des Buddhismus* (Ch. 8, n. 10), pp. 326–90.

26 This text was edited by B. Nanjiō, Otani University Press, Kyōto, 1923 (Bibliotheca Otaniensis, vol. 1), and translated by D. T. Suzuki, Routledge and Sons, London, 1932. Although the latter work claims to be 'translated for the first time from the original Sanskrit', the translation is disconcertingly inaccurate.

27 In chapter 6.

28 In D. T. Suzuki, *Studies in the Lankavatara Sutra*, Routledge and Sons, London, 1930, pp. 17, 19, 96, 102. On the influence of the *Laṅkāvatāra* on Ch'an/Zen see ibid., pp. 44–63, and de Bary (Ch. 16, n. 24), pp. 209f.

29 *Brahmasūtras*, I, 1, 4 (according to Śaṅkara's interpretation); also Rāmānuja, on I, 1, 3, states that *brahman* is only known from the Vedas.

21 STRIKING A BALANCE

1 The story of Mallī is told in chapter 8 of the Prakrit *Nāyādhammakahāo*, the sixth *aṅga* of the Jain canon (among the Śvetāmbaras); a critical edition of the text was published by N. V. Vaidya, Poona, 1940, pp. 90–120. Mallī's words quoted here are found pp. 113, l. 24 – 114, l. 4.

2 Ibid., p. 114, ll. 15–19.

3 Such a story is narrated in the tale of Yaśodhara; in Hariṣeṇa's version, story No. 73, vv. 75–110; for my translation of it see Granoff (Ch. 3, n. 17). A similar story, about a goat sacrificed seven times to the goddess Durgā for his own benefit, with a consequent recollection of past lives, is told as No. 71 (pp. 163–5) by Hariṣeṇa, and in a parallel version in Apabhraṃśa by Śrīcandra in his *Kahakosu* (Ch. 2, n. 15), *sandhi* 29, 1–4.

4 These are the first two chapters of the *Ratnaguṇasaṃcayagāthāḥ*; a critical edition was produced by Yuyama (Ch. 5, n. 31). E. Conze's translation (*The Perfection of Wisdom in Eight Thousand Lines and Its Verse Summary*, Four Seasons Foundation, Bolinas, 1973 (Wheel Series, vol. 1), pp. 9–14) has been superseded by Yuyama's work. On possible links with the Śaila traditions in Āndhra see A. K. Warder, *Indian Buddhism*, Motilal Banarsidass, Delhi, 1960, p. 365.

5 The version in eight thousand *granthas* was edited by R. Mitra for Bibliotheca Indica, Calcutta, 1888, and re-edited by P. L. Vaidya as vol. IV of the Buddhist Sanskrit Texts, Mithila Institute, Darbhanga, 1960, and translated by E. Conze (see previous note). On the compositional history of this text see E. Conze, 'The composition of the *Aṣṭasāhasrikā Prajñāpāramitā*', in: *Thirty Years of Buddhist Studies*, Cassirer, Oxford, 1967, pp. 168–84 (originally published in *Bulletin of the London School of Oriental and African Studies* 14, 1952, pp. 251–62). On the history of

the *Prajñā-Pāramitā* literature in general see E. Conze, 'The development of *Prajñāpāramitā* thought', in: *Thirty Years of Buddhist Studies*, pp. 123–47 (originally published in the Suzuki Festschrift, *Buddhism and Culture*, edited by S. Yamaguchi, Kyōto, 1960, pp. 24–45).

6 Both *Heart* and *Diamond Sūtras* were translated by E. Conze (Ch. 20, n. 15). E. Conze edited the second, *Vajracchedikā, sūtra* for the Serie Orientale Roma, vol. 13, Istituto Italiano per il medio ed estremo Oriente, Rome, 1957. For a critical edition of the Sanskrit text of the former see E. Conze, 'The Prajñāpāramitā-hṛdaya Sūtra', in: *Thirty Years of Buddhist Studies* (see previous note), pp. 148–67 (originally published in the *Journal of the Royal Asiatic Society*, 1948, pp. 33–51).

7 See Ch. 20, n. 28.

8 This *sūtra* is included in E. Conze's *The Short Prajñāpāramitā Texts*, Luzac, London, 1973, p. 201.

9 See above, p. 241.

10 These phrases are frequently used in the first two chapters of the *Ratnaguṇasaṃcayagāthās* (see note 4 above).

11 Ibid., I, 8 and 15.

12 See for instance I. Schloegl, *The Zen Way*, Sheldon Press, London, 1977, particularly pp. 30–60.

13 *Aṣṭasāhasrikā-prajñāpāramitā*, chapter 1 (p. 20 of R. Mitra's edition); quoted from Conze's translation (see note 4 above), p. 90.

14 See note 13 above: p. 14 of R. Mitra's edition, and quoted, with modifications, from Conze's translation, p. 87.

15 Ibid., p. 5 (p. 84).

16 Jaroslav Hašek, *The Good Soldier Švejk and His Fortunes in the World War*, translated by C. Parrot, Penguin Books, Harmondsworth, 1974, p. 420.

17 Ibid., p. 420.

18 This is the *Ratnakūṭa* which, as the *Kāśyapaparivarta*, was incorporated into the Chinese (and Tibetan) mega-*sūtra Mahāratnakūṭa*. It was edited by A. von Staël-Holstein, *The Kāçyapaparivarta – A Mahāyāna Sūtra of the Ratnakūṭa Class*, Commercial Press, [Shanghai], 1926. An English translation of Bodhiruci's Chinese translation (in the *Mahāratnakūṭa*) can be found in G. C. C. Chang, (Ch. 8, n. 20 above), pp. 386–414. The simile referred to here is No. 49 (p. 79) in von Staël-Holstein.

19 Ibid., Nos 52–65 (pp. 82–98). Smaller portions of the Sanskrit text are missing; a German translation of the passage, with the missing portions supplied from the Tibetan, can be found in Frauwallner, *Philosophie des Buddhismus* (Ch. 8, n. 10), pp. 164–70.

20 Ibid., No. 65 (pp. 97f).

21 See Ch. 6, n. 22 above; chapters 1–4, pp. 169–83.

22 Ibid., chapter 2, p. 173.

23 See above, pp. 136ff.

24 For Hašek see note 16 above; for the *Heart Sūtra* see Conze, *Buddhist Wisdom Books* (Ch. 20, n. 15), pp. 75–107; for the Sanskrit text see Conze's *Thirty Years of Buddhist Studies* (note 5 above), p. 150.
25 For a summary of Nāgārjuna's thought, with a selection of translated passages, see E. Frauwallner, *Philosophie des Buddhismus* (Ch. 8, n. 10), pp. 170–217.
26 For instance *dvaita*, 'duality', in *Bṛhadāraṇyaka-Upaniṣad* II, 4, 14 (quoted above, p. 434) and its rejection; for further references see G. A. Jacob, *A Concordance to the Principal Upanishads and Bhagavadgītā*, originally published 1891 and reprinted by Motilal Banarsidass, Delhi, 1963, *sub verbis advaya, -tā, -tāraka, advitīya, -tva, advaita, -tva* and *advaitībhūta.*
27 For references to the rope–snake simile in Śaṅkara's commentary on the *Brahmasūtras* see P. Deussen, *The System of the Vedānta*, translated by C. Johnston, Dover Publications, New York, 1973 (1st edn Open Court, Chicago, 1912), p. 269, note 105.
28 Rāmānuja's commentary on the *Brahmasūtras* I, 1, 3.
29 See above, pp. 445f, 454, with Ch. 20, n. 29.
30 See above, pp. 363f.

22 BEYOND PROSAIC WORDS

1 *(Mūla)Madhyamakakārikā* (edited by L. de la Vallée Poussin, St Petersburg/Leningrad, 1913, Bibliotheca Buddhica, vol. 4), I, 1.
2 The loss of the Sanskrit original of the *Vimalakīrtinirdeśa-sūtra* must be considered as one of the more painful and tragic events in the history of Indian culture. Fortunately we still have Chinese and Tibetan translations of this extraordinary text which É. Lamotte has made available to the Occident, setting an as yet unrivalled standard of translating a Mahāyāna *sūtra*; see his *L'Enseignement de Vimalakīrti*, Museon, Louvain, 1962. In turn, Lamotte's translation was translated into English by S. Boin and published by the Pali Text Society, Routledge and Kegan Paul, London, 1976, as *The Teaching of Vimalakīrti*. The following references to chapter and paragraph apply to both the French original and the English translation.
3 *Vimalakīrtinirdeśa-sūtra*, chapter II, 1–6; cf. also IV, 1.
4 Ibid., IV, 3–8.
5 Ibid., XI, 1.
6 Ibid., III, 62f.
7 Ibid., VI, 15.
8 Ibid., VIII, 1–33.
9 These are explained above, pp. 458–64 *passim*.
10 Umberto Eco, *The Name of the Rose*, translated by W. Weaver, Secker and Warburg, London, 1983, p. 491.
11 Ibid., p. 492 .
12 Ibid. p. 491 (author's italics).

13 Ānandavardhana uses a *prahelikā* in his *Devīśatakam* (see note 39 below), v. 102; Vedāntadeśika, in his *Yādavābhyudaya* (edited by U. Vīrāgha-vācārya, Ubhaya Vedānta Granthamālā, Madras, 1969) canto VI, v. 48.

14 Daṇḍin's *Kāvyādarśa*, III, 113.

15 *Bhāgavata-purāṇa* (Ch. 2, n. 5), X, 22.

16 *Śrī-Govinda-caritra by Mhāībhaṭ*, edited by V. B. Kolte, Arun Prakasan, Malkapur (5th edn), 1972, No. 101 (p. 34 of text). A. Feldhaus has translated the work, as *The Deeds of God in Ṛddhipur*, Oxford University Press, New York/Oxford, 1984.

17 *Śrī-Govinda-caritra* (see note 16 above), No. 112 (p. 38 of text).

18 Ibid., from No. 180 (p. 61 of text).

19 Ibid., No. 181 (ibid.).

20 Ibid., No. 49 (pp. 15f).

21 See Ch. 17, n. 4, p. 244.

22 Ibid., p. 249.

23 The phrase *sa esa nêti nêty ātmā* occurs in *Bṛhadāraṇyaka-Upaniṣad* III, 9, 26, and is repeated IV, 2, 4; 4, 22; 5, 15. Similar is *Bṛhadāraṇyaka-Upaniṣad* II, 3, 6.

24 *Taittirīya-Upaniṣad* II, 4, 1; 9, 1.

25 Translated from: Robert Walser, *Poetenleben – Seeland – Die Rose*, edited by J. Greven, Verlag H. Kossodo, Genf/Hamburg, 1967 ('*Gesamtwerk*', vol. III), pp. 13ff, from: *Brief eines Malers an einen Dichter.*

26 Ibid., pp. 424f, from: *Schwäche und Stärke*. My interpretation of Walser has benefited greatly from W. Lüssi, *Robert Walser – Experiment ohne Wahrheit*, E. Schmidt Verlag, Berlin, 1977 (Philologische Studien und Quellen, vol. 89).

27 Canetti, *Provinz* (Ch. 3, n. 15), pp. 250f.

28 Ibid. p. 251.

29 *Japujī*, poem 19, lines 1–7, translated from '*Sundar Guṭkā*' (date and place of publication unknown), p. 13 (which corresponds to p. 4 in the *Ādi Śrī Gurū Granth Sāhib Jī*); for a full English translation of the *Japujī*, the Sikhs' daily morning prayer, see *The Sacred Writings of the Sikhs*, translated by Trilochan Singh *et alii*, George Allen and Unwin, London, 1973 (originally 1960), pp. 28–51.

30 *Tiruvāymoḻi* VII, 9; cf. *Tiruviruttam* 48. The song is discussed in my *Viraha-bhakti* (Ch. 3, n. 8), pp. 326f.

31 See above, pp. 106f, and Ch. 15, n. 4. The poem is No. 234 in Abbott, 595 in Jāvḍekar; cf. also Nos 74–8 in Abbott, 590, 592ff in Jāvḍekar (her 591 is a truncated variant of Abbott 75).

32 Govardhana (Ch. 2, n. 18), No. 544 (cf. 267, in which her glances through the hole in the fence are compared to a shining fish).

33 Ibid., No. 642.

34 Ibid., No. 536.

35 The passage is found in Bāṇa's *Kādambarī*, pp. 333–42 of M. R. Kāḷe's edition (Bombay, 1924).

36 See above, p. 282.
37 S. Dasgupta, *A History of Indian Philosophy*, vol. III, Cambridge University Press, 1940, p. 119.
38 See my article 'The philosopher as poet: a study of Vedāntadeśika's *Dehalīśastuti*', *Journal of Indian Philosophy* 7 (1979), Dordrecht, pp. 277–325.
39 Ānandavardhana's *Devīśatakam* was edited by P. Sivadatta and V. L. Pansikar for the Kāvyamālā Series, vol. 9, pp. 1–31; there are various reprints, most recently by the Chaukhambha Bharati Academy, Varanasi, 1988. I hope to be able to publish my translation of the text in the not too distant future.

23 IRREDUCIBLE PARTICULARS

1 Canetti (Ch. 3, n. 15) p. 55 (p. 44).
2 See above, p. 224.
3 Nakkaṇṇai's poems are *Puṟanāṉūṟu* (edited by C. Turaicāmi Piḷḷai, South India Saiva Siddhanta Works Publishing Society, Tirunelveli/Madras, vol. I, 1947), Nos. 83–5.
4 See above, Ch. 10, n. 13, and p. 224.
5 See also below, pp. 523f.
6 For a discussion of the medieval controversy between the theoreticians of poetry and the practitioners of *kāvya* see D. Smith, *Ratnākara's Haravijaya – An Introduction to the Sanskrit Court Epic*, Oxford University Press, Delhi, 1985, pp. 37–54.
7 Both have been mentioned previously; see Ch. 5, n. 13 for the text, and n. 25 for an English translation, of the *Subhāṣitaratnakoṣa*, and Ch. 5, n. 23, for the *Saduktikarṇāmṛta*.
8 The *Amaruśatakam* was edited by C. R. Devadhar, Oriental Book Agency, Pune, 1959 (Poona Oriental Series, No. 101). Most of the poems have been translated by L. Siegel in his *Fires of Love – Waters of Peace: Passion and Renunciation in Indian Culture*, University of Hawaii Press, Honolulu, 1983. Textual problems associated with the collection of 'Amaru' are discussed by Ingalls (Ch. 5, n. 25), pp. 44f.
9 No. 55 in Devadhar (see note 8 above).
10 Quoted from Siegel (see note 8 above), p. 11 (No. 102 in Devadhar).
11 D. H. Ingalls, 'A Sanskrit poetry of village and field: Yogeśvara and his fellow poets', *Journal of the American Oriental Society* 74 (1954), pp. 119–31. See also Ingalls (Ch. 5, n. 25), pp. 327–36 and 358–62, for comments and translations from the *Subhāṣitaratnakoṣa*.
12 *Saduktikarṇāmṛta* (Ch. 5, n. 23), No. 2244 (and not found in the earlier *Subhāṣitaratnakoṣa*), ascribed to Vīra (who is otherwise unknown).
13 *Saduktikarṇāmṛta* (Ch. 5, n. 23), No. 1352 (and not found in the earlier *Subhāṣitaratnakoṣa*).
14 Ibid., No. 1342.

15 As R. Gnoli does, in his *The Aesthetic Experience According to Abhinavagupta*, Chowkhamba Sanskrit Studies, vol. 62, Varanasi (2nd edn), 1968.
16 For sources (in Abhinavagupta, *Daśarūpaka*, etc.) see J. L. Masson and M. V. Patwardhan, *Śāntarasa*, Bhandarkar Oriental Research Institute, Pune, 1969, p. 64 with notes.
17 See Masson/Patwardhan (previous note), pp. 48f, 72–5, 161f, etc.
18 For materials see my *Viraha-bhakti* (Ch. 3, n. 8), pp. 561f.
19 For the quotes from the *Caitanyacaritāmṛta* see ibid., pp. 4f.
20 In De's edition of the *Padyāvalī* (Ch. 13, n. 19), the sources are indicated, just as in the *Saduktikarṇāmṛta* (Ch. 5, n. 23) poems also found in the *Padyāvalī* are marked. Sometimes the original wording is actually changed in the *Padyāvalī*. For instance, *Saduktikarṇāmṛta* 624 ('of her friends') is changed in *Padyāvalī* 360 into 'of Rādhā's friends'; and 1032 ('fortunate one!') is changed into 'Kṛṣṇa!' in 187.
21 See my *Viraha-bhakti* (Ch. 3, n. 8), particularly pp. 4f, 8f, 347, 399, 496f, 529.
22 See above, Ch. 8, n. 19.
23 For example, in chapter 19 of Vyaṅkaṭeś Māḍguḷkar's Marathi novel, *Bangarvāḍī*.
24 See above, p. 330.
25 For material and references see above, Ch. 13, ns. 19f, and Ch. 16, n. 27.
26 See my *Viraha-bhakti* (Ch. 3, n. 8), pp. 481–547.
27 *Bhāgavata-purāṇa* X, 33, 17.
28 *Govindaprabhucaritra* (Ch. 22, n. 16), Nos 76, 158, 288, 295. Since the *Bhāgavata-purāṇa* was known to the early Mānbhāvs, such behaviour could easily be interpreted as suggesting that Govindaprabhu (Guṇḍam Rāüḷ) was an incarnation of Kṛṣṇa – which is indeed what the Mānbhāvs believe.
29 See above, p. 486.
30 See my *Viraha-bhakti* (Ch. 3, n. 8), pp. 512–16.
31 This has been demonstrated for a number of chapters in the *Bhāgavata-purāṇa*; see ibid., pp. 510–26 and 647–52.
32 Ibid., pp. 575f, with notes 70–4.
33 A. Feldhaus (Ch. 22, n. 16) has the significant chapter headings 'The mad god of Ṛddhipur' and 'Divine madness'.
34 Material can be found in my *Viraha-bhakti* (Ch. 3, n. 8), pp. 308–468.
35 See above, p. 329.
36 On this Purāṇa see Ch. 2, n. 12.
37 See above, Ch. 7, n. 16.
38 See above, Ch. 7, n. 25.

24 THE HEAD IN THE WORLD

1 On the goddess Naurthā see McKim Marriott, 'Little communities in an indigenous civilization', in: *Village India – Studies in the Little Community*, edited by McKim Marriott, University of Chicago Press, Chicago/London, Phoenix Paperback, 1972, pp. 200–15.

2 A hymn addressed to Perfect Wisdom by Rāhulabhadra is translated in Conze (Ch. 7, n. 25), pp. 147ff, No. 142. Many sculpures of the 'goddess' have been found.

3 Saraha's *Dohākoṣa* in Apabhraṃśa has been edited by M. Shahidullah, *Les chants mystiques de Kāṇha et de Saraha*, Paris, 1928, and by P. C. Bagchi, *Dohākoṣa*, Calcutta, 1938 (Calcutta Sanskrit Series, No. 25c), and translated into English by D. Snellgrove in Conze (Ch. 7, n. 25), pp. 224–39. The present poem is No. 7 (of Snellgrove).

4 Phrases from *dohās* 44, 83, and 97 (in Conze, see previous note 3).

5 The *Pāhuḍadohā* in Apabhraṃśa, attributed to Rāmasiṃha, were edited by Hiralal Jain, Karanja, 1933 (Ambādās Cavare Digambar Jain Granthmālā, vol. 3); the present poem is No. 30. For a French translation see C. Caillat, 'L'Offrande de distiques', *Journal Asiatique* 264 (1976), Paris, pp. 63–95.

6 *Pāhuḍadohā* (see previous note 5), from Nos 31ff.

7 Ibid., No. 160.

8 Ibid., No. 161; very similar in *Paramappapayāsu* (see following note 9) II, 130.

9 *Śrī Yogīndudeva's Paramātmaprakāśa (Paramappapayāsu) – An Apabhraṃśa Work on Jaina Mysticism*, and *Yogasāra* (separately paginated), edited by A. N. Upadhye, Bombay, 1937 (Śrī Rāyachandra Jaina Śāstramālā, vol. 10). The translation is from *Yogasāra* No. 44 and of 47.

10 Ibid., *Paramappapayāsu* II, 177.

11 See above, p. 162.

12 Civavākkiyar, translated in Zvelebil (Ch. 7, n. 20), pp. 84f.

13 Basavaṇṇa, translated by Ramanujan (Ch. 5, n. 34), from No. 125 (p. 76) and No. 586 (p. 85).

14 See above, p. 487.

15 Translated by C. Vaudeville, *Kabīr*, Clarendon Press, Oxford, 1974, p. 263, No. 9.

16 See above, p. 522.

17 On the Bāül see Das Gupta (Ch. 7, n. 19), pp. 157–87; D. Bhattacharya translated a selection of songs: *The Mirror of the Sky – Songs of the Bauls from Bengal*, George Allen and Unwin, London, 1969.

18 See *Lallā-vākyāni, or The Wise Sayings of Lal Dĕd, a Mystic Poetess of Ancient Kashmir*, edited and translated by G. Grierson and L. D. Barnett, Royal Asiatic Society, London, 1920 (Monographs, vol. 17), p. 2.

19 See above, p. 335.
20 See G. Pandey, *The Construction of Communalism in Colonial North India*, Oxford University Press, Delhi, 1990.
21 See above, pp. 293ff.
22 See above, p. 159.
23 See above, p. 161.
24 Mallișeṇasūri's sizeable treatise on the subject, *Syādvādamañjarī*, was translated by F. W. Thomas, *The Flower-Spray of the Quoddammodo Doctrine*, Akademie-Verlag, Berlin, 1960 (Deutsche Akademie der Wissenschaften zu Berlin, Institut für Orientforschung, No. 46).
25 See Hiriyanna (Ch. 19, n. 28), p. 163.
26 On the *kalampakam* as a genre of Tamil poetry see Zvelebil (Ch. 5, n. 28), p. 200; Zvelebil calls it 'rather untidy and bizarre'. I have been working on a translation of Piḷḷai Perumāḷ Aiyaṅkār's *Tiruvaraṅkakkalampakam*.
27 The verses of chapters 97–102 of the *Prapannāmṛta* (Ch. 5, n. 12) add up to a perfect 700.
28 See above, p. 97.
29 See above, pp. 121, 335.
30 See above, p. 106.
31 See above, p. 120.
32 See above, p. 443.
33 See above, pp. 7–11.
34 See Ch. 1, n. 25.
35 See above, pp. 3f, 6, 12, 15.
36 See above, p. 387.
37 Desani (Ch. 17, n. 2), p. 278.

Index